Seasoned Musicians
Playing Beyond the 5th Decade

Seasoned Musicians Playing Beyond the 5th Decade

A Case Study on Symphony Orchestra Lifestyle and Ageing

Warren Brodsky

OXFORD
UNIVERSITY PRESS

OXFORD
UNIVERSITY PRESS

Great Clarendon Street, Oxford, OX2 6DP,
United Kingdom

Oxford University Press is a department of the University of Oxford.
It furthers the University's objective of excellence in research, scholarship,
and education by publishing worldwide. Oxford is a registered trade mark of
Oxford University Press in the UK and in certain other countries.

Published in the United States of America by Oxford University Press
198 Madison Avenue, New York, NY 10016, United States of America

British Library Cataloguing in Publication Data
Data available

Library of Congress Control Number: 2024948013

ISBN 9780198956471

DOI: 10.1093/9780198956501.001.0001

Printed and bound by
CPI Group (UK) Ltd, Croydon, CR0 4YY

Links to third party websites are provided by Oxford in good faith and
for information only. Oxford disclaims any responsibility for the materials
contained in any third party website referenced in this work.

MIX
Paper | Supporting
responsible forestry
FSC® C013604

The manufacturer's authorised representative in the EU for product safety is
Oxford University Press España S.A. of El Parque Empresarial San Fernando de Henares,
Avenida de Castilla, 2 – 28830 Madrid (www.oup.es/en or
product.safety@oup.com). OUP España S.A. also acts as importer into Spain
of products made by the manufacturer.

About The Author

Warren Brodsky is Professor of Music Psychology in the Department of Art History and Visual Culture at Ben-Gurion University of the Negev in Israel. After a short-lived career as a professional Pop/Jazz electric bass-guitarist, Warren completed an Artist Degree (BMus) in Orchestral Percussion, and majored in Early Childhood Musical Development, which led to a Diploma and Certificate of Teaching (K-6) from the Rubin Academy of Music in Jerusalem. Warren trained as a Music Therapist at Hahnemann Medical University in Philadelphia (USA), and during his 10-year clinical career he was Registered, Certified, and Board-Certified in the USA, Registered in the UK, and licensed as a Creative and Expressive Therapist in Israel. Warren completed a PhD in Psychology at Keele University in the UK, and engaged in two Postdoctoral Fellowships at Ben-Gurion University of the Negev. Since then, Warren has been a full-time tenured research staff member.

Professor Warren Brodsky can be reached at: wbrodsky@bgu.ac.il

Dedication

Although this book is published in my name as a single author, many others have been involved in this project. Perhaps too many to mention individually. Yet, one person stands out for his continued encouragement: Wilfried Gruhn (b. 1939).[1] Wilfried is a Violinist, Musicologist, Music Educator, and Professor Emeritus from the Freiburg Music University in Germany.[2] His professional focus is on music education of young children, specifically musical learning. His research approaches involving the cognitive sciences of music led him to investigate the neural foundations of musical learning.

Wilfried supported my study on positive ageing among Orchestra musicians from the outset—even before 2006 when I initiated the designation label term 'Seasoned Musicians'. He engaged in discussions with me during the conceptualization of the study, and then while I developed the materials of the enquiry throughout the first decade of the millennium. Wilfried has indeed been my *partner in crime*. Wilfried paved the way for me to recruit Orchestra musicians in Germany, as well as framed an agreement for an on-site location inside a Concert Hall where I collected data and interviewed orchestra players. He has tirelessly read through draft texts of pre-proposals and proposals; he has been steadfast in reviewing contracts, grant submissions, qualitative data, quantitative findings, and has evaluated the outcomes subsequently presented in this book. Wilfried has provided a stable unfailing passageway for this seemingly infinite journey—all the while providing insights that cut through our never-ending sessions of creative brainstorming and heart-breaking miseries.

Wilfried has remained a constant colleague and collaborator, as well as a cherished friend and confidant. Over the years, he motivated me to continue with this study, and gently pushed me to complete the investigation towards its final destination.

I tip my hat to you, Wilfried!

[1] en.wikipedia.org/wiki/Wilfried_Gruhn
[2] www.wgruhn.de

Acknowledgements

I would hereby like to thank the following people who assisted me along this journey.

Foremost, my PhD mentor John A. Sloboda who suggested in 2003 that I begin conceiving of a topic and start writing (an outline) for a book related to music performance. I discovered that not much had been published about Orchestra musicians, and even less had been written about older-aged musicians. John introduced me to Martin Baum at Oxford University Press, who I contacted for the very first time in December 2006.

Thank you to Richard Paley (master Bassoonist) and A. Mark Clarfield (renowned Geriatrician), both from Jerusalem (Israel). They spent much time with me brainstorming at the very beginning of the process when I first conceived the study. From those sessions, I undertook a small market research (polling study) to find a descriptive label for 'older-aged musicians' that might be more politically acceptable than older-aged musicians—as no one wants to be referred to as 'old'. That procedure resulted in what is now a more acceptable label: Seasoned Musicians.

Several individuals assisted my early attempts to recruit Symphony Orchestra musicians in America. It is indeed a shame that these efforts were unsuccessful. Thank you to Lynne Meloccaro (American Symphony Orchestra), Jan Wilson (League of American Orchestras), and Jay Blumenthal (Associated Musicians of Greater New York, Local 802AFM).

The following individuals tirelessly helped me to set up recruitment meetings, keep track of the participant-player volunteers, and implement the data-collection interviews on-site in each Orchestra Hall during an active research season. Thank you! I could not have done this without your help.

- Israel
  Israel Sinfonietta Beer-Sheva:
  Ofer Sella and Claudia Czobel-Ezra
  Jerusalem Symphony Broadcasting Orchestra:
  Yair Stern
- England
  Hallé Orchestra:
  Stuart Kempster, Simon Turner, Stuart Robinson,
  David Richardson, Carol Marsh, John Summers, and Kay Allen
  BBC Philharmonic Orchestra:
  Richard Wigley, Katherine Jones, Steve Collow, Fiona McIntosh, and Carolin Smith.

- Germany
  Freiburg Philharmonic Orchestra:
  Michael Duhn, Fabrice Bollon, and Wilfried & Erdmuthe Gruhn

Thank you to Donna Abecasis (Israel) who was a 'sounding board' during the early development of the research methodology in the study.

Thank you to Yoav Kessler (Israel) who programmed the E-Prime presentation sequence of events and data collection procedures used for the Finger-Tapping Tasks (described in Chapter 8).

Thank you to Moshe Zorman (Israel) who has served as my 'house-composer' for several empirical investigations. He composed the three pieces (Appendix A) that the Symphony Orchestra musicians played in the *in vivo/in situ* performances (described in Chapters 9 and 10).

Thank you to Amos Boasson and Yossie Arnheim (Israel) who served as external independent judges in the double-blind adjudication process for the Music Performance Evaluation (described in Chapter 10).

Thank you to Ioulia Papageorgi (Cyprus) for all her help—especially for her listening to all of my whining and moaning since 2019! She has been a most welcome colleague, as well as consultant to me in the final stages of the project and book.

Thank you to Dani Machlis (Israel) for the profile picture.

Thank you to those who served as reviewers and commentators of draft portions of the book: Wilfried Gruhn, Richard Paley, and John A. Sloboda.

To the funding agencies who repeatedly rejected my research proposals to explore music engagement across the lifespan and ageing among professional Symphony Orchestra musicians. These included: Israel Social Security 'Keren Manof' (2007), State of Israel Ministry of Health (2007), the Israel Science Foundation (2008, 2018, 2019), and Joy Ventures (2018). Thank you to a host of international collaborators (Co-PIs) of these grant proposals—among them Aaron Williamon (UK) and Wilfried Gruhn (Germany). I hereby declare that as there was no financial support for the field research, data analyses, authorship, or publication of this book, there were no conflicts of interest implementing the study or writing up the research findings thereof.

Finally, thank you to the folks at Oxford University Press. A BIG HUG to Martin Baum (Senior Commissioning Editor, Psychology, Psychiatry, and Neuroscience). Martin has stood by me, and this book project, since 2006. Not to be taken for granted! To Kayley Gilbert who took on the project and saw it through production; also to Michael Mundt. To others at OUP from yesteryear: Carol Maxwell, Charlotte Green-Holloway, and Abby Gross. To copyeditor Rowena Anketell. And to Project Managers (Integra) Nandhini Saravanan and Indumadhi Srinivasan.

Warren Brodsky, Jerusalem Israel, 2024

Contents

List of Figures

List of Tables

List of Abbreviations

α	Cronbach's Alpha reliability test (statistics)
Δ	Delta, difference between two means (statistics)
$\pm$	plus-minus (about) (statistics)
%	Percentage (statistics)
<	less than
>	bigger than
*	< 0.05 (statistics)
**	< 0.01 (statistics)
***	< 0.001 (statistics)
****	< 0.0001 (statistics)
A4	page sized: $8'' \times 12''$
A5	page sized: $8'' \times 6''$
AD	Alzheimer's disease
AIS	Artistic Interpretational Strategies
a.m.	morning daytime hours (00:01-11:59)
ANOVA	Analysis of Variance (statistics)
AS	Auditivity Scale (measures)
bcl	Bass Clarinet (instrument)
bn	Bassoon (instrument)
bpm	beats per minute
BTPS	Basic Technical Performance Strategies
C	Compensation (*SOC*) (Measures)
CDs	compact disks (music format, hardware)
cl	Clarinet (instrument)
CR	Cognitive Reserves (neuropsychology)
d	Cohen's *d* effect size (statistics)
db	Double Bass (contrabass) (instrument)
dbn	Double Bassoon (instrument)
df	Degree of Freedom (statistics)
DNA	Deoxyribonucleic acid, molecule carrying genetic information
DP	Deliberate Practice
DP (*MBI*-DP)	Depersonalization (*MBI*) (measures)
e.g.	for example
EE (*MBI*-EE)	Emotional Exhaustion (MBI) (measures)
ES	Elective Selection (*SOC*) (measures)
et al.	And colleagues; and other author-researchers (citation)
Euro	Euro € (currency)
F	F-test of explained variance (statistics)
F	Female (sex)
fl	Flute (instrument)
FST	Forced Speeded Tapping
FSTAH	Forced Speeded Tapping Alternating Hands

FSTLH	Forced Speeded Tapping Right Hand
FSTRH	Forced Speeded Tapping Right Hand
GB	Gigabyte
GBP	Great Britain pounds £ (currency)
Ghz	Gigahertz
GP	general public (sub-samples)
GTE	greater than or equal to
h	hours (time)
hn	French Horn (instrument)
hrp	Harp (instrument)
i.e.	that is, meaning
ID	Participant's Identification Number
ITIs	Inter-Tap Intervals
KAAS	Keele Assessment of Auditory Style (measures)
KE	Kinaesthetic Engagement
Khz	Kilohertz
L-L	Lifespan-Longings (measures)
LBS	Loss-Based Selection (*SOC*) (measures)
LMOD	Life Management in the Occupational Domain (measures)
LTE	less than or equal to
M	Male (sex)
M (m, MN)	mean, average (statistics)
MAX	maximal range (statistics)
MBI	Maslach Burnout Inventory
MCS	Metacognitive Strategies
Mdn	Median (statistics)
MIHL	Music-Induced Hearing Loss
MNSA	Music Notation Score Analysis (measures)
Mp3	.Mp3 audio (file format)
MPA	Music Performance Anxiety
MPE	Music Performance Evaluation (measures)
MPsE	Music Performance Self-Evaluation (measures)
ms	millisecond (time)
MSe	Error Mean Sum of Squares (statistics)
N (n)	number of people in the sample (or sub-sample)
$N^2{}_P$	Partial Eta Squared, effect size (statistics)
NA	Negative Affect (*PANAS*) (measures)
NIA	National Institute on Aging
NIH	American National Institutes of Health
NIHL	Noise-Induced Hearing Loss
NYC	New York City
O	Optimization (*SOC*) (measures)
ob	Oboe (instrument)
OM	orchestra musicians (sub-samples)
OMC	Orchestra Musicians Committee
p	Probability (statistics)
PA	Positive Affect (*PANAS*) (measures)
PA (*MBI*-PA)	Personal Accomplishment (MBI) (measures)
PANAS	Positive and Negative Affect Schedule
perc	Percussion (instrument)

p.	page (citation)
picc	Piccolo (instrument)
p.m.	afternoon/evening hours (12:00–24:59)
PPT	Preferred Perceptual Tempo
Q1–Q12	questionnaires of the survey booklet (measures)
QEA	Quasi-experimental approach
r	Person Correlation Coefficient (statistics)
s	seconds (time)
SD	Standard Deviation (statistics)
SD	secure digital memory storage card (computer hardware)
SE	Standard Error (statistics)
SESA	Self-Evaluation of Skills and Abilities (measures)
SMT	Spontaneous Motor Tempo
SOC	Selection, Optimization, and Compensation (measures)
t	T-test of variance between two means (statistics)
TAPs	Think Aloud Protocols
TFT	thin-film-transistor liquid-crystal display (computer hardware)
tpt	Trumpet (instrument)
trb	Trombone (instrument)
TV	television
UK	United Kingdom
USA	Unites States of America
va	Viola (instrument)
vc	Cello (instrument)
vn	Violin (instrument)
vs.	versus
wav	.Wav audio (file format)
wk	week (time)

Permissions

I would hereby like to thank the following people for their permission to use materials within this book:

Modern Israeli artist Yair Garbuz (Tel Aviv, Israel) for permission to reproduce his original lithograph titled *The Orchestra* (1998) that appears on the front cover of the book.

Amy Goggins at SAGE (UK) and Jane Ginsborg of the journal *Musicae Scientiae* for permission to reproduce sections from Brodsky (2004, 2011), appearing in Chapters 1 and 2.

Janet Horvath for permission to reproduce sections of her *blog* commentary titled 'Challenges for the Ageing Musician' published in the classical music e-magazine *Interlude* (2019), appearing in Chapter 1.

Claudia Spahn, Bernhard Richter, and Heiner Gembris (Germany) for permission to reproduce an illustration from the book *Musical Development from a Lifespan Perspective* (p. 125), appearing in Chapter 1.

Shoshana 'Shasa' Dobrow for permission to reproduce items of the *Calling* scale, appearing in Chapter 2.

Robert J. Sternberg and Alexandra Lamont of the journal *Psychology of Music* for permission to reproduce the Triangular Love Scale for Musical Instruments (Sternberg, 2021), appearing in Chapter 5 (Table 5.1).

John Wiley and Sons publishers for permission to reproduce material from Brodsky (2006) appearing throughout the book.

Margje van de Wiel (Netherlands) for permission to reprint Table 9.3, appearing in Chapter 9.

Michiko Yoshie for permission to use and reproduce the *Music Performance Evaluation*, appearing in Chapter 10.

Ulman Lindenberger for permission to reproduce Table 11.1 appearing in Chapter 11.

Susanna Scheibe for permission to reproduce Table 11.4 appearing in Chapter 11.

John A. Saloboda for permission to reproduce the *Keele Assessment of Auditory Style* (KAAS) which he and I co-developed in 1993, appearing in Appendix A.

PART I

BACKGROUND AND FOREGROUND

Part I is an introduction to the investigation package. Chapter 1 offers the context and background for the empirical study, as well as providing the rationale for research related to ageing. The chapter introduces longevity among the general population, as well as specifically among musicians. The chapter goes on to describe, in rather full detail, the methods employed throughout the research; it accounts for both quantitative and qualitative methods, the equipment used in the field experiments, and a descriptive portrayal of the Symphony players who participated. Finally, Chapter 1 presents an outline of the book.

Chapter 2 explores music performers. It is logical to perceive *music performance* as its own way of life, including: Deliberate Practice, rehearsals, ensembles, and gigs; camps and residential seminars; masterclasses; Music Conservatories and Academies; auditions; and an Orchestra career. The chapter views the development of Orchestra musicians: familial attitudes towards music traditions and education; music education and instrument tuition; performance experiences including debuts and achievements, competitions, honours, awards, and foreign-travel scholarships. The idea of choosing the music-performance profession is explored. Finally, an estimation of Deliberate Practice over the lifetime will be presented. Chapter 2 brings Part I to a close by focusing on the Symphony Orchestra as an occupational environment, highlighting weekly activities including performing with the Orchestra, Chamber Ensembles, and as a Soloist; rehearsing and Deliberate Practice; and teaching music students.

I should note a few conventions found in the text. When full citation of a vignette is indicated, it appears in a reduced italicised font preceded by the participant's age, sex, and instrument (in parenthesis). This documentation is essential for some readers as it places the words in a specific context of person, age group, and instrument family; the last can be seen as a marker of position in the Orchestra indicating the participant as either a Principal or a Rank-&-File player. Further, I would like to point out that vignettes are presented in ascending ages; the youngest player is presented first while the oldest player is presented last. Such a presentation order may assist the reader's comprehension. Also, it should be noted that only a selection of citations is brought forward for illustrative purposes. Finally, I point out that when names of research associates are mentioned throughout the book, all dates (in parentheses) refer to the year of the cited publication; other descriptions (e.g., academic affiliation, country of activity) denote the information as listed at the time on the cited publication.

1
Rationale, Methodology, and Book Outline

When you attend a live Classical Music concert, or watch an Orchestra performing onstage in a broadcast on TV (or YouTube), have you ever noticed that the players are both younger and older musicians? The younger ones are clearly competent players, having received their position in the Orchestra after a series of auditions and a period of trial—which might have even lasted 12 months or more. But, what about the older players? How do they keep up with the younger ones? After all, the differences of age might range between 20 and 30 years amongst the players. Doesn't age-related wear and tear take a toll on performance-related skills of Orchestra players? Long ago London (1963) commented about this phenomenon:

> One of the aspects of the longevity of musicians that has particularly intrigued observers has been the fact that musicians as a rule continue to be actively productive until almost the very end. This situation contrasts markedly with the population at large where aging is held to be synonymous with vegetating. (p. 160)

This first part of this chapter (sections 1.1–1.4) reviews longevity in general and then specifically among music performers. Given the apparent lack of information on the topic, the rationale for a 'Call' of empirical study on *Seasoned Musicians* is brought to the fore. Thereafter the second part of the chapter (section 1.5) presents the methods used in the field study itself. Finally, the third part of the chapter (section 1.6) outlines the contents of this book.

Rationale For Exploring Seasoned Musicians

1.1 Longevity Revolution

We often talk about *musicianship* within a context of lifespan development.[1] That is, the maturation of musicians is seen as a lifelong process, requiring specific adjustments to changes based on age and environment. Like everyone else, musicians go through a sequence of developmental stages, each unique in structure of musical activity, motivation, and achievements. We might assume, then, that there is an overriding 'model' or 'life cycle' of musicianship, consisting of critical periods over one's lifespan, in which milestones related to artistic mastery and specific career objectives

---

[1] Portions of this chapter were adapted from Brodsky (2011). Reprinted by permission.

Seasoned Musicians Playing Beyond the 5th Decade. Warren Brodsky, Oxford University Press. © Oxford University Press (2025). DOI: 10.1093/9780198956501.003.0001

are attained. But yet, that is truly unknown at this time. Heiner Gembris[2] (2006), the former director of the Institute for Research on Musical Ability at the University of Paderborn (Germany), claims that the idea of musical development as part of general human development—as a lifelong process—has hardly been touched on by researchers of Music Education. 'While we have a rich body of research on the musical development in childhood and adolescence, there are only a small number of investigations on music in adulthood and in the third age' (Gembris, 2008, p. 1). There is a great lack of basic knowledge regarding musical learning, abilities, and interests, as far as adulthood and old age is concerned. One reason for this drawback is that the majority of research studies relating to lifespan music development have focused exclusively on precocious musical beginnings in early childhood (Deliege & Sloboda, 1996; Howe et al., 1998), prodigious adolescents (Howe, 1998; Howe & Sloboda, 1991a; Pruett, 1991; Sloboda, 1991, 1993a), or target factors and component skills of musical excellence leading to musical expertise among young adults (Howe & Sloboda, 1991b; Howe et al., 1995; Sloboda, 1984, 1990, 1993b, 1996; Sloboda & Davidson, 1996; Sloboda et al., 1996). There is but one exception which offers a much broader perspective on lifelong development of music performance skill. In 1975, Maria Manturzewska, a music psychologist and educator from the Institute of Research in Music Education at the Fryderyk Chopin University in Warsaw (Poland), launched a project focused on long-term longitudinal lifespan development and professional careers of contemporary musicians in Poland. Subsequently Manturzewska (1990, 2006) outlined a sequence of development from birth throughout age 75, portraying the lifelong development of professional musicians, describing critical phases in which each reflected a different developmental stage, characterized by typical activities, roles, and tasks. See Table 1.1.

Manturzewska (1990, 2006) felt that musicianship begins about age 5–6, followed by 16 years of systematic training, then passes through critical periods in which public performances and artistic debuts occur, which lead to higher advanced training and attainment of professional diplomas, resulting in levels of mastery acknowledged by a 'virtuoso' status, with the greatest artistic achievements occurring between the ages of 25 and 45 (coinciding with the most efficient psychophysical competence), after which the greatest teaching achievements take place when musicians are finally fatigued from their own concert activity and performance career (thereafter concentrating on the achievements of the next generation of musicians— their protégé students). Manturzewska's model is highly welcome. In fact, it is the only developmental representation of musical activity illustrating a lifelong process. This work was the result of a study with 165 contemporary Polish musicians (including Composers, Conductors, Pianists, Violinists, Woodwind and Brass Instrumentalists, and Singers) between the ages 21 and 89 (born 1890–1960); they

---

[2] I point out that when names are mentioned throughout the book, all dates (in parentheses) refer to the year of publication. All other descriptions (e.g., academic affiliation, country of activity) denote information that was relevant at the time of the cited publication.

Table 1.1 Lifespan Model of Development Stages Among Professional Musicians

Stage	Age	Description
I	1–6	Development of sensory emotional sensitivity; Spontaneous musical expression through musical play
II	6–12	Systematic instruction of musical instrument; Guided musical development of basic technical performance capacities and music knowledge
III	12–20	Formation and development of artistic personality and musical competence within a master–student relationship
IV	20–30	Advanced training and graduation from a music academy or college; searching for employment; Joining of professional community through membership of various ensembles and musical institutions
V	30–45	Professional stabilization and expansion involving performing activity and artistic output
VI	45–55	First signs of physical and psychic fatigue surface; First inklings of inefficiency and lack of ability to learn new repertoire; Change in musical interests from individual career-orientation to more general focus on pedagogical issues
VII	55–70	Teaching phase; Increasing sense of social responsibility within the music culture
VIII	70–75	Retirement from professional activity; Taking on representative functions including adjudicator at jury-based competitions, and honorary titles within civic committees, sociopolitical organizations, and granting foundations

Data Source: Manturzewska (1990/2006), Gembris (2023)

were interviewed between the years 1976 and 1980 (Gembris, 2006, 2023). Among these were 30–35 outstanding 'prize-winners' of international music competitions, and 130–135 'basic ordinary Polish citizens involved in musical activity', randomly selected from listings of the Polish Music Society. Yet, perhaps we might ponder if some form of cultural bias might have tainted the findings of this study? Moreover, we could wonder if during the past 50 years health services have significantly contributed to a 'longevity revolution' resulting in older adults remaining in the workforce longer than Manturzewska reported. Especially when looking at today's musicians, they are professionally active well past the reported retirement age of 50 years. And finally, given the defined criterion of subgroups (e.g., outstanding music soloists *versus* everyday musicians who were not necessarily professional performers), covering a very wide assortment of musicians (e.g., Composers, Conductors, Performers, Teachers, Instrumentalists, Vocalists, as well as a host of amateurs), then perhaps one needs to ask: How ecologically valid and reliable is such a model in reference to professional music performers as full-time contract Symphony Orchestra players?

Today, at least as far as industrialized societies are concerned, we are able to prevent most illness, disability, and death associated with chronic disease by taking advantage of the medical and health services readily available to us in the community. On the other hand, for those living in Third World cultures, life expectancy remains very low. In retrospect, those who were born in the United States in the early

1900s had a life expectancy of only about 50 years. But then, through great improvements in science and technology during the last half of the 20th century, those born in America were seen to live past 70 years of age. Namely, the US population under age 65 tripled, and those above age 65 increased by a factor of 11 (National Institute on Aging, 2006); the actual number of seniors grew from 3.1 million in 1900 to 33.2 million in 1994—and this number is expected to more than double by the mid-21st century.

Data from the American National Institutes of Health (NIH) indicate that men's life expectancy in the year 2002 was 74.5 years while women's life expectancy was 79.9 years. The NIH asserts that by year 2030, the number of older Americans will be roughly 70 million people. This means that there will be a greater proportion of seniors compared to the rest of the population. By 2030 one in every five Americans will be above 60 years old, and by 2050 in the USA alone the population above age 65 is expected to rise to 88 million people. Further, the NIH claims that 8.5% of people worldwide—617 million—who are currently over age 65, will jump to 17% by 2050. In the United Kingdom, the number of older people is also on the rise; statistics from government offices in London claim that by the year 2071 there will be more than 21 million residents over 65 years old, and more than 9 million residents over age 80 (GOScience, 2008).

However, the main issue here is not that we are living longer, but that we have extended our professional active careers by several years. The National Institute on Aging (2006) reported that we are remaining in the workforce for a significantly longer number of years—more than in any other previous time period in history. One area where this presence is specifically noticeable is in the Performing Arts.

1.2 Ageing Among Music Performers

London (1963) was perhaps one of the first Gerontologists to point out that many Composers and Conductors were musically active way beyond what had been the normal accepted period of professional vocation. In fact, they were even active till the day they passed away (listing in alphabetical order): Ansermet (86), Beecham (82), Bloch (79), Charpentier (96), Damrosch (88), Delius (71), Dohnányi (86), Glière (81), Grainger (81), Ives (86), Kodály (85), Koussevitsky (71), Mascagni (82), Mengelberg (80), Milhaud (82), Montemezzi (77), Monteux (89), Munch (77), Paray (93), R. Strauss (85), Reiner (75), Riegger (77), Schoenberg (77), Sibelius (92), Stokowski (95), Stravinsky (89), Varèse (82), Vaughan Williams (86), Villa-Lobos (80), Von Muck (81), Walter (86), and Weingartner (79). London was highly insightful, and perhaps the very first to have perceived: 'There obviously must be more to the ecology of longevity [among musicians] than just the autogenous psychophysiological protection from the diseases of stress, especially when at one time the mortality trends of musicians were the reverse' (p. 161).

For some time, the public has witnessed many *Grand Masters* who continued to perform and astound audiences well into their final year of life. In 1999, neurologist Richard J. Lederman from the Cleveland Clinic in Ohio (USA), an expert on medical problems of performing musicians, described several musicians who were legendary not only for their levels of virtuosity but also for their career longevity. Among the acclaimed soloists he described (and their ages at the time of their death, in ascending order), were:

- Georg Solti (80); Hungarian-born British Orchestral and Operatic Conductor, and long-serving music director of the Chicago Symphony Orchestra
- Herbert von Karajan (85); Austrian Principal Conductor of the Berlin Philharmonic
- Vladimir Horowitz (86); Russian-American classical virtuoso Pianist
- Rudolf Serkin (87); Bohemian-born American classical Pianist, and great 20th-century interpreter of Beethoven
- Nathan Mironovich Milstein (87); Ukrainian-born American virtuoso Violinist
- Claudio Arrau León (88); Chilean Pianist known for his unique interpretations of repertoire from Baroque to 20th-century composers
- Arturo Toscanini (89); Italian Conductor, and one of the most acclaimed musicians of the late 19th–20th century
- Arthur Rubinstein (95); Polish-American classical Pianist, widely regarded as one of the greatest pianists of all time
- Leopold Anthony Stokowski (95); Polish-English Conductor of the early and mid-20th century, having a long association with the Philadelphia Orchestra and the Disney film *Fantasia*
- Pau 'Pablo' Casals (96); Spanish Composer and Conductor, regarded as the pre-eminent Cellist of the first half of the 20th century
- Mieczysław Horszowski (99); Polish-American Pianist, having had one of the longest careers in the history of the performing arts lasting nine decades

Yet, even classically trained Orchestra musicians themselves are bewildered over virtuosi Grand Masters, Conductors, and Composers. Below is a comment from a 60-year-old Orchestra player:[3]

---

[3] When full citations are indicated, these appear in a reduced font preceded by the participant's age, sex, and instrument in parentheses. This documentation is essential (for some readers) as it places the words in a specific context of person, age group, and instrument family. The abbreviations for instrumentation in the Symphony Orchestra use a shorthand system. Nonetheless, there is no standardized version of this shorthand. That is, different Composers and Publishers throughout the history of music have used different acronyms to represent each instrument. In this book I have used the following more common set of abbreviations for each instrument: 'vn' (violin); 'va' (viola); 'vc' (cello); 'db' (double bass); 'fl' (flute); 'picc' (piccolo); 'cl' (clarinet); 'bcl' (bass clarinet); 'ob' (oboe); 'bn' (bassoon); 'dbn' (double bassoon); 'tpt' (trumpet); 'hn' (French horn); 'trb' (trombone); 'hrp' (harp); and 'perc' (percussion).

(60y, M, bn)   *I remember hearing a story from a colleague who saw Arthur Rubinstein in his late 80s. At the time my friend was a student in the academy. He told a story, that all the students came to see a Masterclass. The students were told this might be the last time you ever see Rubinstein alive. My colleague told me that he sat as close to him as the distance of 5 feet. So, he could really see his hands. And, while this student was not a Piano major, Rubinstein as a persona was very interesting to him. Several assistants brought Rubinstein to the Piano. The story was that he looked like a dishevelled old man, had the jitters, he just couldn't even hear the people who were assisting him. He sat down at the Piano, and somebody else had to move the seat up or down because he couldn't turn the levers. My friend said to me he was thinking: 'Isn't it a shame that we actually see this kind of a Master like this because it just ruins your memory'. But, then, the minute they opened up the Piano [fallboard, keylid], Rubinstein became alive, and played things that you just never heard before. Then, one of the top students was brought out for this Masterclass. She played a piece, and Rubinstein said: 'Oh, you must play the G# in measure 127!' And it was like that the whole time; his memory was there, and everything in him was there. It wasn't just he knew how to play, it was like he understood everything that was going on. Then the minute they took him off the platform, and while everyone was still clapping, fell back into that muddle that he came out with.*

    I myself saw Klemperer conducting Beethoven in London when I was a student. He was 90-something. He hardly did any movements. He had to be helped onstage, helped offstage, and sat the whole time. And he just didn't seem to be doing much. I mean there was sort of a few movements like this, but nothing much more. But the playing was just amazing. Quite extraordinary. And they couldn't have played like that if they just thought he was gone. Something was happening, I remember thinking: 'It was amazing!'

I need to point out that the above echoes observations of older musicians in the Jazz genre as well. In this connection, Lyness (2017) states that many 'young bandmates of both Armstrong and Ellington noted how each might appear tired and old waiting in the wings, but would spring to life with youthful energy as [they] took the stage and interacted with the audience' (p. 1297). Another young(er) 40-year-old player questioned the phenomena relating to Seasoned Musicians as 'anomalies' that she could not understand.

(39y, F, cl)   *I [am thinking about] this particular colleague who reached a point when he realized: 'Yeah, if I don't stop this soon, it's going to become difficult.' He wanted to leave the moment he felt incapable of delivering. He reached retirement age. But I think he was aware that soon it was going to become harder, and that this was really the right moment to go: 'I should stop before I fall off it.' In my previous Orchestra we had Pavarotti come and sing with us very late in life. Really, he shouldn't have been there. It was such a struggle for him. What a shame. But, I haven't seen age-related deterioration so close by me in the Orchestra, but I've seen it with other Wind players [in other Orchestras]. You know, people who were my old teachers, various people who've gone on and on and on. Actually, these people were still playing. It was as if their lifeblood; they just didn't want to give it up. I suppose what I'm really saying is, that some of the players are anomalies. It is quite a phenomenon!*

Music Performance has long ago been identified as an occupation committed towards its more seasoned members. There are hundreds of vignettes about the *Grandfathers of Rock 'n' Roll* (e.g., Lyness, 2017). Among those who are still composing, recording, and occasionally performing onstage at the time of this writing (in alphabetical order, with age and birth year) are:

- Animals (Eric Burdon, 83, b. 1941)
- Beach Boys (Brian Wilson, 82, b. 1942; Mike Love, 83, b. 1941)
- Beatles (Paul McCartney, 82, b. 1942; Ringo Starr, 84, b. 1940)
- Billy Joel (75, b. 1949)
- Bob Dylan (83, b. 1941)
- Bruce Springsteen (75, b. 1949)
- Carlos Santana (77, b. 1947)
- Carole King (82, b. 1942)
- Crosby, Stills, Nash & Young (Stephen Stills, 79, b. 1945; Graham Nash, 82, b. 1942; Neil Young, 79, b. 1945)
- Elton John (77, b. 1947)
- Eric Clapton (79, b. 1945)
- Fleetwood Mac (Mick Fleetwood, 77, b. 1947; John McVie, 79, b. 1945; Stevie Nicks, 75, b. 1948; Lindsey Buckingham, 75, b. 1949)
- Frankie Valli (90, b. 1934)
- Grateful Dead (Phil Lesh, 85, b. 1940; Bob Weir, 77, b. 1947)
- Joni Mitchell (81, b. 1943)
- Led Zeppelin (Jimmy Page, 80, b. 1944; John Paul Jones, 78, b. 1946; Robert Plant, 76, b. 1948)
- Neil Diamond (83, b. 1941)
- Ozzy Osbourne (76, b. 1948)
- Pink Floyd (Roger Waters, 81, b. 1943)
- Phil Collins (73, b. 1951)
- Rod Stewart (80, b. 1945)
- Rolling Stones (Mick Jagger, 81, b. 1943; Keith Richards, 81, b. 1943; Ronnie Wood, 77, b. 1947; Bill Wyman, 88, b. 1936)
- Simon & Garfunkel (Paul Simon, 83, b. 1941; Art Garfunkel, 83, b. 1941)
- Smokey Robinson (84, b. 1940)
- Sting (73, b. 1951)
- Who (Roger Daltrey, 80, b. 1944; Pete Townshend, 79, b. 1945)

I point out that older players from Blues, Jazz, Pop, and Folk genres are not often described in research reports. There are, however, a host of studies employing methodologies such as biography and autobiography, ethnography and auto-ethnography, as well as musicological and music performance studies (e.g., Bennett & Hodkinson, 2012; Jennings & Gardner, 2012; Lyness, 2017). One more recent paper by A. Mark Clarfield (2023), former director of the Medical School for International Health and head of the Centre for Global Health of the Faculty of Health Sciences at Ben-Gurion University of the Negev (Israel), described the recuperation efforts of ageing Folk Music hero Joni Mitchell in the aftermath of a brain aneurism which affected her ability to speak, sing, play the Guitar, and even walk. There was a special issue of the journal *Popular Music* (2012, Volume 31, Issue 2) titled 'As time goes by: Music, dance and ageing'. Some of those papers focus on ageing audiences of popular music, and analyse the place of ageing popular musicians through responses of critics and audiences. Certainly, the music backgrounds of Blues, Jazz, Pop, Rock, and Folk musicians are far too unique and different than common; their demographic factors greatly contribute to weakened sample homogeneity. As a result, it is all the more impossible to interpret findings of studies employing popular musicians because such variances often create confounding variables among the data.

On the other hand, players trained in Western Classical concert-music genres are far more alike than they are different. For example, they all undergo a similar development, have completed a standardized training programme, acquired comparable knowledge, and have mastered common proficiencies (see Chapter 2, section 2.1). In the late 1980s, David W. E. Smith (1988, 1989), from Northwestern University Medical School in Chicago (USA), published a groundbreaking study in which 14 retired Orchestra members between the ages of 55 and 90 were interviewed; they were from what was referred to as 'one of America's greatest symphony Orchestras'— presumably players from the Chicago Symphony Orchestra (CSO). The interesting point here is that these players had had an average 41 years of full-time employment as professional music performers ($SD = 9.10$, Range 23–57), of which roughly 35 years ($SD = 8.75$, Range 22–50) were with the CSO. While Smith reported the average age of retirement to be 67 years old ($SD = 7.69$, Range 47–78), this figure actually points to the fact that 42% of the sample retired well beyond the more acceptable age of retirement (e.g., $M_{Age} = 73$ years, $SD = 3.06$, Range 69–78). It is true, that although Smith's study is comprised of an extremely small number of individuals, it still highlights that as a group, Orchestra players retained active careers 35% longer than non-musician populations as reported for American Workforce Participation Rates for older adults (National Institute on Aging, 2006). A validation of Smith's findings was published in the February 2000 issue of *Allegro* (a monthly magazine for members of the Local 802 NYC Musician Union); clinical social worker Jackelyn Frost (2000) points to evidence from the union's listings indicating that most Orchestral musicians were retiring beyond the average American age of retirement at the turn of the millennium which was 61.5 years old.

As Smith (1989) noted, and then later confirmed by Hensen (1994), from the mid-1980s it became an accepted practice with contractual and legal ramifications not to forcibly end the careers of Orchestra players before age 70. The only exception to the law was a situation whereby it was deemed that a player could no longer perform adequately; in such cases performance levels were then judged by a peer-review committee. Nonetheless, many people, even from within the music community, disapproved and condemned such union policies. On the one hand these policies were meant to protect senior Symphony musicians, while on the other hand musicians could be publicly challenged to defend themselves by having to audition for a jury in order to prove that they could still meet the standards and traditions of their Orchestra. Many readers with a music-performance background will already have experienced auditions; no doubt these can be humiliating. But, when forced to defend oneself in an Orchestra after years of service, the process is not only undignified, but can also be fatal by damaging one's reputation. Alice G. Brandfon-brenner, a physician who specialized in the treatment of performing musicians, was very outspoken about the custom. Brandfonbrenner was the co-founder of *PAMA* (Performing Arts Medicine Association, USA) and founding editor of the journal *Medical Problems of Performing Artists* (*MPPA*). In an open editorial commentary, Brandfonbrenner affirmed that common sense should prevail among Orchestra players; they should be smart enough to 'hang it up' when they no longer have the right stuff before the world knows that they have 'lost it' (Brandfonbrenner, 2003).

Yet, Smith (1988) found that the rate of turnover in the Orchestra studied was between 3% and 6% per year. We might understand this statistic to mean that the older players were not often forced to retire. Perhaps, such a low level of substitution was because of the 'value' placed on Seasoned Musicians by both the section leaders themselves and the managements. Accordingly, seasoned players were viewed as having "experience of playing a vast literature of symphonic music under a variety of conductors [. . .] familiarity, understanding, and skill that the best young players cannot match" (p. 238).

(44y, F, vn)	*I only really saw it once or twice that people were almost forced out of their jobs. But to be honest they had problems all through their career. Then again, even if this was once or twice over my 23-year career, and considering I was in two Orchestras with 100 or so people in each Orchestra, then that's less than 1% change per year. Maybe we are more protected. I am aware of people in office positions losing their jobs; they become redundant. But no one in an Orchestra will ever be made redundant. So, we sort of have this perceived idea that nobody ever lost their job in an Orchestra. I don't know if that's entirely true. But then again, if you think that over a 23-year period, with over 100 people in each Orchestra, and roughly five times a year new players are joining the ranks (i.e., there is always some turnover), then 5 × 23 is another 100. So, you're talking maybe about 2 out of 350 people per year. That's hardly anything compared to other professions.*
(47y, M, trb)	*It is better for Orchestras to have older players than younger players because they're the ones that know how to blend and are the team players. Older players are experienced players who know what happens in special places. A young player has just learned the music; has worked on the difficulties of the piece from the score. But for example, if there is a Ritardando which is not written, which can happen when there's a singer singing difficult stuff, [the older players] would watch him. So, it's very important to have these players. I don't really know what makes a great Orchestra like the Berlin Philharmonic; they have fantastic players, and at least 50% are over 40 years, with many others above 50 years old. They have a usual ageing process there—they don't kick anybody out. Even those who leave [on their own] continue to play in [other] professional Orchestras. So, for sure [Orchestras] like to have some 'young bloods' around them. And while they like to say: 'Oh, he's playing great!', they also say: 'Oh, he has to learn a little bit, and needs to get used to everything.'*

Most certainly, unlike other occupations in today's workforce, the music-performance profession does not become obsolete because of an ever-present array of emerging knowledge, sophisticated new technologies, or shifts in consumer behaviour patterns. Moreover, while the repertoire of the Symphony Orchestra has indeed changed over the years, and concert seasons now incorporate programmes featuring contemporary compositions (written by the most youthful of composers) as well as integrating more popular melodies (written by songwriters and tune-masters of Tin Pan Alley), the *musical classics* have remained the same for several hundred years (Botstein, 1996). Most Orchestra players will admit that what was once considered difficult modern music of the avant-garde requiring exceptional dexterity, is now looked upon simply as mainstream. Also, although we witness great advancements in digital processing and an ongoing increasing capability of professional reproduction sound quality within home-based PC-computer music recording and editing packages, the performance stage arena—the actual pit and concert platform—has remained essentially unchanged for over 180 years since the birth of the modern Symphony Orchestra in the mid-nineteenth century (Knight, 2006). This is not the case for many more popular music genres. In an essay on 'Ageing and Popular Music', an entry in the *Encyclopedia of Gerontology and Popular Ageing*, Elliott (2019) underlined age-appropriateness of musicians as based on music genres. Accordingly: "one or more of their most identifiable aspects—be it musical style, volume, dress, or dance—has been so forcefully associated with cultures of display among younger people that to engage in the genre as an older participant is considered inappropriate or 'deviant'" (p. 2). But not so for Western Classical Music! Perhaps, the field of music performance, and the Orchestra itself, is rather predisposed to stability and continuity.

(33y, F, bn/dbn)   *Well certainly the Orchestra hasn't changed in about 400 years. On one hand there's a feeling today that we have to get rid of the older players, but on the other hand the Orchestra is an organization that services older people because it's an organization from yesteryear. It's the older players that keep the Orchestra alive. Because the Orchestra is an old-time organization. There is always gonna be a Conductor who, when if everybody plays well, is gonna take the credit. And if it's not as good as it should be, the Conductor will always blame the Orchestra. You're always gonna have 1st Principal players, and a 1st Desk that threatens everybody else and (perhaps at best) challenges them. There may be a few things that are changing (like the number of women players), but in general the Orchestra is a tradition that goes back hundreds of years.*

Hence, to a certain (and perhaps even disproportionate) degree, Western Classical Music relies upon the more senior seasoned players. David W. E. Smith (1989) concluded that the Orchestra setting is a *great place to grow old*.

Ironically, more than 36% of people who are 65 years old suffer from one or more of seven chronic conditions. The American Geriatrics Society (2007) listed these as: Arthritis, High Blood Pressure, Heart Disease, Diabetes, Lung Disease, Stroke, and Cancer. Furthermore, the incidence of involvement with one or more of these conditions is as high as 80% for people above the age of 70. Undoubtedly, ageing means that time takes a toll on the organs and systems in the body.

(58y, M, va)   *I do have diabetes, and I feel that when my sugar is too high it is difficult to play on stage. First, I perspire more. Then, lately I feel like I have less vitality and am tired more.*

Cavanaugh (1997) points to the fact that these might engage the cardiovascular system, bones, muscles and joints, the digestive system, kidneys, bladder and urinary tract, brain and nervous system, eyes, ears, teeth, skin, nails and hair, sleep cycle, weight, and sexuality. Furthermore, age-related effects on one's mental abilities might include: insults to basic episodic memory processes, relational memory and recollection, and/or semantic memory. Ageing can also cause deficits for specific memory as well as an increase in false memories, not to mention the more generalized syndromes such as Dementia and Alzheimer's disease. Therefore, the overriding question we must ask ourselves is:

How do Orchestra musicians retain their high level of functional music abilities well beyond the 5th Decade?

Undoubtedly, musicians have developed aptitudes, and a host of 'almost super-human' cognitive-motor skills (Parry, 2004; Rink, 2002). And, such facilities are continuously interacting, moment by moment, with a multitude of music-driven affective states and emotions (Chaffin & Lemieux, 2004; Connolly & Williamon, 2004).

(55y, M, perc)   *I really don't understand it. It is true that compared to how we played when we were younger, we should not be able to play as we do today. Yet, we are still in an Orchestra; maybe even one of the best in all Europe. But by all logic maybe we shouldn't be able to do what we do. Yes, we might still be able to play, but perhaps not at the level that other people are paying to come see us play. And that we're able to keep up those very highly toned skills, when most other people my age have trouble walking and fall down steps. So how do we musicians do it? Well, I don't know.*

One explanation might be that, as a group of people, music performers are simply more resilient to the effects of ageing than the general population. Another explanation might account for the systematic musical training that players undergo across their lifespan development. Or perhaps, there is some aspect of the profession as a *lifestyle* that immunizes players from the vicissitudes of ageing more than members of other occupational regimens.

1.3 The Effects of Music on Ageing

Although we have little information about the effects of ageing on professional Orchestra musicians, the outcomes of music engagement with older adult populations have been known for some time (Park, 2015). There are many literature reviews focusing on the general contribution of music to positive ageing (e.g., Bruhn, 2002; Charcur et al., 2022; Clift et al., 2010b; Hays et al., 2002). Programmes of Music Education for seniors have also promoted music instrument lessons (Bugos et al., 2007; Creech et al., 2013; Hallam et al., 2012; Jordan, 2019; Mansens et al., 2018; Perkins & Williamon, 2014), Choir ensembles (Clift et al., 2010a; Johnson et al., 2017; Joseph & Southcott, 2018; Lamont et al., 2018; Maury & Rickard, 2022; Southcott, 2009; Wise et al., 1992), public group singing and vocal lessons (Davidson et al., 2014; Hillman, 2002), and band/orchestra practice (Coffman, 2002; MacRitchie & Garrido, 2019). Wilfried Gruhn, a former professor of Music Education and a researcher on the neurobiology of learning from the Freiburg Music University (Germany), referred to teaching music at the other end of the spectrum (i.e., the 3rd and 4th Age of Human Development) as *Music Geragogy* (Gruhn, 2021). Others highlight Music Therapy clinical interventions for the elderly (e.g., Bright, 1980; Gibbons, 1988; Palmer, 1989; Smith & Lipe, 1991), and cognitive benefits from a musical activity in older adults (e.g., Abrahan et al., 2019). Further, one special issue of *Psychomusicology: Music, Mind, & Brain* (2002, Volume 18) examined the shortfalls of music perception among the elderly, highlighting the importance of music-performance groups for seniors. Park (2015) contended that musical activities contribute to improving quality of life in older people by increasing psychological well-being and decreasing anxiety and depression.

> There is a great potential using music as part of a cost-effective strategy to promote the well-being of healthy community-dwelling older people as well as institutionalized older adults with Dementia. Participating in musical activities, from simply listening to music to more active engagements in singing or playing musical instruments, can be one of the most effective non-verbal communication methods for older people with varying degrees of physical and mental capacities. (pp. 260–261)

Worth mentioning here are several commercial efforts and popular 'self-help' books that advocate healthy ageing through amateur chamber-music playing. One such book was written by Ada P. Kahn (1999) titled: *Keeping the Beat: Healthy Ageing Through Amateur Chamber Music Playing*. This text promotes the joys of tuning up mature minds and bodies through participation in music-making. Further, Don D. Coffman inspired an American movement known as *New Horizons Bands* for senior-citizen novices; Coffman developed a vast literature on the topic (e.g., Coffman, 2002; Coffman & Adamek, 1999; Coffman & Levey, 1997). Even the National Association for Music Education (MENC, USA) commissioned a Special Interest Group to examine how music teachers might provide more meaningful music experiences in such a way that all individuals could continue to participate in music performance in later life. *MENC* developed guidebooks for teachers (e.g., Jellison, 2000), and hosted a national workshop titled 'Music and Lifelong Learning' (September, 2007). In the United Kingdom, music was seen to make a significant contribution to living happily and healthily in old age; *Orchestras Live* provided projects that address the concerns of an ageing population. As music has long been seen to provide physiological benefits, live Orchestral music seems to have a power to stimulate and motivate. The report of the UK All-Party Parliamentary Group on Arts, Health and Wellbeing (2017), titled *Creative Health: The Arts for Health and Wellbeing*, detailed the significant impact of the arts on maintaining mental and physical fitness, aiding recovery, and supporting longer lives. Music engagement, then, has been seen as helping to meet the major challenges facing ageing. For example, the *Hear and Now* project of the London Philharmonia with people who were diagnosed as suffering from Dementia whereby music seems to have had the ability to retrieve memories that were thought to have been lost forever.

1.4 Filling the Gap: A 'Call' for Empirical Study

Nonetheless, the above-mentioned efforts do not widen our knowledge about senior-aged Orchestra musicians. A comprehensive survey of the literature will indicate that a limited number of studies have been executed among Symphony Orchestra players as participants. Among the topics are:

a) Skills, such as aural skills, musical skills, and handedness: Aggleton et al., 1994; Brodsky et al., 1999; Langer et al., 2009.
b) Practice and rehearsal regimens: Biasutti, 2013; Galvao, 2000.
c) Orchestra life, career, and employment: Allmendinger et al., 1996; Carter, 1995/1996; Dobson & Gaunt, 2015; Fassang, 2006; Fetter, 1993; Gaunt & Dobson, 2014; Hendricks, 2014; Henson, 1994; Kivimaki & Jokinen, 1994; Olbertz, 2006; Parasuraman & Nachman, 1987; Sergeant & Himonides, 2019.
d) Community work projects: Abels & Hafeli, 2014; Gaunt & Dobson, 2014.
e) Neuroscience, brain, and psychophysiology: Sluming et al., 2007; Theorell et al., 2007.
f) Acoustics, sound levels, and hearing: Babin, 1999; Carterette & Kendall, 1996; Eaton & Gillis, 2002; Emmerich et al., 2008; Hasson et al., 2009; Kahari et al., 2001; Woolford et al., 1988.
g) Health, mental health, and prevention of injury: Bartel & Thompson, 1995; Brandfonbrener, 1997; Brodsky, 1995, 2000, 2006; Brodsky & Sloboda, 1997a; Cohen & Bodner, 2019; Cohen & Ginsborg, 2021; Dillinger, 1997; Felger, 2014; Fry, 1986a, 1986b; Gembris et al., 2018; Harper, 2002; Holst et al., 2011; James, 1984, 2000; Kenny & Ackermann, 2015; Kenny et al., 2014, 2016; Langerdorfer et al., 2006; Mathews & Mathewa, 1993; Middlestadt & Fishbein, 1989; Parasuraman & Purohit, 2000; Piperek, 1981; Ricket et al., 2013, 2014a, 2014b; Smith, 1992; Steptoe & Fidler, 1987; Voltmer et al., 2012; Whelan, 1994; Yueng et al., 1999.

Despite the above initiatives, we simply know very little about old(er) musicians. According to Jeffri (2007), no one has tackled the unique and urgent needs of artists as they grow old. As an industry based on the lives and talents of the people in it, there is little information about the condition of its members in the profession as they age. Among the few studies focusing on music across the lifespan, are Brandfonbrener, 2003; Brodsky, 2011; Gembris & Heye, 2014; Kenny & Ackermann, 2017;

Kenny et al., 2018; MacRichie & Garrido, 2019; Smith, 1988, 1989. One much-welcomed book was *Musical Aptitude from a Lifespan Perspective* edited by Gembris (2006); this volume consists of nine papers originally presented at a 2002 international conference (of the same name). Another is a 2009 publication by Rineke Smilde from Hanze University of Applied Sciences in Groningen (the Netherlands) titled: *Musicians as Lifelong Learners: Discovery through Biography*. An additional set of articles can be found in the journal *Medical Problems of Performing Artists*; a special issue to ageing (1999, Volume 14) contained four clinical case vignettes. Finally, there are roughly a dozen papers among various medical and social science journals (e.g., Barton, 2004). But, for the most part, all of these highlight 'underperformance' and 'loss of skill' illustrating age-related deficits to music performance; they do not explore possible explanations for how players are able to maintain their skills despite ageing. In short, the literature that does exist on old(er) players generally shows the *ill effects of ageing* on music performance. For example:

a) Deficiencies of rhythmic timing: Krampe et al., 2001.
b) Deficits to fine motor movement: Krampe, 2002.
c) Discrepancies of visual perception: Kadrmas et al., 1996.
d) Losses of hearing: Behar et al., 2006; Henoch & Chesky, 1999.
e) Insufficiencies of voice: Sataloff, 1992.
f) Impairments of central and peripheral nervous system: Lederman, 1999.
g) Damage subsequent to conditions such as arthritis: Dawson, 1999; Hoppmann & Ekman, 1999.

I would like to point out that there are a few wonderful books written by Orchestra players on life as a professional player within a Symphony Orchestra (e.g., Cottrell, 2004; Danziger, 1995; Davis, 2004). These are based not only on casual conversations, but also on more formal verbal discourse between the author and other players within the same Orchestra (i.e., *insider research*). But yet, these authors specifically refrain from engaging with issues considered 'taboo' (such as performance nerves and effects of ageing). So perhaps, another reason we know very little about old(er) musicians is simply because musicians themselves do not discuss such matters as they view these as *off-limits*. Hence, not only is little known about Seasoned Musicians who are still in the Orchestra, but the same players who could have passed on helpful information to young(er) players continue to remain silent.

Nevertheless, another reason for our lack of knowledge about the vocation and members of the profession is that researchers themselves do not often recruit professional full-time contract Symphony Orchestra players in their investigations. Undoubtedly, Orchestra musicians are exceptionally hard to motivate and subsequently engage (i.e., recruit) in time-demanding non-music-performance tasks such as participating in empirically based research projects. We might also assume that there has been no great interest in ageing among Seasoned Musicians. As the ageing process invariably involves deteriorating levels of previously acquired skill, the subject of ageing is often considered a topic that is not open for discussion among performing musicians. But yet, old(er) players are much more prevalent today among the roster of Orchestra members than in previous times. Anecdotal evidence points out that roughly 40% of all Orchestra musicians are currently above 50 years old. It is interesting to note that the *International Musician* magazine, the official publication of the American Federation of Musicians of the United States and Canada (AFM), documented that among the more than 100,000 subscribers in 2010 was a subset of 40,280 (40%) who had been playing for over 30 years, of which 62% ($n = 24,910$) had been a registered union member for at least 30 years, and 59% ($n = 23,850$) were between 40 and 55 years old. I suggest that more research efforts need to focus on performing musicians who have maintained a professional career well into the 5th Decade of their lifespan. Such efforts are inevitable, if for no other reason than because performing musicians are living to an old(er) age, extending their phase of active music-making well beyond what was once considered time to withdraw from effective professional activity. Subsequently, there are just as many *seasoned musician*s on the concert stage as there are *aspiring young talents* (Brand-fonbrener, 2003). It is a gross oversight to disregard seasoned music performers who have persevered regardless of the human ageing process. There is a serious need for attention to be placed on those who *still can perform* music despite their age! Here is a comment from one participant Orchestra player in the current study:

(41y, M, va)   *So, while there may be 50% who experience a decline and are in the process of leaving the Orchestra, there are still another 50% of the players who stay on and that doesn't happen to them. Some claim the percentage of players over 50 years old are around 40%. Especially in America because by law they can't be fired till they approach 70— so they get an extra 5 years unless they are deteriorating. I think that is amazing. In this country it's 65 years old. So, it might be different in the UK or in Germany. But overall, the statistics show that about 30% of the roster of all full-time contract players in Orchestras are over 50. Clearly that doesn't mean they'll make it past [age] 60. Still, you're not talking about a small phenomenon, even when you say that 50% of them will not be able to continue. I would agree that at least 20% of the Orchestra players are going to make it to 65. Effectively, if you have an 80-player Orchestra, that's about 16–20 people. That's a lot of people.*

Below is a very interesting *blog* commentary published in the classical music e-magazine *Interlude*, titled: 'Challenges for the Aging Musician'. Author Janet Horvath (2019) previously published a 2010 guidebook for musicians on preventing injury (Horvath, 2010). Horvath had been the associate principal Cellist for the Minnesota Orchestra for 32 years (1980–2012). The following is an excerpt from the annotation:

Challenges for the Aging Musician

Playing a musical instrument is an amazing endeavor. It's thrilling when a performance is everything we want it to be and the audience erupts in applause. If we've conveyed the beauty, meaning, and emotion of the music, and not the physical effort, we're gratified. Behind the scenes though, every time we pick up our instruments, we are challenged on every level. Mastering an instrument requires much more than innate ability. Developing precision, coordination, fluency, and speed, requires hours of diligent practice, concentration, and discipline, while enduring performance anxiety, the stress of auditions, and a highly competitive environment.

Somehow, we are able to cope with these challenges. In fact, we are willing to do anything to bring off our performances, even to the point of self-destruction!

Many of us are unaware of the mishaps that may occur along the way. Playing a musical instrument is physically taxing. Despite our best intentions we're at risk of injury due to several factors: unusual and awkward postures, long hours, endless repetition, and poor ergonomics such as ill-fitting chairs or equipment.

Unlike professional athletes and dancers who rarely continue at the elite level beyond their mid-30s, musicians have unusually long careers. It's not uncommon for a musician to play in an Orchestra three decades or more— not including the years of study and playing in student or amateur groups. I've lost count how many times I've performed Tchaikovsky Symphony No. 4, with its pages of tremolo, or very long works such as Shostakovich's complex, confounding 70-minute Symphony No. 7. People retire after 30 years in other careers! How do we keep it up?

Ageing poses unique challenges for the musician. When our bodies become less resilient it's more difficult to adapt to the strenuous nature of our professions. We're more prone to injury in part due to muscle, bone, tendon, and ligament changes when our bodies slow down. Ageing causes bones to become less stable, and the strength, size, and endurance of muscle tissue erodes. With time joints become less resistant to wear and tear, in part due to the fact that our cartilage—the tissue that

cushions the tips of the bones in our joints— loses water, making joints more vulnerable to injury from repetitive motion and stress. Less flexible joints can cause us to lose range of motion.

Body composition changes as we age. Body fat increases, while muscle mass decreases. Older musicians might feel the need to practice more to maintain the high levels expected of us just to 'keep up', at a time when individuals in other professions are 'winding down'. We might also become de-conditioned, even though we know we should exercise more to maintain strength and fluidity.

All of these issues contribute to reaching maximum exposure—a physical therapy term that indicates when muscles, ligaments, and tendons have broken down to the point they cannot function properly, when tissues reach the apex or the limit of what they are capable of.

Each individual's maximum exposure varies according to their age, style of playing, posture, training, fitness levels, body size and build, and the number of years of playing. These individuals suffer from pervasive muscle fatigue, back pain, shoulder pain, chronic injuries, and a host of other issues.

Our technique is more sluggish, our memory is not always dependable, and we are tighter and weaker than when we were younger, making some passages more difficult to execute. We may also find we don't hear or see as well as we used to. Somehow, we continue our grueling and physically demanding schedules despite these changes.

An older musician as a result may feel replaceable, undervalued, and threatened by new talent coming in, especially if we notice our technique declining, further derailing our performance.

(Reprinted by permission of the author)

Expert performers devote most of their lives to attaining the highest levels of performance in a highly constrained activity; they start at very young ages, and the duration and intensity for their sustained training far exceeds the range of other activities pursued by individuals in the normal population. Expert and exceptional performances have been shown to be mediated by cognitive and perceptual-motor skills, and by domain-specific physiological and anatomical adaptations (Ericsson & Lehmann, 1996). But yet, as mentioned above, it is rather uncommon for studies to undertake a *lifespan* perspective about music performers; albeit there are many who have professed they have done so! One exception that needs to be mentioned here was implemented by Claudia Spahn and Bernhard Richter (2006), former co-directors of the Freiburg Institute of Music Medicine (Germany). In their exploration of the singing voice across the lifespan, the researchers advanced a developmental model of the music-performance career. See Figure 1.1. It must be said that musicians are different from other occupations as far as career trajectories are concerned. For example, unlike athletes and dancers, professional musicians are capable—and to some extent expected—of providing high performance over a long period of 30–40 years or more. Only between the ages of 45 and 55 are the first signs of physical and psychological exhaustion, as well as a decrease of efficiency, seen. As illustrated in Figure 1.1, there are different trajectories for Vocalists *versus* Instrumentalists. Accordingly, the onset of an Instrumentalist career begins younger and ends later compared to Vocalists. That is, Instrumentalists reach their artistic maturity between the ages of 15 and 24, while Singers achieve the same stage between 23 and 30 years old. Perhaps the reasons for such variances are related to hormonal fluctuations that could easily delay the onset of a singing career and/or cause eventual vocal frailties occurring in later years. Moreover, the transition from employment to retirement is different for Instrumentalists compared to Vocalists. Gembris (2013) claims that some musicians retire earlier (e.g., Singers) while others (e.g., Orchestra players) retire much later. In addition, there are also differences between the instruments themselves as far as longevity and retirement are concerned. For example, Smith (1988) observed that Wind and Brass players retire in their 60s, while String players continue throughout their 70s. Nonetheless, it needs to be pointed out that few research initiatives have actually explored music-performance careers in late adulthood. To my knowledge (at the time of this writing) with the exception of Ralf T. Krampe (2006), previously from the Laboratory of Experimental Psychology at KU Leuven (Belgium), no one has attempted to grapple with the topic of maintaining musical performance skills among professional musicians at an old(er) age.

Regrettably, even findings from investigations that purportedly recruited 'musicians' or 'professional music performers' are very limited in scope. Perhaps one reason is because the inclusion criteria of the target population is misleading. For example, a Canadian research team led by Claud Alain et al. (2014) presented evidence from the scientific literature about the benefits of musical training on aural perceptual and cognitive skills among children and young adults. Although their

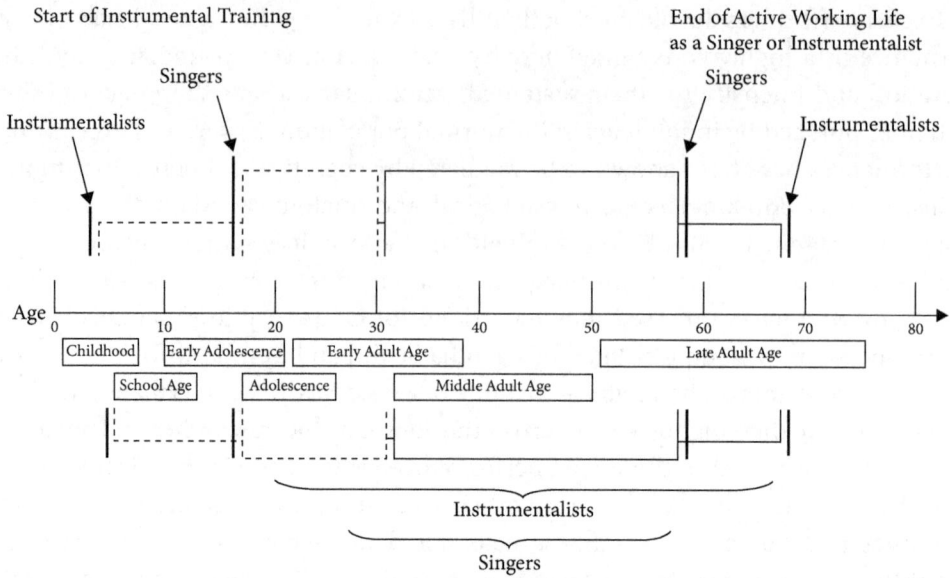

Figure 1.1 Model of Lifespan Music-Performance Career
Source: Spahn and Richter (2006). Reprinted with permission.

full intention was specifically to target the hearing and auditory brain, and therefore the results were published in the journal *Hearing Research*, the findings are unfortunately positioned as reflecting 'an overall benefit of musical training on the aging brain'. This more general assumption may simply be because of the very nature the authors have titled their article. To further understand the benefits of *lifelong musicianship* to our central auditory processing, Alain et al. investigated several studies focusing on concurrent sound segregation and its underlying cortical neural correlates. They claim to have found evidence from the neuroscience literature showing that musical training and lifelong musicianship enhance cognitive abilities. For instance, musicians aged between 45 and 65 executed auditory working memory tasks better than age-matched controls. The researchers claimed that the findings suggest musical training might create a cognitive reserve, which can then delay age-related cognitive declines even in non-musical tasks. But neither the authors nor subsequent readers actually questioned: 'Who were the participants in those studies?' 'How old were they?' 'What was the extent of music training or music performance engagement among participants?' 'Are those recruited valid ecological proxies representing musicians?' Namely, were the participants in the studies analysed by Alain et al. which led them to their conclusions, based on samples of young children learning musical instruments, teenagers, 18-year-old young-adult novice-musicians, 20-year-old young-adult music-amateurs, 30-year-old semi-professional musicians, or actual full-time professional music performers between 25 and 60 years old? Having said that, the highly cited take-away message is thus:

Musicianship is associated with neuro-plastic changes in the auditory brainstem responses, auditory cortex, motor cortex, visuo-spatial brain areas, as well as in higher-order brain areas involved in working memory and executive functions. Differences between musicians and non-musicians are due to training rather than genetic differences. [. . .] Given that musical training seems to strengthen acuity for basic auditory features, and affects performance on some complex auditory processes, it stands to reason that music engagement may prove to be an effective regimen to maintain or even improve listening skills in older adults. (p. 168)

As the study aligns itself within the context of *ageing* by virtue of its title and suggested focus on *lifelong musicianship*, there are many clinicians and researchers who embrace the report as evidence for enlisting music engagement to aid rehabilitation and rejuvenation of the elderly; and some even highlight the pertinent research-based advantages of musicians *versus* non-musicians. But are the rewards of music engagement *bona fide* evidence when considering old(er) musicians? Alain et al. themselves stated that the study of old(er) musicians *would be* particularly relevant to understanding the declines that often emerge with age. Further they wondered: *Can* music reduce the detrimental effects of normal ageing? Regrettably, such highly astute perceptions do not surface in the writings by those citing this study.

Another example is a study titled 'Keeping brains young with making music' by Lars Rogenmoser et al. (2019) from the Music, Neuroimaging, and Stroke Recovery Laboratory in the Department of Neurology at Beth Israel Deaconess Medical Center and Harvard Medical School (USA). The research team questioned whether or not music-making has a potential age-protecting effect on the brain. They examined anatomical magnetic resonance images among three different samples of participants based on their lifetime experience for music-making. For example, they compared between non-musicians, amateur musicians, and professional musicians. The findings indicated that all musicians had lower scores (e.g., younger brains) than non-musicians. The implication, then, is: Lifelong music-making triggers age-decelerating effects on the brain. This is a hugely important finding as far as resilience to the ill effects of ageing is concerned! Nonetheless, are such findings ecologically valid? Rogenmoser et al. defined professional musicians as either performing artists, full-time music teachers, or full-time conservatory students. Are these samples equivalent? Do these samples reflect a homogeneous representative group (proxy) for full-time 'professional' musicians? It is interesting to note that a later investigation by Matziorinis et al. (2022) failed to replicate Rogenmoser et al.'s findings.

Therefore, perhaps we need to look a little closer at differences between amateur musicians and professional musicians. There is evidence not only that individual differences tend to increase throughout life, but that individual differences already exist during childhood and adolescence; these expand in early adulthood and continuously increase in later life. Gembris (2013) states that obviously when professional musicians are compared to amateurs (untrained in music), differences are not simply regarding the amount of time spent in practice, nor the number of musical experiences accumulated over decades, nor vast differences in their levels of performance. Rather, while professional musicians increase their musical activities and achievements after the 2nd Decade of life, there is a general decrease in these same parameters for amateurs; that is, a continuing inverse correlation in the following years to come. Moreover, although professional musicians maintain their achieved high levels, amateur musicians—who are also members of a large array of professions, pursuits, interests, hobbies, and motivations—invest much of their time and energy in activities outside music performance. Therefore, the normally degenerative progression, as far as music performance is concerned, is a normative consequence. Gembris points out that this itself means the developmental processes of professional musicians *versus* amateurs are on an opposite trajectory.

The issue being forwarded here is the undeniable need to enlist real-world musicians when investigating aspects of music development and performance. The argument is actually not so new in concept. Over 25 years ago, in his groundbreaking publication outlining 30 years of investigation on musicians' temperament titled *The Musical Temperament: Psychology and Personality of Musicians*, Anthony E. Kemp (1996), former director of Music Education at the University of Reading (UK), noted that the real question between musicians *versus* non-musicians is not the *degree* (of engagement) but rather the *qualia* (depth of focus). Some studies (e.g., Rodrigues et al., 2013) do implement a high level of rigour when recruiting ecologically valid samples of musicians. Hence, in an effort to fill the gap, the current study exclusively recruited professional full-time contract Symphony Orchestra players to investigate *lifestyle and ageing* within the music performance profession.

Positive ageing is often seen as *successful ageing*. Daatland (2005) claimed that successful ageing "has to do with the road (process) more than the destination (end state)" (pp. 375–376). Moreover, as a vocation and lifestyle, the Symphony Orchestra seems to provide all the ingredients necessary for *well-being*. Steverink and Lindberg (2006) outlined a three-factor model highlighting the basic needs of human well-being: Affection, Behavioural Confirmation, and Status. Accordingly, Affection could be fulfilled when players feel liked, trusted, accepted, and empathized within their section and the overall Orchestra. Behavioural Confirmation would refer to players feeling they play their part well, contributing to a more common goal of expert music performance, and that they were useful as a constituent element in the success of the group effort. Status would be fulfilled by the respect players receive and offer each other within their section and beyond. This notion has been examined in more depth employing a brief multidimensional measure of *flourishing* referred to as the PERMA-Profiler (Butler & Kern, 2016); subsequently, the PERMA-Profiler was used with a sample of Classically trained musicians (Ascenso et al., 2018). Finally, readers should be aware of a specific perspective resounding throughout the pages of this book (outlined in detail in Chapter 11): *creative resilience.*

METHODS OF THE STUDY

1.5 The Interviews: A Case Study

This book is the scientific report of an interview study. The study can be seen as part of a wider case study focusing on professional Symphony Orchestra musicians. In his book *Real World Research*, Colin Robson (1993) from Huddersfield Polytechnic (UK), wrote that a *case study* is a strategy which involves an empirical investigation of a particular contemporary phenomena within its real-life context of a group or institution using multiple sources of evidence. Robson distinguished between strategies and tactics; a *strategy* refers to the general broad orientation addressing the research questions under investigation, whereas *tactics* are the specific methods of investigation. Further, *real world research* was outlined as employing hybrid designs which combine aspects of two or more traditional strategies; for example, using a survey within one or more case studies. Case studies can cover a single individual case, a set of individual cases (often referred to as a collective case study), or a specific community or social group (such as an occupational group). Case studies often describe and analyse activities and/or relationships. In general, case studies allow for data collection employing various means, including: observation (passive unobtrusive observation), interviews (using a standardized set of questions or a semi-structured interview guide specifying key topics), written documents, standardized tests (scales, repertory grids), projective methods, storytelling, life histories, role play, gaming, as well as recordings and transcriptions (from audio and video files). Robson was adamant that multiple sources of evidence commonly bring forward quantitative data (e.g., experiments, quasi-experiments, and surveys), as well as qualitative data (e.g., interviews). Accordingly, case studies are highly appropriate for exploration; the researcher can find out what is happening, seek new insights, ask questions, and assess phenomena in a new light. By incorporating a survey within a case study, researchers can collect descriptive data portraying profiles of people, events, or situations. By integrating experiments or quasi-experimental methods within a case study, researchers can collect explanatory data to illuminate problems or situations.

The current *interview study* serves as a means to explore the attitudes, perceptions, and experiences of professional full-time contract Symphony Orchestra musicians. The resultant conversations that occurred during the research seasons among five Orchestras in three countries (see full description below) allowed the players to explain certain aspects of their lives in their own words. The face-to-face interviews offered the possibility of modifying the line of enquiry, following up interesting responses, and investigating underlying motives in a way that postal and other self-administered questionnaires could not. Robson (1993) asserted that semi-structured interviews, where the interviewer has worked out a set of questions in advance, are far more functional than fixed structured interviews. A semi-structured interview platform allows the researcher to freely modify the order of topics based upon perception of what seems to be most appropriate in the context of the conversation; researchers can change the way questions are worded, give an ample number of explanations, and even modify or leave out some topics based on the appropriateness and flow of the conversation.

Clearly, the transcripts of the interviews, alongside other quantitative data that were completed by the players in the form of an 11-measure 12-page questionnaire booklet (see full description below), are a *multi-strategy approach.* In their 2021 book *Performing Music Research*, Aaron Williamon and colleagues from the Royal College of Music in London (UK), claimed that multi-strategy research is typically used to address a research question, solve a problem, or view a phenomenon from different perspectives. Multi-strategy research uses words to add further meaning to numbers, such as those that surface from survey questionnaires and/or standardized assessment measures. Accordingly, the multi-strategy format is especially warranted "when a research question cannot be answered using a single type of methodology and when the researchers seek multiple types of insight into one phenomenon" (Williamson et al., 2021, p. 47). The current study placed equal weight on both qualitative and quantitative methodologies, whereby information of an exploratory and/or explanatory nature is combined. The investigation considered narrative discourse conversation, and content-analyses of interviews and written materials, as well as descriptions of specific observations—all towards a synthesis of a storied account of the phenomenon being studied (e.g., Orchestra Lifestyle). In addition, the investigation analysed audio recordings of music performance (*in vivo/in situ* performances). All data was considered regardless of the methods used to generate responses. Williamon et al. claim that such a platform reflects a *concurrent triangulation design* whereby both qualitative and quantitative approaches are undertaken independently but simultaneously during the same single stage of research. Each addresses the same research questions, but each from a different perspective.

1.5.1 Recruitment Procedure

Initially, dozens of Orchestra managements across the USA, England, and Europe were contacted. Letters were sent seeking permission to communicate with a representative of each Orchestra members' committee (OMC). Many Orchestra managements were not open to the idea of conducting a research study inside the Halls of their organization, and thereafter declined the initiative. Orchestra managements in United States required written permission from the American Federation of Musicians prior to any correspondence with representatives of management or OMCs. Consequently, several days were spent in the Union Offices of the Local 802AFM

(Associated Federation of Musicians of Greater New York). I had assured the Union Manager that all collected data would remain anonymous. I had agreed to sign an affidavit transferring the final decision of which data would be included in this book to the Union. I had offered ultimate editorial privileges for all texts to be published to the Union Manager. Nonetheless, all of these guarantees and efforts were frowned upon. I was refused access to Orchestra players in the Greater New York Tri-State Area (potentially over 150 professional performing organizations). In retrospect, the Union reps, the Orchestra managements, and subsequently the players themselves, all seemed terrified as to what might surface from an interview study on the *taboo* topic of 'ageing'. It was feared that perhaps even just one player could lose their position as a result of 'opening up'. Nonetheless, some Orchestra managements outside the USA not only granted permission to approach OMCs, but also supplied the names and contact information of all elected representatives. These managements assisted in scheduling on-site meetings with the OMCs. Two of these Orchestras were in England: the *BBC Philharmonic Orchestra* (Manchester) and the *Hallé Orchestra* (Manchester). Two of the Orchestras were in Israel: the *Jerusalem Symphony Broadcasting Orchestra* (Jerusalem) and the *Israel Sinfonietta Orchestra* (Beer-Sheva). One Orchestra was in Germany: the *Freiburg Philharmonic Orchestra* (Freiburg). These five5 Orchestras were actively involved in advancing the study.

The above organizations fully complied in providing an environment for the collection of data from inside the Orchestras. With the help of the OMCs, detailed flyers were handed out to all Orchestra members (roughly 450 players), announcing a future public meeting on-site in their performance hall. These meetings were held in Orchestra lounges, *green rooms*, and the actual rehearsal Halls. The meetings were scheduled prior to, or immediately following, a full Tutti rehearsal. Attendance was on a voluntary basis. I point out that about half of each Orchestra attended (roughly 200 players). During a 20-minute session, while standing in front of the players without the enhancement of an audiovisual PowerPoint™ presentation, the concept of the proposed study was introduced; stages of the investigation were outlined, and a 2-year timeline was presented. These informative *Briefing & Recruiting Meetings* took place roughly 1 year prior to the planned active research phase. The players who were interested in receiving more information offered their contact details on a sign-up sheet. Then, these players were sent additional details via email. Further information sheets (as hard copies) were sent to the Orchestra administration offices. OMC representatives pinned these announcement flyers on bulletin boards specifically targeting the Orchestra members, and placed stacks on central coffee tables and lamp-side tables inside *Green Rooms*. Two months after the initial Briefing & Recruiting Meetings, a list of participant players from each Orchestra was finalized; all players who volunteered were accepted. Personal contact with each Orchestra player was maintained throughout the next 10 months via email. The dates of a 10-day on-site active phase of data collection was scheduled by each

OMC. Scheduling of each *research season* accounted for each Orchestra's calendar of travel (national and international touring dates), rehearsals (major performances with guest conductors), periods of yearly maintenance (for building and performance Hall as well as for musical instruments), and for Union-mandated vacation time.

Two months before each research season, OMCs were sent sealed envelopes for every participating player. Each A4 (8″ × 12″) envelope contained another smaller A5 (8″ × 6″) envelope, with the following documents:

a) Information Sheet
b) Consent Form To Participate in the study
c) 12-page Booklet consisting of 11 standardized questionnaires (fully detailed in Table 1.3).

All of these above-mentioned materials were anonymous. They were marked in advanced with a pre-assigned multiple-digit personal identification number (PIN). Specific digits of the PIN reflected the country and city of the Orchestra (international calling code), the Orchestra name, as well as the participant's number. For example, a hypothetical PIN could have been 44–020-LSO-012. This would have indicated: England (44), London (020), London Symphony Orchestra (LSO), participant #12 (012).

1.5.2 The Research Sample

The final research sample (referred to as the *full corpus*) was comprised of a total $N = 52$ professional full-time contract Orchestra players recruited from five professional Symphony Orchestras. Although the Orchestras were located in three countries (i.e., England, Germany, and Israel), the players themselves were born in more than 13 locations from around the world, including: Asia ($n = 1$, 2%: Singapore = 1); Central Europe ($n = 11$, 22%: France = 2, Germany = 8, Ireland =1); Eastern Europe ($n = 11$, 22%: Poland = 2, Romania = 2, Ukraine = 1, Russia = 6); the Middle East ($n = 3$, 6%: Israel = 3); the United Kingdom ($n = 23$, 44%: England = 20, Scotland = 2, Australia = 1); and the United States ($n = 3$, 6%). On average, the players were 48 years old ($SD = 10.12$, $Mdn = 51$, Range 27–64); they were born between the years 1946 and 1983. The sample reflects a normal sample of professional full-time contract Orchestra musicians. As an example, Gembris and Heye (2014) provided information from $N = 2536$ Orchestra musicians of 132 publicly funded orchestras (Kulturorchestern) in Germany; the German Orchestra musicians were reported to be on average 45 years old (Range 20–69). Among the participating players in the current study were 29 (56%) males. The majority ($n = 43$, 83%) self-reported to be right-hand dominant (based on the hand they employed for writing with a pen and holding a toothbrush); a few ($n = 4$, 8%) reported to be left-hand dominant. On this topic Jancke et al. (1997) reported that left- or mixed-handedness in musicians is only slightly (4–6%) higher than non-musician samples. It should be noted that no formal exam of handedness was implemented.

The full corpus consisted of 34 (65%) players from the String section (Violin = 16, Viola = 7, Cello = 8, Double Bass = 3); 11 players (22%) from the Woodwind section (Flute = 3, Clarinet = 3, Oboe = 1, Bassoon = 4); 4 (8%) players from the Brass section (Trumpet = 2, French Horn = 1, Trombone = 1); 2 (4%) Harp players; and 1 (2%) Percussion player (Xylophone = 1). The positions of employment as reported by the players were: Concertmaster = 1, Leader = 1, Principal = 16 (31%), Co-Principal = 2, Sub-Principal = 11 (21%), and Rank-&-File Players = 21 (40%). It should be noted that in some Orchestras the 'Concertmaster' is referred to as the 'Leader', 'Section Leaders' are referred to as 'Principals', 'Principals' are referred to as '1sts' (or 'Number 1s'), 'Sub-Principals' are referred to as '2nds' (or 'Number 2s'), and 'Rank-&-File' Tutti players are referred to as 'Section Players'.

All participant-players volunteered one year in advance of the data collection. They signed an 'Informed Consent Form to Participate', completed an 11-measure 12-page booklet of standardized questionnaires (see section 1.6.3.3, Table 1.3), and took part in a pre-scheduled 2-hour individual session (see section 1.6.3.1). The sessions were comprised of conversation, a tapping exercise (see section 1.6.3.2, described in Chapter 8), and two *in vivo/in situ* music performances (see section 1.6.3.2, described in Chapter 10). Each Orchestra player received $55 USD cash payment as compensation for participating in the study; at the time of data collection the equivalent was to £40 GBP or €50 Euro.

I point out here that a smaller number of players are indicated in various analyses presented throughout the book; these samples are referred to as a *dataset*. Each analysis in each chapter will also describe the pertinent dataset. Although this level of detail may seem tedious to some readers, others may view such an account as fundamental.

Finally, a second sample of $N = 6$ retired players was recruited from two of the Symphony Orchestras participating in the sample (see Chapter 12). These musicians were on average 67 years old ($SD = 3.39$, Range 63–72). They had retired between the ages of 58 and 63 ($M_{Age} = 60$, $SD = 1.9$); they had been employed with a contract position for an average 31 years ($SD = 6.25$, Range 23–37). The sample of retired players consisted of 4 females and 2 males, who for the most part (83%) played String instruments.

1.5.3 Methods, Materials, and Equipment of the Study

1.5.3.1 Semi-Structured Interview

The first method of collecting data was qualitative in nature through a single individual 2-hour interview session held on-site in each Orchestra's rehearsal hall. The current study employed a semi-structured interview format as an overarching template.

Few studies publish the full inventory of questions they employed to guide their interview study. One exception is the Orchestra Members' Semi-Structured Interview Protocol by MacRitchie and Garrido (2019) that was adapted from Hendricks (2014); this inventory was not suitable for the goals of the current study. Hence, a predetermined set of principal themes for the interview was developed; these were conceived as 'considerations of ageing for music performance'. All of the listed issues were acquired from comprehensive texts on music performance, including: Gordon (2006), Parncutt and McPherson (2002), Rink (2002), and Williamon (2004). See Table 1.2. As can be seen in Table 1.2, there are 6 main themes and 60 sub-themes. This kind of pre-planning—which some refer to as an *interview schedule*—was not only a guide-map for every 2-hour session, but provided the underpinning of a standardized focal point of attention on all topics to be covered with every participant. Although highly specific in focus, the template outlined in Table 1.2 also allowed the freedom, flexibility, and spontaneity to respond to each musician personally. I point out that sometimes it was important to question a player for the sake of clarification, and sometimes it was necessary to ask a player to provide more information than what was initially said. Such a template endorsed a more rigorous structure, whereby the same level of identical conversation could be retained for each and every individual.

The interviews consisted of introductory remarks including an explanation of the interview. Then, issues of confidentiality, and the presence of audio recording equipment were outlined. The main body of the interview was implemented as two 40-minute segments of conversation. In between these, there were two more active performance tasks (described below in section 1.5.3.2; see also Chapters 8–10). Finally, a standardized closure statement was made.

Table 1.2 Interview Template: Considerations of Ageing for Music Performance

Themes	Topics of Consideration	Subtopics of Discussion
Theme I	**Mental**	1. Brain Mechanisms, Information Processing 2. Mental Skills, Attention, Concentration 3. Memory and Memorizing Music 4. Keeping Preparation Fresh and Focused 5. Improvising 6. Structural Representation of Music (Flexibility—Stability) 7. Types of Errors (Structure-Preserving, Structure-Violating) 8. Automaticity
Theme II	**Motor and Physical**	1. Physical Challenge and Demands Physical Fitness 2. Dealing with Repetition and Drill 3. Practice (Individual, Ensemble) 4. Kinaesthetic Memory, Memorized Performances 5. Performance Preparation, Preparing for Performance 6. Rehearsing

Themes	Topics of Consideration	Subtopics of Discussion
		7. Body Movement Communicating with the Body in Performance
		8. Overall Tempo, Tempo Fluctuation
		9. Accuracy, Psychomotor Speed
		10. Coordination (Between Limbs, Different Players)
		11. Use of Relaxation Techniques and Breathing
		12. Physiological Considerations (e.g., Fatigue, Endurance during Performance or Travel
		13. Hearing/Seeing the Conductor or Score
		14. Repetitive Stress Injuries, Tremor (At Rest, Postural or Kinetic)
Theme III	**Emotional**	1. Motivation Performance and Spiritual Life
		2. Emotional Communication Performance and Human Interaction
		3. Creativity Originality
		4. Discipline, Artistic Integrity, and Commitment
		5. Performance Anxiety, Performance Nerves, Stage Fright, Drugs
		6. Dispositional Traits, Relationships Among Players
		7. Work Satisfaction
		8. Boredom, Regret
		9. Sense of Responsibility/Vocation/Meaning
		10. Generalized Stress
		11. Emotional Involvement in Performance
		12. Emotional Components of Instrument
		13. Gender Issues
Theme IV	**Musical**	1. Expression Music, Expressivity, Communication
		2. Musical Competence, Intonation, Playing in Time, Sight-Reading
		3. Musical Interpretation, Music Analysis
		4. Musical Potential
		5. Performance: Piano, Strings, Winds, Percussion, Solo Voice, Conducting
		6. Technical Considerations (e.g., Control and Maintenance of Articulation, Dynamics, Rhythm, Timbre, Attack, Tone Quality)
		7. Dealing with New Repertoire, Restricted Repertoire)
		8. Contemporary Music
		9. Improvisation
		10. Adaptation to Conductors' Interpretation and Demands
		11. Solo vs Section Playing
		12. Opportunities for Chamber/Solo Career
		13. Position in Orchestra
Theme V	**Environmental**	1. Work Environmental Influences
		2. Working Conditions, Score Size
		3. Competitive/Isolated Environment
		4. Contribution to Community (Education, Charity)
		5. Public's Expectations
		6. Combining Personal Life with Work/Travel
		7. Cultural and Socio-Economic Considerations (e.g., Social Status/Prestige, Support from Institutions)
Theme VI	**Organizational and Financial**	1. Job Security
		2. Hierarchy According to Competence
		3. Specialization
		4. Evaluation
		5. Advancement and Mobility ('Entrapment')
		6. Organizational Involvement

The interviews were digitally audio recorded with an *H2 Handy Portable Stereo Digital Recorder* (ZOOM). This model features W-XY microphone patterns with four microphone capsules and signal processing allowing front (90 cardioid) and rear (120 cardioid) polar patterns. The microphone was positioned in between the researcher and the participating Orchestra musician, enabling clear audio recording of the conversation. Namely, the full interview session was recorded (front and rear) as a 2-channel audio file employing a 44.1 khz WAV format at a 16-bit resolution. Each individual interview was initially deposited to a 2GB SD memory storage card, and then subsequently downloaded to a computer hard drive. The audio files were itemized (employing PIN number) with a date/time stamp (of the recording), and the file size. For example (hypothetically):

44–020-LSO-012   19Jun2010at14:20   15.08MB

44–020-LSO-015   20Jun2010at08:00   17.08MB

The contents of the conversations that occurred in the interviews were analysed from verbatim transcriptions. These are delineated in Part II of the book (see Chapters 3–7).

1. 5.3.2 Performance Tasks

During the interview sessions, the participants engaged in two performance tasks. These are outlined in Part III of the book (see Chapters 8–10). The Psychomotor Finger-Tapping Tasks (see Chapter 8) were a series of five isochronous exercises presented on an *IBM Thinkpad X31* laptop computer (Intel Pentium™ M, 1.7GHz processor) with a 12″ TFT display. They were:

a) Self-paced tapping at a spontaneous tapping rate
b) Self-paced tapping at a preferred rate
c) Speeded uni-manual single-finger tapping with the right hand
d) Speeded uni-manual single-finger tapping with the left hand
e) Bimanual alternate-finger (right–left, right–left) tapping.

The tasks were programmed and executed with *EPrime* software (Psychological Software Tools, PST). *EPrime* is a comprehensive stimulus presentation platform used to design experimental studies, and then run experiments while collecting timed response data. A proprietary sequence of events was programmed specifically for the investigation. Among other events logged and recorded were Inter-Tap Intervals (ITIs).

The Music Performance Task (see Chapter 10) was based on an original music piece composed specifically for the study by Israeli Symphonic and Operatic Composer Moshe Zorman (see 'Concert Program Notes' description of the pieces on the Cover Note preceding Part III). A very high level of music-performance skill was demanded from the participant-players to execute the piece; the player's utmost attention to technical detail and musical articulation-expression was required. I point out that Zorman composed three stylistically similar versions for the study: (1) Strings (also Harp); (2) Woodwinds (also Xylophone); and (3) Brass. The music notation was scored as individual parts for all 16 Orchestra instruments. See Appendix A.

The two active performance tasks (i.e., psychomotor and music performance) were seen as Quasi-Experimental studies. The *quasi-experimental approach* (QEA) is a valuable method. Clearly *QEAs* are platforms that attempt to liberate the empirical experiment in an effort to cope more realistically with conditions outside a laboratory. *QEAs* are highly similar to lab-based experimental methods with the exception that there may be no possibility of random assignment to experimental conditions, and most often there is no possibility for comparison or control groups (Robson, 1993).

1.5.3.3 Questionnaire Booklet

Another methodology of data collection was quantitative in nature; this was through an 11-measure 12-page survey booklet. The booklet consisted of 11 standardized questionnaires and assessment measures. See Table 1.3. On the cover of the booklet was a 'Thank You' note to the players for agreeing to participate in the research study. The participants were reminded that all questionnaires were anonymous; they were instructed to complete all the questions in the booklet, not to skip any questions, nor to leave any item blank. The booklet was received and completed in advance of the individual single 2-hour pre-scheduled interview session. As a result, there was ample opportunity to scan through each booklet, and to find items lacking responses (i.e., missing data); each participant was requested to fill in any missing data during the first few minutes of the interview before moving on to the planned topics of discussion (as listed in Table 1.2). The questionnaire survey booklet was concerned with facts, behaviours, beliefs, and attitudes of the participating professional Symphony Orchestra musicians. There was no real interest in any specific individual per se, but rather on profiles and generalized statistics drawn from the total sample or a dataset. The questionnaire survey booklet was seen more as a research strategy than a method or technique. The cover note also detailed the further stages of the study, including:

a) Attendance at a single pre-scheduled 2-hour interview consisting of conversation on relevant subjects
b) Participation in a computerized finger-tapping game
c) Participation in recording a piece of music scored as a part for their own instrument; the participating musician players were asked to bring their own specific instrument to the interview.

Table 1.3 Measures of the 12-Page Questionnaire Survey Booklet

Item	Title	Description
Q1	***Orchestra Musicians Bio Sketch*** (Chapter 2)	Developed by Brodsky 1. General Descriptive Information: age, gender, musical instrument, position in the Orchestra 2. Parental Family Environment: place of birth, year of birth, attitude of family (grandparents, parents and/or siblings) towards music tradition and music education 3. Education: beginning of music education, course of music education, music achievements and difficulties, and teachers (coaches, masters, and mentors) 4. Professional Experiences: First public performances (debut), achievements and obstacles, music competitions, foreign travel and scholarships, honours and awards 5. Choice of music profession: personal contracts with eminent musicians (performers, conductors, and Orchestras)
Q2	***Estimation of Livelong Deliberate Practice*** (Chapter 2)	Developed by Brodsky 1. Stages and Ages: <10, 10–19, 20–29, 30–39, 40–49, During last decade During past year
Q3	***Weekly Hours of Engagement*** (Chapter 2)	Developed by Brodsky 1. Music Activities: Performing in Orchestra, ensembles, solos Rehearsing Practising Teaching 2. Number of Pupils per Week: 1–9, 10–20, 20–30
Q4	***Self-Evaluation of Skills and Abilities*** (SESA) (Chapter 11)	Developed by Brodsky 1. Motor Abilities: skills related to playing an instrument 2. Hearing Abilities: skills related to notational audiation 3. Inter-Musical Abilities: skills related to playing with others 4. Intra-Musical Abilities: skills related to interpretation and expressiveness
Q5	***Positive and Negative Affect Scale*** (PANAS) (Chapter 11)	Watson et al. (1988)
Q6	***Selection, Optimization, and Compensation*** (SOC) (Chapter 11)	Baltes et al. (1999a)
Q7	***Maslach Burnout Inventory*** (MBI) (Chapter 11)	Maslach and Jackson (1981/1986); Maslach and Leiter (2008) *Orchestra Musicians Survey* adapted from *MBI* for professional Symphony Orchestra musicians by Brodsky in 1993 (Brodsky, 1995, 1996; Brodsky & Sloboda, 1997a, 1997b)
Q8	***Lifespan-Longing*** (L-L) (Chapter 11)	Baltes (1997) *Life Longing for a Soloist Career* adapted from L-L for professional Symphony Orchestra musicians by Brodsky

Item	Title	Description
Q9	*Life Management in the Occupational Domain* (LMOD) (Chapter 11)	Weise et al. (2002)
Q10	*The Social Circle* (Chapter 11)	Developed by Brodsky 1. Acquaintance with Orchestra musicians aged 30–50, 50–60, 65+ 2. Acquaintance with retired Orchestra musicians 3. Acquaintance with retired non-musician retirees
Q11	*Music Performance Self-Evaluation* (MPsE) (Chapter 10)	Yoshie et al. (2009a, 2009b) 1. Artistic Expression 2. Temporal Accuracy 3. Technical Accuracy

As can be seen in Table 1.3, several of the measures were developed specifically for the current study (Q1, Q2, Q3, Q4, Q10). Further, there were standardized assessments (Q5, Q6, Q9, Q11). Finally, some of the measures were adaptations (Q7, Q8). These later versions altered the texts by considering the occupational nature of the sample. Williamon et al. (2021) highlight that such adaptations are usually the case within Music Science Research. Some of the measures listed in Table 1.3 provide descriptive qualitative data in the form of Free-text responses (Q1, Q10). Other measures supply quantitative nominal data responses of a *categorical nature* (Q2, Q3, Q6); and several others deliver quantitative nominal data responses of an *ordinal nature* (Q4, Q5, Q7, Q8, Q9, Q11). Furthermore, the booklet employs several response types, including: Forced Choice response (agree/disagree), Closed Questions, and Open Questions. The booklet also asked respondents to deposit Diaries (i.e., free-text transcriptions of their personal history), as well as Scales and Tests, Attitudinal Measures (using summated Likert-type scale ratings), and Semantic Differential scales (designed to explore a series of bipolar ratings).

INTRODUCTION TO THE BOOK

1.6 The Book

From the outset of the current research initiative, I had an *a priori conception* that the various themes identified, coded, and analysed in the interview sessions would need to be part of a more comprehensive context—involving at times the entire corpus as well as several smaller datasets—employing both quantitative and qualitative data analyses. Namely, that the depth and complexity might be lost if reported within several journal articles adhering to strict word limits (< 4,000 words, inclusive). Therefore, I had conceived of an extensive volume as answering the needs of an investigation exploring this under-researched topic of music engagement across the lifespan, especially emphasizing ageing among Symphony Orchestra players.

Ironically, the materials presented herein seem to have become my own lifelong journey. From the initial presentation of the idea to receiving a letter of commission from Oxford University Press, to active research seasons in three countries with five Orchestras collecting data from the players, to analysing transcripts and writing draft chapters, till completion of a full text—all tallied—18–20 years have gone by! Albeit, the actual writing of the text itself was four years. It is perhaps not at all a coincidence that the researcher-author had to mature in age as a prerequisite to understanding what the participants themselves said about their own processes of ageing within a music-performance context. For several years, little was done with the materials collected. The interviews were transcribed (verbatim) from audio files; the music performances (recordings) were cropped and labelled as *prima vista* or Post-Practice performances; the 11-measure 12-page booklet survey data were entered in a statistics package (*Statistica*, StatSoft). Essentially, all materials were impeccably 'wrapped up' and placed in storage. In the interim, I developed a research niche intersecting the fields of Music Psychology and Traffic Psychology; a comprehensive picture of the findings that surfaced can be seen elsewhere (e.g., Brodsky, 2015). Then, during the Covid-19 Pandemic (March 2020), when all other active research endeavours were cancelled because of forced quarantines and lockdowns, I began to reread the interview transcripts. I listened to the full set of audio files, one by one, covering the entire 2-hour sessions of all 52 Orchestra players—and the additional 6 retired players. Ten years had passed since the interviews!

There do seem to be some positive benefits of living with complex data for a long time! My renewed listening seemed to have provided more clarity than I had had at the time of data collection. I wonder if some research topics on human behaviour just simply need time to *mature* for a more meaningful picture of the investigation to surface. Anecdotal evidence does demonstrate that concepts in science may take years to cultivate. After all, research-based theories are not like cooking a meal—following a written recipe using ingredients bought in a supermarket. Empirical science is more often experienced as finding a treasure on an unchartered isle! While discovery can indeed take a few hours, in some cases coming to a full understanding may take several years, and then a period of empirical validation might require several more years. It would seem that even Isaac Newton (1643–1727) spent several years thinking about astronomical motions of celestial objects; albeit, only when seeing an apple fall from a tree did Newton experience the actual 'aha' moment which inspired him to come to magnificent insights leading to the world-changing end-product known as *Newton's Law of Gravitational Force-Pull*.

1.6.1 Outline of the Book

The book is divided into four parts. Part I (Chapters 1–2) delineates the *background and foreground* of the Orchestra musician. After the current introductory chapter, Chapter 2 on being and becoming an Orchestra musician follows. The development of Orchestra musicians will be sketched, including: familial attitudes towards music traditions and education; music education and instrument tuition; performance experiences such as debuts and achievements, competitions, honours, rewards, and foreign travel scholarships; choosing the music-performance profession; and the estimation of Deliberate Practice over the lifetime. Finally, the chapter will focus on the Symphony Orchestra as an occupational environment, highlighting players' weekly activity (e.g., performing Orchestra, performing ensembles, performing solo rehearsing, Deliberate Practice, and teaching).

Part II (Chapters 3–7) outlines the various *considerations of ageing in a music-performance career*. Chapter 3 is about the mental considerations: mental skills, information processing, memory and memorizing music; attention and keeping preparation fresh and focused. Chapter 4 is about the motor considerations: physical challenges and demands physical fitness; dealing with repetition, drill, and practice; rehearsing and preparing for performances; kinaesthetic memory and memorized performances; body movement and communicating with the body in performance; and tempo, accuracy, fluctuation, and psychomotor speed. Thereafter, Chapter 5 highlights the emotional considerations, including: motivation, performance, and spiritual life; emotional communication; performance and human interaction; creativity and originality; discipline, artistic integrity, and commitment; performance nerves and anxieties; dispositional traits; relationships among players as well as emotional bonds with an instrument; and gender issues. Chapter 6 continues with musical considerations: music expressivity and structural communication; musical competence (such as playing in tune, playing in time, Sight-Reading, music analysis and interpretation); and musical potential. Finally, Chapter 7 closes Part II with the environmental considerations: work environment and working conditions; Orchestral position; and job security.

Part III (Chapters 8–10) targets *music performance*—empirical tasks specifically undertaken and reported in this book. Chapter 8 reports the perceptual motor finger-tapping task. Chapter 9 reports a thematic analysis of Think Aloud Protocols during a period of Deliberate Practice to polish a music performance from glitches and snags that may have previously surfaced—in an attempt to overcome malfunctions, anomalies, and near-errors of fingering or articulation. Then, Chapter 10 reports both *prima vista* Sight-Reading and a Post-Practice music-performance task; these were self-evaluated by the performers, as well as critiqued by independent external double-blind judges.

The final Part IV (Chapters 11–13) is about *finding some meaning* in the study of Seasoned Musicians. Chapter 11 offers a profile of Seasoned Musicians, including:

self-evaluation of skills and abilities (motor, inner hearing, inter-musical, intra-musical); mood and emotion; stress and Orchestral life; a behavioural inventory of positive ageing; assessment of 'life-longing' (regretful sentiment for a Soloist career lost); feelings of success, reaching potential, and satisfaction in the occupational domain (including indices of burnout); and one's social circle involving currently employed players as well as retired players (specifically looking at incidence of Dementia and Alzheimer's disease). Chapter 12 presents reports from retired Symphony Orchestra musicians, looking back at their development and years as a career-driven music performer. Finally, Chapter 13 presents a concluding statement on 'Musical Gerontivity', and summarizes the complete investigation package.

1.6.2 Intentions of the Book

It is my intention to present a case study among a sample of professional full-time contract players of Symphony Orchestras in which half of the sample have *played beyond the 5th Decade*. The investigation package attempts to explore the resilience of Seasoned Musicians to the vicissitudes of ageing, suggesting a more positive successful process of ageing than previously conceived. I point out that, from the onset, a fundamental basic element of the book, somewhat reflecting a 'contract' between the author and the reader, is that the contents herein have never been published before in the scientific journal literature. Some colleagues have noted (in personal communications) that publishing the data and findings herein as chapters of a book rather than within the annals of the scientific journal literature, can only be seen as my dishonourable attempt to sidestep the more accepted rigorous blind peer-review processes. To seek a *free pass*. A degree of incompetence on my part. To this notion, I humbly reply by quoting Quincy Jones:[4] "UNDERSTAND THE POWER OF BEING UNDERESTIMATED" (Jones, 2022, p. 172). At the time of writing, the current case study stands alone as far as depth, breadth, and reliability compared to any other previously published description of professional full-time contract Symphony Orchestra players. Most specifically, the perceptions of how music performers adapt to the ill effects of ageing perhaps reveal a picture illustrating higher levels of resilience than usually depicted among the general population. Such a portrayal has never before appeared in print. It is also important to point out that a *secondary gain* of this investigation, although somewhat hidden between the lines of the texts and vignettes, is that it undeniably serves in an effort to answer the more ultimate question:

What can Seasoned Musicians tell us about lifelong music engagement?

---

[4] Legendary American record producer, songwriter, composer, arranger, and film and television producer. Jones's career spans over 70 years, with 28 Grammy Awards (out of 80 nominations). Jones (1933-2024) had been presented with several Humanitarian Awards by world leaders, over 10 Honorary Doctorates, and received the National Medal of Arts from an American President.

2

On Becoming and Being an Orchestra Musician

This chapter is about becoming and being an Orchestra musician; namely, the development of Orchestra musicians. The chapter will touch on familial attitudes towards music traditions, music education and instrument tuition, performance experiences (including debuts and achievements, competitions, honours, rewards, and foreign-travel scholarships), choosing the music-performance profession, and an estimation of Deliberate Practice (DP) over the lifespan. In addition, the chapter details the Symphony Orchestra as an occupational environment, highlighting players' weekly activity (such as performing, rehearsing, and teaching). Nonetheless, before the development of Symphony Orchestra players comes to the surface, I would like to raise a more general question: *Who is a musician?*

2.1 Prologue

An overriding number of the public consider musicians to be professionals who write, arrange, orchestrate, conduct, and perform musical compositions. This is what seems to have been passed down for generations. Yet, perhaps, the reality is far from this truth!

As a youngster I frequented musical instrument stores. In those days many of the neighbourhood retailers were simply referred to as 'Guitar Shops'. Once having spotted a guitar that interested me, a salesman would come over to demonstrate the instrument. Then I could hear the sound, as well as experience the typical music styles that could be performed with it. I remember being impressed by the prowess of these guitarist-salesmen. The way they played boosted my imagination, and of course gave me a feeling that maybe even I could become a great player if I just owned that instrument! Throughout my life, whether I was seeking to purchase an Acoustic Guitar, Classical Guitar, Electric Jazz Guitar, Electric Rock Guitar, Ukulele, Guitalele, Electric Bass-Guitar, Double Bass, Electronic Keyboard, Upright Piano, Spinet Piano, Drum-Set, Cymbals, Electronic Drum-Set, Orchestra Percussion Instruments (e.g., Xylophone, Vibraphone, Snare Drum), Educational Percussion Instruments, Autoharp, Folk Harp, Recorder, or Flute—I always witnessed salespeople performing on an instrument. They always took me on a journey across a wide gamut of music repertoire, in a number of music genres and performance styles, all with the utmost skill and passion that demonstrated the highest

Seasoned Musicians Playing Beyond the 5th Decade. Warren Brodsky, Oxford University Press. © Oxford University Press (2025). DOI: 10.1093/9780198956501.003.0002

levels of performance skills that could be imagined! After expressing my appreciation for such showmanship, on many occasions I would enquire about the location of their upcoming concert. For the most part, I received the same answer: 'Oh no! I used to be a musician. I once wanted to be a musician. But today I just sell musical instruments!' Indeed, that answer always confused me! Sometime in my late twenties, I began to wonder:

> *Isn't there a difference between who you are (such as identifying yourself as being a musician), and what you actually do to make a living (such as composing, arranging, orchestrating, conducting, performing, teaching, therapizing, researching, or just selling instruments)? Aren't all of these people musicians?*

In their landmark book *Musical Identities*, editors MacDonald et al. (2002) put forth the notion that all people have both an identity involving music and a musical identity. One's identity with music does not exclusively entertain music-performance activities, but can also be defined through musical preferences and musical beliefs. On the other hand, musical identities are based on external and observable activities and experiences, as well as membership in groups involving music. One's musical identity is affected by parental expectations, and to some extent, parent–child coalitions regarding musical development. Moreover, there are specific aspects of musical identity for all performing musicians; these interact with one's self-identity as a young musician, and then later with one's inclination to assume a performer's identity. Accordingly, these highlight the role of self-perception in the development of music-performance skills.

I point out that over the years I have befriended many musicians. Some of them were classmates at a Music Conservatory, Music High School, Army Entertainment Band, Army Orchestra Marching Band, and Music Academy (College). Some of these musicians eventually became professional Doctors, Lawyers, Psychologists, Teachers, and even High-Tech Computer Programmers. A few of them may have continued to maintain a degree of music-performance ability—but not all of them! And, from time to time some may even have joined an Orchestra, Chamber Ensemble, Jazz Big Band, or Rock Group. When I asked a few of them their thoughts about being a musician, most said: 'Oh no! I used to be a musician. I once wanted to be a musician. But I am now just a — —' (Lawyer, Doctor, Psychologist, Teacher, Computer guy, etc.).

2.1.1 Musicianship Is for Life

Long ago, Jane Davidson (2002), formerly from the Department of Music at the University of Sheffield (UK), claimed that musical potential and achievement are quite possible among the vast majority of people—actually about 95% of the general population. Accordingly, this applies to musical skills (e.g., Sloboda et al., 1994a). Such a stance pits the role of biology against environmental influences. Or, as it is better known: the *nature versus nurture* debate. This concept itself led to much heated discussion in the 1994 July issue of *The Psychologist* (e.g., Davies, 1994; Hargreaves, 1994; Radford, 1994; Sloboda et al., 1994b; Torff & Winner, 1994). While not taking a side for or against the above argument, nor investing more in an examination of the possible 'norms' for developing the physical and mental capacities of musicality, I do feel that the term *musician* needs to be seen as something more generative. That is, I believe, that the term *musician* describes any individual who emerged as having an intimate primary relationship to sound and music from early childhood. Gembris (2006) relates to this as *musical aptitude*:

> *The potential to perceive and shape sounds and tones, and the resulting ability to communicate sense, meaning and feelings, [which] exists already in the earliest stages of human life, maybe even some weeks before birth and can be maintained until very old age.* (p. 11)

Some individuals may eventually develop music-performance skills. And some may even rise to a level reflecting high abilities and expertise. Yet, others may not! Nonetheless, most musicians seem to have had music-related memories going back to periods of infancy and toddlerhood. Some may even recall their mother's testimony of prenatal (*in utero*) 'musicality'.

(38y, M, bn/dbn)   *I do remember being surrounded by music from an early age and going to concerts very young. Nobody told me to sing. My mom told me I could whistle before I was talking, I don't know what age that was. But something was being wired in the brain; or maybe it was pre-wired and I just fulfilled what I was supposed to do. My mom used to take me to concerts, and I saw there what I wanted to do. [In my mind] I was playing along, playing instruments, and singing. I always had quite good mathematical ability (and that came out at school and university). But, maths didn't really do it for me. I just went off and decided [playing in an Orchestra] is what I wanted to do.*

French neurologist Jean-Martin Charcot (1825–1893) believed that people could be distinguished by their cognitive sensory preferences. He labelled individuals as *visuels*, *moteurs*, and *auditifs*.[1] *Auditifs* use the auditory channel as a continuous source of input to the psychic structure, and even in adulthood this overriding style may continue to play a prominent role in one's emotional exchange with the outside world. Some psychoanalytic developmental theorists (e.g., Nass, 1971, 1975; Noy, 1968, 1990) conceived of *auditivity* as originating from early hearing experiences during the preverbal infantile stage. Accordingly, this sensory style was used as a means of adapting to and mastering reality. Eventually, persons whose primary sensory mode led to an overall auditory orientation might perceive interactions in the environment slightly differently than those who are predominately visual. It is clear that the indication here is not just one's 'constitution', but also one's ongoing

---

[1] This material has been adapted from previously published papers by Brodsky (1990, 1997, 2004). Reprinted with permission.

development and predisposition as based on an *Auditory Style* (for more details, see Brodsky, 2004).

We should consider how early infantile and childhood musical experiences shape abilities. For example, during the bonding process proprioceptive, kinaesthetic, tactile, and vestibular stimulation are all coupled to auditory and visual modes. How might these experiences be different for *auditifs* within the schema of maturation (as effecting further developmental milestones and primary affect)? Infant musicality certainly plays a later role in the development of communication, speech, and language; these are all subsequent to a number of preverbal interactions including babbling, lullabies, rhythmic games, finger- and hand-clapping songs, as well as the singing of children's songs—all of which are considered to be *childlore*; that is, the musical folklore of children (Brodsky & Sulkin, 2011; Campbell, 1998). Finally, the presence of music in the home and at concert venues (i.e., receptive listening), as well as music-making (e.g., actual parent–child active engagement with an instrument), are of the utmost importance at early ages of development.

Is Auditory Style similar to other conceptions of temperament or personality styles? Is there a classification system to assess one's degree of involvement? In 1993, with John A. Sloboda, the eminent music psychologist of the late 20th and early 21st century who was the founding director of the Unit for the Study of Musical Skill and Development at Keele University (UK), I (Brodsky, 2004) developed such an assessment measure: The *Keele Assessment of Auditory Style* (KAAS) (see Appendix B). *KAAS* is a 61-item self-report questionnaire targeting behaviours based on retrospective memory across three critical periods of human development: Child-Youngster (4–12 years old); Teenager (13–18 years old); and Adult (>18 years old). *KAAS* employs a 5-point Likert scale to rate responses (1 = 'Never'; 5 = 'Always'), with an option to mark 'nought' (zero = 0) for items the respondent couldn't remember or for those items that did not seem relevant. Among the 61 items is a 38-item subscale reflecting more general behaviours related to sound, referred to as the *Auditivity Scale* (AS). In addition, there is a second 23-item subscale for specific music engagement such as playing an instrument. Among a heterogeneous sample of respondents ($N = 254$; $M_{Age} = 37$, $SD = 9.95$; Males = 53%), *AS* was found to be normally distributed: $M_{AS} = 117$, $SD = 0.47$, Range 63–168. Hence, *Auditivity* was not rooted in the development of musical ability nor in formal musical instrument training. Yet, when comparing *AS* scores by dividing the sample into two subgroups (professional Symphony Orchestra musicians [OM] *versus* individuals from the general public [GP]) the musicians demonstrated statistically significantly higher Auditivity Scale scores: $OM_{(n = 156)}$ $M_{AS} = 122$, $SD = 17.8$; $GP_{(n = 98)}$ $M_{AS} = 110$, $SD = 15.9$; $t = 5.14$, $df = 252$, $p < 0.0001$.

The Auditivity Scale seems to highlight behavioural attitudes, and to some extent may even predict aspects of music engagement. Many of those with the highest scores had been involved with formal musical instrument lessons already in early childhood, occupying themselves with hours of practice, and subsequently became music performers. Some even entered the profession as a full-time contract Symphony Orchestra musician.

(60y, F, vc)   *Music was my first language. Before I learned to write and to read in my mother language, I learned to write and read music notation. Yes! I knew how to write notation before I could write letters. So, Music is my initial mother tongue—in a way it's the first language I learned. I don't know how many musicians are like that. I never talked about this [before].*

Yet, not all of those with an intimate primary relationship to sound and music in early childhood become professional Music Performers. Some may acquire training as a Composer, Arranger, Orchestrator, or Conductor of music. Others, perhaps, train to be a Teacher of a musical instrument (Studio Teaching), or general classroom music instruction in Elementary School or High School, or a Lecturer of music in Colleges or Universities. Still others may have trained in non-music-related professions, such as Clinical Arts (Psychology and Social Work), Education, Empirical Science, Law, Medicine, and Technology. But for all of these people, *auditivity* may have remained an overarching orientation throughout their lifespan. Gembris (2006) feels that musical aptitude is the potential to perceive and shape sounds and tones. A lifespan perspective of musical development implies that such aptitudes exist already in the earlier stages of human life, perhaps even before birth, and can be maintained until very old age. Yet, as Gembris points out, such a perspective also accounts for the fact that music abilities are subject to strong changes during the course of one's life.

Music is indeed in the heart and soul of each and every *auditif*. Many go on to play an instrument, and are versed in knowledge of Music Theory and Music History. But the majority do not become professional music performers of the concert platform. However, does that mean that they should be excluded from identifying themselves as a *musician*? My position here is that the term *musician* is more of a general descriptor for all who participate in the music profession. See Table 2.1, which illustrates that not every musician is a full-time professional performer, and definitely most performing musicians are not Symphony Orchestra players. Statistically speaking, I would estimate that the incidence of musicians who actually become full-time top-professional music performers is close to 1:100,000, and even less are those Western Classical music performers who achieve the performance levels that meet the requirements (e.g., auditions and trials) to earn and maintain a full-time contract position in a professional Symphony Orchestra. That is, I estimate the incidence of professional Classical musicians newly joining the ranks of a professional Symphony Orchestra as full-time contract players (per geographical region) to be as low as 1:1000. Based on Gagne and McPherson (2016) who denote the IQ Distribution, the *SD* equivalents of such estimates would be 4.3 *SD*s and 3.0 *SD*s respectively. Ericsson (1996) has referred to the 5 Levels of Music Performance for comparative purposes: Club, District, National, International, and World Class. See Figure 2.1. Accordingly, these are not absolute levels of performance, but rather based on relative standards to determine performance requirements at each level. Ericsson noted that these can increase and decrease over different periods of time.

Certainly anyone might be able to occupy themselves in many of the subspecialities listed in Table 2.1 without ever having felt intimately connected to sound

Table 2.1 Subspecialities of the Music Profession

Music Performer, Performing Artist	Music Educator Tutor (private individuals, groups)
Music Vocalist	Music Teacher Elementary School
Music Accompanist (in support of Singers, Choirs, and Instrumentalists)	Music Teacher High School Music (marching bands,choirs, musicals)
Music Composer	Music College Instructor
Music Conductor Music Theorist	Music Computer Specialist (programs, programming,applications)
Music Copyist (notating by handwriting or computer program applications)	Music Editor (curator, playlists, mixes, syncing to film)
Music Director	Musical Instrument Builder
Music Orchestrator	Musical Instrument Repair and Restoration Specialist
Music Arranger	Piano Tuner
Music Producer	Musical Instrument Mechanic (guitar technician)
Music Promoter	
Music Public Relations Manager	Music Journalist (magazines, newspaper)
Music Advertising Specialist	Music Blogger
Music Industry Specialist (design, production, marketing, and distribution)	Music Critic
Music Recording Engineer, Sound Technician	Music Publisher Music Store Manager, Music Store Salespeople
Music Audio Specialist (Studio or Home-Based)	Music Supervisor (Licensing Specialist)
Music Disc Jockey (radio, events, parties)	Music Lawyer, Music Union Specialist
Music Broadcaster (presenter on radio or television)	Music Therapist
Music Photographer (covering live concerts, portraits, band promos)	Musicologist, Ethnomusicologist (Scholarly Historian), Academic of Music
Music Librarian (books, media)	Music Psychologist, Music Cognitive Scientist, Music Researcher

and music. For example, fulfilling the position of a Music Librarian might simply befall a general librarian as an opportunity of employment. Yet, as an undergraduate student at the Jerusalem Rubin Music Academy (in the 1970s), I do recollect the legendary academy librarian Claude Abravanel (1924–2012). Claude was a Swiss-Israeli Pianist (trained by Constantin Lipatti in Geneva and Yvonne Lefébure in Paris), as well as a Composer (trained by Arthur Honegger in Paris). I remember that any student could hum him an instrument part of any Symphony composed in the last 200 years, and he would simply go to the 'stacks' to retrieve a pocket score (i.e., a miniature handy pocket-sized booklet edition). Who would have thought that a Music Library would engage as manager someone as highly trained and proficient in music performance and composition as he?

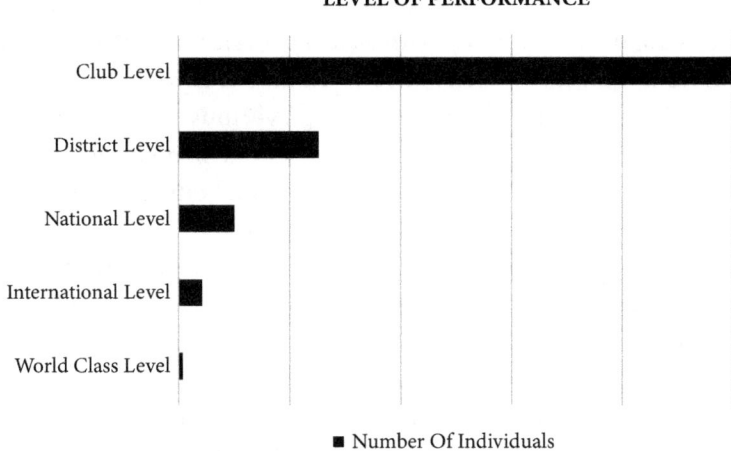

LEVEL OF PERFORMANCE

Figure 2.1 Incidence of Music Expertise

Data Source: Ericsson (1996)

(50y, M, vn)   *There is someone in this Orchestra who studied and trained as a Doctor. I remember that while I was at Juilliard, I also studied one year at Yale; there was a guy there I used to play a lot with who was doing a Master's Degree in Business Computing. I remember thinking: 'How strange! I am just into Music' (although I did have few other interests). But now I look back and think: 'What a smart guy.' Because he was able to make money doing computers as well as play in an Orchestra. For me, you are either 'in' or 'out' [of music and the Orchestra]. Yet, there were times when this guy wasn't employed as an Orchestra player, and when that happened he could rely on skills from another profession.*

I also believe that one does not ever lose their 'badge' of musicianship. It is true that for the most part many non-performing musicians may have given up any attempt to realize their long-ago childhood aspirations to become a music performer. In a very interesting report, Koch (2006) engaged a group of finalists and 1st Prize-Winners from the 'Musical Youth' Competition (*Jugend musiziert*, Germany); 15 years later he was able to locate 51 out of 60 musicians (85%). The study found that 78% were regularly employed as musicians; under 50% performed in Top German (European) professional full-time contract Orchestras; 11% with the Berlin Philharmonic Orchestra or Bavarian Radio Symphony Orchestra, 43% with the Bavarian State Orchestra and Bremen Philharmonic State Orchestra; 26% performed in semi-professional freelance Orchestras. Many taught at a Music Academy. Yet, 20% did not continue professionally in any music-related profession, but rather were employed as an Investment Banker, Journalist, Nurse, Physician, or Teacher. Accordingly, the majority of respondents considered that their earlier intensive music activity was worthwhile—having had realized their ambitions and dreams. Do these individuals still see themselves—at least in their heart—as musicians? Perhaps! But there are people I have come across who deny affiliation to their past musicianship. They contend to have 'moved on'; even when considering they had invested more than 15 years in musical instrument training, which indicates an estimated accumulated 2,000 to 5,000 hours of DP (based on Ericsson, 1996; Hambrick et al., 2014). In addition, many had participated in Chamber Ensembles, Orchestras, and other bands; and some learned formal courses on various topics such as Music Theory, Music Analysis, and Music History. Perhaps their perception had much to do with the more widely socially accepted viewpoint that being a musician is exclusive to being a Music Performer, Composer, or Conductor.

One question raised by Balbag et al. (2014) is whether those who self-select into the Music Performance profession are fundamentally different from those who do not. Are differences between musicians and non-musicians due to musical training (i.e., environment)? Or, perhaps the issue is more about pre-existing biology (i.e., innate differences of brain structure or function)? Long ago Marchant-Haycox and Wilson (1992) found that musicians seem to be more alike than different; they targeted personality! The point being forwarded here is that the term *musician* includes even those who deny their musicianship—because they did not reach the performance levels required for a stage career. Studies on emotional responses to music (e.g., Sloboda, 1992) reveal that individuals with a lifelong commitment to music are far more likely to report key emotional experiences in response to musical content during early childhood than those who never learned a musical instrument beyond an initial stage.

So, do all *auditifs* feel a consuming meaningful passion for the music domain? In this connection Dobrow (2013; Dobrow & Tosti-Kharas, 2011) examined one's *Music Calling*. This seven-year study recruited 450 High school music students. The longitudinal time-frame of the study spanned between high school and college, when participants took their initial steps toward pursuing a professional music career. The variables for music, education, and family backgrounds were controlled. The findings indicate that Vocalists start out with a higher Calling than Instrumentalists; those with the highest Calling registered as Music Majors at their chosen College. Dobrow (2013) viewed *Calling* as a stable unchanging construct, contending that "once people find their calling, it acts as a cause rather than as a consequence of positive outcomes" (pp. 444–445). Music Calling was assessed using a 12-item scale. Dobrow's scale (Dobrow 2013; Dobrow & Tosti-Kharas, 2011) was found to be valid and reliable ($\alpha = 0.89$). Among the items are:

- I am passionate about playing my instrument/singing, and I feel a sense of destiny about being a musician
- Music is always in my mind in some way, even when I am not playing music or practising
- I enjoy playing music more than anything else, as music gives me immense personal satisfaction
- I would sacrifice everything to be a musician, and I would continue being a musician even in the face of severe obstacles
- I describe myself to others as a musician, and I know that being a musician will always be part of my life.

The perception of Calling occurs before fully committing to a professional identity (see section 2.2.1.3). According to Dobrow, although many young musicians may have felt like misfits in high school, they reported that they were more socially comfortable among other musicians, and could express their true selves. It is of interest to note that music ability is not necessarily related to one's initial Calling. That is, behavioural involvement, which refers to doing activities associated with the Calling domain, is often independent of actual ability. The findings do support the notion that one's perception on Music Calling does change over time; despite behavioural involvement and social comfortability, decreases in one's Music Calling could occur when considering one's level of music proficiency.

So, now I ask the following question: Do those with an intimate primary relationship to sound and music in early childhood (i.e., *auditifs*) demonstrate higher levels of *Calling* in the music domain? Dobrow (2013) wonders: Do Music Callings pre-exist to identifying oneself as a performing musician? Then: Is a higher Calling a prerequisite for becoming a professional musician? As stated previously, professional Symphony Orchestra musicians demonstrated higher *KAAS AS* scores than the general public. Further, Brodsky (2004) used a median split of *AS* scores to divide the sample of Orchestra players (i.e., the bottom 50% *versus* the top 50%); Brodsky found that Orchestra players with higher *AS* scores were also statistically significantly higher on 17 out of 23 items (74%) of the second *KAAS* subscale indicating specific music engagement. See Table 2.2.

Table 2.2 Behaviours of Orchestra Players with Higher Auditivity Scale Scores

#	Selected Items of KAAS Music Engagement Scale
1	As a child I produced expressive sounds on my instruments
2	As a child I felt emotional 'power' or 'comfort' while producing sounds
4	As a child I often attempted to imitate other musicians
5	As a child I attempted to 'show off' with my instrument
6	As a child I felt 'different' from other children not learning any instrument
7	As an adolescent I played my instrument while sad, lonely, or apprehensive
8	As an adolescent I felt that my parent's approval was dependent on my music mastery
9	As an adolescent I felt that my performance proficiency reflected my control over my life
10	As an adolescent I felt that my musical talent and preoccupation justified my general lack of motivation to overcome academic demands
11	As an adolescent I felt that music-making was a vehicle to escape into my private world, counteracting poor relationships among peers and other social interactions
12	As an adult I feel that music rekindles the 'childlike' part of my soul
13	As an adult I feel that I need to perform with someone in order to understand them
14	As an adult I feel 'lost' if I am unable to hear my sound distinctly from the rest of the Orchestra
15	As an adult I feel 'assaulted' by discrepancies of intonation
16	As an adult I feel I often enter a trance-like state when practising on my own
17	As an adult I hear internal sounds when I imagine notation.

Source: Brodsky (2004), reprinted with permission

To summarize thus far, becoming and being an Orchestra musician may be related to a host of variables. For example, one's intimate primary relationship to sound and music in early childhood. Or, one's perceived Music Calling. Others speak of music-related (i.e., music-relevant) aptitudes; or being 'musical' (i.e., mastery of musical competencies, musical giftedness, or natural musical potential). Gagne and McPherson (2016) took the nomenclature a step further by initiating the expression *musilinked*. For sure, when looking at Table 2.1 it is clear that Music Performers are one of the many subspecialities that together forge the Music Profession. Nonetheless, as all subsequent chapters in this book target professional full-time contract Symphony Orchestra players, the following sections of this chapter offer details extensively sketching a profile outlining *who they are* and *where they came from*.

2.2 Symphony Orchestra Musicians

2.2.1 Development Towards Expertise

This section presents a general biographical sketch of Symphony Orchestra players. To my knowledge, there is only one such outline in the academic literature: Manturzewska (1990, 2006). There have been limited studies about pupils in music-specialist high schools (e.g., Howe & Sloboda, 1991a; Sloboda, 1991; Sloboda & Howe, 1991), a few papers about students in Music Academies, and some articles concerning Virtuosi Soloist Pianists and Violinists (e.g., Krampe & Ericsson, 1996), as well as Musical Prodigies (e.g., McPherson, 2016). All of these offer partial descriptive information. One study that did involve Orchestra musicians (albeit using a mixture of professional and amateur players) was Hendricks (2014); that study put forward a protocol examining musical background of family, formal music instruction, musical friends and associates, motivation for joining the Symphony Orchestra, history of involvement with the Orchestra and other ensemble experience, self-regulatory practice habits, and personal preparation for Orchestra concerts. But still, at the time of this writing, I am not aware of a biographical examination of professional full-time contract Symphony Orchestra musicians. Moreover, to my knowledge there has been no investigation of Seasoned Musicians published in the scientific journal literature. The below outline describes the age of onset, the number of years of formal lessons, familial attitudes (support) for music education and formal tuition, musical instrument training in educational settings, performance experiences (such as age of first debut, and first Orchestra position), as well as being the recipient of honours and achievements (i.e., awards from competitions and contests). Finally, I calculate the age at which these players consciously chose the 'Orchestra' (representing a more mindful cognizant Music Calling) as the vocation of their career. In addition, estimations of Deliberate Practice across the lifespan are presented. Finally various activities of professional involvement that bring together music performance as a *way of life* (e.g., Deliberate Practice, rehearsals, ensembles, private studio instruction, and College-level group music teaching) are assessed. Some of these topics have been adapted from Manturzewska's interview platform.

To reiterate: The current research sample was comprised of $N = 52$ full-time contract Orchestra players recruited from five professional Symphony Orchestras located in three countries. These players were 56% males, between 27 and 64 years old ($M_{Age} = 48$, $SD = 10.12$, $Mdn = 51$), born between the years 1946 and 1983. Among them were members of the String (65%), Woodwind (22%), and Brass (8%) sections, as well as Harp (2%), and a Percussion player. These players were contracted as Principals and Sub-Principals (60%), as well as Rank-&-File section players (40%).

2.2.1.1 Family Environment and Development

For many years there has been a *folk myth* that great musicians ultimately arise from within musical family dynasties. In the Classical Music genre a few examples are: Bach (Wilhelm Friedemann, Johann Christian, and Carl Philipp Emanuel, sons of Johann Sebastian), Mozart (Wolfgang Amadeus, son of Leopold), Haydn (Alois Anton Polzelli, son of Joseph, and Johann Michael, younger brother of Joseph), Mendelssohn (Fanny Hensel, sister of Felix), and Strauss (Johann-Schani, son of Johann). In the Pop Music genre a few examples are: Cash (Rosanne, daughter of Johnny), Cole (Natalie, daughter of Nat King), Cyrus (Miley, daughter of Billy-Ray), Guthrie (Arlo, son of Woody), Wilson (Connie and Wendy, daughters of Brian), Iglesias (Enrique, son of Julio), Jones (Nora, daughter of Ravi Shankar), Marley (Ziggy, son of Bob), Minnelli (Liza, daughter of Judy Garland), Starkey (Zak, son of Ringo), Lennon (Julian, son of John), and Williams (Hank Jr., son of Hank Sr.). And so . . . there is an Urban Legend!

As can be seen in the vignette below, it has often been believed (even by Orchestra musicians) that 60% of professional musicians are born with suitable familial DNA to achieve musical prominence, and are subsequently raised in an environment that specifically enhances music education and music ability. Albeit, it is often also acknowledged that such an inheritance places great expectations on offspring and siblings to meet familial traditions. Namely, anecdotal evidence seems to point out that only 25%–40% of professional musicians actually surface from nought— on their own! Some studies seem to perpetuate such myths. For example, Hearn (1972) reported that the musicians ($n = 37$) participating in that sample were early beginners who took lessons as early as 5 years of age, with a number (but no details?) stating that their parents were also musicians. Hern did claim that these participants were mostly (but no details?) members of the Kansas City Philharmonic Orchestra. Another example was Manturzewska (1990, 2006) who reported that among the total $N = 165$ sample, 93% ($n = 148$) were descendants of families having some form of music tradition: "only 5% of the musicians came from families with no musical tradition or showed no evidence of musical talents" (2006, p. 27). Moreover, that

50% followed in the footsteps of their father, while 25% followed the career trajectory of the mother; albeit there is no mention of the other 25%. In the sample there were Polish Soloist Prize-Winners ($n = 30$–35), as well as everyday citizens with music experience ($n = 130$–135). Manturzewska claimed that almost all came from towns, with none coming from small rural villages. Part of the difficulty with this issue is that children raised in a musical home are certainly going to receive more musical input, feedback, and encouragement than children raised in a non-musical family. Yet, as Levitin (2012) affirms, DNA only goes so far: "self-reports of world-class musicians [. . .] point strongly to the view that practice accounts for a significant proportion of the variance in who becomes an expert musician and who does not" (p. 635).

In general, the players in the current sample reported that they themselves were the only (singular) professional musician in the family—to the best of their recollections going back at least three generations. Only $n = 13$ (25%) listed a grandparent, parent, or sibling as a professional musician. More frequently (58%, $n = 30$) players noted that among their family was someone who might have been considered to be a moderate amateur musician, having played one of several instruments such as: Accordion, Church Organ, Guitar, Piano, Recorder, but only rarely an Orchestral String or Wind instrument. More often family members sang in a Church Choir or participated in a local village theatre.

(29y, F, vn)   *I started Violin when I was 7 [years old]. Some start really early, like 3–4. We don't start school till we are 7. So, that's when I started. There are six professional musicians in my family. It is a family disease. My parents are professional musicians. My dad, my sisters, few of my cousins, my auntie and uncle, are all professional musicians. So, I knew what it was like, including the pressure. I don't know how many musicians come from musical families. It's really difficult for me to think of a figure. But in Poland, probably the majority come from a musical family, or at least a family where somebody played an instrument. The way our education works is that we are already very professionally orientated from the beginning. There aren't many who take music 'just for fun' as a hobby. In this country, there's loads of people who play for a year or two and then give up; at least they have some sort of taste of what it's like to play a musical instrument. In Poland even if you want to go to an afternoon music school you have to take an entrance exam (including singing or playing) to prove that you already have the talent. So it's really difficult for me to put it in figures. Worldwide, I would maybe say 60% [of performing musicians come] from a musical family, and 40% [do not come from a musical family].*

The majority of players ($n = 43$, 83%) in the current sample claimed that one parent encouraged them to become a music performer. These accounts echo findings from a large-scale investigation published in the annals of the *British Journal of Developmental Psychology* (Davidson et al., 1996) on parental influences in the development of musical ability. Davidson et al.'s research concluded that parents, siblings, and other guardians have a critical role in developing skills of engagement. Foremost, the highest-achieving group was supported most frequently and consistently by their parents; on the other hand it was not uncommon for children to give up learning a musical instrument because they did not receive sufficient parental support. In the current sample, many players stated that one parent supported their pursuits by vowing to cover the financial costs of private tuition and musical instruments. Albeit, many players did note that they were themselves expected to contribute their share of the costs by entering performance competitions to obtain Prize Money—which could then be allocated towards scholarships and procuring better instruments. Some players indicated that the overriding message in their family was: 'If you want to pursue musical training and follow a music career, then you'd better stand on your own two feet.' Such a message was reported long ago by Pruett (2004) who discussed the *good-enough* parent within the context of raising a musical child. The participating players recalled that such a message was made clear to them already in late childhood.

(47y, M, trb)   *I'm definitely sure that I was blessed. [Laughs.] As if God said: 'OK, I give you Trombone, you just play it!' I come from a small village. My parents loved music. Here is my true story:*

I went to this small local Brass Band rehearsal. I wanted to play the Trumpet. I thought about Jazz Trumpet. There was this very nice Trumpet player and other great guys; I wanted to be one [like them]. But, they had too many Trumpet players, and needed Trombones. So, they gave me a Trombone. I was 8 years old. I came home crying! Now, that's really young for a Trombone; my arms were even too short. I couldn't even reach. Today, there are small ¾ instruments for 8-year-olds. So I was crying when I came home, and said: 'Oh, see what they gave me! I wanted Trumpet!' But, then, I started to play a little bit; I could play instantly a little piece. I went marching through the house, and my mother was happy. So, I stayed with the Trombone—but not for my mother! From the beginning I had a small group: Clarinet, Trumpet, Drums, Trombone, and perhaps Tuba; we played together in this room of my friend. That's how I grew up with a Brass Band. [Here], the Brass Bands are not that good, but it's part of village life—so people are really proud to be part of that as it has a cultural meaning. The Marching Bands in the USA are more like playing on the football field. We don't do that—we do concerts! Then, later I made it to the big group; there were 65 musicians in my home-town band. A lot of those really good players made it as professionals. My embouchure was very good. I still have my etudes [notebook] with the year written on the pages because my teacher always wrote down the exact date. I had a good height, I could play pretty easily in high range. It just worked out and I'm really thankful!

(50y, M, vn)   *My mother was a professional Pianist, graduate and a teacher at Juilliard [New York, USA]. I was also a Juilliard graduate. But she did much less working in her career than I do probably because she was a mother who raised kids in the 60s–70s. Back then it was much more acceptable for a woman performer to give up her career for the sake of her children. I was always very into music, but she often said that one of the turning points for me was in my teen years. I wasn't sure. I thought maybe I'd be a Journalist. I consulted with her, and she said: 'If you feel like you have to do it, then you have to do it! If it's a burning desire, then you should do it!' But she also added: 'It's very hard!' But, being in an Orchestra [versus being a Soloist] might be a better way not to lose the passion.*

Within the 11-measure 12-page questionnaire booklet (see Chapter 1, section 1.6.3.3, Table 1.3 [Q1]), the players in the current sample self-reported their retrospective memories of childhood in a handwritten biographical account. Moreover, roughly a third of these players further appended an additional page of supplementary detailed narratives.[2] Gruhn (2021) points out that early musical development

---

[2] It should be noted that a few of the players did not offer extensive details as written accounts. Therefore, sample size (i.e., number of participants and percentage of the omnibus sample) is provided in parentheses of each parameter discussed.

usually starts with the voice; among infants, early musical guidance revolves around establishing and strengthening of the singing voice. But yet, as "early vocal development exhibits large individual differences according to infants' musical-aptitude and environmental stimulation [...] it is quite problematic to indicate concrete dates and ages when children start using their singing voice" (p. 89). Therefore, most players offer information in their historical chronicles about the 'age of onset' for learning an instrument. As recalled by the participating players, they often began playing an instrument before the age of 6 years old ($M_{\text{Age} (n\,=\,48,\,92\%)} = 7$, $SD = 2.66$, $Mdn = 6$, Range 3–16). Starting at a young age may clearly be an extremely important factor in the development of a music performer. For example, Hambrick et al. (2014) and Hambrick and Tucker-Drob (2015) suggested evidence demonstrating that there may be a critical period for acquiring complex music skills (just as there may be for acquiring language). This finding resonates with Manturzewska (1990, 2006) who claimed that the musicians in that sample had started their musical instruction at between 5 and 6 years old.

The participating players frequently mentioned that the first instrument they played was not their final 'main' orchestral instrument. As young children they often began learning to play music with a Recorder or a Piano. Hence, when they outlined their formal engagement with musical instrument lessons, they usually mentioned an average of five teachers who provided them with their more formal weekly lessons, spread out over a 10-year period of development to their 18th Birthday ($M_{\text{Years} (n\,=\,34,\,65\%)} = 10.38$, $SD = 2.79$, $Mdn = 10$, Range 6–18). Manturzewska (1990, 2006) noted that the data collected from the 92 Polish musicians in that study found that it took about 16 years of systematic musical training to become prepared as a professional music performer.

(40y, F, vn)	*I was kind of a late bloomer, so there were things about Violinists that I only found out about much later. Yes, I started at age 4, but I quit early on. Then when I started to play again, I wasn't so serious. So, those late teens when a lot of my colleagues spent time isolated in practice for 6 hours [a day], I didn't really do that. And, I didn't go to [music] summer-camps, nor studied with this and that teacher. Also, my first couple of years in [Music] College I probably didn't have the best possible teacher. So a lot of things I only discovered in my mid–late 20s or even 30s.*
(47y, F, vn)	*I started late with the Violin. I played Piano first, and then I started Violin at 13. I just loved it. Maybe by the time I was 15–16 years old, it was clear to me that I wanted to be a Violinist. I thought: This is the profession I want to be in for the rest of my life. I just loved the Violin. The sound of it! Not to be a Soloist. No, never! I wanted to play in the Orchestra. I was playing together with my sister and my grandfather; my sister played Piano, and he played Cello. We all played some Trios. I was in a school Orchestra and I just loved it. I was so excited whenever I went there. I thought it was great to be part of the Orchestra. I even remember the first piece I ever played in an Orchestra: Titus Overture [the opera seria La clemenza di Tito (The Clemency of Titus), K 621, written by Austrian composer Wolfgang Amadeus Mozart, 1756–1791]. That's what grabbed me! Yes. I was just sitting there, and I just loved it!*
(60y, M, cl)	*I play this instrument because when I wanted to begin learning an instrument I [originally] wanted something different, but my family couldn't afford it. So I was given this one [i.e., the Clarinet] especially since I was tall and had long fingers.*

I point out that Smilde (2006, 2009) observed that, especially in childhood, informal learning was a very important mode of learning music. For example, participation in a 'community of practice' was central to music development. Collaborative music-making, whether that be singing together with a Choir, or playing instruments together in a Wind Band, Chamber Ensemble, or Orchestra, were all seen to be of great significance to children and adolescents. Such participatory learning—guided by a Teacher or Conductor who was encouraging as a mentor—led to strong intrinsic motivation. There is evidence by Davidson (1999, 2002; Davidson et al., 1995–1996) showing that, after the age of 11, many children did not need external sources for motivation; they developed very strong intrinsic links with their instrument that took over from parent–teacher roles regarding success of learning. Eventually, their sense of self was interconnected to playing their musical instrument.

Researchers (e.g., Farnam, 2016) who have studied high achievement among musicians find many similarities between the backgrounds of professional musicians. All seem to agree that professional musicians developed their own musical identity and commitment, and are highly self-motivated to the point of obsession. Kemp (1995) claimed that musicians behave "as if they were unable to separate their developing self-perception from that of being a musician" (p. 35). All of the participating players in the current study mentioned that their parents were interested in music, encouraged them, and were engaged in musical recreation (e.g., concerts, listening to music at home, getting their children involved in private lessons). They all remembered their first music teacher as being warm and friendly. Encouragement from their peers, especially those who like them were interested in music, helped with further motivation. They also recalled having had many opportunities to perform.

Based on the written accounts, the players in the current sample reported that their first 'public' appearance occurred at about their 10th Birthday ($M_{\text{Age}\,(n\,=\,40,\,77\%)}$ = 13, SD = 3.93, Mdn = 13.5, Range 5–20). I point out that such performances were not always considered to be the *debut* as many players often declared that such a designation was (at least in their minds) reserved for a specific time and place—usually identified as their first professional 'Solo Recital' or 'coming out' event in their Orchestra. In the sample studied by Manturzewska (1990, 2006) players reported that their debut was between 8 and 9 years old. It is interesting to note that the players in the current study recounted that their first 'orchestral position' occurred about their 15th Birthday ($M_{\text{Age}\,(n\,=\,22,\,42\%)}$ = 16.5, SD = 4.17, Mdn = 15.5, Range 10–26). These posts were usually when they were permanent members of a School Ensemble or local Municipal Youth Orchestra. Further, almost all players recalled having participated in a World Tour as a member of the National Youth Orchestra from their country of birth.

Only a few of the participating players (n = 5, 10%) reported to have attended a Music Conservatory as an elementary-school setting. Many more (n = 15, 29%) claimed to have been educated at home by a parent. Usually, a father or mother had trained the child on their first (and sometimes second) instrument, as well as having taught them to read music notation. The narratives point out that only a third ($n = 16$, 31%) of the sample attended a specialist Music High School. This is quite contrary to other reports: Bullerjahn et al. (2020) found that 57% of the participants reported to attend music schools as children, and that 16% were taught by a private teacher. Nevertheless, almost all of the participating players ($n = 48$, 92%) in the current study reported to have completed a music-related Bachelor's Degree, while just over a third ($n = 20$, 38%) had completed an advanced postgraduate music degree programme.

One interesting detail in the participating players' historical chronicles is that as children and teen musicians, only half ($n = 26$, 50%) had won a financial prize in a competitive performance contest. Accordingly, these winnings were allocated to the costs of private tuition, music courses, summer camps, international travel to masterclasses, and for higher-quality musical instruments. Moreover, as an adult (e.g., Academy student or Orchestra player) less than half ($n = 20$, 39%) had won a prize in a competitive performance tournament. In short, the Symphony Orchestra players in the current sample declared that they did not often engage in performance competitions and contests throughout their lifespan. This finding seems to oppose some research outcomes. For example, MacNamara et al. (2006) studied eight professional Soloists. All were (1) self-motivated from an early age; (2) had a sense of identity given by music; (3) highly dedicated to practising their craft; and (4) throughout their years of developing music skills were engaged in—and won—performance contests. Another example is Ruthsatz et al. (2008) who reanalysed Ericsson's (1996, 1997, 1998, 2000, 2004) original data; this data revealed that the 1st group of *Elite Violinists* won more open competitions (67%) from the time they were 8 years old than the 2nd Level Violinists (54%), while the lowest group of Violinists won significantly far less (18%). Finally, in a survey study by Bullerjahn et al. (2020) $N = 1143$ musicians ($M_{Age} = 15$, $SD = 2.1$, Range 9–24; 62% female) all participated in *Jugend musiziert*—the most important musical competition for highly gifted young musicians in Germany. Accordingly, preparing for a music competition like *Jugend musiziert* requires much practice (both independent Deliberate Practice as well as with teachers), and therefore those at this National Level are considered as having the highest musical expertise. Perhaps the variances between these samples (e.g., Bullerjahn et al., MacNamara et al., and Ruthsatz et al.) versus the participating players in the current study actually reflect differences between *Virtuosi Soloists* and *Expert Orchestra Musicians*? This notion is in line with Krampe (2006) who felt that, unlike music experts, Virtuosi Violinists and Pianists start much younger, worked with fewer teachers, encountered the most influential teacher at an early age (who was usually an internationally famed Master), took part in public appearances early on (such as Concert Debuts), as well as participated and succeeded at major international competitions (typically winning their first major prize before age 18).

2.2.1.2 Deliberate Practice (DP)

Within the survey booklet completed by all participants (see Chapter 1, section 1.6.3.3, Table 1.3 [Q2]) each player reported their estimated hours of DP across their lifetime. Such estimates have been reported in the past by many researchers (e.g., Clarke, 2002; Krampe & Ericsson, 1995) to be highly valid as a form of retrospective memory: Test–Retest reliabilities ±0.80 are considered to be *good* or *better* (Hambrick et al., 2014). Ericsson (1996, 1998) claimed that the Reliability of an accumulated lifetime practice at different test periods has typically been found to range between $\alpha = 0.70$ and $\alpha = 0.80$. DP is defined as "a highly structured activity with the explicit goal of improving some aspect of performance" (Reid, 2002, p. 111). DP is seen as a problem-solving activity whereby the musician identifies a problem and then finds a means of eliminating it.

From commencement (onset) of learning an instrument through to 10 years of age, the current participating players reported an average ±3 hours per week of DP ($M_{DP\,(3-10yrs)} = 3.6_{h/wk}$, $SD = 4.22$, $Mdn = 3.0$, Range 0–24). Then, between the ages of 10 and 20 years old, the amount of weekly DP more than doubled to ±11 hours per week ($M_{DP\,(10-20yrs)} = 11.33_{h/wk}$, $SD = 6.71$, $Mdn = 12$, Range 0–24). Together, these suggest an overall total number of DP hours throughout 21 years of age to be more than the *10,000-Hour Threshold* for performance expertise—as reported in the literature (Ericsson, 1996, 1997, 2004; Krampe & Ericsson, 1996). Namely, the overall 17-year period of DP was: $M_{DP\,(3-20yrs)} = 14{,}744_{TotHrs}$, $SD = 8373$, $Mdn = 13{,}832$, Range 0–33,592.

One renowned expert on the psychology of performance is Eric Clarke, formerly from the University of Sheffield (UK). Clarke emphasized that expert music abilities do not develop overnight. Accordingly, by the time the best performers have reached the age of 21, they are likely to have spent over 10,000 hours practising their instrument (Clarke, 2002). This level of DP is quite separate from the time players devote to other aspects of formal music education—as well as to the more informal aspects and other music components, which were referred to as 'musical enculturation'. A number of other studies (e.g., Ericsson et al., 1993; Sloboda et al., 1996) have shown that the most effective activity for acquiring musical skill is DP. Those studies have mostly recruited young Elite Soloists, demonstrating a clear relationship between the accumulated hours spent engaging in formal practice with their subsequent achievements. Ericsson (2000) elucidates that the best music students had started between 6 and 7 years old, and amassed between 7,500 and 10,000 hours of formal practice by the age of 18–20 years; while those who achieved lower performance-related scores had accumulated under half of these total hours. Further, there seems to be extensive empirical evidence for a *10-Year Rule* in a wide range of domains; many investigators have proposed that expertise in a domain would be obtained virtually automatically after 10 years of experience as the benefit of extended experience seems so obvious. Yet surprisingly, many researchers (e.g., Ackerman, 2014; Gobet & Campitelli, 2007; Hambrick & Tucker-Drob, 2015; Hambrick et al., 2014;

Macnamara et al., 2014; Platz et al., 2014) negate such claims, mentioning a host of scientific reviews showing that length and amount of domain-related experience is a relatively weak predictor of performance level. Accordingly, DP may be a variable which does not explain more than 30% of the variance. Finally, several players of the current sample not only spoke about normal DP, but also mentioned excessive practice regimes as having ill effects on one's body.

(33y, F, bn/dbn)   *Then again, there is also overpractice. You can practise so much that the embouchure falls apart. The muscles [simply] can't hold it together; you can't control it anymore. Like the lips losing air. After the summer vacation, if you didn't practise for a while, you don't have the muscles. After half an hour it sounds horrible, you're losing air, and you can't maintain the pressure. So, you have to know what your limit of practice is. There's no need to practise six hours. It is important to maintain the quality, and to practise the things you have to practise. But within limitations.*

(33y, M, va)   *I see people practising hours outside [rehearsal times] trying to maintain or to learn the notes. Whereas the way I've coped is by learning my technique and my Sight-Reading. [My Sight-Reading] is good enough that within any two-and-a-half-day period, I can play any piece on a concert level—even if I haven't ever seen the piece before. I never take [the music] home. That was a conscious decision, to make my Sight-Reading skills good enough. Many people think they have to do 17 hours a day to make it good. You can enjoy Deliberate Practice. You can enjoy the fact that you're getting better by sorting out a technical problem. My technique is at a level to cope with whatever I need to do. I try to do [my practising] within the Orchestra [rehearsal]. On long passages when there's nothing happening, I can sit there and kind of really practise when [the conductor is] talking to other people. I found there's enough time while I'm seated to actually [rehearse] without an instrument sounding aloud.*

(59y, M, va)   *I think that people who start to have less and less skill is because they're not even practising 1 hour a day! I don't mean being in rehearsal, I mean [Deliberate] Practice. I do think that some practice very much—maybe even too much! And I think that young colleagues who don't have much experience either practise more, or they think they should practise even more. But, if you are practising in an economic way you could save much work. Even if you have to learn new things, you need to practise intelligently, without too much wear and tear. I remember as a student (some 40 years ago) many Asian music students practised 8 hours per day; they repeated things over and over—not the usual 10 times but 100 times. Maybe physical training is necessary to keep the muscles in form; that's the sportive part of the work. But if you want to learn a piece, it's enough to think about it and then play one time!*

In the book *Musical Prodigies*, Gary E. McPherson (2016), formerly director of the Melbourne Conservatorium of Music (Australia), stated that not all musicians accumulate the requisite 10,000 hours of Deliberate Practice leading to mastery of Virtuosi talent to perform on the stage. Much earlier, Ericsson et al. (1993) hypothesized that personality factors may have an indirect effect on the acquisition of expert performance through DP. That is, some individuals are more predisposed towards DP, and that would allow those individuals to sustain very high levels of DP for extended periods. Bonneville-Roussy et al. (2011) found that a personality factor reflecting 'persistence' in accomplishing long-term goals also predicted one's level of engagement in DP.

In an exciting study, Hambrick and Ticker-Drob (2015) investigated gene–environment correlation and interaction with respect to musical accomplishment.

Accordingly, genetic effects on music practice may be quite astonishing, given that practice is conventionally conceptualized as an environmental variable. Is it likely that genetically influenced gifts for music could prime some children to dedicate themselves to music practice? Whereas the lack of such genetic gifts might drive other children to quit practising early on or never even begin? Do children with genetic gifts for music evoke more reinforcement from parents and teachers, subsequently leading them to be even more motivated to practise? The results indicated that although genetically influenced propensities towards engaging in practice may account for some of the genetic influences on music accomplishment, they were not sufficient in themselves to explain motivations and eventual music accomplishments. Yet, the difference in heritability of accomplishment between those who practised and those who did not, was 58% ($p < .01$). Thus, Gene x Practice interactions not only persist, but can be strengthened. Therefore, it would seem that DP (i.e., a proxy for music lessons) is associated with the expression of genetic influences on music accomplishment.

There are two distinct viewpoints about music experts. One is that experts are *born*: innate ability puts a limit on the ultimate level of performance that a person can reach through training. The second is that experts are *made*: individual differences in performance can be explained in terms of training. These studies seem to provide some evidence suggesting that either individually or together, genetic potential and/or one's developing personality could be an important part of the expert-performance puzzle accounting for variances in DP. Levitin (2012) suggested that among the factors that cause some children to practise more than others are goal-directedness, self-confidence, innate reflexes, finger speed, motor coordination, auditory memory, and auditory structuring abilities. Moreover, there are contributing environmental factors, such as "having a teacher or family member who encourages or motivates the child and having access to musical stimulation and musical instruments" (p. 635).

DP must continue throughout the career of a professional Symphony Orchestra musician. Krampe (2006) found that in a retrospective study among Violinists from Top Berlin Orchestras, between the ages of 18 and 22 there was a drop-off in DP which levelled off at age 26. Krampe assumed that such a decrease reflected the surrender to Soloist ambitions in order to secure a position in a prestigious Orchestra (see Chapter 11, section 11.2.2). Such a change in life goals could also be seen as adaptation of time investment for other activities. Krampe concluded that DP remained fairly stable throughout middle adulthood till retirement—roughly till the musicians were 55 years old. In the current sample of Symphony Orchestra musicians, these players reported that between the ages of 20 and 29 years (the *2nd Decade*) they continued their individual weekly practice implemented outside regularly scheduled group Orchestra rehearsals with a slightly higher frequency than had been reported when they were 10–20 years old: $M_{DP (2nd Dec)} = 16.35_{h/wk}$, $SD = 10.68$, $Mdn = 14$, Range 1–49. Then, between the ages of 30 and 39 years (the

3rd Decade) there was a gradual reduction of practice implemented outside regularly scheduled group Orchestra rehearsals equal to less than half of the hours they reported for the previous decade: $M_{DP\ (3rd\ Dec)} = 7.51_{h/wk}$, $SD = 6.89$, $Mdn = 5.75$, Range 0–36. Finally, between the ages of 40 and 49 years (the *4th Decade*) individual practice implemented outside regularly scheduled group Orchestra rehearsals was again halved in frequency from the levels reported for the decade prior: $M_{DP\ (4th\ Dec)} = 4.57_{h/wk}$, $SD = 4.76$, $Mdn = 4$, Range 0–17.

(43y, F, vn)	*I haven't sat down to practise much [lately]. When I first got the job I did much more practising, for the sake of practising, than I do now. I mean, today I just go over little bits and bobs. If there's something really hard at work I'll take it home—especially if I have a concert. I don't want to lie or say: 'Oh I practise at least an hour or two a day.' Because I don't! I can't quantify it. I suppose on an average, [I practise] 1–2 hours most days, but [now] about 3 hours a week. But, I'd do more if I've got something [specific to practise].*
(47y, M, trb)	*Practice? Yeah, I [still] have to work on it. I have to do my daily drills and stuff. I do have one day off [a week] that I don't play. But, when we have a rehearsal at 10 o'clock, I'm [usually] here at the latest by 9:15. I do my practising here when I come early. I don't play at home. I used to practise (between ages 20 and 30) about 1–2 hours a day, 6 days a week. Then for the last 10 years, on average 1 hour a day, 5 days a week. Every day I practise; I warm up before a rehearsal, and rehearse the stuff I need for my job. I have to keep the same standard.*

Long-term DP of a musical instrument is a cognitively demanding activity that might moderate age-related cognitive decline. Such effects may possibly be explained by "improved neural efficiency of general control networks, allowing cognitively active individuals to better cope with age-related neural changes" (Amer et al., 2013, p. 6). It should be noted that the current sample reported an average ±7 hours of DP per week across the last 20-year period ($SD = 5.46$, $Mdn = 5$, Range 0–24). Specifically, for the past 12 months prior to the active research season of interviews, the current sample of players reported an average ±6 hours per week of DP ($SD = 5.39$, $Mdn = 5$, Range 0–21). In summing up all of the above, the current participating players' recollection of DP over their entire career was estimated as an average ±8-hours of DP per week ($SD = 3.82$, $Mdn = 7.57$, Range 1–18) for *every week of every year across the whole working life* of an Orchestra player. That would mean more than 5 Decades of maintaining performance abilities as a world-class Symphony Orchestra player.

(50y, M, vn)	*Sometimes I get the sense that some people [want to be in an Orchestra] because they did it from a young age. There wasn't really anything else that spoke to them, so they kept on going with the instrument. For example, when you've been at it for so long, you are very single-minded, very focused, and there's nothing else you know. I often wonder if there really isn't any other way? [The expectation is] that the [student] player spends an average 3–4 hours a day [practising] outside of rehearsal time or classes. And then there are summer camps and studies. And, an average 3–4 hours a day means that some days are more like 5–6 hours. And you're isolated by yourself, practising Scales, Arpeggios, or whatever. That takes a toll; it puts a mark on your social life, and your whole development. One question I often ask is about the price: 'Is this the price musicians have to pay?' That is, I wonder: 'Is that the price society wants us to pay, so that they can buy a ticket to see and hear an Orchestra (or Soloist) perform?'*

(57y, F, vc)   *I do know some players where there is a problem; I have played with them for many years, and I know their performance is declining. But I don't think it has to do with age! We often think that because we are rehearsing every day we don't need to practise. So, we basically stop practising—Deliberate Practice. And some think that even if they don't practise, then whatever [technique] they had will remain. But that is not the case. It is like sport: if you don't work out you lose your skills. Some feel that if they were once good enough, then, they will always be good enough. I now have evidence that you need to practise. Practice can be at home, or in the hall (before or after the rehearsals). I don't mean to practise the part you need to play, but to work on the instrument itself! Sometimes I play with Quartets and Quintets; I need to work on these parts alone at home for hours. I learn more about music in order to be more musical. If you don't practise these parts, then no one will want to play with you. Playing Duets, Trios, etc., is like playing a Solo; you can't hide behind the massive sound of the Orchestra. You need to put in the time to be able to play Chamber Music. I did have a period [for about 8 years] when I didn't practise. I neglected my instrument. I came to rehearsals, but didn't pick up the instrument in between. I also stopped playing outside of the Orchestra. Then, after a few years, I felt disabled; my intonation had degraded. Without practising, the intonation of a string instrument gets worse. It is impossible to play clean in the Orchestra if you don't practise outside of the Orchestra. After 10 years I returned to the music. My level of performance slowly came back.*

(60y, F, vc)   *I think we can keep the skills because we work on them. Especially for those who are 50+ years old, we need to continue practising. [I don't mean] rehearsals, but practice! I have had a few periods in life when I didn't engage in daily practice; then [I felt a] reduction in ability. I usually practise 4–5 hours a day, every day! When I don't have a lot of time, I practise only 2 hours a day. It's part of my lifestyle. I also need to spend time to hear myself, to fix mistakes, and to work on Orchestra parts.*

Deliberate Practice does explain a considerable amount of the variance in music performance. Hambrick et al. (2014) claimed that calculating DP may be necessary to account for why some people become experts while others fail to do so. But is this the whole story? Other factors (already mentioned above) may be heritable genetics, personality, and starting age. Yet, the historical chronicles of the current sample also seem to point to at least one other milestone in the development of Orchestra players. I point out that this 'variable' is as yet undocumented—having never been taken into account by other researchers in the literature. Namely: *Coming of Age.* That is, the 'age of intent', or the point in development at which one makes a conscious declaration to themselves—and to others—that they intend to become an *Orchestra Player.* This may be quite an important milestone! This has somewhat been referred to as cognizance of one's *Music Calling.*

2.2.1.3 Becoming an Orchestra Player

Many players point out that there are immeasurable differences between Soloists and Orchestra musicians. Accordingly, a Soloist practises and then reproduces what has been practised to the utmost highest possible level. There is excitement in the performance. A Soloist's greatest ability is their expertise to reproduce the sound they intended to perform—each and every time they are on the Concert platform. On the other hand, a Symphony Orchestra player might practise their own individual part for hours, but in the end, it is the group sound of all players performing one piece together that is heard. It is not their individual contribution, but rather the collective sound! This is a new event—each and every time the Orchestra performs the piece. Moreover, being a Soloist fundamentally differs from being part of a large Orchestra in terms of public exposure, demands, and psychosocial stressors. A study implemented by Détári et al. (2020) demonstrated that among 110 players of Symphony Orchestras in Norway, the feeling of having less control over the environment was greater among musicians who were either Soloists or members of Chamber Music Ensembles than any other vocation. This lack of control might be attributed to having to play under the close supervision and command of a Sub-Principal, Principal Section Leader, or Conductor/Music Director. To some extent, Orchestra players lose their independent preferred playing style, as well as their personal approach to music expression—simply by having to fit into a well-balanced uniform group-sound. "It is easy for us to feel we are an insignificant cog in an unappreciated note factory. But then, once in a blue moon, we will feel effortlessly in control of our instruments, which will no longer be an appendage we hold onto for dear life but instead will become fused naturally to our bodies" (Davis, 2004, p. 15).

Yet, there is a total lack of congruence between how a player is educated and their subsequent work in an Orchestra. Typically, a musician's education focuses on their development as a Solo performer, and emphasizes a more creative and aesthetic dimension of their musicianship. On the other hand, becoming and being a Symphony Orchestra musician requires teamwork, thus subordinating individual creativity and independence. Sternbach (1993, 1995) remarked that because most instrumentalists are trained for Solo playing, Orchestral work can be something of a disappointment. While studying elite performers, Krampe and Ericsson (1996) concluded that only the most outstanding players are able to pursue a Soloist career while the remaining expert musicians engage in other types of music-related jobs; the most popular being playing in professional Orchestras or Teaching musicians to play an instrument. While both of these aforementioned may be less prestigious careers, nonetheless they are a more predictable way of life. Brodsky (2006) reported that some Orchestra players view membership with a Symphony Orchestra as "the final surrender of the ambition to join the ranks of celebrated world-class Soloists" (p. 673). But yet, these same players admitted that there are many constructive reasons to pursue an Orchestra career, such as "socializing with like-minded people, camaraderie, teamwork, solidarity and friendship" (p. 687).

Certainly, the education of musicians should prepare them for specific aspects of the career. But for many this is not the case. This situation was explicitly investigated by Langner (2004) who examined String players' need to overcome discrepancies between instrumental training as a Soloist against the requirements of work employment in an Orchestra. The truth is that Orchestral musicians have to be able to switch between various behaviours; from supporting other players, to following other players, to leading other players (Davis, 2004). So how do so many players perform together, each on their own individual instrument, in complete synchrony? Davis feels that playing in an Orchestra is a process whereby collective talents are placed into one output. Hence, to be an Orchestra player, musicians need to have a host of skills beyond mastery of their specific instrument. Orchestra players clearly have to subordinate themselves and their perceptions about the music to a Conductor. Moreover, players from different sections (e.g., String, Wind) or positions (e.g., Principals, Tutti) are each required to meet different sets of demands (Gembris, 2006). Habibi et al. (2014) assert that performing in any sort of group format requires each musician to carefully attend to different aspects of the sound produced by the other musicians. Clearly, that includes intonation, timing, and dynamics. Collective music-making strengthens group cohesion by forcing participants to orient their attention to a shared temporal framework. Moreover, each player is required to connect emotionally with others, integrating the intended emotional impact with their own playing. Hence, as Davis points out, more than mastery and sheer talent, Orchestra musicians need ambition, discipline, attention to detail, intelligence, objective self-criticism, a sense of confidence and pride, and flexibility. Moreover, as Orchestral work-life requires close proximity and intense relationships, players must develop capabilities of cooperation and unselfishness.

(29y, F, vn) *I would have been a bit afraid if at college I was classified as being [either] a Soloist or an Orchestra musician. I wish I would have had better training in Orchestra playing. Yet, I don't regret having doing all those Concertos or Caprices cause they were so much fun to play. And if I were to say from the very beginning that I wanted to be an Orchestra player, I might never have played those solos!*

(30y, F, vn) *They should train you for what you need on the job. So, if 80% or more of professional musicians are gonna be playing in Orchestras, they need to train you as a player. But they try to develop your skills to be as high as possible, and even higher than what you need for an Orchestra. In Orchestras you have players who come with phenomenal techniques. But then, they just kind of get lost in the band. Those kind of 'Paganini' skills [Niccolò Paganini, celebrated virtuoso Violinist, 1782–1840] are not gonna help you in an Orchestra. If your skills are that high you don't have to worry about the technical side. That's certainly an advantage. But, there seems to be a link between the time you spend practising and the skills you develop.*

(39y, F, cl) *Is there any other profession that works like an Orchestra? On the one hand it is the group effort that makes the outcome, But on the other, each person is doing their own thing, regardless of what the next person is doing. Is there any other profession that involves you being a contributor to a group outcome, that requires you to do everything simultaneously? Well I suppose one could see a synchronized team swimming like Water Dancing. Or maybe Ballet. So, perhaps some might say that in an Orchestra it's not what I do that matters. But my role is Principal Clarinet; I do have moments where I become the 'star'. But nobody is going to say: 'That Clarinettist was great but the rest of the Orchestra was horrible.' That collective camaraderie is a whole different experience. How much does that offer a 'protective measure' of resilience? The fact that everybody has a certain responsibility to contribute keeps you going and agile, and is part of the occupational lifestyle.*

(57y, F, vn) *I believe that everyone has his or her own sound (expressed by their instrument). That sound is an expression of one's personality. Now the problem is that when you play in an Orchestra you need to blend in. That is, you need to lose your own personal sound. You cannot stand out—neither in volume nor colour. The ideal is that everyone will sound the same (especially Tutti players). Most of the time I won't even hear myself unless I am playing something else. There is a chance, then, that a player will lose themselves [metaphorically speaking]. That is why a player has to work independently at home—to try to come back to their own characteristic music personality. Their personal sonority and intonation. Then, when they regroup, and listen to all the others they will still be bringing something of themselves that no one else has. That is what builds the Orchestra. So, someone who doesn't practise, loses their technique, and loses a bit of their own music personality. But that has nothing to do with age!*

(60y, F, vc)   *Most people in a service profession do not share [their services] online simultaneously. An academic writes articles for others; but readers are not there watching them write! Or, when you go into a restaurant, the chef is not there sharing his food with you; he's usually in the back making food while someone else brings it out [to the table]. There aren't many professions where you actually do what you do with others, and then do it in front of people simultaneously at the same time. Even a painter who wants to share his art with people is not there with them while he's making art; people only see the finished product. But that's different when we play a concert. And this makes it very precious. But [also puts] a tremendous weight on the responsibility when playing with an Orchestra. I never really wanted to be Soloist. Perhaps I never even wanted to be in an Orchestra. I just wanted to play with others in Chamber Music groups.*

It is highly interesting to note that the participating musicians in the current sample reported to be aware that they *chose* to be an Orchestra player as their professional career already when they were at a very young age. Many wrote in their narratives: I always knew I wanted to be in an Orchestra . . . to be part of that sound. Davis (2004) claims that musicians should do some 'soul searching' if they really want to perform music as a career. There should be no doubts! One needs to *crave* to be an Orchestra musician. It must be more important than anything else in the world. It must be an obsession; inconceivable that one could consider any other profession.

(59y, M, fl/picc)   *Growing up during my early music education, I was placed in an Orchestra at a very, very young age. I was already in a Symphony Orchestra after only three years of playing an instrument. I was petrified when I saw so many people. But I really loved playing with all of them. The togetherness. They were a group that supported each other. I enjoyed the social side of the Orchestra. I won't apologize for that! I live an Orchestra lifestyle. I had learned many Solo pieces (with Piano accompaniment) such as Sonatas and Concertos; I used these in exams and auditions. I never really wanted to be a Soloist. It was the socialization among the Orchestra members. It's not just that there are many people. But there are so many other people 'like me'. Many groups (e.g., football clubs or industrial organizations) also get together after work, go out for drinks, and perhaps also have intimate relations with each other (i.e., couples). The key difference with an Orchestra is we also have an opportunity to play together, to make music as a group. I even enjoy Chamber Music (e.g., Quintets) more than the Orchestra as it is even more intimate; there is even more of a chance for me to express myself than in the Orchestra. Also, don't forget that when I play, I am not playing for cement walls. There are people! My instrument is a Solo instrument, and I am playing for someone. As if I am saying: 'Listen to me, what do you think?' When I play I am specifically looking for the eyes of a person. I am playing to someone. When someone in a break says: 'Wow, that was great!', then I enjoy it even more. When you learn to play an instrument, it is like learning to drive in a parking lot. Eventually you have to learn to drive in traffic. You learn by playing in the Orchestra.*

(60y, M, cl)   *I often look at my instrument simply as a stick with holes. Today, I less look at the instrument as being special. As a musician, you realize that it is really not important if you play Clarinet or Flute or Trumpet! Because each and every one of us plays their part in a social setting, this microcosm. I always enjoy hearing one of my colleagues play their instrument. For example, when I play the Beethoven Violin Concerto [Violin Concerto in D major, Op. 61, written in 1806 by German composer Ludwig van Beethoven, 1770–1827] and there are Woodwind solo parts that sound so nice together, there is nothing else in the repertoire that sounds like that! I have great pleasure and pride that I can partake in producing that sound. So when I hold my instrument, I don't think too much as a Clarinet player, but rather as a compatriot to the Orchestra sound.*

Accordingly, the players in the current study recalled that their decision to become an Orchestra player had already surfaced as 'a more conscious declaration' by their 15th Birthday ($M_{Age\ (n\ =\ 46,\ 89\%)}$ = 18, SD = 4.65, Mdn = 17, Range 8–30). The reader should look again at the range! Some declared this as early as 8 years old! This is what I refer to as the *coming-of-age* event. It was the collective sound, and the feeling of making music together. This finding is similar (but different) to Dobrow's (2013) musicians who started making career decisions by the end of High school—when they became aware of their *Music Calling* (see section 2.1.1). Some of the participating players in the current sample wrote that they chose the Orchestra as a vocational setting after realizing that they could not achieve the performance levels required to be a Soloist. Others wrote that the Orchestra offered them a performance alternative—as they had experienced overwhelming anxiety when performing with the spotlight exclusively upon them as a Soloist (see Chapter 5, section 5.3.1). Finally, some players noted that the Orchestra seemed to be the most applicable environment for a musician with a family (i.e., a parent of young children); albeit these players described struggling and juggling between performance-related obligations and family responsibilities, and found difficulties in meeting financial commitments based on remuneration as a Symphony Orchestra player. These latter sentiments were also reported by MacNamara et al. (2006).

(43y, F, vn)   *Well it can be difficult to get into an Orchestra. It's not as easy as that. It's not like if I can't [play solo] then I should definitely [play in an Orchestra]. Because, I mean, we've seen how many people go for one position, and then when you're in the section you also have different trialists for that one position. So, it's not a given that you're just gonna walk into an orchestral job. And I remember the day I got the job—I was so proud! This is the only Orchestra I've ever been with. I was just basically out [of college]; I'd done a couple of postgraduate years. I am not saying this is considered to be the best Orchestra in the area. It's funny how people in the public perceive us [versus another Orchestra in the city] to be rivals. Actually, quite a number of people in both Orchestras are either going out [dating] or actually married. Our Orchestra does a lot of new music whereas the other one does more outside [live] broadcasts of popular music. So, I do think we have different audiences.*

(47y, M, trb)   *I'm really happy that I have this job. Tell me of jobs like this where we get paid for being onstage and playing in a performance. We get a big applause afterwards. I'm really happy to be part of that. Can I understand musicians that don't want to be in an Orchestra? Sure! To play in an Orchestra as a Trombone player is totally different than to be a Viola [Tutti] player. Some feel that they took an Orchestra job, but should have been a Solo player. Not me! I never wanted to be a Solo player. I played some Solos in my Brass Band when I was young, but I was so nervous that I almost had an anxiety attack.*

(47y, F, vn)   *I never wanted to be a Soloist, I always wanted to be in the Orchestra. It was clear for me that I wouldn't have a chance [to be a soloist] because I started late with the Violin. I played some small Solo concerts, but that wasn't my goal. Playing Chamber Music was a great thing for me. Chamber is still really my favourite form of making music.*

(49y, F, vn)   *I realized [at age 25] I couldn't be a Soloist. Foremost it is very difficult! You need to practise [all the time], and I am a woman [with a] family and children. Yes! I was already married with children back then [when I auditioned for this Orchestra].*

(49y, M, vn)   *Do I see the Orchestra as a compromise because as a musician I had trained to be a Soloist? On the one hand: 'Yes!' But on the other hand the Orchestra offers many benefits, including steady work and salary, as well as [feeling at] home. Yet, Orchestra work is not suitable for every musician, just as much as being a Soloist is not suitable for every musician. When I was very young, I was considered a prodigy. I already understood then that Orchestra life was what I wanted. So it was never a compromise, but rather a choice! Obviously, not all musicians have the privilege to make that kind of choice. Out of all of the Concertmaster Leaders that I know (from around the world in major European and North American Orchestras), 90% could have been world-class Soloists—but of the 2nd tier not the 1st top level. Those who could have been among the top-ranking soloists are the 10 Leaders [Concertmasters] of the Top-Ten Orchestras in the world. For them it was certainly a compromise! Unfortunately, among musicians the hierarchy is: (1) Soloist; (2) Chamber Ensemble Player; (3) Orchestra Musician; and (4) Music Teacher.*

(55y, M, bn)   *It was my decision to [become a musician, an Orchestra player, and then] join the ranks of this Orchestra. I have to live with my decisions. I didn't think I felt that when I was younger that there might be consequences. Today I feel it was a major decision! I'm happy that I'm a musician. That I wake up in the morning and I play music. But 35–40 years later, I'm unhappy with the fact that I've put myself in a position where I have no chance of financial security. That's upsetting for me as being a long-time career professional. It's upsetting to me that I want to be able to leave some kind of inheritance to my kids, and I cannot do that because of the profession that I chose [when I was a teenager].*

(56y, F, vn)   *I never wanted to be a Soloist even though I had the potential to do so. I think that all players between 25 and 50 years of age receive so much from playing in an Orchestra (which is just as much, if not more, than playing Solo). A good Orchestra, with good people, a good Conductor, and good concert programmes, gives great satisfaction and growth. That is what an Orchestra is all about. You are never alone! And, this is not something that happens only when you get to my age. I always felt that way from the first day of my first Orchestra in the Conservatory. Some say it is like a family, or a group, or a collective. Ensemble playing is far superior to playing Solo. We all start out as Soloists, but not everyone can play with others. I always know how I feel at the same time [as do the other players around me]. I never play alone.*

(57y, F, vc)   *I wanted to be in an Orchestra already from a young age. But, I think there are players who should never [have been accepted] to play for an Orchestra. They play because they feel they have no other choice. Maybe they wanted to be a Soloist, but they became an Orchestra player. Some enter the Orchestra, and then after 5–6 years realize it is not for them. I really don't think that most of the players here thought they were going to be [long-term career-track] Orchestra players. Maybe they didn't even want to be here, but they needed income. I never wanted to be a Soloist. I understood that that I was not fully engaged nor [could I] live up to the challenges to achieve the required level. By the time I realized what I never did (at a younger age) I was too old; life was not open any more for that kind of commitment. So being a Soloist was out of the question. I just didn't have the proper foundation. I always loved Chamber Music and Ensemble playing. Especially the solidarity of group perfor-mance. Some like being alone; they want the spotlight. Yet truly, not everyone can be a Soloist. Others enjoy being among the group. I had enjoyed all kinds of Ensembles from Duets onwards. I loved the vast repertoire, with endless possibilities of all instru-ments playing together. And, I always loved the Orchestra—also as someone seated in the audience! I remember as a young 15-year-old student going to the Philhar-monic, sitting among all of the voices that the composer wrote. I loved it! Even today I sit and listen to the Winds behind me, and hear all of the harmonies. It makes me feel good!*

(59y, M, va)   *Did I want to be an Orchestra player? I actually come from a family where every-one in my family were scientists—grandfathers, father, and siblings. My father was a Mathematician, my older brother a Biologist, and my second brother was also a Math-ematician. My father studied in the 1920s at a time when you didn't just study one subject; he learned Mathematics, Physics, Counterpoint, and Composing, He was a well-playing dilettante [amateur]. He composed, and could improvise very well on the Piano. So, we all also played instruments. The first time I played Viola was at the age of 11. We had a Flute Quartet in the family; a father with 3 sons. I did quite well very early on. But it was self-evident that none of us would ever get to [be a] professional musician—that was out of our way of thinking. On the one hand it was natural that everyone played, but on the other hand [it was clear that] you went off to study something scientific. When my father died I was 17. I thought about what profession I wanted to choose. I was not sure about anything. I had listened to many Operas from the age of 13, but only heard Symphony Concerts with an Orchestra at the age 17. At that time I had just decided to [be a] professional musician. My father was dead, and he couldn't say: 'No!' I think there is no typical way young musicians decide to become professional. I was just lucky to go to this city where there was a very good famous Viola teacher. It went well, and I chose this way [of life and profession]. It was just fate. But, I never wanted to be a Soloist. I always wanted to be an Orchestra player.*

Indeed, achieving and sustaining a position as a member of a Symphony Orchestra is widely looked upon with considerable admiration. Landing a contract with a top-level professional organization requires competitive auditions, many years of preparation, and considerable perseverance. Those who 'make it' in the performance world are often revered by those seeking entry to the profession (Brodsky, 2006).

2.3 The Orchestra as an Occupational Environment

Two issues surfaced from the narratives about the Orchestra as an occupational environment. The first relates to the various types of activities that preoccupy Orchestra musicians. The second relates to different profiles of the Orchestras themselves.

2.3.1 Portfolio Players

Within the survey booklet (see Chapter 1, section 1.6.3.3, Table 1.3 [Q3]) each player reported their weekly activities, involving: (a) music performance (e.g., in the Orchestra as a contract player, external Chamber Ensembles, and Solo recitals); (b) rehearsing (with the Orchestra); (c) practising (DP at home or in the Hall prior to rehearsals); and (d) teaching (studio teaching of an instrument, or in College classrooms). Several researchers (e.g., Mills, 2004; Mills & Smith, 2006) refer to such multiplicity of activity among musicians as becoming a *portfolio player*. Accordingly, for about 20 years between 1979 and 1995, there was a decrease (−48%) in professional musicians who could actually sustain a job in just one area—while at the same time there was an increase (+71%) in the phenomenon of having to be involved in two or more areas of work. Smilde (2006, 2009) noted that the nature of a musician's career has changed. Perhaps Orchestra players do have a job for life—or at least as long as they can perform up to standards. But yet, for the most part in today's economic atmosphere, musicians also need to develop Portfolio Careers. Namely, players must function within different contexts, taking on various roles, such as:

Accompanist, Arranger, Coach, Composer, Editor, Leader, Mentor, Performer, and Teacher. These may be overlapping, and seem to be relevant in all genres of music. Smilde identified more than 50 multifaceted-but-related roles and skills, referring to areas of engagement for present-day musicians. For a list of subspecialities among the Music Profession, the reader is referred back to Table 2.1. Today's professional music performers need to develop entrepreneurship, as well as other generic skills, and these also include abilities to interact appropriately with potential students, music directors, music presenters, and music promoters. The changing nature of a musician's career requires them to be lifelong learners of adaptive strategies for transferable skill development.

We do need to put into context that the accepted practice for full-time employment ranges between 35 and 45 hours per week (as outlined by the US Federal Labor Standards Act, FLSA). Accordingly, a 40-hour work week reflects the most common standard of employment. As can be seen below, professional full-time contract Symphony Orchestra musicians in the current research sample reported an average 38:30 hours per week of engagement and employment. Obviously, the major difference between the music-performance vocation and most other occupations has to do with how 'business hours' are defined. The more traditional outlook of business hours is that the most prevalent hours of business are between 9.00 a.m. and 5.00 p.m., Monday to Friday. That standard represents a workweek consisting of five 8-hour days. Yet, such an occupational lifestyle is typically unusual for the working music performer. Foremost, the majority of music performances, especially within Symphony Orchestras, are characteristically scheduled in evening hours after 8.00 p.m. (20.00). Then, most concerts occur during the weekend (on a Friday and Saturday) as these evenings are the most applicable time frame for the general public to purchase tickets as the audience seated in the Concert venue auditorium. On this topic Détári et al. (2020) claim:

> The sporadic schedule of musicians can be compared to shift workers. Shift work is defined as work undertaken in 'nonstandard' hours, late evening or night hours, work on weekends, and irregular working hours in general. Being out of synchronization with the rest of society, meaning that their work, leisure, and sleep times are skewed compared to the general population, can make it challenging to organize a day, corrupt social well-being, and negatively impact interpersonal relationships. (p. 8)

Such a sentiment is reflected by the player below.

(40y, F, vn)   *The Orchestra is a very social place; I have friends there. That's one of the things that I like about it. That it's steady and social. It's not just a job where people also work at home glued to the computer all day. So actually, I am saying that one of the aspects of the profession is that the Orchestra is a way of life that allows you to be more 'immune' to ageing. In many professions as you get older you become more isolated, but that's not the case in an Orchestra. The Orchestra has a lifestyle built into it. In other professions friends pick up and move away, but in an Orchestra there's always a group that you're with, travel with, and see every day. It's not like in an office where you see 2–3 people a day. Rather you're with 70 people all the time. Yet, that is also kind of incestuous. [Laughs.] I wouldn't necessarily say that most of the people in the Orchestra are married to the Orchestra—in the sense that that's who they are and that's where they go. But we do spend more time with our Desk Partner than our marital partner. Most players do have lives outside the Orchestra. We work less than 8–9 hours a day which is the amount a lot of office workers are employed. But the main problem is time management. One challenge for me is that while we have a lot of performances, we have much fewer rehearsals. Hours-wise, it is perhaps just a little more per week. The biggest problems is always that work is scheduled in the evenings. So while I may have the whole day free and I can do whatever I want, in the evening I work from 7 to 10 p.m. It is a little bit of a problem to have social life with people who are not in the Orchestra. A lot of players marry other players [from the same Orchestra or beyond]. Funny, I once worked in an Orchestra where 5–6 people were related in one way or another.*

In the survey questionnaire booklet, the participating Symphony Orchestra players indicated the number of hours per week they were engaged or employed in various professional music-performance activities. Using a numeric representation spanning between 0 and 40+ hours per week, each player indicated the frequency they engaged in each activity. The array of numbers was: 0, <1, 1–4, 5–8, 9–12, 13–16, 17–20, 21–30, 31–40, 40+. Then, the original responses were recoded as *median* values (0, 0.5, 2.5, 6.5, 10.5, 14.5, 18.8, 25, 35, 45). The findings reflect the responses of $n = 44$ Symphony Orchestra musicians; this dataset is 85% of the omnibus total sample whereby missing data resulted by a few players who did not fully comply.

2.3.1.1 Performance

The players reported to perform music onstage for an average ±11 hours per week: (a) Orchestra ($M_{h/wk} = 9{:}30$, $SD = 5.8$, Range 3–35); (b) freelance with external Chamber Music ensembles ($M_{h/wk} = 1{:}00$, $SD = 1.68$, Range 0–7); and (c) Solo recitals ($M_{h/wk} < 1{:}00$, $SD = 0.81$, Range 0–3).

2.3.1.2 Rehearsal and Practice

The players reported to rehearse inside the Orchestra hall, and practise outside Orchestra rehearsals, for an average of ±24 hours per week: (a) Orchestra ($M_{h/wk} = 18{:}30$, $SD = 6.8$, Range 0–35); and (b) Deliberate Practice ($M_{h/wk} = 5{:}45$, $SD = 4.58$, Range 0–19).

2.3.1.3 Teaching

The players reported to Teach music to individual students (instrument lessons), or College-level classroom courses, for an average of ±3 hours per week ($M_{h/wk} = 3{:}67$, $SD = 4.98$, Range 0–25). They reported to engage with an average ±3 students per week, who they see on an individual basis in their private studio teaching a musical instrument ($M_{pupils/wk} = 3.34$, $SD = 4.11$, Range 0–15).

(60y, F, vc)   *I did say that I chose the Orchestra as a way of life. I was once a well-known Soloist. Being in the Orchestra isn't the same as being a Soloist as far as musical level is concerned. Yes, I did really think that for a couple of years. But then after some time I understood that it's also a different kind of responsibility. I tried to find an integrative approach to understand that Orchestra playing is one language in a very wholesome general way, and being a Soloist is a totally different way to play. So, I try to keep both ways. I am now invited for 3–4 recitals [a year]. I can switch from one language to the other. It's difficult, and you always feel that one thing takes time away from the other. But I always work on these integrative processes. And it helps me by taking time off from the Orchestra to do Solo Recitals. I have always tried to find the perfect combination; the right proportions of playing in an Orchestra, Solos, Chamber Music, and Teaching.*

2.3.2 Working Orchestras

The professional Symphony Orchestra is a unique workplace. Orchestra members are superb musicians; they are among the fortunate few who were able to contract a full-time position in Western Classical Music. As an organization, professional Symphony Orchestras are highly complex. Previously in Chapter 1 (see section 1.2) a study by Smith (1988, 1989) was introduced. That study interviewed 14 retired Orchestra members of the Chicago Symphony Orchestra (CSO). The players had been active members of an Orchestra for roughly 41 years, of which the last 35 years had been with the CSO. As Smith noted, and was then later confirmed by Henson (1994), as a work environment, vocation, and profession, the Orchestra is considered to be a *great place to grow old*. That sentiment can be seen in the statements of six retired players from two Symphony Orchestras (see Chapter 12).

In a landmark study, Allmendinger et al. (1996) solicited 81 professional Symphony Orchestra musicians from the former East Germany, the former West Germany, the United States of America, and the United Kingdom. See Table 2.3. In total, 78 Orchestras participated in that survey. The data was collected between 1990 and 1991. The participating Orchestras were both Concert and Broadcast Orchestras; a few orchestras exclusively performed specialized repertoire such as Operas and Pops. Among those participating in the study were the Boston Symphony and the New York Philharmonic Orchestra. Unlike Smith (1988, 1989) who studied retired players greater than 60 years old, Allmendinger et al.'s sample included young(er) players less than 40 years old. As can be seen in Table 2.3 the players served in the same position of their present Orchestra for an average 14 years. Their length of tenure was 17.5 years while the mean length of service for Principals and Assistant/Co-Principals was 17.15 years. These data are highly similar to British Orchestras (e.g., Sergeant & Himonides, 2019). Allmendinger et al.'s typical player had been employed previously by two Orchestras before moving to their present Orchestra. The researchers note that while most new arrivals to a major Orchestra came from another Orchestra, new arrivals to a regional Orchestra either came directly from a College or had been an experienced Freelancer. Allmendinger et al. outline the typical career pattern of Orchestra players:

Table 2.3 Descriptives of Players in 81 Orchestras (in the 1990s)

	East Germany	West Germany	USA	UK	Total	
					M	*SD*
Average Age of the Players	42.0	41.0	44.0	37.0	41.0	(2.94)
Years in Current Orchestra	19.8	15.3	15.1	10.9	15.3	(3.64)
Years in Current Position	18.1	15.3	15.1	10.9	13.8	(3.56)
Number of Previous Orchestras	1.9	2.4	2.2	2.0	2.1	(0.22)

Data Source: Allmendinger et al. (1996)

- As a young player out of College they begin to play with a regional Orchestra (as a freelancer reliever)
- After a few years they gain an audition with a major Orchestra
- They undergo several rounds (e.g., 2–3 stages), and then if successful, are employed on a trial basis
- Eventually, after 1–2 years of performing with the Orchestra, a permanent full-time contract is offered.

Accordingly, most players who move to a major Orchestra may change Orchestras one more time. But for the most part, they settled down and continue in the same position in the same Orchestra until retirement. Symphony Orchestra playing is not a profession characterized by a great deal of career movement (see Chapter 7, section 7.3.4). Allmendinger et al. note that at the other end of the career, the most common reason for departure from a major Orchestra (53%) was either retirement or death.

Knight (2006) outlines Orchestras as adhering to one of two sizes. The Chamber Orchestra is between 24 and 35 players, consisting of: 11–22 Strings, 12 Winds & Brass, and Percussion. The Symphony Orchestra is between 70 and 110 members, consisting of: 60+ Strings; 30+Winds & Brass including Piccolo, Cor Anglais, and Tuba; Percussion; and Harp. Some Orchestras also perform as a Radio Broadcasting Orchestra. Most Orchestras perform in Halls designed for concerts. The purpose of the Hall is for the Orchestra to assemble for rehearsals and performances. Professional Orchestras tend to rehearse and perform several times a week. Although most Orchestras perform in closed spaces, outdoor performances do occur. While there is not one standard of absolute seating arrangement, both Chamber and Symphony Orchestras employ very similar seating positions that have been traditionally employed for the past 300 years; albeit, some modern pieces demand specific 'spatial' seating arrangements.

The variances in work-related scheduling (which subsequently indicate different levels of rehearsal, practice, and performance engagement) were often the subject of conversation among the current sample of participating players. In fact, some consider this factor when contemplating future contracts that involve an audition procedure for an open position. Players often felt more 'vulnerable' in terms of demands when playing for an Orchestra whose repertoire mostly contained Modern Contemporary Music. According to Détári et al. (2020) who studied Orchestra players in Norway, there is a liability attributed to the fact that special instrumental techniques are often associated with Contemporary Music—and hence there is a need for more practice time if and when transferring to such an organization.

(38y, M, bn/dbn) *Some Orchestras seem to be well known for their scheduling of a one-off single (major) performance per week, while other Orchestral environments involve as many as five concerts per week.*

(60y, F, vc) *The training period is never finished, it never ends! That's the point. I don't know if it's special for an Orchestra musician, but I can tell you that there is a tremendous training from week to week, year to year, throughout the years. There is always new repertoire [that one needs] to adapt. [Some do think] we play the same thing every year. No, we do not! We are the Radio [Broadcasting] Orchestra. Most of the time, we learn new pieces. Here and there, there are some Brahms, Mahler, or Tchaikovsky that we've played already—but that's exceptional. That's one difference for a Radio Orchestra compared to a Philharmonic Orchestra.*

Finally, several players spoke about vast differences between the Orchestras depending on the location (e.g., country, culture, etc.). Orchestra players often have professional work experiences in different countries—as mobility is somewhat built into the music performance profession. Players are often subcontracted as 'extras' and 'relievers'. Sometimes there are open positions at an Orchestra in a foreign country—and that requires repeated auditions and trials, as well as residing elsewhere.

(61y, M, fl/picc) *An interesting aspect relates to Sight-Reading. It has always been a necessary tool [here], much more so than in Europe or America. Because here we have a Deputy System. It's frustrating because you may have a job in the Orchestra, but if you wanted to put in a deputy, you could do so. Let's say we had a Tuesday–Wednesday rehearsal with a Thursday evening concert. If on the Wednesday a really nice student came in (as a freelancer paid for hours engaged), I could say [to the Principal Leader]: 'I'm putting in a dep for that [concert].' Someone to cover for me—a deputy. In that case I would pay them myself privately. I would receive my fee from the Orchestra for being there [even if] I wasn't there; I'd pay the fee of the dep when actually I would've been off earning more somewhere else (e.g., at the studios). And this was very prevalent already from the 1930s—very much to the frustration of management. There's a story about a Conductor who on the first day rehearsed the Orchestra, but then on second day half the players had changed. He asked: 'Where's my Orchestra?' and was told they sent in deputies [freelancers]. On the final rehearsal the Conductor recognized just one player—a Double Bass player— who'd been through all his rehearsals. He went up to him saying: 'Thank you so much, you've remained loyal to me, thank you for being here. You're the only person who hasn't sent in a deputy. Thank you so much.' The player replied: 'Well don't worry, I won't be doing the concert!' Traditionally that's the way the system worked. You had to be able to Sight-Read; you just turned up and Sight-Read. Players [in this country] are good Sight-Readers. Whereas in Germany you might start rehearsals on a Tuesday [for four days of rehearsals] for a concert on Friday. Typically, you don't have to Sight-Read there. You turn up and gradually get the hang of it; by the time of the concert you've learned the piece.*

2.4 Discussion and Summary

This chapter offers a retrospective perspective on how musicians become Orchestra players. The depiction is very different from other previous studies presented in the literature. For example, Farnam (2016) outlined a study exploring the 'characteristics' of music performers, seeking causes for *lifelong musicianship*. Farnam recruited $N = 10$ Lifelong Musicians who were 35–60 years of age. Those musicians reported to have played music from childhood well into adulthood, but yet and unlike the players in the current study, they all had separate careers in conjunction with being active musicians. Nonetheless, Farnam uncovered 14 themes targeting life experiences and social factors that were accountable for one experiencing 'lifelong engagement in music'. These were:

- Learning Music by Ear by spending hundreds or thousands of hours listening to recordings and copying what was heard.
- Music Performance engagement that is related to personal dynamics, receiving attention or recognition for musical accomplishments and ability.
- Motivational Factors responsible for continued interest in music, such as euphoric responses from the audience.
- Distinct Memories of non-traditional music experiences, playing in music ensembles not affiliated with School Band or School Choir.
- Early Childhood Memories of music of listening to music with a parent while in a car.

Although these characteristics and developmental themes provide some insights, unfortunately they are not relevant to Western Classical Musicians—especially to full-time contract Symphony Orchestra players.

So how did the current participating musicians become Orchestra players? The data of the 11-measure 12-page questionnaire booklet details the overall development of the current musicians in the sample from early childhood throughout early adulthood. For the most part, they did not come from families of professional musicians. Albeit, many of the families were viewed as having a huge appreciation for music. In some cases there were family members who were quite good amateur players. Usually, a single parent was identified as the one who encouraged, supported, and emotionally accompanied them throughout their development from age 6; nonetheless, some players reported to have begun at an earlier age of 3. In general, the players reported to have had five main teachers for their instrument before age 20. Their first public appearance occurred by age 10. Less than half reported to have participated in local, national, or international instrument competitions. The players recalled having invested roughly 14,744 hours of DP by the time they reached age 20. They continued to engage in DP 8 hours per week every week throughout their career—sometimes for as long as 5 Decades when they were well in their 60s. The players mention that they consciously chose the Orchestra profession by age 15; nonetheless, some claimed they had already decided to live out their lives as an Orchestra player as early as when they were 8 years old. Many sat on the stage as a permanent positioned member in a National Youth Orchestra already at age 15. All players completed a College-level music degree.

The current participating musicians reported that their standard Orchestra Lifestyle consists of: performing, rehearsing, and practising:

- Performing with the Orchestra 3–35 hours per week
- Performing as a Freelance-Reliever with external Orchestras, Chamber Music Ensembles, or as a Soloist 0–7 hours per week
- Rehearsing with the Orchestra 0–35 hours a week
- Deliberate Practice 0–35 hours a week
- Teaching College-level courses 0–25 hours a week
- Teaching Studio instrument lessons 0–15 hours

PART II

THE INTERVIEW STUDY

Part II includes transcripts of the single 2-hour interview session among 48 professional full-time contract players from five Symphony Orchestras in three countries (see Chapter 1, section 1.6.2). I point out that four players (7.7% of the omnibus $N = 52$ full sample) cancelled their participation in the pre-scheduled interview. While sitting side by side with each individual participant (see Chapter 1, section 1.6.3), employing a predetermined script of topics to direct the dialogue (see Chapter 1, Table 1.2), each participant-player was asked to imagine the session *as if* it were a conversation in a café. Every session began with the same pre-scripted story:

Imagine that I am a younger player seeking your advice as a much more experienced seasoned player. The advice you offer me is not necessarily just from your own personal perspective, but also from what you may have heard from other players in the Orchestra about situations they experienced.

Let's think about ageing as something that happens to all of us, not just to musicians. Ageing happens to our bodies and our minds. We might understand that as we age all kinds of things happen to us. And, it's logical to say that you can't do the same things you could have done 20 years ago, perhaps because of wear and tear. As a metaphor: buying a car. You buy it, and then take enormous care of it. You buff it and clean it. You take it to the garage for maintenance and repair. But just by using it every day for 5–10 years, time will take its toll. Just out of steady use, it's getting older, and starting to break down, no matter how well you take care of it.

Our body and our mind are sort of the same. So, one could only question, by all other logic, you shouldn't be able to do what you do in the Orchestra. It's really amazing to keep the skills you've developed for so many years. But, one would assume that as you get older, you don't have the same flexibility and dexterity, and your mind isn't as bright as it was. By the time athletes are 30 years old, they have to give up their careers; their bodies just can't maintain what is needed. Professional dancers finish their stage performance careers at roughly 25 years of age; maybe one or two do move on. But, basically there are no Ballet dancers on the platform at the age of 50—still dancing onstage like they did when they were 20 or 30 years old. And so, we [in the scientific community] are baffled: How can Orchestra players continue to play beyond 50 years old, and [I added with some extra enunciation] they sound as good as they did when they were 35 or 40 years old? Hence, the main question is: How do you keep it up? How do you do it? Even if your opinion might be: Well, actually we don't! That's what I want to hear!

It has been previously pointed out that qualitative approaches are particularly well suited for the subjective world of the music performer (Cottrell, 2004; Kingsbury, 1998/2001; Williamon et al., 2021). Accordingly, *Ethnography* is associated with the study of culture. The goal is to describe the cultural practices of certain people whereby the researcher aims to 'get inside' the way a group of people see the world. The analysis focuses on understanding the lived experiences of Orchestra players, and how these relate to (or differ from) other musicians. Such studies are typically carried out over periods of many months (or many years), allowing researchers time to become immersed in the culture that is being studied. Williamon et al. (2021) contend that usually such studies are conducted on-site in the culture being studied, making use of interviews, with the researcher "engaging in a lot of hanging around, soaking up every detail" (pp. 33–34). Previously, Kvale (1996) felt that just hanging out in the environment where the interviews are to be conducted will give the researcher a taste of the local language, the daily routines, and the social structures. Nonetheless, Imreh and Crawford (2002) point out that it may just never be possible for musicians to really feel free or relaxed enough to talk about themselves without fear of losing the confidence of the interviewer—and subsequently the readers of printed interviews. Given that public confidence is usually reflected in annual subscriptions, Concert ticket sales, and revenues from recordings, such fear is quite genuine. Williamon et al. (2021) further claim that Ethnography is the prime strategy to be used when seeking "to understand musical cultures such as educational institutions and Orchestras" (p. 34).

Part II (Chapters 3–7) presents the reflections and considerations of professional full-time contract Symphony Orchestra musicians on the many aspects of music performance, and on a music-performance career. As little material can be found in the literature about Symphony Orchestra lifestyle, it seems warranted to present some more general data—even if not necessarily related to ageing.

A digital audio recording of the interviews was undertaken for every musician. Each verbal record was transcribed verbatim (i.e., word for word). Only a few interviews were conducted in the Hebrew language, and even then, portions of the conversations (such as idioms and phrases) were mentioned in the English language. These were translated from Hebrew to English—as close as possible to the original. Nonetheless, I acknowledge that when transferring an oral verbal means of communication (i.e., spoken Hebrew) to a more formal printed text (i.e., transcribed English), the process of linguistic analysis may be intuitive, and at times, even interpretative. The qualitative analysis of all documents involved a total of four overpasses for each vignette. The analyses included: conceptualization, classification, and categorization. These procedures enriched the research by identifying themes leading to an improved understanding of meaning illuminating further interpretation. That is, the material was sorted inductively, suggesting particular topics. Then a coding procedure was applied—following the rules of structured content analysis—combining inductive and deductive coding.

The process led to categories that subsequently defined the chapters presented here in Part II; these were a combined inductive (empirical) and deductive (theoretical) approach for understanding the players' statements and associations (e.g., semantic meanings). The coding process consisted of two main steps: categorization and reduction. In the first step, the primary documents were read, segmented, and organized according to a coding scheme. In the second step, relations were determined by category. Namely, the analyses moved from open coding, to axial coding (identifying relationships between codes to generate subthemes), to selective coding of themes which were then grouped into concepts to generate theories.

At the beginning of the coding process, I read the participants' thoughts several times in order to attain a higher level of familiarity with the raw data. The coding began with the selection of text quotations relevant to the research. During the categorization, different answers were recognized and I assigned codes for partitioning the data; carefully rereading of the text was undertaken in order to avoid redundancies and repetitions of the same participant. During the reduction step the codes were sorted into six categories: Mental, Motor, Emotional, Musical, Environmental, and Organizational. The codes and categories were later validated by an independent reader. All contrasts (and ambiguities) were dealt with.

As described earlier (in Chapter 1, section 1.6), the chapters in Part II present data from a set of individual cases, referred to as a *collective case study* among a specific occupational group within its real-life context. Robson (1993) referred to this strategy as *real-world research*. In general, the players did consider the context of ageing among Symphony Orchestra musicians. Below is an example from the transcripts of one 47-year-old player as he remembers himself in a younger time period recollecting a story about a Seasoned Musician:

(47y, M, vc)   *When I joined the World Philharmonic Orchestra (my first job), I'd sit next to an old Australian chap, who learned with Pablo Casals [1876–1973, a Spanish/Puerto Rican Cellist]. He was just hilarious. He wore these rustic old boots, and swore madly. But he was an incredible musician, and he taught me so much. When I joined, in the early '70s, the guy was 72. He had studied with Béla Bartók in Budapest [1881–1945, a Hungarian composer]. And this guy was completely 'doolally'. We'd do this thing [to him] where you'd get a polystyrene cup with coffee, and if you pushed it along the floor hard enough it kind of looked like it was bubbling. He'd say: 'Christ, that coffee's bubbling away like an acid'. Of course, he thought it was still boiling. He completely and utterly couldn't accept the fact that it was a joke. And we did stuff like that [to him] all the time. Once we did an encore and said: 'Bows down' (because it was a Pizzicato encore). So, he put his bow down on the floor. And of course, the last note was Arco! And you could see in his face: 'How the hell am I going to get the bow [back] in my hand?' Instead of just picking it up, he tried to kick it. On a certain level he was 'away with the fairies'. But, when it came to the actual job of playing notes, interpreting music, or meeting the Conductor's demands—he was fearless! And staying in Tempo and everything. That's the person you'd think is not going to be able to keep up: 'How could that 72-year-old keep up with me?' But, he was way ahead of me. Nonetheless, there are other older players that you can see they have a bit of shaking when they start to play. Some even walk up the stairs of stage and fall on the last step because they can't lift their feet. But yet for the most part, once they are onstage, every single note and motor-motion is there!*

Chapter 3 is about the mental considerations: mental skills, information processing, memory and memorizing music; attention and keeping preparation fresh and focused. Chapter 4 is about the motor considerations: physical challenges and physical fitness; dealing with repetition, drill, and practice; rehearsing and preparing for performances; kinaesthetic memory and memorized performances; body movement and communicating with the body in performance; and tempo, accuracy, fluctuation, and psychomotor speed. Thereafter, Chapter 5 highlights the emotional considerations, including: motivation, performance, and spiritual life; emotional communication; performance and human interaction; creativity and originality; discipline, artistic integrity, and commitment; performance nerves and anxieties; dispositional traits; and relationships among players. Chapter 6 continues with musical considerations: music expressivity and structural communication; musical competence such as playing in tune, playing in time, Sight-Reading, music analysis and interpretation; and musical potential. Finally, Chapter 7 follows with the environmental and organizational considerations: work environment, working conditions, and job security.

Orchestras are often looked upon as a group of people working together in an intimate manner towards efficiently creating an emotional product—at a specific moment right in front of our eyes. We often view players as being 'colleagues', or perhaps a 'bunch of friends' at play with each other, or perhaps a group of like-minded artisans. At least to us—the public—Symphony Orchestra musicians open their minds and hearts, bearing their souls, in a collective group effort to express something bigger than mundane human daily experiences. But yet, there is also a tradition among Orchestra players not to share intimate feelings with each other—specifically those issues related to insecurity or weakness. Never!

(33y, F, bn/dbn)   *[Sometimes I need to] talk to someone. I say: 'Please help me.' Because if you're a person from outside [the Orchestra] you can see a lot. And that's also the point with my boyfriend. I can tell him: 'You know what? I trust you and I'm able to tell you I have a problem.' Because as a musician in an Orchestra you don't share! You can't! It's a kind of a concurrence. No one wants to show there is a problem, because if you tell someone that you have a problem, then one day, they might use it against you. And [an Orchestra] is not really a relationship of trust. That may be why many players didn't want to come here [to participate in the current research study]. There's only six of us. Maybe [the others] didn't want to come because they didn't want to talk; didn't want to open up.*

The above vignette also illustrates the fact that the participants in the study might not have been a random representative sample of everyday professional full-time contract Symphony Orchestra musicians. That is, perhaps the more typical Orchestra player would not have agreed to participate in a format requiring them to engage in personal discussions containing self-discovery, leading to insights on a rather intimate issue. Especially so, when the subject matter is considered to be *taboo*—as is the topic of ageing! This was my previous experience when I investigated Music Performance Anxieties (e.g., Brodsky, 1995, 1996, 2000, 2006; Brodsky & Sloboda, 1997a, 1997b; Brodsky et al., 1994).

I reiterate here a few conventions found in the text. I often reflect (and paraphrase) the words of several players at one time. However, as pointed out earlier, full citations appear in a reduced italicized font preceded by the participant's age, sex, and instrument. This documentation is essential as it places the words in a specific context of person, age group, and instrument family. Further, I would like to point out that vignettes are always presented in *ascending* order of age; the youngest player is presented first while the oldest player is presented last. Also, it should be noted that only a selection of citations is brought forward for illustrative purposes. Lastly, some of the chapters are somewhat split in layout; the more general aspects of Orchestra Life are presented first, and then specific aspects of each topic are brought to light within the context of ageing.

Finally, I note that Part II is mostly based on the transcripts as transcribed from the audio files of each 2-hour interview. This literary style is not the same as those found in the chapters of Parts I, III, and IV (which are heavily supplemented by the scientific-journal literature and tables of empirical data). Therefore, Part II can be seen as an account of what players say about themselves—as has never ever been told before. It is truly their story!

3

Mental Considerations for Positive Ageing Among Orchestra Players

3.1 Introduction

The first topic of discussion with every player related to the mental skills of music performance including: information processing, memory, memorizing music, focus and attention, Sight-Reading, preparation, and practice. See Chapter 1, section 1.6.3.1, Table 1.2, Theme I. The participant-players were asked to specifically consider the possibility that age-related declines might affect them like all other everyday people without formal musical background. But then, when specifically in the 'performance arena' (whether that be in a Rehearsal Hall or the Concert Platform), do they feel that their mental skills and abilities are different than when they function 'offstage'?

At first, the contemplation of age-related effects confused some of the players—perhaps even causing a few to feel uneasy—claiming that they see 'no effects of age'. Namely, that deficiencies, if occurring among performing musicians, can simply be explained as pertaining to a host of other variables. Among other reasons delineated were: a period of absence from the Orchestra; one's character, overall disposition, and personality; long-term chronic illness and physical injury; levels of exhaustion and stress; lack of experience and talent; orchestral position or occupational routines; and substance abuse.

(36y, F, tpt)   *So, I don't really see a problem with my mental abilities as I'm getting older. I think it has stayed the same. I think I'm coping with the job. If you're asking me to think about ageing and other people, I know one above 50 who's having problems. But, I don't think these are age-related. Every player could have problems, just like any person. There are so many different factors. I think there's an addiction factor going on. You know, you don't know how much could be age (and it's just his age that would be affecting things), or how much it would be the other problem (alcohol). So, I don't know. Subsequently, there's problems with concentration. The person was a drinker 25 years ago, and didn't adapt to getting older.*

(37y, M, va)   *I don't think that any problems of concentration and attention among 50-year-old Orchestra players have anything to do with age. Rather, it's about personality. Those with vitality keep their mental abilities.*

(39y, F, cl)   *I do see players who I think their level has slipped, but there are some remarkable examples of people who still seem able to do it. And I think it's a lot about physically trying to maintain yourself. When I was appointed for the Principal vacancy, there was this Co-Principal Clarinet player who had been [playing] a lot of 1st Clarinet while they were looking to appoint someone. He incredibly managed to just carry on*

Seasoned Musicians Playing Beyond the 5th Decade. Warren Brodsky, Oxford University Press. © Oxford University Press (2025).
DOI: 10.1093/9780198956501.003.0003

playing very, very well right up until retirement. How do I think he did that? Well I think physically he seemed fine with playing; didn't really struggle with the physical demands of playing, or had any injuries. He just seemed to have an incredibly relaxed stress-free attitude about it. That was just his personality; he was very much able to do the job [and then] walk away from it. I didn't really notice any deterioration. But, I can think of one [other] guy who had to be off for a little while for a hip operation. [This] obviously wasn't playing-related. But I do remember quite well that when he came back, he was saying: 'What is so strange is that everyone else around me now seems so incredibly fast; they seem to be able to read the music and to absorb what the Conductor wants very, very quickly.' So, I think in a way, having a break from it makes it difficult. I also experienced that myself with maternity leave. Coming back to playing, then, I noticed a sort of dip in my own concentration and ability to keep up with the players around me. I could still play, and that came back. But, it was that the mental reading that has to do with levels of exhaustion especially when you're looking after young children. It took a while to refocus. I don't feel that there is any change as you're getting older; but I do feel that there is a change on all skills when you disengage from the Orchestra and then come back to it. I mean, even when the Orchestra goes on vacation, we come back in September and there is a sense of cranking up again.

(41y, M, vc)   *My understanding is that some of the issues that we are talking about also have something to do with position and experience, and not necessarily with age. There may be a correlation between experience and age in the sense that the more experience you have, the older you would be. People tend to think that the older you are, the more your mental facilities are weakened. What I am saying is that you don't see that happening at all. Because you can very easily find examples of people like my Section Leader who got the job when he was 25, and he's way sharper than me even though I was nearly 15 years older than him. I don't see the age being a deficit in mental skills of performance. We're talking about guys who are 50 or 60 years old. They're just as sharp in these kinds of skills as they would have been 30 years before.*

(47y, F, vn)   *I really don't see older players than me falling apart—even though we presume that as we get older our mind starts to fail us and we forget things. I don't know how to explain that. True by the time that you're 50, you'll already have been in the profession 35 years (since you were age 15). Perhaps, it is because the music is the one and only thing in life.*

(56y, F, vn)   *I personally think that mental issues do begin to rise about age 50. My point is that many players do not feel young anymore, and are not willing to work on themselves. So, it is really not about age, but character or disposition. For example, I am finding it more difficult to memorize the scores when I play Solos. Today it is acceptable to use a music stand. I think someone who practises 7 hours a day wouldn't have this problem. Therefore, I feel that someone older in age needs to understand they will have memory problems—but not because they have aged, but because they don't practise as much. I think that any player who is well, does not make mistakes as a result of ageing. One needs to practise!*

(57y, F, vn)   *As a performer reaching age 60, thinking about the effects of ageing on mental skills, the first [thing] is that if a player feels young then they need to think they are young. I never thought about age. One doesn't look at the mirror on all of these things.*

(58y, M, va)   *I think that whatever happens to Orchestra players after 50 years of age is more personal—not related to age per se. I have diabetes. I had problems with sight that were problematic until I was able to find solutions. I think that problems after 50 is not the age itself. Just thinking about it is frightening. But basically, the age itself does not affect mental abilities. I don't find myself forgetting things, or have difficulty concentrating during a performance. Quite to the opposite. It has everything to do with experience in the Orchestra and one's relationship with other players.*

(59y, M, fl/picc)   *People assume that there is a breakdown in the mental aspects because of ageing. But I don't feel anything. I think that [we] do one thing for such a long time, and expand so much energy and repeated practice over our lifetime. If you were a younger player, and asked me: 'How did I survive, because you want to survive,' then I would say: 'Come early before the rehearsals; be motivated to practise; don't walk in and open the instrument case without doing some type of warm-up; listen to repertoire, open up your ears and mind to music; and discover something in the music you are playing. Then, you will never burn out!'*

(64y, M, tpt)   *I don't find for myself any major problem. Each person ages differently, and the more active you remain, the better chance you have of remaining mentally intact. The majority of people I see, especially at the age of retirement, don't have a problem. Maybe there's some concentration things, but that's a part of our job; we have to concentrate. It's not an effect of ageing, [but rather] you become accustomed to doing something, you don't think about it. And if you don't stay focused, that lack of concentration can cause mistakes. But it's not a matter that you're mentally unable. It's a matter that you have relaxed to the point that you don't [concentrate]. Perhaps this is a tendency if you play the same piece all the time. You say: 'I've done that 100 times, so no problem!' Then, you don't pay attention anymore.*

Nonetheless, some participant-players did bring out that while they do not recognize the ill effects of ageing inside the Orchestra, things might be occurring outside the Orchestra setting. Namely, there was a feeling that at least within the context of music performance, there are no age-related declines of mental abilities.

(40y, F, vn)   *[For me] the only thing that may be a difference [of age] is remembering people's names. Or, knowing if I met them before. But I wonder if that just has to do with the number of people I've met up till now.*

(47y, M, vc)   *Maybe when you're younger, you're a little more naïve. Now I'm looking in between the notes and not at the specific notes. I am less focused where to put my fingers or how I'm playing, but more focused on the music. When I'm performing, I feel there are no effects of ageing. But, when I'm not playing, I do recognize sometimes [things do happen to me]. For example, if my wife would ask me a question, like: 'What would you say, if...', sometimes I might reply as though I've already done it. But, clearly I haven't done it yet! So, I think that possibly my mind wanders. But when it comes to being behind the Cello in the Orchestra, I feel a specific clarity. So perhaps the effects of ageing might happen to a musician in a non-music context. But, it doesn't affect them at all in their area of expertise.*

(52y, M, db)   *I remember some [phone] numbers, but I have difficulty with names. Yet, in music I don't have any problem. I feel that I'm a better musician now than 23 years ago.*

(56y, M, va)   *From my experience, it is quite possible to be less attentive and forgetful with all kinds of things in other areas of life, but not the area of my expertise. I may forget to call someone, or to do something. But over the years I have been focused on listening and learning the repertoire. I have played Symphonies and Operas by heart. There is quite a difference between one's field of expertise and daily life (where obviously, one's age and ageing is just like everybody else). When I am involved with music, there is nothing else on my mind. A player is looking at notation, performing an instrument, in synchrony with others, and looking at a Conductor for expressive and timing directions.*

(55y, F, fl)   *I definitely find it hard to just concentrate on reading a book, but not in music. Maybe then, just like everybody else, ageing affects you similarly but not in the Orchestra. Perhaps in the Orchestra you have developed skills that overcompensate for the ageing process. Or maybe you could just put it: 'When something's so close to your heart, it sort of fires you up.' The music keeps you awake! There's a certain passion that brings you into music as a child, and it keeps you going. It sort of keeps you floating along this route of skill development, personality development, and throughout your career.*

(61y, F, vn)   *It is interesting to note that while I might not have good memory for phone numbers, music is something different. From an early age we learn to pay attention and focus on the black-and-white dots among five lines and four spaces. We learn to cut out all other [cognitive] noise when we practise—and that goes the same for Orchestra rehearsals.*

3.2 Considering the Mental Skills of Musical Performance

Below are some comments of the participating Symphony Orchestra musicians about their mental skills of music performance. These do not necessarily consider the ill effects of ageing.

3.2.1 Focus, Concentration, and Mental Agility

Collectively, the players portrayed the concept that one enters a 'performance zone'. This could be a Rehearsal Hall, a Recording Studio, or a Concert Platform stage in front of an audience. These events demand the players to be as focused as ultimately possible. Apologies are unacceptable! Some refer to having *concentration stamina* for performance. Others speak of a specific 'mindset' that is associated with being a musician performer.

(52y, M, vc)   *There are infinite colours when playing strings. You are making thousands of decisions, every minute. How much pressure to apply, how much Vibrato, etc. It isn't tiring because of the level of concentration needed. It's more enlightening! It's like sculpting or painting a new drawing every few minutes.*

(54y, F, vc)   *Perhaps, outside of the Orchestra I'm one person, but the minute I walk in the Rehearsal Hall there's like a switch and now I'm in 'Orchestra Mode'. It's always been really important to me that I equip myself well. I set a standard for myself below which I don't want to go. So, from that point of view, there's a certain mindset about coming into the studio. And it has been that way for a long time. It's not a conscious thing. But all of a sudden you switch. Outside, or in the house, I could forget where I put my keys. Or I might leave clothes at the cleaners. But when you walk in here, there's no way that you're gonna forget your notes!*

(60y, M, bn)   *What's so nice about live music is that it's not perfection, but I just try to keep on making it 'good' or 'interesting'. I was always interested in that. I try not to apologize if it hasn't gone the same as last time, or if it didn't go well.*

Many Symphony Orchestra players do not see their specific performance behaviours as necessarily related to age *per se*. To them, with ageing there is repeated exposure and experience resulting in a higher degree of competence. But then again, musical expertise is not just increased levels of technical mastery. Musicians themselves feel that *making music* is beyond one's adeptness for specialized well-practised mechanics. Rather, music performance demands a host of mental proficiencies that are needed to turn the production of sound into a sonic art form.

(52y, M, vc)   *You can have a younger player that has these abilities. But, there are both younger and older players that don't have a clue. All they are interested in is getting the right notes, the right rhythm, and the right tempo.*

For the most part, the Symphony Orchestra players relate to having been involved in music learning from a very early age (see Chapter 2, section 2.2.1.1). They wonder, and to some extent very much believe, that their brain has been wired differently than others who have not been engaged with music learning and playing an instrument to the same extent that they did when they were children. The participant-players talk of their superior abilities for multitasking and split attention. In addition, there is a notion that they have highly developed capabilities for processing a multitude of simultaneous inputs and incoming signals that others do not command (especially those people without more than 10 years of formal music training).

(29y, F, vn)   *I know these [older members of the Orchestra] that when a Conductor might say: 'Let's start from . . .[here]' are still just setting up their instrument. When everyone starts to play, they catch up after a few seconds. Also, there are some that fiddle with their cell phones, and a Conductor might say: 'Let's start from . . .[here]' They don't even look for the place [in the score] but just start playing in the right spot. So, while they are texting, they still subconsciously know what the Conductor is talking about, and what's going on! What I found with having this job, [is that] you develop slightly more multitasking [abilities] with experience.*

(35y, F, vn)   *You have to concentrate. I know that all this is going on simultaneously. You're wondering about your intonation, or about the intonation of the person next to you. Your ear is constantly adjusting [to] what you're hearing. And, you need to look at the Conductor and at the Leader—[all] while trying to work it all out.*

(39y, F, cl)   *I don't actually think that as I get older the skills I've developed begin to fall apart. But I do feel I have to invest more in order to maintain it. How do I explain there are no age-related declines? It's just having that ongoing incredible level of mental stimulation each day. Outside of Orchestras you see older people who somehow manage to keep going and are incredibly alert mentally who just have an awful lot of stimulation. My own father-in-law is a History academic; he's in his mid-80s now, and he's just as bright as a button. But, I don't honestly believe that the type of stimulation he's getting (reading, lecturing, and conferencing) is the same as what the Orchestra offers. I think there's probably something about the sort of speed of stimulation that we're receiving. We're getting a temporal flow of information, having to react incredibly quickly to instructions from a Conductor, and from listening to other colleagues around you. Although most of the information is aural, there is quite a high percentage of time you're watching tiny gestures from a Conductor. I'd say that I'm probably a bit more visually dependent than some of my colleagues. We're responding to these split-second aural stimulations. What's very challenging for the brain being in an Orchestra, is being able to listen to yourself whilst at the same time listening to other people. I mean that's an incredible discipline. Somehow, sort of dividing yourself—looking for feedback as to how and what you're playing, while at the same time feeding into the noises that are coming from all around you. It's quite easy just to listen to other people, and in a way you are not able to hear yourself at the same time. I mean that's an incredible operation for the brain—and that is a huge difference between a Soloist and an Orchestra player.*

(64y, M, tpt)   *Information processing? I get directions from the Principal, the Section Leader, and the Conductor. There is a clear difference between mental flexibility and performance flexibility. Mental flexibility would be an understanding of what they want; performance flexibility would be being able to do it. Playing in a section is a matter of matching.*

One idea that surfaced from time to time during the interviews was the feeling that even other musicians, who might play a variety of music genres from Classical to Country music styles, are not really aware of what happens inside an Orchestra. Namely, professional full-time contract Symphony Orchestra players see themselves as being a different breed of performing musician. On the one hand they are similar to all others, but on the other hand they are uniquely different. From their perspective they are different from world-acclaimed Soloists, Chamber Music Ensembles, Opera Pit-Orchestras, Broadway Theatre Musical Show Bands,

Hollywood Bowl Production Orchestras, In-House Studio Recording Orchestras, and Junior Orchestras (e.g., National Youth Orchestras, Collegiate, Academy, and Young Philharmonic Orchestras). Moreover, the Orchestra players claimed to be different than professional Opera Singers and Choir groups, as well as other members of Orchestras such as Freelancer, Amateur, and Semi-Professional (reliever) players. Most certainly, professional full-time contract Symphony Orchestra players claim to be unlike Jazz Artistes, Rock Bands, Pop Stars, and most other music celebrities. This feeling seems to be part of an overall (but rarely spoken-about) *mindset*.

(60y, F, vc)   *I am a good example of someone who is 60 years old, the Principal of my section, already 45 years as a professional—having started playing at age 4. How do I do it? I think the main point is the mental aspect! There is no problem for an Orchestra player to pay attention or to remember various things from memory. I grew up from very early childhood being trained, and understood that [I wanted] to play music and to become a musician. Very early I felt that to become a professional musician one had to involve oneself completely; to work on the mental and physical side—the coordination—with the emotional side. If you want to build up a permanent level, you have to do it every day; you have to take the challenge every day to become better and better. This is how I grew up. And I think I never stopped to be this way. When I was 39 years old, [I had a] difficult time adjust[ing] because it's a special language to play in an Orchestra— compared to being a Soloist. I felt it as a challenge to renew myself from week to week. Each week, a new programme [needed] to be ready within three days for a direct live broadcast. And I felt that to do it [I needed] to adapt. The difficult thing for me, in the beginning, was to play each week at least with one different Conductor which I didn't choose, who came with their [own] conception; I was compelled to play in their rhythm, with their [interpretation] of the music. This helps you to be able to renew your life. Each concert needs to be your 'personal concert'. You don't necessarily have to feel the need to convey a personal message, because you play with 60–80 others. And the audience won't hear you personally [anyway]. But prepare it emotionally from the heart, as if it is your own personal concert.*

Symphony Orchestra musicians indeed feel that they need to be prepared. But how does one do that? Some players practise more, while others practise less. Some players practise at home in-between scheduled rehearsals, while others feel that practice time actually occurs during the Orchestra rehearsals themselves (see Chapter 2, section 2.3.1.2). Practice can lead to pleasure in music performance. Many of the players pointed out that by being prepared they assure themselves that they can fit into the collective group effort. But, like many other pleasures in life, 'more' is not necessarily 'better'! There is a notion that much practice should be mental without an instrument in hand. Finally, several players claimed that although experience has taught them well, many times a younger, fairly less experienced Conductor comes along who claims that the Orchestra players should forget what they have learned and experienced before, as now they will be led to higher heights and insights.

(44y, F, vn)   *It's bizarre, the [older] people [in the Orchestra] are not always connecting with other players. They're playing their own way, but as an individual—not joining in. To a certain degree, I can see myself doing that sometimes. I'll just play it, because I know how to play it; I'll be less receptive to what the Conductor wants to do. The people who're doing that, do not feel they know better, but are actually resisting. They're saying: 'Who's that guy to come and tell me when to come in.' Most people's abilities don't go down that much. Maybe a little bit! But, practising 8 hours a day at college goes a long way! I don't think my playing has gone horrendously down. And I don't think other people's playing has either. It's not that as we get older we become decrepit. But, it is impossible to think you can play as well as you did 25 years ago. Being in the Orchestra means you come in, you play your piece, you shut the case, and you go home. Most of us don't go home and practise anymore.*

(60y, M, cl)   *I have 45 years of experience in the Orchestra. [Some people] think that we continue all of these years as if nothing has happened to us. Because, statistically speaking, the difference is not significant. I am not sure that I play today the way I did when I was 30 years old. But I would say the key is: Mental Rehearsal. This is what kept me safe. It has decreased all of the motor problems that arise out of overtaxing the motor system. It increased the pleasure of performing music. Too much use of the motor system is like overcooking a stew. When you over-practise you can also learn and relearn the same mistakes again and again. Clearly, when you practise there is a 'sport-like element' that is very positive in nature; we are often focused more on the resultant motor movements than the actual music itself. Yet, when we put the instrument aside, we can deal with the 'idea' as well as the 'ideal'. So even though other players (especially among my age group 60 years old) claim that the most important thing is to practise with their instrument, my opinion is that the most important thing is to practise without my instrument.*

(64y, M, tpt)   *You need to listen beyond your own part. You might not have the whole score in front of you, but you do have the whole score in your mind. You should have learned the piece already. You should come to rehearsals prepared. If I come to a piece that I've never played before, most definitely I'll take a look. But, it depends on what I'm playing. When I'm playing 1st Desk, my preparation is different than when I'm playing 3rd Desk. I am also Assistant Principal so I go back and forth playing 2nd Desk. When we were playing the Bartók Concerto for Orchestra [Sz. 116, BB 123, written in 1943 by Hungarian composer Béla Bartók, 1881–1945], one guy was not making the entrances. I said: 'You don't know the piece!' He replied: 'Yeah, yeah, I know the piece, I've listened to it.' I said: 'No you don't know the piece! You may think you do because you can whistle it; you know what your part is, and what the notes are. But, you have to know what comes before, and what goes after. From where you take the part to where you put the part. Because it's not just your thing. Music has to do with a process. It starts in the upper left-hand corner and this is the lower right-hand corner. What happens between these two corners is the music. And you have to be aware of what's going on in order to put your part where it needs to be. You need to know what it goes along with. Who's doing what. Whether this is a secondary part, or a primary part. Not just within your section, but the whole Orchestra. That's what makes a good Orchestra player.' Indeed there are players that are good players but they just can't fit in. I shouldn't say 'can't', but for one reason or another they just 'don't'!*

3.2.2 Preparation, Score-Reading, and Motor Memory

How do musicians incorporate preparation (e.g., practice) into their everyday lifestyle? All Orchestra players have a very personal and illuminating story. For the most part, these are all somewhat 'behind-the-scenes' pictures that are never revealed to others.

(43y, F, vn)   *When I was at university I had to practise 'cause you've got deadlines. And I suppose that's really why the further [I got] into the job the less voluntary practice I've done. My husband is a Principal; obviously he has to practise more than I do (as he plays lots of Solos). Often, if he says he's got to practise, that will actually motivate me to*

practise more. But then I begin to think: 'Shall I go and clean the house?' I have practised more since being married to him. And, I always feel good about myself after I've done it. I feel like I've done some good exercise.

(61y, F, vn)   *As a more seasoned player, I can relate to the mental considerations of music performance. For example, my memory is quite average. But what makes all of the difference
in this profession, is: 'How much does a player enjoy his work?' So, if the player loves
the profession, and wants to stay in it, [they] will find a way to steer around the obstacles. Although many [players] have families, they have to put aside time to practise. It
might sound very trivial, but with ageing one has to be more proactive in making more
efforts to practise.*

A lot of musicians Sight-Read during Orchestra rehearsals. Sight-Reading seems
to be a mental process based on pattern recognition. In a previous study, Brodsky
and Kessler (2017) claimed that music experts know how to activate the right knowledge at the right time. That is, Symphony Orchestra players have highly rich and
coherent knowledge of configurations (e.g., rhythms, melodies, and harmonies),
allowing for immediate access to strategies, skills, and control mechanisms as necessary to play their instrument. Subsequently, music performers apply their hands and
fingers, formulating a host of well-learned patterns. This is what many Orchestra
players assume happens to them during Sight-Reading. They see patterns, recognize them, and employ specific hand arrangements that were once worked out
beforehand—*pun intended!* As these patterns are recurring, many Orchestra musicians feel they do not really engage any sort of 'memory' at all. But rather, they
experience the phenomenon as instinctive, intuitive, and autonomous. They often
refer to Sight-Reading *as if* a specific kind of motor or kinaesthetic memory.

(52y, M, vc)   *Our memory seems to be focused on one task, and only on one task for 6–7 days a
week. If we don't see a piece of music that's tricky from one year to another, it would
just take me 5 minutes to just work out what my fingerings were [back then years
ago]. That's motor memory. There's only a dozen pieces that come up over the years,
where I need to take music home in advance to fully prep my part. But the motor
memory and fingering is in there—it's automatic. In this Orchestra only 25% of the
pieces are new; we'll give the first performance [premiere], but then we'll never see
the piece again.*

(61y, M, fl/picc)   *Part of the problem is translating what you see on the page to what comes out of
your instrument. It's not hearing the music inside by looking at the page. It's the
fingerings.*

Several players expressed having difficulty with their music-memory and/or
Sight-Reading proficiencies. As Symphony Orchestra musicians always read notation from a scored part, the feeling is that over the years they may have disregarded
the skills needed to memorize music repertoire. Further, that Sight-Reading is an
aptitude that some players acquire at a very high level, while others, regardless of
their age or the number of years' experience, continue to struggle with it throughout
their years of tenure in the Orchestra.

(29y, F, vn)   *I'm actually stressed about my Sight-Reading. Most players here Sight-Read on an
amazing level. Obviously, I'm more used to it now. But when I first came here, I was like:
'How can they do that?' Even in College Orchestras, almost everyone could Sight-Read
on the spot. I couldn't really do that! Many people say they always been good Sight-
Readers. Most of the time I take the music home, and I know that the others don't do
that. Then when I sit next to them, even after I have practised, they are not worse than
me even though they are Sight-Reading. As most of them are older than me, it might
also be a matter of experience.*

(43y, F, vn)   *I think the memory thing is a bit difficult, because we don't have to memorize music. It's not something you have to do as an orchestral player. In our particular Orchestra, we play a lot of new music. Other Orchestras play much more of the traditional 'Classical Hits' repertoire. So, our Sight-Reading is going to be better as we're used to reading notes that we've not seen before.*

(60y, M, cl)   *The topic of memory is very problematic. Thirteen years ago I was the Soloist for a Mozart Concerto with this Orchestra. I had played that piece when I was 20 years old, but then eventually got to play the piece with this Orchestra at age 46. The question arose: 'Should I play onstage with music notation or not?' The whole dilemma is this: When you play with music notation it gives you a sense of security. But yet, when you place the music notation aside, you can communicate much more to the audience. Then on the day of the concert, while I was reading I wasn't sure what I was reading: Was it the notes? Or: The place in the part? Or: Was I reading my own marks of expressiveness? So, maybe the score causes more confusion than help? Moreover, at our age, the multifocal [aspect of vision] begins to bother. So, on the one hand the score is over there and you look over there, on the other hand you can't really see the notes the way you did when you originally learned the piece when you were young.*

(60y, F, vc)   *When I was in my 20s or 30s I was afraid that as I get older I might not be able to memorize new things. So, all these years I've been learning new languages to help to keep my memory fresh; to help my mental abilities. Maybe some things do get a little bit more difficult to learn—so I need a little bit more time for preparation.*

3.2.3 Choosing to Be a Professional Symphony Musician

Many players comment about having chosen the Orchestra profession (see Chapter 2, section 2.2.1.3). As can be seen from various vignettes throughout this book (see Chapter 5), some chose 'out of passion', and still experience the passion every time they perform. Nonetheless, for others there seemed not to have been any other choice. To some extent, those players even belittle the occupation, albeit understanding that their developed skills on an expert level allow them to be among this highly cherished vocation and subsequently earn a monthly income.

(40y, F, vn)   *The first year I worked in an Opera Orchestra was very stressful. I had only played one Opera before that. Opera and Ballet repertoires were completely unfamiliar as I'd played before in a lot of Youth Orchestras. That first year I learned how to watch the Conductor. [Since then] I've played as a Concertmaster and Principal for short periods of time, but [those are] not the same frame of mind as a Tutti player.*

(53y, M, vn)   *When I was about to graduate from high school, my Professor asked me: 'What do you do now?' And I said: 'I don't know exactly.' And he said to me: 'Of course you will study music.' So, I studied music, and that was it! When I was ready to play my final recital there was a colleague from [this] Orchestra who heard me play; he asked me to join them as they were looking for three players for the 1st Violins. I auditioned, and the rest is history! I didn't decide to join an Orchestra by myself; I didn't know anything about the profession. It wasn't a 'right decision'. It wasn't a decision that 'life brought to me'. There was no time in my life that I said: 'This is what I wanna do!' Yet, I've now been in the Orchestra since I was 25.*

(55y, M, bn)   *When I was younger I was just happy to be playing music. Now, I'm happy to be playing music. But, it's become more of a business than it should be! This last month I've been putting in more than 3 to 4 hours a day to practise as I'm gonna audition for a Philharmonic Orchestra. At my age! I am tortured by the thought of doing an audition right now. But I can't not do it. My Orchestra is failing and could go bankrupt at any minute now. Yet, I don't believe they are going to give me the job even if I play better than everyone else—because of my age. There's a list of pieces I have to play. I've performed each and every one of these with this Orchestra numerous times. So, there's no surprises. Next week I have to play one of them: Tchaikovsky's 6th [Symphony No. 6 in B minor, Op. 74, known as the 'Pathétique', written in 1893 by Russian composer Pyotr Ilyich Tchaikovsky, 1840–1893]. But, when you're on stage in a big hall, with the Basses and Cellos, you come in on a soft low note. It's much easier not to have to play quite so soft. Tchaikovsky wrote 4 p's [pppp, 'pianississississimo']. But, in the audition when you don't hear those Basses surrounding you with this chord underneath you, it's much harder! Do I actually play it as if I'm playing in the Orchestra (so try to imagine the Orchestra around me)? Or: Do I play it like a Solo? While I'm enjoying my own playing and the music that I'm making, I'm not sure if I can play at the highest level at the audition. I am terribly worried about it; I think about it when I go to bed at night, and when I wake up in the morning. I feel I'm in good shape, but I haven't played an audition for over 25 years. I also know many of the other people who are auditioning against me; a whole bunch of kids in their 20s. I have to play an audition against several of my own students. What if one of them gets it, and I don't! [Author's Note: See Chapter 13, section 13.2 on this topic.]*

3.3   Considering the Effects of Ageing on Mental Skills of Music Performance

This section presents the participating Symphony Orchestra musicians' thoughts on the mental skills employed during music performance—considering the ill effects of ageing. The conversations targeted nine topics, collectively labelled 'Theme 1: Mental' (see Chapter 1, section 1.6.3.1, Table 1.2).

3.3.1   Focus, Concentration Stamina, Mental Agility, Information Processing, Widening Horizons, and Automaticity

In general, the participating Orchestra musicians claimed that their mental skills have not decreased as time goes on. Rather, they seem to have actually become better with age. There is an overall emphasis that novice players need to undergo a period of orientation to the profession and their specific job as defined by their orchestral position. The perception is that their increased abilities result from a widening awareness about the music itself. Subsequently, many new insights are gained from repeated music exposure and experience, which seemingly were not available beforehand. Namely, the participants believe that to some extent, they had been 'blind-sighted' through previous music training schemes at Music Conservatories, Music High School, and Music Colleges (i.e., Academies).

(33y, M, va)   *If one wants to play 'devil's advocate' one could say: 'These [older] guys should not able to concentrate and pay attention in a very focused Concert; they should just forget where they are, and what they're doing.' But that is not the case. I don't know how to explain it. It could be that a Concert is a very special situation because there's 1,000+ people in the audience directing their focus at the 80–100 players onstage. The audience is giving a huge amount of energy to the Orchestra who are picking up on that; it's enabling us to rise up as a collective group. So, there's no reason why an older player shouldn't be in the flow as much as a younger player. The whole experience pushes everyone along.*

(33y, F, bn/dbn)   *I think it's not true that as players get older their music performance becomes more difficult. When you are younger, you're more nervous and concerned about 'What do the other colleagues think?' Or: 'What's your status (your position) in the Orchestra?' I do think that as you get older you become more calm and secure, and then more open to the music experience. I think you're able to concentrate more, and take away all other (cognitive) noise.*

(35y, F, vn)   *I think there's such a consistency between what we do and ageing; being older means having experienced a lot of the repertoire many times before. I've been professional now for 10 years. I do think my ability to concentrate and focus has gotten better. From discussions with others who are older, I would say that you get to a certain point, and then it kind of stays the same. You build up this stamina. Year, after year, after year, of constantly working in a certain way; challenging your brain with different musics, different Conductors, different Concert Halls, different countries. It's never exactly the same! There are little adjustments all the time depending on the acoustics, hall temperature, Conductor's mood, how you're feeling, and so on. All of these can change the atmosphere, which changes the way people react. There are hundreds of variables: the phone rings, somebody's music is not on the stand, you've forgotten your shoes, you can't remember if the parking meter is going to run out, your strings are about to snap, the Conductor suddenly takes it really fast. Any of these things can be on your mind while you're playing.*

(36y, F, tpt)   *I think in my everyday life that I totally forget about the 'time'. It's got worse [as I age]. But my attention to my music? Not at all! I don't think about anything else when I'm playing. I'm just focused on the sound I'm making, and what I want to do. But obviously in everyday life there's so many other things: 'I gotta pick up my child from school. What are the dates of school holidays? I've got to find childcare for next week!'*

(41y, M, va)   *As I age, I actually find it easier! The older I get, the more comfortable I feel with things going on in my life. So, there aren't a million and one things struggling for space in my head that can prevent me from concentrating on the job. I feel more comfortable about my abilities to do the job. That's not necessarily to say that my playing is any better, because it's not as good physically. But mentally, it's easier to focus. I am more secure in myself as a member of the Orchestra, and my ability to play together with the rest of my section. You go through this learning curve, and you learn to cope better in this big machine. After nearly 20 years, I would say I'm a pretty good 'cog' [in the wheel]. Moreover, I would say the most forgetful players, the ones who are the most absent-minded and who have the most trouble concentrating, are the younger ones. Some of them just came out of College; they are in awe of the whole professional experience. I do understand the age-related physical decline, but I can't explain the fact that despite the ageing process some players are able to continue doing their job. The only thing I can think of is it has something to do with the job itself. Certainly, I feel that my mental faculties for the job have improved in the last 20 years.*

(47y, M, vc)   *There is some type of thinking that as players get older, you have to get rid of them. That they are more of a liability! But actually, it might be more of an asset to have experienced mature players who look at music differently than younger players. I'm talking about working Orchestra players. I'm now better at paying attention than I was then. As a young man I was much more easily distracted. Today, I am able to be more attentive and focused. As the Principal I have a whole different set of responsibilities; I started doing this job as the Principal 20 years ago!*

(52y, M, db)   *We are told that as we get older, we sort of forget things, and the mental things that go on in the mind (e.g., concentration and attention) become even less. But actually I don't think so. In my case it's gotten better! My brain knows now how I have to concentrate. I think that getting older was actually better for my musical skills.*

(55y, M, perc)   *As a musician I think I'm better now than when I was younger—especially at remembering notes. I remember the shapes because I can't read it! You have to look down at the instrument. You've got 2–4 mallets in your hands, and you just hit the keys [Xylophone, Vibraphone, or Marimba]. I was dreadful when I was in my 20s. No! I don't think that now, past 50 years old, my abilities to focus, concentrate, or pay attention have gotten worse.*

The participating players felt that their capabilities of attention and stamina for longer periods of concentration are indeed superior at old(er) ages compared to what they remember having had experienced in earlier years. Further, their mental agility has become increasingly more flexible and adaptive—especially multitasking! Most specifically, their 'eye–hand span' (i.e., the ability to read a bar or more of notation ahead of the bar currently being played) has extended in length as they have matured. Further still, their aptitude for information processing is most efficient; their perspective on the music has widened with experience, especially their capability to take in more of the actual content itself. In short, the players feel that when they were young(er) they were exclusively focused on the notes! Nonetheless, the ageing process has subsequently provided experience whereby they could learn to focus 'beyond the notes'. Namely, there is a developmental process to *making music* along with other like-minded musicians in the Symphony Orchestra that is matchless in comparison to all other opportunities and formats of performing music previously experienced.

(38y, M, bn/dbn) *I don't feel at all that my mental skills have gotten worse, but rather are even getting better. I think my listening ability is definitely better. I really like the mental agility that is developing; to slot right in, and be spot on. I am concentrating more than 10 years ago. I'm learning all the time now, whereas I might not have even been aware of the 4th Horn 10 years ago. Maybe, it's not that I didn't hear it, but that it didn't register. So, I'm just able to do a lot more multitasking [e.g., concurrent music analyses] and am getting more information from the notes.*

(40y, F, vn) *How does one keep their mind limber? The older I get, the more experience I get. The better I Sight-Read, the more quickly I learn pieces. The more I remember what was done in the Rehearsal Hall, the more I remember what to do on the Concert Stage. Things come a lot more naturally. And the pieces that I've played before, come back very easily. When I compare myself [to a younger time] it's only gotten better. In the past 20 years I've been playing in the Orchestra, I've become more fluent. It does seem to go against what we know about getting older. Paying attention and concentrating is a challenge at any age, but I don't see a significant difference. I don't even see people 5 years older in my section [having problems]. I think every person can have an 'on' day and an 'off' day. That has nothing to do with age. Regarding lapses of attention or concentration (when your mind goes somewhere else), as you get older that does not become more problematic. I think the only thing that's changed (but for the positive) is that I now know which places need my full attention.*

(41y, M, vc) *I think that as you get older there is some sort of process of widening one's perspective. I think that when you're younger you are extremely focused on what you yourself are doing. So, it's about playing all notes, playing what's on the page. As I've got older, I've became aware of everything else that's going on in the Orchestra. What that probably means in terms of real focus, is that you can sometimes be more easily distracted. It's a trade-off. I do see it as a benefit of getting older rather than as a problem.*

(43y, F, db) *When you're younger you concentrate more on playing the right notes and being with the person next to you. Now, I am concentrating on the overall ensemble. You start hearing different things as you learn pieces better. Your horizon broadens, and you see yourself more as part of the bigger thing. I mean young players often sail into the rests on their own. I don't feel that as I've gotten older my ability to pay attention and concentrate has gotten worse. Perhaps it hasn't actually gotten 'better', but maybe 'wiser' is the right word.*

(60y, M, bn) *I think I am just as focused after 37 years have gone by. I certainly don't think I thought particularly hard about how to play the notes when I first joined. But today, I have to think harder because it's harder to play. Basically, things I thought were easy, actually get more difficult. Things I thought were difficult, keep being difficult. I do think I have to concentrate more now; not because it's more difficult to concentrate, but because I'm seeing so much more in the music. I analyse more! So, I'm not saying I have to concentrate more because as I get older I have more problems of concentration. But actually, I'm looking more in-between the notes.*

(64y, M, tpt)   *My strategy to try to keep myself focused and concentrated is just to pay attention to the music. Not necessarily analysing, but you should always hear something new. Even in things you've played a number of times there's always some kind of counterpoint that you may not have heard before.*

One interesting point brought up by many players was that as they aged and consequently gained more experience, they also learned to be more economical with time. What they mean is that the duration of time they engage in determined mental effort becomes far less; with experience they discovered when it is necessary to expend energy (i.e., focus), as well as when they can withdraw for a break period (i.e., easing-off relaxation). Yet, all the while remaining aware of the music surroundings. Some talk discreetly of counting bars. Others assert that many previously developed and expertly practised abilities seem to be executed *as if* independent and autonomous processes. Hence, a number of skills and capabilities in the music performance *toolkit* seem to be implemented unconsciously and with far less mental effort than what was remembered to have occurred earlier during young(er) years in the music-performance profession. Albeit, there was also a certain feeling that in earlier years, the more technical aspects of playing an instrument were seemingly on a higher level. Therefore, while ageing seems to have advanced strategies reflecting increased economy of mental facilities, there is also a notion that with ageing the player has lost a fraction of highly developed competencies.

(29y, F, vn)   *Different people in my section react quite differently. I don't really think it has to do with the age. Some of them have been playing in the Orchestra for 5 years, and some for 20. I don't think that the older players have less concentration or pay less attention. If anything, they probably [can more efficiently] split their attention. I found that when I was on trial I had to concentrate quite a lot. If you are not needed, then you can drift away and give your mind a bit of a rest. Some slightly older players aren't concentrating, but it doesn't seem to affect their playing.*

(47y, M, trb)   *When I first joined the Orchestra everything was so new. I was concentrating on how to play and not to make mistakes. For me as a Trombone player counting is very important. You just have to get used to counting. A big thing that happened to me over the years is that counting became automatic! I can talk [to you] and even count at the same time. It is not that I feel time—I count! I count sometimes with fingers, or in my mind. It is not only among Trombone players, but many musicians who have lots of rests—count! They're not looking at the music to see what the Violins are playing, and [by that] then they know when to come in at a specific measure. Something that comes over the time; you just mentally, automatically, and unconsciously, count!*

(47y, F, vn)   *I can concentrate, pay attention, and remember things better now than 22 years ago! I think there's kind of a filter that allows you not to put in all of your concentration from the beginning till the end. You get a sense where you have to concentrate and to focus, and then you can relax in-between. And I think when you are young, you concentrate the whole time. You lose lots of energy! So, over time, you learn to be more economical. You have to develop some type of a strategy when to concentrate, and when to take a step back. So, 22 years later, I think that I'm better with the mental work of music performance.*

(52y, M, vc) *As you get older you are more focused and more attentive. You can switch in and out of focus more quickly. It's not so much getting older per se, but rather gaining experience in the Orchestra.*

(59y, M, va) *I think it is important, to be aware of things. Many people understand what it means to be more economical with physical work. Too much force, too much muscle, too much energy. Being more economical with your mind means not using too many thoughts to manage things.*

With ageing comes retrospective awareness. Many players spoke of their career stages that had been somewhat framed by evolving phases of life that (at least outwardly) seem to have defined their being. For example, they account for various life circumstances (such as marriage, childbirth, raising children, job relocation). In their opinion these often caused havoc with their mental (and sometimes physical) ability to maintain their orchestral position. They speak of the great efforts that are required for them to 'crawl back' to the required standards as a member of a professional Symphony Orchestra. A basic contention is that one's level of function as a player has much more to do with one's character than it does with age—and that the consequences of life's circumstances are related both to one's make-up (e.g., disposition and personality) as well as to one's emotional state at the time an event seems to have occurred.

(52y, M, vc) *People go through different stages in life. When they are new to the Orchestra they are already focused. Over the years they get married, and suddenly, they're up at 5 o'clock in the morning coming to work wretched. You can't stay focused. I have a blank of about 8 years when I had my child; I came to work and I just went through the motions. But I didn't actually (mentally) know what the hell was going on. I just did what I had to do, and then I went home. Then there's a later stage when you kind of start refocusing on your career. That's suddenly become important again—until retirement. You go through these different stages in life, and [some of them make it] very hard to stay focused.*

(54y, F, vc) *I have obviously survived to this point (31 years in the Orchestra). I hope I will make it to retirement age. I think I'm still able to focus and concentrate as well as I ever could. Possibly better! But I think the factor that plays into how well I do it is affected by what sort of emotional state I'm in. I don't think that as I've gotten older, my concentration has become worse than say 20 years ago. I know where to focus my attention. And so, I can approach things in a much more succinct and organized way when I'm preparing material. I don't really feel that there are any mental effects of ageing on my musicianship. As far as to the type of errors, if they are any, they're not worst for age. But I did go through a rocky period in my personal life when there was some illness, and I had several periods of time off. My concentration was absolutely terrible then; I made loads of totally unnecessary mistakes, and there were several periods that were really tricky for my own self-confidence.*

(59y, M, fl/picc) *Attention in rehearsals does not get worse, but sometimes life circumstances get in the way and take up space. I am always thinking about how I did something in the past. I think about how I did the fingering, articulation, breathing, tonguing, etc. I want to be at least as good as I was the last time I played the same piece. I am always looking [at the markings in the score] to see how I did it. Maybe I can find an even better way to play the piece [this time].This is what keeps one's mind agile.*

On the other hand, a few players did express sentiments of weakening skills and abilities; they acknowledge to have age-related decline. Decreased mental stamina with increased fatigue is mentioned. Some players state that as they aged they seem to get more confused more often than when they were young(er) players. Confusion occurs when faced with a more difficult section of a newly learned passage in a newly composed piece. One player even recalled feeling paralysed while playing a piece with the Orchestra on the Concert Platform while in clear view of the attending public audience. Several players noticed that they have less patience in rehearsals and in performances when the pieces are repeated over and over and over again (more than 20 times during the last 30 years).

(47y, M, hn)	*As far as concentration, I feel I've had to apply more and more self-discipline to maintain the same standard. I've been slightly muddled by what's happened to me in this Orchestra. The Orchestra seems to have been doing better now. So I wonder: Am I having just to try a lot harder as I get older? Or: Is the Orchestra getting much better around me? It just seems to me that my behaviour in the past was poor, and it's better now. But I don't know if I've had to do that because the Orchestra's changed, or my attitude has changed.*
(52y, M, vc)	*I think that among older musicians, their sense of confusion [on the stage] will be [about] the same as it is for when they drive a car: the elderly are fine driving when things are straightforward but not so [much] if they hit a very busy roundabout or are in a strange city. The chances of getting confused are there for all musicians. There are times when I can't physically move, 'cause I can't figure out in my head what I should be playing. I don't know if that's just having a 'senior moment', or whether that's just the way I'm trained. If I don't know what I'm supposed to be playing, then I just don't play anything. It feels as if being paralysed in space and time!*
(53y, M, hrp)	*I haven't noticed any deterioration. I always had the tendency to be a bit absent-minded. Especially playing the Harp, you've got ages and ages to wait before you come in. And it's very easy to let your mind wander. But in general, I don't feel that my age has affected my playing compared to 20 or 30 years ago. Except that sometimes at the end of a long concert I'm more fatigued than I used to be.*
(54y, M, cl/bcl)	*I feel the mental skills have become worse as I've aged. Things like memory, paying attention, and staying concentrated, are all more difficult. When I was younger, I sat up from a 3rd Desk to the 2nd Desk, and from the 2nd Desk to the 1st Desk. But, these days I find that stepping up is more and more difficult.*
(54y, M, va)	*The problem of being alert is my major problem. I think the only thing is to have more coffee before the morning rehearsal. It's a pity, but I have to depend on that compared to 10 or 15 years ago. I do feel it is a problem as I'm getting older. But I think it is both because of age and because I have played some of these pieces so many times that I don't have as much patience!*
(61y, M, fl/picc)	*Possibly my abilities to concentrate, pay attention, and be focused have changed as I got older. You hear that sometimes other players are bored by the pieces they're playing. They'll run through their shopping list while they're actually play-ing. I think I may have done [that] when I was younger, but I don't think I do that now! Maybe it's because I'm frightened that I might actually lose concentra-tion, or make a mistake, or embarrass myself. Today, I make more efforts to be focused. So, if these [mental] things do change, it is so gradual that you don't really notice.*

3.3.2 Mishaps, Slips, Errors, and Memory Issues

The rule of thumb among Orchestra musicians seems to be that there is no room for errors—neither among Young(er) Players nor among old(er) Seasoned Musicians. On the other hand, it is recognized that all musicians occasionally make mistakes simply because the nature of music performance is that music is performed live!

(60y, M, bn)   *You can hear where the inaccuracy is. So that's how your brain coaches the fingers. I don't think: 'Oh, I'm now gonna play an Ab, must make sure that I push that finger, before, in front of that one.' But, if you play slowly enough with your fingers you can hear the mistake and then you can put it right. One of my philosophies is: As long as I can recognize I've made a mistake, then I know what to practise.*

Errors and mistakes are an integral part of the 'tension' of music performance—as well as the excitement of a music-related stage event. It is the *chill & thrill*: 'Can they do it!' We might wonder if there are different types of mistakes. For example, do Young(er) Players typically make certain varieties of errors compared to Seasoned Musicians? This is actually one of the questions investigated in the Music-Performance Assessment described in Chapter 10. Many players claim that errors can occur as a 'slip of mind' or as momentary 'lack of concentration' or 'lapse in judgement'. Some of the Orchestra players mentioned 'logical mistakes', which do not necessarily cause havoc to the piece—referring to *structure-preserving errors*. Further, there are unreasonable or 'irrational mistakes' not even related to the music itself, which do cause havoc to the piece—referring to *structure-violating errors*. Players report that some mishaps remain on the level of solely affecting one individual player—albeit perhaps seriously embarrassing them as mishaps occurring in public. Nonetheless, players also account for mishaps that cause repercussions involving other players; they refer to these as *dropping a domino* (after the 'Domino Effect'), whereby one action causes a chain of reactions each following in succession. Although many players affirm the notion that errors and mishaps do not increase with age, they do recollect that the type of mistakes they made when they were young(er) were more often related to content (e.g., when they did not get the right notes in the right places at the right time). Yet, 20 years later, they find that they more often fall prey to distraction as a result of cognitive noise (i.e., having more on their mind that takes away from the music performance) with many non-performance-related intrusions in their mind (including aspects of Music Theory Analyses of the contents).

(50y, M, vn)   *I do feel the types of errors I make are different now at the age of 50 than when I was 30 or 40 years old. It could be that I was sharper then; getting the first-time hard passage on a higher level than I do now.*

(52y, M, vc)   *I don't find that as I get older I make more errors. There is no room for errors! But it does happen and some Conductors make a big deal about this. Yet, we all make mistakes. Musicians wouldn't make fun or harangue another player about it; the next time it could be them. It's just ignored. Or, accepted as part of the live human element of music. Certainly, I've seen younger players come offstage in tears because they have made a very public error. My only word of comfort to them would be: 'It's not going to be your last, don't make a thing about it.' And I'll laugh or joke about the mistakes I've made the last 30 years while playing professionally. We do need to try to avoid seriously embarrassing moments. But, this happens less often as you get older because you are more aware of where these places can happen. Perhaps in a rehearsal of a first-time run-through you might experience a so-called 'senior moment'. It is very rare, but it can happen! And that has nothing to do with age, but rather it is a slip of mind, or lack of concentration. Yet, there is no 'time' or 'age' when you can say it happens more [often]. It might be that some people are less prone to these errors than others. For example, playing a piece of music and missing a repeat! I can go through a week's rehearsal and know exactly where the repeats are, and then when I'm doing a performance I'll totally miss it, even though I've done the rehearsals. There are plenty of times, thinking back to my youth, sitting with an older player, when the two of us missed a repeat sign, and we had to go back but neither one of us could find the sign where we should have gotten back to. So, we sort of just 'bus along' until the piece actually finishes.*

(55y, M, bn)   *I'm more aware that I can make mistakes, and also more embarrassed. Everyone knows that mistakes happen. But now it's more like: 'I don't want to make that mistake—that logical mistake.' I think I probably make less mistakes today. Because I've been in the Orchestra for over 30 years and consider myself one of the senior players. It makes me much angrier than it did 20 years ago to make mistakes! Now, if I make a mistake, I think: 'I have a certain reputation to keep up!' Or: 'Maybe there's a little bit of slippage.'*

(55y, M, perc)   *Just last year in the middle of a piece, the whole Orchestra stopped. It stopped! I missed it! I went back and played the Trio again. We never ever play a Trio twice. I went back and played the Trio again! Unfortunately, it was in a concert where there were at least 10,000 people. I was playing the Snare Drum. And I went for it: 'I'm really gonna go for this.' And I did! I played these 8 bars. Everybody stopped. It all stopped! They actually stopped, because that was the end of the piece! And I was the only one playing! I know this piece. I love all that military music [like] Semper Fidelis [composed in 1888] by American composer John Philip Sousa [1854–1932]. And there's a big Snare Drum break in it. It's one of those great marches in the repertoire. It's got big Bass Drum, Cymbals, and Snare Drum. But it's in the Trio. And then the tune comes back. I missed the feeling completely. The audience didn't realize it either. But, the whole Orchestra did and were crying with laughter. I mean, it sounded great! I was really pleased with it. It was terrific! It sounded fantastic! I kept going. I played my 8-bar phrase. And that was it! Then, everybody clapped! You just have to step back with calm. You have to prepare as best as you can. We all hit wrong notes. It's a percentages game: you only get about 95%–99% at best!*

(59y, M, va)   *A musician shouldn't do a mistake twice. One has to know exactly where that mistake was, and make sure not to do it a second time.*

It is interesting to note that many Symphony Orchestra players put the blame for performance errors on the 'face-type' of the music notation (e.g., scores that lack clarity, or scores which are not printed in a user-friendly graphic format, or scores that use a specific font itself). I note here that a previous study (Brodsky & Kessler, 2017) demonstrated the ill effects of *beam slope* (e.g., incline/decline) on the perceptive skills of professional music readers. In addition, several players spoke of Conductors, who are viewed as causing errors simply because they do not properly indicate signs with clear manual or facial gestures at the required time.

(43y, F, vn)   *In fact, just now we were doing some modern stuff and a lot of it's written badly. Quite difficult to read. With handwritten stuff, you can find yourself making mistakes purely because of spatial awareness and spatial perception. A handwritten score is not regular. Whereas when it's printed you know how long a bar is gonna be. If it's written out in standard bars, then that has some meaning; the clarity of the ink on the page is undeniable. And that has to do with beaming as well. There are so many times I can think of that we've corporately made the same mistake because of ignorantly printed music; where the beams are incorrect and subsequently all players do the wrong rhythm or play too many notes.*

(55y, M, bn)   *A 'mistake' is playing a wrong note. You'd hear it in the audience even if you didn't play my instrument. I made a mistake last night. A counting mistake; counting rests. A non-playing mistake. I didn't get into my entrance on time! It was just stupid. I counted a bar rest of 4 instead of 2. Now, other people got messed up because I didn't get that entrance right; it was a section of the piece that wasn't good. It wasn't just my fault, because the Conductor should have given me a cue at that moment. I looked up to him for help, but I didn't get help there. So, [in the end] it was my mistake. It was also this Solo thing; it was sort of a 2-second hold, and if someone was really listening to the piece they'd know that something should have been happening there. Do they know it was me? No! It's a piece that nobody knows. Things just sort of fell into place, but probably [only after] 6 or 7 seconds. But, a 7-second pause is a long time; two bars! Probably more like 8 seconds. It was a moment that I lost that I was really looking forward to playing. Because it was a thing I played really well. I was happy about the way I played it [in rehearsals]. But, I screwed it up. I was partially upset because other people were relying on me to come in. Maybe, I wasn't concentrating very much. Maybe I wasn't focused enough. The Conductor should have given me a cue at that moment.*

3.3.3 Score-Reading, Sight-Reading, Preparation, Motor Memory, and Memorizing Music

Several participant-players spoke about their waning Sight-Reading abilities. They felt that as they aged, their responses during Sight-Reading (i.e., the coordinated efforts between their brain, eyes, and fingers) have slowed down. This notion is highly subjective in nature as there is no evidence to support such perceptions. Yet, many Young(er) Players stated that such is the reason why Seasoned Musicians are reticent to receive newly composed pieces that have not as yet been premiered (or recorded previously).

(43y, F, vn)   *Some tend to think of getting old and losing it. Personally, I don't think so. I think Sight-Reading new stuff was always something that I enjoyed. I'd say Sight-Reading doesn't change with age, nor does it get worse throughout one's lifetime career.*

(49y, M, vn)   *It is not enough just to practise [in rehearsals] no matter how many hours per day one puts in. Look, when a player is accepted after an audition and a trial period, they're in good shape. But ultimately, and for everyone, there will be a decline. It is inevitable. The answer, then, is: daily renewal. One needs to play Scales, Études, and other materials (like Concerti) that you will never ever play in a Symphony Orchestra every day. Twenty hours a week of Orchestra rehearsals is not enough—not even for maintenance!*

(54y, F, vc)   *I know that I don't react as quickly if I am in a situation where I have to Sight-Read. I'm not somebody who finds it very easy [to brag] about my skills. But I know that as a younger player I could Sight-Read very well. Yet now, I can't Sight-Read very well. My brain just doesn't work as quickly. So, I'm putting it down to age. I think the first 10 years of my Orchestra job relied a lot of my Sight-Reading ability. The turnover of music was so quick.*

Perhaps, score-reading also depends on Orchestra environment. For example, some Orchestras predominantly perform the more well-known standard 'Hits' repertoire repeatedly throughout the season. In these cases players rely much more on their memory of pieces. Yet, other Orchestras regularly premiere newly composed pieces (sometimes on a monthly basis). These different working environments, reflecting a somewhat different tradition, may directly contribute to players' abilities (and maintenance) for Sight-Reading skills.

(41y, M, va)   *Perhaps an older player in a different Orchestra would be much more reluctant when handed a fresh piece off the writer's block than an older player here. Here we're used to seeing new pieces all the time. So, I would say a 60-year-old in this Orchestra is used to getting something brand new every couple of weeks. But elsewhere, they'll feel much more comfortable playing repertoire they've seen 10, 20, or 100 times.*

Balancing that, is the fact that when that happens to them, they'll have twice as much rehearsal time than we would get. That's why they keep giving premieres to us! Yes, there is a possibility that we could get someone in an audition who is really good at the standard repertoire, but then not so good at Sight-Reading new pieces.

(49y, F, vn)   *Now I am in this Orchestra almost 18 years. There are virtually no new pieces. This situation makes me indifferent. I am not sure if I play automatically or not. I don't even need to look at the score. That doesn't mean if I got something new I couldn't play the score. I play from notation (i.e., reading) much better than I did 25 years ago. Also, I now understand the materials better and faster. Truthfully, I think right now I am at the peak of my performance.*

Most players seem to point out that with their increased experience across time, kinaesthetic memory—which is undoubtedly the memory for motor patterns, hand positions, and combinations of finger sequences—not only remains intact but actually escalates to higher proficiency. Subsequently, players have become exceptionally delicate with greater expertise in execution.

(41y, M, vc)   *I might be playing a Symphony which I've played a lot of times before; there is definitely a physical muscle-memory thing going on. Even if you talk about Solos, and how you memorize things, part of it is muscle memory. I don't think my memory or concentration skills are becoming more difficult as I get older. I'm not sure if it's improving necessarily, because I remember from the age of 16 years old I had already been told that my memory was better than average! Sometimes it feels like I'm on automatic pilot—especially when we play a piece which we've played 60 times. I'm often amazed there's a hard passage that just comes out right without thinking about it! It's not a 100%, but it's fairly close. That's kinaesthetic memory.*

(55y, F, fl)   *I haven't seen a decrease in kinaesthetic memory. I've got a brilliant finger-memory. I can remember just about everything that I've ever played. I'm not sure if that is like a photographic memory (when you look at the music [just] once, and you know it). I also remember the sound—what it sounded like before!*

(56y, M, va)   *I believe that my mental skills have become even better with age. I have no explanation for this, as it does conflict with what we know about ageing. Perhaps this has to do with experience. On the one hand, if you were to show me a piece I haven't seen for more than 8–9 years, I would clearly remember how to play it. But yet, I can't even remember a phone number! A lot has to do with my first experience with the piece. After all, the ability and skill allows you to replicate things (like finger patterns).*

Some of the participating players stated that, as they age, the preparation of pieces for stage performance has become easier; it takes less time to master. They assert this phenomenon to be the result of familiarity, as well as to motor proficiency. A few claimed that such expertise is subsequent to the intensification of cognitive organization that seems to have surfaced over the years. Some mention a 'neural synchronization process'. Almost all players state that as far as they are concerned, their music memory is much more efficient than it had been many years previously.

(43y, F, db)   *As you get older certain things get easier. Like playing the same pieces over and over again. So, basically if 15 years ago you've sorted out a piece really well, and could play it from memory, then you don't have to do that much work on it ever again. I mean, the brain sees notes and lots of accidentals, and then the hands and the fingers just do it! I haven't noticed that as I get older I lose that kind of kinaesthetic memory. But, when we get something really modern, or something that we don't know at all, then I have to take the piece apart. It's between you and the notes again; the first Sight-Reading is always a bit of a challenge.*

(52y, M, db)   *Now, it's easier to remember fingering and the music. I take out a score that I've played before, and the music just pops out! I would say it takes me less time to prepare a piece than before. But even new pieces look like many pieces I've played before. When I have to play chords (double stops or triple stops), I now feel that the coordination between my brain and my body is easier.*

(59y, M, va)   *Yes! When we get older, everybody starts to have problems with their mental abilities. I think I forget words. But what about music? In my younger days I could play pieces by heart, but nowadays I wouldn't do that because there would be some lacks. Yet there is no problem remembering the fingering. And, when we play an Opera that we played 10 years ago, most things are still there. I think lots of things work because they are all reflexes. If you have to think about it, it's already too late!*

(61y, M, fl/picc)   *I don't know if as I've gotten older my mental agility has become more difficult. Some things I find easier. I mean, when I first played some pieces I'd spend hours and hours and hours playing them for weeks. Nowadays, I just turn up at first rehearsal and I'm fine for the Concert Performance. It might be that my mental abilities have improved, or simply, the job's got easier.*

Concerning the topic of practice, many players expressed a widely accepted concept that one needs to put in the time to maintain both mental and physical skills. Practice is seen as an ongoing patterned behaviour occurring throughout one's entire lifespan (see Chapter 2, section 2.2.1.2). Moreover, that with ageing and experience, players have learned to be more economical with their practice time. They have adopted strategies which allow much more rehearsal, repetition, and exercise to be accomplished mentally without causing undue strain to the mechanical physical body. In addition, there is a notion that as players mature, having accumulated a wealth of experience by learning new pieces from a wide range of repertoires, styles, and time periods, they have also developed the propensity to examine the content of music directly. They can execute musicological analyses on the structural representations of music concurrently while Sight-Reading the text as well as when actually performing on their instrument. Finally, the musicians felt they could absorb the music instantaneously; they can place it in various types of memory at countless levels of intensity, including: short-term buffers, long-term storage, phonological recall, and kinaesthetic tactile-like reminiscence. Accordingly, these all stem from an integration of supplementary perceptual channels and aptitudes. One of these, first empirically examined in the Psychology research literature by Brodsky et al. (1999, 2003, 2008), is referred to as *Notational Audiation* (after theoretical conceptualizations by Gordon, 1975, 1993).

(33y, F, bn/dbn)   *I think you really have to practise. By practising you will get better. If you're not practising, you won't improve. I think that those who are getting older and not practising have problems. Practising is the key to being able to maintain your musical abilities throughout life.*

(41y, M, vc)   *I think that my basic Sight-Reading was much better when I was younger; I wasn't playing the standard repertoire at the time. I was getting through a huge range of repertoires then, and I wasn't preparing each piece as I do now. So, I had to be quicker and more accurate. I definitely Sight-Read worse now, but I think today it goes through a more complicated process. I think it doesn't directly go through my eyes to my fingers. Now, I think it's rooted through something a little bit more musical—maybe a bit more analytic. Today I'm very into the phrasing and expression, and the sort of sound I want. When I was younger, I was more mechanical with less semantic meaning going on. It wasn't completely without meaning, but it was more like you'd pushed the button!*

(55y, M, db)   *I don't see any difference in my ability to understand or absorb music materials as a result of my age. In the past, I practised music of the same piece so many times that I actually learned it by heart, but there is no need for that intensity today.*

(58y, M, va)   *It is now harder for me to remember pieces by memory. When I was younger I used to play Solo performances and auditions from memory. But as we only use music notation on the stage it has been a long time since I had to memorize materials. This seems to have caused me to be less secure about my abilities to remember pieces by heart. I am now aware that my Sight-Reading is not as good as others. So, I need to take the score [home] and learn the text. But this was the same 20 years ago; it is not related to age!*

(59y, M, fl/picc)   *Memory does not get worse. The more I learn and play, the more I remember. If a piece comes up from many years ago, I will immediately remember where the hard parts are; the parts I had to practise more often then. Now I need to practise even less because I will remember how I fixed these problems back then.*

(60y, F, vc)   *Maybe, when I learn new pieces now I'm learning them differently at the age of 60 than when I was 30. First, there is an experience of learning a new piece. I analyse it, I absorb it—immediately on many different levels. My motor coordination of breathing is different now than 20 years ago. Thirty years ago, it may have been biologically easier, although I don't think that the motor aspects of my playing are less agile than 20 years ago.*

(61y, F, vn)   *Practice is the only thing that makes the difference if a player will survive! One cannot come into the rehearsals without being prepared. So obviously, the way to steer around an obstacle when it comes up is to work harder. Kinaesthetic memory of the fingers will be better with more work; it will also lead to automaticity.*

3.3.4 Boredom and Fatigue

Many of the participating musicians stated that as they aged they often experience far less boredom in rehearsals than previously. Accordingly, over time they discovered tactics to occupy themselves, including 'mind games' with which they can contemplate strategies to improve their music performances.

(47y, M, vc)   *I used to get very bored very quickly in rehearsals. I don't anymore as I'm able to find things in rehearsal to occupy my mind. For example, working out ways to improve how I'm playing a passage. Thinking: 'How can I make a more beautiful sound? How can I make a more intense sound? How can I change my Vibrato speed?' Twenty years ago I'd be playing these passages, sitting back in my chair, just playing it. But now I'm trying to improve the music.*

(50y, M, vn)   *I once worked with this Concertmaster who told the following: 'Instead of thinking that this is the 123rd time you're playing this Symphony, try to look at it as something that you'd really love to conduct if you were up there.'*

Yet, many Symphony Orchestra players note that as they get old(er) they experience exhaustion and fatigue more frequently and intensely. Some questioned whether or not such feelings were because of ageing itself, or whether they stemmed from *repeated exposure* of the music being rehearsed. Several players claimed that when music is inspiring (e.g., emotionally moving), there is no fatigue, and in such cases they might even go home wanting to engage in more practice.

(52y, M, db) *I get a little bit more tired and fatigued now than when I was younger. I get tired more during rehearsals, get bored more, get upset more. Maybe, because I've played this five times. But yet, I am aware that every time [I play the piece] there are things that become clearer to me. I don't think this happens because of age, but because I have more repertoire [experience]. Very often I need to wait for 2½ hours, sitting very quiet, until we are finished. Sometimes we talk [among ourselves said in a whispering voice]; but if the Conductor sees that, you can get punished!*

(52y, M, vc) *An 8-hour-a-day rehearsal does cause fatigue. We often need periods of rest. That is the intensive lifestyle of an Orchestra musician! I do feel more fatigued if I've had a really crap week when we've been playing badly. But, if it was a good day of music-making, then I could have been playing for every possible minute of that day; not really feel fatigued but rather inspired. Then, I'd go home, pick up the Cello, and try and do a bit more playing.*

While discussing boredom, a much more serious line of content emerged. Although most Symphony Orchestra musicians have played the standard repertoire of Western Classical Music at least a dozen times, many players allude to circumstances in which Guest Conductors enter their Rehearsal Hall and insist that their own interpretation is the 'best' way, instructing all players how to express the music to be performed differently than they have done in the past. The transcripts reveal a phenomenon whereby reactions and sentiments of players might have much more to do with 'disregard' and 'contempt' than 'lethargy' and 'exhaustion'. Finally, several players recognize the fact that verbal expressions of 'boredom' or 'scorn' are very infectious. Many recall being 'swept away' by others sitting in their proximity who openly and very quietly (under their breath) express discontent and anger.

(47y, F, vn) *I think it's a problem if you get bored; this is something that you should avoid. In a rehearsal, you need [to] listen to the others, to keep your interest in what they are doing. I am in the 2nd Violins; a Rank-&-File player. How do I keep myself passionately involved? Sometimes we have great Conductors, and there's not one minute of boredness. Sometimes, it's really hard to not get bored—then the best thing is to think of something different. Not to think negative. Not to join in complaining. A lot of people complain about Conductors; they look at each other, roll their eyes, and get in a bad mood. But if you can, think about the beautiful music in front of you!*

(54y, M, va) *First of all is the ability to enjoy a piece of music. I find that as long as there's an audience in the hall, I still get quite inspired. I find it exciting to play concerts, just as much as 30 years ago. Very often it also depends on the Conductor. For instance, if one has a very [ordinary] Conductor, it's more difficult to keep concentration. That does get worse as you get older. Our Orchestra job is 80% rehearsals and 20% concerts. One can assume, then, that players are probably bored for roughly 80% of the time. If there's a good Conductor, and it's fascinating to follow him to see how he develops the music, then you can keep up your interest. It could be that when we're younger we're not involved in the music content; we're more focused on technical aspects. But then as you get older there's less of a challenge to play. The way to keep it fresh is 'music analysis'. A good musician should be able to think of harmonies, counterpoint, how things are connected, and listen to the orchestration. That is, to focus on details that you've never noticed.*

(55y, M, db) *Maybe the secret is to always discover something new! I don't believe anyone can take in all that there is to hear in a Symphony. It takes time! Each exposure consists of new players, and a new Conductor. One problem is that most players, who have played the repertoire several times before, feel they know the pieces better than the Conductor. So, they play automatically based on some cultural practices of their previous experiences.*

3.3.5 Coping with Cognitive Noise

Many of the musicians specifically stated that as they aged they felt a decrease in mental stress. For some players this feeling related to experience itself. That is, knowing 'what' and 'how' to play seems to build self-confidence in one's performance skills. From self-confidence comes *reassurance*. In a sense, reassurance means *insurance*! That means one can rely on their skills in all sorts of music-performance situations. Nonetheless, other players do clearly mention that with ageing there is also a much higher intensity of non-music-performance-related tension and anxiety. These may have more to do with concerns about psychosocial aspects of life in general, including: physical health, well-being, and finances. Nevertheless, the *Orchestra* (including all proxies such as the Rehearsal Hall, the occupational environment, and actual body of colleagues) offers players great solace! In most cases, the participant-players assert that the Orchestra unequivocally provides them with a more peaceful state of mind.

(47y, M, trb) *Stress is a very important thing in doing this job. What I have found over the years is that when there's too much going on around you, you have too much in your head; you can't really concentrate on the music. If you're unable to close down those things in your mind, then [you should] count bars. I am not talking about Music Performance Anxiety. I am talking about being able to clear your mind of everything else in life. Just be with the music! It gets easier as you get older, because over time, you feel you can rely on the sound.*

(55y, F, fl) *I'm definitely a better player today than I was 10 years ago. I would say that the job's harder today than it was 10 years ago. It's harder to concentrate sometimes. Actually, I have a real problem in keeping awake. I'm exhausted a lot of the time because of various life-stresses. Sometimes, when I get completely chock-a-blocked [from tension] I fall asleep. It might also have to do with age. But actually, being at work is the place where I feel the most structure in my life. It is a relief for me to get to work. I feel like I'm at home in the Orchestra. This is the place I feel most comfortable!*

3.3.6 Orchestra Life and Orchestra Environment

The last variable that surfaced from the discussions on mental considerations of music performance was *House Tradition*. Accordingly, each specific Orchestra has a 'glorified' local custom. Namely, an unspoken and uncontended prerogative of the Conductor/Music Director and Management. The attempt to keep such customs over time for all future generations of the specific Orchestra! There are particular conventions, most often viewed as institutional standards for each Orchestra. These have been in place since its foundation. These might compel some players to practise more in an effort to increase their level of preparation in order to perform more efficiently. But yet, such traditions are also often employed as fear tactics, used to threaten those who do not seem to be 'pulling their weight'. These players are often referred to as *dead wood*.

(44y, F, vn) *Particularly in this Orchestra, it's the variety of music that keeps you on your toes. I think more and more nowadays, you can't afford to not be able to play. Otherwise, you could lose your job. Sometimes the repertoire I need to play one week has been played so many dozens of times before. But there are still certain pieces that I need to think about as they are really difficult pieces with complicated rhythms.*

(49y, M, vn)   *Foremost, I believe that ageing makes it more difficult to deal with routines. When you're young every single first concert with a specific Conductor is a 'high'. But then later on in life when you are coming to age 50, and already [have experienced] 30 years onstage, you understand that it is rare for you to feel a 'musical peak'. Thus, you realize that you always have to renew yourself. I think one has to turn inward, and ask: Am I doing the maximum to perform my part? Is my playing in line with those in front and behind me? Is my playing aesthetically pleasing?*

(54y, M, cl/bcl)   *In a previous Orchestra it was very rare that we did concerts in the afternoon. But, when I came here the tradition was that we did a lot of light broadcasts (recordings) in the afternoon. I found that quite hard as I was never going out live on the radio in an afternoon but rather always in the evening. That time [slot] is quite hard compared with what I was used to. I am not sure that that's something that had to do with age at the time. Now after six years here, I feel I'm getting used to it. So, perhaps the different types of Orchestra environment also need to be considered as a variant that affects ageing!*

Several players spoke of changes within the Orchestra over the years while they have been a member in the same organization. Some modifications were for the better, while others were not seen to be very positive. Changes in Orchestras are always subsequent to political, social, and economic conditions of society. Specifically, over the past decades, Orchestra managements more often book 'in-house local' Concert venues as these generate increased income as there are less costs involved (e.g., less transportation, travel). The players mention that such (intensive) schedules have also boosted unnecessary pressure on the players themselves.

(47y, M, hn)   *I've been here for the last 12 years! [It seems that each year] the goalposts have moved further ahead. I really think the Orchestra has changed since I got here. I have had to get a lot more self-discipline to cope with that. It's not all just down to age. To be absolutely honest, I've been running flat out just to stay where I am. What I feel is it's been an incredible sort of race, just to keep my place in the Orchestra. For the time being, I've been successful. They say: 'You're only as good as your last concert.' That's really the way. Well it's not entirely true. But, in the minds of your colleagues [and management] that's true! As soon as you mess up, and let them down, that's who you are! I'm talking about mental stamina—something I've been better with in the past. I have been found to be nodding off at the back of the Orchestra, not paying too much attention. But as far as my other skills are concerned, I can play as well as I did when I was younger. I mean it's all technique!*

3.4 Discussion and Summary

The present chapter explored orchestral lifestyle and the Symphony Orchestra environment within the context of age-related ill effects on mental skills. From the onset of the study, the basic contention was that ageing might cause havoc with focus of attention, concentration, stamina, mental agility, and information processing. Or perhaps, ageing simply serves as a trigger for increased errors, slips, and memory failures. Or, that ageing contributes to boredom and fatigue.

The participating Orchestra musicians in the study claimed that their mental skills have not weakened or deteriorated as time goes on. Actually, they report to have become better with age. They claim not to experience mental deficits or other declines of their mental skill set involving concentration, focus of attention, attention span, score-reading, Sight-Reading, memory, eye–hand span, mental flexibility, automaticity, and mental stamina. Of course, there were a few exceptions in which players did mention shortcomings in some of these skills.

(52y, M, vc)   *I think mental agility is the ability to scan, take in information, and to sort it quickly. You learn to do it more quickly as you gain more experience. Partially because you can't put in all the practice hours anymore, so the motor elements are done in your head. As you read music you need to scan ahead, get information in advance of actually playing it. The better Sight-Readers can be a bar ahead. Sometimes on a good day I can be a couple of bars ahead. It can get a bit confusing because you're actually reading ahead and playing something else—sometimes with different accidentals. I play the Cello and often we are divided into different parts; two players on the top part, three players on the bottom. But, it changes all the time. So, all of a sudden, the music line will expand to four or five parts, and you have got to quickly single out which part you need to play.*

(55y, M, bn)   *How is it that I'm over 55 obviously not really forgetting things, still able to stay concentrated and focused? Well, actually it's more difficult to stay focused onstage! I just find it's more difficult to track the notes down, which means I can't focus on looking at the Conductor as much as I used to. In the old standards your hands know where they're going. But when you're playing new pieces, I find it a little more difficult to take in full phrases at a time; to be able to look down at the phrase, get it, look at the Conductor, look around, and listen to other people. I am saying that my 'eye–hand span' has closed up a little bit. Technically it means seeing smaller chunks. I adapt by looking at the music notation longer. I found myself more focused on the dots on the page than I ever was. It's probably something more general as I also find that when I drive I look longer away from the road (to change the channel or answer a phone call). I think it's much harder today to filter out my life when I'm onstage. But, it's easier to play music today. For example, I played Prokofiev 3rd Symphony last night [Symphony No. 3 in C minor, 'The Fiery Angel', Op. 44, written in 1928 by Russian composer Sergei Prokofiev 1891–1953]. I've never played this before. But, I've played enough music of 1928 from Paris, music of Prokofiev, and other Russian music. So, I already have a lot of information that I can utilize. Actually, I'm beginning to wonder if I'm getting more to an age where I'm more of a risk to myself and others—not because I'm playing on a less than acceptable level, but because a lot of other things come to my mind while I'm playing!*

The overall perception of the participant-players was that there was no real decrease in practice regimens or stage performances because of age-related declines in mental capabilities. Quite to the contrary, the Symphony Orchestra players felt that ageing was a benefit, and that maturity brought about competence from experience. For the most part, these Symphony Orchestra players asserted that they were no longer reading notes but were highly engaged in making music. Nonetheless, it was conveyed that sometimes such a widening of horizons might cause distraction. The players spoke of specific problems with memorizing scores—but yet, this waning may be unrelated to age. Perhaps, memorizing music is a lost aptitude from yesteryear as it is not part of an Orchestra musician's skill set. Finally, akin to all other people, ageing does come with an expectancy that abilities will decrease to some extent. But, among the Orchestra players in the current study such declines to mental skills were not apparent in the performance arena. When deteriorations are mentioned, these seem much more often to be related to other variables and life circumstances outside the Orchestra rather than ageing itself.

4

Motor Considerations for Positive Ageing Among Orchestra Players

4.1 Introduction

The second topic of discussion in the single 2-hour interview session related to motor skills of music performance, including: physical challenges and demands, physical fitness, dealing with repetition drills and practice, rehearsing and preparing, kinaesthetic and motor memory, memorizing performances, communicating with the body, tempo accuracy, pace fluctuation, and psychomotor speed. See Chapter 1, section 1.6.3.1, Table 1.2, Theme II. The players were asked to consider the possibility that ageing-related declines might affect them like all other everyday people without formal musical background. But, then when they are specifically in the performance arena of a Rehearsal Hall or on the Concert Platform, do their physical motor skills and abilities function somewhat differently than when they are offstage?

Foremost, an important issue that surfaced from the transcripts related to the concept of *maintenance*. For many years, my personal view on this topic was that positive successful ageing has everything to do with 'maintaining skills'. Specifically, that maintenance is essentially a process requiring adaptation to emerging life circumstances; changes that need to occur because of maturation. Accordingly, periods of late(r) adulthood bring forth age-related depreciations that tend to arise from time to time. Hence, the challenge of a professional full-time contract Symphony Orchestra player would be simply to retain their level of skill by way of practice.

(53y, M, vn) *On average, I practise an hour a day, every day! It's so important to keep my skills and technique up, and if I wouldn't do this, I'd have a 15%–20% loss rather than my current 2%–3% loss. If someone doesn't practise, the loss could be more than 20%. There are people in the Orchestra who are about 50 years old and they don't practise anymore. You can really hear the difference.*

(55y, M, db) *In general, I do know that as people get older their motor abilities get worse. But, I don't think my motor abilities and skills have declined significantly. Yet, they are not the same as I do not practise that much. When I was in the Academy, I practised 5 to 6 hours a day; later I practised 2 to 3 hours a day. Now, I practise only when a specific piece requires me to do so. Maybe I look at it that I just want to maintain enough to remain in the game. The Orchestra is daily work (8 a.m. to 5 p.m.), and then every so often there is an evening concert. Right now, I am Assistant Principal; this is just fine with me. It is enough!*

(59y, M, va) *I practise 1 hour a day for all 5 days a week. But I don't have to practise every day to keep me in form. I don't have to practise as much as I did years before. I mean some weeks I might have 2 hours just one day, and then 2 days nothing. But on average, that's*

Seasoned Musicians Playing Beyond the 5th Decade. Warren Brodsky, Oxford University Press. © Oxford University Press (2025). DOI: 10.1093/9780198956501.003.0004

enough to maintain standards. I think if I were a Soloist, with one big concert per week, then I would have to practise much more. But for the work I have to do in the Orchestra that's not necessary. The main thing is to keep things in form.

Nonetheless, what came to the surface in the discussions is the notion that if a player maintains their acquired level of skill as developed yesteryear, then essentially they are only conserving a skill set that was mastered over a short period of time—such as a year or two while at the Music Academy. This skill set can then be for the duration of the next 30 years! Players do highlight a much different concept of maintenance over a Symphony Orchestra musician's career than the former concept as it does not meet the requirements. Namely, it is necessary for a player to constantly and consistently increase their skill perfection simply because the Orchestra as an organization steadily upgrades itself. That is, by employing young(er) newcomers who continuously raise the 'bar' of Orchestral performance, the Orchestra is taking in those who are technically more efficient than was previously acceptable as the 'audition standard' for entry to the Orchestra.

(52y, M, vc)   *There are those that will sit on their laurels and they can think: 'Well I've got 30 years' experience.' But actually, they've got 1 year's experience they've been using for 30 years. You can't sit still in this. There are good older players, and there are bad older players. So, when the Philadelphia Orchestra fired all older players in an effort to entice younger audiences to engage with them as subscribers, it had everything to do with age, and nothing to do with players. There may even be a benefit of retaining the more seasoned players—if you keep the right ones. Incompetence has nothing to do with age. You can get just as much incompetence with a bad appointment made [to a] 25-year-old. So, when one passes the 5th Decade, there isn't anything one has to consider to 'maintain the career'. But, I guess 'maintain' is the keyword. If I wanted a promotion, or to switch Orchestras, I'd have to start committing myself to some serious work. So, 'maintaining' a career means staying a member of the current Orchestra at the current position. But, bear in mind that in this country there are no short-term contracts; we're all on a continuing contract until the day we die or retire. So, there is no annual review or audition. I see myself as a musician that is happy in my work, with what I have. I don't need to change. So basically, I'm maintaining my position and my lifestyle. I wouldn't want my performance to be any less than it is now, or any less than it was 20 years ago. You can't say that my level of performance 20 years ago was adequate and I don't have to improve more. Yet the Orchestra does improve! There are youngsters joining all the time; they are better than we were 20 years ago. For you to maintain you have to keep up! That may be a problem for seasoned musicians who joined 30 years ago when the performance of the Orchestra was at a certain level. Whereas now, as new blood is coming in, one can't just maintain the same level. To maintain the career, players have to improve; the new blood is bringing everybody to a higher level all the time. There will be some that say that they have a contract and they don't care. So, perhaps the player isn't getting worse, but just they didn't improve enough to fit in with the Orchestra as it's coming up. We're playing the same music we played 20 years ago, so the pieces haven't changed! And what we play (our part) hasn't changed! It's just that other players have gotten better!*

Many players offered quite nice general comments about the physical motor side of music performance in a Symphony Orchestra. These are worth highlighting— albeit these vignettes may not necessarily relate to the ill effects of ageing.

(33y, M, va)	*One thing that I see in the Orchestra as a physical issue is bad backs; bodies wear out. We do get more tired, we do get more aches and pains. A few [players] had to stop in their late 40s because of other problems—not RSI [repetitive strain injury].*
(41y, M, vc)	*I think long coach journeys, airline flights, the strains of being on tour, staying up late, and generally being zoomed all over a continent, tend to toll more as you get older. I mean you're a bit stiff and out of shape. Although players don't really talk about the subject of getting older, how it affects your playing does come up occasionally. Yes, we're all worried about that. I once heard someone talk about the music performer as being a heightened highly-tuned athlete. But athletes are working to the absolute maximum of their physical ability while we're not! Even when we play a 3-hour programme, and the cardiovascular strain on our heart is overwhelming, I don't think we're working at the limits of our physical endurance. The sort of body movement that we make is more about fine-motor control than absolute strain or speed.*
(43y, F, vn)	*We do tend to think that as we get older our bodies fall apart; maybe not in a really severe way, but certainly motor agility and accuracy. Do we fumble or stumble a little bit more?*
(43y, F, db)	*On the one hand, I do feel that as I'm getting older my motor skills have gotten worse. But on the other hand, I don't think I've gotten worse. The amount of practice I do is enough to see me through what we're doing on a day-to-day basis. I enjoy playing in the Orchestra; I wouldn't push to do Solo stuff. I'm No. 3 [Rank-&-File].*
(52y, M, vc)	*Different musicians have different physical needs depending on their position in the Orchestra. Position in the Orchestra IS the big thing. The people playing the Solo positions will be doing more practice, while in the lower ranks abilities do remain simply because we don't have to do Solos publicly. So, most people can get by with very little practice. Some people practise on the job; they use the rehearsal time to focus on their own elements. Others take the music home. That is sometimes looked upon as a sign of weakness. I think in the case of a younger player who had to spend time prepping all the time, it would just indicate that their reading skills and their mental agility aren't really strong enough. [An Orchestra player needs] to get an enormous amount of information that comes flooding during the day, assimilate it, know what's relevant, apply it, and retain it!*

In general, when raising the issue of ageing among players, several related to *longevity*. Many indicated having knowledge of others with physical motor prowess over long(er) periods of time. While some mentioned well-known players, others talked about those who were especially close to them (e.g., parents, siblings, teachers, or previous mentors). Such longevity, in their opinion, is an indication that after players undergo a periodic review, they can adapt and renew their technique for the next several years to come. Such capabilities also mean knowing *when not to play*; how not to put undue stress on the mechanical structures of their body.

(29y, F, vn)	*I know of some players in their 50s approaching 60s [who are] still capable of playing up to a really high standard. I don't know how they do that. I mean, we all do things that can be seen as a 'senior moment', such as knocking over a cup of coffee. But do they forget things like making a late entrance in a piece? Do they play every other 16th note? Well, perhaps some people do. It is especially easier in the String section because there are so many of us. But in the Wind section, when there is just one person to a part, the quality of their playing, their abilities, and their musicality are really amazing. It's probably a matter of experience and hard work; lots of practice just to maintain these high standards.*
(35y, F, vn)	*You wouldn't think musicians are slowing down. When they have an entrance, it's gotta be spot on. Do they have the same motor skills they had 20–30 years prior? The folks in the back of the 2nd Violins are a little bit older; do they play differently from the*

younger players? I think things do change [because of age]. My father played [professionally] up to age 60; but, he wasn't playing the same as when he was at 30. It's a sharpness that fades! It's not precision, because you can still play rhythmically as precisely as before, as well as still play in tune. But there's just a fading spark; a tiny loss of agility, and not necessarily accuracy. I suppose we're talking about deviations of milliseconds. But you can hear it. You just feel you're not the player that you were. I don't think it is enough to make management comment. They don't make people retire early, but they also don't particularly want people carrying on for too long! It is so minute that most players simply continue through to retirement. Today, there are five musicians in their 70s that are playing. Our Leader is in his late 50s and he's playing like he always did. I don't know how he feels when he plays, or how much he has to work to play. He doesn't sound like he's a different player than 15 years ago when I first heard him. If technique went from 0 to 100, then somebody who began their career with a score of 95 might have a much better chance of getting to 60 [years old] simply because their technique was so much better than someone who began their career with a score of 85.

(36y, F, tpt)   *If you look at people like my old teacher from Scotland, he's been playing Trumpet all his life. He's come up to retirement age, and he's still playing absolutely fantastically. He's very much [about] the ethos: 'Don't do anything out of your comfort zone!' Like he'll never do Piccolo Trumpet work. He'll never do any Jazz stuff. He knows what he has to do, and he'll never venture out of that. That's how he kept longevity. Look at some of the great Trumpet players: Maurice Murphy [1935–2010, principal trumpet of the London Symphony Orchestra]; he went on till his 80s—still in top form! But again, those players were very clear what ventures to take on, and what to steer clear of. So, I'm saying that they've been able to learn to adapt in an older age. I think experience has taught me that if I want to continue, there're things I need to do as a Trumpet player— especially to limit the abuse of actual muscles used that can damage embouchure.*

(52y, M, vc)   *Ability to sit in the same position for many hours is just part of the job. There's a particular age where the body appears to change; it is about age 30. Almost everyone I know will go to about [age] 30 playing without thinking about it. And then at some point, they get some minor injuries (such as a Repetitive Strain or Trapped Nerve). These cause them to review their playing [habits]. Sometimes this requires a bit of medication, or a bit of time off. It happens to most players in their 40s. It's not like a midlife crisis, but it is sort of like a midterm musical-physical review that is necessary because of the physical changes in one's body.*

(54y, M, va)   *Sitting for long hours is more difficult as one gets older. But, I don't think it's a problem. I don't feel myself slowing down in any way. My father is 80 now! He doesn't play [Piano] in the same technical bravura as he did when he was younger. But he manages quite difficult Romantic pieces. So, the amount that one loses technique is minimal. I am not talking about Soloists. I think I could continue to play in this Orchestra until 80.*

During the interviews it became clear that although many players do see physical motor declines among a few Symphony Orchestra musicians, such reductions may not necessarily be related to ageing per se. Rather, these deteriorations are more often a result of other circumstances, for example: tensions of marriage, separation and divorce, remarriage, giving birth, and relocation of residence. Further, they revealed that the ill effects of ageing might reflect how one deals with 'life' when things happen. Several players also relate to practice/lack of practice as one of the main reasons for performance-related declines. Finally, one player claimed there to be *divine intervention* or 'sanctified determination' behind the degradation of motor skills. I have noted such an attitude previously (Brodsky, 1995, 2006) as an affirmation by some players who believe in being 'Blessed' (or not) by the Lord.

(30y, F, vn)   *In general, people are having families later after establishing a career first. Not just female players! That makes demands as far as family life is concerned. There's definitely a correlation here as there is less time to practise.*

(37y, M, va)   *I actually know players [age] 60+ that play really great! They have been in the profession for at least 40 years. So how do they do it? It is the Almighty God. He gives his Blessing and then Man can do anything. So, a player who does not maintain his or her abilities is because they are not in a solemn dialogue with God. The Almighty allows one to choose. If they do not choose well (e.g., do not engage in the passion and love for God's music through deliberate practice and performance), then they will not succeed in professional longevity. I believe that if the Almighty wants you to succeed, and if you have the passion for the profession, then you will.*

(41y, M, va)   *I don't feel I play as I did before. Although I may have lost some physical skills, others tend not to deteriorate. I think it affected my muscular agility; that last degree of bow-control [needed for] a vibrato. It just gets a little bit rougher around the edges. It's never really the fingering and accuracy. It's more something like the speed of the trill. It can be the ability to produce the various types of tone colour that you would want during a piece. That kind of control goes. This kind of thing relates to life. Particularly if you've got family, you don't have as much time to devote to keeping these things in top condition. So, I think somebody who's maybe on their own (or doesn't have children), has a little bit more time for 2–3 hours' practice after work every day. I get home from work, and I'm knackered. Then, I need to see my wife, the children, help with the homework, and do some housework.*

(43y, F, db)   *I've been through a tough time recently. In the last 3 years I've left home. I am with a new partner, and moved to a new place in the countryside. Without a doubt I'd like to enjoy that as well. But you can't say that out loud among your colleagues in the Orchestra. I'm sure that if I did more practice I would be better. It's not that I don't enjoy the music, and I don't enjoy getting it right. It's just that some people work to live while others live to work. I work because it pays the salary!*

(55y, M, db)   *While I do see my elderly mother doing everything much slower, I don't feel that at my age my motor abilities have slowed down. But it is interesting that I notice I now enjoy to play more pieces in slower tempi than faster ones. Especially in the Orchestra, I like when it takes longer for the sound to come out and envelop everyone. To hear all of the chords; sometimes when it is too fast we lose something. Perhaps my kinaesthetic [or] finger memory has declined a tad, but I would claim that it is because of my lack of practice, and not because of my age.*

(60y, M, bn)   *Four years ago, the management had a bit of a talk with me; they thought that my playing wasn't as good as it should be. They initiated a formal process. There were lots of things going on: I'd left my children some couple of years before, remarrying, and renovating a new home. These must have got in the way. I probably hadn't taken on board enough of how much all that affected me. A number of years later, my playing was suffering. I don't remember particularly how [the management] put it, but [it was] formal and [involved] the union! I was a bit offended. But I love the Orchestra very much. So, I changed some aspects of my playing—including reeds. I must admit, it was also very much a question of my attitude.*

A few players viewed occupational stress as the cause of physical motor deteriorations. Stress is associated to responsibilities of a Symphony Orchestra position (such as Sub-Principal or Principal Section Leader). Stress can also surface from being on tour, travelling to locations that are far from the Rehearsal Hall, and being away from family and home for extended periods of time (See Chapter 7, section 7.2.2).

(36y, F, tpt)   *I'm going to see a physiotherapist; someone that deals with players. I don't really think at the moment it's Nerve Entrapment or anything like that. But, I'm always preparing a side of caution if I feel anything is not quite right that's gonna prohibit me doing my job.*

(47y, M, hn)   *People say that I've got one of the hardest jobs in the Orchestra: 1ˢᵗ Horn. I am always exposed. It's the kind of job Conductors worry about. A huge amount of responsibility. Horn players tend not to last that long. In recent years, there's only been a few 1st Horns that made it to pension age. But, if you go back to the 70s, they tended to fall to the wayside sooner. [For example], my predecessor left here by the time he was 50!*

(61y, M, fl/picc)   *I have seen older people trip while going up steps, or knock over a coffee cup. Is that because they're not careful, or because of [age-related] depth perception? If when we play there is a little bit more difficulty, it would be understandable. But yet, if we were not entirely good with our fingers, then we wouldn't be here. I do find some things like technical finger-patterns don't work as well as they used to. I have to spend a bit more of time looking at patterns; this might just be a Scale or an Arpeggio that I might find that I'm fluffing. I've noticed that I do get tired more than I used to. When I joined the band I was 27 [years old]. I remember we quite often had an 'away day' concert involving travelling from the city—sometimes as much as 105 miles taking 2 hours' bus travel time in each direction. And then after the concert we'd get back at midnight. I'd go to bed at 1 a.m., and get up at lunchtime the next day. Of course, now I get more tired; but when I'm tired, that's when I get a bit stupid and knock over cups of coffee.*

Even for those who feel they have noticed 'slippage' of intonation over time, they do not necessarily connect such occurrences to age-related declines.

(30y, F, vn)   *I know about 15 people who have significant loss of pitch accuracy. I have known them for some 10–15 years. It's very hard to put the reason to it. Professionals like me tend to be working all the time. Whereas other musicians outside of the Orchestra might not be doing an awful lot of playing. You think that some players actually don't adjust notes the way they used to. They seem happier to sit on notes that are somewhat out of tune. I'm not so sure if there is a significant 'loss of tune' ability when players become 50–60 years old [or its temperament].*

Finally, there is a notion that certain music styles, and perhaps even specific orchestrations by particular composers, can cause increased physical stress and fatigue. All of these viewpoints strengthen the idea that motor difficulties of music performance are not necessarily related to ageing.

(38y, M, bn/dbn)   *It's really difficult to compare [myself] now with [how I was] 10 years ago because I was doing a different job. Maybe I'm putting more in now, and concentrating on the content more than I used to. So, it's not really because of age. Also, I find at the end of a day, especially when playing highly dissonant tense [modern] music, I am very tired!*

(43y, F, db)   *I have heard others speak about the effects of ageing on their motor skills. They talk about issues of technique, feeling that they've slowed up, or are not able to hit the right notes at the right time. I feel that the only thing is: synchronization between the hand and the bow. It's not the same! And, that's purely down to practice—not because of age! I do take more time over things, and not because I can't do them as fast. The Bass is one of those instruments that you actually cannot physically possible play all the notes. Because when it's too fast you just can't shift; all the distances are simply too huge. So, you find a way to economize. And [whispers to the researcher very, very quietly]: 'Conductors don't hear the difference either'. You can still make it sound as if all the notes are there without actually playing them all. It's just because the instrument speaks so incredibly slowly, that if you're playing at a certain speed, you're actually playing faster than the vibrations. So, you go for certain notes that are important to the rhythm (in a busy pattern). This is certainly not something that we openly talk about.*

(49y, F, vn)   *I know that older people behave in a slower manner. But honestly, I do not feel anything! There are things that I don't play of a virtuoso nature anymore. Virtuosity is something I once did in my life. I am much more interested in playing some very difficult orchestral passages that have to be learned well to play.*

In general, when considering age-related declines, players still feel that old(er), more experienced Seasoned Musicians are an asset to the Symphony Orchestra over Young(er) Players. This is true even when they consider that Young(er) Players have better motor abilities with an overall stronger technique than Seasoned Musicians. See Chapter 8 and Chapter 10 which demonstrate that all players (regardless of age) have similar motor abilities.

(33y, M, va)   *Sometimes we are playing (so softly) that it's like not playing at all. We go through the motions. But, for all 10 people in our section we make less sound than one person does. So, there is a bit of one odd person who does stick out in moments like that. They're not the older person! Rather the younger player! I think that as your technical skills decrease, your ability to play in an Orchestra increases. And so, although young players seem to be able to play anything, they do come in at the wrong bar. They're focused more on 'me' or on 'the music' and don't think about the 'collective group'. Older players never come in at the wrong place. That is partly because they've done the repertoire before. But also partly because they're more sensitive to the people around them.*

4.2   Considering the Motor Skills of Musical performance

4.2.1   Physical Challenges and Demands

Several players related to the physical challenges of music performance as they aged. They spoke about required adjustments of their body (such as changing different postures), and about adapting their instrument (such as using straps and other props). Further, some spoke about various types of coping mechanisms including curative efforts that they use as an intervention for their motor capabilities.

(36y, F, tpt)   *I don't think my lips have given in. To me things have gotten a lot easier in the last 10 years. I've had to change my style from when I was at College where I trained as a Solo player. But in the Orchestra, everything has to change including my sound and projection! So, maybe the actual muscles I'm using now have developed over the years. When you've got a Conductor in front of you, you have to be adaptable to fulfil their wishes. I had an idea of what I wanted to sound like [back then], and that obviously wouldn't configure with what was in mind [for me here]. I play 2nd Trumpet and most often I need to balance the chords—which (to be honest) was out of my capabilities at the beginning. But as the years went on, I developed the strength to cope with it. Yet now, I think I can feel problems coming on. Just this last month I've actually started to notice problems with [my] hand. But I'm not sure it's age-related. I think it's more an issue of posture. We never really have time to relax; we're always on the edge of our seat. You just get one shot at it!*

(60y, M, bn)   *I used to think nothing about posture when I was a student. I looked at myself in the mirror and I thought I look fairly normal. I had a shoulder strap, and a particular way of holding the Bassoon when I was young. I decided that to get decent breathing it's important to have some sort of curvature of the back, the hollow of the back (the concave bit). But, as soon as you do that, you have less room for breathing! I thought that if you hang the Bassoon on that shoulder, the reed goes down lower. For about 8–10 years [I had] no problem, then suddenly I had a real problem—a terrible frozen shoulder. I couldn't play! I was awake for 3–4 days without any sleep. I went to Osteopaths, Craniologists, and all sorts. Eventually, I learned that what I'd been doing was pulling the muscles; I was pulling my head this way, and then this [shoulder] went that way. Everyone has got tales about their physical journey in an Orchestra. I discovered Alexander technique; I didn't believe in [that] before, but now I go quite regularly. I think a lot about the body more than I used to: How not to push and pull; to have muscles toned but not fighting against each other. If you want to stay in the job, you need [to] adapt!*

4.2.2 Deliberate Practice, Performance Preparation, and Mental Rehearsal

The players spoke about the motor aspects of Deliberate Practice (DP). They related to how much practice is 'safe' for maintaining longevity. And perhaps, how much practice can be done without the instrument in their hands (or between their lips). One revelation that surfaced was that some players have music not only in their 'mind's ear' (referred to as Sub-Vocalization or Phonological Memory) but also in their 'mind's body' (which is described more as a Kinaesthetic-like Motor Memory). Many readers might relate to these simply as *Mental Rehearsal*. But I would like to point out that the players seem to be referring to a form of unconscious behavioural preoccupation *as if* physically making music. These feelings are no doubt autonomous, uncontrollable, and somewhat perseverative by nature. The sense is that the experience of motor actions continues to be felt well beyond the actual context of music performance. Kemp (1996) referred to a dispositional typology based on sensory preference for audition that may be seen as an overall orientation to both internal and external worlds. As discussed earlier (see Chapter 2, section 2.1.1), Brodsky (1990, 1997, 2004) tested and revealed the enduring representations of *Auditory Style* using the term *auditivity* as a marker for this behavioural profile that is conceived as having developed across sequential stages from childhood throughout adulthood.

(36y, F, tpt)   *I may be wrong, but I'm of the opinion that embouchure longevity has more to do with how much you look after your lip. There's been lots of people who've gone from periods of doing hardly any practice to preparing for a Concerto—and that was the point when things started to go wrong. So, they went from 'getting-by' practice which is roughly 1 hour a day, to practising a full 4 to 5 hours a day. Then, maybe a year or two later, it's all completely collapsed. So, my way of thinking is you've got to be sensible about just how much you take on.*

(55y, F, fl)   *I'm rehearsing without playing. You can do a lot of good just by doing the fingering as rehearsal. I do it all the time actually. I'm even doing that now while I'm talking to you! I am practising something I've got to play later on. Actually, I do it without realizing it. Just going over the fingering passage that I find tricky in my mind. So, I'm talking to you—seemingly attentive—but I'm also playing a D major scale in Thirds downwards at the moment. Perhaps each of these is in another bit of my brain. It could be with my fingers, or on my knees. It's wherever my hands happen to be at the moment. It's a minute sensation; I don't have to actually move the fingers—it's just a little jitter. I probably do this more than I realize. I'm doing it all the time when I sit still. So, obviously it's something that's unconscious! Only once in my life did I actually realize I was doing this; I was talking to my last boyfriend and found myself practising. If there's something that I've got to play, it's in the back of my mind the whole time, and my motor programme is in operation without my conscious control. [Author's Note: For the past 15 minutes she has been fingering the claps of a Flute. I ask: 'So what are you playing now?' A bit surprised that someone has attentively understood she was practising and not simply moving fingers at random, she replies: I'm playing Mahler—the scale at the end of the Mahler V, (Symphony No. 5, written in 1901-1902, by Austro-Bohemian composer Gustav Mahler, 1860–1911).] [Laughs.] Yeah. I'm not thinking about it. [While it seemed that she was very interested and even insightful towards the topic of conversation, she also knew exactly what she was 'playing'—and this was clearly not the same piece from 20 minutes earlier. She says:] I'm several people! I can split off from a human face-to-face verbal interaction and engage in internalized imaginal mental performance, while at the same time being externally attentive.*

(60y, M, cl)   *I do a lot of practising. But there was a period of time that I drastically reduced working with the instrument as I developed another way of working. If there was something that welded my advancement, it was by me working without the instrument. Last week we had to play the 'Pathétique' [Symphony No. 6 in B minor, Op. 74, written in 1893 by Russian composer Pyotr Ilyich Tchaikovsky, 1840–1893]. In this work there is a slow Clarinet solo. What I did was to sing (in my head) the most important sections of my part, and I asked myself: 'How do I want to express this part?' I tried to imagine expressing the section each time differently. I played some notes a bit longer: 'How does that sound?' I imagined myself playing different dynamics, and even breathing differently. The very next day when I got to the Orchestra rehearsal, my whole part was perfect.*

(60y, M, bn)   *To be fair, I don't do a huge amount of practice. My philosophy has always been to do as much Deliberate Practice as I possibly can, but in as short a period of time as possible. I do not understand people who practise for 5 hours. I mean, you just cannot concentrate. I've been playing 1st Bassoon since I joined the Orchestra.*

4.3 Considering the Effects of Ageing on Motor Skills of Music Performance

This section presents the Orchestra musicians' thoughts on their music-related motor skills and abilities during music performance as they consider the ageing process. They accounted for most of the 15 topics labelled 'Theme II: Motor & Physical' as seen in Table 1.2 (Chapter 1, section 1.6.3.1).

4.3.1 Physical Challenges and Demands, Physical Fitness, Muscular Agility, Control and Coordination, Psychomotor Speed, Breathing, Intonation Accuracy, and Synchrony

Foremost, when considering the ill effects of ageing on music performance, many players simply felt that in the meantime they have been spared from specific declines and frailty. Therefore for them, there is really not too much to talk about.

(35y, F, vn)   *Some people believe that the technical level that you attain when you leave College, is the best you're ever gonna be. While lacking experience, you've been practising 8 hours a day. You can't do that in the Orchestra. So, maybe some players feel that they'll never be as good as before their first job (upon finishing College). But I don't believe that! Technique isn't how good you are as a player, but rather the naturalness of the movements, and your posture, and how you cope to withstand the stresses up to 40 years of playing. When players run into problems and technical injuries, that is an indication that their technique hasn't been able to sustain them.*

(36y, F, tpt)   *I don't think that physical issues have anything to do with ageing. I don't feel that as players become older there may be problems with motor control. As far as I am concerned, I haven't experienced anything!*

(47y, M, trb)   *The most important muscle for me is around the mouth. Does the coordination between my hand and my embouchure become weaker and more difficult as I get older? When I was a student, I would practise 3 to 4 hours a day, and then it would hurt! Muscles do get sour [sore], and it does take days for them to get back. But it's more or less the same for me [in other aspects of my life]; I know if I want to be in shape to run for an hour, I have to work on that. I have to build up stamina.*

(47y, F, vn)   *I don't think that as I'm getting older I am slowing down. Certainly not tempo, nor my reaction time. I am also not slower to learn things. Thinking about other people in the Orchestra, it depends on the person. Some people who [are less active] do start to get slower earlier than people who are more active. I ride my bike every day, and I'm in a fitness centre where I train. I'm glad that I don't have anything I can complain about. But there are people my age (and maybe a little bit older) that have aches in their arms and back. I don't see much of a difference between those who are 28 [years old] and those that are 50 [years old]. Nobody comes in late [in the music] because of their age. I even feel my accuracy is getting better. Also, my feeling for rhythm is better now.*

(49y, F, vn)   *Some time ago our Music Director decreed that all players have to do an [assessment procedure]. I heard some of the 60-year-olds; they were quite good! I didn't hear any problems of coordination. Quite to the opposite! I can now do things more accurately with much less strength (and tension) than I needed before. I can remember only one player in the Orchestra who had coordination problems; but that might have been health-related (rather than age-related).*

(50y, M, vn)   *I actually think that since I came 21 years ago, my playing has improved. My playing used to be a bit heavier. That may not be related to age, but perhaps was partly from my own unawareness. There's always something that is never quite good enough that needs to be sorted out!*

(52y, M, vc)   *People have different needs, and as you get older you know what your needs are. I don't know any 60-year-old musician who is fine on the stage but then suddenly behaves like an 'old man' (walking slower, taking longer to do things, etc.) when they step down off the stage. I feel the same now as I did when I was 18 [years old]. There may be some little Celloistic things that I could do when I was 18 that I can't do now—but not many! Yet, there are a lot more things that I can do now that I couldn't do then.*

(54y, M, va)   *I don't think that I am having any problems with motor or physical issues. And, it doesn't bother me to sit through the Concert for more than an hour before I can get up for a break. I am not aware of coordination problems between my bowing and my fingering of the Viola. I am not more fatigued in a Concert than I used to be. I don't have a lot of stress, tension, or anxiety. When I was younger the tension was greater; so perhaps, one can say that actually there is an advantage of getting older.*

(57y, F, vc)   *What do I do to enable myself to play as I did when I first started 23 years ago? I renewed practising after a period that I didn't practise. At the time I was really into Flamenco dancing. When I began practising again, I played a whole lot of repertoire we do not play in the Orchestra. I actually feel that I play better now than I did when I first joined the band. I also feel that my kinaesthetic memory is better. Nonetheless,*

I do think that coordination is more of a problem with ageing as I see that occurring among others in my surroundings. We do know that as people get older their 'tempo of life' is slower; it takes longer to get up, to get dressed, to shower, to prepare food (e.g., breakfast), etc. But for me personally, Flamenco dancing, which requires coordinating hands, feet, body, and fingers, actually helped my instrument playing.

(57y, F, vn)   *As far as music is concerned I have no problem with motor processes slowing down nor with tempo. Whatever is written is what I play. I also do not have problems working in synchrony with others. But I certainly have problems with time management at home—it takes me longer to do things!*

(58y, M, va)   *There is no problem of being a music performer after age 50! Perhaps ageing only has to do with technique. If one doesn't practise, then one can't play. But then again, I could say the same about players of age 30 or 40.*

(61y, M, fl/picc)   *I can't give you an explanation why I don't see any problems with my motor skills. I guess the explanation you're looking for is: 'How can musicians do it (at older ages) while other professionals (of the same age) in other fields, can't?' Are musicians a different breed of human? Well, I wouldn't have thought so. No! But, I can't explain it! Hypothetically, is it possible that Orchestra players age just as much as anyone else when outside the Orchestra, but when inside the occupational setting of the Orchestra, the effects of age are not as great or don't exist at all? I have often wondered if playing in an Orchestra actually does keep you young and active.*

Thus far, although many players feel that they do not experience any consequences of age-related motor declines in the music-performance arena, they do point out that they have experienced an increase in duration of the time needed to prepare themselves in the morning before leaving for Orchestra rehearsals. That is, the players mention there seems to be a more general slowing down of their time management in the home environment. They also note to have experienced decreased eyesight. Yet, to the contrary, most of the players assert that their physical abilities and motor skills related to music performance have simply improved over the years. Declines, if they had occurred, were no more than a microsecond reaction; and even then such weaknesses of intensity or accuracy were no more than shortcomings that are not worth mentioning. On the other hand, as can be seen in the vignettes below, when considering age-related declines of music-performance skills, many participant-players do admit to have been afflicted. Some ill effects could be very slight such as fatigue, while others seem to be more devastating, including severe pains in hands and fingers. In some cases players noted that music performance had to be slightly modified in an effort to adjust to changing circumstances of ageing; for example, seeking new adaptive techniques, or developing a more functional body/hand position. Because of the importance of the testimonials here in this specific section, I have included an increased proportion of vignettes offering a wider range of ages and instruments than in previous sections.

(33y, M, va)   *By all logic, a player aged 55 or 60 shouldn't be able to play the way they do. We think of old age as when people get slower (e.g., walk slower, talk slower), but yet they're playing! Sometimes I do notice a little bit of slowdown in older players. Like in the tremolo sections. I'm experiencing [that] myself; if I'm not feeling completely relaxed I can't seem to get as fast a tremolo as I once did. So, it's really not a major* *slowdown, but there are some circumstances that you can feel. The other thing is vibrato; it tends to get wider and slower. One thing I've noticed about the older people in the Orchestra [is] they never come in on time. They learn when not to play. So, I think there is a decline; it's very slight but noticeable. For example, a Conductor goes like [that] and everyone gets ready to play, but the older people come in fractionally behind others, possibly as much as a 32nd note. Well it depends on the Tempo. It might not be noticeable to the audience, but from within the Orchestra if you're sitting next to someone you can see they've lost a little bit of their technique. Intonation and rhythm has gone a bit haywire. Since I've joined they've got rid of about 5 people; not because of their age [but] because of their inability. They had to go through some kind of a trial; they do cut the 'dead wood'. [Some are] paid off. But, in a sense, they could have fought it, and said: 'No! I don't wanna go, I want a re-audition.' I've also seen Leaders going to the back of a section under duress (albeit, retaining their Leader's salary). So, I do feel that older players are slowing up. It's not a general, but on specific types of repetitive movements like tremolo, vibrato, and trills. But other than that, I don't see anything else—except a slight deafness!*

(33y, F, bn/dbn) *I know that as people become 70 [years old] they start to walk slower, and start doing things slower. Actually, I do see some of my colleagues who are [age] 60+ where everything they do is slow! The way they walk, their reaction [time], and sometimes while they're playing music too. The interesting point is the change in sound quality. They are nearly at the age of retirement; they're not really able to play with a beautiful sound. Actually, for the Woodwinds the sound does change. And if they are not practising, you can really hear it! Even if they practised, the issue is biological; you can't control it, It just happens! I think that muscles lose their strength even if you work on them. I don't know if there's a [way] to work against the physical [decline of ageing].*

(38y, M, bn/dbn) *I can imagine that the older players would have difficulties with some types of motor skills. I mean people do get Rheumatism or Arthritic Finger. Possibly someone like that would be able to play at the proper level. However, if you're putting in more effort, then you might play slower. I can imagine that older players would have difficulties with some types of motor skills.*

(39y, F, cl) *We would suspect that motor abilities do fall apart with age. One can see physical abilities and motor skills of everyday people who are 50 or 60 [years old] getting worse. For example, sometimes they just trip walking up the steps, just lifting their foot for that extra half-inch. But here one sees some intricate work. I think players do maintain that, but I also think there is deterioration with finger agility. But yet, I have noticed that the older players around me are on an acceptable level. I don't think they have the same motor dexterity that they'd had had. They're not falling off things, nor tripping up in passages. It's the difference of level between being a Professional Sportsman versus being an Olympic Athlete. Unfortunately, we do compare ourselves today to when we had that Olympic-type Soloist level. I mean there might not necessarily be deterioration, but rather we simply compare [ourselves] to a time when we were younger and did much more practising. But it could also be that we're ageing, and things are slowing down. You might see entrances that aren't quite right. Or, trills and vibrato that aren't quite there. When you come out of the Conservatory you've been putting in 5 hours of practice per day. But as you get older, you just sort of turn up and do the job on an acceptable level. So, I find it quite hard to distinguish between the two; ageing-related declines versus decreased performance level resulting from lack of practice.*

There are so many people in our Orchestra who are injured. We have lost a few Violinists due to injuries. Not all are over 50. I do notice that some of the players who have managed to carry on are actually incredibly physically fit and have really put in the effort. On a personal note: I'm well aware of what I do [to my body]. Particularly, my Clarinet is very, very heavy; that's the [brand] I've chosen because of the sound. But it's a real issue. Physically there is a lot of strain on my body. I wasn't wearing a sling (strap) because that is terrible for your neck. Most Clarinettists do not wear one; I think quite a lot of American players do, but not so many here. It's hopeless as it just puts more weight right round your neck. You know, I'm not gonna be playing when I'm 50 [years old] if I'm like that all day. So, for me it's not just the [mental] stress side of it, but the physical side of it now is about maintaining myself NOW [raises her voice to enunciate the word 'Now']. That means Alexander [technique], swimming, running, and an Osteopath; I'm aware of many colleagues who physically can't carry on doing what they're doing. And the people around me who have managed to carry on playing, who are not suffering from injuries; they have invested much into physical maintenance. I could well see myself in 10 years with a shoulder injury because of the sheer weight and the awkwardness of how I spend my day sitting in rehearsals, let alone lugging around a 4-litre [8.8-pound] toolbox. I do feel that my whole physical investment is absolutely crucial to get to be able to carry on doing this. I've searched high and low for an instrument that is lighter that will have the same sound.

(40y, F, vn)   I don't see a lot of older players around me with declines. But I didn't know them before. It does seem like their coordination is a little bit off, but I would assume that listening to one of those people playing would still be very impressive. If you think about it though, the Violin is so small; the difference between something that's in tune or out of tune could be just 2mm. So, maybe they'd be off that 1.5mm. It could be that a leading tone needs to be just a little sharper, or the Bow bounces a little bit when it shouldn't. Maybe the coordination is a tiny bit off, so the fingers and the Bow don't move quite as efficient as they should. In other words, players do not decline that much at all! The idea that somebody would come along and ask a player to defend themselves because they are too much of a risk to keep in the Orchestra is less than 10%. Ninety per cent will remain in the band and get to pension age. But, in other countries Orchestras are quite young; when they expand they take in more and more players who are recent graduates. I think maybe the Violin is an easier instrument to play [till retirement age] as opposed to Brass or Woodwind instruments. I remember a Trumpet player friend of mine saying that he wanted to play [gigs] as much as possible to put away as much [money] as he could for retirement—he knew his lips would go early. It seems the Violin is more about precision than brute force.

(41y, M, vc)   Looking at the motor-physical considerations, I can only say that in my own playing I have less power (i.e., natural physical strength) than I had when I was 25 [years old]. But I have so much more mental control over it. I Bow better now than when I was 25. It's this trade-off stamina thing.

(41y, M, va)   The decline thus far is gradual; I don't know if it's gonna continue. I have seen players who were 50+ who did deteriorate to a point where they entered a procedure of early retirement. Whether it's lips, or Bow control, or whatever. There are a few who manage to retain the quality of their playing all the way through to the end. I can think of one who used to be our Number 2 (1st Violins) who kept his standard right up to the end. At any point he could've been asked to Lead if the Leader went off to do a Solo. In my own section there's someone who managed to keep things going till she retired. She was as good as ever! Yet, at least a few others definitely have marked a decline in their last few years; large enough that they began to be a problem in the ensemble. I think one was quite happy to go so as not to embarrass himself. The physical things I'm talking about do not go as far as tempo fluctuations, or slowing down to the point that they just can't keep up. I do notice 1 or 2 players who are certainly a number of years older, who stumble over more notes than perhaps they would have done 10–20 years ago. And sometimes the coordination between the Bow and the fingers change. It isn't quite as clean as it used to be. I think the audience wouldn't notice because the overall affect is still pretty clean and tight. [But] if they were to play Solo, without the masking of others, it probably would be noticeable.

(47y, M, hn)   The oral musculature (embouchure) is something that can weaken with age. But not necessarily for everyone. I think there's almost nothing else apart from that, that I need to maintain in the context of getting older. Everything is factored in to *maintaining the standard. Even what I eat or drink! When I was younger, I didn't bother with that part. So, I've learned things about nutrition and fitness programmes. That is, eating food that can help rebuild muscles. So, I'm doing these things differently today than the way I did them when I was in my 30s. I'm saying that I need to be able to adapt my life in a more positive way in order to maintain the career. But also, I feel I have to do better now than I ever did in the past because of my Principal position in this Orchestra, So much more is expected of me. When I turned 40 I wasn't too bothered, but now that I am moving towards 50, I can't deny it, I've gone grey! I've got to apply more and more self-discipline to practising, as well as in my personal life.*

(49y, M, vn)   *When I first started I saw hand and back problems among the older players. It was very common. Now, I see the same among the younger players. The older players who complain are in their 60s (not in their 50s). After playing 30 years in a specific position, the body adapts and is accustomed to it. But then, the body starts to break down after 30 years. With ageing there is also more fatigue. I am much more tired after rehearsals and concerts than I was in the past. Then, I could have continued to play all night.*

(52y, M, db)   *I get tired earlier than [before]. But, my playing is the same—there's no difference! Fifteen years ago I could play for 3 hours. Now I can't. Sometimes when I play these really long pieces, I think: 'It's enough, I'm really tired!' I am onstage for more than 2 hours; I can't just walk out. With some pieces it's very easy, and the power you need is balanced throughout the piece. But sometimes, after only 15 minutes you feel tired. My back aches! When we have 4–6 hours of rehearsals I do feel problems in my legs and my seat [i.e., rear end]. I practise now about 1 hour per day, every day. But, really it depends on the piece. Some days I have to practise 2–3 hours when I have to play a big Opera. But, then when we have easy pieces, I can play without practising; I come half an hour before rehearsals, and just warm up. I do think that the practice has helped me retain my skills; if I don't practise during a week, then the week after I'd feel 'OK'. When I'm off from the Orchestra for a 2–3-week holiday, I come back looking forward to playing. Although I have noticed older people have slowed down, I don't think that I have. I don't feel that trills are getting slower. But, that's what it means to be a musician; you have to do the same exact thing, over and over again, whether it be slow or whether it be fast, no matter whether you are young or old.*

(53y, M, vn)   *I don't think my technique is the same as when I was young. My technique is perhaps less by 7%–8%. People don't tell me that. I just know by myself. Foremost, I make a difference between the physical technique [versus] the beauty of sound. I think the greater problem [of ageing] is the sound! My sound (the tone quality) of my playing has gotten worse. For me, the Orchestra profession was ideal; I was not the type who went to the stage to 'present' himself to the public. I had a little bit of fear from being a Soloist. [But] in the Orchestra I was in a group. I also think my speed is 2%–3% less than before.*

(54y, M, cl/bcl)   *I definitely feel the motor side (technique and agility) is not what it once was. I've never played as well as when [I did] in those early days leaving College about 30 years old. I feel that for a really long time, I'm just treading water. Honestly, not really getting better on those things I never did well in the first place. If I found things difficult then, now I find them even more difficult. I mean, I'm playing up to standard—or they wouldn't allow me to continue. It's not like it's falling apart. But yet I feel that the weakness I always had as a player is even more difficult to keep on top of now. [Laughs.] I put in a lot of effort, and sometimes I feel it is wasted 'cause it isn't, actually, get any better. I presume it is an age thing. Yet, when I'm playing with the Orchestra, my entrances are a 100%; the vibrato and trills are just as good! I do think that when you think about older people you sort of feel that they're walking slower—and they've slowed up in lots of other things. I know I'm not as quick to learn [new pieces] as I was once; it takes me longer.*

(55y, M, bn)   *One would think that for someone who's been playing in the Orchestra for 30 years, there is great wear and tear (like what occurs among Ballet dancers or athletes). Well, I just find that what I have to do is to warm up before I can walk onstage. If I did not warm up it would take me much longer to actually feel my fingers. Sometimes, I may walk onstage without warming up for a rehearsal. But for a concert, I need a half-an-hour to warm up with the instrument. Once warmed up, the fingers will just move; they play pieces that I've played before. I know that as we get older we slow down, but I have not yet experienced problems with tempo or rhythms. I don't feel any speed or dexterity problem. But I don't have that 'driving' tempo that I used to have. Also, it's harder for me to sit in a chair; my posture isn't as good as it was when I was younger. That is, I sit back in the chair more often now; I don't have that energy to really sit up at the edge of my chair to play endlessly all day long. On the other hand, I feel that my lungs are better now; it's easier to open up. I have a deeper sound, and its more natural. I don't feel any great pain from playing, and I have no back problems. But I do think [all the older players] are not as limber.*

(55y, F, fl)   *Certainly, you see older people walk, and think, and talk slower. But, does that happen to musicians? My body's quite stiff, but my fingers aren't. I still have the same level of technique. If there's anything particularly difficult, it might require some practice, but not much! We rehearse so much, and I practise in the breaks. I don't feel there's been any detriment in my motor skills at all. [But] I have noticed a slowing-down in my tongue. I used to have a super-fast single-tongue; I couldn't go 160 [bpm] with my single-tongue anymore. In the last 10 years I've had to learn double-tonguing. I used to be able to keep up trills or tremolos forever.*

(56y, M, va)   *I think today I play just as well, if not better, then I did 20–30 years ago. Clearly there is wear and tear. There are pieces that I feel fatigued [playing]; I have to practise just to keep up. Practice is one of the factors in survival. I don't know if colleagues who might be declining in their performance if it is simply because they don't practise. I don't have any problems with speed (i.e., tempo). I also don't see problems in learning new pieces—not the time it takes to get organized, nor my responses.*

(58y, M, va)   *The truth is, I have experienced feeling the slowdown of my hands and fingers; problems with specific [hand] positions and touch. Already from about a year ago! That was a time when I stopped practising 2 or 3 hours a day. Practising does give you security, and the feeling that your fingers are agile. I still play some scales as a warm-up. Nowadays, I find that when a rehearsal is boring, I get more fatigued. It is much different than having a difficult rehearsal rather than an intense workout with a good conductor. Also, after a good performance it takes me much longer to come down [e.g., heightened arousal] and to fall asleep.*

(59y, M, va)   *I am very lucky that my body (and my general health) is working nearly perfect. I just have some backache. It's very [unnatural] what we do. Is it luck? Or, do I do some things that allowed me to maintain my body? You need be more economical with the instrument; not to use too much force. When you open up the music, your fingers just move like they have their own memory. Overall, I think reflexes don't change, and automaticity doesn't get worse. Passages and scales that require much more dexterity (like trills) seem to become even better every year. I do not find myself getting slower with things outside of music; but some things might take me more time to do than it did before!*

(60y, M, bn)   *I think physically something has fallen apart. I'm finding the higher notes more difficult than I used to. I mean you can't exactly say to the Conductor: 'I'm sorry, I'm 60, I can't play that . . .' But, it just comes out with a bit more wobble. I should do more [practice] and I probably don't. I certainly think very hard about it: getting the pressure and embouchure just right. But it was always difficult. I'm not talking about a 15%–30% difference [i.e., variance between then and now], but something really tiny like differences of 1%–4%. You wouldn't even hear it! I've had a lot of problems with my teeth. But besides my oral musculature, my hands, accuracy, tempo, breathing, fatigue, and kinaesthetic memory, have not at all gotten worse.*

(61y, F, vn)   *As far as I am concerned, the only motor problem that comes up with age is back problems. Some chairs have caused me pains and aches. But my age has also caused me to practise while seated. When I was a student I used to practise in a standing position for 4 or 5 hours a day. I can't do that anymore. Now when I practise I have to have a break after 1 hour; it is a break for my hands as well as*

for my head. I usually reach a level of fatigue much sooner than before. The break is usually for an hour itself. Therefore, a 2-hour practice regime has become a 3-hour session. Orchestra rehearsals are different; we can have a 3-hour rehearsal, and then a 20-minute break. But during the actual rehearsal, you never play all of the time. The Conductor often works with a specific player or section. Also, there is a possibility that ageing has caused a slight coordination problem between the right [and] left hands (i.e., between the Bow and fingering).

(64y, M, tpt)   *As we get older, and certainly above [age] 50, there's wear and tear on the system. This is just natural. It's not just among musicians, but other professionals using fine-motor coordination. The question is: 'What is your starting point?' As far as the decline is concerned, for somebody who got to a very high level, the decline might be greater than someone who never got to that level to begin with. That's why you need to take a look at players from different sections. Most times you see String players lasting longer than Wind players—because of the physical demands. But if you're working efficiently, it's not as strenuous. I took a year off from the Orchestra in 1984 to study with Vincent Cichowicz [a Trumpet player from the Chicago Symphony Orchestra, and teacher] at Northwestern University in Chicago [USA]. The things that I learned from him helped me develop and added years to my playing. Today, the physical drain is real. My lips take longer to warm up in the morning. After a hard Concert it takes me longer to get loosened up; and it takes longer for my lips to recover. I'm Assistant Principal Trumpet, so I don't have the demands that I had when I was Principal Trumpet. As far as the speed is concerned, I don't think there's a big difference. As far as range is concerned there's some minute differences. Now, close to the retirement age, I feel that I perform pretty much on the level that I had 30 years ago. I may actually be playing better! Over time you learn how to play more efficiently. Look: If you need 10 pounds per square inch to produce a certain product, and you find that you can produce the same product with 7 pounds per square inch, then the lack of effort allows you to work for longer. So, actually I do feel physically and motorically better now than I did before. But, I do note that I started to take a nap in the afternoon before a concert (already 3 years ago). I never did that before! I don't attribute this as much to the age as I do to conditioning.*

4.3.2 Performance-Related Accumulative Disorders, Repetitive Strain Injury, Eyesight and Hearing, and Interventions

The last subtopics of discussion relating to the motor skills of music performance considered injuries and mediation for conditions that arose over an orchestral career. Many players claimed to have had some form of playing-related ailment that needed repair. These include: degradation of finger control, Repetitive Strain Injury (RSI), cramps–tension–spasms in back and legs, soreness of tendons and nerve endings, and a weakened spine. Moreover, many players mentioned decreased hearing abilities, Tinnitus, and poor eyesight. The players noted that they did engage in a host of treatments to manage the ill effects of ageing on music performance, including: exercise, massages, Osteopathy, Orthopaedic care, and pharmaceuticals (i.e., prescriptions from a general physician). In addition, players revealed they partake in various movement-based programmes such as Alexander technique, dance (Salsa, Flamenco), and Yoga. For deficits of hearing, earplugs and sound filters were preferable (albeit many also stated they could not get used to playing with these while onstage). For losses in eyesight, diverse types of optical lenses (e.g., reverse multifocals) were employed, as well as having score parts reprinted in a larger notation font. Finally, some players stated that they had no choice but to decrease their participation in actual music performances (e.g., practice and stage venues).

(29y, F, vn)	*Most of the players have playing-related injuries. I've had problems myself. So I'm aware and try to take good care of myself. I like doing some therapies and getting more exercise. Mostly massage, but I have thought about going to an Osteopath. I need to relax a bit more. I am not so worried about my hearing. We do have specially designed earplugs. I used them the other week. There is a Bell [i.e., Church Bells also referred to as 'Chimes'] in one of the movements of Symphonie Fantastique [a 5-movement symphony, Op. 14, written in 1830 by French composer Hector Berlioz, 1803–1869]. It was right behind me, and with the earplugs I was fine. The young players are more willing to try them (than those who have been here a long time). You can still hear pitch, and if you play the Violin the vibrations go from your jaw into your skull.*
(33y, F, bn/dbn)	*It's really important to do some bodywork. Just recently I had problems with my back. Now for the past 6 weeks I still have pain, and the muscles are tense. I went to Orthopaedic treatment.*
(38y, M, bn/dbn)	*As you get older your mind might still be clear as a bell, but there is physical degradation in the fingers. I do have pains in my fingers, arms, and body. But that's just from actually playing my instrument; a repetitive physical strain. It doesn't have to do necessarily with age—although it might be due to this accumulative thing. And maybe repetitive pain becomes worse as you get older. But, when we think about old people, we usually think that they have slowed-down. But I am not aware of players above 50 [years old] who play slower. I do think that there's potential for trills and vibratos to go bad with age.*
(47y, M, trb)	*I see my parents (in their late 70s) walking slower and doing things slower. I don't see Orchestra musicians similarly. There's one guy (already 65 and will retire soon) who had trouble with hearing. I will have trouble with hearing too as I have really bad Tinnitus in the right ear. I do often wear filters (hearing protector earplugs for musicians), but actually, it's too late! I use ER 15s or 25s [Etymotic Research filter earplugs for musicians]. But, you don't want to play soft pieces with [these] in your ears. Younger players should get used to them to save their ears [hearing]. It's very loud in an Orchestra pit; it's really narrow, and we do not play very soft. So, for String players who are sitting right in front of the Brass section, earplugs definitely have a protective function. For me it's always the Timpani on my right side behind me; that's why I have the troubles with my right ear.*
(49y, F, vn)	*I do feel that the chairs are not comfortable—more now than ever before. And that has something to do with my inability to concentrate. Sitting for long periods of time does affect my spine. This is something known to all Orchestra players.*
(52y, M, vc)	*It's not so much that when you reach [age] 50 you've already gone through it all (a decade ago) and have already adjusted. You can still get little injuries, albeit you now know more about how to deal with it! Like a football (soccer) player who was injured at some point their career, even if they stop at 30, they'll suffer some long-term damage. One big physical challenge as you get older are your eyes; many members of the Orchestra go to the library for enlargements of music to use in rehearsals and in the concert.*

(56y, M, va)   *Personally, the only effect of age that I need [to address] is different optical lenses; one to read [the score] and another to watch the Conductor. Sometimes I ask the librarian for [large-]size pages. [I have also noticed that] notation with blue ink does not bother me [as much as the standard black notes on white paper].*

(57y, F, vn)   *Ageing has had a physical effect on me. This whole past year has involved a chronic infection of my tendons (and nerve endings); both hands and one leg. It hurts when I play. Doctors have said this may be from a hormonal imbalance, or perhaps from the lack of calcium. They told me to reduce the amount of playing I do. There are no other suggestions. I also have problems of fatigue and breathing (e.g., steady stable heart rate as a result of my sleep disorder). I don't fall asleep during the rehearsals or concerts, but I no longer breathe along with the phrases [as I used to do].*

(57y, F, vc)   *Generally speaking, musicians do not have [great] coordination of their body, and therefore, with time they might develop problems. I suggest Yoga or perhaps learning to dance Salsa or Flamenco [styles].*

(60y, M, cl)   *Nowadays, what keeps me from working efficiently is the 'bodily peel'—that is, the package of the body; I believe that I have the wrappings of a 61-year-old body with a 25-year-old mind. I have intense back problems of the spine in my back. Sometimes, I have cramps, tension, or even spasms in my back or legs. I don't think one can say that Orchestral musicians suffer more from backaches than trashmen (who lift garbage cans all day long). Yet, there is something about sitting all day long during rehearsals and holding an instrument (which is a continuous steady physical tension). But, the issue of an instrument is all the more acute at later ages. As time moves forward, it is much more difficult to deal with the differences between the ever-deteriorating skeletal wrapping and the greater-than-ever-improving mental insights that surface from lifelong musical experience.*

4.4 Discussion and summary

Roughly a third of the participant-players claimed that ageing has not at all afflicted their physical abilities or their motor-skill set. Further, they declared that their kinaesthetic memory has not declined, that expressing music with their body during music performance is just as fluid as ever, that their ability to control and maintain tempo in a steady state (as well as following tempo fluctuations)—are all intact. Moreover, the participating players noted that pitch accuracy, as well as hand positioning and finger agility, are all up to par on the same levels as when they were 20 or 30 years old.

(43y, F, vn)   *I have seen players 50–60 years old playing the Violin, and the impression is they are just as great as they must have been 25 years ago. I have heard that people compare musicians to athletes. Then again, when you think about it, athletes finish their career by age 30; they can't continue on a professional level. So how do we do it? I don't know! I mean some can drive a car at [age] 65 or 70; [even though] I wouldn't want to get in the car with them. Yet, when they get on stage they could still be this phenomenal player. I can't explain it. Maybe because we've been doing it all our life! We know to play automatically—like riding a bicycle. You don't think about your legs, hands, or steering. But then again, I know that as we get older, some coordinated movements do become worse. The fatigue, repeated stress, injuries, all kinds of tremors that happen. I guess these do happen to musicians as well, but not necessarily does it affect the way we're playing.*

(53y, M, hrp)   *My motor skills don't seem to be wearing out yet. Not my ability to play, not the fingering (i.e., getting the notes right), nor dealing with repetition. It's hard for me to say, but I feel that my motor skills are just as good as they were 20 years ago. I am just as agile as I was back then. I haven't come across passages I could play 20 years ago that I can't play now. I don't feel my body is slowing up. Although generally, I find it takes me longer to get ready to go to work in the morning. [Laughs.] But once I'm there: 'No problem!' There is a possibility that as we get older, the effects of ageing [can be] found elsewhere (just like anybody else). But not so much in our professional environment or on the platform. I haven't felt any noticeable deterioration related to ageing—apart from my eyesight!*

(59y, M, fl/picc)   *As a player nearing 60 years old I believe that I play at least as good as I did when I was 30 years old. That is because I have practised all of these years, and have done warm-ups before rehearsals and concerts. I don't think my motor control has weakened at all. But when I get an entirely new piece I do think my responses are slower; I used to learn the piece much faster (but not necessarily better). I try to compensate for this 'debility' by sitting much longer to learn the piece before rehearsals. I believe that ageing musicians do not have to worry about coordination, kinaesthetic memory, or speed (tempo); maybe when I am past 60 years old I won't think like that! But, I don't think there is another motor-related profession where one can be a professional for 30 or 40 years maintaining intact motor skills.*

Nonetheless, the majority of the players in the sample do mention age-related ill effects and declines on some level. The vignettes clearly indicate that Orchestra musicians felt that many players have come to an age where they have weaker eyesight, and an overall increase in general fatigue that often overwhelms them. Tiredness is experienced in Deliberate Practice, daytime Orchestra rehearsals, and night-time stage venue concerts. The players find themselves needing more time: more time to learn new music pieces, more time for warm-ups before rehearsals and Concerts, and longer breaks to refresh themselves or relieve their bladder. In addition, they note they require increased time for post-concert recovery of their lips and hand muscles. The players also talk about needing increased durations of time to calm down from higher levels of adrenaline (Post-Performance Arousal) after an evening event, than what was required when they were young(er).

(54y, F, vc)   *Questions about [age-related declines on] technique are relevant to me as I have had a lot of muscular-skeletal problems over the years. I think it all comes down to experience! I mean I've got a bit of arthritis finger; sometimes it's very painful to use. I have to be careful with my elbows; I wear a brace on my elbow. But I've learnt how to decrease the damage to my system. When I prepare something, I go about it in a completely different way now than when I was a younger player. I don't think my age has ever stopped me when it comes to performance, because I've learned how to approach technical issues better. It's the compensations you make, the approach, and the understanding how your own body works. It's knowing where the weaknesses are; they're all the time changing as you get older! It's being able to adapt.*

Players often spoke about the increasing difficulty of sitting in a chair. For example, regarding the absolute effort it takes to sit on the edge of the seat for long periods of time, to remain in that optimal seated posture to hold a musical instrument, has become more and more problematic. Aches and pains are more frequent. The players related to backaches, musculoskeletal aches, twinges of the buttocks, stiffness of the body, and pains in finger joints. There is a general lack of agility and flexibility; a more general decrease in natural power (physical strength). Further, players mentioned a decrease in stamina, weaker muscles, slowing down, and decrease of control over tongue and lips (embouchure). Wind players clearly talk about the difficulty in producing higher-range notes, while string players discuss the difficult of synchrony between the bow (right hand) and the fingers (left hand). Further there is an ever-increasing inability to physically relax effectively prior to repetitive movement of technical embellishments (such as tremolos, vibrato, and trills). Some players mentioned that they avoid adjacent pitches in multiple-note fast-paced passages. Sometimes there may be changes in sound quality, and the accuracy of the score may be slightly less than what is written—albeit still evaluated to be between 90% and 99% true to text! Finally, players of an advanced age may demonstrate slower reaction times as seen in flawed entrances, with lags estimated to be a 64th or 32nd note. Yet, when all is considered, as one player so eloquently portrayed:

> *Ageing, among Symphony Orchestra players, just seems to have caused a situation whereby yester year's elite Olympic Athletes simply remain to be expert Professional Sportsmen.*

Therefore, the overall picture does seem to be one in which old(er) Seasoned Musicians continue to perform on an acceptable level to retain their position in a Symphony Orchestra.

(56y, F, vn)   *I really don't see any motor considerations after passing age 50. I don't have any problems of sitting long hours [i.e., bladder issues]; but some of my girlfriends here do. I think hand position (fingering) is more of an artistic issue; age doesn't matter at all. Each player needs to choose what works for them. Albeit, as the Section Leader I will sometimes declare which string I want to hear a certain note. I also don't see any difference in my breathing [compared to] when I was younger. I don't think that I have naturally slowed down. I play the tempo that is required (as written on the piece). I definitely need more rest time after the rehearsals (in daytime) and after performances (at night-time). I am more fatigued because if it is a heavy piece (with difficult time changes or meter changes) that causes much greater physical stress. That is, I need more time to refresh myself than I did before. There is also stress and tension in holding an instrument (so it won't fall), and playing the instrument is all about body tension. One needs to develop a lot of physical control to keep tension to a minimum.*

(60y, F, vc)   *Taking on the role of 'Devil's Advocate': If some people [in the Orchestra] above age 55 claim not to be able to drive the way they used to at [age] 30 (as far as reaction time is concerned), then how should these same people be able to keep up in the Orchestra with the necessary motor skills as they do? Don't forget, we are still playing with microsecond reaction time because if we weren't we wouldn't be here. Especially me, as Principal Cellist! So, even when I say some player's timing is a little bit off, it's only microsecond timing. It's not like somebody's coming in a quarter note later. How do I explain how am I able to keep the dexterity, the motor coordination between my 2 hands, and my eye–hand synchrony for some 40+ years? I don't know. I know people that it doesn't happen to them at all. It may be inevitable that the body breaks down; that the motor does undergo wear and tear. By the time we get to 50 [years old] there is natural damage from the usage; a depreciation of functionality. Common sense would say that there has to be some kind of decrease in physical ability. Older people do begin to do everything more slowly. But I can't envision musicians playing less than the required tempo. Yet, I do know some players who actually perform fewer notes than are written in the score [as a partial compensation for flaws in ability]. And, perhaps some players prefer to move back [in the section] to play a less challenging part. But when I listen to the older String players, they are playing the same notes, but maybe not with the same intensity, or accuracy of intonation.*

Seasoned Musicians play very, very well. The evidence of this can be found in Chapter 10. Their performance is highly impressive to the ticket-buying audience of concertgoers. If there is any incapacity at all, then most players would estimate such declines to reflect roughly 1%–3%. Namely, even when old(er) aged Symphony Orchestra players experience the ill effects of ageing on their music performance they seem to be executing their performance capabilities at roughly 97%–99% of proficiency even after 35 years of daily wear and tear in a highly vigorous motor-demanding profession.

5

Emotional Considerations for Positive Ageing Among Orchestra Players

5.1 Introduction

The third topic of discussion in the single 2-hour interview session related to the Emotional Considerations of music performance. See Chapter 1, section 1.6.3.1, Table 1.2, Theme III. Initially, some of the players were puzzled about this topic. Namely, there seems to be some confusion between aspects of music performance that involve the more cerebral intellectual mind versus the more emotive impassioned heart. For example, motivation and discipline are often related to practice regimes, while emotional communication is often related to articulation on an instrument. Players conveyed a preconceived impression:

(56y, M, va)   *Does age affect the emotional side of the performer? This is a difficult question. [Long pause.] I wonder if the emotional side of things means 'engagement' or 'excitement'. You have emotional engagement whether you want or not; it is the music itself! That has nothing to do with age. Excitement is a different thing. I was excited the first time I played with an Orchestra; I had to be much more careful and attentive to my responses. Of course, this all has to do with motivation. When I play pieces that I really like, the emotional elements will be higher. What about communication? Does age affect a player's ability of musical communication during music performance? I think age has nothing to do with it! There are some pieces that I get more excited to play now than I did before. But there are also pieces that I have played so many times that I just get bored with them!*

During the discussions, several emotional aspects and attitudes were enumerated as a list consisting of 13 subtopics (as presented in Table 1.2). Among these were: motivation, music performance, and spiritual life; emotional communication; performance and human interaction; creativity and originality; discipline, artistic integrity, and commitment; performance nerves and anxieties; dispositional traits; relationships among players and bonding with an instrument, as well as issues of gender. As was the case in the previous two topics (Chapters 3–4), the players were asked to speak generally on the current theme, as well as to specifically consider the possibility that on the one hand ageing-related declines might affect musicians like all others without formal musical background, but on the other hand that when they are specifically in the performance arena (e.g., a Rehearsal Hall or on the Concert Platform) their emotional facilities and capabilities may be somewhat different than when offstage.

Seasoned Musicians Playing Beyond the 5th Decade. Warren Brodsky, Oxford University Press. © Oxford University Press (2025).
DOI: 10.1093/9780198956501.003.0005

The friendly face-to-face atmosphere of the interview situation allowed most participants to express themselves without fear of judgement or retaliation. In general, the young(er) players saw the old(er) musician as being somewhat more affected by ageing than they usually speak about. To the best of their recollections, they have observed declines in emotion (i.e., disengagement) among the old(er) players.

(27y, F, ob)   *The [older] guys in the Orchestra just sit there. They show no emotion! Sometimes we are playing the most exciting pieces. I don't really know if this changes with age, but it interests me because I want to know how players keep their emotional excitement when they play the same thing a few hundred times during their career. I guess what I am asking is: When do they stop playing out of passion and it becomes just a job? I recently spoke to a senior player who sits near me. He said: 'You have to come in every day and do what is expected of you—no more, no less!' Yet, I feel that I need to come in, and play my heart out with all of the passion that there is in me. I don't want to feel that the audience bought a ticket without getting the best there is. That's fraud! I remember once playing the second movement of Tchaikovsky IV [Symphony No. 4 in F minor, Op. 36, written 1877–1878 by Russian composer Pyotr Ilyich Tchaikovsky, 1840–1893]; it has a really very beautiful Oboe solo. For some reason during the performance I wasn't 'there' in the hall. I found myself talking to myself: Now change the sound, take a little more time, articulate more, change the dynamic. [Author's Note: The subject of inner self-talk among Orchestra players has been detailed by Brodsky, 2006.] When the solo was over, everyone said: 'Wow, that was really great!' Yet, I felt it was simply a deception as those were simply techniques I had learned to express emotion. The guy I spoke to, said: 'Well you have to learn to trick everyone because you can't always put yourself out on the limb and die on the stage or you will burn out! That is what it means to be a performer.' I wondered if his statement was somehow influenced by his age? Maybe I do need to learn more balance! I wonder if that comes from age.*

Nonetheless, some players emphasized a much wider perspective. The focus of discussion moved tangentially from a more personal 'excitement' and 'appreciation' for music and the performance profession, to more global issues. For example, some talked about personal wonderment at having developed specialized music skills, allowing entrance to a profession that provides the means for lifelong financial support, but then they went on to speculate about a much bleaker future if circumstances were to occur in which they couldn't retain their musical talents subsequent to burnout, physical disability, or even a tragic event.

(29y, F, vn)   *Yeah, I think that age does affect emotions, tolerance, patience, spirituality, and so on. I'm still at the stage when I am quite excited about what I'm doing. But I can see many older people in the Orchestra who quite often moan about everything. They are never happy! Whenever the Conductor comes, they will criticize anything; they even find some sort of fault with the best of Soloists. I don't know if it comes from the fact that they have been in the job for 20–30 years; they just can't find excitement anymore. For me, making music is one of the greatest passions in my life. So, why are they [the older players] still here if they aren't happy with the job? Well, because it's a relatively well-paid stable job that gives you a full pension. Unfortunately, the way most of us train is that we can't do anything else; we just don't have another skill set. I sometimes wonder what would happen to me [if I couldn't play anymore]? What could I do in life?*

(41y, M, vc)   *I hope I never give up. There are times that I think I'm going to stay here for the next 20 years, and there are times that I feel that I just can't be bothered with it anymore!*

> Then I ask [myself]: What would I do? Maybe I'd go into the food industry; I'm a good cook! One of my friends is not sure that as a Brass player he'll make it till 60 [years of age]. He claims he's more likely [to have] physical limitations. Not that he's worried about it, it is just a part of his life. This happens less to String players.

(47y, M, hn)   If I had to stop playing, for whatever reason, I don't know if I would find something else to do—like another career. I can't just let go of it—the idea of wanting to do it. So I'm still here. Yes, maybe obsessed. I still want to do it. It's very important to me. I suppose that [if] I stopped working in the Orchestra, after 2 weeks I'd think: Something's missing!

(56y, F, vn)   But I have thought in the past, what would happen if there was a time I couldn't play my instrument? I think I could become a writer; either a newspaper writer or an author of literature. I have already written in local newspapers under the pseudonym 'Metha Zubinah'. [Author's Note: This is a play on the name of Indian-born Conductor Zubin Mehta, b. 1936.]

Finally, there were some players who felt that ageing happens to musicians much to the same extent as it does to everyone else, but yet the ill effects of ageing are minimal and not relevant to music performance—certainly not to performing musicians in an orchestral environment.

(53y, M, hrp)   I think I do find myself feeling more intolerant of people and losing patience. I've never thought about it having to do with age, but now I'd say it's quite possible! That does happen with ageing! But it does not apply to my work environment. I wonder if there could be a possibility that Orchestra players will feel the effects of ageing outside of Orchestra environment—almost like everybody else—but yet inside there's no effects at all.

5.2 Considering the Emotional Skills of Musical performance

The participating musicians commented about the emotional aspects of music performance. While the aim was indeed to focus on ageing, I do point out that some of the vignettes below illustrate Orchestra Lifestyle, not necessarily considering age. The reader should note that the positive-toned vignettes are presented first, and then those of a more negative nature follow. Namely, in addition to highly energetic attitudes on emotional involvement and passion, many players also point to the fact that they have 'lost their passion' and actually feel frustration; they no longer experience the 'shiver up the spine'! Some players mentioned lower levels of tolerance towards others, boredom, and emotional fatigue.

5.2.1 Positive Passion, Motivation, Emotional Involvement, and Satisfaction

Many players expressed the notion that they are still very passionate about the music, and still feel highly motivated.

(43y, F, db) *As I get older the passion and emotional involvement is there just as much as it's always been. But I do get a lot more frustrated if it's not happening; especially if it's a tough Conductor or if people don't play well together. I get frustrated much more now when we're rehearsing for the sake of rehearsing; especially when the Orchestra knows the piece really well [as opposed to when] there's an inexperienced Conductor [who personally needs the rehearsal]. Maybe I have a lower threshold of tolerance now!*

(44y, F, vn) *As you get older you become less inspired by people that come and go. Possibly it would take somebody very special for me to say: Wow that was a fantastic Soloist! We haven't had one of those in a while!*

(47y, M, trb) *As I'm getting older I don't feel less passionate about the music. I've been in this Orchestra more than 20 years. I am proud to be a member of this Orchestra. Symphony Concerts are rehearsed and played just once! I like my job, and so I don't have troubles with being bored in boring rehearsals. However, 'passionate' is a strong word. I would prefer to say: I like to play!*

(47y, F, vn) *I'm a really passionate Orchestra player and Chamber Music player. For some it's just a job; they come here, play, and then go home. Some leave their instrument here—all the time! They don't practise at home. When I say that for some it's just a job, I mean they get more bored, are always complaining, and not very happy with the job. Yes, perhaps they have really good technical skills to be in the Orchestra; many of them are really talented. But they don't really love the music.*

(53y, M, hrp) *As I've gotten older I absolutely don't have less motivation, less creativity, less inspiration, or less emotional involvement. I may even have more! It depends on what we're playing and how it's going. I wouldn't say these aren't related to ageing. But [they have] to do with the piece, the Conductor, and if my colleagues are playing well. We all sort of feed off each other. [On the one hand] you are not really motivated to learn your piece, but you don't want to show up at work not being able to play. As far as inspiration—like getting shivers up my spine—I'd say it's about the same. The emotional involvement and excitement is just the same even though I've played so many of the pieces before.*

(53y, M, vn) *As I get older I am not bored. I am still very passionate about music. I am still very interested in the music. I still have this feeling in my heart when I play. It is the same as when I was younger—or even more! For me playing in the Orchestra isn't just a job. Maybe [orchestral performance] was never an obsession, but it was 'just the right thing for me'. As I get older I do get tired more than I did 10–15 years ago. For example, if I play an Opera till 10–11 p.m., I feel that the last 15–20 minutes is just too much; it's late and I want to go home to bed. When I was young that wasn't a problem. Yet, when I do get home, now I find I need much more time to calm down.*

(59y, M, fl/picc) *I still have passion. How did I manage to maintain passion? On the one hand I don't think the age affects musicality or passion for music at all. On the other hand, [ageing] can pull you outside of music [e.g., towards cynicism and burnout]. But, that can be because you get tired after 30–40 years in the business. And that is why one needs to practise every day. Practice maintains you. I see other older players who also practise every day; they have the insight that without the regimen of daily practice, they would've become cynical, burned out, or lose their passion for music.*

As mentioned above, the matter of the repertoire they perform, and the level of repeated multiple exposure, is often conveyed as having an influence on *valence* (direction) and *intensity* (energy) of motivation and passion. Namely, in the players' opinions, music coverage can increase emotional engagement for some players, while it can also decrease emotional involvement for others.

(35y, F, vn) *I don't think that older players feel less inspired, have less motivation, are more bored, or less satisfied. I suppose as you get older, your life takes over. When you're fresh out of College, all you think about is playing. But then as you age, other parts of life become as intense as is the Orchestra—like your children! I do think the older players often sit back! They know the repertoire, know what's coming up, and don't have to practise as much. I've now been 10 years in this Orchestra; I've probably played some things 2–3 times. The impression that many have is that if a piece I've played already comes up, then, I'm not as motivated as I would have been as before. But actually, I enjoy it more! Maybe, there's something about previous exposure that allows me to be more emotionally involved the next time round. In our Orchestra we don't repeat much. But when we play something that I know, it's such a relief as I can play without being on the edge of my seat.*

(38y, M, bn/dbn)   *I do not have less emotional inspiration, or less involvement in the music because of ageing. I'm very moved by music that I play. I don't really see huge changes [related to ageing]. [But it] depends on the music! It's not just a matter of I've played something 5–15 times already. Some music moves me more than other music, and will continue to move me! Other pieces just haven't really had much of an effect on me—at any point. Maybe that's sacrilegious; although I tend to enjoy playing them, they're not such a treat anymore.*

(43y, F, vn)   *I suppose when you're younger, everything's new and you're learning more. So, you're more likely to be motivated and interested in new experiences. Perhaps motivation is not related to age, but rather to experience. On the one hand, you could say that someone who is 30 has perhaps 10 years of musical experience, and someone who's 40 could have 20 [years]. Yet maybe [one person's] 10 years of musical experience is much richer than [another person's] 20 years' experience.*

(52y, M, vc)   *As I get older I don't find it difficult to be motivated, nor do I need to force myself to be excited for a performance every night. But I know the chances of making a really serious mistake are actually multiplied when you've [played the same piece] 10, 20, or 100 times. You've really got to stay focused no matter how many times you've done it before.*

(60y, M, bn)   *Do I find myself less emotionally involved in the music because of my age? [For] some pieces of music I would say: Yes, but not necessarily. I've given some fantastic performances recently. I often say to myself that there will be 12 concerts that I remember throughout my life. I keep adding to this so-called 'Big 12'. I still go home and bore the wife silly about how it was! Yet, some pieces that I used to think were wonderful, and that gave me shivers up my spine, just don't do it for me anymore. I don't think that is because of experience or age, but rather repetition and exposure. Generally, I think that the amount of exposure you have to certain pieces causes a situation that you just don't feel it any more.*

The transcripts illustrate that as participant-players gained more experience, they not only became more proficient but also developed a greater understanding for the music itself. Several players claimed that this kind of *awakening* deepens emotional pleasure from each performance, often causing them to be even more inspired. Yet, such an awareness can also *strain and stain* one's previous naïvety regarding music passion and intimacy. Several players mentioned having lost passion, subsequently affecting their emotional drive, which at times even tainted their self-perceived level of satisfaction. More specifically, players claimed that multiple repeated exposure over many years seems to have coloured one's experience of excitement, and feeling the shivers up the spine. Hence, one's levels of arousal, involving the all-ultimate adrenaline rush, are not the same as they remembered in the past.

(33y, F, bn/dbn)   *I think some have the lost patience for making music, for hearing new things or new impressions. When you're young and just get into an Orchestra, you have lots of energy and really want to play new projects. I don't think that as you get older you become less passionate about music or performing music. But, it depends on your attitude and overall personality. Players my age (and even some who are younger) might already have that attitude. I know of one player who left the Orchestra because she lost the passion at 33 years old. She lost the drive! No matter how old you are, if you still love music then you still have the passion to perform it.*

(40y, F, vn)   *I haven't had problems with staying motivated. I am not sure if it gets better or worse as you get older. Does one get more emotionally distant [with age]? Unfortunately, I see the attitude of my older colleagues who seem to be really discouraged. Previously some [of them] won international competitions and some were Concertmasters. Now they're all Tutti payers (having auditioned for the Principal position but didn't get it). I'm now playing Symphony repertoire that I've not seen for many years; I'm discovering new things in them as I'm hearing them differently. So, perhaps one way not to be bored with the long hours of rehearsal is to try to see new things that you haven't seen before. When you practise just your part, you don't hear what the other instruments are doing. So, to be more emotionally involved means to try to listen to what else is going on with the other instruments.*

(41y, M, vc)   *Nowadays, I think I am less easily swept away by music than I used to be. I don't get 'shivers up the spine' or 'tingles in the fingers' as easily as I used to. I remember that when I first joined the Orchestra it happened an awful lot, Now it takes something really special for it to happen. So, it's a trade-off! Having said that, one could say that music isn't just technical; lots of emotions are going on! So, the argument, is: Are we feeling the emotion ourselves? Or: Are we just creating the emotion for the audience? I don't think about it as an illusion, I think it's real. But, perhaps we're the Puppet Master pulling the strings, and not actually feeling it ourselves. And I think that's one of the reasons that it's easy to get swept away when you're younger; you identify more of what's coming out. I think that as you get older, you're a little bit more aware of what you actually need to do for the end result.*

(47y, M, vc)   *From my point of view, I think that the emotional issues, like motivation, satisfaction, and so on, are less of a problem as one gets older. Maybe one finally understands what one is doing. When I first started I took it for granted! My mother was a Celloist; I obviously got some of her genes. So, there was a kind of ability, and I could play the Cello [early]. I got this job, and I took it for granted. But definitely as I got older, I've taken it less and less for granted! I've enjoyed it more and more. I got more pleasure from playing my Cello [in the Orchestra] in the last few years than I did in the first 20 [years].*

(50y, M, vn)   *If a person is generally unhappy or unsatisfied, well then they'll bring it to work with them. So, even if the work situation is excellent, they'll always find something to complain about. How do you keep the passion alive after being in the profession 40 years? You just have to feel the music. Don't look at it so much as a job, but really try to be connected emotionally to the music—even if you've played the piece 400 times! When I was younger it was easier to get more excited. Maybe it is more difficult as you get older to get an emotional high from the music or the music performance. That level of arousal! I am also not sure if, as you age, you're more in control or less in control of [arousal]? So, how do you keep the inspiration going? Well it can be that you also have to have things going on outside the Orchestra. I would say: Do something else in music outside of the orchestra—like listen to music (not Classical) to help broaden horizons, hear new sounds, as well as to appreciate other great players.*

(57y, F, vc)   *I feel all the more depth of energy in the music. But, there are many players of my age who feel burned out. Sometimes I also feel weariness and fatigue. I had a 10-year period when I learned Flamenco dancing. At that time I did not maintain the [orchestral] standards required. Honestly, I didn't really care! Maybe others around me suffered. It was not that I hated the music, but I was just somewhere else (outside of the Orchestra). But then, I came back to myself as a player. Some players actually hate music; they are just waiting for their pension, counting the days and the minutes. Not me!*

One subject that often surfaced concerns listening to music outside the Orchestra: Concerts in the community, the radio, and CDs. The players were fairly split in opinion. Half felt that one cannot be passionately involved in the music-performance profession and a musician's lifestyle without listening to music 'all the time'. The other half felt that one needs a rest from the noise (i.e., both the physical sound and the cognitive involvement) which is necessary to achieve a more balanced well-being. Hence, some players were adamant that the absence of listening to music outside the orchestra is clearly a symptom of burnout. This issue is discussed in more detail in section 5.3. Others feel this behaviour is associated to reduced integrity and lack of conviction to the music vocation.

(33y, M, va)   *I don't listen to any Classical music at home. I think that is the norm among the Orchestra players. I'll be quite happy to have an evening without listening to music reading a book. Most people have this picture that the reason we are here is because of this passion with music. So, it just can't be a job. And I know that's impossible, because a lot of players do say: 'It's my job.' Most outsiders say: 'If there's anybody that's really involved with music, it's you guys!' Yet, some of us go home and don't want to hear anything. Nothing! When you're young, I suppose the options are: Follow your dream, and try and become a professional musician, or give up on the dream but still enjoy music. Yet, many people who do follow the dream end up not really enjoying music. They do it because they're good at it. They do it because they don't know anything else. And many of them say: 'I love my job.' But, when asked: 'Do you also listen to music when you go home?', they might say: 'No! If I have to practise then I hear more music, but other than that: No!' So, there's no music in their life outside of Orchestra work hours. Because by joining an Orchestra, they've taken something that's so intimate and passionate, and turned it into a career/job. Maybe, the problem is: How do you rekindle the initial passion that brought you here to begin with?*

(59y, M, fl/picc)   *Many players who are burnt out never even listen to music anymore. In my opinion these players are not interested anymore in creativity and have no passion. But I still have passion. Outside of the Orchestra I listen to a lot of Classical music and even other styles (e.g., Folk, Religious, Pop). I like wearing headphones and listening to YouTube. I still buy CDs to listen to, and take them with me in the car during driving trips. But it is never like it used to be; once we sat quietly [in our living rooms] and listened to music. Life is so much more complicated now, there is no time to just sit and listen.*

(61y, F, vn)   *I rarely listen to music from radio or CDs. That sounds like a contradiction because the best advice I could give to a young player to maintain oneself in the Orchestra is: Practise and do not lose the passion for music! Music performance is a way of life; it's not just a job. But, one can't be involved in music all the time because [music] requires focus of attention. I do find that I need to rest when I go home. I actually see no connection between ageing and musical emotional engagement. The passion is the same no matter what the age may be. It depends on you, rather than on your age! Nonetheless, it may be that as you age [the music] takes up more of your energy. For example, our last concert was so beautiful—I really enjoyed performing even more than I can remember for a long time. But, the next morning I was so tired during the rehearsal! I don't remember that feeling when I was younger; I could have played out my heart and soul, and I was up and ready for the rehearsal the next morning as if nothing happened to me. But, not today!*

(64y, M, tpt)   *Does one become hardened and less emotionally involved in music as you become older? Well . . . [Sighs and waits a long while.] I'd say: For you to stay passionate about the music, you have to be emotionally involved! Look: For a Brass player to play Haydn or Mozart it can be very dry. You've got three notes to play. But you need play them like you're in the 1st Violins. You have to be in tune with what everyone else is doing, and have the same phrase structure in order to be properly supportive. So, I can't subscribe that one would be less emotionally involved because of age. One might assume that with large amounts of experience and repeated exposure, the passion wouldn't be there anymore. Whether it's because one gets bored with the pieces, or one feels they've already played a piece 100 times, there's no great adrenalin rush! And, most assume that players will play simply because they're getting paid for it. But that isn't really true. You still have to be involved in the music in order to keep it alive. I personally listen to music outside of the Orchestra. I go to concerts to hear people play. And not only Orchestra stuff but a very wide range. Music is still very much a part of my life. I don't know many players who do not listen to music anymore because they feel they have so much music every day that they want to go home and just hear quiet. That kind of attitude could reflect levels of burnout. The question is: Are those who are more involved in music outside of the Orchestra less affected? In other words: Is resilience to ageing related to the Orchestra profession, or are there less effects of ageing among professional Orchestra musicians and therefore they are more involved outside?*

5.2.2 Negative Passion, Motivation, Emotional Involvement, and Satisfaction

Many players claimed that as they age they feel they have lost the passion and motivation. This notion has recently been somewhat mentioned in the literature. For example, Détári et al. (2020) note that musicians lose motivation once music performance becomes a form of employment. In the current study, some participating players demonstrated to be far too fatigued and drained to be emotionally involved in music performance. Subsequently, they claimed to receive less satisfaction from performance, and hence the Orchestra environment has become viewed more as a *job* than as an adored *lifestyle*. One of the intervening variables that came up from time-to-time was the repertoire. This issue has to do with the actual programme the Orchestra is required to perform. Perhaps, then, decisions by Management and Music Directors when selecting repertoire for programmes should consider more than marketability and ticket sales.

(41y, M, vc)   *The emotional considerations that need to be discussed are: being bored, not finding motivation, and [having] no inspiration from the work you're doing. Let's say you're doing a 'Pops' concert for the 7th time, or a 'Kids' concerts for the 10th time—all within the same 2-week period; that is extremely difficult! It is definitely somewhat age-related to feel frustrated by that kind of programming.*

(41y, M, va)   *I would probably say that on average players [aged] 50+ have less motivation towards the job than younger players. If you have less motivation, then you'd have less satisfaction. So how [why] do orchestra players keep coming [every day]? To be honest, I don't know. Maybe some simply think: I'm just counting the years before my pension starts. Or: It's become a job. I think I can separate between my work in the Orchestra ('it's just a job') and the performance ('that piece is gonna be great' or 'it's gonna be great working with this Guest Conductor'). So, you probably get to a point where there is a sort of run-of-the-mill feeling to come to work in the same building with the same colleagues and with the same Principal Conductor. But then, if something new comes along, it really excites you! For example, I'll be doing one very exciting piece this week. I have only played it twice; this week will be my third time in 20 years of being a professional Orchestra musician.*

(49y, F, vn)   *I am more tired and fatigued than before. I get tired when the pieces are not interesting. Unfortunately, much more often than before I am not drawn into the music. Before the proportions were 80:20 (interesting versus uninteresting); today it is just the opposite [20:80]. I have played Mozart's Symphony No. 40 [G minor, K 550, written in 1788 by Austrian composer Wolfgang Amadeus Mozart, 1756–1791] a million times. After all of those performances, how can anyone find something interesting in that music? It would take a really talented Conductor to do something new with that music! So, I don't always feel engaged to the same emotional extent as once before. I do believe that as a result of ageing it is more difficult to express emotion. Also, there is less motivation, less satisfaction, and more fatigue. When we were younger, we were very motivated to audition for better jobs (e.g., a higher positions) in other Orchestras. But, at some point you just learn: That is it! You became slightly apathetic. Most of the time I feel 'stuck' [i.e., emotionally constricted] as far as my own potential.*

(50y, M, vn)   *The fantasy seems to be that it's not so difficult to get into an Orchestra. You just have to be a good player: if you have the skills you'll get through the audition. Yet, it's more difficult to remain here—to survive! I recognize that with time one does become jaded and that is the burnout thing. I mean I see people in the Orchestra who actually arrive with the attitude: Today is one less day to the pension. And don't forget there are always other younger people who are trying to get in to the Orchestra, and hence by doing so, they are actually pushing you out.*

(52y, M, db)   *I feel I'm not really as satisfied as when I was younger. When I came here, I had no idea about working [conditions], or salary, or orchestral life. I thought I'd start at 8 a.m. and finish by 5 p.m. But now, after all of these years, it's not really about the money, the work[ing] conditions, or the pension. It's about the passion! When I started, music was a passion; it was all my passion. But not anymore! I haven't found a lot in the music that allows me to be fresh and excited again. So, maybe I should find something that isn't music? But, I can't do anything else at [age] 54. I have to get along with the job till I retire at 66—and that means 13 more years! I'm not really less passionate about music in general, but about the music I'm playing in the Orchestra. I hear music and I think it's really beautiful music. But then when someone says: 'You don't play it very good!' Or: 'You have to play it like this!' Well then, the thrill is gone. [Laughs about referencing an actual well-known song by American Blues singer Riley 'BB' King, 1925–2015.] When I hear the music it's very emotional and beautiful. But then, when we have to practise . . . [that is] the minute I receive it in notation . . . then it's just a piece. I mean when you just hear the music, it's not work! But, when they hand it to you, it's work! Perhaps when I was younger everything was new; everything was very exciting and very emotional. But as I got older, it became: This isn't love any more, it's work!*

(56y, F, vn)   *All my life I believed the most important thing for a player is not to lose the 'willingness' or the 'want' to work. That is [the drive] to make music. This is the most important aspect. That is clearly more difficult after age 50. I would say that 99% of the people in the Orchestra [above 50] feel that work is no longer interesting. They already know, have heard, and seen everything! I sometimes have to remind myself that when I feel that way, music's always interesting—it's like a puzzle. Yet, sometimes I feel lost. One can lose the 'light in their eyes'. So, to younger players I would say: If you give yourself to music, all of your life, you won't lose sight of it! Keep loving music! Watch concerts, listen to music recordings. Think about it because this is your life. The love of your life—like a partner! Don't lose that. There are those in the Orchestra who have lost it! They come and go, sit and play with no emotional involvement. They just want to get by, and avoid getting thrown out.*

(57y, F, vn)   *There are some players who are 60+ years old and they don't seem to care anymore. They don't even try to maintain themselves (through Deliberate Practice). Most of them say that they have less time as they need to spend more and more time with their grandchildren. But the truth is, they are simply less engaged with the music. Maybe they are 'broken'. Or, simply burnt out.*

It is very disconcerting to hear players relate to highly fatal aspects of ageing on passion and emotional involvement in music performance. Most specifically, in a rather unprecedented fashion—and to my knowledge for the first time ever presented in the academic scientific literature—below are a few examples of sentiments among world-class Symphony Orchestra players who, in an open and honest dialogue, disclose emotions explicitly describing their heartfelt impressions about the music-performance vocation as having become a form of *prostitution*.

(55y, F, fl)

There's a certain passion that brings you into music as a child, and it keeps you going along this route of skill development, personality development, and then career. But the minute it became fused with the everyday job and playing things that you really don't like, and having Conductors or Composers who force you to act in certain ways that don't fulfil your musical potential, and you're all the time putting your head down by just accepting it, then you've become a Prostitute! It brings in the money. So, when there's no passion anymore for music, you also don't listen to music when you go home. It's just not there!

(60y, M, cl)

There are those among us who use the term Prostitution. Yes, it is Prostitution in the sense that we do everything with everybody at any price. More than that, the whole profession has become one in which you take the most passionate and intimate act [of making music], and it becomes something you do every day all day long. Perhaps then, it is impossible to even be emotionally involved. So, when the intimate passion becomes employment, maybe there is something to be said for the use of the term 'Prostitute'. And maybe a Prostitute acts out of 'emotional castration' (i.e., doesn't even get involved emotionally at all). Today, the Orchestra environment has become predictable and ordinary; like [the fast-food giant] McDonald's. These [restaurants] pop up in all sorts of places, including historical sites in cities that need preservation. Like putting a McDonald's in place of a museum at Ground Zero [where the Twin Towers stood before 9/11]. Today, even Beethoven's 'Eroica' [Symphony No. 3, E♭major, Op 55, written 1802–1804 by German composer Ludwig van Beethoven, 1770–1827] is not very 'heroic' anymore! Someone comes along and they don't give a damn; they just make [conducting] movements with their arms. Nothing happens! So, the issue is when you take the most passionate intimate experience you know, and turn that into employment—an everyday daily experience that does not involve the levels of emotional engagement for the type of activity that is involved—isn't that Prostitution?

(64y, M, tpt)

I have also heard players talk about the fact that as they grow older they feel more and more like a 'Prostitute'—being forced to play pieces that they are not really interested in playing. They are forced to perform for money! I know what some players mean that when you take something you're so passionate about—which most likely is what brought you into the music-performance field to begin with—and then in the Orchestra you end up playing without passion. Players use the metaphor of a Prostitute because in their imagination those people can no longer enjoy having sex in their personal lives as they turned that kind of intimate passion into something that they do for money. For me personally, I don't see that! And, I don't see it as being age-related. This can happen with younger players too! I don't go as far as calling it Prostitution. But the requirements as a professional are clearly different than when you are an amateur. An amateur can say he's gonna have fun doing this, and then does it! Whereas the professional says: OK. It's got to be this, and got to be that. So, that happens when you take your avocation and make it a profession.

5.2.3 Discipline, Artistic Integrity, and Commitment; Conviction and Motivation; Sense of Responsibility; Dedication and Pride; Dispositional Traits; Vocational Meaning; and Boredom

The participating players often spoke about their professional commitment, conviction to the Orchestra, and tolerance for others in the Band. In fact, it was difficult for them to separate those feelings from other emotions such as passion and motivation. Discussions often led to portrayals of 'artistic integrity' and 'dedication' to the music itself. Players mentioned having a great drive to perform at the highest possible level, requiring them to improve themselves constantly through practice and rehearsal. They expressed great pride when performances met the standards that they felt reflects artistic expectations—even when the music materials covered were not as artistically interesting or challenging as they would have wished them to be. Often, the young(er) players brought out that the old(er) players have 'lost it'—while the same is frequently conveyed by the old(er) players about the young(er) players. Finally, it is widely perceived that multiple performances of the same pool of more popular pieces are a source for developing 'lack of conviction' and 'lack of pride'.

(35y, F, vn)   *Saturday night's concert was so really difficult. We didn't have that much rehearsal, so it was quite stressful. I mean it was good music! But, the audience was only half full. I am not sure if it does something to our motivation when the Hall is empty. We all try to play well no matter how many people are there.*

(36y, F, tpt)   *Emotional things [in music performance] go up and down all the time. That has nothing to do with age. However, I do see older players with less conviction—they complain all the time; more negative vibes come from them. Probably because they have been doing the same programmes for some time now; maybe the 15th time of playing a particular piece. But, I don't see that on myself. I think I'm probably more tolerant now than I was 10 years ago. Some things used to annoy me when I first started—like people who were not as dedicated as I was.*

(39y, F, cl)   *What I find really hard to believe is that I've been in this job for 9 years and I still don't feel I am good enough. Yet, I am the Leader [of my section]. I think that the constant striving [to be better] is what keeps us going. I suppose with music there's never a sense ever of having arrived! I think Orchestra musicians do tend to be fairly self-effacing. I don't know if that's perhaps a bit to do with our whole culture, and how the Arts are viewed. I believe the Berlin Philharmonic Orchestra would assess themselves higher in skill proficiency than we would. It's how we view ourselves as an Orchestra. I mean this is a great Orchestra, but no one is saying we're like the Berlin Phil. For a long time a previous Music Director/Conductor told the players that they were dreadful; I'm sure that feeds into the way people view themselves. I've gone through a patch of just trying to remember that I am one of the best Clarinettists in this country! But at the same time, I am very determined to keep going, and to keep striving.*

(40y, F, vn)   *As I get older, and have more years of seniority, I really think I'm in the minority! I see my older colleagues bored with some of the works that they played a million times, but [on the other hand] they are also very resistant to anything new. [Maybe] some of the non-standard things that we play I also don't find appealing, but I'm still kind of grateful for the opportunity. I'd say there is resistance to more modern music and to the Conductor [who chooses them]. A good Orchestra (and Music Director) will find a balance between the old, the new, and the special. Players don't need to end up playing all nine Beethoven Symphonies every season across their 30-year career. Perhaps once in a while there can be a new Opera, a Pops concert (e.g., Broadway musicals), or a recording session with a well-known vocalist.*

(41y, M, vc)   *I have no idea how many times we've played '1812' [the Solemn Overture, Op. 49 in E^b major, written in 1880 by Russian composer Pyotr Ilyich Tchaikovsky, 1840–1893]. Or how many times we've played 'Pomp and Circumstance' [Military Marches, Op. 39, written in 1904 by English composer Edward William Elgar, 1857–1934]. So, I do think there is a repertoire thing—as well as a standard thing! Concerts that do not go well cause much frustration.*

(41y, M, va)   *I do think that as we get older, we become less tolerant, more bored, and less satisfied with life and work. The older players are the 'grumpier' ones. But you'd be surprised at how many of the younger [players] are influenced and taken in by some gripes. I've been guilty of that myself over the years! When you're new in the job, and you don't know where you are—or who's who—and then somebody who seems nice and friendly takes you in. Before you know it, you're agreeing with all sorts of rubbish that is spouted at you. You don't know who they're talking about, but you find yourself hating the Principals. It's passed on! I don't think it's entirely true that as you age you become less tolerant; there's at least as much intolerance among the younger players as there is among the older players.*

(47y, F, vn)   *The only thing I see that may have to do with age is that some people get more bored if they play the same Operas too many times. For example: Hansel and Gretel [a fairy-tale opera, written 1891–1892 by German composer Engelbert Humperdinck, 1854–1921]. We have played that Opera three times. I do love the piece, but some [other players] really get bored, and they just don't have the will to get involved in the music anymore. I think that some even get tired of coming here; they have lost motivation. The just sit there. Maybe, [that does have to do] with ageing! It's very important to have an inner feeling that you are worth sitting here!*

(47y, M, trb)   *A lot of people have told me I could have reached a much better Orchestra. I say: I like what I'm doing. But, perhaps I could've done much more. Yet, in my own job there's always something I can learn, and there's always something that I can do. I'm happy to have this job.*

(49y, F, vn)   *When I open up the instrument case, I enter into another dimension. I always play all of the notes to the best of my ability. When I find the music uninteresting, does that mean that I have no passion? Maybe!*

(52y, M, vc)   *Motivation is not an issue. The fear of embarrassment and making a mistake is enough to keep you motivated; [it is] self-preservation. Your own pride keeps you motivated. But ultimately doing the concert is about professional pride! People are paying for the concert. Even when we do a more distant out-in-the-sticks for the non-paying public concert, it needs to be handled right. Maybe we don't rehearse [for those] as much as we usually do for a major-city venue. But that doesn't mean we shouldn't give the best performance we can.*

(54y, F, vc)   *I've always been a very organized person, very conscientious, and I tend to every detail. If I can [I will always] be well prepared for my job! I'm diligent about looking at stuff in advance. I know I can perform better and deliver the goods better when I'm prepared. That is how I like to operate. I do not like to fly by the seat of my pants.*

(56y, F, vn)   *No, I don't feel that as I age I have less patience for a Guest Conductor. If the Conductor is good, then they are good. But, I am less patient with a mediocre Conductor.*

(59, M, va)   *How do you keep the music fresh as you get older? You've played so many different pieces, some more than three times. And some [were already] boring from the first time. So then, the question is: How can I play them after 15 years? Well . . . it's my work! Sometimes I have to play things I don't like. There are some (older) players whose minds have been the same for the last 30 years. But if you love music, then there are things [like Mozart] that one can play thousands of times and love them even more as time goes on.*

(61y, F, vn)   *I think motivation to play, to practise, and to come to work, is affected by ageing. After age 50, players are much more tired and burned out. By that age we have been in the Orchestra for 25 years or more! Not necessarily does that mean that Seasoned Players don't want to come to work. I personally would be very happy to have a break [for a few weeks]. But some Conductors inspire enjoyment, that brings on great motivation. Other times, especially when the material is far from interesting, decreases motivation. We all still come to work [ready to work] because there is a certain professionalism in the routine!*

One explanation for age-related declines that is often mentioned among the players is: *personality*. Players point to 'temperament' or 'dispositional constitution' as factors responsible for triggering emotional reactions to music, the music performance, and the orchestra as a profession. Accordingly, emotional considerations for music performance are related to the individual. Hence, age-related ill effects on artistic integrity and conviction are distinctly per single case. Specifically, we cannot speak about Symphony Orchestra musicians in a more generalized fashion with regard to authenticity, truthfulness, and morality towards their profession. These vary per player, and are not at all related to age!

(43y, F, vn)   *From my own experience, and [from that of] other musicians, as we get older we do not become bored more. Nor do we become overly excited because we're all the time playing something that has an emotional content. If these do happen, then it's more to do with personality than one's age. So, for instance, there may be players who are bitter at age 28, while others become bitter as they approach 60. We all have bad weeks. But the truth is that Orchestra players really complain; I mean there's always a 'moaner'. It's a group of 190 people; we can't all be the same. But, I love my job now as much as I did when I first joined. And when we do a really special concert, I'll still leave the platform thinking: This is why I do this job. You know, sometimes I can get unbelievably stressed about a particular piece. It might be an exposed bit for the 1st Violins. But then if a concert goes really well, I think: Actually, it was worth all that pain. To do something as special as this. And I'm really glad I think it's special, because if I were cynical it would be really sad. I'm with this Orchestra nearly 25 years. I can definitely say that those people who are moaners and cynical are not necessarily the older ones. I don't think ageing has anything to do with it. When I see the cynicism in someone young aged 30 after only 5 years in the Orchestra, it really makes me cross. I think: When I was your age and hadn't been in the job that long, I was so happy, and felt lucky as everything was new and exciting. And, already you're being 'uuff' about everything. That sort of thing can get you down, especially if your desk partner is that person. So, I would say it's got nothing to do with age, but rather it's a personality trait.*

(58y, M, va)   *I don't think that there are effects of ageing on the emotional issues of music performance. Nonetheless, I know that older people become less patient and care less about things. But, I am just as patient regarding others. That hasn't changed much with my age. So, maybe it has to do more with personality? There are those who can't work together with a stand-partner. But that has nothing to do with ageing. I do get bored sometimes, but it depends on the piece and Conductor. When that happens, I try to remember that I have the responsibility of playing as best as possible. I am a professional who has to do the job.*

Some players mention disillusionment, bitterness, and cynicism. For them, the Orchestra has indeed become a *job*. Perhaps, it is not like any other profession. But yet, in their minds the Orchestra has become a preoccupation whose sole purpose is to generate the financial means of supporting a family, that hopefully will continue till their age of retirement.

(30y, F, vn)   *There are some boring days. You don't want to go to work as it's not a great repertoire [day]. No one's really thinking: Let's work as hard as we can. But I think the younger players would stick with it longer, because when you get older you become more disillusioned.*

(33y, M, va)	*I really look at the Orchestra as a more stable way to have income and sustain a family. It is what paid for our home [mortgage].*
(43y, F, db)	*One thing that isn't positive in nature about getting older as an Orchestra player, is that you get a lot more cynical about everything. I presume when I first got here I was excited about everything. But today I hear some of the young players say: 'Oh, this is so exciting, we're playing X.' And I say: 'No, actually it's not that exciting to play X.' That is really why I would love to go on a 50% [half-time position]. I don't wanna do the dire weeks anymore, I just wanna do the good weeks. I want to choose what I want to play, and give the rest to another person I'm sharing it with. I know some old players who are still really loving it; you can definitely see that in their playing. But I also know some who are cynical; they are not as good players. I think it affects your posture; if you're hanging in a chair like that, you can't really play the Violin well enough. So, I do think that we have to work on our attitude. But sometimes it is very hard to do that— especially when you're sitting in a little hellhole of a place, about 2 hours away, in a Sports Hall with no acoustics, and with some very young Conductor. There's nothing musical taking place at all!*
(44y, F, vn)	*For lots of players, it's just a job. We all move into the profession out of passion. But, after a while, you say: It's my job! I personally don't go home anymore and turn on the radio, or listen to music CDs as much as I used to. Maybe because I've had so much of it. Yet, I still think we're very lucky to do a job that is very enjoyable.*
(50y, M, vn)	*As I get older I find it more and more wearing to work with mediocre incompetent Conductors and Soloists. The older I get, the harder it is, because I feel I have less patience. I try to see myself as competent. It's just very wearing when you have to work with somebody who's not competent—especially Conductors! When I was younger I didn't feel that way. Maybe, I was more respectful; I would have looked up more to senior players, Soloists, and Conductors. So, there is definitely a lack of patience, and that is definitely an issue of age. At this point, I am much more confident in my own competence.*
(53y, M, hrp)	*Actually, I forgot my music last Saturday, and I had to get a taxi driver to bring it. I mean something like that really threw me, because I missed one of the pieces in the rehearsal. I just didn't have the music for the Encore. So, I was really stressed because I hadn't done the full morning rehearsal. I told the Conductor that I was waiting for the music. He was relieved when the music did come, and that I was able to play. Yet, I think that if he had got angry, and said something (that could have affected my whole evening), I would probably have thought: What an annoying man . . . You know . . . these things do happen to everybody!'*

5.2.4 Camaraderie, Orchestral Allegiance and Devotion, Relationships and Coupling Among Players, and Affective Bonding with an Instrument

As seen above in vignettes, many of the participating players described a loving relationship towards their Orchestra. For most musicians, the players in the orchestra are an alternative family! Nonetheless, several did speak about how societal attitudes have changed regarding all kinds of 'playful' but yet socially unacceptable (and, sometimes, blatantly 'naughty') conduct involving mischievous and/or sexual behaviour. Many players feel that age (and ageing) doesn't really enter into the equation as far as camaraderie is concerned. But rather, they seem to acknowledge that social ties have everything to do with one's ability to perform music. What really matters is: how well you play your instrument; and how well you support your other teammates in your section.

(35y, F, vn)   *I am here 4 years as a Rank-&-File player. It is my second time with this Orchestra. I left [the first time] because I married an American, and we moved there. But I am back now! I quite enjoy it, and it's quite a challenge. I love the people I work with.*

(38y, M, bn/dbn)   *This is my favourite [Orchestra] setting of all the jobs that I've had. I've been here 18 months; you could say I'm still in a Honeymoon phase. I'm more optimistic about this band compared to other Orchestras. I'm still loving it, and highly motivated. I imagine that 5 years from now I'll still be loving it! One explanation might be that we do spend a lot of time together; there's a lot of camaraderie here which hasn't necessarily been the case in other Orchestras. Here it doesn't feel like anybody's trying particularly hard to 'outdo' anybody else. We do get on very well.*

(43y, F, db)   *When I first joined the Orchestra there were certainly a lot of affairs going on. Maybe some people were in relationships already before they joined. We're constantly sort of sitting on top of each other in the back of the bus . . . Well you know! Then, when you go touring, people relax! Years ago, there was a lot more bed-hopping than there is today! Sure, society has changed, and people look at things differently now. I think people used to drink a lot more before their playing—and that kind of just loosened things up. I remember one time there was a punch-up over a woman on one of our tours—of course that would have been grounds for instant dismissal. This guy was mitring this lady; he kept talking to her and she kept making it clear that she didn't want anything to do with him. It was about 4 o'clock in the morning, and then a punch was thrown. Maybe society looks differently at the openness of sexual relationships today than it did years ago. I think there's just so many women in the band now; [but] no good-looking blokes! I mean, when I came in there were still a lot of women in the band, but there were an awful lot more men. And now, I think more than half are women. And there's not as many younger men coming in! As the men get older, there's just less activity, and less attraction. I certainly wouldn't fancy anybody in the Orchestra—but I probably would have many years ago.*

(44y, F, vn)   *There is a sort of friendship in the Orchestra—a social aspect—that you don't necessary get in another job. But, I think that Orchestra musicians have changed over the last few decades; it's not the same! We used to go and socialize a lot more; nobody gets a drink now! I remember we'd do these ridiculous things. We'd even throw Water Balloons out of hotel windows. [But] everyone's so sensible nowadays. In some ways it's probably good as we did do irresponsible things. Yet what I'm getting at is the fact that with this more mature attitude some of the camaraderie's been lost. Some of the community spirit seems to have gone.*

(47y, M, vc)   *Once you settle down in an Orchestra, you usually think that this is what you're going to be doing until pension. I love playing in this Orchestra. I have been approached by other Orchestras; I do play with other Orchestras sometimes as a guest. I still do solos (somewhat to prove myself I've still got it). But there's no desire for me to move.*

(52y, M, vc)   *Years ago we didn't have mobile phones to play games with behind our Cellos. We couldn't text our mates on the other side of the Orchestra. [Nowadays] you can send rude messages to each other! Some players might take to drawing cartoons of the Conductor. These then start filtering their way around the Orchestra. Others get on with their social lives by using mobile phone Apps. But years ago, we could barely take out a newspaper, or read a book, as those were also frowned upon in many Orchestras. Today, when everybody seems to be really pissed off, that's when I start looking around to see who actually looks the most pissed off! Then I say to myself: Well, they're not going to last. They're going to be screaming out of the door in 5 minutes.*

(54y, F, vc)   *I would say that a lot has changed as far as more acceptable social behaviour is concerned. The drinking is totally different. Touring behaviours have changed! Certainly, various aspects of liaisons have changed. But what I'm really saying is that ageing isn't equal for all players. There's a gender issue as well. I am not quite saying that part of my place in the Orchestra, or the social network in the Orchestra, had to do with how many suitors I may have been able to attract. It was more along the lines of the interactions of people; the amount of time people were 'interested' (I use that word loosely) in communication or just being near. What I'm saying is that age especially among women ... Well, attractiveness is also something to do with how one sees it in the context of ageing. So, men sort of look at certain aspects of women differently. I would presume that the younger men would look at certain aspects of women differently than the older man. I have seen it happen so many times. A new young person, who happens to be a woman, comes into the Orchestra; there's just this sort of level of response! So, in the end, maintaining your place amongst all that, as you get older, you just jolly well got to be great at what you do. That may be the case in the world at large, but then again, Orchestral life is very different! And [if you are a woman] the way to maintain yourself, and keep value and worth, is to rely on those musical skills! So, in the end, you're not [just seen as a] woman, but as a fellow Orchestra player.*

(55y, F, fl)   *I think part of Orchestra life is not looking at one's age—but rather looking at skills. Maybe that's what allows you to grow old in an Orchestra. My friends in this Orchestra do tend to be a lot younger than me. Yet, I don't think of them as being younger than me, but rather as me being as young as them. [Laughs.] I hope they don't somehow unconsciously think of me as the 'old lady'. I certainly don't play like an old lady! So, maybe that is what it all comes down to. Age really has no meaning; it all comes down to how you play! As long as you're playing spot on, nobody really cares how old you are. The older players aren't saying: 'Oh, it's just a young kid!' I don't know if there is any other profession that works like this. I've got friends who aren't in the music profession, and they think that the older musicians are mentally youthful. I don't know how to explain that. Because my life revolves around music and musicians, so most of my friends are musicians. That is the camaraderie among Orchestra players! No matter where you came from, no matter what your age, no matter the race, religion, gender, sexual preference, or whatever—we all have something in common. It's the music that cuts to the core! It's not just: We're all mates. But, sitting in the Hall during a rehearsal is just so riveting and all-engaging! It is intense! It's not just a team effort, but it's a team effort that involves music. Everyone that comes to it are like-minded people who speak the language of music. You've got the music and you've got the team. But, then there's me and the music. My sound and my instrument. And then there's my sound that either meshes with the other people's sound—or not! What you hear is your sound in the music that you're playing, and how that sits with everybody else's sound. The fact that you're playing an instrument, and I'm playing an instrument, and each one is doing their own part, it then becomes a third thing. It is more than a joint effort. If you're playing one line, and I'm playing another line a third above, what we hear isn't my line or your line, but rather a certain type of harmony. You can't pull it apart again, 'cause it made something new.*

(60y, M, bn)   *I particularly love this Orchestra; I mean it's been my life. I've gone through three marriages, but I'm still married to this Orchestra. So, maybe I'm too married to the Orchestra?*

5.2.4.1 Relationships and Coupling Among Players

Relationships among musicians have often been of great interest to the public. Musician couples are often featured in the press—especially the Tabloids. These couples consistently provide content for the electronic media (such as Channel 'E!' Entertainment). Among the long list of Pop Music couples that have occupied the hearts and minds of the public, are: June Carter and Johnny Cash, Jennifer Lopez and Marc Anthony, Beyoncé and Jay-Z, Whitney Houston and Bobby Brown, Mick Jagger and Marianne Faithfull, Ike and Tina Turner, Carly Simon and James Taylor, Stevie Nicks and Lindsey Buckingham, Paul Kantner and Grace Slick, Sonny and

Cher—to name just a few! Well-known couples among Jazz players have also been quite abundant: Peggy Lee and Dave Barbour, John and Alice Coltrane, Max Roach and Abby Lincoln, Ella Fitzgerald and Ray Brown. Finally, Western Classical Music has also hosted various well-known couples: Johann Sebastian Bach and Anna Magdalena, Wolfgang Amadeus Mozart and Constanza Weber, Robert and Clara Schumann, Gioachino Rossini and Isabella Colbran, Gustav and Alma Mahler, Benjamin Britten and Peter Pears, Mstislav Rostropovich and Galina Vishnevskaya, Daniel Barenboim and Jacqueline du Pré, Leonard Bernstein and Felicia María Cohn Montealegre. Yet for the most part, what have been reported in the press, musicological biographies, screen documentaries, and TV docudramas, are exclusively legendary stories about great icons—who are no doubt famous 'star' personages of the Music Stage. Perhaps there is something about such couplings that epitomize the public's curiosity with relationships among those who share something special (e.g., talent, fame, fortune) that most common people do not have? Or maybe, we are simply captivated by couples who seem even more invested in each other's musical art form and stage-performance lifestyle. The public wants to witness the daily unfolding storyline in a similar way as viewers today watch Reality TV. Whatever the case may be, we do need to question, if removing the publicized *drama* (surrounding the romances, courtships, marriages, pregnancies, children, extramarital affairs, breakups, and divorces), how much of the phenomenon is actually related to the *music* itself: Is there more about the music itself that engenders coupling? Kemp (1996) drew the following conclusion:

> *Musicians possess an auditory dominance, which is not only essential for the development of musical giftedness, but may also exercise the effect of separating the musician from others from whom they feel fundamentally different* (p. 45).

When Jane Davidson (2002) studied the emerging music identity, she noted several key attributes that emerge which mark participation in music as the principal determinant of self-concept, the critical means of expression and of intimacy. Accordingly, the emotional and motivational aspects of personality enable them not only to sustain their love for music, but also to feel that music is the stabilizing factor in their life—a form of psychological balance. Davidson concluded that music performers see music as highly integrated with self. This notion gives credence to the ethos about music performers as not having boundaries that differentiate between *who they are* and *what they do*! That is, the *performer* and the *performance* are one and the same entity.

(33y, F, bn/dbn)   *Musicians often say: 'You're only as good as your next performance.' But, as you never really know how good your next performance is going to be, you are never really sure how good you are! Why should it be like that? I think we connect the value of a person with the way they play the instrument. I wonder, what comes first? I bet it all [comes together] at the same time. So, there's the performer, and there's the performance. As we grow up, the performer and the performance become one.*

To my knowledge, little has ever been written about family life among everyday Symphony Orchestra musicians. One reason may simply be that there is little-to-no public interest in reporting such details. After all, Orchestra players are everyday working musicians! Indeed, they are not celebrity superstar idols. Nonetheless, relationships among the Orchestra players have always (but discreetly) been talked about. Many players laugh about the Orchestra as an 'incestuous' environment, recalling a host of liaisons among players. Some vignettes have already described such references. For example:

> When I first joined the Orchestra there were certainly a lot of affairs going on. [. . .] We're constantly sitting on top of each other in the back of the bus. [. . .] Well you know! Then, when you go touring, people relax. Years ago, there was a lot more bed-hopping than there is today! Society has changed, and people look at things differently now.

Further, when viewing their careers in retrospect (see Chapter 12), several retired Symphony Orchestra players recalled memories, such as:

> "I don't know if there were as many liaisons as people like to make out of it! Yet, in the early days when we were on tour, there was always noise in the corridors, doors slamming, and all the rest of it. It was all a party—the bed-hopping and drinking!"

> "I was playing then at a time period when various behaviours were acceptable—boozing and bed-hopping. There were stories in the Daily Tabloids claiming that these were essentially coping mechanisms for the pressures of stage performances. But, I can definitely say that couple-swapping did go on. I had an affair with somebody in the Orchestra, and when we were on tour we stayed together. It wasn't really partner- (wife-) swapping. I just fell in love."

> "If you are married and you work together, then you have to make it work. If it's not gonna work, then one of you will have to leave the Orchestra!"

It is interesting that the participating players in the current study openly discussed the issue of coupling amongst players. Moreover, several players attempted to reach deeper insights about *why* performing musicians—almost exclusively—develop relationships with other performing musicians.

(33y, F, bn/dbn)   *My boyfriend is a musician—also a Bassoon player. Sometimes that is really fun, and sometimes it's a little bit difficult. Sometimes there's a little bit of competition, as we are very different. He does things that I can't do, so it's like a catalyst. We read together. [Laughs.] And sometimes, we just play together. I've improved a lot by living with another Bassoon player. Actually, I cannot tell you how important is it for me to have an intimate relationship with somebody who's a musician. Because I've always only been with musicians. I think it's because of our lifestyle which is not very stable. We work at such different time schedules than other people. So, it's convenient. And, I think you need someone who understands what you are doing! It's not just the passion for music. Music is a very huge part of my life, and I dedicate many hours for practising, playing, and making reeds. I think if you have someone telling you: 'You've already practised for one hour, please finish now!' then, it's not possible. But also, I feel it's a kind of a soul connection. Maybe being a musician changed my character. I don't know what was first: Personality for making music? Or did my personality change by me making music from a young age? Or, maybe it all happens at the same time. Maybe that's why musicians are so different. I started Bassoon at 11. So, that wasn't exactly when your personality is formed. So I wonder: Is [being together with musicians] just convenience? Or, is it a necessity? Because the only people that you could really ever communicate with on the same emotional level, is another musician!*

My first Bassoon teacher taught me how important it is that I have fun. The Bassoon became my very best friend. Just having an hour a day together when you're becoming a woman; maybe you don't understand the world, but you have a friend in your hands. And it has always been a pleasure for me to play. And now with my boyfriend, it's just that I can see another side of his personality through the instrument. He takes it so very seriously; he's really into the details—a different kind of playing! He works more from the brain, while I work more from the heart. So, there's always this kind of conflict, and we see our personalities more clearly while we are playing. And of course, you can hear that in the music too. I am not just talking about the personalities in the sense of caring for the instrument, the approach to learning a piece, the fingerings, and other stuff. You can actually hear it in the music: two different personalities in our music performances [albeit on the same instrument]. The difference is not because he and I play different lines [like in a duet]. If we played the exact same line, one would hear a different character and tonal expression. But there is a difference: my version would be more spontaneous, and maybe not in the music style! He's Spanish (Catalan) and I am German, so it should be the exact opposite; he should be very hot and passionate from the heart; I should be very cold and methodical. Maybe that's why I chose a Spanish boyfriend! He does tell me: 'You know, what you played here was beautiful, but it wasn't in the style of this composer.' Because he thought about [the music style], and I'm not really thinking about it; I'm just playing, having fun with the music!

All my boyfriends have played music with me. I was always able to understand them better when we were playing music. It was an important part of understanding who they are and what happens between us. I was once with a Pianist. I think it was different because we played two different instruments, and there wasn't this kind of competition. We played concerts together, and it was very comfortable. I really relied on him, and it was very easy to work together. We didn't need to talk so much, we just fit together emotionally.

(41y, M, va)   *My wife doesn't play; she works in the Health Services. Yes, that's really a standard deviation from the [others in the] Orchestra. I think there are only one or two who are married outside of the profession. There are few who had married players, but since have left the profession and developed a second career. Yet, the amount of people who actually married someone who wasn't a player to begin with is a very small percentage.*

(43y, F, db)   *My current partner plays a lot of music himself in the house; he's more of a Blues-Folk Keyboard player and Guitarist. Can I imagine having a partner that was not a musician? A sort of a regular bloke? Well, my previous partner was not only a good amateur Horn player (who sometimes played in an Orchestra), but was also a Structural Engineer. And that's what I think blew us up! Is there something about a musician that only another musician can understand? I think so! Music is foremost a language. I'm not sure how much of what I'm actually doing is taken in by my desk partner, or to the Bassoonist sitting in front of me. We're certainly communicating and listening to each other. So, to understand a musician, you have to understand music. I do feel I couldn't have a relationship with someone who doesn't understand my language. So, perhaps that's why most musicians have relationships with other musicians. There are many who look at the Orchestra as incestuous. If it is, then it is not so much because the schedule is so tight that one cannot meet other people outside of the music circle. But rather because we need people to understand who we are.*

(50y, M, vn)   *I used to do Concerts with my wife; she's a Pianist and Cellist. We did do that even though other people said to us that [performing together] could be dangerous [to our relationship].*

(52y, M, db)   *My wife is a musician too—a Singer and Piano player. She teaches in school and at the Music Academy. Sometimes she turns pages in the Concerts; sometimes I turn pages for her when she plays. I love to hear her play! But we don't play together often. I do think that many musicians (from Orchestras) marry other musicians; you like people who are doing the same thing as you are doing. Also, we can talk about it. If you married someone that didn't know how to play then you couldn't talk about it on the same level. I started playing Electric Bass-Guitar at a local school band when I was 14 years old; it was a '75 Fender Jazzbass and a Vox amplifier. [The same amps used by the Beatles.] Partly I played Electric Bass then because all of the girls ran after you; I played Rock 'n' Roll. Even my wife was interested in me [back then] because I was a musician.*

(53y, M, vn)   *My wife is a musician; she plays a little bit on Guitar. Not a professional, but we are in a Country band. [Laughs.] I can't really play Fiddle music, but they wanted me to try. But as I'm a trained Classical Musician, I don't really improvise. We do play together as non-professional Folk/Pop musicians; the band isn't that good! [Laughs.] Orchestra life for me is a job, it's a place you go to work. Most people in the Orchestra are my colleagues—not my friends! True, there are people who get married with others in the Orchestra. In my group [2nd Violins] there is one couple, and another one who married a Trumpet player. But for me, it would have been horrible; I'm glad that I can go home, and there's my private life. But if my wife was an Orchestra musician too, it would've been more difficult. It's important for me to have a person at home who can give me [something] from outside of the Orchestra.*

(54y, F, vc)   *I can't conceive of having a partner who wasn't a player. All my partners (boyfriends) have been musicians. In part it is because of the circles that I move in. Once you become a member of an Orchestra, it's quite difficult to meet other people. You've got a very time-consuming schedule. And practice! I think the opportunities to meet people outside of music are incredibly limited. Also, I think being a musician—and certainly being an Orchestra musician—when you're in a partnership, you have to have somebody who has some measure of understanding about what your life is like. It is not the same as ordinary people. I mean now I've got lots of friends who aren't musicians. I met many of these just by being a mom (e.g., nursery school). And I really like that. But in friendships with musicians there's just something you don't need to go into. An unspoken understanding! I do think that you can have a relationship with someone who doesn't speak your language. Music is a language of its own! My partner had a post in the Orchestra for 24 years. When he left the Orchestra it was a terrible time for both of us. For him to give up music performance; for me it was a loss of what I felt he was able to express through music (that he couldn't necessarily express in words). I remember things that he played; when I was sitting there in my section, I heard everything [he played] even though there was more than one [Brass] player. I always heard his sound! We're still together. It was all very tangled up having a relationship with somebody in the Orchestra, when both of us had stressful [Principal] positions.*

(55y, F, fl)   *My husband was a musician in another Orchestra. But I did have boyfriends who weren't musicians; [looking back, I can say that] it is a big barrier! When something is so close to your soul, it doesn't work if the other person doesn't get it! Then, I honestly don't know what they don't get. It could be that they don't get the music itself, or how one can be so involved in it. It's a barrier to developing the relationship to a higher level. Music is a language. So, someone that doesn't speak music is like trying to have a relationship with someone who doesn't speak English (e.g., only speaking Spanish). I mean there are lots of musicians who marry other musicians who don't speak the same language. But they have music in common! Music is more of a language; it is the emotional side as well as the content. The fact that they can't say words to each other is a problem—but not as much as someone who doesn't understand music. I'm thinking back in my life that the people that I felt really close to were only those who I could share my love for music.*

(57y, F, vc)   *In many countries there seems to be roughly 60%–70% couples among the players (many of whom are married). I think it is not so adaptive as both would need to keep to the same hours. I wonder who takes care of the children when both parents are onstage? Who takes care of the children when both parents are on tour? Actually, I do have some experience with this as my husband is also a player in this Orchestra; he has worked here for 26 years (3 years more than me). We met at a gig before I joined this Orchestra.*

(59y, M, va)   *My wife is a musician. But she didn't play in an Orchestra because of having three children. She teaches Cello. You asked if there a reason that musicians always marry musicians. When you're in a Music Academy, the people you get to know are musicians. Maybe there's something about being a musician that you can only experience, express, and share your deep emotions—with another musician. So, if you are married and your partner doesn't estimate what you do, and what you feel about it, it won't work. The partner has to feel that you love what you are doing. She doesn't have to do it as well as you do, but she has to understand and support what you love to do. We have played together! Maybe too seldom, maybe too little! It seems to be important for a relationship among musicians.*

(60y, M, bn)   *It's been a big thing in my life marrying musicians. Most Orchestra musicians marry musicians. I used to say that my first wife was not a musician—she was a Singer. [Laughs.] My second wife was a Horn player; quite a good musician. Wife number 3 played the Flute; she was an extra player here. But she didn't get a job in this Orchestra. She should of [gotten it]. So, she joined the Fire Service; she has given up music altogether—a full-time Firefighter. I am in aura of her. So, she doesn't play at all now. That's been emotional for both of us. I've been wary of talking about work because she isn't part of it anymore.*

(60y, F, vc)   *I don't know if the only way for me to really understand another person is to [actually] play with them. It's certainly a much deeper understanding playing with musicians on a certain level than to communicate verbally. But most of my meaningful relationships were not with [professional] musicians. Rather, they were people who were just connected to music, who played a few years. Namely, [they had] sensitivity [but] were not necessarily professional musicians. Yet, they were people who understood a lot about music. Well, music is this intimate language.*

5.2.4.2 Affective Bonding with an Instrument

The final emotional consideration on the subtopic of relationships among Orchestra players that was discussed concerns affective bonding with one's instrument; it can become a unique intimate love attachment. As can be seen in one of the vignettes above, a 33-year-old female bassoon player declared:

The bassoon became my very best friend. Just having an hour a day together when you're becoming a woman. Maybe you don't understand the world, but you have a friend in your hands.

In this case, perhaps we need to ask the question: What does 'best friend' mean? The *Oxford English Dictionary* defines *friend* as a person with whom one has developed a close and informal relationship of mutual trust and intimacy; (more generally) a close acquaintance. Accordingly, that means *friendship* is inclusive to animate living and breathing objects such as human beings or pet animals. That would, therefore, exclude inanimate objects such as musical instruments. Nonetheless, *Merriam-Webster's Dictionary* defines *friend* as one who is attached to another by affection or esteem. Accordingly, this latter definition might include inanimate objects such as musical instruments. Especially when providing a causal relationship of affection and esteem. Such a causal relationship could clearly exist when the production of a highly pleasing sound leading to efficient and repeated success in performing music over long periods across one's lifetime triggers higher levels of confidence, self-esteem, self-pride, and affection from one's communal environment.

(60y, M, cl)   *This is not a special instrument; not so expensive! I bought it a year and half ago in Paris. At the time it was €2,800 when I could have bought another one for €5,000. But it is a good instrument. Conductors like my playing because of the sound I can make and the way I articulate phrases. Musicianship is very much because of hard work—not because of the instrument. But it is an instrument that can take me for a ride; I feel that as a vehicle I can express the maximum spectrum that I have at my command. Unlike other players who might convey that they would be in mourning had their instrument been stolen, I am not sure that I would be like that—even though I see this particular instrument as an extension of 'me'. Yet, I am aware that it takes me a rather long time to sell an instrument. And when I am done with one, it takes me a long time to 'say goodbye'. When I do sell it, I say: Thank you for all of the time I had had with you over the years!*

In a recent paper by an American Psychologist of Human Development from Cornell University (USA), Robert J. Sternberg put forward a theoretical platform with which we might assess love attachments to musical instruments. Sternberg was previously well known for his *Triarchic Theory of Intelligence*, as well as for several prominent models on Creativity, Thinking Styles, Leadership, and Love. Accordingly, Sternberg (2021) recognized that all musicians have a relationship with their musical instrument; musicians' affect seems to vary along a gamut of emotions from 'hate' to 'dislike' through 'like' to 'love'. I point out that at the time of publication Sternberg conceded that this theory was solely based on hearsay, but was founded on previously published empirically based examinations of human love-relationships referred to as *The Triangular Theory of Love* (Sternberg, 1986). Sternberg's notion is that a musician's love for their musical instrument bears resemblance to the same merits of love that people have towards other people. Namely, the same factors that cultivate love towards an intimate partner are those that influence one's relationship with their own musical instrument. The structure of love for a musical instrument is portrayed as being based on three components: Intimacy, Passion, and Commitment.

a) Intimacy is expressed by feelings of emotional closeness, connection, understanding, emotional support, and communication. Intimacy gives the feeling of connection. Accordingly, a musical instrument is then far more than the sum of all its mechanical parts. The more one feels emotionally connected to the musical instrument, the more that the instrument is actually felt *as if* part of oneself. This is similar to the way as one feels towards their intimate human partner.

b) Passion is intense arousal (e.g., pleasure, delight, and even ecstasy). The same feeling as when a person is driven to be close to their human partner. This reflects the romance one has with their musical instrument. Especially when that object (be it a human person or musical instrument) is absent, there is a feeling of heightened tension and such infatuations have no reprieve.

c) Commitment is a cognitive-based ethos in which a person devotes themselves to another human partner evermore. The feeling is similar in nature to the commitment one has to their musical instrument. A specific musical instrument is not only deep-rooted in one's life but can become an extension of one's life-being (e.g., music performance and Orchestral Lifestyle).

To tease out his model, Sternbeg (2021) designed a self-report assessment measure referred to as the *Triangular Love Scale for Musical Instruments*. See Table 5.1. As can be seen in the table, the assessment measure features three 8-item component sub-scales. As mentioned above, the sub-scales are Intimacy, Passion, and Commitment. Respondents complete the assessment by scoring each item with a 5-level response scale (1 = Not at All True of Me, 5 = Always True of Me). By summation, each sub-scale score can range between 8 and 40. The sub-scale scores are indicative of the intensity of one's love attraction to their musical instrument; the higher the score, the more intense the bonding with their instrument. Sternberg (2021) emphasized:

Playing the instrument can carry one to a different mental and emotional world than one quite can achieve in any other way. A fine instrument played well can help to create a bond between player and instrument that, like a romantic relationship, just cannot quite be achieved in any other way. (p. 1750)

Intimacy, Passion, and Commitment seem to apply to musical instruments as well as to human partners. Some players may feel that their musical instrument does offer them an intimate way to communicate with themselves (intrapersonal) as well as to an audience (interpersonal); but yet, they seem to have no particular Passion or Commitment. A love romance emanates from a combination of Intimacy and Passion. Sternberg states that although many usually think of a romance as being between two humans, it can also occur between a musician player and their musical instrument. That kind of love comes about when one not only feels a sense of closeness and connection to a musical instrument, but also feels intensely passionate about it. Accordingly, the players who are romantically attached to their instrument tend to feel a sense of pride, joy, and attachment; an enduring sense of connection with feelings of warmth and contentment. Some players may be committed to their instrument because it is *valuable* (i.e., a monetary perspective), or because it is a *gift* (that is, in a spiritual sense finding the right instrument is never looked upon as happenstance but rather as predestined). Moreover, such commitments to a musical instrument may reflect expectations that come with proprietorship (e.g., having to

Table 5.1 Triangular Love Scale for Musical Instruments

	Sub-scales	Items	Score[1]
A	**Intimacy**	1. I feel emotionally connected to my ——.	
		2. I feel that I can communicate my feelings in a unique way through my ——.	
		3. I find that playing my —— provides me with emotional support.	
		4. When I'm down, I turn to playing my —— to lift my mood.	
		5. I feel I understand my —— and how to bring the best sound out of it.	
		6. I value my —— greatly in my life.	
		7. I experience great happiness from my ——.	
		8. I feel a certain warmth toward my ——.	
		Sub-scale Score	
B	**Passion**	1. There is almost nothing more important to me than my ——.	
		2. I cannot imagine my life without my ——.	
		3. I adore my ——.	
		4. I find myself thinking about my —— frequently during the day.	
		5. Just seeing my —— is exciting for me.	
		6. I find my —— beautiful physically.	
		7. I idealize my ——.	
		8. There is something almost 'magical' about my relationship with my ——.	
		Sub-scale Score	
C	**Commitment**	1. I feel a strong sense of responsibility for my ——.	
		2. I expect my love for my —— to last for the rest of my life.	
		3. I view my relationship with my —— as permanent.	
		4. My —— never lets me down.	
		5. I have decided I love my ——.	
		6. I view my relationship with my —— as a carefully thought-out decision.	
		7. I would not let anything get in the way of my relationship with my ——.	
		8. I have confidence in my relationship with my ——.	
		Sub-scale Score	

[1] Scores: 1 = Not at All True; 2 = Rarely True; 3 = Sometimes True; 4 = **Often True**; 5 = Always True. Adapted from: Sternberg (2021). Reprinted with permission

fulfil the artistic potential by passion of the specific instrument that has been placed in their hands). Finally, after many years of companionship, much like some human relationships, one cannot ever imagine a period of disengagement or parting (i.e., separation, divorce, or widowhood).

Many players do speak about the importance of their instrument, as well as performing on their specific musical instrument as part of their day-to-day life. Many players can't even see themselves as being anything else but an Orchestra player of their instrument genre (i.e., String, Woodwind, Brass, etc.), or of the specific musical instrument they use in the Orchestra. One player even reported to have attempted to 'force' herself to break off ties from her instrument (i.e., a trial separation) which is constantly by her side, no more than at an arm's length.

(27y, F, ob)   *I was once 4 months without my instrument. I went to Tibet. It was an interesting experience. I tried to see how long I could live without it. After 4 months I returned [home] because of the instrument! Well perhaps not [exactly because of] the Oboe, but rather not being able to play [Classical Music with my Oboe] with others. I just couldn't live without it.*

(54y, F, vc)   *When I was 45 I gave birth to my daughter. But I never thought I'd be able to do it. I was ambivalent about having children because I didn't see how I could possibly keep my job—and have a child. For such a long period of time, my self-esteem and self-belief was totally bound up in my job—and my instrument. I am only a Cello player! There's no separation between the performer and the performance. So, who am I without my Cello? I just couldn't imagine a situation where my Cello wasn't all of my life. To just be: 'Mommy'.*

The majority of musicians claim to feel their musical instrument is associated with a deep emotional meaning, reflecting an intense intimate bonding. Many players even ascribe human-like features to their musical instrument. Most crown their instrument with a *name* (beyond the manufacturer's brand name or the name of the master craftsman who made it). In addition, they characterize their musical instrument by *sex* (referring to 'he' or 'she' and 'him' or 'her') as well as by *gender* (labelling the sound texture, reverberation envelope, or touch response as being typically 'masculine' or 'feminine'). Many of the players stated they could not even fathom the loss of their instrument, and those who have already undergone such an experience describe the aftermath as involving intense feelings and moods reflecting deep sorrow similar to when someone has actually passed away, reminiscing about a period of mourning.

It is rather unfortunate that the *Triangular Love Scale for Musical Instruments* was unavailable when the 11-measure 12-page booklet (see Chapter 1, section 1.6.3.3, Table 1.3) was developed for the current study with Symphony Orchestra players. Nonetheless, a rather different approach was employed as a method to explore the same concept. Below is a selection of examples from players responding to a specific hypothetical scenario that was presented to them during the 2-hour interview session. The purpose of this was to pin the bond with one's inanimate musical instrument against an animate human object. The participating players were asked to respond to the following situation:

You are on a cruise-ship passenger ocean-liner vacation. The boat quickly begins to sink (like the Titanic). With there being only a few seconds for you to get out of your cabin room, would you grab the hand of your companion or clutch the case handle of your musical instrument?

There were many different kinds of responses to this postulated sequence of events. Some players were quite shocked by the imaginary storyline. A few were even angered at the proposition! There were some who simply replied that the situation was preposterous because they would never go on a vacation that involved a boat! Others giggled at the thought, and then pondered what would they do! To have to make a forced choice between their lifelong musical instrument and their intimate romantic human partner. On the face of it, for some players this is not an easy decision. Some exhibited post-response nervous laughter as they were very surprised (and perhaps even mortified) to have heard aloud their somewhat semi-conscious immediate response of the projected behaviour. Yet, many were very clear: There really is no question at all in their mind!

(35y, F, vn)   *I don't know what I'd do if my Violin was stolen! Maybe go into mourning? Because I identify with the sound. It is me! Another Violin is completely different. I've always played on this Violin with this Bow. [Then when asked: 'If you happened to be on vacation on a boat with your husband, and the boat starts to sink, who/what would you grab first?' She begins laughing hysterically, for a long time . . . about 3 minutes.] Oh . . . it's a . . . umm . . . [Laughs again and again, with a wide smile on face]. It's funny, because it's not worth a lot of money, not got a value! So, the thing is that I would never be able to find a Violin like this. No! I could never replace it. It's the sound! If a Violin doesn't sound like me anymore, it's very weird. I'm not obsessive about it. I don't keep it close to me, carry it around with me all the time. But it's not very far away from me. Ever! I'll be careful about it. [Laughs again, but in the end does not answer the question.]*

(60y, F, vc)   *If I were on the Titanic, and the boat was going down, with only having a few seconds to grab either the person I was with or my Cello, I would definitely save the person. Nonetheless, I do sometimes feel the Cello is me! It's a part of me that I just can't leave behind. I know that! But, as difficult as it is, one can buy a new Cello, but not a person! I have already been in different crisis situations like this. Foremost, I saw my Cello burn in a car accident, and then another time my Cello was stolen from my apartment in Paris. These were very deep crises—very traumatic! It was like mourning. Definitely! I mean [in the first instance], thank God no person was hurt. A friend of mine and myself were in a car between Paris and Brussels driving to a recital; we ran from the car while the car burned, and the Cello burned! When I took it out, it was like something . . . not really a [charred] body, but something close to it. And I had to transport the remains to Geneva because the insurance company was there. It was horrible. It was as close to [transporting a dead body] as could be. It took me more than 5 months to buy a new Cello. During that time, I played on different Celli because I had Concerts and contracts. It was a very difficult period. A few years later the second incidence happened. A different Cello was stolen from my apartment in Paris. I gave a Concert Recital in Paris, with two different instruments; one French and one Italian. I had wanted to sell the Italian one, but my friends all said that I sound so beautiful with it. So, I hadn't sold it yet. A few days later, I was in an Orchestra rehearsal with the French Cello when my Italian Cello was stolen; it was taken right out of my apartment. They never found it again—not even Scotland Yard or InterPol. That one had its own identity: Mandelli made it! [Guglielmo Secondo Camillo Mandelli, known to the Violin world as 'Camillo di Calco', 1873–1956, with instruments labelled 'Camillo Mandelli', 'Camillo da Calco', or 'Camillo Mandelli di Calco']. There is no [serial] number because each one is unique. All it had [on the label inside the body] was the name, the city, and the year it was built. I was told the* *criminals were from the Far East who specialize in stealing special instruments; it was the only thing they came and took from my apartment. Probably, somebody saw it at the Concert! It was worth about $50,000. I do think about that Cello [sound] all the time. What I play on now is much more expensive, but then it's more about the emotional attachment. I had to learn that it's [just] an instrument. Then again, you're always looking for something which is as close as possible to your inner voice; and that is from some former instrument that you remember [in your mind's ear].*

(60y, M, bn)   *If I were on the Titanic, and had a second to grab either my instrument or my wife, there is no question! This instrument has been with me for 30 years and it's like an extension of who I am and that's it! I'm extremely attached to that. Some players would say that if their instrument was stolen or lost they would go through mourning just like if they lost a person. I couldn't imagine buying a new instrument. It just couldn't have the same maturity as the one I use. It's phenomenally particular for me. It's 105 years old. It's not because it's old, [but rather] it's a very unusual Bassoon. It's not even like the other great Heckels of the 1930s. [Heckel is a manufacturer of Woodwind instruments based in Wiesbaden Germany founded in 1831 by Johann Adam Heckel.]*

Well. . . now as a second thought, I do think I would take my (3rd) wife first!

5.2.5 Spirituality and Creativity in the Orchestra

The interview transcripts demonstrated that for the most part the players simply enjoy speaking about 'Spirituality'. Among the topics that arose in the discussions were: the Spirituality of Music and the Spirituality of Music Performance. The players felt that Spirituality is the recognition of a sense or belief in 'something greater than oneself'. That is, Spirituality signifies something *divine* in nature. Yet, players seem often to confuse between two different concepts: Spirituality *versus* Passion.

(52y, M, vc)   *There's a point where if you try too hard to achieve that great spiritual thing, you affect your performance in other ways. What I'm saying is that I've learned and adopted a more overall approach, that I won't sacrifice accuracy for some spirituality. Sometimes you can go for the excitement and lose accuracy. I just try and take a more rounded approach of giving a semblance of excitement but maintaining accuracy.*

Liljeholm-Johansson and Theorell (2003) claimed that Spirituality as a phenomenon in the occupational life of Orchestra musicians is difficult to capture in scientific studies:

> Spirituality represents something that is at the same time grandiose, outside of normality, and stressful because the occupation also has many everyday work problems. When the divine aspect is disregarded, three factors seem to be important to orchestra musicians— ambitions/quality perceptions, collaboration, and health. (p. 143)

Yet, several players openly spoke of Spirituality as a feeling that puts forward an answer to questions about the 'meaning and purpose of life', or the 'mysteries of human existence' in general. For them, the spirituality of music can be seen in the fact that music has been of such great constant importance to them as players throughout their whole life. They reveal that Spirituality is at times felt through the *magical* feeling that comes over them when they perform on the platform in front of an audience.

(33y, M, va)   *I would say that the spirituality of work [in an Orchestra] depends very much on the individual. It is not necessarily whether they're older or younger. I have a feeling that age does change people. Some people become more spiritual [with ageing], while others become jaded (not getting as much out of the experience as others). But some people will be able to transcend, and get a lot from experience regardless of their age (gaining much more in their 40s than they did in their 20s). So, there might actually be an asset to the fact that you're an older musician.*

(36y, F, tpt)   *I think my emotional spiritual musical life gets better with age; but I can't really explain that. Maybe as you get older you just have more appreciation for life and for music. I mean if it wasn't for music, I don't know where I'd be. So, it did sort of save me. Music gave me a way to believe in myself, and to find a more stable way to control life!*

(55y, M, bn)   *I don't think I've lost the magic; I still feel a certain passion and spirituality when I play. As I get older, it has not 'dulled down'. I still think that there's a certain magic involved in making the sound, to interpret something, to communicate it, and to please myself through sound. I now realize that it's as much about pleasing me as it's about pleasing others! I used to think that I was doing something for the audience when I was younger. But today I don't think the audience understands as much or even cares as much. However, I still like to try to move the audience.*

During the interview, discussions also focused on 'Creativity'. Creativity is very much a topic of contention among Orchestra musicians. On the one hand, players would like to think they have great potential for Creative Expression. Undoubtedly, the processes of Creativity are traditionally what musicians have been trained to engage in as performers. On the other hand, all participant-players admit that Orchestra musicians are expected to simply 'fit in' to a large community of others. Olbertz (2006) stated: "Orchestra musicians do not create art; instead they use their craft on already existing pieces of music in order to bring them to life" (p. 55). The players note that one's individual Creativity needs to be sacrificed for the greater good of the communal collaborative effort. This cognitive shift is essential if players wish to achieve higher levels of Orchestral performance.

(33y, F, bn/dbn)   *I find that there's still just a little bit of space for creativity in what I do. Well, if you're going to play in an Orchestra section, you have always to adjust to the other people. You can't do whatever you want. You have to play together, and you have to do it in a certain way. But we have possibilities to be creative like in Chamber Music! Yet, even in a Symphony you can change things, little things, although it's not [substantial]. You won't ever give your interpretation, because a Music Director [Leader and Conductor] all do that for the group.*

(33y, M, va)   *I have been with the Orchestra now for 10 years. I think it takes a long time to settle into an Orchestra as you don't feel particularly comfortable at the beginning. It certainly takes time to embrace what you have to do to fit in. Look: You're pushed as a student to be a professional Soloist. And then you're brought into this situation and you're told: 'Play down, play down.' There is no individuality; you need just to do what you're told. I used to think of myself as just being a part of a big machine. But I've kind of come to realize that the 'Act of Creation' is in everything that is within the parameters set by the Composer, the Conductor, and my Section Leader. I do my job to the best of my ability, and that itself can satisfy my creativity.*

(47y, M, trb)   *I have a real problem with being creative [in the Orchestra]. That's why I play Jazz. Creativity is not part of our job. In our job we're about 2% creative, and then only when we have a Solo in a piece; for the Trombone that can be as much as 16 bars! There you can be creative—you can make your own line there. But the rest of the time you have just to play what's written and be precise. Sure! We're all great musicians; we can play everything! But, we can [only] play anything that's on the paper. There are those who say: 'There's no sound on the paper, it's just black and white. Hence, the paper is just an interpretation of what the Composer had in his mind.' But Orchestra traditions mean we rely on the [interpretation] of the Conductor. So, this is what makes me think about where's the creativity? There's a lot of tradition [to be considered when interpreting music]. Maybe you have a greater understanding with more experience. That is something younger players wouldn't have. So, being an older player, or Conductor, gives you a big advantage.*

(55y, M, db)   *I admit that I was never really creative. I never really thought that I need to be creative in my playing in the Orchestra. Each Conductor sees the piece differently. So, Rank-&-File players all need to play the same way—we need to follow directions, and adapt to one another. This does become easier as one gets older. You stop trying to be an individual, and more often just try to be one of the group. Look! Every player comes from a different country, and a different teacher. Every player feels they know best. And then, you have to understand that when playing in a big ensemble of musicians, what you've learned [in the Music Academy college as a Soloist] is not relevant for the collective.*

5.2.6 Emotional Communication in Music Performance

Ironically, the players were undecided about what 'emotional communication' within the context of music performance actually means. Some of them implied that expressive body motion <u>is</u> the only way for them to express emotional communication in music performance. This concept has also been noted previously by Goodchild et al. (2019). Other participating players claim that orchestral communication in performance can only occur when at a particular moment the whole group comes together during the execution of a piece. When that happens, it is not necessarily because of the Conductor *per se*. Namely, emotional communication in music performance is something that does happen as a result of one feeling a more *communal kindred spirit* based on the timing of harmonic structure and sonar-like echoes between sections. At times these reflect long-existing Orchestra traditions. Yet, others felt that emotional communication in music performance is sharing the music not only between the players themselves, but also with those people seated in the audience. Communicating affect in music performance, then, relates to how players are able to 'articulate' emotion. Such a notion also means to generate Passion.

(30y, F, vn)   *I would say that younger players move their body more. Although, if you get a player who moves an awful lot that doesn't really go down well. You actually talk about 'telegraph poles' in the Orchestra. There's a certain amount of movement you can achieve on a chair. Orchestra players tend to move in a certain way—like in directions of bows. But sometimes you see a certain movement, and some players [are] going the other way; that doesn't feel right! I'm talking about expressive body-movement. I think you would find it in all String players, and perhaps Wind players too. Maybe it's less taboo among younger players; when the older players were younger they were told: 'You don't do that!' Today, the younger players definitely recruit their body to help them express the music. Perhaps one could say it's a form of freedom, that they were less prohibited. However, the older players would just say: 'Don't [play] that way.'*

(43y, F, db)   *One day, it just happened in the performance without talking about it, the whole Orchestra just decided: 'We've had enough of this nonsense!' The performance really took off! The Orchestra played a lot faster than the Conductor was conducting—and it was really exciting! It was Brahms IV [Symphony No. 4 in E minor, Op. 98, written in 1884 by German composer Johannes Brahms, 1833–1897]. It was the Bass section that pushed everybody; the Horns immediately took up, and then everybody else just fell in line. We were suddenly aware that we could make a difference. It's great when that happens. It is this force that goes on in the Orchestra. But, that takes a lot of playing together with the same people. The old ones basically passing the beat on to the young ones; that's something that you can't teach. And that means that 86 people on the stage are communicating; they all feel the same way, where that beat falls!*

(56y, M, va)   *Expressivity seems to be harder as I mature; it becomes more difficult with age. I mean, I don't have the same expressivity as I did once. Or perhaps, I have a different kind now. I mean that many look at expression as 'extraversion' (i.e., how a player moves their body, and their facial expressions during a performance). But not only is this not the case among Orchestra players, but I personally am against such expressions during performance—especially when it becomes a focus of attention. But, the audience loves this kind of behaviour. Yet, for me expressivity actually means something else. With age, phrasing has become more internal than when I was younger; it is not as 'open'. For example, Sforzando doesn't have to be so pressured like a bombardment. Articulation needs to be internalized and focused outwards in a more functional manner. I think all of this expressive communication in music does have to do with age.*

(60y, F, vc)   *It's very important to share (emotion) in each concert—even within an Orchestra! I'm sitting in front, so it's more [evident]. I see the people and I play for them! So, it's about sharing! If there was no one sitting in the seats I would play differently. The concert experience helps me communicate the utmost emotion—much more than if I'm playing in a recording studio.*

5.2.7 Ageing-Related Adaptation to Emotions in Music Performance

The participant-players spoke about the fact that you also need to *disengage* from emotion as you age. Two aspects were outlined: (a) after having had years of experience, it seems to take much more intensity during a performance to bring about that wave of excitement, that feeling of a 'high' which is referred to as an 'adrenaline rush'; and (b) during a performance when higher states of arousal or excitement are experienced, the affect lingers on all the more afterwards (i.e., Post-Performance Arousal), taking much more time to dissipate. Accordingly, one way to adapt to both of these extremes is to learn to control one's emotions. It is best on the one hand not to be detached from emotion all together, while on the other hand not to be swept away by emotion. This wisdom comes from experience gained by ageing—a concept more prevalent in discussions among the Seasoned Musicians. The interview transcripts also indicate that players recalled earlier times in which they were highly resistant to specific repertoire, but now after several years of experience, they have adapted with a more reasonable attitude for the same pieces; perhaps that reflects a form of emotional resilience! Finally, other aspects of optimizing for ageing were to practise more often—in an effort to raise one's own level of performance (i.e., reducing risks), as well as to increase awareness of the other parts (i.e., to have better command, one needs to listen beyond one's own part).

(41y, M, va)   *Emotional involvement is quite complex! I think you develop the ability to 'disengage' yourself emotionally—especially as you can get stuck emotionally in the performance. When you're young you can't help it; if it's a highly charged performance you are sucked in whether you like it or not. But, the older you get, [the more] you develop the ability to decide if you need to remain [engaged or] detached. It sounds like a very calculated thing. I think you develop more control over your emotions. You need to remain rooted on the ground because there's a danger you might get swept away, and then something unpredictable can happen, and you're off somewhere else! But that doesn't mean that when you're playing a piece that you don't get emotionally involved. Having said that, I would say that as you get older, you are less inspired. I think that's partly down to the fact that the longer you've been in the job you've seen more things. You're not seeing anything for the first time anymore. Yet, a new Conductor can come along, and he's absolutely amazing; or perhaps an amazing Soloist. Both of these can inspire you.*

(47y, M, vc)   *Each person has to adapt to a set of circumstances that they feel is going to facilitate their needs. For example, when I first started out, I'd couldn't bear Beethoven. I hated it! I don't know why! But, over the years I have learned to love it. Yet, there are still some Composers who I cannot abide; that music just rubs me the wrong way. Before when we'd be playing those kinds of pieces, I would have been [slouched down] in my chair thinking about the football match, or about some movie I was going to see that night, or what kind of wine I was going to drink when I got home. But now I have definitely worked out a way to overcome that.*

(49y, M, vn)   *I think the emotional issues are very personal. Not at all related to ageing. If you are a positive person, then with the age you will continue to find aspects that turn you on and give you the 'push' for more. During my first 10 years in the Orchestra I couldn't care at all how I was compared to the rest: how loud I played, the coloration, the fitting-in, the give-and-take. [Author's Note: the participant is the Concertmaster and Leader 1st Violins.] I didn't care about the intermusical relationship at all. It took me many years to be able to listen to the background—to balance myself to the section, and have the Orchestra behind me. These proficiencies needed to be developed. That takes years, and maturity! So, there is always some benefit for Seasoned Players. I am now [nearing] my 50s, and I believe that the next 10 years will be my most difficult. It is not so much the music per se, but when the musical expression includes both affective and physical fatigue, then the expression can be expressionless. To win the battle one must develop a critical analytic attitude. It is not enough to say: I played it. It was good enough. It's over. Done, next! But rather, ask: Was it good enough? Was it clean enough? One needs to hear the wider soundscape: What do others do when I am playing my part? How can I craft that line in a way that rejuvenates? So, perhaps there are ages when you are more concentrated on yourself. Then after a certain age, you must concentrate on everyone else.*

(55y, M, bn)   *I think now when I play something, [it's] more emotional. Before it was more about getting through it; learning the piece, learning the notes. [Now] I know the notes, I know the piece. So, I think: How does the Composer want it? How can I play it perfectly? How can I really show the emotion? So, definitely I'd say that in younger years I was more interested in technical aspects of the music, and now I'm more interested in expressive aspects. I feel that onstage if I have a solo part, I experiment much more than I did before. Because I know I've done it. I can get through it. I'm not as crazy playing Bassoon onstage as before! I don't 'let it rip' as much as I did! I used to enjoy the feeling of 'letting it rip'. Now, I feel: OK, play it right! I am still out there to impress people. I definitely got that exhibitionistic side when I'm up on stage; I want to show off. I'm a performer! There's a reason I chose this business, and sometimes I like to show off my talent. I know better. I like to slam things down, to put it down, and tell people: This is how it should be done. I enjoy that!*

(59y, M, va)   *I don't think I have any problems in expressing emotion or feeling emotion as I got older. I feel I have even become more passionate. I'm 1st Viola player. So, I have to play all the Solos. In former days that was rather difficult for me—the nerves and anxiety! I was [anticipating] those Solos with a bit of fear. And that's [knocks on a wooden table] better than before. Maybe that is experience of life, or as the expression goes: 'Wisdom of the Old People'. When you get older, a good thing is that you're calmer. Maybe because you don't have to prove anything to anybody! But one of the big problems of our profession is that you always have to [prove] something to your colleagues. Everybody knows how it has to sound, and how it has to work. If there's a tiny little bit that's not very good, no one will say anything. But they know! Some players have this problem more than others. They sit on the 'ejection seat' every time they play. It's dangerous as everybody looks, and anyone can 'press on the button'. Look: A basketball player may actually only throw the ball 10 times—but if he gets it in the basket 3 times he is considered great [even though that is only a 30% success rate]. An Orchestra player can play 20,000–50,000 notes, but then gets one wrong note, and people would say: 'He's not so good anymore.'*

5.2.8 Gender-Related Issues in the Orchestra

The topic of gender-related issues in the Orchestra came up during the interviews; it was not an easy subject for discussion. While innate musical talent is certainly more or less spread evenly between men and women, historically Symphony Orchestras have been exclusively male ensembles. The entrance of women into Orchestras goes back to the 1970s; it was a slow and stressful process (Allmendinger et al., 1996). The procedure of placing a screen in front of musicians who were auditioning for openings in Symphony Orchestras greatly contributed to an increase (between 30% and 50%) in the number of women who were successful in securing a position (Goldin & Rouse, 2000). Accordingly, the practice of *blind* auditions had become widely adopted over a 20-year period (1970–1990). It is now a standard practice accepted worldwide. Subsequently, by year 2000 there was an increase (between 25% and 46%) of women members in both North American and European professional Symphony Orchestras. Nowadays, as Orchestras are almost evenly split between the sexes, many players feel the topics of gender are no longer relevant for discussion. Nonetheless, among the issues that surfaced in the discussions were: pregnancies, family, ageing, and stereotypical gender-identification of musical instruments.

(33y, F, bn/db) *I have never spoken to other women players about our changing bodies, pregnancy, or how [being a woman] affects how I play. I never talked about it not even when I was younger. It's not that it's taboo. We just never talk about these things. Of course, our whole body changes, and these also change the way we [Woodwinds] breathe. Just having a bigger mass, the embouchure changes a bit. Everything's [bigger]! Maybe I'm just imagining, but I think there's always a kind of pressure on women if they get pregnant. We once had an Oboe player who really had problems—she couldn't play because the muscles weren't working anymore while she was pregnant. She should have come back [after she gave birth], but she just stayed away for three years with the first child. Then she got [pregnant again]. She never returned [to the Orchestra].*

(36y, F, tpt) *I was between 10 and 12 [years old] when I started playing. Music was the only thing that I could do. It just seemed to click for me! You know everything was [falling apart] when I got an old bashed-up Cornet. My parents were splitting up, and things were going really bad at that time. [Music] was the only thing that I could focus on; it just kept me. It was something I knew I could do; I could latch on to it! Perhaps because it was a loud instrument, and I could scream! I never walked into a room [with] the sun hitting off the bells of all these Brass instruments, saying: Wow! But, I couldn't actually play the thing for about two months. Yet, I made my mind up that I was gonna learn to play. That was strange especially for a girl! I didn't know any female Trumpet players; there's not many in [Orchestra] jobs. It's usually referred to as a masculine instrument. I think it's the history: The tradition of Brass players [in the UK] were all colliery miners down in the pits; in their social clubs were the Brass Bands. [Author's Note: In the USA, the male soldiers from the Military Bands* after the Civil War led the way to playing the Trumpet especially in New York and New Orleans.] And I think from there, obviously you've got those skills that then were transferred into Orchestral life. It's only been quite a modern thing that girls were given the opportunity [to join an Orchestra as a Trumpet player]. Back then when I was young, it didn't cross my mind at all that it's a boy's instrument—at least until I actually got into the band. And then it was like: Oh, there's no girls here! But, then there were loads of boys around you!

(39y, F, cl)   I was playing while pregnant. Played up until around sort of 5 or 6 weeks before giving birth. It was a challenge! The first time around, before I had a child, I had a fantastic Alexander technique teacher. I worked so much with her that by the end of it my breathing was even better than it had ever been. I mean I got through longer [music] phrases than I would have done before. My second time around was not so good because I didn't have the same time to invest in Alexander [technique]. So actually, by the end of it, it was a bit harder to play and maintain [the standards]. The first time round I came back after 8 months. I felt reasonably invincible. I thought: I've given birth, I look after a child. If I can do that then I can surely get up onstage and play anything for anybody! Shortly after coming back I performed the Mozart Concerto [K 622, in A major, written in 1791 by Austrian composer Wolfgang Amadeus Mozart, 1756–1791] on an instrument that was special—an 'extended' clarinet (which was very new to me). I didn't get to [preparing] it till about a week before; I thought I was invincible. But, the second one . . . Oh no! That was a completely different matter. I took another [second] 7 months out. For the next couple of years, I had difficulties with concentration and with nerves. I was just so much more tired. You know, you've got two of them!

I think as you have more life experience, you get a bit more perspective. You can see your work in a wider picture, and for me that reduced some of the stress of work. Having children has open my eyes to many things. I had my first child at [age] 35. I would have liked it to a bit earlier, but for a working woman [in an Orchestra], that's quite acceptable. But since then, [the Orchestra] doesn't matter quite as much. I mean I love it, but I've moved a little bit away, partly because I know it's not as important as my family. On a day-to-day level, I'm not sure I can make the separation between 'The Performer' and 'The Mom' (or 'The Spouse')? Gosh that's a tough call! If I'm feeling low about my playing then it does affect the other aspects of my life. Yet, in general, I think becoming a mom, and having a family, has helped me reduce my stress, and put the demands of my music performance career in perspective.

(43y, F, db)   I hear that one of the ladies in this study said: 'It's much more difficult to get older in the Orchestra as a woman than it is as a man!' [Author's note: This is indeed an indication that sometimes participants shared the contents of their interviews with each other.] I've never heard that before, but she's right! When you get older as a woman, the men stop looking at you—you become a little bit more invisible. All of a sudden, a younger woman player comes [to audition for the band] and all the men in the Orchestra are looking at her; the other women are quite less attractive to the men as we get older. The men are such good mates to me. But the lack of attraction is not there, 'cause we're getting older. Age has never stopped me; I mean my partner is 18 years older than me. I've always gone for older men. But as far as what that lady said: Yes! It is something I had noticed right on the first day I came to the Orchestra over 20 years ago. I thought: Blimey, these ladies look knackered! Look! I'm not a great one for make-up because I tend to be allergic towards a lot of things. I think there were some ladies in the band then who also would never have put on make-up. And, it does show under the lights. I said to myself: Am I gonna look like this in 20 years? Is that what this job does to you? Yet, with the men, it doesn't really seem to matter how wrinkled or tired-looking they are. But if a woman doesn't look after herself, then the men aren't gonna be that interested. To be honest I don't think that anybody in this Orchestra is checking out people in that kind of way anymore. I know that the lads (in the Horns and Percussion sections) will always go like this [raises her eyebrows up and down]. It's not serious—it just breaks up the monotony.

(47y, F, vn)

As you get older, giving birth and having children, is quite different while you're in an Orchestra. Perhaps when you're younger, you don't think about that. You could have had maternity leave from the Orchestra, and then you come back. But, if you don't play for a couple of months after you give birth, it is more difficult getting back in shape. When I was pregnant with my first daughter, I felt some pressure not to be away for a long time. I took just one year. Today, everybody takes 3 years off; that's what I did with my third child. You don't get paid, but they have to take you back. I know that there are some who think about this aspect when they bring in a new player; if it's a woman, she might become pregnant in a couple of years, leave, and then they have to bring a substitute till she returns. If she returns? Although this does bring some disorganization in to the Orchestra, it's really OK. Yes! I think it's getting less and less, because many more women trying to get a job in the Orchestra only want to play for the Orchestra [i.e., they don't really want to have children]. Moreover, there are less men in the orchestra; I don't know why. Are less men going to Music College? Has the Violin become a typical woman's instrument? I am not talking about just the Strings—also with other instruments. When I first came here, the Winds were mostly men, and now it's about 40% women. For every man who left the Orchestra, a new player came in who was a woman. I think [Orchestra] is a very good job for a woman—especially if you want to have children and continue working full time. I worked full time while I raised three children! I was alone with the children for a long time. It worked. I could organize it. Some women take a half-time position with [small] children; I think that is ideal. With my first child, I felt some pressure to come back early. Nobody asked about problems I might have had at home. There was never too much interest. Even the women in the Orchestra [never said a word]. I think the children you have are your private thing, and you shouldn't talk too much about this here. I don't know if that's good, or if it's the way it should be. I never wanted to have any privileges just because of [being a working mom with babies and] having small children. But orchestra work is not really easy when you have children. As you get older, and you have more children, it becomes more difficult.

(54y, F, vc)

Someone wrote in an article somewhere that: 'The Orchestra is a great place to grow old'. [Author's Note: see Chapter 1: Smith, 1989]. I don't know if I agree with that! I think there are difficulties for women growing older in the Orchestra. For example, when I had a child, I didn't stop playing the minute I got pregnant. Holding this Cello in a very strategic place! I carried right on till about 3 weeks before [giving birth], and came back just under 6 months [after giving birth]. It was very difficult the first year because of the fatigue. I was never anything other but completely and utterly exhausted for about 18 months. I didn't get a lot of help from my partner (who at the time was also a player in this Orchestra).

While an Orchestra is a fantastic place to have relationships and friendships that span generations, I think there are difficulties of getting older as a woman when as a younger person you are viewed very differently by men. As women grow older, they tend to become more invisible than the younger women who've got all their attractions (and the things that men desire). I think from a personal point of view, it's one reason why the doing of my job—the actual daily playing of the notes in the right place—is very important. Because it's a compensation; [a way] to be respected amongst one's peers of all ages of both genders. From my experience, as a young woman in the Orchestra I had a lot of attention; mostly because I was a younger woman and not necessarily because I was a half-decent Cellist. Men can be very shallow! So I think it can be a great place to grow old, but I think there's another edge to it. You are in the spotlight, being viewed, looked at, and judged. I know that some of the women feel threatened more by the younger women joining the Orchestra; [more so] than the men would be of a younger man [joining the Orchestra]. Also, I think a lot of younger players do not have a ready-made respect for older players. When I was a youngster, I respected the older players [especially the women] simply because they were doing that job a bloody sight longer than I had. And they had a lot to offer. There was a great example when I joined the Orchestra, of somebody who was about [to] retire (she was approaching age 60) and she was No. 2 in the 2nd Violins. Now I know that she was held in the most high esteem, and that is really what I've aspired along my way—if I make it to the grand old age of 59 in the Orchestra. I hold this person as a role model. For me she was the epitome of the right sort of professionalism: she was great, had poise, and dignity. And the gents never looked at her as a woman. She was their Violinist! She was loved universally by both genders. But there was no doubt about it. For all of us, she was . . . (and I hate using the word): an 'older woman'! You know, she was retiring for goodness' sake. You can't get away from it. But, we're talking about 20 years ago, when respect was a different thing altogether

5.3 Considering Emotional Health in Music Performance

5.3.1 Performance Nerves and Anxieties, Stage Fright, and Drugs and Alcohol

All music performers are affected by the general stresses related to having to perform under conditions of high adrenaline flow. More than 30 years ago Sternbach (1993, 1995) claimed that the factors present in the lives of professional musicians generate a *total stress quotient* well beyond what might be expected. These contribute to a lifestyle of overwhelming stress unique to the music profession. Today, most clinicians and researchers employ the label *Music Performance Anxiety* (MPA) as a more generic term to umbrella all the previously accepted nomenclature, including 'Performance Anxiety' and 'Stage Fright' (e.g., Cohen & Bodner, 2019; Kenny & Ackermann, 2015; Kenny et al., 2014, 2016). Years ago, other classifications were also employed to describe the tensions in performance, such as: 'Musical Performance Stress', 'Psychological Stress of Musicians', 'Anxiety in Musical Performance', 'Career Stress in Musicians', and 'Musicians' Stress'. The first to adopt a concept that all of the above circumstances are not independent was the British psychologist pioneer in Behavioural Medicine and Health Psychology, Andrew Steptoe, former director of St George's Hospital Medical School in London (UK). Accordingly, Steptoe (1989) claimed that all of these need to be considered in conjunction in order to develop a comprehensive approach to stress management. Based on Steptoe and others who post-dated his conception (e.g., Hamilton, 1995; Marchant-Haycox & Wilson, 1992), a more comprehensive generic classification was proposed. MPA has received major attention as a factor for poor health among performing musicians. For example, studies with Music Academy (i.e., College) students report significantly higher levels of anxiety than even those of professionals in high-risk vocations. The majority self-reported the causes of MPA as: inadequate preparation, pressure from self, general lack of confidence, difficult repertoire, and excessive physical arousal. Summarizing the research literature, Ascenso et al. (2017, 2018) found that women players are 3 times more likely to experience MPA than men players, and Soloists demonstrate higher MPA scores than Chamber Ensemble or Symphony Orchestra players. Accordingly, when adding physical injury to MPA, performing musicians are often associated with having higher levels of general psychological ill-being (e.g., prevalence of mental distress).

Brodsky (1996) brought forth the notion of a *Performers' Stress Syndrome* (PSS), with designated prefixes that account for modality specific idiosyncrasies: PSS among musicians (M-PSS), PSS among dancers (D-PSS), and PSS among theatre actors (T-PSS). Brodsky (1995, 1996, 1999) claimed that different degrees of intensity could specify the type of problem, and hence dictate, to some extent, the intervention package needed to manage the stress. See Figure 5.1. This concept was similar to other models developed by the American Psychological Association delineated in the *Diagnostic and Statistical Manual of Mental Disorders* (DSM). Brodsky conceptualized that clinicians should be able to differentiate stress and tension *versus* anxiety and panic states by accounting for chronic versus acute circumstances. By employing a continuum of psychologically related problems, clinicians could identify the nature of a more normative *career stress* (degree #1, M-PSS.1) that is an integral part of the performance occupation (in the same manner that Sports Psychologists have always viewed stress states among competitive athletes) *versus* the more extreme pathological *stage fright* (degree #4, M-PSS.4). Brodsky further conducted a clinical trial intervention outcome study specifically designed and implemented with professional full-time contract Symphony Orchestra musicians. The players were randomly assigned to one of three psychotherapeutic treatment groups; two intervention platforms were enhanced by music listening, with one of the two also applying whole-body music-generated acoustic vibrotactile stimulation. The clinical-trial intervention demonstrated positive outcomes (Brodsky, 1995, 2000, 2006; Brodsky & Sloboda, 1997a, 1997b), and the new diagnostic label (M-PSS) was received as a valuable novel contribution to the field of Performing Arts Medicine (e.g., *Congrès International des Arts et de la Médicine, International Conference on the Arts and Medic*ine in Lyons, France, 1996; and the *6th European Congress on Performing Arts Medicine and Physiology of Music* in Berlin, Germany, 1998; see also Brodsky, 1999). In retrospect, Herman and Clark (2023) stated that it was rather unfortunate that both (i.e., the clinical intervention model and the new diagnostic label) were eclipsed by more popular trends presented in the literature, and hence were neither really acknowledged by other researchers nor incorporated in treatment procedures among performing musicians by clinical psychotherapists.

Several participant-players in the current study mentioned to be tormented by MPA from time to time. For them, it clearly doesn't get better with age! A few players spoke about suffering more at a time when they had been Freelance players constantly auditioning for a position. But, once they won a more stable and secure contract, their specific anxieties and feelings of uncertainty about the future subsided. Some players conveyed narratives about their use of alcohol as a routine

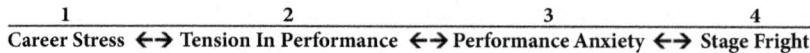

Figure 5.1 Continuum of Psychologically Related Problems Among Professional Musicians

Source: Brodsky (1995, 1996, 1999). Reprinted with permission.

intervention means to cope. Others mentioned pharmaceutic agents such as beta-adrenoceptor blocking agents (e.g., Inderal, Propranolol, Metoprolol, and Levatol) as their choice intervention for dealing with MPA. I note here that readers should see Nelson (2017) for a brief note on the benefits and risks of Beta Blockers. However, many of the players were adamant that they never (neither in the past nor nowadays) suffered from MPA. They feel that involvement with MPA has all the more to do with Orchestra position than any other variable. Soloists and Principals are afflicted more than Tutti section players. Finally, some players insist that specific pieces raise nervousness—and these are somewhat based on memories of a previous experience involving situations which caused the player to employ a precarious manoeuvre that, in the end, saved them from public embarrassment.

Furthermore, within the discussions on the emotion-related aspects of a music performance Orchestra career (see section 5.2), many players conveyed perceptions of not having attained their expected potential. They noted that they often had feelings of apathy, burnout, and depression. Finally, many players stated that the more publicly known allegory known as *Fear of Failure* is actually no more than a 'cover story' for the real-life much more potentially self-defeating behaviour referred to as *Fear of Success*.

(30y, F, vn)   *We're more aware of health risks now. I read a book written by an Orchestra player named Richard Davis [Becoming An Orchestral Musician: A Guide For Aspiring Professionals. London: de la Mare Publishers Limited, 2004]. [The book] talks about Beta Blockers, claiming they have more of a negative impact than a positive one; they take your anxiety edge off as well as your emotional edge. It calms your head, and blunts your affect. If you look forward and anticipate playing, both excited but a bit scared, with Beta Blockers you don't have all that. I think that playing onstage is a risk, and if you take away the risk, it's not the same experience. You don't need to take away the risk, you need to develop coping skills. When somebody wins a competition as the best Violinist in the world, I'd wanna know that they did it because of skill on their own, and not because some medication or steroids helped them.*

(36y, F, tpt)   *I went through Stage Fright to a point where I couldn't actually produce a note. I had a Principal Brass [Leader] at the time who was very specific what he wanted from the No. 2 player: I wasn't allowed to come in with him at the same time; I wasn't allowed to play louder than him. So given these [and other] restrictions, I was even afraid to actually play. He would take me aside and reprimand me. That left me with the feeling of I don't know what to do. Once he left the Orchestra things got a bit easier for me. With this new Principal, I actually felt I can get back and try and play the way I wanna play. I'm fairly sure everyone has gone through [something like this] at some point. But no one will talk about it!*

(40y, F, vn)   *Tutti players rarely have stress or Performance Anxiety in the Orchestra. When you're a part of a bigger group, unless you come in very loudly during a rest or make a mistake, most of the time what you do is not noticeable. So, as a Tutti player I never have anxiety in the Orchestra. But the nerves do go up and down in an audition. Until my middle-to-late 20s I never got nervous at all. Orchestra auditions require you to play a Solo repertoire (which is never played again once [you] get the job). I actually felt more comfortable when playing music from a Concerto than Orchestra excerpts. I don't really know why [it started]! I think it's just the fact that your colleagues are sitting there judging you. They're not listening to you, but judging you, and giving a verdict. I think that's what makes it so stressful.*

(41y, M, vc)   *Performance Anxiety, Stage Fright, and stresses should become easier with experience. Thankfully, I don't suffer from these. But I definitely have had my moments, and perhaps that does change with age. I probably had it worse when I was Freelancing looking for jobs. Not knowing what was going on, nor having a sense of stability. So, that led me to be much more nervous. So, now as a contract-player, I'm much less stressed. You know who you're sitting next to, you know the Conductor, you know the Hall, what you've done, and what you have to do! This kind of stability allows you to deal with nerves. By the way, I consider nervousness before a Concert to be a good thing—to a degree! It certainly helps your awareness. It may depend on how and where it peaks. But, the idea of a heightened state during a concert is definitely good!*

(43y, F, vn)   *Some use Alcohol to cope with stress. But I find it makes me worse! If I get really stressed about [a piece], I tend to go through a detox for a few days (or a week) where I just drink Herbal Tea and Tonic Water. But, it works for me! I don't think that nerves get better with age. I think that for me it's got worse! I suppose I was quite lucky. I didn't think about [nerves] till I'd had the job for a few years. Then, somebody else in the 2nd Violin section sitting near me said she got really nervous about a particular bit. And it was almost like: Oh, that's a good idea! I'll get nervous now. It's just contagious, and it was horrible! This week's programme is stuff that we don't know; I feel that if you don't know the piece then you can't have to worry about it. So that's good. But Violinists that have been here for a while all have certain pieces that 'put the willies up them'! For me it's usually when I have to play really quietly because it's really difficult to play quietly when there are so many of us on the stage. If you're playing, and the Conductor goes like that to you [she makes a sour face], your instant reaction is to tense up. I don't think Conductors realize the effect they have.*

(44y, F, vn)   *I'm just a Rank-&-File player with the 1st Violin section. That's another ball of contention because I was (and am now) a better player than that. But, because I have problems performing in front of people, that really denied me the opportunities to move up. Basically, I became dependent on Alcohol to get up on the stage. So, I had to give up a Leader's career! I was 'pissed' [i.e., drunk] at trials. I'd miss beats, wouldn't come in on time, and even play in the wrong key. I just didn't feel as if I could play without some kind of chemical enhancement. And yet, I had been the Leader of a National Youth Orchestra when I was younger, and Leader of [several] different Orchestras. I did solo stuff [with world-class Orchestras] like the Mendelssohn Violin Concerto [in E minor, Op. 6, written between 1838 and 1844 by German composer Felix Mendelssohn Bartholdy, 1809–1847]. I could have done so much more. But, I'm only just getting to the point that I feel that I can play in front of people without needing something. I don't want to be bitter, nonetheless, I do feel like I've missed so many opportunities.*

(47y, M, vc)   *I've got a big Solo to play within the Orchestra. But that's kind of in my comfort zone. That is what I am paid to do. I won't be any of the less nervous for it. It won't take me to the level of anxiety that playing a Concerto does. Yet, if I had to do Don Quixote [Op. 35, written in 1897 by the German composer Richard Strauss, 1864–1949] I'd be sweating in a corner somewhere. But I would still make myself play that because I have to have self-respect in my own playing. Do I need the thrill of the risk-taking and high adrenaline? When I am on a stage playing a Concerto, I am aware that I'm taking a risk; I am playing above my comfort zone. If it goes wrong, I'd look like an idiot. So, there is a 'Fear of Failure'. But, a lot of musicians also have the 'Fear of Success'. I was taking an audition two weeks ago for the Leader's job here. There was this one guy [who auditioned]; he was good, but he wasn't great! Not quite at the right level of being the Leader of this Orchestra. When I spoke to the Piano accompanist, he said that in the room before coming onstage, it was just the most sublime-staggering beautiful playing that he'd ever heard from a candidate. But then when the guy came [out to the stage], the Pianist thought: What's he doing? He's obviously a high-up player in a Violin section from one of the better Orchestras. He succumbed to 'Fear of Success'. A lot of players just don't make it through the audition. At times, they self-defeat themselves; [afterall], once you get through it—then you have to maintain it!*

(47y, M, hn)   *I worry because I find myself tending to drink. When I have a very intense day, and I'm concentrating very hard, the best thing in the world is a nice big drink. But it's very damaging because it effects the ability of my muscles to regenerate themselves, and it's very bad news because of what it does to the growth hormones; just stops them working. So whatever damage you've done to your embouchure [pointing to his lips],* it won't fix itself fast by morning. I have to play the Horn, and I can never stop thinking about them. It's always there in the back of my mind.

(50y, M, vn)   I would say most of the musicians here smoke [cigarettes]. After an hour [of playing] they're already getting itchy to smoke. So, during the break (first half of a concert) I go out to talk to someone, and it's like a smoke chamber. I think that [smoking] is also partly connected to nerves; many of the players feel nervous when they have a Solo. I definitely have problems with the nerves. It's actually an interesting question about 'coping'—because over the past 4 months I was put in the position of Assistant Concertmaster. I've done that before [in other Orchestras]. I play Tutti here, but now suddenly I also have a 10-measure Solo. I definitely felt the nerves at the beginning, but it becomes less and less with experience. Until now I haven't really used any pills! Just once during the past 30 years (2 years ago) I took half of a Beta Blocker before a concert. I felt the nerves, but didn't have the jitters. I remember feeling: Wow, that really works. I could see using it if I had an audition! But I would hate to resort to that every time I had a Solo.

(53y, M, hrp)   I am not sure if performance nerves (or performance anxiety) gets better or worse with age. I think you just learn to cope. And the fact that you've played something so many times and it hasn't been such a disaster [laughs], is sort of somehow reassuring. Yeah, so if it didn't go wrong last time, why would it go wrong this time? I cope through nutrition. I avoid any form of caffeine (e.g., tea, coffee, chocolate) on a performance day. I also avoid stimulants because just the situation itself will stimulate me enough to hamper concentration. The same with too much sugar. I don't think that this changes with age. I've always known since I was in my early 20s not to have tea or coffee on the day of the concert. Then I added a few other things as I went along. What to avoid wasn't something that I was aware of 25 years ago; it's something I've gradually worked out over the years with experience.

I've been playing in Orchestras now for 31 years, and I can't think of people who have retired early because they can't play properly because they're old. But rather, they have gone [because of] Alcohol and other problems. I am not sure how often a player either leaves on their own, or how often the management asks one to leave—when it's not related to level of playing. I can only think of one instance where that happened because somebody's behaviour was generally aggressive and impossible to deal with— although their performance level was always spot on technically (i.e., their standard was still OK)—but yet they just weren't fitting in.

(53y, M, vn)   Sixteen years ago, I had a phobia while in the Orchestra. I had the fear of playing long notes in slow movements towards the end of the section. There'd be this vibrato-shaky-kind-of-sound. I had fear to play this note—an anxiety which was later defined to me by a mental-health professional as a 'phobia'. It's much better now! But it was a hard time for me. I went to two psychiatrists. The first one offered a Talk Therapy—that didn't work! The second one offered a Behavioural Therapy—that worked better! But, it seems difficult to treat this special anxiety behaviour. I think the best treatment was just 'time'; it took me 3 or 4 years to get over the issue! They were very hard [years]. Now it's gone. I think what made me afraid was that people would hear me shaking. I also took Beta Blockers—but that didn't work for me.

(60y, M, bn)   People say to me I look nervous. They ask if I want to take a Beta Blocker. I just say: 'No. It's good that I am nervous because there are good aspects to nervousness.' I just kept telling myself at the time, that the more I'm nervous the more it's heightened my senses about this particular bit and playing those notes.

5.3.2 Burnout, Chronic Fatigue, Depression, Failing Potential, and Fear of Success

As seen above, the transcripts illustrate that some players convey a perception of not having achieved the Orchestra position that they had expected to attain. At times they mention having developed affective states of fatigue, burnout, and depression.

Although the myth that 'Fear of Failure' is what unconsciously drives most musicians, it has been rebuffed by pointing to 'Fear of Success' as the more potent and dangerous mental state. The topic of 'listening to music after hours' has resurfaced, but this time this phenomenon is clearly associated to Burnout.

(33y, F, bn/dbn)   *For a long time in an Orchestra it seems to be working. But, then it begins taking [up all] your energy. You notice that somehow, you're mentally getting more depressed—like your spirit is a little bit lower, and you're getting more bored. Yes! You get more bored in the Orchestra as you get older. It depends if you have the energy to stay lively—to search for some adventures. And I think if you start having this Depression, then your body will also begin to have problems.*

(36y, F, tpt)   *I always felt there should be a mentoring system in the Orchestra. That younger players should have an older mentor. Because it just seems so often that we've had young 'superstars' come in, and very quickly within a few years something's happened to blow them off course. And the older guys here, they've obviously been through it themselves. You know, just to have a confidant that you can rely on, and to trust! Part of the problem is that when you deal with issues that are 'taboo' people don't want to talk about them! The younger players have no way to get information. They don't know who to talk to 'cause they're embarrassed to ask. And, they're even more so embarrassed because when they finally do ask, [that] they hear an older player say: 'We don't think about it.' Or: 'You don't talk about it.' Part of the problem is that the people who have the years of experience, don't share it! If the older players would be willing to be there [then younger players might learn how to adapt].*

(47y, F, vn)   *I hope I haven't achieved my full musical potential yet. My goal is to play more Chamber Music now. I'm always afraid to lose the courage to play Solo concerts, as I really want to be a Soloist in a Chamber Ensemble. It may have something to do with me being a Tutti player. I've thought about why most of the 2nd Violin players love it, while the 1st Violin players don't like playing Chamber Music. Maybe because we are always in the 'big pool', and don't have such difficult parts. We don't have so many notes to play, and the notes [we play] are in the middle. The 1st Violinists have so many more notes to play. All the 1st Violin players are 'Prima Donnas' by character; they have more stress, frustration, bad moods, and body problems. I personally don't really listen to music outside of the Orchestra—definitely not to Classical music. I may go to a Chamber concert, and sometimes hear the radio.*

(54y, M, va)   *I do think it's only natural to get fed up if you've been doing it so much. This lack of motivation comes out in different ways. I just don't want to have to play in rehearsals anymore. Yes! I would call this situation: Burnout. I do believe that Orchestra players get more burned out as they get older. My expectations of orchestral life were never met! I thought I would've gotten a better position. I didn't think I would've had to fight to get a [Tutti] position. I had imagined it would be only once (or twice) throughout the 29 years I'm in this Orchestra! I do get jealous of people who get more gigs than me. It's not only a question of extra money, but rather opportunities to play more. Sometimes I play with Chamber Ensembles, and occasionally there has been a recording. I still haven't lost my love of playing. But, it's not easy to take other steps to increase your marketability; there's so much competition. In a way, I feel that this gets worse as you get older—the frustration that rarely you meet expectations of what you had wanted. I chose to be a professional when I was about 21 years old; I joined this Orchestra from an advertisement in the paper.*

(54y, F, vc)   *I didn't get less motivated over the years, but there's been a lot of frustration between me and the Management. I know that people do become cynical; I'm cynical in a sort of Political sense. But I don't think I'm cynical when it comes to my own personal involvement in the music. I'm not a hardened embittered person. I've certainly been hurt on a more personal level that caused me to become very solitary in the Orchestra.*

I'm coming out of it now. I don't think I'm ever going to be somebody who just doesn't care. While I've been a player here, there have been quite a lot of ups and downs. Getting through those periods has been tricky. My personal life hasn't gone smoothly; I have been depressed and stressed for more than a month or two. It has had a very negative effect on how I'm able to concentrate. I think that overcoming that [has been hard]. Yet, I do have a different attitude now than when I first started; a different way of approaching things.

(58y, M, va)   *Lately, my job satisfaction depends on the pieces (repertoire) we play, and of course the Conductor. I must say it also has to do with responses from my colleagues. There are many who say (under their breath, with animated faces): 'This is not acceptable.' Or: 'This was not good!' Those attitudes influence my feelings of satisfaction with this Orchestra. I still see the Orchestra as a family. Other players may be burnt out and are not living up to the responsibility that I would be proud of in my family. But I can't say anything to them; I am a Tutti player—not a Principal.*

(59y, M, fl/picc)   *At the beginning of my career here we all talked about the 'music' during our breaks. We spoke about what we played, how the recording sounded, [about] some Soloist, or some concert. When we played the same programme three times a week, during the breaks we'd discuss if the second time was better than the first, and anticipated the third performance to make it much better than those before it. Today, we only play one performance, and it is over! No one talks about the music anymore! If you take any concert programme of any Orchestra from the 1990s, and then a concert programme from today's season, there'd be no comparison. There are no longer any musical challenges. Once, there was a much bigger investment in great Conductors, great pieces, and better Halls. Attendance was bigger, and there were many more concerts per week. I am more bored of being an orchestral player. My way of dealing with that is to look for other stimuli. When I go home, I listen to music! I know a lot of players who claim to have heard enough music at work so they don't want to listen to music [at home] at all. For me, that is a sign of burnout!*

(60y, M, cl)   *You know, I am so overdosed with music that when I get home I don't listen anymore to music. I don't feel I'm burned out. But rather, I have a more general fatigue. The management does not bring in younger replacement players for those that retired. Therefore the intensity of performance is far greater than it was years ago when the section was bigger. Basically we go through the motions, but never really reach the maximum artistic output that we'd expect of ourselves. Have I reached my full potential [after 35+ years in this Orchestra]? I am not sure! I should arrive at rehearsals and concerts feeling much more relaxed. Yet, almost everyone is already tired before the first note. I do feel there is an effect of ageing on my performance. The minute you realize that your body is not the same as it was at age 40, you begin to feel stress and anxiety. That seems to have a knock-on effect on my memory too.*

5.3.3 Post-Performance Arousal

The final topic of discussion concerning the emotional aspects related to music performance was Post-Performance Arousal. Many players mentioned the fact that as they aged they consistently remained awake longer after a Symphony Orchestra concert performance had ended. It takes a much longer duration of time to calm down than it had in the past. Sometimes, Post-Performance Arousal even lingers on throughout the early morning hours of the next day. This was a very different experience than what they were familiar with in the earlier years of their Orchestral career. More than anything else, such perceptions brought on feelings of debilitation.

(49y, M, vn)   *Today, although the level of arousal during a concert is the same, now I take it different than I did in the past. The arousal was [once] like: POW! Like fountains! But with time, you learn to balance it out. Ageing (or experience) allows for more control. While calming down after a performance is not so different for players aged 50–60, but after 60 it is definitely more of an issue! The younger players are off to a pub (because the 'high' stays longer), but those [aged] 60 are in their car [going home] with the highs long gone.*

(50y, M, vn)   *I notice that sometimes when I come home I have to stay awake longer after the Concert. When I was young I stayed up late, but then I would also get up later. Now I can't just go to sleep right after the concert because there is that 'high'! So, then it can take 90 minutes just to calm down, and I eventually fall asleep by 1 a.m. Today, I do all kinds of relaxation exercises and meditation to help me come down. When I was younger I went out more with the lads. I wasn't married then! So, what I am saying is that even if the actual adrenalin-rush (that level of arousal) peaks, and it takes the same amount of time to come down, the way of coping with it as I'm getting older is very different. Other people in the Orchestra claim they can't go to sleep until 2–3 a.m. after a concert. They say: 'How can you go to sleep after that concert when you're so excited!' But of course, everyone has their own way [to deal with it].*

(53y, M, hrp)   *It is interesting to think about the possibility that coping with stress may get better. [Even] with pieces you've played so many times you can still get a bit uptight. I would say that the problem of stress and nerves is far more likely to have an influence on one's performance than [anything else]. So, I would assume and really expect that in another 10 years I will be in the same state as I am today. On the other hand, I think I'm probably more fatigued than I used to be. Not necessarily during the concert, but after the concert! Music performance has more of a toll on me as I age. I mean sometimes, it can take me a long time to unwind. I know I will have to stay up a while before I go to bed. And I don't know if this happens to my colleagues as well. We don't talk about things like that. [Laughs.]*

(59y, M, va)   *After the Concerts I have a lot of adrenaline. As I got older, I think it hasn't changed. There is the same level of excitement, and same problem of falling asleep. I like those hours after the performances to be alone. I have a glass of Wine! My sleeping time is about 1 a.m. nearly every day. Operas are finished about 10.30 p.m., so I'm at home about 11.30 p.m. And then I have [another] 2 hours before I can fall asleep. It was always like that for me. But my wife is an early riser/starter in the morning. And we always had differences in sleep-wake cycles. Everybody knows about that! When the children were small, she got up early to feed them. But I always started working in the Orchestra at 10 a.m.*

(61y, F, vn)   *It takes me longer now to come down and fall asleep [after a Concert]. Many times, I can't fall asleep at all. It can take me about 2 hours to come down from the adrenalin. I don't take anything to help. I don't have any exercises that I have learned. I am not one to go to Bars or Pubs—I don't drink! The truth is that when I was about 25 years old, I also had problems sleeping after a great performance. But I could always still get myself together and function in the rehearsal the next morning. Nowadays, I feel I need a day off between an evening concert and the next morning rehearsal. I have trouble concentrating on new material as I still seem to 'be there' [in the aura of the night beforehand]. It is the lingering feeling of excitement and passion. I don't speak about these things with my friends in the Orchestra. It is far too personal [taboo] to share these things with colleagues.*

5.4 Discussion and Summary

This chapter dealt with emotional aspects of music performance that need to be considered within the context of ageing. The effect of passion was discussed; emotions of both positive and negative valances were offered by the players. They spoke about passion, motivation, involvement, and satisfaction all within the context of ageing.

(54y, F, vc)   *I think that as you get older one's emotional involvement, motivation, and satisfaction becomes better. Sure, there are some performances that are like: I played it before and so I'm just doing it because I have to. But, it's the unique set of circumstances that comprise each concert: Who is the Conductor? Where is the venue? Who are the audience? No concert ever truly repeats itself. It is interesting to talk about how you are supposed to keep passion alive after 38 years of work. Well, first of all, I don't have to work harder for the lust of it! It's just there; music has always had the power to move me from my earliest days. One of my earliest memories is of hearing a Brandenburg Concerto [written in 1721 by German composer Johann Sebastian Bach, 1685–1750]. [I remember] crying because it was just so beautiful! Some of my mom's friends who were there, said: 'Aww, are you missing your daddy?' because he was at work. And I sort of said: 'Yes!' But it was the music. I think it's within you. Whatever experiences I have had in my professional life have not done anything to make it disappear. If anything, I think music has more power now because of life experience, and the connection [that surfaces] between what is expressed in music and life itself.*

The players often spoke of discipline, artistic integrity, commitment, and conviction. They expressed their sense of responsibility, dedication, and pride to be in an Orchestra. But yet, the other side of these is a sense that all can be lost at any time because of wear and tear.

(55y, M, db)   *Yes, I do think that ageing has influenced my passion for music and music performance. I do think it is more difficult to be gratified from Orchestra work as I get older. Everything is so repetitive. But, I am still here because I can't see myself finding a new profession; I can't see myself changing Orchestras. And by the way, I am not sure any Orchestra would take a player my age—except as a Reliever, Substitute, or an Extra for a specific piece. So, the passion is not there! But, I still love to play! Also, my expectations of something big happening isn't there anymore. I am more realistic. Whatever we play is only 'good enough'. It was the best that could have been performed. I may sound as if I'm burned out. Obviously I have some physical and emotional fatigue. And, definitely less motivation! Somewhere along the line, you lose it! It is not that I would suffer for the next 10 years till pension. But clearly, I have the feeling of: This is it! This is what I was able to achieve. I have no more [occupational] dreams! I reached the point of what I can, and there is no more!' In the beginning I did have greater expectations and motivation. I had thought I would be able to reach a much greater Orchestra. I had entered competitive auditions 2–3 times, and even made the finals. Those Orchestras would have paid higher salaries, but also I would have been required to work twice as hard as I do now. So, in retrospect, maybe this Orchestra is quite comfortable. I do love this Orchestra!*

(60y, F, vc)   *There's a difference between loving music and loving to come to work every day in the Orchestra to play. Perhaps one would think there's a lot of burnout and frustration. I love all the aspects of being a musician. I play in the Orchestra; it's definitely about self-esteem and self-respect. I play on the highest possible level; even if it's not always the utmost perfection. I try to do it, and I fight for it. I practise! I am always judging myself, being very self-critical. I started as a Soloist, came here [to the Orchestra], but continue to play Solo performances. It's about giving a Concert. So, it doesn't matter if it's with an Orchestra, or if you're alone, or with a small Chamber Group. You can't grasp music. You can't take hold of it. It's just in the heart and soul of the people. And this is what makes music performance so very precious. But this [also puts] a tremendous weight of responsibility on the player at a concert. This is what makes performing more than a way to make a living! It's a way of integrity. Artistic integrity!*

As stated above, one of the more unique topics discussed in the chapter has to do with camaraderie, orchestral allegiance and devotion, relationships, and coupling among players. These have not ever, to my knowledge, been documented before in the academic literature. In the current study the participating players were forthright and outspoken on these topics; they were candid with their descriptions of how personal and orchestra lifestyles collided in ways that do not occur in any other profession.

(47y, F, vn)   *My husband is a musician in this Orchestra. But, we are not together anymore. From my point of view, why do most musicians marry other musicians? Well I don't think all do. There is a percentage that I know didn't marry other musicians. Some musicians may feel it is helpful when you marry a musician, but in my case [laughs] it wasn't! Yet, it might be helpful because you understand each other. I think that musicians are very special. So, it could be really good to get a better understanding for the problems each one has—because everybody has to deal with their instrument. Also, understanding what you experience in music [is essential]. People that marry (or have a relationship with someone who's not a musician) may find difficulty because the other person doesn't understand what it means to practise, to rehearse, or what you feel like when making music. I did have some relationships with people who were not musicians, and I had always the feeling that something was missing. A big part of my heart that I couldn't share. And that bothered me. So, what's it like to have an ex-husband in the Orchestra? Uugh! We don't really talk too much. Yes, I realize that in most other professions, you would barely stay in the same building as your ex-husband [or wife]. If you worked in a bank or a store, and you were married to someone and then separated, and they were still there, you would just go to another bank or store [branch]. But this happens in Orchestras all the time! With us it wasn't such a problem; we got divorced because it just didn't work. There was not too much hurt from either side. But I know there are some colleagues in similar situations who have really great problems with that. I just don't know if as we get older does it become better—as the [year of] divorce gets further away—does it become better? Or the fact that you still have to play and tour together make it worse. Maybe you just get used to that. With [my ex-husband] I don't have a problem. But it is true that socially, you're still part of this very intense group, and that's a part of Orchestra life that you don't find in any other profession. You have to deal with it. You can't just walk into another Orchestra and play there. I can't think of any other profession that the life of that profession is so intense, and there are so many other levels that contaminate your professional life as well. But as a player in an Orchestra, you can't say: I'd like to play in a different section, so the two shall never meet'—because all of the sections play together in an Orchestra. If you don't change your job before age 30, then you will most likely stay in the same place [till retirement].*

The chapter went on to highlight affective bonding with a musical instrument. Sternberg's (2021) *Triangular Love Scale for Musical Instruments* was described, and the concept was somewhat replicated in the current study; this later self-report assessment measure is a highly novel approach that as yet has not been incorporated in research studies. The majority of musicians reflected having an intense intimate bonding to their musical instrument. Many described them as having human-like features relating to them with a first (given) name, sex, and gender. Players stated that they would deal with the loss of their instrument with deep sorrow in a similar fashion as when someone has actually passed away.

The chapter touched on discussions with players about Spirituality and Creativity. In addition, emotional communication in music performance, as well as ageing-related adaptation to emotions in music performance were presented. Then, gender-related issues in the orchestra were brought up.

Finally, the chapter looked at emotional health, considering music performance within the context of ageing. Listening to music outside the orchestra resurfaced as an indication of Burnout. Among other topics discussed by the players, were: performance nerves and anxieties, Stage Fright, Drugs and Alcohol, Burnout, Chronic Fatigue, Depression, failing potential, Fear of Success, and Post-Performance Arousal. As was seen in the vignettes, players' opinions vary to a great extent, as does the severity of involvement.

(47y, M, trb) *I don't listen to music outside of the Orchestra. It's not so much than I'm not listening to music, but I'd rather listen to quiet. I don't need music being in the background. When I'm on the job I'm really into it, I really follow what's going on. When my colleagues are playing, even if I don't see them, I know who's playing by their sound; who's playing 1st French Horn just by listening. I can also hear how they feel: If they're in good shape or not. Or: If they have trouble. Or: If something hurts. Or: If something has happened. I mean I play in the Orchestra 5–6 days a week. So, why do I need to listen to music when I go home?*

Losing a tooth would definitely affect my embouchure! That is fatal for a Wind player! But, what is much more dangerous, and happens very often to quite a lot of people, is some kind of crisis in playing. Look: In the morning rehearsal, mostly in a pretty easy spot, it's just not happening! You try to play a really simple part, and you just lose it! Totally mess it up. You don't know what's happening. You don't understand. You haven't got a clue what that was. Most of the time your colleagues are laughing because they didn't expect it either. Then you're sitting there, at first laughing also, and then you start thinking: What happened there? If this happens once again, or twice again, then you're in trouble. Now [turning to the interviewer, he says:] I ask you to whistle with your mouth! If that doesn't work, what would you do? You'd haven't got a clue! You just learned to do it. You know how to do it. But, you don't have any idea what you're doing. It's the same with us! I bet I do know more about the mechanics of [the] mouth, lips, and teeth than you do. But if you're in a situation that you lose an ability you had before, you're really in trouble. But, you have to find a way to get rid of that problem.

(52y, M, db) *I don't feel really 'OK' today. [I have felt this way for] a long time. Actually, I'm now on a 'down' waiting to be picked 'up' again. It's more [about] family. It effects my mental state, but I don't know if it effects my playing. Gradually, I felt burned out! When you came here a year ago, I was in a better state. You asked for participants to interview, and I signed up. I don't think I would have [volunteered] today! I'm a little bit [fed up] with music and work; lots of stress and anxiety. It depends on the pressure in the Orchestra from the Conductor. Sometimes we have Conductors who are really [hostile] and scream: 'PLAY THAT!' There are other Conductors who say: 'Very good. Play it once more.' I wasn't upset or stressed about playing here by myself [referring to the in vivo performance, see Chapter 10] because I don't have nothing to lose! But, [right now] I'm not really satisfied with the final version that I just played! I still had wrong notes— but I'm not bothered by it too much as in the Orchestra you have to get used to hearing wrong notes, and then go on. But other things in the Orchestra do cause me stress. I have to admit it's getting a little bit worse [as I get older]. I know there is a myth that it should get better as you have experience because you can play it. But, that's not true. So, how does it get worse? The pressure comes from [the fear] you will lose your face [self-confidence and further embarrassment] in front of the other musicians. Sometimes you play very good, and everyone says: 'Cool, very good!' Then you have to play every time as good as that first time! So perhaps it is better not to play so good because then they won't expect you next time to play better. I learnt a long time ago that many think about 'Fear of Failure'. But actually, and many musicians won't really admit it, but we are more afraid to succeed! Look: If I'm very good once then everyone would expect me to be that good next time. And if I'm good next time, they would expect me to be even better the time after that. Maybe part of me can't lose face after 30 years in the Orchestra. In the beginning, you could say: 'Well, what do you want? I'm just young and inexperienced.' But, after 30 years in the Orchestra it's much worse to lose face than after 2 years in the Orchestra. Also, they might be saying: 'He's getting old, he can't play as good as he was, and we have new players [auditioning].' So, I think you start to feel the pressure of your age. I don't really think that if I make a mistake once or twice they're gonna ask me to leave the Orchestra. It is just more of a social embarrassment, rather than fear of losing your job.*

(52y, M, vc)   *Performance stress (anxiety and stage fright) is like carsickness. Everyone says: 'You'll grow out of it!' But I jolly well didn't! It's there! Maybe some people can cope with it better than others. There are times when it's worse and I have to deal with it. But, it's the way you handle it that matters; whether it be medication, drugs, or Alcohol. In my experience, I am not sure that it changes with age. In fact, if anything, it can get worse. It has to do with individual concerts; sometimes you want to give a good concert on the day, and you have pressure on yourself. There are other times you're at ease; you just go in and do the job well. I don't think it is age-related. People can think themselves into a crisis whether they're 20 or 50+ [years old]. But, as a player gets older they just deal with it differently. Different from what they would have done when they were younger. When I joined, the afternoon Pint [of beer] was a given. Now, consumption of Alcohol during the day, or before a concert, is an absolute 'No-No'! This has changed significantly, and not just in this Orchestra. That also applies to all sorts of boisterous behaviour. We used to be allowed to smoke in rehearsals—now you can't even smoke in the building!*

(55y, M, db)   *When I auditioned I found myself suffering from 'excitement'; Performance Anxieties didn't seem to go away as I gained more experience with age. It is interesting that you don't think anyone else has the same thing as you. It is a traumatic experience and so you don't share or talk about it. Perhaps, it is a fear that you are not going to be good enough. Or perhaps, that you will make a mistake and be blacklisted. From this fear of making a mistake you can lose self-confidence. I did have auditions when I was a student that were better. But some audition experiences were worse; in some my hands jittered. But, I never took medication (pharmaceuticals). I believe that Performance Anxieties are emotional; a form of inferiority, feeling that something bad can happen to you.*

6

Music Performance Considerations for Positive Ageing Among Orchestra Players

6.1 Introduction

The fourth topic of discussion in the single two-hour interview session considered music-performance skills. See Chapter 1, section 1.6.3.1, Table 1.2, Theme IV. The participating players were asked to contemplate the ill effects of ageing on various aspects of music performance, such as: music expressivity and structural communication, musical competence and technical considerations (e.g., control and maintenance for playing in tune, playing in time, articulation, sight-reading, music analysis, and interpretation), as well as dealing with repertoire (e.g., a restricted repertoire pool and learning new contemporary music), adaptation to Conductors' interpretation and demands, one's position in the Orchestra, opportunities for playing as a Soloist and in smaller Chamber Ensembles, and achieving one's musical potential. As was the case in the previous topics of discussion (i.e., Chapters 3–5), the players were asked to speak generally on the current theme, as well as to specifically focus on the possibility that age-related declines do affect musicians in areas related to music abilities and/or their music-performance skills.

6.2 Abilities and Skill Set

6.2.1 Music Skills and Reaching One's Potential

For the most part, the Orchestra players spoke about the more general topics of music performance, and distinguished between music *abilities* and music-performance *skills*. They wholeheartedly believed that there was nothing to talk about, as ageing has no effect at all on music abilities! Nevertheless, regarding one's music-performance skill set, an issue that did often surface was: *weakened tone colour*. Almost all of the players were quite sure that they are even better musicians now, and hence superior music performers, than when they were young(er). Their depiction of 'younger' times was often 20 or 30 years earlier. The players perceived that not only were they more competent as far as rhythm (time) and intonation (pitch) are concerned, but that they were also far more proficient with synchronous music analysis in real time which subsequently leads them to higher levels of understanding and interpretation. Undoubtedly, being at an old(er) age

Seasoned Musicians Playing Beyond the 5th Decade. Warren Brodsky, Oxford University Press. © Oxford University Press (2025).
DOI: 10.1093/9780198956501.003.0006

having accumulated great experience even leads to further learning of newer materials in a much more expedient manner. Finally, the players conveyed a feeling that as they aged they became all the more sensitive, communicative, expressive, and articulate with the music they performed.

Yet, players did misperceive the concept of 'musical potential'. The idea of *achieving one's potential* within the Orchestra vocation was far too vague for them to grasp! Several wondered if the intention was the 'music' itself. Or, does the concept mean that there might still be room for improving one's music abilities and/or music-performance skill set? Or, perhaps the concept of reaching one's potential reflects *moving further* within the profession (i.e., onwards and upwards within the Orchestra). For the most part, it seems that understanding how one achieves one's occupational potential reflects several parameters:

a) Orchestra Membership (e.g., moving from an amateur Orchestra, to a semi-professional Orchestra, to a professional Orchestra)
b) Employment Conditions (e.g., moving from serving as an occasional extra-reliever, to a part-time freelancer, to a permanent full-time contract player)
c) Orchestra Position (e.g., moving from the backrow Rank-&-File players, to a Sub-Leader, to a Principal Section Leader)
d) Orchestra Placement (e.g., transitioning from a 3rd Desk position, to a 2nd Desk position, to a 1st Desk position)
e) Orchestra Section (e.g., moving from the 2nd Violin section, to the 1st Violin section).

All players agreed that the Orchestra is indeed a hierarchical organization whereby the higher ranks direct the lower ranks. But, unlike any other grade-based institution, the ranks of Orchestra membership are not in the least awarded on the basis of tenure superiority or years of experience (which somewhat reflects age), but rather are based on applied abilities and performance proficiencies (which are traditionally seen as related to talents and skills). Therefore, Orchestra musicians do not necessarily aspire to reaching higher levels of actualizing their potential as do so many other persons in other vocations. As can be seen below in one vignette, players are sometimes simply relieved to be, and hence remain, *small potatoes*! But yet, using the same metaphor, they still aspire to be: *the best damn potatoes one could possibly serve on a dinner plate*! It is interesting to see that one player openly and explicitly conveyed her feelings of having reached her peak as a Symphony Orchestra player at age 61. Accordingly, there is no more that she can achieve, and therefore her sole concern now is simply to safeguard her current talents and proficiencies.

(30y, F, vn)   *Among older players there's less work-satisfaction. They're much less motivated and less involved in their music performance. Maybe when you've played the same piece five times, it doesn't have the same thrill that it did the first time. You'd probably hear greater enthusiasm from a younger player. Yet, younger players may not actually produce as good of a product, in the sense of an Orchestral product. Because there are very subtle (String) sounds, and ways of playing in an Orchestra that younger players aren't particularly taught to play.*

(40y, F, vn)   *When I consider the ageing process on musical aspects, I think all of it gets better! It's all experience—if you've done it before then it's better! Like what you put into the music—interpretation and expression—and being able to live up to what you feel is your musical potential, self-confidence. Those definitely get better. Because as you experience more things in your life, you become more complex. As when you have more depth as a human being, it goes into the music. But also, you know how to make an accent; you know what sounds good, and what doesn't sound good.*

(52y, M, db)   *I don't feel that my interpretation has changed as I've gotten older. It could be that it's even gotten better because of experience. Perhaps I feel the phrases, because I've played a lot of phrases that are similar. I feel that I express myself in the Orchestra the same as when I was younger. Sometimes, I play just the notes. But when I play Solo there is much more expression. I don't think I have reached my musical potential. I think there could be more. The truth is that as time goes on, I feel more that I'll never reach it. That doesn't sadden me; I think that's life!*

(53y, M, vn)   *I do think my musical abilities become better as I age; but these are not the same as my skills. I understand abilities as: to listen, to hear, to comprehend, to interpret, and to analyse. I listen better now than when I was a young 25 [year-old]. Also, my understanding of music, to see the structure of music, is so much better now. I don't think this is only because of getting older, or by becoming more mature. It's also experience!*

(55y, F, fl)   *I think as I get older I get better at the musical things, such as musical competence and musical expressivity. Not sure about Sight-Reading. What does musical potential mean?*

(55y, M, bn)   *I think the musical aspects of playing in an Orchestra become easier with age. Things like interpretation and keeping time; these are the more specific musical aspects of making music. I even feel that my intonation is better than it ever was. I've learnt more about my instrument. Sometimes when I sit next to somebody else I think that his intonation has completely failed—but he's the same age as I am.*

(57y, F, vc)   *In my opinion, as we age we become even more musical. With age you become more sensitive, you can feel deeper levels of musical expression. But that is really only if you still love it!*

(61y, F, vn)   *I think that musical expression and musical communication become better with ageing. The more experience, the better it is! It is also easier to learn new music; more experience means better understanding of the text. Also, more experience contributes to a player's understanding of a Conductor. As far as 'potential' is concerned, I feel that now is the furthest I can go. Whatever music skills I have achieved (by 55 years of age) is all that I can achieve. There is no further potential. I have reached the peak. However, that doesn't mean it can't be maintained. So, my current job is to retain whatever I have.*

6.2.2 Orchestral Skill Set and Reaching Potential

The players were asked to refocus their thoughts from more general aspects about music ability and skill to a specific outlook on playing in a Symphony Orchestra. After all, most Orchestra musicians admit that their set of tangible Orchestra-specific skills are not those associated with *playing the right notes at the right time*. Those skills are a given! There is no player in any Orchestra who would have received an offer with a full-time contract to join a professional Symphony Orchestra had they not undergone several auditions and trial periods in which they consistently and repeatedly demonstrated themselves to be a highly proficient expert music performer with absolute control over their musical instrument.

(39y, F, cl)   *Many players say that they had to learn how to be an Orchestra player. That is, when they came out of school [Music College] they had a very different mindset. And there's certainly something to be said about differences between 'joining' an Orchestra and 'being' in an Orchestra. And I'm not just talking about the Tutti players, but rather also about the Principals (where it's also very different than being a Soloist). I mean you're collaborating with everybody sitting around you. That requires a certain openness. Not just in how you're listening, but in your whole personality. You need to be willing to work and blend with other people. It is very different from standing at the front [as a Soloist].*

(47y, M, trb)   *What makes the difference between a good [Solo] Trombonist, and a good Orchestra Trombone player? You have to think as an Orchestra player; that is, you have to think in group sound. Especially as a Trombone player, you're not responsible very much for Soloistic stuff. You're more responsible for a whole group sound. It's not important to play super-super-loud because most of the time the Trombones are even louder than everyone else—except the Trumpets. It is very important to play very, very soft. So, you have to get a good mixture. And most of the things we have to play in the Orchestra you already know anyway; you needed them as orchestral excerpts for auditions. I mean you are technically able to do an Orchestra job. So, I think it's very important to understand: there is a difference between being a good musician, and being a good Orchestra player. Now that doesn't mean that Orchestra players aren't good musicians! The other side is there are great Soloists. I teach in the [Music] University and there are great Trombone players there. But when they start playing with a Piano [accompanist] they have to learn it's a Duet. Yes, they are the Soloist. But they have to react to the Piano; when to start, when to breathe, how to go on, what tempo to play, etc. Very often they forget that there's a Duet going on. You can feel if a player isn't able to blend with the Piano, or just going on, and doesn't care. They may even be in the same synchrony, but they don't blend. So, what I'm saying is that a good musician will know how to play with other people. Just being with them at the same place, in the same time, won't necessarily [mean] blend with them.*

(58y, M, va)   *Being an Orchestra musician is a totally different profession than being a Soloist. Not that one is better. In general all music performers do the same thing. But what is special about the Orchestra profession is learning to listen to what is going on around you in order not to stand out too much; it involves being patient and to compromise. This is not the same for Soloists where they can take the executive lead, and do not have to fit in with others. Essentially, that means Orchestra players have to have a specific personality type. The problem is that we do not train Orchestra musicians in the Music Academy, but rather we train musicians to be Soloists.*

(59y, M, fl/picc)   *I am aware that others seem to feel that all of a sudden, a young virtuoso Music Academy graduate comes along and pushes everyone of the same instrument aside. But it is really not like that. Playing in an Orchestra is much more than just having an excellent technique. One can be an amazing Soloist, but the Orchestra requires special performance techniques. Knowing your part and position within the section is not as easy [as one tends to think it is], and you have to know how to fit in. Perhaps an Orchestra player can be a good Soloist, but a great Soloist cannot necessarily be a good Orchestra player.*

6.2.2.1 Sectional Membership

The first subtopic to come up was seeing oneself more as an associate collaborator (e.g., a bandmate team-member in a section) than as an individual musician Soloist. Many players reminisced about their years of music-performance training. Some underwent training during early childhood at Music Conservatories taking part in numerous Recitals, and later in music-specialist High schools, summer camps (consisting of endless competitions and contests), a Music College or Music Academy involving a never-ending number of presentations, performances, Concerts, and then further auditions for a position as a music performer. All of these were under the auspices of becoming and being a world-class Soloist. The biographical accounts of the current sample were detailed earlier (see Chapter 2, section 2.2.1). But today, the players assert that *fitting in*, fulfilling one's part of the

music score, and being aware of what the other members and instruments are contributing to the overall collective sound, are of the utmost importance. Finally, the
adeptness of taking directions from others (e.g., Section Leaders, Principals, and
a Conductor/Music Director)—in an effort to realize the best interpretation of the
music being performed—is simply a must! Yet, this latter statement is also somewhat
contentious among the Seasoned Musicians.

(36y, F, tpt)   *I don't know if age has affected my playing. It might be experience! I know I've got better
at balancing the chords; you know, the middle part of chords. I'm not so bothered about
what sort of accolades I get. Whereas when I first joined I think I was a bit preoccupied
about having to prove myself—to be the best! Now, I'm there more for the group. So, I
probably was a bit more of a 'maverick' at the beginning trying to prove what I can do.*

(43y, F, vn)   *I was just thinking if I could remember how I used to play. I first got the job when
I was 23 [years old]. I think I've definitely learnt how to react to different Conductors better now than 20 years ago. It's very different being at a Music College
and playing with those Orchestras [compared to] being in a professional Orchestra.
I think [it takes time to] get used to dealing with different quirks of some Conductors. It can get really annoying having to know how to interpret the beat. I mentor
students who come from College; they sit with me at my desk, and it's really interesting how almost all of them have trouble playing as part of a corporate group.
One of the problems is that all students everywhere in the world are trained to be
Soloists. There is no Orchestral training. I suppose we all think that if [you] can't
be a Soloist [then you can] settle for doing the Orchestra thing. It's always been like
that!*

(47y, F, vn)   *My ability of intonation and playing in time is easier now. I know I said that the
younger players would have a better tone, but they wouldn't play in time. Some just
play too early. They don't look too much at the 1st Desk player. Younger players don't
fit in as much. I don't feel my age at all. I think I just love it like I loved it 20 years
ago. Am I playing like I did 20 years ago? No! I think I'm playing better. I can read
and react faster, and see what's important. I feel that as I get older my interpretation, analysis, and Sight-Reading gets better! I understand the piece better, and it's
easier.*

(47y, M, trb)   *What is difficult in the beginning [of an Orchestra career] is to react to the pulse of the
Conductor. [The scores say] where to play, but what the Orchestra does is a different
thing. In the beginning you're always early or always late. When the Conductor goes like
this [demonstrates a downbeat by waving arms] it really is like a 16th note afterwards.
It has to be, because otherwise, if you play right on time, he has no chance to show
where he wants to go. So, he always conducts in advance; you have this millisecond
of space like a reaction time. The Conductor is always before the beat, and we have
to play on the beat, so there's always a lag. It just happens. Nobody decides that. It is
tradition! Some Orchestras are before, some are after, some are faster, some are slower.
You go with the breath of your colleagues, you don't go with the Conductor. You learn
that as you go on.*

(52y, M, vc)   *I don't think there are musical aspects one has to consider as you get older. I wouldn't
give any younger person advice about music interpretation. But then, when we have
youngsters, there are a lot of times when I might say: 'You need to do that a bit shorter'
(because they have played 'too long' and they don't hear when everyone else has played
it 'short').*

(54y, F, vc)   *Some of the real skills for Orchestra playing are so subtle, and not about whether you
can play the notes. An Orchestra player needs to be able to fit in, and to be aware in
a way that Soloists can't necessarily measure. It's just an approach of corporate unity.
One of the reasons that I wanted to stay so long [in this Orchestra] is that there is a
level of quality and depth that you don't always find in every Orchestra. I want to do
my job as well as I possibly could. There is a sense of responsibility. I sit at the front; it
is my job! But there's also people at the back doing their job incredibly well. We work
alongside each other.*

(54y, M, va)   *Have I reached my maximal potential? I know that my potential is limited. For instance, it could be very difficult for me to play a Concerto. But on the other hand, I haven't given up improving [as far as being a player] in the Orchestra field. I thought my problem at rehearsals was simply keeping up the attention. I thought sloppy intonation in rehearsals was a result from me not paying attention. But now I do more checking [of my part] before the concerts. I don't just come onstage without playing a bit—I mean practising before the concert in each performance Hall [venue] itself!*

6.2.2.2 The Wall of Sound

The second subtopic to surface in the discussion of this theme was about the experience of sitting among 80 Orchestra players listening to that collective sound! One can, and often does, lose their sense of aural identity. Namely, their sonic self-image that has accompanied them from the earliest of childhood memories, throughout their mature periods of late adulthood. It is masked! There is a 'wall of sound'.[1] This is all the more apparent for Tutti section players. Some saw the issue as differences between the sections, or as contrasts between Soloist-Principals (such as Wind players) *versus* Rank-&-File players (such as String Tutti players). Players refer to idiosyncratic and stereotypical temperaments and performance styles that have been noted over time as 'mythical portrayals' of particular instrumentalists. Accordingly, many portray Principals as those behaving in an emotionally outgoing exhibitionist manner compared to the more reserved Tutti players. Actually, this has been the topic of study of Kemp (1996) who deconstructed the component constituents of personality in order to examine factors such as introversion, independence, sensitivity, anxiety, and gender roles among musicians. Then in his effort to reverse-engineer these factors, Kemp reconstructed the characteristic profiles of instrumental Orchestra players, Keyboard players, Vocalist-Singers, Conductors, Composers, and Music Teachers.

(41y, M, vc)   *I think it's quite possible to lose yourself when you play among 80 musicians in an Orchestra. Because you're 1/80. It is even more so in the String section where you are a Rank-&-File [player]. That can be a positive thing 'cause you can also hide among them, whereas a Principal Solo player (e.g., Woodwinds, Brass) can't because if they don't play there's no one else there. Technically a String player might not play a few bars if they're not sure what to play, but they're covered by the others. On the other hand, because you're all moving as a group, there's a feeling that if you're even a millisecond early or late to everybody else in the group, then that's very very obvious. That wouldn't matter too much if you were a Soloist; people would probably think that your performance phrasing was an articulate emotive way of playing. Yet, to us it would seem like a massive event. People can get quite stressed by that! The number of times I've seen people come off stage who say: 'Oh my God, did you hear that?' To which I would say: 'Well No! I was sitting right behind you, and didn't hear a thing.'*

(47y, M, vc)   *I think temperament has got a lot to do with Solo work versus the Orchestra as an approach to performance. The same can be said about performing as a lifestyle. I think if you got any chance of being a Soloist, you have to be gregarious, and a bit of a show-*

---

[1] The 'Wall of Sound' is a music production formula developed by American record producer Phil Spector at Gold Star Studios in the 1960s. He orchestrated massive teams of session musicians, latter known as 'The Wrecking Crew'.

off. I [also] do solo work. I'm sitting up as Principal Cello. So I don't mind people hearing me play. But I do that in order to maintain my levels within the Orchestra; not because I get a massive buzz out of it. Obviously, you've got to have the ability to sustain a career as a Soloist. It is temperament!

(47y, M, trb)   *What I'm saying is that to be a musician is a different thing than being an Orchestra player. To have an Orchestra routine is totally different than to be a great Soloist. So I'm saying that you could be a great musician but a poor Orchestra player. I think the most important thing for an Orchestra player, and it doesn't matter what instrument, is to be able to be a team player. With some people that gets better with age. But some people never learn. They always feel like a Soloist, and they say: 'OK, this is where I play, this is the one, and you [i.e., the Conductor] better follow me because I don't care.' It is personality! And perhaps sometimes you want people like that—those that are arrogant—at least on stage in a performance. For example, a Principal Horn may behave like: 'I have to play now, and I don't care about blending. This is very difficult, and I have to play.' The Conductor will then follow [the Horn] and the rest [of us] will follow [the Conductor].*

(49y, F, vn)   *I don't think the music itself becomes harder as we age! If the player does their work, then: 'No!' I don't understand why they say (or feel) that when a player reaches 60 [years old] they should retire! When I first came to this Orchestra there was a player who sat next to me. He was 70 years old. He played with great intonation (pitch precision) and was always in time (rhythmic precision). All except his colour! I mean, as a player you don't hear yourself, your own individual sound. We try to fit in and create a collective sound. The sound for Mozart is much different than the sound for Debussy. So essentially, we lose our own personal sound in favour for the collective one. But you must also learn to get it back by practising at home. So, I am saying he lost his own sound. God willing I will be able to play like him when I will reach 70! Today, my main concern is just maintenance!*

(60y, F, vc)   *We have to take more responsibility. As far as expression goes, that certainly gets better as you get older. Sometimes the Orchestra prevents me from expressing as much as I can in the music. Even though I am a Section Leader, I still can't stick out; I'm not supposed to make myself celebrated! Sometimes I can give more when I play the solos. But playing in the Orchestra is collective! It gets artistically better as I mature.*

Tutti players often claimed to be content as a section player, and were highly proud of the group effort to create the 'wall of sound'. They see their contribution as one to strengthen the 'wall' for the overall goodness of the Orchestra. They work to create, and then recreate, the same collective sound for each and every piece, in each and every Concert performance, at each and every venue Hall—near and far.

(54y, M, va)   *I am a Tutti player. I'd like it to be more, but there is an advantage of being 'small potatoes'! There's less tension. There should be five Violas, but right now we're only four. That makes it more challenging, and keeps my interest high. [Often] the Violas are divided; two play one [line] and the other two [play another line]. I do accept the fact that while I'm good, there are a lot of others who are considerably better. As I get older, it does become more difficult to step up and take over as the Section Leader which requires me to play Solos; but on the other hand, I like the challenge!*

(54y, F, vc)   *I like to talk about the very, very high level of my section. But, the section is only a part of the Orchestra. Your responsibility is not only to support the people of your section as that's the sound that you represent, but it is also the sound we bring to the Orchestra. It is not you and the Orchestra as a section, [but rather] you in the Orchestra. These are inexplicably, undeniably, totally linked: What I do; What I give; What I'm part of; and the Person I am. Yet, there is a possibility that someone could be very happy with their section, but not with the Orchestra.*

(60y, F, vc)   *If I were a Tutti player sitting further back, would I feel different? I guess the question is: How much of dealing with ageing has to do with Orchestra position? I do think it might be more difficult to deal with problems of ageing sitting among the Tutti. But when you are a Leader [like me], you naturally take more responsibility, and you have to be at the top [of your game]. I feel that there are people who are also in my group that are less reactive in their playing; they [take] less initiative when playing, and sometimes none at all. They put themselves on my shoulders, and do not exist by themselves. So, I imagine that ageing will affect them differently. Being a Principal Section Leader was very helpful in keeping me young.*

6.2.2.3 Conductors, Management, and Power Structure

Many Orchestra players stated that the 'Conductor' is a highly potent and potential component leading to severe emotional reactions. In the vignettes below, players mention that by ageing they have finally been able to clear away any pressures they previously had in which they felt compelled to prove to themselves and others that they were proficient. Now, they are far more open and emotionally available to work alongside a Conductor-Music Director or even an external Guest Conductor. Often Guest Conductors come steadfast to the podium, insisting that they wish to try a new approach that reflects their more personal preferred artistic interpretation. Yet, many young(er) players outright claim that it is the old(er) musicians who are far too set in their ways to do so; those players refuse to adapt to such directives. The truth is that many highly experienced Seasoned Musicians did express the notion that through their abundant years of service in the orchestra, they simply know *what is best for the performance*! Hence perhaps such an unyielding, and on some level even obstinate, stance simply has to do with experience. But the other aspect may be simply one of perceived 'social leadership'. That is, the long-standing members of the group, usually referred to as the *old guard*, see themselves as a band of legionnaires, unwilling to accept alternatives in their effort to preserve the vocation and the music traditions—as were passed on to them by previous generations of musicians from the same Orchestra.

The players also voiced a notion that Management and Orchestral executives have become more business-compliant. They more often implement policies for selecting repertoires, programming, Guest Conductors, Soloists, and even Music Directors, as based on economic considerations rather than on values such as music quality, artistic excellence, and cultural significance.

(30y, F, vn)	*Some days my awareness is pretty good. On the days that a [Guest] Conductor makes us repeat something more times than we really need to, I feel bored. I don't believe Orchestras should be an 'educational project', or that we be used as a training platform [for young Conductors]. The way things run, whether [that is] because of a Conductor or the Leader, will always lead to resentment, disillusionment, and resistance. But for the most part, these kind of emotions are not seen among the younger players.*
(36y, F, tpt)	*I think, for me, that musical aspects of music performance got better with age. I'm not so preoccupied [anymore] with what I want to fulfil. So, I've learned to adapt a little bit. It used to confuse me quite a bit when I first joined at age 23. It used to quite frustrate me that I never seemed to be able to fulfil the musical wishes of the Conductor. Now it seems a lot easier. I'm not so caught up in it so much anymore. I seem to be [playing along] with [the Conductor] most of the time. I know exactly what they want from my role.*

(41y, M, vc)   *I've been doing this for 20 years. I'm not new to all of this. And I've got a little bit of experience behind my opinions. So, why should we listen to somebody [e.g., a Guest Conductor] that doesn't really know anything? I think the older you get, the power structure in an Orchestra where 80 people are being told what to do by one person, becomes more and more [potent for conflicts]—unless that one person has something worthwhile to say, and says it in the right way! The older you get, the more frustrated you get of being bossed around. It doesn't matter whether the Conductor is a young kid or an old guy. If they don't know anything, you can sense that there is a tide against them. And I find that I've become extremely difficult as I get older. My attitude has hardened and I'm less tolerant!*

(44y, F, vn)   *I think as you get older, players are less adaptive to the Conductor's instructions. Younger players adapt better while the older ones are less adaptive to the Conductor's changes. The older players are more set in their ways, and a bit jaded with their attitude towards the Conductor. Whereas you should be excited when a new person comes in. But, as soon as they put a foot in the wrong place, the older players are making jokes at the back of the Orchestra. The Conductor is not really aware that players may be drawing cartoons or sending text messages. For example, one day we got this Austrian Guest Composer [as a Conductor]. We thought he would be very young guy, but when he walked in he looked to be in his late 80s. That sweet little old guy had a much younger, well-preserved, blond wife who looked about 65. Within minutes jokes were going around. I guess it's cruel, but it made everybody laugh. You get that with older players—it wouldn't happen with younger players.*

(54y, M, va)   *Interpreting the Conductor's demands does not become more difficult as I age. Some people might be more set in their ways. They may think: 'I don't care what he wants, I will do it like this.' As an Orchestra musician I have to be open to different things, all kinds of different approaches. Variety should be more interesting for an Orchestra musician who has more experience. Greater repertoires and more challenging pieces are not as frequent; the Orchestra is rather limited financially at the moment. [The management] has to be careful with the budget. The more interesting pieces require a higher payment for performances; more Royalty fees. I know that Conductors choose pieces (older versus newer) according to Royalty fees. For example, it is expensive to play Stravinsky or Shostakovich, whereas Ravel is easier to perform (because he died at age 37). Lots of music is gradually getting out of the Royalty cycle. It is usually 70 years: 35 years of Royalties for the Composer, and then the inheritors get another 35 years of Royalties. That is why Mozart lives forever; not only because of his inspiration, but also because his music is free!*

(54y, M, cl/bcl)   *Quite recently a Conductor came in with a completely unknown Orchestra piece that we're recording. It was a big famous Conductor. So I thought I'd better have a look at the score. It was for Bass Clarinet in [the key of] A written in a Bass Clef. It was horrendously difficult to just know what note you were supposed to be playing. As simple as that! And some of it went on continuous for a full page of Arpeggios. I had to write some of it out, so I could more or less play it. The Conductor obviously had performed it somewhere, and had a bad time with whoever was playing Bass Clarinet. So, he just said to me: 'OK, Bass Clarinet, come in here: Play that!' I played about three bars of it. He said: 'Could you just play that.' I played a few more bars. Then he said: 'No, no, no! Keep going. Play it all!' If I hadn't looked at it previously, there was no way, no matter how good you were, no matter who you were. No one could have been able to play it from Sight-Reading! I could have said to him: 'I'm sorry, I'll get that for tomorrow. Give me some time and I'll practise it.' But not necessarily would he have been happy. Yet he would have had to accept that. We do get a Conductor now and again who says: 'No, I want to hear it now! Work it out, now.' But I mean, there's no point! In an Orchestra like this one, the players would have just revolted. In two cases we've actually got rid of a Conductor saying: 'No, we're not being treated like that.' Especially since some Guest Conductors are here for a week; they're just passing through. They can just make you feel like you are nothing, and that feeling lasts the whole rest of the year. That can ruin your mental stability.*

(55y, M, db)   *One problem is that most players, who have played the repertoire several times before, feel they know the pieces better than the Conductor. They don't allow themselves to flow with someone trying to give a new interpretation of the piece. Perhaps it has to do with temperament (of some players). Do these players get burned out sooner than those who can flow more easily? Perhaps it has to do with a grudge, contempt, disregard, or even insult.*

(60y, F, vc)   *Do I become better at interpreting the Conductor and the music itself as I become older? [The truth is, that] I don't interpret the Conductor, but I am always connected with the music. It's not really about adapting to the Conductor or what he's saying. This is not my utmost goal. The moment I play in the Orchestra I try to fulfil the music according to the Conductor. But it's always about music! Sometimes I correct the Conductor through my own playing! That means that many times we have Conductors who are not as good as others. There were those who allowed us to play as the high-level professional artistic musicians we are. Yet sometimes, we do play in spite of them—as best as we can!*

(60y, M, cl)   *I have spent years playing great music repertoire conducted by Masters with great Solo artists on the platform. But, nowadays because of budget cuts [there are only] second-grade pieces, second-rate Conductors, and second-tiered artists. Subsequently, the actual motivation to perform, and the spirituality of the occasion, has been drastically cut down. Music doesn't give anything anymore. Look, in 1975, when I was only 25 years old, I first played the 'Emperor' Concerto [Piano Concerto No. 5, E♭ major, Op. 73, written in 1809 by German composer Ludwig van Beethoven, 1770–1827]. The guy who played piano was Arthur Rubinstein [1887–1982, Polish-American virtuosi pianist]. It was something that was meant to be bigger than life. But today, the feeling is that the 'Emperor' is just another standard selection; it is just another regular piece of the repertoire. That angers me to no end as we are no longer interested in creating Art. Rather, we all let it go by as part of 'survival' [i.e., keeping the Orchestra floating, and making it through to pension]. This week we're are playing a light programme of selected pieces from Broadway musicals. The problem with these Pop-oriented programmes is in many cases the Conductors are also Pop-related personas. They have no idea how to conduct an Orchestra; they wave their hands, and mostly get confused about their right versus left hand. Sometimes they drag the tempo down; we all need to watch the Leader who takes over keeping time by giving entrances with his head. Also, many of these type of programmes involve a Review Rhythm-Section; those are basically Pop players who do not know how to play with an Orchestra [e.g., Drummers, Electric Guitarists, Electric Bass Guitarists, Saxophonists]. This week there's a guy who usually plays Piano for Theatrical productions (either as a Soloist or with a small Combo); his entrances are always too early, and his Ritardando are always as if he suddenly gets to a junction and slams on the breaks. We have played this programme in the past with the same Conductor; the management likes it because [his name on the ad posters] sells tickets. But, he always brings his own hand-notated scores with his arrangements of the pieces; they always have the same kind of mistakes on them which we corrected in rehearsals last time but he never corrected them for the next time. So, we have developed a sort of cynical (black) humour response to the management who have given the podium to someone who can't take charge of an Orchestra nor bring out the music. But we know that the audience buys tickets for this level of musical performance. That is what the management eventually wants! Not a musical art form of the highest possible level, but rather economic success of substandard programmes. The same goes for the Music Directors of Orchestras; today management looks for someone whose name and branding will be great for public relations and marketing.*

6.2.2.4 Desk Partners

The final subject to surface in discussion about ageing-related effects on music performance was unforeseen. Actually, this subtopic was not even among the issues listed for Theme IV (see Chapter 1, Table 1.2) which was employed as a guide for the interview sessions. The topic was a highly emotional aspect of Orchestra membership. To my knowledge, this topic has never been mentioned in the academic scientific literature about Orchestral players and/or their Lifestyle. The subtopic refers to *desk partners*. The issue relates not only to compatibility of personalities, functionality of cooperation, tonal fusion, and articulatory blend but also to emotional longevity and loyalty. All of these impact other aspects of ageing in the sense of growing old(er) together over years of Orchestral performance activity. Having to deal with the loss of one's desk partner may eventually occur with time. The players note that having to deal with this kind of loss is highly traumatic! An Orchestra player could lose their desk partner if they relocate to another Orchestra—or when they retire after more than 30 years of service. There is the possibility of an unexpected passing (death) due to illness. While it was not the main undertone of many players, a few did raise the possibility that the loss of their desk partner could cause them to consider withdrawing from the Orchestra themselves—albeit such actions may not be so viable for most players below the age of 50 years old.

(54y, F, vc)   *In the [Orchestra] organization you come in and see the same people day in and day out. I've sat next to my desk partner for 30 years. If I didn't have a good relationship with the person sitting next to me, enjoying what that person contributed, it would've absolutely coloured everything about my job. I'm closer to that person for more hours a day than my own partner—or his wife. I am not saying here that such a closeness affects certain types of boundaries or things like that. We are both very very lucky to have each other, and I feel appreciated by him very much so. And if my [desk] partner leaves, to go to another Orchestra, it would obviously change my job radically. Not that I couldn't go on. I would have to deal with whatever [i.e., whoever] came along. I don't think it's possible that someone would just stop playing because their desk partner left. I mean it depends on the state of your career, what your responsibilities are, what your financial situation is. I would be very, very upset if I had to continue my job after he decided to leave. I would miss his presence, contribution, and playing. But, it is not the same as a divorce, or like mourning someone who passed on. But, as far as another partner, it's just that it takes time to make relationships. A lot of things come with experience. I was only in the Orchestra a year before he joined. You know 30 years ago when you're in your 20s, is not like I am now in my 50s. So, your whole wheel of life and life experience is very different to what it was then. The way I view relationships, as the way I viewed everything then, is very different to how I see them now.*

(60y, F, vc)   *I think a very important human aspect of playing in Orchestra is that it requires a good level of communication with the same neighbour of the same stand [i.e., desk partner]. A permanent challenge is to make it harmonic, and to do the utmost in honour [of the music and composer]. We need to coordinate with the 1st [Principal] players [and desk partner] all kinds of aspects of the playing. [Music performance] is not something natural; it's something you have to work for and try to analyse how to behave. This is a very positive aspect you learn in an Orchestra over the years.*

(60y, M, bn)   *I absolutely adore the guy sitting next to me. Twenty-five years he's sat next to me. How on earth he's coped with me for so long I don't know. And yet, you know, he can play fantastically. Maybe we over-accommodate each other all the time. We're always: 'OK, you do that, and I'll do that.' So if I decided not to do that quite so much, I'd be a little bit truer to myself. I know it puts him under stress when I don't play the right notes in the right order. So, perhaps I'd better get that sorted out rather than looking after him. But of course, I'd look after him as he looks after me!*

6.3 Discussion and Summary

This chapter dealt with music-performance aspects of the vocation that possibly need to be reflected upon when considering the issue of ageing. The participating players were resolute that an orchestra musician's skill set is absolutely not solely their ability to play the notes per se, but rather their capability to fit in. First to coordinate with their desk partner, then with their section, and then subsequently with the whole Orchestra. Of utmost importance is the ability to blend in an effort to create a group sound.

(64y, M, tpt)   *Speaking to a younger player I would say: 'You wouldn't have gotten into this Orchestra if you didn't have the skills. But, you won't be able to last long on your musical and performance skills alone. You have to learn other behaviours. One of these is learning to adapt, to accept that it's not just you in the Orchestra, it's not just your opinion that makes the difference. To play within a section, to raise the collective, to make the performance achieve a higher level, you have to accept what everybody else is saying (e.g., the Leaders). If you don't have that kind of flexibility, or if you're not willing to accept [others' input], that will cause you emotional strife. You may even have to leave the profession!' To be a good Orchestra player you have to know what is going on in the other sections. There are players who are good players but they just can't fit in. Actually, I wouldn't say 'can't', but for one reason or another they just 'don't' [or 'won't']. Maybe it is personality or character. There was a wonderful Violinist who played in the Orchestra many years ago. The guy was a great player; he had a wonderful sound. The problem, though, was that you heard him! He didn't play within his section. You could hear his section, and you could also hear his sound. And while his phrasing was magnificent, [it] did not necessarily fit with the section. Nor did the section always fit with him. And he wasn't the Principal player who would've been in a position to say: 'OK, do it my way.' He stayed in the Orchestra for maybe a year. As a 1st Woodwind or Brass player this kind of thing is more acceptable (because we stand out anyhow). But as a section Tutti player?*

As seen in the chapter, the players related to flexibility—an awareness about cohesiveness for the section and the Orchestra. Yet many do see that this essential mindset is at the expense of giving up one's self-perceived expectations of achieving one's potential. Most players talk about the costs of staying in the same orchestra for many years. On the one hand much effort is placed in practice-related efforts to maintain skills, but on the other hand they subsequently remain in the same place at the same level that was offered them with their initial contract. The truth is that few players ever move forward and upward in an Orchestra. Rank-&-File players seldom become Sub-Leaders or Principals; few players ever move from a 4th desk to a 3rd desk or from a 2nd desk to a 1st desk. Rarely do players from the 2nd Violin section move to the 1st Violin section. Actually, the majority of players mention that after the age of 35, they would not even have been accepted for an audition in any other orchestra—except perhaps in their own current organization. Therefore, Orchestra musicians learn very early in their career path that they have little to aspire to as far as reaching higher levels of actualizing any potential beyond their initial tenured contract position.

Almost all players spoke about becoming a collaborator—a bandmate team-member in an Orchestra section. This ultimately means taking directions from others, including: Section Leaders, Principals, and Conductors. Much discussion—usually in the tone of an argumentative debate or disputed contention—centred around the Conductor. Especially Guest Conductors! In a Symphony Orchestra the Music Director is a far more important component to work life than is usually spoken about. For example, they serve several roles:

a) Figurehead who represents the Orchestra in a more symbolic way
b) Leader who guides and motivates the players to achieve the Orchestra's goals
c) Liaison who acts as a go-between the players on the inside, and the general public, National Arts NGOs, and wealthy donors on the outside.

As a professional manager, the Music Director-Conductor has to have great knowledge of the relevant principles, practices, and procedures required in the domain. They are responsible for achieving the objectives leading to completion of projects within the organization. This responsibility usually includes accountability for human, material, and financial resources allocated to the Orchestra. These concepts are clearly seen in the vignettes of the players.

(33y, M, va)   *If there was a really great concert, they'd say it was because of the Conductor. If the concert didn't go so well, they'd say it was because of the Orchestra. But it's neither way . . . it is the Conductor [in both conditions]! You get these Guest Conductors who could be really great people, or they could be real . . . (you know)! They sort of walk in as if they're your boss now, and you always have to say: 'Yes, Sir.' You'd could say my allegiance should be exclusively to the Principal Conductor because he's here for a long period of time; he is the Ambassador of our Orchestra. But some guy comes in for a piece, a day, or a week, and then behave like they are a 'Gift To Mankind'. I don't know any other type of organization where that happens. [The Orchestra] is a really strange set-up. But it has to be in order to work. The hierarchy is foremost you have a Principal Conductor; he's your boss. Then, all of a sudden because the Principal Conductor isn't there, you have to have someone else who's Leading. Our current Principal Conductor has been here for 10 years [usually contracts last 3–5 years], and he's just signed for another 5 years. That's a very long time. But he has his own ideas. He has got rid of people; he 'rocked the boat'. Ten years on, he's still very well respected, and the Orchestra is really strong. He's a great ambassador: he does the talk, he does the politics, he does the business (e.g., gets donations to keep the Orchestra going). And, he's an amazing musician! He has a very good idea about every piece that comes up. He brings in amazing Singers (that we wouldn't have access to otherwise). And, he gets us to give these very amazing performances.*

As stated earlier, the Conductor is a highly emotional component of a music performance career. All 80–100 players of a Symphonic Orchestra continually need to acclimatize, and adjust their performance exclusively for one sole personality. This is the ethos that they need to satisfy day after day, week after week, month after month, year after year! So, we might ask, as players age, does it become easier to forfeit their hard-earned knowledge gained through years of music-performance experience? Namely, with an expanded ripeness of expertise, do Symphony Orchestra musicians develop more mature attitudes and perspectives towards leadership and authority allowing for the presence of different (but equally worthy) artistic interpretations? Some players claim that as they age they feel they are more tolerant and compliant. But not all! For others, tensions seem to remain highly impassioned, and even dual-edged!

(53y, M, vn)   *I think my ability to adapt to the Conductor has gotten better as I got older. Yeah, I do think I'm a good Orchestra musician; all my Orchestra skills have all gotten better during my professional life. Even new repertoire is not more difficult for me to learn. I am just as flexible and open to new ideas as I was 25 years ago. For example, a Conductor might say: 'You should play without vibrato.' Some players don't like that. They would think: 'Don't tell me how to play, I've been doing this for 22 years!' I think the Conductor has a certain sound in their mind; it is our job to give this sound. I have no trouble with that. The Conductor's job is interpretation! Yet, it is true that when a young Conductor comes along, some players do say: 'Here's a young Conductor who's only 28 years young. What do they know about music? We can tell them how to play a Mozart or Beethoven symphony.' But, I do not necessarily think like that? Well . . . at least not at first! I'm always curious about a new Conductor. First I want to hear what they want. [But I do get] angry if we play something else than what is written in the score. I will ask: 'Does it have any meaning? Does the Composer want something specific that is not in the notes?' And I do expect the Conductor to know the difference. But, if I see they are surprised, then, I will have problems with the dirigent [conducting], as well as actually having less respect from that point on!*

(55y, M, bn)   *It is much easier now to understand, and adapt, to the Conductors' interpretations and demands. I'm much more open! I understand today that there are many ways to do something. So, it's much easier to adapt—because I can take what he wants and do it my way. In a sense I can find a way to play that should be acceptable to him and to me. Look, some Conductors ask for something and most players just think: I know better. Sometimes a young Conductor asks you to play in a certain way, and you think to yourself: This is really stupid. Then you have two choices: (a) You can say: 'Yes', and then keep on playing it your way anyway. Most likely the Conductor wouldn't even know the difference! They do have certain expectations that you're just gonna do it. Or: (b) There's a degree of how far I wanna go with a Conductor who I think is an idiot. So, I'll just 'overdo' what he wants—just to piss him off! And why not! Look: You want it short, then, I'll play it really short. If you want to be an idiot (because it really shouldn't be short), and you demand me to play short, then you're an idiot! So, I'll play it really, really, really short! I can do that! It is a whole game. This is definitely something that gets worse as you get older—especially because you're less patient, and more cynical. As much as I'd like to help young Conductors, and it's the right thing to do to help them get better, sometimes it's unbearable! Sometimes you wonder why are they standing in front of us. After all, we've played these pieces more times than the Conductor has even conducted them. An older Conductor would have done it many times, and therefore would've had a better idea of how it goes.*

7

Environmental and Organizational Considerations for Positive Ageing Among Orchestra Players

7.1 Introduction

The last two topics of discussion in the single 2-hour interview sessions were environmental and organizational considerations of music performance. The full list of 13 subtopics of the discussions was previously presented in Table 1.2, Themes V–VI (see Chapter 1, section 1.6.3.1). Among these were work environment, working conditions, orchestral position, and job security. Some of these topics have already surfaced previously (i.e., Chapters 3–6), for example, issues concerning score, the influence of work schedules, as well as travel. More detailed discussions about family, hierarchical ranking in the Orchestra, periodic evaluations of performance abilities, and managerial policy becoming more businesslike are mentioned below.

7.2 Performance-Related Environmental Considerations

7.2.1 Rehearsal Halls and Stage Platforms

Foremost, work environment issues were brought up. Players spoke about the Halls: the actual performance spaces and the stage platforms. The most common issues that surfaced included: eyesight (lighting), hearing (noise exposure), seating (chairs), and rest breaks (recess for toileting). The participating players were asked to relate to these aspects that perhaps become more problematic as they mature. Are these all considerations for ageing among Orchestra musicians? Some players claimed that such issues do not affect them at all. But others felt that over time they have succumbed to an ever-more increasing unsympathetic environment. They convey an understanding that perhaps the environment may not really be much more hard-hitting itself, but rather that as they aged they themselves have become more intolerant of the environment. Ageing ultimately means having to compromise on personal, professional, and artistic aspects of the daily milieu.

In general, poor lighting and inadequately printed scores seem to affect players' eyesight. Many musicians report wearing *reversed* bifocal or *inverted* progressive multifocal optical lenses whereby the top portion is used for the close reading of

Seasoned Musicians Playing Beyond the 5th Decade. Warren Brodsky, Oxford University Press. © Oxford University Press (2025).
DOI: 10.1093/9780198956501.003.0007

notation whereas the bottom portion is used for longer-distance observation of the Conductor. Many players also reveal that they have developed hearing losses subsequent to high-intensity exposure involving peak volumes and long overdosed durations of sound; referred to as Noise-Induced Hearing Loss (NIHL, see Behroozi & Luz, 1997; Chasin, 2006a; Einhorn, 2006; Hart et al., 1987)—specifically known among professional musicians as Music-Induced Hearing Loss (MIHL, see Chasin, 2006b; Eaton & Gillis, 2002; Emmerich et al., 2008; McBride et al., 1992; Woolford et al., 1988). Many players mention that they have tried earplugs to reduce sonic levels and extreme audio plateaus (using *ER* brand 'hearing protectors' with filter-caps decreasing intensities by −15dBs). But for the most part, the use of such protective measures during stage performances has been reported to be unsuccessful for Orchestra players. Yet, the topic is quite controversial because the literature has long ago claimed *ER15*s to be the most efficient means of cover (e.g., Chasin & Chong, 1992; Niquette, 2006; Santucci, 1990, 2006). Therefore, Orchestra managements and other institutions of music performance (such as Music Academies and Colleges) supply these as a preventative measure—which has in the meantime also become a legal mandate of the occupational health industry as regulated by insurance companies). Further, orthopaedic seats are found inside rehearsal halls. Nonetheless, these anatomically correct chairs are never shipped to concert venues. Hence the participating players (in all five Orchestras of the current sample) reported performing in Halls where they are forced to sit on substandard seats, causing a host of musculoskeletal pains.

Moreover, some players complained that as they aged they developed slight inabilities in controlling detrusor muscles; as a result they need to remove themselves from the Orchestra more often in order to relieve their bladder. On the one hand many players did mention that their experiences have taught them to limit liquid intake before Concerts; while on the other hand they know that a minimum of fluids is required to counteract dehydration that could possibly cause other issues within a performance. Finally, rehearsal time is often mentioned; apparently players are dismayed that Conductors do not release those who are not necessary for the section being prepared; in general Conductors are quite deficient in pre-planning how they will work on a piece.

(29y, F, vn)   *I am not sure if as we get older the environment causes players to have problems with working: sitting, nutrition, touring, lights, vision, etc. I think probably it used to be like that very much in the past, especially with the lighting. Opera [pit] players have always complained about the lack of light affecting their vision. But, we are more aware of the effect it can have on us, so the management tries their best to give us the facilities. Even chairs that can completely adjust for anyone, with each leg being fully independent so you can raise/lower them as you want, and move the back up/down or far/close to your body—as well as make the seat higher/lower. Yet, we can't take the chairs on tour. Also, our names are not on the chairs; in my Tutti section we rotate a lot! It's like being in the kindergarten—you get a new chair all the time. I'm usually Chair #9, but for this week's programme I am sitting in Chair #6. I do recall all the markers so I can adjust each chair to be the same.*

(36y, F, tpt)   *I've noticed some of the older players have problems with their bladder; they can't sit through the first half and have to get off the stage. So, I know some older players that do worry [about that]. If we've got a long Symphony to do, then that's the first thing they'll say: 'We better not drink.' I don't think it's more with Wind players than String players; it's probably just something with ageing across the board.*

(38y, M, bn/dbn)   *I do feel very tired at the end of a week's work, and sometimes even at the end of the day's work. I know it is not because I had a lot to do playing-wise. But because the environment that we're in is very loud. I do wear earplugs: ER9s and ER15s (which the Orchestra supplied a few years ago). I use them sometimes depending on where I'm sitting on the stage. I can pop them in for particular passages. But I can't play with them if I have to play quietly, but if it's really loud I can. [The problem is] if it suddenly becomes quiet, with all the heavy Brass dropping out, and I'm left there with just a few other people on my own, then I can't have them in for that loud passage just prior; there simply is no time to take them out! I've tried putting only one in ear and not the other. I haven't actually tried using them without the attenuator (filter). But I find it very difficult playing with earplugs because I have a reed in my mouth vibrating. Even though the ERs are probably better than all others, they're still dreadful with something vibrating in your mouth. It's not the same as a fiddle player who is just literally hearing everything turned down.*

(41y, M, vc)   *I'm not convinced that my hearing is that great [anymore]. Yet, my ability to hear across the Orchestra (e.g., selective focus of hearing) is definitely better than it's ever been. Perhaps I know what to listen to more; I only need to hear a small fragment to reconstruct [the whole thing] in my head when playing. But it's funny ... if I hear a sentence [words] I sometimes don't know what's being said! Also, I find it is now increasingly more difficult to hear somebody saying something in the audio track of a movie—my ability to filter out [the noise] and comprehend. [Author's Note: The Cocktail Party Effect is a phenomenon of the brain, an ability to focus one's auditory attention on a particular stimulus while filtering out a range of other stimuli—like focusing on a single conversation in a noisy room. This requires listeners to have the ability to both segregate different stimuli into different streams, and subsequently decide which streams are most pertinent to them. One of the ill effects of ageing is a decrease in ability to segregation aural streams. See Getzmann et al. (2017)].*

(47y, F, vn)   *The work environment and working conditions are certainly better organized than before. The seating, chairs, lighting (e.g., lamps), buses—have all improved. [These are] not more difficult as I age!*

(47y, M, trb)   *About 10 years ago I started wearing glasses; that made life easier. I only use glasses in the Orchestra. That was the first thing I discovered about getting older! Now we have lights on our music stands, and for the [Opera] Pit. Also, we now have really great chairs; they spent a lot of money to give us something good to sit on. These do make you feel that the management really cares about you. But the Pit is very narrow; it's really difficult to sit in a good position and see your [music] stand.*

(49y, F, vn)   *I am not sure if chairs, stage, AC, and technical matters are related to age. But the chairs are very important. The environment also needs to be nice with lighting and flowers! But, our ears never have a break! Even when there is an official break, there is always someone practising on the stage; people are practising everywhere! So, I mean there is never silence! Never!*

(52y, M, vc)   *The only thing you have to be careful about as you get older is degeneration of eyesight; you might need a bit more light, and need [to move] the music [stand] further away or closer [depending on your eyes]. But, these are things you have to deal with in real life anyway. I need glasses to read the newspaper; I need glasses to read music. If I forget them, I'm not lost, and I cope! Walking up onstage [is not a consideration]. I don't find that the older players have difficulty sitting throughout the whole first half—they don't have to get offstage to go to the toilet. Although we do joke about it! When you know there's a long piece to play, then fluid intake might be modified. I don't think it affects everybody, but perhaps more so the older men than the older women! I am not saying that a lot of the men have bladder problems, but as men get older, they just feel the need to go to the toilet more often.*

(53y, M, vn)   *As I get older the Orchestra environment is more difficult. My eyes, and the lights, and bladder [are worse] than earlier. In general, I have glasses for the distance and glasses for [reading] the notes. But, when you sit in the Orchestra, I have no glasses for the distance between things. I don't see as good as earlier, and I'm more near-sighted. And when the light [onstage] is not bright, it's more difficult. Also, the notation itself has become problematic; sometimes you play with very small notes, or many notes on one side [left side pages] with Piano staves on the other. The printing sometimes causes problems. I have difficulties to take in all of this amount of information. I also write marks [texts and symbols] on the music notation. Actually, we already get our notation with most of the markings already on them (from somebody else in a different Orchestra from another country in another language). And the next player [in another Orchestra] will get this [same] score with my markings as well. But, the Conductor could say that he doesn't want it that way, but wants something else. And then what do you do? First, we discuss if it's really his opinion, and if he says so, then we make changes to the score! Most scores are rented; we can see lots of fingerings on the scores. In some, a player crossed all this out from the user before them. [Laughs.] Sometimes by mistake someone crosses out a note! [Laughs.] I don't know what would Debussy say about that! Here someone crossed out a sign to do a Pizzicato. Actually I do think we play that note. I did it automatically.*

(53y, M, hrp)   *Lots of times I just sit around and get more and more bored 'cause I'm not doing anything; I'm just totally out of it after 15 minutes. I mean sometimes I can be in a 2-hour rehearsal and I don't play for the first hour. And I'm paid, so I just have to sit there. I can't say: 'I'll come back in an hour.' I mean if you know you're not gonna be needed for an hour, [the Conductor] can say that. But mostly they don't know whether they're going to get to your bit or not. It's not always obvious that you're going to wait an hour. Many Conductors do not walk in and say: 'Look, I'm gonna be now working with the Strings, so you and all the others can come back in an hour.' If a piece has lots of different movements, and you know which movement you're in, then you may know they're gonna do the 3rd and 4th movements after the break. You may not be needed till then—so you [can leave and] don't have to come back till after the break. But, if it's a long piece, with no subdivision, and you don't play till the end, a Conductor could just say: 'I wanna hear the end now.' He might be going through it, or he might start at the beginning; he might rehearse each 100 bars and spend an hour on each. Then, you're waiting for your bit at the end. You can't walk out in case he suddenly decides to go through the whole thing.*

(54y, M, cl/bcl)   *The only environmental issue that seems to be more difficult as I'm getting older is my eyes. I have never linked between ageing and playing music. I mean I don't have bladder problems (like some men who then have to worry about that as they get older). So, I don't feel that by passing the 50-year mark, the years have done something that I now have to be really careful. As far as I am concerned, as long as you're practising, everything else will fall into place.*

(55y, M, bn)   *Definitely they give us the wrong kind of chairs. The fact that I have a different chair every day, with different angles and heights, annoys me to no end. Or that I have a dirty music stand in front of me makes me feel disrespected. When I walk onstage for a concert, and I see chairs in a straight line that truly shows me there's no care about production. Maybe the actual working conditions are not becoming worse per se, but as I get older it's more difficult to overlook the flaws.*

(55y, F, fl)   *I don't think lighting or seating get worse as you go along. But seeing the music is harder. That's why I've got these special glasses. [Shows the researcher a pair of optical lenses.] They're bifocals—but upside-down. Nobody I know has got these. I invented them! That's the Conductor bit, and this the music bit. I also have a hearing loss, but I haven't noticed any difference in how it affects my playing. I have hearing tests because of European legislation. I've got ER15s hearing protectors. I hate them! I have tried, but just can't gauge my own performance properly. I was told once that I should try to use them without the caps on—without the filters. Maybe I should have gotten the ER9s. But when I was fitted they gave me ER15s 'cause I play Piccolo. I've got a hearing loss within that top octave.*

(56y, M, va)	*Regarding the physical environment, such as Hall, chairs, lighting, etc., this does not get any harder with ageing. On the other hand, one does begin to feel some level of fatigue when having to sit long hours in rehearsals.111*
(56y, F, vn)	*The stage, stairs, lighting, and AC/heating are all good. I am still young! Who said that being 56 is old? I just want to say that I am very lucky! [I don't have any] age-related difficulties with the Orchestra work environment. I sometimes need glasses; I have problems with distance [vision]. This distance is ideal! [Demonstrates.] This is the distance of a music stand; therefore I am without glasses. If I need to see the Conductor, then, I can't see him. What bothers me the most is when things are not on a professional level. For example, most of the time we are given orthopaedic chairs. Some better, some worse. But if I am given a plastic chair (like balcony or restaurant furniture), then I won't play! I need to be comfortable to play. I do see others who have problems in sitting, or having to wait to use the bathroom. Look, when playing a Symphony, Orchestra players hold their instruments in unnatural positions. This causes a strain on them; it's not just sitting, but sitting holding the instrument—and sitting 'holding it in' [not being able to relieve your bladder].*
(58y, M, va)	*There are a lot of environmental considerations for Orchestra musicians after [the age of] 50. For example, AC. In younger years I was able to suffer quietly, but not now! Sometimes also the lighting. I used to have to wear glasses to see the Conductor; but after a Cataract operation, that has all been settled.*
(59y, M, va)	*I don't think the environment or the lifestyle has become more difficult as I've gotten older. Not the rehearsal rooms, seats, stands, lights, or even the hours. I'm nearly 40 years in this Orchestra, and those circumstances have changed for the better slowly and surely.*
(59y, M, fl/picc)	*In my experience, the only environmental issue that might be affected by ageing is eyesight! We get score notation parts that are too small. I immediately ask the librarian to recopy them in a bigger resolution size. But, our present Music Director hands out scores printed in blue; blue inked notes [i.e., commentaries] on them. The lines are really small—they are from Boosey & Hawkes publishers. Though they are not handscript, they are not printed well enough to see clearly. I can't really play by reading them; I have to learn everything by rote. Therefore, as we get older, visual crispness seems to go down. And, multifocal lenses really don't work; we need better lenses for reading scores, but then we can't really see the Conductor!*
(60y, M, cl)	*You know, right now I deal with eyesight much better than before. I moved over to multifocal lenses; my reading and performance became better. Before I had to choose between reading the score and seeing the Conductor. I always felt a need to see the Conductor's face for timing entrances and other feedback.*
(60y, F, vc)	*Some of the environmental and working conditions of the Orchestra do become more difficult as I get older—like getting onstage or sitting in a chair. The lighting for sure! The management do economize on lights during rehearsals, but it is not the same for a 2–3-hour concert. Some years ago I started to have eyesight problems, and needed to put glasses on—that may be normal for ageing anyhow! My hearing is fine; perhaps even more sensitive as I now suffer more from noise. This certainly is the case for ageing. Maybe it's about nervous sensitivity too! Perhaps, I've become a more nervous person with age, but I don't think that affects the way I play.*
(61y, F, vn)	*At my age the lighting and seating are much more difficult and critical.*

7.2.2 Travelling and Touring

One issue that surfaced quite often in the interviews regards travel and touring. It seems that these aspects need to be considered much more carefully as a factor of ageing among Symphony Orchestra musicians. The participating players mentioned several sides to the issue. First, the mode of transportation (e.g., sitting for hours on a bus or plane) is no longer seen as viable. Second, the distance itself (an indication of the required time away from family members and household responsibilities) is highly distressing. Finally, the once infamous *touring mode* (referring to a set of behaviours that promote indiscretions as one feels *out of sight out of mind* from others) has been drastically reformed over the past few decades. Touring Mode is discussed elsewhere (see Chapter 5, section 5.2.4, and Chapter 12). Today, players simply cannot act wayward, mischievous, or promiscuous as that is no longer socially acceptable or tolerated. Nonetheless, the players do reveal many 'celebrated folk tales' (what we might see more as *urban legends*) about the Orchestra players of yesteryear. Many of the more Seasoned Musicians also recalled 'real-life' stories about their colleagues (and of course that might mean themselves!) depicting the more frolicking nature of what was considered conventional behaviour in the earlier years of their career.

(39y, F, cl)	*The environment of the Orchestra does get harder to deal with as you get older (e.g., seating, lighting). Touring takes its toll! Fortunately, in this particular Orchestra we hardly go away. It's just much more about sitting on a bus, being out of town, and all the flying. Especially if you have children!*
(40y, F, vn)	*Some of my colleagues are dying to go on tours, the more trips the better! It's not because they're not married or have no children. It's because they do have families! Look: you stay in a hotel, and everything is taken care of for you. You don't need to cook, you don't need to clean, the kids aren't there (so you don't need to worry about picking them up). You go and have fun. And you also get paid a little bit more. But, I've travelled so much in my life, that I don't love the tours. In fact, last year we had a 1-week trip tour which I tried really hard to get out of going; I had just come back from the United States [doing a series of Solo recitals].*
(41y, M, vc)	*There may be some players who need to consider seating, reading, nutrition, and bladder, as they get older. I think the thing that definitely has an impact on me is touring—especially sitting on buses! Maybe it's not that much to worry about, but I think it's probably an ever-increasing frustration. Yet, I can't imagine that stopping me from playing in the Orchestra.*
(47y, M, hn)	*I just think tours are becoming more of an issue of self-discipline. It is more of a challenge than they used to [be]. I am thinking that there's booze everywhere; and not a drop to drink [for me]. So, I just have to put myself to bed with some exercise. I need to be very careful because I've noticed I can't recover [well] if I stay up late [drinking] compared to when I was younger. I just have to look after myself now. Not that I was a 'party animal' when I was younger, but I liked hanging out in bars late at night. So, I don't dread touring, but I don't look forward to them anymore.*
(47y, F, vn)	*Right now, touring is getting better again. There were some years where it was really hard when the children were small; I had to organize babysitters which was really hard and expensive. I had to leave them, and to hope that everything would be fine when I come back. But now, it's getting much more relaxed because the kids are getting older.*
(52y, M, vc)	*I don't think that one's ability to combine personal life with work tours changes as you get older. Going on tour is exciting when you're younger. Then, in a middle [of your professional life] you don't want to go on tour at all—'cause you've got family and you're getting 'ripped' by your other half about childcare. Finally, a little later, it's great to go away, to get out of the house; to have a bit of freedom, and to party with your friends. As we've gotten older, the 'touring rules' have changed— specifically you've left bed-hopping. But the 'touring mode' stays the same. Some players might*

be a bit 'under the thumb' at home; so when they go on tour it's their time to 'let go'! Travelling can be a time to 'let your hair down'. For me it's my chance to have a nice meal with friends. But for others it is more difficult to pack up, and to get on and off the busses. Some prefer to be at home; they will try and get out of tours as much as they can. Sometimes it has to do with the needs of your other half. By the way, I hear that there are some with wives who don't like them [going] away; so, they'll do as much as they can to get off [the tour]. I don't know the percentage of players that marry someone out of the profession; [but I think] most of the people from this Orchestra are married to someone in the profession. [Author's Note: For more on relationships and coupling among players, see Chapter 5, section 5.2.4.1.] There is certainly one [woman] player who is married to an ex-Orchestra player who doesn't like her going away at all; he claims he knows what goes on during the tour. Perhaps what he perceives as going on during tours [is because he remembers what he himself did on tours during his career].

(53y, M, hrp)   *Jet lag seems to affect me far more now than it did when I was younger. It takes me longer to be able to put myself together than it used to. Last year we went to America; we started on the West Coast. I actually fell asleep during the first piece (which I didn't play in it for the first 20 minutes). Yes! I actually fell asleep on the stage! But, I woke up in time! Subconsciously, I recognized the bits before I needed to play. In general, the Harp does always have long interims. In this particular piece, I come in near the end to play some sort of quasi-Medieval little Ditty thing that was some special effect near the end of a 25-minute piece. Maybe I should have brought a newspaper, or played a game on my cell phone. Something to keep me busy as I often do for rehearsals. Yet, sometimes you can become so absorbed that you can miss your entry altogether.*

(54y, M, cl/bcl)   *I actually enjoy touring more now than I did when I was younger. Simply because my family are all now grown up—and my wife doesn't mind too much if I'm away for a week. When the kids were younger I found it quite difficult—I didn't like that aspect of it. But now, she's sort of relieved when I'm not there for a while.*

7.3 Performance-Related Organizational Considerations

7.3.1 Work Employment Conditions

The participating players spoke about specific problematic working conditions, such as: number of hours per week they are scheduled to play; application of sick days; aspects of control and decision-making by Management; the elected Orchestra Members Committee; financial issues including retirement and pension; expectations of the occupation; and cultural geopolitical differences that surface between players (based on their country of birth and music training). The main issue that repeatedly came up was *remuneration*. The players conveyed feelings that although they work multiple hours as a highly skilled expert professional, the payment they receive is barely above the minimum wage—which is of equal value to an apprentice-trainee labourer. Moreover, there are no increases in the base salary (e.g., a pay scale system) linked to Education, Academic Degree, advanced professional training, or Seniority (i.e., years of experience). Over time, such a policy seems to lead to apathy, and encourages indifference with associated outcomes related to task-diligence and work-persistence. The players claim that if they do not engage in other part-time work (e.g., Teaching a musical instrument or classes, or Freelance gigs outside the

Orchestra), they could not possibly earn enough income to cover maintenance costs (i.e., living expenses).

Finally, it is rather heartbreaking to read one specific vignette of a 60-year-old Clarinettist who has been employed for more than 30 years in the same Orchestra; he would have wished to retire early at age 60 while he still feels young enough to enjoy the oncoming *3rd Age* (a descriptive label for the period of life between 'middle age' and 'old age' when one can still be very active). The situation is such that Orchestra managements prefer not to release players if they are 'still functioning at the highest performance levels' as required by the Orchestra. Accordingly, this player conveys a position that it seems rather absurd that you work hard during a 30-year career, whereby you maintain performance abilities and skills on expert levels, and then Management won't allow you to withdraw respectably; but rather they seem to prefer to delay retirement until performance levels have deteriorated, when subsequently, one might endure a more-than-humiliating experience onstage.

(40y, F, vn)	*For a Tutti player, I'd say environmental and occupational considerations are bigger challenges to survive in the Orchestra than the actual playing. If you're already in an Orchestra it means you know how to play. The challenge, then, is all this other stuff. The schedule here in this Orchestra is one of the reasons I haven't even auditioned for another Orchestra. I know [other Orchestras] work a lot more than we do, but they also get paid a significant amount more than we do. So, it's a trade-off. Yet, my salary is a challenge as it is half of what I earned in my former Orchestra.*
(47y, M, trb)	*As you get older, you need more financial security as you have children that are getting older. You have to give them more money. I don't ever think that I shouldn't have become an Orchestra player simply because we work a lot of time without extra pay. I think I'm really lucky to have this job! I also teach at the University for extra money; together [both incomes] is like that of an Orchestra in a bigger house. The extra salary gives me financial freedom. We do less travel (out of the country), and less 'modern' repertoire.*
(49y, F, vn)	*Perhaps when we were younger, we really never paid much attention to our Social or Pension rights. But as we aged, we began to look at those aspects. It is rather a joke to speak about financial security among professional performing musicians. My monthly salary is just above minimum wage! And, I have a child in College! You think about how we started as young children, and acquired formal education; most [players] have two degrees [BMus and MMus] while some have three [a final DMus or PhD]. Further, we all have extra-collegiate training, and at least 30 years of on-the-job experience by the time we are 50 [years old]. That is the reason why so many of us need to play 'gigs' for extra cash; we want to be like other 'normal' people! People often ask me: 'You play Violin? Is that really your work?' I really do hope that I will be able to withstand time [ageing] and maintain my ability until retirement. Playing in an Orchestra doesn't really give the feeling of working [employment]. It requires a certain minimum; I sit opposite the conductor, watch, and don't have to think too much. I sit opposite the score, and play.*
(52y, M, db)	*The organizational side, such as job security, and management, has occasionally become more difficult as I get older. Sometimes I feel that they [abuse me] because in one week there is so much to do—with no breaks—not even one day off. I never thought about this when I started. Most of the time our week consists of 5–6 calls [i.e., rehearsals]. You do hear players complaining. At the moment I have a lot of pressures at home; while that's not [related to] the Orchestra, I do feel that it's everything altogether.*

(53y, M, vn)   *I am the 1st Principal player of the 2nd Violins; I have been in this Orchestra now 29 years. I know that even if someone's skills are very bad it's very difficult to [retire them] out of the Orchestra. I remember two cases: One was a player who was already 62 years old and wanted early pension; he went to the Chief [Music Director] saying 'I don't feel that I'm good enough [anymore]', and he was allowed to go. The other one who was a Woodwind player had problems with his hand, but he wanted to stay, and the Chief said: 'No!' He didn't fight!*

(54y, M, va)   *I think there's frustration from the salary; it doesn't get better as you age. Maybe I had more expectations when I was younger. Relatively speaking, the salary seems to have been somewhat better at the beginning! Although stereotypically [men are] supposed to be the main breadwinners, [the Orchestra] is not a very good job [for men]. I earn less than my wife who's a teacher, and we all know that they don't earn a respectable salary.*

(55y, M, bn)   *I'm much more angry about the conditions now. About the fact that I made my career here! That I have very little financial remuneration from all the efforts that I put in. I feel that for my services I've very little financial satisfaction.*

(57y, F, vc)   *Here they don't tell a player to retire. There are countries that already begin to retire players after 50 years of age. Here, some players last as long as age 70. I know one player who shakes and often plays out of tune. But they keep him, and won't tell him to retire. He does succeed in playing his part, but he is no longer on the level of the Orchestra.*

(59y, M, va)   *Well, I do have back problems, but I haven't been sick [off work] not even for one day in 40 years. There are two different kinds of people in the Orchestra. One wakes up in the morning, coughs, and then phones in sick; the others (more like me) don't! I was not ill—not even one day! Now, there are some pieces that have to be played by only one Viola player or a Cellist. In most cases, there will be another player who prepares as a substitute (if needed). But, everyone knows I'll never get sick, so they don't even waste their time rehearsing. [Laughs.] I hope it will be the same over the next (my last) 5 years.*

(59y, M, fl/picc)   *I believe that a player of [age] 60–65 will be able to play as they did when they were 35 years old. But if not, then it is time for them to retire. For me, rehearsals and performances are mental. If I ever get to the point where I play out of pitch, then I will ask the management to place me more in the back [of the section]. But, not to remove me [i.e., forced retirement] as that is not fair after all the years that I have been a loyal player of this Orchestra.*

(60y, M, cl)   *Some players ask for early retirement. I did that! But the management doesn't agree to retire someone who still has their chops—even if they've become emotionally detached. But, if I'd play with a lot of mistakes, the management would then release me! Players don't really do that! More often players behave in some unacceptable manner (like being late, calling in sick, or not showing up). Namely, players are retired more for disciplinary issues than musical faults. So here is the paradox: You work for years to build up your skills. Then maintain them for 5 Decades. And, when you have had enough and want to retire, management says: 'You're too good!' So, it all seems to work against you! Hence, the message seems to be: Don't try to be a good player till the end, and think you will be able to retire honourably. But rather, be a poor member of the Orchestra in order to give good cause for the management to offer you a better retirement package—to get rid of you as soon as possible. Yet, I think it should be different! When a player comes forward and says: 'I have been a loyal player for 33 years, but I have back problems, or pains and aches', then management should give their Blessing! I said: 'Let me go when I am in a good state (i.e., emotionally and motorically performing well) rather than wait till I make a fool of myself in front of all the others [players and public] who will then only remember me as someone who was once a good player but lost it.'*

(61y, M, fl/picc)   *It is hard work! You have to put in your hours of practice. The interesting thing is: If it really is your way of life, if it is your vocation, if it's what you do, if you're a musician primarily (and everything else secondly), then, you'll find the means of*

> doing that. *Because you want to do that! That's what you do! But, if you think: Maybe I should have become something else, then, you might reach a point where you say: I don't wanna work at this anymore. Hopefully, most people do want to maintain the standard. That's the way it works. I mean this Orchestra is changing rapidly all the time. There is a sense that, if you don't cut the mustard, it won't last!*

(64y, M, tpt)   *Unfortunately, after 30 years of work I see the Orchestra being destroyed! And a product to which I was proud to be connected has become something less. The Orchestra is not the same. It went from being 94 players filling the Halls three times a week, to a 70-piece Orchestra that can't even fill a small venue once a week. Look: there were cutbacks, and everybody says the audience is getting smaller. But, there are still large big-name Orchestras that also have had cutbacks, and are filling the Halls. So, my frustration with administration is one thing, but work satisfaction—about with what goes onstage at the time at the Concert—is something quite different! There are some who say: 'Well, they're not paying more than that, so I'm not going to practise.' Or: 'I don't have to bother if that's all they're paying me to do!' I don't think that [these kind of] attitudes develop with age? I've seen it also with younger players. I mean because of the salary [amount] they have already stopped practising, and continually look to move on to a different Orchestra.*

7.3.2 Auditions, Trials, and Job Security

The participating players spoke about the process of becoming an Orchestra player—from auditioning, through multiple trial periods which can take between weeks and months at a time, to receiving a final offer with a full-time contract. They relate to the *politics* involved in the procedure, as foremost having to be referred and recommended (i.e., 'befriended') by another player from the Orchestra. Players often undergo several auditions in different Orchestras in parallel. To earn decent wages, professional Classical musicians often serve as extras (e.g., relievers) in other Symphony Orchestras, as well as in Ensembles and Bands. Accordingly, one acknowledged problem is 'leakage'. Namely, although auditions are supposed to be anonymous and hence implemented behind a screen (see Chapter 5, section 5.2.8), the names of candidates and outcome-decisions of auditions can eventually leak out to the community. Further, players often state that the procedures are not always based on music *skill* (e.g., an indication that the position will go to the best of the lot), but rather on the notion of *fit* (an indication of suitability between the applicant and the section advertising an open position). The players often mentioned that even today they may/may not feel secure in their current position. This was especially pertinent for those approaching a more advanced age of 50 years old. They denote differences between music-performance organizations regarding the structure of salaries, and they often express an understanding that they have compromised their level of income from what they could have received had they been employed by a different Orchestra. In retrospect, some players regret having accepted the long-lasting security of their current contract, including job permanence of a tenured position: the conditions written on their binding financial package were those awarded yesteryear which are not so attractive in today's job market. This notion is similar to what Dobrow (2013) found in a study about job satisfaction among professional Classical Music musicians; even though they had aspired and anticipated to be performing in a professional Orchestra—which was considered to be their 'dream job'—those musicians who *won* an Orchestra job expressed relatively low levels of job satisfaction. Accordingly, Dobrow found that out of 13 occupations outlined in the study, Symphony Orchestra musicians ranked 7th in job satisfaction—just below Federal Prison guards.

Yet, in a previous survey by Olbertz (2006) findings did not support any hypothesis that musicians would see their profession in a negative light. Recruiting a representative sample of Orchestra players (N=150; M_{Age} = 40; 60% string, 40% wind; 70% male), Olbertz found that 80% reported to be *content* with their jobs— almost all of them said they would 'choose the same profession all over again'. That percentage (m = 70%) was just above all other vocations, including: Library Science Medicine, Police, and Teachers. Yet, on the other hand, Olbertz did find that 15% felt the job does not allow them to attain their full potential; 43% would like to have more creative and artistic input; 60% reported that they do not see any prospects for promotion; and 32% felt that the limited possibilities of promotion restrict individual development. The reality is that the professional Orchestra vocation offers little opportunities for occupational advancement, and the critical period for advancement is usually seen as 'optimal' until age 35; auditions demand virtuoso performance-levels which, unfortunately, it is believed cannot be maintained after age 35. Olbertz clearly states that once the musician has entered the orchestra, they leave the Soloist benchmark behind—be it knowingly or unknowingly.

Finally, several participant-players in the current study mentioned how societal consumption of music has changed audiences. For example, there has been a shift from *live* music exposure (i.e., authentic performances inside Concert Halls) to *digital formats* such as pre-recorded content heard via audio reproduction hardware. In addition, today there are hundreds of 'free' online music streaming services and mobile apps.

(33y, M, va)	*Orchestras here work on a trial system which has its pros and cons. But that means that people get jobs because of who they know rather than how they play. And you might even get to a couple of weeks' work in the job, and then six other people come in and get a couple of weeks' work (in place of you). In the end, the Leader chooses a couple to come back, and then depending on personalities, and what other people say, one player is chosen.*
(35y, F, vn)	*The Orchestra has become different since the last time I was here as a player. The Conductor changed, and the repertoire has become different; for my taste it has not be fantastic for the Orchestra. This Conductor is due to finish, and I am looking forward to the next one. I've had to audition to come back [after giving birth, and one postnatal year off]. The fact I was here before did not give me any advantage; everybody has to audition. I actually auditioned here three times: first time while I was a student as a Freelance Violinist for a position with 2nd Violins; second time for a position with the 1st Violins (which is a requirement to join that section); third time when rejoining after giving birth. It's the policy that all jobs have to be open; so if it was advertised then you interview and audition. There is no advantage of coming from inside the Orchestra; you still have to prove that you're better than the other people applying for the same job.*

(39y, F, cl)   *If I were auditioning people for a position, would I be listening to how well they play? Or: would I be trying to imagine (assess) them as a person whose gonna be part of my section sitting next to me for long periods of times? To be honest, a lot of auditions are done behind a screen; only then do they come and do a trial in the Orchestra. So you get a bit more of a sense of whether [or not] that person is going to be able to integrate and to be part of your team. Of course we're looking for the best players. But it's very hard to not take into consideration personality—whether somebody's going to fit in your team. So, if you had two candidates who theoretically were about at the same level, what would make the difference whether they get offered their position is their personality. That is, non-musical characteristics which are very much an integral part of how people play. We all play who we are; everyone gives a certain impression of their personality through their playing. Somebody once told me: 'Playing is a mirror of your soul.'*

(41y, M, va)   *There's a good deal of understanding between the [different] Orchestras that our roles are different, as well as the requirements for appointing players. Obviously, there's a lot of overlap. If [someone is] turned down by our Orchestra, the chances are they'd be trying at a second Orchestra at the same time anyway. Generally, one rejection doesn't affect your odds with the other Orchestra. But, if you start getting turned down by 5–8 or more different Orchestras, then there's a problem. I think the music profession is quite incestuous. Word does get around, and people would know. There is quite a lot of leakage between the musicians. On the other hand, because auditions are done behind screens, it's not always possible to know who it was; in this Orchestra there's an awful lot of emphasis on confidentiality. So, if someone fails an audition, chances are that that's as far as it goes. Unless the player (candidate) told their friends. But there could also be someone who is indiscreet; obviously while the judges wouldn't say anything, if one was taken into an admin office then somebody there might see you.*

(50y, M, vn)   *When we sit on audition panels [as judges] it seems that we like the same thing. I'm sure that one reason our section has grown to be what it is, is that we all seem to value the same sort of things. It is not simply skill; we don't necessarily appoint the red-hottest player. We have always appointed people who fit! At first you are not sure, but then you do know because they do a trial in the Orchestra. A trial could be anything from a week to a month, or even months on end. Depends what the post is. A Rank-&-File player would probably only have a 1–2 weeks, and we would do 2–6 trials [different applicants]; then there might not be a decision for 3–4 months. It would be considerably longer for a more senior position because the actual trial period would go on more; the decision would be based on a very wide variety of repertoires. If the position was the No. 2 (or one of the higher desks), the trial period could be several months more than that. You'd give everybody who passed the audition a similar amount of time. And then out of that initial trial, you would choose if there was a clear outright front-runner. You would then invite them back and they'd do a bit more. If you're still finding it difficult to decide between them, you'd give them all a bit more until it becomes clearer who if any of them are shortlisted for this position. During this process, they'd all be allowed to audition for any other Orchestra as there's no contract yet. Generally speaking, as they're Freelancers they'd might have to go do other work because that is their means of earning a living. There's no way you could come here and do 2 weeks [or months at a time] and not do anything else. They're paid for whatever they do; recognized rates for specifics (e.g., rehearsals, recordings, Concerts, travel, etc.) which is regulated by the Musicians' Union.*

(56y, F, vn)   *Last year I looked at my financial contracts, and my pension [package]. I think no one will ask me to leave the Orchestra early [because of ageing] as my level of playing is one of the highest here. I am proud of my position—second only to the Concertmaster. Hence, I am certain I will be here for many more years.*

(61y, M, fl/picc)   *In this Orchestra there is an annual salary (your contract), and if all goes well you have a job for life. There is a feeling that you're employed by a Society [i.e., a business organization]. If the Orchestra has got problems financially, it's not the players' issue; it's for the Management and the Board to sort out. You're safe here. We don't have the same kind of pressure you find in [other big city Orchestras] where you might be paid a small retainer, but basically if you want to earn money you need to do the work. In those cases, the only way the Orchestra gets the work is to do engagements. Therefore, the players are motivated to keep standards very high; there's a great sense of competition to get more work in order for you to get your commission on the number of performed engagements per month. So, sometimes they'll work three sessions a day, every day, for a month. Some players might not survive depending how high the standard of the Orchestra is! Some players' standard has slipped. It is ultimately up to the players, the Principals, the Leader, the Conductor, and the Management. I remember a couple years ago seeing a programme on television about the Berlin Philharmonic. They interviewed some of the older members, people in their 50s and beyond. They said: 'You know, it seems I don't know whether or not I can maintain this seat much longer, because the standard is so high!' Maintaining such standards are a challenge!*

The profession has definitely changed in the past few decades. I remember seeing a photograph from the 1950s which was taken outside the Musicians' Union office in Soho (London). In those days there were so many more job opportunities for musicians. You could literally turn up at 10 o'clock on a Monday morning; there would be about 200 musicians queuing up outside looking for work. And someone would say: 'We need an Orchestra in X cinema! We need an Orchestra in Y studio!' By 11 o'clock there would be work for everyone; all were gone from the street corner, and they all got a week's work. There were so many Orchestras and little Bands playing all over the place. Back then, if you wanted music you couldn't turn on a machine [a phonograph vinyl LP record player, or FM stereo radio, or cassette tape machine, or CD disk player, or MP3 player, or Smartphone app with Bluetooth speakers]. You had to have musicians! That's the way it worked. I mean in those days there were both good Orchestras as well as lots of pretty average ones. You could just earn a good living as a 'jobbing' musician.

7.3.3 Orchestral Hierarchy

Within the interview the participating players raised issues about Orchestra hierarchy. Accordingly, each Orchestra section has its own structure. These might be referred to as 1sts (Section Leaders), 2nds (Principals), 3rds (Sub-Principals), etc. Orchestral hierarchy also means a player takes on specific responsibility for the sound produced by all others in their section. The Leaders ensure fitting together and producing one overall part of the music composition. When the players mentioned being appointed to the Orchestra, they conveyed that during their initial period after the trial(s) there was usually another Orchestra member who served as a 'mentor' for them to better acclimatize to the section. These players suggested how to function in a more adaptive manner. The conversations usually pointed out issues about *ranking* in the Orchestra. Namely, in the Orchestra, positions are not at all based on chronological age, seniority, tenure, or years of experience. Nor is ranking based on actual skill. Rather, many of the players claimed that there is yet another factor involved in gaining appointments which they refer to as *musical age* or 'musical performance maturity'. This factor is one's ability to hear and execute the most correct sonority. Further, it seems that the most suitable and befitting 'qualia' is the one that reflects the timely *sound traditions* of each specific Orchestra. This is more often the reason why some players are retained as Principals and Section Leaders in the Orchestra.

(33y, F, bn/dbn)	*I once received a phone call to play a gig. The guy said: 'I'm searching for a 1st Bassoonist. Can you give me some numbers? I know in the Orchestra you're playing 2nd so you can't do it.' And I thought: This is incredible. I can play everything. And that's exactly what I hate about the structure of an Orchestra. The people who play well, are only allowed to do so if they are in a Leader position. But if I play very well as 2nd Bassoon, no one is interested. This kind of structure is not working anymore; I think it's really from the Middle Ages.*
(39y, F, cl)	*I have been with this Orchestra now for 9 years. I've seen players come and go! When you first get to an Orchestra, there may be another player who serves as mentor (e.g., someone that takes you in and shows you the ropes). But, it depends a little bit where you're sitting. Perhaps if you come in at the back desk of the Violins, you might have someone to help settle you in. But, I came in as the 1st Clarinet Section Leader. Even though I was quite young, I was expected to lead and shape my section—rather than have somebody help me. But, I was quite lucky as the chap sitting next to me was close to retirement and quite experienced. I suppose in a way he acted as a mentor to me. You know he'd done this job for many, many years and was still fantastic. He was the Co-Principal while there was a Principal vacancy. So, he had been 1st Clarinet a lot, covering the job while they were looking to appoint someone. He'd also played 2nd Clarinet; he really knew what the job involved. He had managed to carry on playing very, very well right up until retirement. Just incredible.*
(41y, M, vc)	*I am the 2nd Cello. It's called a Principal [position] because there is a Section Leader (1st Cello) and then the 2nd Cello. I think the amount of responsibility one can take for what's going on, does change things. Most people are not aware of the rank[ing system]. So, there's the Leader of the Orchestra (Concertmaster), Section Leaders, Section Principals, Section Sub-Principals, and then Rank-&-File players. My job is an interesting one because I have to fit in with whatever my Principal chooses to do, as well as whatever my Section Leader chooses to do. Although I might have a little bit more say (and a little bit more opportunity), most of the time I'm basically not officially doing any more than the Rank-&-File players. But, when [the 1st Cello] is not here, then I do have to stand up. So, I do the leading role, and then that does rub off on the way I play as 2nd.*
(47y, M, trb)	*Being Co-principal 2nd Brass player is always like I have an eye on the 1st [Principal] Trombone [position]. You think: I could do that! But sometimes you may also think: I'm so happy I don't have to play that! Like the Bolero [one-movement orchestral piece composed in 1928 by French composer Maurice Ravel, 1875–1937]. I remember saying: 'I'm so happy that I'm 2nd!' It is true the 1sts get a little bit more payment, but it's not worth it. I mean, it's the image. So to be Principal is always: He's the man. But I'm happy, I have a job! I'm here. I don't need more pressure. What I do is fine, I love what I do. I don't have to become the Head of Department. I don't have to be 1st! I feel that I am a good team player. And one of my biggest qualities is to get the group working; we have a really good relationship—the four of us. We do a lot of Chamber Music together.*
(50y, M, vn)	*In the end it is not just about skill or age. But rather respect. I think to get real respect, there are other factors than one's skill. The actual doing of the job, acquitting yourself in a situation. You might have a Leader that's much younger than you. But for real harmony, and the extra pleasure that comes from a very good amicable relationship, there has to be more than just skill!*
(52y, M, db)	*We have 5 Double Bass players. I am the 2nd on the 1st Stand, which means sometimes I have to be the 1st when the Principal is sick (or when he doesn't want to play). We also have a lot of pieces that are not played by all of us together; some pieces only require 2–3 [players]. That means we have to talk [negotiate] 'you do this piece and I'll do that piece'.*
(64y, M, tpt)	*Foremost, 'chronological age' is not the important factor; it is the 'musical age'; whether the person hears it, and whether they can do it. I do sometimes go and say something to a player in the back rows; our working dynamic is very good. There's no issue of: I have much more experience than you, so what I say should have a lot*

more weight. New players who just come into the Orchestra are full of themselves. They think they know the way to do it. Our Hollywood fantasy leads us to believe that in most organizations, the more experience you have is deemed to be highly valuable. That is, giving one's opinion, and then people accepting that opinion, because you have 20–30 years [seniority]. That, maybe, should be the case! But, that doesn't necessarily work in an Orchestra. Although you yourself might be the most experienced senior person in your section, it's the Section Leader who has the job; they set the tone and standards. So, some may think that being in an Orchestra means always having to yield. I wouldn't go that far. I never felt the need to inflate my ego by saying: I've been here longer. For sure, this kind of behaviour is actually a very positive way of adapting, and being able to survive. Otherwise I could end up fighting all the time; maybe even taking on a whole lot of emotional stress, and getting burned out.

7.3.4 Advancement and Mobility (Entrapment)

Many players mentioned advancement procedures and mobility within the Orchestra profession as being highly limited. Promotion may bring on awards such as increased salary and a more lucrative package of financial benefits. But it also invariably involves more tension and stress, as well as demanding increased daily practice. In an interesting study by Allmendinger et al. (1996), satisfaction towards inherent opportunities of growth within a Symphony Orchestra was ranked as 9th out of 13 professions; that was acknowledged as being 'fairly low'. See Table 7.1. Albeit, readers should note the placement of Chamber Music, which was listed in 1st Place above all other occupations—in regard to satisfaction for advancement opportunities. Perhaps part of the issue may be that the prospect of advancement among

Table 7.1 Satisfaction for Occupational Advancement Opportunities

Rank	Occupation
1	Professional String Quartet
2	Mental Health Treatment Teams
3	Beer Sales and Delivery Teams
4	Industrial Production Teams
5	Economic Analysts (Federal Government)
6	Airline Cockpit Crews
7	Airline Flight Attendants
8	Federal Prison Guards
9	**Symphony Orchestra Musicians**
10	Operating Room Nurses
11	Semiconductor Fabrication Teams
12	Professional Hockey Team
13	Amateur Theatre Company

Data Source: Allmendinger et al. (1996)

Symphony Orchestra players almost always require mobility. Namely, players usually need to move to a new organization (Orchestra), and most often such a move also requires relocation to a new city—and many times to a different country. For example, although the participating players in the current study were recruited from three countries (i.e., England, Germany, and Israel), the players themselves were born, educated, and worked in a host of countries from around the world, including (in alphabetical order): Australia, England, France, Germany, Ireland, Israel, Poland, Romania, Russia, Scotland, Singapore, Ukraine, and the United States of America. On this topic, Sterns and Miklos (1995) described three types of career pattern:

a) *Homesteaders* are individuals who stay in the same job (profession) for their entire career
b) *Transformers* are individuals who change their job (profession) once, either early in the career after a trial period, or later in the career once feeling they have become well established and financially free
c) *Explorers* are individuals who change careers several times over a lifespan.

Allmendinger et al. (1996) reported that most players were generally satisfied with their position in the Symphony Orchestra. Nonetheless, they concluded that the lower average number of departures each year from Orchestras indicates that there is not much career mobility within the Symphony Orchestra as a vocation. For example, when considering that a full-scale Symphony Orchestra consists of 80–90 players, while a full-scale Philharmonic Orchestra is slightly larger with about 100–120 players, then perhaps just under 50% (40–45 members) will ultimately have no opportunity for advancement during their 30-year career—especially the Tutti Rank-&-File players.

(29y, F, vn)	*It is strange that when you audition you are expected to play Solo repertoire. But once you get into the Orchestra you never play those pieces again. And that's what I find fascinating about the people that have been in the job for a long time who try to move on somewhere else. After 10 years of playing in an Orchestra, then suddenly for them to stand alone in the middle of the room and play on their own, it must be really stressful! They have to practise 7–8 hours a day before auditions. Normally there is not much time to prepare—maybe a day or two—unless the position is highly advertised. Even then [it is no more than] a month beforehand.*
(30y, F, vn)	*Some players are excited by the career ahead, but then there is disappointment. Especially if you're a Tutti String player. The chances of promotion are very slim. Look, your friends from school [outside the music-performance profession] expect promotions along their career. Further, [they expect] an increase in their earning salary more towards the end. Yet, that's not so much the case in Orchestras. I think that starts to 'bite' later on. There are plenty of players, some frighteningly young, who come in as they are keen to work, but then become disillusioned.*
(33y, M, va)	*I know I'm quite a unique person for an Orchestra player; I don't fit in the normal musician profile. I do have a problem with my long hair. Sometimes the people behind ask me to tie it because they can't see the conductor. But I tell them: 'Just move.' I think that I wasn't given a numbered position about 5 years ago because 'my face doesn't fit'. So, I'm a Rank-&-File player. We have four Sub-Principals in*

the Violas, and I went for the 3rd and 4th position. I auditioned but was told before that most likely I wouldn't get it even if I was the best player (which no doubt I was). The Leader of my Section told me it is discrimination. So, I took it to the Union and the Board; they wouldn't do anything. Especially in this Orchestra, not many people progress through the ranks. In order for me to progress I'd have to go to another Orchestra. But, I don't want that anymore. I've given that up because of my lifestyle choices. Now it quite suits me sitting at the back as I can do what I want; I've got more free time. I can even take a 10% cut of my contract (i.e., unpaid holiday) when I want. I don't struggle anymore with personalities of the people in the front. I also really like the variety we do here. It's stable in this job climate [of unemployment]. Yet, I do feel that in some ways I've compromised. The weird thing is that the person who got the 4th Desk position [that I auditioned for] was another Rank-&-File player who has a severe hearing loss in one ear—he always comes in early or late!

(33y, F, bn/dbn)   I think that the age of people entering the Orchestra is something like 27–28 years old. In earlier days it was like 18. The great famous Bassoon players were really young when they started, and now they're all older. I hear [turns to the researcher-interviewer] that you often ask the players: 'How many years have you been in this Orchestra?' I assume most would say 22–28 years. But, have you ever thought to ask them: 'Why didn't you think of ever going to another Orchestra?' They would probably say: 'Once you're past 35–36 years old you can't move. You're locked in! You can't go anywhere else.' That means that you only have a certain amount of years that you can try to be mobile. But there's something about not being able to move that either makes you happy and content, or not! Whether you want to or not, you're forced to be happy with what you have. Because there's no other possibility.

(43y, F, db)   I'm in my 18th year now at the Orchestra. I would say that I've learned to survive thus far. I hope to retire from this Orchestra as I'm not gonna be moving on now. The problem is that the audition process [requires] you to play Concertos. That's something that we don't do! So, hanging over the Bass and practising Concertos for hours a day, I couldn't do with my back. There is some talk about changing the audition procedure to ask for Orchestra excerpts only. This will give people from the section a chance to move up, and also make it easier for established players in other Orchestras to go for the job without the fear of having to play a Concerto. When you get past a certain age (maybe 35 years old) when auditioning doesn't quite come as easy as it did before, there's no way to place yourself back on the market again. So, if this change in audition procedure does take place, then I could probably think about mobility.

(54y, M, cl/bcl)   I'm in an Orchestra that's always doing Premieres and things like that. So, I mean, coming here was much harder 'cause I hardly ever played anything [newly composed]. I mean I've been here 30 years. I had the opportunity to leave [my previous Orchestra] after I'd been there for 10 years; but I didn't go because of family reasons, children, etc. I sort of regret it. But, now this current Orchestra, I could join without moving house [as it was in the same city I live in]. I thought it was a job I'd like. I'd already been there too long. I wish I'd done it [earlier]. I feel [the move] has given me a new lease on life; it is difficult because I don't know the pieces. This Orchestra has given me a reason to keep practising the bloody thing after all this time. When you look at a part you think: I have to practise that . . . especially as it came out in 1974. And you think: In what other line of work would I still be trying to improve myself after 40 years of occupational employment?'

(55y, M, bn)   I feel really totally trapped right now; as you get older that becomes more of an issue. Part of the reason players do many auditions is not necessarily because they want to move to another Orchestra, but as compensation for the feeling that they've been trapped for so many years. So, it's your way out! It is also an opportunity to get your act together—analysing your level of playing. Honestly, I don't really want [another] job, and play with [different] people. I am happy to stay here, and then will go early to pension.

(55y, F, fl)	*[Sighs.] I was very lucky. My life turned round when I joined this Orchestra 8 years ago. I mean I didn't mind [the previous Orchestra], but it's much more fulfilling here. I started here at 47; it is rare that they take someone that old. I mean, it shouldn't really matter how old you are. Either you have the goods or you don't! Let's say there was an opening, and I was sitting in an audition, if a phenomenal 50-year old player came along, I suppose a lot of it depends on whether they're gonna work well with us. That's what they did for me! [Laughs.] Normally you don't get applicants that age. Usually, someone who's still around at 50 (or older) has been with their Orchestra for[ever]. But, it does happen that people get tired of their Orchestra and want to go elsewhere. That's what happened to me! I don't think I'm that much of an exception—but I can't think of another player example of my age. I mean maybe a Principal Player might come from another band. But, Principals tend to be the young ones; the ones who can do a shit-hot audition. Not like me . . . but I did have to do a load of trials!*
(58y, M, va)	*The problem is that Section Principals do not change often and that means there is no upward promotions. I really don't have any more aspirations to take on more responsibility. Sometimes I do sit up as a replacement (when my Principal is not available). Twice I had attempted to move on (and upwards) taking part in auditions with other Orchestras (18–20 years ago). But, at the time there was no money for a superior position. So, I auditioned here, and have since been the Assistant [2nd]. There was a time when the environment was much more competitive. There was a feeling that younger players were trying to pinch my position. But not now. I mean it is always possible. That is the name of the game in an Orchestra. But I am ready for a competitive audition. I am willing to fight for the place. I feel that I still have potential; that I haven't reached my limitations yet as far as playing my instrument is concerned. But in the Orchestra, it is already too late. I have had this position now for 18 years, and I never tried to advance to a higher position since.*
(64y, M, tpt)	*If you can't function within the reality as it exists, then you have to either change the reality or you must leave. That's the only way to survive in the Orchestra; learn how to adapt through some kind of a compromise. There have been players who've come through the Orchestra, who've been here for a year or two. They leave because it was too much of a compromise. For the older players, once you're in the Orchestra for 30 years, you're not gonna go anywhere—except to stop! After the age of 30 (maybe age 35 in some exceptional cases) you're also not gonna be invited to an audition anymore. In the Orchestra you are essentially 'locked in' the same position already from the age of 40.*

7.4 Personal and Social Considerations

When the topic of combining personal and social aspects with home life came to the surface, the players spoke about many different issues. Among those mentioned most frequently were: food and nutrition; working hours and family routines; access to medical care; and merging Deliberate Practice within a more domestic environment.

7.4.1 Integration of Personal Life with Work

7.4.1.1 Food and Nutrition

Learning how to eat wisely before a music performance is a serious business! The players mentioned that the issue is not simply the amount (i.e., feeling heavy onstage), but rather, learning to limit specific food groups (e.g., no curries that contain tomatoes and peppers, sauces like salsa, and spicy foods). Experience has taught players to decrease specific foods that lead to higher levels of stomach acid which subsequently increases the chances of experiencing heartburn while onstage in live performances.

(36y, F, tpt)	*I know there are satires [i.e., parodies or lampoon comedies] about elderly Brass players having problems of indigestion: as they blow out on one side it comes out the other side. But, this has always been the case. I couldn't eat a big heavy meat meal before a Concert. But, that has nothing to do with ageing!*
(38y, M, bn/dbn)	*There isn't anything I can't eat now before a Concert compared to 10 years ago as I [became] a Vegetarian. I don't feel I have to make more effort to keep fit.*
(47y, M, trb)	*Especially as a Brass player I watch what I eat so my mouth doesn't become dry, nor get indigestion (and gas). I don't eat too much garlic before I play. That is [not because of ageing, but rather] to be gentle to my colleagues who are sitting very close to me.*
(53y, M, hrp)	*I usually have a good meal before a Concert as we have a 2-hour break between rehearsal and Concert. It's not often easy to find somewhere that caters for Vegetarians especially within the time [frame]. So quite often I'll take stuff with me such as precooked pasta. But then I eat it cold! I have to avoid anything too spicy, because if I'm a little bit nervous it will really give me terrible indigestion throughout the concert. Over the years I've learned what works best.*
(54y, M, cl/bcl)	*Only my nutrition has changed over the years! I tend not to have big meals before a concert. I mean when I was younger I used to go out and have a curry [a heavy hot meal with sauces] before a show. And sometimes, I'd sit there thinking: Oh, I wish I hadn't done that. I mean it was just a dumb thing to go out and have dinner and then rush back and do the Concert when you're bloated which affects the way you play. But that's not because of ageing; it's because of experience.*
(56y, M, va)	*I must say that over the years, one does need to adapt food intake. I am not certain that that has something to do with music performance per se, but rather human ageing.*
(60y, F, vc)	*I don't have to watch what I eat before a concert more than I did when I was younger. All my life I ate very little before a concert. It was never about age, but rather about discipline. I felt I had to feel light, but shouldn't become hungry during the concert. When I was very young, I twice almost fainted onstage because I hadn't eaten. You learn from experience!*

7.4.1.2 Family Life

Family life is especially hard when young children are involved. For some Orchestra players the issue is related to time management. There is a constant juggle between the ongoing physical maintenance of babies, toddlers, younger children, and child-care routines—and Orchestra schedules. The compromises one needs to make as an Orchestra player seem to be unavoidable. There are long hours of rehearsal, and also having to travel away from the family for Concert tours (sometimes in foreign countries). Moreover, the activity life of an Orchestra player covers working hours that do not mirror those of other people in the community. Therefore to some extent, Orchestra musicians are viewed as antisocial—especially as far as the needs of one's partner are concerned. Music performers work when all others are free from employment. The players themselves, as well as their families, need to adjust to irregular working patterns as these have an effect on daytime childcare rosters as well as on nocturnal sleep cycles. On this topic Détári et al. (2020) found that within their sample of 110 professional Symphony Orchestra musicians in Norway, significantly more family–work conflicts were reported than among any other profession of the general workforce.

(39y, F, cl)   *I go home feeling stiff. My neck's in the wrong place. You know I'm much more suscepti-ble to injury. In the long term this isn't gonna be very sustainable. So, that's quite a big part for me to be approaching 40 [years old]. Trying to understand how the age affects my physical ability. How I have certain losses, and how to compensate. Now having a full-time job [in the Orchestra], the challenge is what can I do physically. I also have to hold my 2-year-old who wants to be carried a lot. I've got to invest in tools now so I don't injure myself. I've seen several people in the Orchestra who were unable to play anymore [after having children]. The challenge is that both my family and my playing are physically very demanding.*

(43y, F, db)   *The problem with this job is that it's very time-consuming. It requires very antiso-cial hours, and you're knackered all the time. So, you're sitting onstage and you're dreaming about what else you could be doing. And then when you get home you're so knackered that you don't do anything. I mean the actual hours [of an Orchestra position] on paper are not that bad. But if you're coming back from somewhere at half past midnight, you're not gonna be jumping out of bed at 7 a.m. in the morning to go for a 2-hour run. It does take its toll!*

(47y, F, vn)   *I have a family with three children. I have a completely different life outside of the [Orchestra]. For me it's just being with them, educating my children. The [Orchestra] is a completely different world. When I'm here, I try to forget my home; when I'm at home I try to forget the Orchestra. I think for me it's just a perfect profession. But I have noticed that colleagues who don't have a family are more often off sick than I am. I don't know if it would fulfil me if I only had the Orchestra as a family or if the centre of my life was just playing in the Orchestra.*

(53y, M, vn)   *Union contracts certainly define everything. So, I don't think about the way the Orches-tra is organized or administrated. But job security, salary, vacation days are all the more difficult for me as I get older. Yet, I do think some of it does depend on family. We work in the evening, we work over the weekend. My family—wife and children—and all my acquaintances, all have the evenings and weekends free. But I don't! If they want to meet up with friends on a Saturday afternoon, I can't go! They often go to others at 6 p.m., and I have a concert or Opera at 7:30 p.m.; so I can't go! When I was young, I wasn't so tired after 10 p.m. But now, I see that the social life of persons around me, and my life, are not equal. Some people think that an Orchestra player's social life is the Orchestra. But, it's not like that! It might've been easier if it was. If all of your friends, and everybody that was important to you, was with the Orchestra, then it cer-tainly might make life easier. Many things you do in the evening you wouldn't do in the early afternoon. For example, to go out for a drink [is something] you usually do in the evening. And I can't do that if I'm in the Theatre. Orchestra players have a certain lifestyle. We don't have a normal 40-hour work week. We come to work 7–9 times a week. A normal worker comes every day at 8 a.m. in the morning and leaves at 5 p.m. Sometimes, I don't work 6 days a week, but only 4 days. That is why other people seem to see me as on vacation all the time. My children are now older. But there's no dif-ference to be an Orchestra player now compared to when the kids were younger—my wife [always] took care of them then. Outside of the Orchestra my hobbies are reading, jogging, and Ballroom Dancing (with my wife).*

(56y, F, vn)   *As far as being able to integrate personal life and Orchestra life, I think that ageing offers you certain experience. So now it is actually easier than before. My children have grown up, and less dependent on me being in the home as a caretaker.*

7.4.1.3 Health and Medical Care

While the players clearly stated that they receive most everyday services of health care, many mentioned that aspects of medical care are so much more essential for them than the everyday public. Accordingly, some medical procedures could actually threaten their livelihood as a professional music performer. For example, a 50-year-old male Horn player explicitly discussed a very much 'ordinary' dental practice of removing a Wisdom Tooth. I note that roughly 85% of the population have experienced having had their 3rd Molars removed from their mouth. Yet, such a procedure essentially represents a risk of losing some muscle tone—his embouchure (i.e., lip control). In that case, perhaps dental work could cause his career to end prematurely. Other aspects raised were water retention and sleeping abnormalities. It does seem that a variety of health-related issues become even more apparent as one ages, and medical care is even more of a concern among the Seasoned Musicians than among the Young(er) Players.

(47y, M, hn)	*My teeth are beginning to go, so that's on my horizon. The Wisdom Teeth. If they take them out, then I can lose some feeling which can affect a nerve. So, that's an end point. The only thing I can do is put it off. The dentist says: 'It is what it is—they have to come out.' And I say: 'When I am in agony they'll come out!' The last time I spoke to [a dental specialist] the odds of this ending my career were like 1 out of 200. That isn't very good! A 1-out-of-200 chance of losing some feeling from the brain to the embouchure [is kind of high]. Although that might not seem to be so much, it's enough for me to be worried about it!*
(47y, M, trb)	*I do have to watch my mouth and teeth. You know, as we get older we all have problems with our teeth. And everything you do to them changes your embouchure. When I go to the dentist, they make a copy of my dents with this gum—to make sure if I would have an accident they could rebuild them. But I'm pretty positive, so I don't think about it too much. If it would happen, I have good insurance. Yet, I don't have special insurance on my mouth like some famous Soloist Pianists do on their hands. But, it is more or less the same. If I would lose a tooth, I couldn't do my job!*
(54y, M, va)	*Getting up at night might affect one's ability to play in rehearsals. I have to have an afternoon rest, as that way evening concerts are easier. We usually finish our concerts at 10:30–11:00 p.m. Afterwards, it takes me a long time to calm down. But, I don't think falling asleep after the Concert has become more difficult as I get older. We usually eat out [in a restaurant] after the Concerts.*
(56y, M, va)	*Maybe it is biorhythm, [but I have noticed] that there are those who need to use the bathroom more often, Not like me! I do feel more tired in the morning hours. Perhaps because over the years I have adapted to be more active in the evening hours (and even in the late hours of early morning). Once I used to rise early to practise, and now I can't do that. Not that I sleep more hours (because I don't sleep well at all).*
(59y, M, fl/picc)	*I am more careful about what I eat (in general), and especially before a concert. I also watch what I drink—so as not to have to run offstage to the bathroom which becomes more frequent as one gets older. The metabolism is not the same as it was when I was younger. The real problem is the rehearsals; these should be limited to a 90-minute time slot, so it shouldn't matter too much. During the concerts I have no problem [of bathroom breaks].*

7.4.1.4 Deliberate Practice

Players often talked about home-based practice between other domestic responsibilities and activities. Further, DP is often mentioned as a trigger for clashes between personal domestic life and the profession. For example, a family vacation should provide players with a well-needed break away from the heavy demands of the Orchestra; it is a time to 'unwind', and to give their utmost attention to loved ones. Yet, all players are aware of what is required to get back to shape in the aftermath of a break. Such thoughts are persistent, and do not dissipate when a player goes away for *R&R* (i.e., rest and relaxation).

(47y, M, hn)   *When I look at the [list of pieces we will play this] season, I say: Well that is a very hard piece. I found it hard 20 years ago. I will have to be prepared for it. If I can't play it, then I shouldn't be sitting here in this job. Look, the schedule is out the year before, so you always need to prepare in advance. In most Orchestras, if there's a really big major concert, they have to plan it at least one year prior. So, you do know exactly [what's coming up]. For example, I've been ringing my management to find out what I'm playing on September 4th. [Author's Note: The interview took place in the month of March, 6 months prior to the month in question.] I'm quite worried about that. They don't know yet, but I've got a holiday in August. So, I need to know, before I go off. I need to plan: How am I going to take a Horn with me? How much practice am I gonna do? But [right now] I don't know what I'm gonna have to play when I get back. It could be Mahler 1 [Symphony No. 1 in D major composed 1887–1888 by Austro-Bohemian Romantic composer Gustav Mahler, 1860–1911]; that one is incredibly hard. It would just completely change my summer. I am looking forward to this vacation. Especially, I wanted to put [the Horn] away for 2 weeks. Look: last summer I had a vacation and I put it away for 2 weeks. But it does take you a long time (even months) to come back to the level that you're happy with. But then [after that vacation] I took the family to Italy. I was practising in Italy. That was awkward, and it wasn't really good-quality practice. By the time I had to play something really hard, although I was in good-enough form to manage, there was something that wasn't good enough. Some people said: 'You shouldn't have done it [i.e., gone away]. Why do that if it's gonna take so much time to get back?' Yes. It is a case that I needed it. I did need to stop playing for 2 weeks. Just for my sanity, as well as my physical well-being, and that of my family. So, that's why I felt I had to do it. But these two sides didn't coincide!*

7.4.2 Social Aspects of Being an Orchestra Musician

One final topic the players spoke about at length related to the more social aspects of Orchestra employment and lifestyle. These were concerns about public perceptions and expectancies of Symphony Orchestras: Who is an Orchestra player? What do they do? Who is covering the expenses of the organization? How long should players remain on the concert stage? Players conveyed the notion that there is a certain absurdity as to how they are subjected to the same questions over and over, time and again. For example: 'So, what do you really do?' As if being asked to justify what is their 'genuine' job. Clearly playing a musical instrument for a major Symphony Orchestra is no more than a passionate hobby! In addition, the players comment about public opinion claiming that musicians shouldn't continue to occupy their seats in an Orchestra beyond the 4th Decade. Such an outlook supposedly reflects an ethical issue: old(er) players who stay longer cause there to be fewer tenured-track positions available for young(er) players! After all, newer young(er) players are the future generations of the Orchestra. The participating players raised the question whether such perceptions are no more than bigoted prejudiced and slanted views which could only be referred to as *ageism*. Finally, they mentioned that there seems to be *anecdotal evidence*[1]

---

[1] See 'Why are young people not listening to classical music?' by Shelby Britt. At https://offthehookarts.org/18119-2/.

suggesting a rather negative attitude towards Classical Music as a music culture solely for 'old people'. Such sentiments alert Orchestra managements to a need for old(er) players to be removed from an Orchestra's roster; that younger ticket-buying audiences simply prefer not to see old(er) music performers on the Concert stage—but rather prefer to view young(er) more virile acrobatic players on the platform.

(40y, F, vn)	*I have often found myself having to explain to people what we do [in the Orchestra] and why it's so valuable. Something in our society, and the lack of education [among the public] is a source of great concern.*
(49y, F, vn)	*People often ask me: 'You play Violin? Is that really your work?'*
(52y, M, vc)	*There isn't a difference between players who are getting older as far as the public is concerned? The public hears the thing as a whole. My contribution as a Cellist certainly isn't major; I'm part of a 10-person group. You may find that Oboists have a different take on the matter. So, my main consideration is simply to do my job— while [as far as I am concerned] the public is just there!*
(55y, M, bn)	*I feel the community [i.e., society] has definitely changed throughout my career. I mean how the community sees me as a Classical Player. Thirty years ago to be a Classical Musician was seen as important. I feel that today we're less important in the grand scope of things. People are less excited when I say I'm a Classical Musician. They think I'm crazy to actually do it. Long ago, people used to say: 'What do you really do?' Or: 'Music playing is a sort of hobby, so what do you really do?' And while that perception had changed for some time, it has come back again. I think people of my peers appreciate the fact that I did what I wanted to do. That I wasn't pigeonholed to do something that I wasn't prepared to do. That I chose a dream, and followed my dream. But now they also say: 'I have to [accept] the consequences'; that there are things that I can't do because I earn a lot less than my friends. That's the consequence I have to accept.*
(58y, M, va)	*I didn't want to be a professional musician. I wanted to be a Doctor or Biologist. It just happened; I got a job in an Orchestra. One thing led to another, and I was supporting myself as a player. I went to study in an Academy, and just stayed in the profession. Looking back, if I had to do it all over again, I would have said: Don't become an Orchestra performer. I think society looks at us as simple folk, one of the herd, and not as a 'personality'—which is how they view Soloists.*
(61y, M, fl/picc)	*You often hear people [from the public] say: 'What this Orchestra needs are lots of good young players.' You know, it's a rather sad assumption that although older players might have experience, they haven't got so much 'get-up-and-go'. I think people assume that when you do it a long time, you get stuck in your ways; that you're not open to new ideas, or that you haven't got a flexible outlook. Well, possibly that's true to some extent! It's human nature to get a bit set in your ways as you age. Also, there may be something in assuming that old players will often say: 'There's only one right way of doing it . . . and that's the way I've always done it.' So, given that view, if we did have all younger players in the Orchestra then we would be better. I just don't know where [that expectation] comes from. It's just not true in my opinion. I mean I think older players are more of an asset than a liability. Especially their experience brings lots of different views from what they've gained about how to do things over the years.*

In continuation of the sentiments above, several players also mentioned that there were better times in the past when being a performing musician of Western Classical Music was an admired and even respected contribution to society. But today, there are some players who have experienced members of society with views of an Orchestra as being no more than a lavish extravagant and affluent expense paid by local Regional Councils and Municipalities through everyday taxpayers' hard-earned money. Therefore, in some more hardened times, Orchestras should be cut back or terminated altogether.

(47y, F, vn)   *There were some years when I was afraid I'd lose my job. A few years ago, there wasn't a good atmosphere in our town; the Council went against the Theatre, and everybody [in the Orchestra] got a little bit scared. Then, when another Orchestra moved to town [a Radio Broadcasting Orchestra], there were public discussions suggesting that our [Symphony] Orchestra be reduced. Honestly, I didn't really believe that they could close the Orchestra [founded in 1887]. But it was a bad atmosphere. Everybody discussed the Orchestra [costs versus value]. There were several years I had the feeling that my job was just some kind of luxury. That didn't feel good for me. And, as there were some productions that weren't very good at that time, I didn't feel so comfortable. But, today, I'm really proud of the Orchestra and the Theatre. It makes very much sense for us to work here. I now have the feeling that we are doing very important work for the town—and for the world! What I do is for the betterment of society.*

7.5 Discussion and Summary

The current chapter explored work environment, working conditions, orchestral position, and job security. The first topic to be raised was the actual rehearsal Halls and stage platforms. The players were candid about these as being quite harsh and, to some extent, triggering frailties that surface from ageing.

(50y, M, vn)   *The physical demands of sitting, being able to get through performances has not changed so much. But, lighting is often extremely annoying for me. Often there are spotlights that should be working, but are burned out. They claim to fix them but they don't work properly. Spotlights can make a huge difference on how you perceive the page. You put the stand between players where one person sits here and one here. So, you're really not looking at the page in a healthy way. And sometimes your stand-partner tends to pull it towards them. And they may even be sitting in a way that blocks the page. So, if you're in a Hall where the lighting is not good, and you have to look at the Conductor as well, and it's at night when people are more tired . . . Well then, as you're getting older, and your eyes are changing, it gets more difficult. Further, I would say that for me, being able to sit in chairs has not become more difficult. But, I've been in the Orchestra (now 20 years), and I've heard people who are now 60 [years old] saying: 'When I was like you (a bit younger), it wasn't so hard for me to sit through the concert.' Now, when forced to sit onstage where the first half is unusually long (about 100 minutes without a break), some players start shouting: 'I just can't take it! My ass is hurting.' Maybe it is muscular-skeletal, or circulation. Perhaps needing to go to the toilet. I don't have those problems. Yet, some people just walk out of rehearsals in the middle of a piece. [The Union rules are that] you have to sit in a rehearsal for up to 1:20 [hours]. Yet, some say: 'But I take this pill (a diuretic) for blood pressure. Therefore: I can't do that.' Then, they are allowed to walk out. Sometimes somebody says something, but often nobody says anything. Yet, if I am being very honest, in a live performance, which can be an 1:30 hours per half, no one does that!*

Players mentioned issues of declining eyesight and hearing impairments, as well as physical fatigue. Much was said about working schedules, evening hours, and weekends. In addition, travel (e.g., overnight venues and touring) was raised as a factor that creates a more destructive and even hostile atmosphere.

(43y, F, db)   *Some Orchestras get twice as much rehearsal time, and are a lot slower than we are. That's what I felt when I came here 20 years ago. Quite often we do a concert in the evening [only after] a 3-hour rehearsal in the afternoon. We rehearse Tuesday and Wednesday for 3 hours, and then there's a concert Wednesday night (which is repeated on Thursday night). There might be a rehearsal on Thursday afternoon. On Friday we'll be going out of town somewhere to play. On Saturday we'll be doing 'Film Night' in the local Hall (i.e., a completely different programme with a different Conductor). And then on Sunday we'll be doing an afternoon 'Kids Concert'. In the evening [on Sunday] we repeat the Wednesday night Concert programme! We're only allowed to work 25 playing hours a week; these are 'on-call' hours [as regulated by the Union]. Sometimes it's a real juggling act to fit it all in. Basically, we need to play as many Concerts as possible for the ticket-buying audience. This is just the way to keep the Orchestra floating.*

(49y, M, vn)   *Seasoned Musicians are those between 55 and 65 years of age. In America they talk about 'dead wood' as a metaphor for players getting on to age 60. Some players retire before that time because they can't play any longer, or simply, because they are burnt out. Don't forget, an Orchestra player has no other choices. Six hours of rehearsal is playing for 6 hours. You can't stop, get up, take a break, answer a phone call, or have a sandwich—and then come back to your desk. You can't come in late, and then add on an extra hour at the end of the day. Even a driver can make a rest-stop. Here, there is nothing like that. A Beethoven Symphony that is an hour . . . is an hour! There is nowhere to stop, and then continue in another 5–10 minutes. Moreover, the profession is very public. Not just public in the sense that the audience is watching you on the stage, but public in the sense that when you work (even in a so-called isolated rehearsal space) it is in front of everyone else. There are no private moments. Orchestra players are always 'under the microscope'.*

(52y, M, db)   *Work conditions are definitely more problematic as I get older. First, it's the reading: the eyes are getting [weaker], and after 15–20 years I started to wear glasses. Second, I'm losing my hearing (a little bit). Also, I'm more sensitive to loudness changes in the Orchestra. I try to use earplugs, but I can't play with them as good as without earplugs. I've used ER filters. Many Violin players use −9dbl [in the left ear] and −15dbl [in the right ear]—so one side gets more sound! Percussion players use −25s as the −15s aren't enough for them. Anyway, some people say that only 2% of playing is based on hearing via your ears—but that doesn't make sense to me. I think [it's more like] 80%. For example, Gary Karr [American classical Double Bass virtuoso, b. 1941] says the rest is 'proprioceptive' because by the time your ears hear it, your fingers are already playing the next notes. I think that may be right for him as a soloist, but as we have to play with each other together, we have to hear the other instruments. Perhaps I don't hear much [of myself], but I hear the whole music, and hear the sounds if they vibrate together.*

(54y, M, va)   *The working conditions are not so difficult for me now; not the lighting, or the heat/AC. Of course, having to read, my eyes became worse as I got older. It's become more difficult to see the notes and the Conductor. I know that my [prescription] becomes larger, but there's no proof that that is because of actual playing. But definitely, I see that all the older players have glasses. I also do have a personal problem with my bladder; albeit I can sit through long rehearsals and performances. I just try to ignore it! I don't think it's ever happened that I had to get up in the middle or walk offstage in a performance. But, I do know other players that that has happen to them—but only in rehearsals!*

The chapter touches on work employment conditions. Further, the players discussed periodic evaluations, and relations with Management, viewing them as assuming a more businesslike character. Hierarchical rankings in the Orchestra were placed into the mix. Advancement and mobility were especially hot topics of discussion.

(55y, M, bn)   *I can look at the [upcoming] audition as an experiment. If it works it's fine—it'll give me other options. If it doesn't, then I tried, and that's the end of it. I just don't know yet if I can live with that. Some people have 'Fear of Failure'. Others have 'Fear of Success'. I'm not sure which one I feel. But I don't want to turn around in another few years and say: 'I had that opportunity, and I should have taken it.' I've been waiting for some guy [in that Orchestra] to retire for years; I know I'm a better player than he was. And, it's a shame this didn't happen 10 years ago; if it had happened 20 years ago, maybe I wasn't ready then. Maybe it was politics. It is bad politics this time already too! There's another player, that all the players in the Orchestra want; some other guy because he's . . . you know [younger]. He is also a good player. But I think I can do a better job than him. So, is it already a done deal? I don't know. I'm going into this to prove to myself (and to other people) that I am the better player—even if again they don't take me!*

(58y, M, va)   *From an organization point of view, I think the Orchestra offers less financial security [pension and retirement payment] than other organizations. And that has changed over the years. In younger years either I didn't think about it, or I was naïve about the topic. Foremost, there have been quite a lot of layoffs in the Orchestra recently. Some of the players were just a little older than I am now. Maybe, when I was younger and players left the Orchestra, we all assumed they simply retired—that they were not fired. There really is no reason to get rid of the Seasoned Musicians. For the last 20 years I am [also] the Orchestra inspector; I am in charge of discipline, and keeping the peace among the Ranks. I am also the elected Orchestra representative assistant to the manager. I do much administrative work and arrange technical aspects (such as timetables, ordering cars and buses for Concerts outside of the city, speaking with people, recruiting extra players when a piece requires them, etc.). I do this extra work as a bonus to my salary. It is not easy because it places me in-between the players and the management. It also takes many hours of preparation, and that keeps me away from practising. How did I survive till now getting to age 60? One has to play. To play a lot! To participate in auditions. To be more active [in ensembles]. To be sociable with Orchestra members (and the management). Why didn't I leave the Orchestra earlier? Maybe because I am lazy! This is what I know; the Orchestra is familiar. I have been in this Orchestra for the last 3 Decades!*

(60y, F, vc)   *Previously I had played 2 years in a Swiss Orchestra as Principal Cello. I was also a Soloist with several Concert Recitals pre-booked in advance! Then when I was 39 years old, I emigrated here and became an Orchestra player [appointed as the Cello Section Leader]. The first years were very difficult because I had to deal with a different music-performance language and different Orchestral style. I had to learn to lead without really showing I am leading as not to provoke resistance. I had to learn to unify the people to play the same voice as much as possible, rather than impose something different on them. Finally, I had to learn that I was obliged to play with people I didn't choose, and to do the utmost to play well together. Orchestra positions are vital. Those sitting in the back (Tutti players) have nowhere to go except 'out' [of the job]. Yet, as a Principal player you can always go further back. Does that give me a little bit more security knowing that I could let go of the Leader position to play 2nd Cello or move further back as a Tutti player? Perhaps. I know that as a Principal Section Leader I will make it till 65 (i.e., retire from the Orchestra). But, my answer is quite clear: No, I would not like to continue to play in the Orchestra if I was not the Leader. If I could not be the Principal anymore, I would leave.*

Personal and family responsibilities were intertwined with the professional work life of a Symphony Orchestra player. Nutrition and even medical care were touched upon as problematic aspects that need to be considered. Finally, social perspectives were listed as causing turmoil. The Orchestra profession has passed through several periods in History alternating between being cherished and being guffawed at. As can be seen in the vignettes, these social perceptions most certainly do affect the music performer—and even more they cause emotional havoc as players age.

(61y, M, fl/picc)   *For some players it's been a job, while for others it's vocation. I've often said: To do this you're got to love it! Because if you don't, if it's not your blood, it's not a pleasant profession. It's [actually] hard work and there could be many unpleasant challenges. You've got to want to do it, and find ways of coping. There are things which make me unhappy. When I'll eventually retire, I won't miss all the travelling, the politics, some of the people, and some of the Conductors. But there is a lot that I will miss. I will miss walking out on to that platform, knowing that I'm somebody important. That what I'm about to do really matters, that it can be life-changing to 2,500 people if it's a really good concert! I do believe that music is very important; the spiritual side [of life]. People who come to the Orchestra are optimistic and confident they're going to get a good product. And they may go away feeling that that piece affected them; their heart and emotions. The poetry in music takes them away from the humdrum. But how does working in an Orchestra keep you young? Maybe because of the social aspect (comradery). Or, because it's music and it's passionate. Or, because it does something to your brain. I certainly feel as a musician in the Orchestra that I have some status; that I must be special. Maybe it's foolish, but I feel that way. I feel that I have a purpose here [on Earth], and it is quite an achievement for me to do this. Maybe that keeps me young. Perhaps it's not so much that I'm an Orchestra player per se, but because I'm the one playing the music!*

PART III

PERFORMANCE ANALYSIS

Part III presents materials related to actual performance skills and abilities of Symphony Orchestra musicians. Chapter 8 outlines perceptual motor abilities; these are presented as tapping tasks performed on a computer to collect timing data. Then, two chapters on music performance are presented. Chapter 9 is concerned with Deliberate Practice after *prima vista* Sight-Reading of an original piece employing a *Think Aloud Protocol*. Then Chapter 10 describes the musical performances through the players' own self-evaluation, as well as highlighting an external independent double-blind judging procedure.

The Composer

The music piece was commissioned to Israeli Symphonic Composer Moshe Zorman (b. 1952).[1] Moshe has served as 'house composer' for most of the Music Science research studies I have implemented across my 25-year academic career. Moshe has written over 120 original works, in all music genres. Among his works (at the time of writing, 2024) are: 11 Operas; 6 Symphonic pieces; 5 Concertos; 10 Cantatas for Choir, Soloists, and Orchestra; 20 Choral works; 5 Ballets; 30 Chamber Ensemble pieces; 8 Song Cycles; and 14 compositions for Pianoforte. Moshe has arranged over 1,000 compositions in all styles, including: Popular, Jazz, Symphonic, and Vocal genres. His works have been performed by musicians and ensembles around the world, including the Israeli Philharmonic Orchestra under the baton of Zubin Mehta, the Baltimore Symphony under the baton of Sergiu Comissiona, the BBC National Orchestra of Wales, and the Swedish Mezzo-Soprano Anne Sofie von Otter. Moshe received the *Lifetime Achievement Award* (2023) on behalf of the 'Authors, Composers, and Music Publishers in Israel' (ACUM) society.

---

[1] Biography of Moshe Zorman can be found on the official home page, *Israel Music Institute* (IMI): https://www.imi.org.il/Moshe-Zorman-Israel-Music-Institute?language=eng as well as at *The Music Cathedra*: https://www.musiccathedra.com/moshe-zorman-english.

The Music

The music piece performed by all participating players was composed specifically for the current study. Previously, Bangert et al. (2015) selected a piece for Sight-Reading based on its technical and musical challenges. Accordingly, all participants confirmed that they had not seen, played, or heard the piece before; nor could they identify the Composer's name. Hence, Bangert et al. asserted that their findings enable them to infer the basis on which the players made decisions (e.g., 'How to practise' and 'How to perform') in the absence of complete information from the score. Ericsson and Lehmann (1996) had claimed that one of the marks of expert performers is that they can display their superior performances on demand—including within the boundaries of a laboratory—by which they can be subjected to scientific analysis. Nonetheless, the current investigation attempted to put in place an even higher level of rigour regarding the music piece that was offered to professional Orchestra musicians.

The music stimuli commissioned specifically for the current investigation was based on the following requirements: (1) *anonymity* to ensure that none of the musicians could have had previous exposure or experience performing the music; and (2) *ecological validity* confirming that the *in vivo/in situ* performance piece would be suitable for professional full-time contract Orchestra musicians. That is, the piece serving as empirical stimuli needed to be considered by the players as they do other Western Classical Music. Such a notion is completely opposite to what has been employed in other studies; many other studies employed musical stimuli comprised of 7–11-note melodies (e.g., Meinz & Salthouse, 1998). On the one hand, the music piece was intended to be technically difficult enough to ensure it would be a challenge for music experts such as professional full-time contract Symphony Orchestra players; namely, it was not to be a piece for Conservatory youngsters or Music College students. On the other hand, the intention was that the piece could realistically be improved within a very limited time of Deliberate Practice (e.g., a ±10-minute duration). It was imperative not to present the players with a piece that could either be insulting or over-frustrating. There was a notion that participating players would not feel one of these sentiments:

> You've giving me something that I could have played when I was 13. I'm a professional Symphony Orchestra musician, and this is what you're bringing me?

Or:

> I can't even play it! You should have given me this score to take home in order to learn; I would have come in today playing it very nicely.

As per the empirical requirements, a very high level of music-performance skill was required to execute the piece, demanding the players' utmost attention to technical detail and musical articulation-expression.

(33y, F, bn/dbn)   *When I played this piece, I was proud that I made it! But on the other hand, I'm not satisfied because I know I didn't have the solution for the rhythm. So, you can see it both ways.*

(60y, F, vc)   *Maybe I'm too critical. But I can't help it. Sometimes I know the performance I just gave was far from being perfect. But I tried to improve it a little bit within the given time. I think it's probably rather realistic. I know that I didn't perform great differences between Mezzo Forte, Forte, and Pianissimo in the end. I did at least one wrong note; but I didn't do it again the second time round! It's not a recording for the radio but just a test!*

Three similar versions—each an independent complete stand-alone *miniature*—were composed for the study. Each consisted of the appropriate notation and performance markings for one of five instrument families (Strings, Woodwinds, Brass, Harp, and Keyboard Percussion). In total, 15 scores were prepared for all orchestra instruments as individual parts. See Appendix A. These include: Strings (Violin, Viola, Cello, Double Bass); Woodwinds (Flute, Oboe, Clarinet in B^b, Bassoon); Brass (Horn in F, Trumpet in B^b, Alto Saxophone, Trombone, Tuba); Harp; and Percussion (Xylophone). In general, the scores consist of an average 60 bar measures, graphically presented in staved notation on two A4 pages. In performance tempo (crochet/quarter note = 120bpm) the duration of each piece was roughly 02:30 minutes.

Musicological details, as conveyed by the composer, indicate that the music was not composed in a specific key or tonality (such as C major, A minor, or the Dorian mode). But rather, the music flows freely. Nonetheless, there are clear central tones and melodic motives, as well as stylistic rhythmic figures, which together bring forth a tight unity and structure. Every miniature piece employs several changes in metre, and these changes offer the varied dynamic characters for each of the internal sections. A similar configuration can be found for each piece; these are structured as a three-section A–B–C format, with a different character, and specific pitfalls, in each section.

Strings

The form is A1–A2, B, Coda. The piece exemplifies motion, articulation, and characteristics of string instruments (such as Double Stops), as well as use of the Bow. Each score, for each of the four instruments in the String family, is a duplicate. Yet, each was transcribed for the appropriate register of the specific instrument. In addition, this piece was transcribed for Orchestra Harp. The sections are:

- A1 (measures 1–9) Opening with Double Stops
- A2 (measures 9–28) Dolce
- B (measures 29–41) Leggiero with Triplets
- Coda (measures 42–51)

Woodwinds

The form is A–B–C. The piece exemplifies the character of Woodwind instruments (such as articulatory control, including Tonguing techniques like Staccato, Legato, and Double-Tonguing), as well as musical phrasing and dynamic ranges in the higher registers. Each score, for each of the four instruments in the Woodwind family, is a duplicate. Yet, each was transcribed for the appropriate register of the specific instrument. In addition, this piece was transcribed for Orchestra Xylophone (incorporating rolling techniques, i.e., tremolos, used to lengthen the duration of tones).

- A (measures 1–20) Leggiero
- B (measures 20–37) Lyrical Expression
- C (measures 38–55) Meno Mosso, slower feeling with the ending left open (e.g., musical text ends with a feeling of uncertainty).

Brass

The form is A–B–A+Coda. The piece exemplifies the character of Brass instruments (such as percussive flutter, Double-Tonguing, broken chords, and Fanfare playing). Each score, for each of the four instruments in the Brass family, is a duplicate. Yet, each was transcribed for the appropriate register of the specific instrument.

- A (measures 1–19) Marcato/Bravura, Leggiero
- B (measures 20–47) Dolce
- A+Coda (measures 48–66)

8

Psychomotor Tapping

8.1 Introduction

The timing of fine motor movement has been extensively explored in the study of lifespan cognitive and motor development. Thompson et al. (2015) bring out that the ability to tap consistently to a beat emerges in early childhood, and then has a developmental trajectory with improvements into early adulthood. But, among older adults, rhythmic control and tapping asynchrony become more variable. In fact, many researchers (e.g., Greene & Williams, 1993; Krampe et al., 2001) claim that slowing of the central clock, as well as additional factors, can explain age-related changes regarding timing variability. Thompson et al. highlight the fact that older adults demonstrate some deficits in motor coordination including balance and gait, revealing the slowdown of human movement. Accordingly:

> *Ageing is associated with decreased brain connectivity, degeneration of neurotransmitter systems [. . .] a loss of synchronous firing throughout the auditory system [and] a loss in neural synchrony [that] may be a key contributor to the older adults' reduced ability to entrain to a beat, especially given the established link between tapping performance and subcortical neural synchrony.* (p. 9)

Finally, age-related changes in speed and accuracy of timing control have been associated to basic aspects of information processing including attention and executive functions.

8.1.1 Finger-Tapping and Musical Experience

The *Dynamic Attending* theory postulated by Mari Riess Jones (1976, 1990) of the Psychology Department at Ohio State University (USA) predicts a gradual slowing of internal periodicity with increased age. The conceptual viewpoint, as examined through self-paced finger-tapping tasks in which the spontaneous or 'preferred' tapping rate (pace or tempo), has been tested across different age groups (e.g., Drake et al., 2000; McAuley et al., 2006). However, only partial support for the hypothesis was found elsewhere (e.g., Andrews et al., 1998; Salthouse, 1996). Nonetheless, many models of cognitive ageing have typically described a rise-and-decline pattern for the performance in a vast amount of motor and cognitive functions over the lifespan; these promote a general factor account for movement timing, assuming that most

Seasoned Musicians Playing Beyond the 5th Decade. Warren Brodsky, Oxford University Press. © Oxford University Press (2025).
DOI: 10.1093/9780198956501.003.0008

age-related differences in performance have a single common cause associated to an overall reduction in timing control and processing speed (e.g., Cepeda et al., 2001). But yet, research by Thompson et al. (2015) has shown that such shortfalls in tapping synchrony may less than dwindle for individuals with music experience. They investigated beat synchronization through a uniform assessment of tapping, and reported to have found that those with musical experience track with greater synchronization ability throughout life. Namely, although the ability to move consistently to a beat seems to improve across the lifespan, and while in old(er) adulthood this ability somewhat falls, Thompson et al. provided evidence that musical experience is a causal factor for lower tapping variability and lower mean tap asynchrony (i.e., increased beat alignment) during paced synchronization.

Ralf T. Krampe and colleagues, at the time from the Max Planck Institute of Human Development (Germany), focused on timing control as an adaptation to specific internal and external performance constraints (Krampe & Ericsson, 1996; Krampe et al., 2000, 2001, 2002, 2005; for a review, see Krampe, 2002). They found that internal constraints (e.g., age and musical expertise) were associated to processing capacity affecting fine motor movement. Regarding the effect of internal constraints on the different components of motor skill, Krampe and Ericsson (1996) provided support for a *selective maintenance* account, which assumes that certain skills would not show age-related decline because of domain-specific mechanisms acquired and maintained through Deliberate Practice (DP). In their experiments, Krampe and Ericsson employed a wide range of tasks with four groups of Pianists: Young(er) Amateurs, Young(er) Experts, Old(er) Amateurs, and Old(er) Experts. They employed maximum repetitive tapping rate, speeded multiple-finger, and bimanual alternate-hand finger-tapping tasks. In the Old(er) Amateur Musician subgroup, they found age-related effects in speeded multiple finger-tapping and bimanual coordination tasks (similar to non-specific general psychometric and reaction rated tests). In contrast, Old(er) Professional Pianists showed normal age-related declines in general measures of processing speed, while negative age-effects were reduced (or fully absent) in expertise-related tasks. Moreover, variabilities were similar for both Young(er) 18–21-year-old and Old(er) 67–73-year-old adults. Given that isochronous tapping is seen as the most direct measure for the efficiency of the internal clock, these findings indicate age-graded stability of low-level timing mechanisms. Taken together, the findings point to crossover interaction patterns of age, expertise, and capacity (Krampe, 2002). In general, these early studies found that the degree of maintenance of skills (albeit, relevant to Piano performance) was predicted by the amount of DP during late adulthood.

Later studies by Krampe (e.g., Krampe et al., 2001, 2002) demonstrated that age-related declines of motor skill were modifiable through practice, and that age-related changes were not observed for tapping in two groups of Amateur Pianists (i.e., 19–30-year-olds *versus* 60–81-year-olds). Hence, the researchers proposed that musical expertise does reduce variabilities caused by ageing; a finding that is consistent with previous literature showing an effect of musical expertise on maximal tapping rates (e.g., Keele et al., 1985). Further, Krampe (2002) provided evidence for expertise-specific adaptations in processes underlying motor movements seen in bimanual coordination and timing tasks. Namely, another perspective was forwarded: individual differences in fine motor performance are based on outcomes of long-term adaptations to external task situational demands and age. Finally, Norton et al. (2005) pointed to instrumental training as improving finger-tapping speed, which is quite understandable given that developing techniques on an instrument involves fine motor coordination. Yet, Krampe underscored wide discrepancies between published studies employing repetitive tapping, whereby many seem to suggest findings pointing to age-related variability—viewed as negative effects of age. It is of specific relevance here to mention Frost (2000), who may have been the only researcher to purposely study ageing among Concert Musicians. Frost found that these musicians retained finger-tapping speed and general reaction time *as if* they were in the years of their youth; Frost claimed that finger-tapping tasks are primarily measures of *coordination* rather than of *muscle function*.

8.1.1.1 Interhemispheric Transfer

We should note that the prevalence of right-, left-, and mixed-handedness has often been examined as a means to highlight expected variances in cerebral dominance based on intensive hand-skill training among musicians. Accordingly, hand-skill can be seen as a measure of handedness; handedness is thought to illuminate neurodevelopment. Some studies have found that *interhemispheric transfer*, the capacity for information transfer between right- and left-brain hemispheres, progressively improves until around 10–14 years of age when they reach optimal levels of adult performance (Piccirilli et al., 2020). But then, roughly around the 6th Decade of human maturity, a progressive decline in performance is also seen to occur with atrophy of the Corpus Callosum. Nonetheless, as Massimo Piccirilli and colleagues from the University of Perugia (Italy) point out, there is an associated link between the structure of the Corpus Callosum and musical training. That is, systematic DP with a musical instrument commencing from an early age over many years, can trigger plastic changes in the Corpus Callosum whereby those with extensive musical training have been found with a larger Corpus Callosum (i.e., increased volume of cell weight and size) as well as more efficient White Matter organization. Consequently, these researchers found that among $N = 65$ old(er) professional Classical Musicians ($M_{Age} = 69$, Range 56–90) there were significantly fewer errors during a *fingertip cross-localization test* than age-matched control subjects. Hence, Piccirilli et al. claimed to have found a relationship between music playing, music-induced changes in plasticity, and maintenance of developmental gains—despite ageing.

8.1.1.2 Asymmetry

Conceptually, *Asymmetry* is represented on a continuous scale, and has been thought to be stable even after extensive practice. Albeit, both hands do show improvements after training. In a landmark study, Lutz Jancke (Jancke et al., 1997), then of the Heinrich Heine University in Düsseldorf (Germany), questioned if the degree of hand-skill asymmetry would be reduced in right-hand-dominant musicians. Their study examined if, as a result of musical instrument training, there would be a reduced degree of right-hand superiority. They hypothesized that due to intensive hand-skill training, musicians would differ from non-musicians; their more skilful use of the non-dominant hand might interfere with hand preference for certain tasks. Jancke and colleagues also sought to shed light on the degree of hand-skill asymmetry as co-dependent on the age of commencement of musical training (see Chapter 2, section 2.2.1.1), as well as on choice of musical instrument (e.g., Strings *versus* Piano). Their findings were unequivocal: (a) hand-skill asymmetry was highly linked to the age one began their musical training; and (b) hand-skill asymmetry was associated to the instrument learned. Nonetheless, the researchers did not find a relationship between hand-skill asymmetry and duration of musical training. Yet, in an earlier study, Christman (1993) demonstrated that musicians playing either String or Woodwind instruments exhibited a decreased degree of hand preference than musicians playing Keyboard instruments. It should be pointed out that all of these studies seem to be indicating that changes in fine distal hand/finger motor skills occur subsequent to training regimes, and that these are essentially psychomotor manual skills strengthened by DP. Most specifically, that the reduced degree of right-hand superiority is seen as the left hand *gaining* equivalent strengths and parallel independence, rather than as the right hand *losing* its dominance.

8.2 The Current Study

Within the two-hour interview session, each Orchestra player completed two performance-related tasks. There was an *in vivo/in situ* music performance (see Chapters 9 and 10). Moreover, there was a *psychomotor finger-tapping* exercise. The participating players were aware of the performance components in advance, and each signed informed consent for collecting timing data; they also granted permission for audio recording of the two-part music-performance exercise.

In the finger-tapping exercise, five isochronous finger-tapping tasks were employed (see section 8.2.2.2). *Isochronous tapping* involves repetitions of the same target interval. These included: self-paced tapping at spontaneous and preferred rates; speeded uni-manual single-finger-tapping (for each hand); and bimanual alternate-hand finger-tapping. Shammi et al. (1998) point out that single-finger-tapping and alternate-hand finger-tapping are tasks that require psychomotor consistency for efficient performance. Accordingly, Shammi et al. found age-related increased diversity among old(er) non-musician participants for self-paced preferred rates of finger-tapping. Moreover, Krampe et al. (2001) found that while uni-manual single-finger-tapping was comparable for young(er) and old(er) Pianists, there were differences in the maximum tempo of alternating-hand finger-tapping (with slower bpms for the old(er) players).

8.2.1 Participants

In total there were $N = 48$ Orchestra players who participated in the two-hour interviews. In only one case was the finger-tapping exercise omitted. Unfortunately, a glitch in a command line (i.e., a technical programming error) was found at a later date that had caused the data of nine musicians to be overwritten. The remaining $n = 38$ participants were all full-time contract Orchestra players recruited from five professional Symphony Orchestras. Although the Orchestras were located in three countries (England, Germany, and Israel), the players themselves were born in over 13 locations around the world. The sample consisted of 23 (58%) Strings, 9 (24%) Woodwinds, 3 (8%) Brass, 2 (5%) Harps, and 1 (3%) Percussion (Xylophone) players. Among the players were 23 (61%) males; they were on average 49 years old ($SD = 9.87$, Range 27–64) born between the years 1947 and 1983.

8.2.2 Methods

8.2.2.1 Procedure and Equipment

The tasks in the finger-tapping study were presented as five blocks (referred to as 'trials'). The trials were presented on an IBM *Thinkpad-X31* laptop computer (Intel Pentium™ M, 1.7GHz processor) with a 12″ TFT display. The tasks were programmed and executed with *EPrime-1* (Psychological Software Tools, PST). EPrime is a comprehensive stimulus presentation platform used to design experimental studies and to run experiments that collect and save timed-response data. A proprietary sequence of events was programmed specifically for the investigation; among other events logged, were Inter-Tap Intervals (ITIs).

Participants were asked to tap regularly with their forefingers on a laptop computer, either on the right *alt* 'alternate' keyboard key, or left *ctrl* 'control' keyboard key, or both (depending on the specific task). The instructions for every task appeared on the monitor screen as a Textbox in English. Participants were given ample time to read the instructions, and if needed, received further explanations orally to fully understand each task. Within the interview session, the complete finger-tapping exercise lasted about 15 minutes; it was strategically placed between two 40-minute segments of verbal discussion.

8.2.2.2 Empirical Tasks

The specific tasks (i.e., trials) used in the study were adapted from many investigations as reported in the literature, including: Drake et al. (2000), Jancke et al. (1997), Kemper et al. (2003), Krampe and Ericsson (1996), McAuley et al. (2006), and Shammi et al. (1998). The five finger-tapping tasks (trials) were:

a) *Spontaneous Motor Tempo* (SMT). Trial-1: Participants were asked to finger-tap regularly for half a minute (30s), while maintaining a constant interval between successive taps. They were asked to finger-tap with a smooth gesture, at their most comfortable, favourite, natural rate of finger-tapping, maintaining a constant interval between successive finger taps. They were told to tap at a rate that was 'just right'—neither too fast or too slow. The task was self-paced.

b) *Preferred Perceptual Tempo* (PPT). Trial-2: Participants were asked to finger-tap regularly for approximately half a minute (30s) at a rate that seemed most appropriate for the well-known song 'Happy Birthday to You' (see Figure 8.1) as they mentally imagined it, perhaps humming to themselves without external audiation. They were asked to finger-tap while maintaining a constant interval between successive finger taps. The task was self-paced.

c) *Forced Speeded Tapping Right Hand* (FSTRH). Trial-3: Participants were asked to finger-tap uni-manually with their right forefinger for approximately half a minute (30s) as rapidly as possible. They were asked to finger-tap while maintaining a constant interval between successive finger taps. It is presumed that participants could not physically finger-tap quicker, and hence, this trial reflects upper limits. In almost all cases this was the dominant hand. The task was self-paced.

d) *Forced Speeded Tapping Left Hand* (FSTLH). Trial-4: Participants were asked to finger-tap uni-manually with their left forefinger for approximately half a minute (30s) as rapidly as possible. They were asked to finger-tap while maintaining a constant interval between successive finger taps. It is presumed that participants could not physically finger-tap quicker, and hence, this trial reflects upper limits. In almost all cases this was the non-dominant hand. The task was self-paced.

e) *Forced Speeded Tapping Alternating Hands* (FSTAH). Trial-5: Participants were asked to finger-tap bimanually, starting with their right and then left forefingers in alternation for approximately half a minute (30s). They were asked to finger-tap as rapidly as possible while maintaining a constant interval between successive finger taps. It is presumed that participants could not physically finger-tap quicker, and hence, this trial reflects upper limits as well as their ability to synchronize bimanually between right and left hands. The task was self-paced.

Figure 8.1 Song: 'Happy Birthday to You'

Written for a 19th-century kindergarten class (in Kentucky, USA) by kindergarten teachers, sisters Mildred J. Hill and Patty Smith titled 'Good Morning to All'. First published: 1893; Copyright free: 2016.

8.2.2.3 Analyses

The analysis of finger-tapping data (in milliseconds, ms) was multi-level by nature. Foremost, it involved an investigation of each participant themselves (e.g., the speed that each participant had finger-tapped), as well as involving the items of each task in each trial (e.g., variability/consistency/stability of finger-tapping performances). The analyses involved the following steps:

a) The first five ITIs were deleted as they might not necessarily reflect steady regular consistent successive finger-taps based on a smooth hand gesture.

b) The last five ITIs were deleted as they might reflect motor manual fatigue.

c) ITI Outliers were deleted as they might reflect untimely finger taps. ITIs outliers were defined as either less than half or more than twice the average ITIs of the same participant; these data were removed from all further analyses.

d) The Average (*M*) and Standard Deviation (*SD*) of ITIs were calculated.

e) The Grand-Mean Average (*M-TotTap*) and Grand-Mean Standard Deviation (*M-SD*) of ITIs were calculated. The former relates to the speed of finger-tapping; the latter relates to the variability and consistency of the ITIs. Then, age-related increases in variability of finger-tapping (i.e., *SD*s of finger-tapping tasks) were investigated. This analysis sought to shed light on the question if variability is a unitary phenomenon that can be seen across all psychomotor finger-tapping tasks.

f) ITIs (ms) were converted to Beats Per Minute (bpm). BPM represents the musical value equal to a quarter note. BPM is the most accepted and well-known indication of *pace* for a temporal string of events (e.g., 'slow' or 'fast' tempo).
   Arithmetical Procedure: *bpm = 60,000/MN ITIs [ms]*
   Explanation: There are 60,000 ms in 1 minute.

g) Hand-skill Asymmetry (ASYM) scores were calculated. This score is independent of music performance (see Chapter 10).
   Arithmetical Procedure: *Asymmetry = (RH—LH) / (RH + LH)*.
   Explanation: RH is the number of finger taps in speeded finger-tapping with the right hand (Trial 3); LH is the number of finger taps in speeded finger-tapping with the left hand (Trial 4). Asymmetry is measured on a linear scale between −1 and +1, whereby hand Symmetry = 0, and hand-dominance falls close to either −1 or +1. Therefore, Asymmetry or superiority for the right hand is a positive value (between .00 and +1), while asymmetry or superiority for the left hand is a negative value (between .00 and −1).

8.2.3 Results

The findings from the psychomotor task are presented in Table 8.1. First, the whole dataset sample (*N* = 38) is presented. But then, in an effort to compare the Young(er)

Table 8.1 Pace Speed (ms and bpm) of Finger-Tapping Tasks: Comparisons Between Young(er) Players *Versus* Seasoned Musicians

Task	Total Musicians (N=38)			Young(er) Players LTE45 (n = 13)			Seasoned Musicians GTE55 (n = 14)			Sig
	M^1	SD	bpm	M^1	SD	bpm	M^1	SD	bpm	p
SMT	721	214	83	757	288	79	643	169	93	
PPT	682	269	88	780	400	77	608	152	99	
FSTRH	178	34	337	173	33	347	188	45	319	
FSTLH	180	29	333	180	31	333	184	36	326	
FSTAH	126	32	476	120	27	500	133	42	451	
TotTap	377	82	159	406	110	148	351	73	171	

^{1}= ITIs in milliseconds (ms)

Players (players less than or equal to the age of 45, LTE45) with the Seasoned Musicians (greater than or equal to the age of 55, GTE55), 2 subsamples were put forward: LTE45 (n = 13, 48%, M_{Age} = 37, SD = 6.39, Range 27–44) *versus* GTE55 (n = 14, 51%, M_{Age} = 58, SD = 2.83, Range 55–64). It should be noted that all Orchestra players who were between these two age subgroups (e.g., 46–54 years old) were not considered in the final analyses in an effort to nullify overlapping that might confound results.

8.2.3.1 Spontaneous Motor Tempo (SMT)

The average finger-tapping tempo of the musicians was *Moderato* tempo (83bpm). As can be seen in Table 8.1, the Young(er) Players tapped slightly slower than the Seasoned Musicians; however, this difference was not statistically significant.

8.2.3.2 Preferred Perceptual Tempo (PPT)

The tempo perceived as the most appropriate pulse beat for the well-known song 'Happy Birthday to You' was 88bpm. That was slightly faster than SMTs. As can be seen in Table 8.1, the Seasoned Musicians players perceived the pace for the 'Happy Birthday to You' song as slightly faster than the Young(er) Players; however, this difference was not statistically significant.

8.2.3.3 Forced Speeded Tapping (FST)

As can be seen in Table 8.1, forced speeded finger-tapping of all three tasks (FSTRH, FSTLH, FSTAH) was performed faster by the Young(er) Players than the Seasoned Musicians. In addition, the Young(er) Players finger-tapped faster with their right hand (FSTRH) than with their left hand (FSTLH), while the Seasoned Musicians demonstrated the exact opposite finger-tapping behaviour. Finally, the Young(er) Players were fastest when alternating between the right and left hands. It should

Table 8.2 Consistency and Variability (SDs) of Finger-Tapping Tasks: Comparisons Between Young(er) Players *Versus* Seasoned Musicians

Task	Total Musicians (*N*=38) M^1	Young(er) Players LTE45 (*n* = 13) M^1	Seasoned Musicians GTE55 (*n* = 14) M^1	Sig *p*
SMT	26.67	25.33	26.18	
PPT	27.79	29.91	26.66	
FSTRH	13.25	14.06	15.05	
FSTLH	15.23	16.76	14.33	
FSTAH	20.30	20.36	21.14	
TotTap	20.65	21.28	20.67	

^{1} = *SD*s of ITIs in milliseconds (ms)

be noted that the tempos of all forced speeded finger-tapping tasks were performed *Prestissimo*—at an extremely fast pace in excess of 200bpm. Yet, all of these differences between the age subgroups were not statistically significant.

To sum up, as far as *pace* is concerned, the Seasoned Musicians performed all psychomotor finger-tapping tasks just as fast as the Young(er) Players—who were sometimes more than 20 years younger.

After examining the general speed of finger-tapping, the analysis turned to assessing *variability* or *consistency* of motor performance (i.e., deviations of tapping). See Table 8.2. As can be seen in Table 8.2, the variability of spontaneous and preferred finger-tapping tempos demonstrated similar ranges of consistency; no statistically significant differences surfaced between the Young(er) Players *versus* the Seasoned Musicians. This finding directly contradicts Shammai et al. (1998), published in the journal *Aging, Neuropsychology, and Cognition*, who found greater diversity in terms of larger *SD*s among the old(er) participants. Accordingly, age-related increases in diversity were greater in the self-paced condition (which is equivalent to both SMT and PPT tasks in the current study). But, perhaps there were various confounding variables that led Shammai et al. to determine unfounded conclusions. For example, at the time they did not consider the possibility that their subjects were not really as expert with proficiencies as required by the empirical task. The participants were *n* = 36 'healthy female volunteers' either recruited through ads in local newspapers (between ages 20 and 35) or from a Geriatric residential living centre (between ages 60 and 75) all residing in Toronto (Canada). Nor was there any recognition (i.e., limitations) that each finger-tapping was administered twice—each under a different empirical condition: self-paced and then externally paced. The second condition required participants to synchronize their finger-tapping to an external 'click-track' heard via a computer-generated beeping sound. Foremost, synchronization to an external 'click' sound is a totally different facility than self-paced finger-tapping. Second, given the time period of the experiment was roughly 1997—while the microcomputer revolution of the 1970s was already in full bloom, the personal computer as a mass-market consumer electronic device had not as yet become a household appliance—hence perhaps the beeping sound of the computer not only generated pacing sounds but also generated higher levels of anxiety as being reminiscent of a soundscape associated to an ICU Hospital room environment. Finally, there may have been much confusion among these 70-year-old elderly participants (born between the years 1920 and 1940) lacking experience with computer-generated audio signals and *earcons*. And finally, unlike the current study in which participants finger-tapped for a total 30s and then rested for 30s while reading instructions of the following task, Shammai et al. had participants finger-tap for each 45s trial—four times in succession—with no (reported) respite. Finally, the current data of all tasks were cleansed by eliminating the first five ITIs and last five ITIs for a more reliable picture of variability and consistency of motor manual performance. Shammai et al. didn't employ such a procedure.

Then, the forced speeded single-hand finger-tapping for right and left hands indicated consistent ITIs. This finding shows the tightening of variability for speeded finger-tapping (i.e., much smaller ITIs) than performed for the spontaneous finger-tapping task. Finally, as can be seen in Table 8.2, forced speeded bimanual alternating-hand finger-tapping was slightly less controlled for all musicians than forced speeded single-hand finger-tapping for either right or left hands. However, these differences were not statistically significant. This is an important finding because the more subjective feeling of many musicians from both age subgroups is that a 'sure sign of ageing' is an ever-so-slight slowing-down of repetitive movements such as found when performing *tremolos*, *vibrato*, and *trills* (see Chapter 4, sections 4.1, 4.3.1, and 4.3.2). Nonetheless, comparing across all three FST tasks (i.e., Trials 3–5), employing a Repeated Measures Analysis of Variance (ANOVA) for *M-SD*, statistically significant differences did surface; but these were not indications of age subgroup. That is, Orchestra players were significantly more in control of forced speeded uni-manual finger-tapping for either the right or left hand than for forced speeded bimanual alternating-hand finger-tapping: $F_{(2, 74)} = 15.72$, $MSe = 31.97$, $p < 0.0000$, $n_p^2 = 0.30$ (considered a large effect size). To sum up, the Seasoned Musicians performed all psychomotor tapping tasks with just as much consistency as did the Young(er) Players—who were sometimes more than 20 years younger.

Although Orchestra players might have self-perceptions of superiority for one hand over the other (referred to as hand-dominance), and such a superiority regards most everyday tasks such as handwriting with a pen or holding a toothbrush, when considering music performance such superiorities for the right or left hand are usually annulled. This annulment is often subsequent to intense DP whereby the non-dominant hand becomes stronger in an effort to work in conjunction with the dominant hand. It should be brought out that Orchestra musicians spend at least 10,000 hours engaged in DP across 17 years, commencing from age 6 throughout maturity to the age of 18 years (see Chapter 2, section 2.2.1.2). The analysis then calculated the number of finger taps (i.e., NTaps) for forced speeded finger-tapping (Tasks 3–4) with both right and left hands. See Table 8.3. As can be seen in Table 8.3, the average number of finger taps (*M*-NTaps) produced for the right hand were generally more than those produced with the left hand. However, these differences were not statistically significant. In addition, the Young(er) Players tapped more frequently with the right hand than the left hand, whereas the Seasoned Musicians tapped with each hand in a similar fashion. Yet again, no statistically significant differences between the age subgroups surfaced.

Table 8.3 Forced Speeded Tapping of Right and Left Hand: Comparisons Between Young(er) Players *Versus* Seasoned Musicians

Task	Total Musicians (*N*=38)		Young(er) Players LTE45 (*N* = 13)		Seasoned Musicians GTE55 (*N* = 14)		Sig
	M[1]	*SD*	*M*[1]	*SD*	*M*[1]	*SD*	*p*
FSTRH	161.87	42.79	177.23	29.25	158.35	44.11	
FSTLH	156.79	36.70	165.62	28.68	157.00	39.91	

[1]= Average Number of Taps (*M*-NTaps)

Finally, asymmetry was calculated. See Table 8.4. Table 8.4 indicates values all above nought (i.e., to the right of 0 zero/naught or '+' values); these reflect a right-hand superiority. Yet, for the most part, these values are extremely close to 0 zero. This, then, is an indication of bilateral symmetry in the development of coordinating both hands. Albeit humans do seem to have innate abilities of hand-dominance, in which both hands are somewhat independent, it is the usual case that one hand is stronger than the other. Hence referred to as the dominant hand. Yet, for the sake of efficient music performance, sometimes all four limbs need to act fully independently with equal strength and synchronicity in a most systematic manner. A few outstanding examples are:

- Concert Pedal Harp: 47 strings for right–left hands; 7 pedals for right–left feet
- DrumKit or Drum Set or Trap Set: 3–6 drums and 2–3 cymbals for right–left hands; bass drum pedal for right foot with hi-hat cymbal pedal for left foot

Table 8.4 Asymmetry of Right and Left Hand: Comparisons Between Young(er) Players *Versus* Seasoned Musicians

Task	Total Musicians (*N*=38)		Young(er) Players LTE45 (*N* = 13)		Seasoned Musicians GTE55 (*N* = 14)		Sig
	M[1]	*SD*	*M*	*SD*	*M*	*SD*	*p*
ASYM	0.009	0.07	0.034	0.05	0.001	0.05	

- Church Pipe Organ: 2 5-octave manual keyboards for right–left hands; 30–32 key pedalboard for right–left feet

The findings of the current study support the notion of music-training-induced symmetry; this was found for all 38 out of 38 players (Range −0.261 to +0.159). It is interesting to note that the indices of asymmetry for the Young(er) Players are very similar to those reported by Jancke et al. (1997) for right-handed musicians ($M = 0.04$, $SD = 0.03$). The subgroup of Seasoned Musicians in the current sample demonstrated even better indices of symmetry—albeit such differences were not statistically significant.

To sum up, beginning as young children and then throughout their teen years of music-skill development, Seasoned Musicians not only advanced their less dominant hand to perform in a synchronous fashion with their more dominant hand, and exercised the performance of specific psychomotor tasks for each hand until they acquired the same level of speed and consistency matching the other more dominant hand in an effort for them to function together, but they were able to retain and maintain such gains well past the 5th Decade of human maturation. Namely, Seasoned Musicians empirically demonstrated symmetry skills at least as well as Young(er) Players who were sometimes 20 or more years younger. Then, in an effort to examine if lack of differences for asymmetry x age might be masked by other demand characteristics (e.g., musical instrument type), an ANOVA was implemented with instrument type entered as a grouping variable for indices of asymmetry. The findings indicate no statistical differences between the musical instrument types: $F_{(2, 35)} = 0.268$, $MSe = 0.005$, $p = 0.97$. Hence, the above findings seem to be both valid and reliable as based on age subgroups.

8.3 Discussion and Summary

Clarke (2002) claimed that "expert performers have remarkable control of performance timing at levels ranging from the individual note to sections or complete pieces" (p. 61). They possess the capacity to judge and even set the tempo of a performance with varying degrees of reliability and reproducibility. Accordingly, some seem to have the tempo equivalent of absolute pitch. But do these change over time?

(43y, F, db)   *I don't know if the younger players will have an easier time [with the tapping exercise] than the older players. I am not sure the younger players will be more steady (less fluctuations) just tapping a beat, than the older players. I am not sure that's something that does change with age. I mean if you consider what we're doing in there, we all have to be pretty accurate. I know from an article I read that as we get older our tapping ability slows down. But then, it said that it doesn't matter if our natural tapping slows down; it's more of a question of the stability. So, let's say that when someone's younger, their most natural tapping was 100bpm, and now when they're older they tap 80bpm. On the one hand that does show you're slowing down, but on the other hand whether or not one is tapping 100 or 80 it should be just that stable. So, my feeling is that age has nothing to do with it. Musicians should be able to be regular tappers at 30 or 70 [years old]—if they're still playing.*

The current findings demonstrate that acquired expertise-specific mechanisms can indeed be retained and maintained well into the 5th Decade by professional full-time contract Symphony Orchestra Seasoned Musicians. This is contrary to Ericsson and Lehmann (1996) who specifically note that the highest achievements in motor skill occur in the 4th Decade between 30 and 40 years old, after which declines are to be expected. As can be seen in the previous chapters, Orchestra players often relate to *maintenance* as having to do with continually upholding a practice regimen outside scheduled Orchestra rehearsals. In this connection, Krampe (2002) was steadfast in conveying the message that preservation of capabilities relates to dexterity within musical proficiency, and that depends on the amount of DP invested at later stages of maturation—especially in the 5th and 6th Decades of life.

Krampe (2006) noted that virtuosic performances of old(er) musicians are not clearly understood. On the one hand, comparative studies with normal adults indicate a systematic age-related decline in cognitive mechanisms, including: reaction time, speed of memory search, general processing speed, and maximum tapping rate. Accordingly, normal adults in their 7th Decade usually need about twice as long to process the same level of information as do adults in their 2nd Decade. But this was not the case for old(er) musicians. Other studies also confirm such findings. For example, Piccirilli et al. (2020) found that professional Classical musicians ($N = 65$, $M_{Age} = 68.9$, $SD = 10.33$, Range 56–90, 65% males) made significantly fewer errors on the *tactile interhemispheric transfer test* (i.e., cross-tapping on the opposite knee to a visually presented stimuli) than did aged matched non-musicians. Yet, in an early study, Krampe and Ericsson (1996) found no difference between 60-year-old professional musicians and old(er) amateur musicians for general cognitive tasks, but they did find differences for expertise-related tasks (such as single-finger-tapping and alternating-hand finger-tapping). The researchers concluded that domain-specific mechanisms come to the surface when examining age-related maintenance of skills; most specifically, that old(er) Concert Pianists were able to maintain their performance skills and abilities at the same levels as young(er) Concert Pianists. Here we need to ask: Are these findings transferable to professional full-time contract Symphony Orchestra players?

We might question if some components, such as speed (i.e., maximal rate of repetitive single-finger-tapping), indicate advantages of age for variability, stability, and consistency of ITIs? As we age we might expect higher variability of ITIs—especially as it is more common to find a more general effect of age-related slowdown. The implication is that age-related differences in variability are an independent consequence of ageing, and not simply a consequence of age-related declines in overall performance (Shammi et al., 1998). In fact, some players see reductions of musical skills among old(er) players, especially when it comes to timing issues. Yet, these players are adamant that the source of such declines is more of an 'emotional' component than actual 'motor' control. For example, one player in the current study stated that she experiences performance declines among a few old(er) players in her section, and these are related to aspects of 'the beat'. Accordingly, she is certain that the real issue is personality, temperament, and dispositional attitude:

(44y, F, vn)   *I am not so sure that the players who are over 55 have more trouble concentrating or paying attention. But, the one thing I've noticed is that as people get older, they rush more for the music. They just come in, and they're not on the beat. The conductor gives it, and quite often I find that [those] who are a bit older, don't really look for the sign, but they feel: 'I know what to do, I'm just gonna come in.' Perhaps because they have no patience. It's not the tempo, [they] just come in before the beat. Possibly, it's a motor-physical thing, but more likely it's an awareness or a personality thing. It's almost as if they're in their own little world. A type of arrogance: 'I am right, and you're late' [referring to the conductor's downbeat].*

The argument being put forward is that in repetitive movement tasks with explicit timing requirements, it may be more efficient (from a research perspective) to examine *variability* of ITIs than *frequency* of number of finger taps produced. For example, Krampe et al. (2001) asserted that variances of timed intervals are attributed more to the variability of the central clock (i.e., fluctuations during peripheral motor implementation) than to maximal speed (i.e., one's ultimate upper limits of pace during performances). Hence, if age-related slowing does affect the central clock, then, variability in timing should be higher in old(er) age. Accordingly, Krampe et al. found maximal single-finger-tapping to be comparable for old(er) and young(er) amateur Pianists, but that there were significant differences for bimanual alternating-hand finger-tapping tasks between the old(er) and young(er) Pianists.

For the most part, findings concerning music-related psychomotor tasks are often 'shared' between various literature sources on Music Development—especially within the annals highlighting the Neuroscience of Music and Ageing. Many citations from investigations seem to form the basis of 'emerging conceptions and theories', referring to what has become a most popular trend: *Lifelong Music Engagement*. But perhaps these need be reconsidered on the basis of ecological validity? I contend there is a great lack thereof! As mentioned in Chapter 1, seniors who have only just begun to engage with music performance in their 6th or 7th Decade of life may clearly demonstrate positive effects of music on physical processes. Many researchers report to have demonstrated that music is a means to regenerate age-related losses. This phenomenon was referred to as *Music Geragogy*. Such activities are certainly highly important for the maintenance of physical motor and cognitive abilities that decline in later life. But yet, I contend that for the most part these findings about musical skill development in later life say little about the effects of *lifelong music engagement*. My position here is that amateur musicians—no matter how long they have learned a musical instrument, no matter how many times a week they engage in a rehearsal, no matter how many times a year (or month or week) they appear onstage—are far from being a valid sample (i.e., a proxy) representing the effects of music across the lifetime of a professional performing musician. As an illustration to my viewpoint here, the following study is brought forth: Thompson et al. (2015) claimed that the ability to move consistently to a beat improves across the lifespan, but yet declines slightly in old(er) adulthood. Accordingly, the research team claimed that the findings of their study provide *further evidence* that musical experience and long-life training causes lower tapping variability and asynchrony. This paper is often cited in the literature as confirmation 'proof' for specific benefits among professional musicians. Thompson et al. stressed the fact that their recruitment procedure was in line with most previous studies that target the effects of musical training; they claim to have adopted a 'stringent inclusion criteria' for recruiting musicians. They report the participants in their study as individuals with:

> a minimum of 3 years of practicing music [to] qualify as having musical experience [. . .] as opposed to the more common case of an individual with just a few years of musical experience. (p. 3)

We then need to ask here: What is the difference between three years of musical experience and *a few* years of musical experience? Is this criterion no more than the preservation of an unreliable benchmark to recruit samples (i.e., proxies) for real-world *bona-fide* musician participants? Therefore, the claims of Thompson et al. to have provided 'evidence' demonstrating musical experience as offsetting age-related declines, and having caused a decrease in finger-tapping variability and asynchrony, may not necessarily be valid. Ironically, Thompson et al. themselves had the foresight to safeguard their conclusions; albeit, many others who cite the paper do not heed their forewarnings. The researchers stated:

> Our participant population did not include any older adults with musical training. As a result we cannot say with certainty whether or not the musical experience correlation with beat synchronization performance is maintained into older age. Given that older adult musicians have superior auditory cognitive skills and more synchronous neural responses to sound than their age matched non-musical experience peers, we predict that older musicians would also have increased beat synchronization performance. (p. 10)

Then, taken on face value, Thompson et al.'s study may have absolutely no relevance to professional music performers who have reached the 3rd or 4th or 5th or 6th Decade—after a *lifetime of musical experience*. At most, Thompson et al. provided a much-needed prediction for future research studies. But they put forward no evidence.

In their stride to investigate professional musicians who have attained the status of being a music performer, many researchers simply target exceptional *Virtuosi Soloists*. Sometimes they are Violinists or Pianists. But, do such Grand Masters of musical technique and artistry offer appropriate models (i.e., proxies) that demonstrate the *resilience* to ageing that might surface from long-term music study, DP, and a lifetime of music performance? Case studies of musical prodigies show that these marvels of music performance are, for all other purposes, independent freelance professionals and 'stars' of the music stage! They do not compare to homogeneous samples of full-time contract Symphony Orchestra players. Orchestra players have all had similar backgrounds, maturational lines, sequences of musical skill and development, and training experiences including Music Conservatoires, Music Summer Camps, National Youth Orchestras, Music Academies, multiple auditions, extended trial periods, and continued re-evaluation performance assessments throughout their career. In short, professional full-time contract Symphony Orchestra musicians do not seem comparable to exceptional Virtuosi Soloists who have been the forefront of Music Science studies on exceptional music talent, training, and lifetime engagement. The concept, serving as the basis of this book, argues that, as a group, professional full-time contract Symphony Orchestra musicians provide the only valid and reliable research sample with whom to investigate *lifelong musical engagement*. This is especially true when teasing out differences between subgroups such as Young(er) Players (LTE45) and Seasoned Musician (GTE55).

The current study found that Spontaneous Motor Tempos (SMTs) were performed (i.e., finger-tapped) at a moderate pace (83bpm); these were stable and consistent across both age subgroups. Preferred Perceptual Tempos (PPTs) were slightly faster (88bpm); these did not significantly vary between the age subgroups. The song 'Happy Birthday to You' proved to be an excellent choice for all musicians to finger-tap a pulse-beat, regardless of their culture; the participants were from 11 countries of birth, eight mother tongues, and three countries of residence. Uni-manual forced-speeded finger-tapping for the right and left hand offers a look at the upper limits of non-specific music-performance psychomotor skills among Orchestra musicians. Finger-tapping was particularly fast (between 326bpm and 347bpm), consisting of 157–177 taps throughout a 30s duration. FSTs were extremely controlled and stable (i.e., *SD*s of ITIs). Consistency of FSTs was seen to be quite similar for both hands regardless of handedness. Bimanual alternating-hand forced-speeded finger-tapping was performed at the fastest possible rate (between 450bpm and 500bpm), but was significantly more variable than uni-manual tasks. Finally, the current study contradicts Peters (1985a, 1985b) who only found 'reduced' hand asymmetry in bimanual alternating-hand finger-tapping tasks for just two out of five Pianists (40%); although those participants were described as skilled subjects, perhaps they might not have been as expert as should have been the case. I note that in the current study, no asymmetry was found for any of the Orchestra musicians in the sample—38 out of 38 players or 100%. This finding was shown to be reliable despite age differences between the musicians.

The current study, then, raises the possibility that although Young(er) Players are more often considered to entertain superior adaptabilities and musical instrument competencies compared to Seasoned Musicians, such assumptions might not actually be a valid representation of the truth.

9

Performing Music, Part A

Think Aloud Protocols

9.1 Introduction

Chapters 9 and 10 examine music expertise in an effort to contribute to the body of knowledge that explores the processes and strategies used in music performance. Specifically, the acquisition of high-level skills. It needs to be pointed out here that most previous research has applied one or two approaches: the *Expert-Performance Approach* which targets top performances that can be objectively measured, and the *Expert-Novice Approach* that compares elite performers and those with intermediate levels of training (e.g., Ericsson, 1996, 1998, 2000; Ericsson & Lehmann, 1996). However, the current study takes on-board another method; examining problems that need to be solved during Deliberate Practice (DP) in order to play a piece as precisely as possible. DP is a task-structured training activity that plays a key role in understanding skill acquisition (Platz et al., 2014), and explains individual differences in expert performance. The current chapter highlights what players do to subdue glitches and snags encountered during a 1st *prima vista* Sight-Reading. The study, then, examines how Symphony Orchestra players adjust their performance for malfunctions, anomalies, and near errors of fingering and/or articulation. The study attempts to focus on strategies used in problem-solving towards performing music at the highest level, but yet within a most limited timespan (±10 minutes) of rehearsal.

Brodsky and Kessler (2017) claimed that *expertise* is the result of activating the right knowledge at the right time. Experts have developed rich and coherent knowledge structures that allow immediate access to the relevant strategies, skills, and control mechanisms. They stated:

> More efficient [performers] are those who are particularly attuned to superordinate structures with consequential economy of coding, and that such processes occur by organizing material into higher-order interrelationships which represent certain regulations and limitations leading to cognitive expectancies. (p. 190)

Van de Wiel (2017) indicated that problem representations guide expert musicians in selectively focusing on relevant information and features in order to assist them to carefully monitor and adapt their performance in an ongoing process enabling them to coordinate thoughts and actions in cognitive processing. Specifically, that:

Seasoned Musicians Playing Beyond the 5th Decade. Warren Brodsky, Oxford University Press. © Oxford University Press (2025).
DOI: 10.1093/9780198956501.003.0009

The evolving mental representations in task performance reflect the content of working memory [whereby] experts update their knowledge and skills by means of study, practice and experience. They enhance learning from their experiences by seeking feedback and reflecting upon their performance to find weak aspects in processes and outcomes that might be improved. Expertise development is a gradual process in which the knowledge and skills needed to plan, monitor and evaluate performance are refined during practice. (p. 114)

Van de Wiel also contended that music performance can only be improved when players search for, and identify, reproducible superior outcomes which can then be used to guide DP. Yet, given the current investigation's particular attention to ageing, it would be imprudent not to pay close attention to the findings of Ralf T. Krampe (2002; Krampe et al., 2001, 2002) formerly from the Center for Lifespan Psychology at the Max Planck Institute for Human Development (Germany) and the Center for Cognitive Study in the Department of Psychology at Potsdam University (Germany). Krampe felt that old(er) musicians simplify complex rhythmic structures by relying on their relatively intact lower-level timing mechanisms, sacrificing complex sequences and executive control operations that overtax their processing capacities. Namely, that there are age-related changes underlying fine-motor movements (e.g., skills related to playing an instrument), and such phenomena can be seen from a developmental perspective—referred to as *adaptation*. A further description of adaptation within the *SOC Model* is presented in Chapter 11. When reading music notation, mental representations are critical because the information contained in a score is rather underspecified with respect to optimal implementation (e.g., fingering and expression). So, might one then ask if the findings reported by Krampe align with old(er) expert Symphony Orchestra musicians? I note that among the most effective techniques that can be used to assess higher-level thinking processes—especially those which involve working memory that can also be enlisted when studying individual differences of the same performance task (variegated by age subgroups)—is the *Think Aloud Protocol*.

9.2 Think Aloud Protocols

Think Aloud Protocols (TAPs) refer to the verbalized account of a subject's mental process, targeting the sequence of cognitive events or thought processes between the introduction of a problem and the final product (Charters, 2003). Accordingly, TAPs try to see into the minds of individuals. Participants are asked to voice the words that surface in their minds as they solve a wide variety of problems, from mathematical equations to visualizing puzzles, from reading a text to composing poetry. TAPs have been denoted by many research teams with various terminologies, for example: 'concurrent verbal protocols', 'thought-listing', *as if* 'thinking aloud', 'inner speech', or as a form of 'self-report'. TAPs can be thought of as a methodology allowing researchers to find out how a person approaches a problem or task, and then describes the problem-solving techniques or interpretations to be used. TAPs have been predominantly used as a research technique in the field of Cognitive Psychology (e.g., Ericsson & Simon, 1980; Hannu & Pallab, 2002; Nisbett & Wilson, 1977). As a tool, TAPs provide insight into the kinds of processes employed to complete tasks, including: decision-making behaviours, conflicts, and strategies (Barkaoui, 2011). In their *Psychological Review* paper, Ericsson and Simon outlined several levels of verbal reports, referred to as 'Think Aloud' or 'Talk Aloud' platforms. See Table 9.1. As can be seen in Table 9.1, TAPs might be directly reproduced from the verbal form as acquired (Level 1), or intermediately recoded into a verbal code as the original information has to be translated from non-verbal stimuli (Level 2), or intermediately recoded after a prerequisite scanning/filtering process occurs (Level 3).

Besides being particularly informative about an individual's global approach to a task, other advantages of TAPs concern the levels of decision-making, and the considerations that govern their decisions. All of these can rise to the surface for scrutiny. Further advantages relate to the fact that TAPs are immediate, thus avoiding problems of information retrieval and/or filtering. It should be noted that what is usually revealed in music-performance investigations has had more to do with what music performers *believe they do* (and what they are concerned with) whereas TAPs more likely reflect what music performers *actually do* (and what they are concerned with).

The breakthrough researcher in the Psychology of Expertise and Human Performance is a Swedish-American, K. Anders Ericsson, from Florida State University (USA). Ericsson stressed the importance for a theoretical basis of Think Aloud methods (Ericsson & Simon, 1980, 1993). TAPs were outlined as an introspective research technique; a conception based on the distinction between *working memory* (whereby concurrent reasoning takes place in a more verbal form) versus *long-term memory* (whereby some of the ideas from working memory are subsequently stored, albeit not necessarily in a verbal form). In agreement is Charters (2003) who asserted that the goal of TAPs research is to obtain a greater comprehension about the processes of working memory. Finally, Guss (2018) pointed out that rather than investigate whether or not a person solved a problem, TAPs permit one to focus on the process of human reasoning while solving problems.

Table 9.1 Levels of Verbal Reporting

Level	Description
I	Verbalization of heeded information and task-directed processes are separate and distinct.
II	Verbalization of heeded information is generated by task-directed processes.
III	Requirements for verbalization of heeded information modify task-directed processes.

Data Source: Ericsson and Simon (1980)

A host of research studies employing TAPs was critically reviewed by Guss (2018). Among these were projects investigating: Business Management, Clinical Psychology and Counselling, Cognition, Discourse Processing, Education, Medicine (Diagnostics and Surgery), Psychology and Law, Software Engineering, Sport Psychology, and Text Comprehension. Another corpus of literature targeting 'verbal-cognitive data' within empirical platforms was assessed by Welsh et al. (2018). In all of these later studies, data was collected *in situ*—simulating real-life situations in Arenas, Fields, Greens, Halls, and Tracks. Among the participants were professional Algebraic Mathematicians and Chess Masters, as well as various elite and super-elite sportsmen executing highly crafted skills, such as: Cyclists, Endurance Runners, Golfers, Rugby coaches, Snooker players, Tennis players, and Trap Shooters. Ericsson and Lehmann (1996) mention: Auditing (fraud detection), Bridge (planning to play a given hand), Chess (best move for a chessboard position), Computer Programmers, Medicine (diagnostics), Physicists (solving diagrams), Scientists (research designs), Sport Judges and Referees (viewing filmed games), and Writers. There is also a study of 'self-talk' employing a Soccer task (Papaioannou et al., 2004). Nonetheless, for the most part, studies among *music performers* have not been listed within the literature reviews evaluating the employment of TAPs; nor has DP of music performance been explored as an empirical platform.

9.3 Verbalization During Deliberate Practice

TAPs have not been highly cited in published literature investigating musical excellence (e.g., Ericsson, 1996; Gordon, 2006; Parncutt & McPherson, 2002; Rink, 2002; Williamon, 2004). Nonetheless, a few studies from Music Education and Music Performance Science literatures (e.g., Barry, 1992; Boucher et al., 2019; Burwell & Shipton, 2013; Oare, 2012; Suzuki & Mitchell, 2022) have mentioned strategic approaches to practice including analysis of verbal protocols. For example, transcription analyses of video recordings taken during student practice. But yet, all of these studies do not directly employ TAPs. There are a few single case studies (e.g., Bangert et al., 2014; Nielsen, 1997a, 1997b), as well as studies with very small samples of less than 10 cases (e.g., Ali, 2010; Deniz, 2012; Grondahl, 1987). In one study Nielson employed a prototype developed by Ericsson and Simon (1980, 1993), delineating two types of verbal reporting: (a) concurrent verbal reports during practice, and (b) retrospective debriefing reports after practice. Further, in studies by Ali and by Deniz verbal protocols were employed as means for either Voice or Piano teachers to understand how their students were comprehending and implementing self-regulated changes during DP for the acquisition of successful performance skills. Finally, Rosenthal et al. (2009) examined the content of transcriptions from videotapes of 18 musicians consisting of: eight 16-year-old High school students, five 23-year-old Music Education undergraduates, and five

48-year-old Music College faculty (labelled as 'professional musicians'). Rosenthal et al. attempted to explain what these musicians were thinking and doing while practising the expressive aspects of a musical composition. Ironically, most studies found in the literature point out that while little is known about the reflective thinking processes of performing musicians, there has been very little value attached to TAPs as a means to explore such procedures.

One incomparable study that needs to be mentioned here was conducted by Chaffin and Imreh (2001) and Chaffin et al. (2002/2012). The investigation followed Gabriela Imreh, a Concert Pianist with an international reputation, during a 10-month period involving 57 practice sessions; 45 sessions were fully recorded, totalling more than 30 hours of DP. All of these sessions document Imreh's efforts to learn the *Presto* (Movement III) from J. S. Bach's *Italian Concerto* (1735, BWV 971) for the Concert stage and for a commercial recording (Connoisseur Society, NY, 1996, CD 4207). The Bach masterpiece consists of 210 bars, lasting roughly 4 minutes at performance tempo. As Imreh practised there were occasional comments, sometimes in just a cryptic manner, but for the most part verbal annotations were clear detailed accounts of goals and the motor strategies employed. From the verbatim transcripts, Chaffin et al. were able to abstract 21 aspects of practice organized into 4 broad dimensions. See Table 9.2. As can be seen in Table 9.2, some aspects

Table 9.2 Practice Dimensions for Music Performance

Dimensions of Practice		Aspects of Practice
1	Basic Aspects	1. Fingering 2. Technique 3. Patterns
2	Interpretational Aspects	4. Phrasing 5. Tempo 6. Dynamics 7. Miscellaneous
3	Performance Aspects	8. Memory 9. Musical Structure 10. Using the Score 11. Attention 12. Expression
4	Metacognitive Aspects	13. Self-Evaluation 14. Affect 15. Learning Processes 16. Research 17. Plans and Strategies 18. Slow Practice 19. Use of Metronome 20. Combating Fatigue 21. Editorial Finesse

Data Source: Chaffin and Imreh (2001); Chaffin et al. (2002/2012)

relate to Basic Instrumental performance skills, while others relate to Music Interpretative skills, and still others relate to the Cognitive Skills required for music performance. Chaffin et al. (2002/2012) concluded that "three quarters of [Imreh's] practice time was spent not in playing, but in thinking" (p. 133). It should be noted that during the study period, Gabriela Imreh also engaged in an additional 30 Concerts involving two different recital programmes, and performed five Concerti with Orchestra—two of them for the first time. This is quite a superhuman feat to begin with! Yet, beyond this case focusing on a verbal data of a Concert Pianist, other studies simply do not exist. Most specifically, there may not even be any studies that recruited Symphony Orchestra players.

TAPs aim to capture processes in performing tasks by prompting the contents of working memory to surface simultaneously during task performance. This means that cognitions can be examined in direct relation to the task, yielding more specific and precise information than interviews, focus groups, *in situ* probing, post-performance recall, or retrospective reports (van de Wiel, 2017). See Table 9.3. As can be seen in Table 9.3, TAPs are highly positive (+) as a process during the *in vivo/in situ* performance tasks. TAPs reduce the participants' opportunity to theorize and rationalize about what they do, and keep the time-delay between processing and verbalizing to an absolute minimum. The rationale behind TAPs as a method is that the verbalized thoughts reflect the evolving mental representations in working memory during task performance.

While some researchers may solely rely on TAPs transcripts as their single source of data, others caution about the incompleteness of TAPs. For example, Barkaoui (2011) puts forward the notion that TAPs data should be seen as an *indicator* of cognitive processes rather than as the *direct evidence* of full realizations. In this

Table 9.3 Advantages and Disadvantages of Qualitative Empirical Strategies

Timing and Method of Strategy	Enhancing Task Performance	Interfering with Task Performance	Inducing Interpretation	Reflection of Working Memory
Before Task				
Interview	–	–	±	–
Focus Group	–	–	±	–
During Task				
Think Aloud	+	±	–	+
Dialogue/Group Discussion	+	–	–	+
Probing	+	+	±	±
After Task				
Free Recall	–	–	–	+
Explanation	–	–	–	+
Retrospective Reporting	–	–	–	+
Probing	–	–	±	±

Source: van de Wiel (2017). Reprinted with permission

respect, Ericsson and Simon (1980, 1993) long ago stressed that Think Aloud data from working memory will always be incomplete, excluding a number of thought processes as they are not held in working memory long enough to be expressed verbally. It should be acknowledged that although the verbalization of thoughts might not change the sequence of actions, or disturb the cognitive processes that the participants engage in, TAPs could slow down processes. Moreover, perhaps in some cases, verbal encoding and vocalization of information could interfere with natural task performance because the increased load on working memory might make it difficult to keep up with the flow of information that needs to be attended. Finally, it should be pointed out that because highly skilled and expert music performance involves cognitive processes that are largely automated, there is also a possibility that TAPs will only reveal those thoughts that consciously come to mind. Therefore, it might be the case that TAPs could illustrate what knowledge is activated, which parts of cognitive processing are automated, and when deliberate analytical thinking is involved in specific tasks.

In light of the above, the literature recommends that studies employing TAPs should take onboard additional sources of information. Namely, *triangulation* as a means to increase credibility of data. For example, Guss (2018) asserts that TAPs should be combined with post-experiment interviews or survey data. It is interesting to note that Chaffin et al. (2002/2012) concluded that while Gabriela Imreh was not able to mention each decision, let alone the reasons for why she chose what she did, "the rest of the story is told by what actually went on at the keyboard" (p. 164). Hence, based on such advice, the current study cropped two recordings of *in vivo* music performances as supplementary sources of data. These recordings were sent to expert Orchestra players as external independent judges for music-performance analyses in a double-blind adjudication procedure (see Chapter 10). In agreement are Suzuki and Mitchell (2022) who strongly stated that "in order to measure the efficacy of practice strategies, it is essential to link them to performance success" (p. 613).

9.4 Description of the Task

The first step of designing a verbal-protocol study is to choose task characteristics and requirements that can reveal expert behaviour under ecologically valid conditions reflecting the essence of the task (Barkaoui, 2011; van de Wiel, 2017). Van de Wiel heeds the warning that employing TAPs in an empirical platform necessitates a highly rigorous design by which only natural task processes and real-life problem representations can be captured by *in situ* conditions. Hence, the formulation of stimuli and simulation conditions is critical as the conditions must be ecologically valid to ensure that reliable behaviour can be revealed. The current study, then, presented professional full-time contract Symphony Orchestra players with a real-world original, totally unknown piece of music for music performance.

This piece was composed specifically for the study by Israeli Symphonic Composer Moshe Zorman. A full description of the piece can be seen in the Cover Note Page preceding Part III.

Initially, the musicians played the piece at first sight, never before having had access to the text—not even visually scanning the score. This is referred to as a *prima vista* performance. For more exact details of the procedure used in the music-performance tasks, see Chapter 10 (sections 10.3.1.2 and 10.3.1.5). Then, before playing the piece for a second final performance, each player received a standardized period of time ±10 minutes for DP. This period was defined as a time to rehearse and resolve performance elements or sections of the piece that they perceived as having been difficult during their first Sight-Reading. DP was considered an effort to improve the performance. During the ±10-minute period, the player might spend time attempting to overcome glitches and snags that previously surfaced, or they might attempt to overcome malfunctions, anomalies, and near errors of fingering or articulation. The players were asked to speak aloud throughout the full duration of the ±10 minutes. Specifically, they were told:

> *Say out loud everything that comes to your mind as you rehearse your instrument part in preparation for the 2nd performance.*

The music participants spoke *as if* talking to themselves. Both TAPs and the music performances were digitally recorded. A description of the audio recording equipment used in the study was outlined in Chapter 1 (see section 1.6.3.1).

Previous research studies present evidence that both quality and quantity of verbalization vary across individuals and groups. It is acknowledged that no information was available as to what could be expected from professional full-time contract Symphony Orchestra players as an occupational group. Barkaoui (2011) reported that some of the participating players in that study did not talk consistently, and remained quiet for quite long periods of time; other participating players simply engaged in a more active monologue with themselves. Hence, there was every possibility that some Orchestra players might target specific practice strategies (see Table 9.2), or that they would focus on explicit dimensions of performance while omitting others. Namely, that some players might concentrate more on Technical aspects (such as Accuracy, Dexterity, Tempo and Rhythm, or Memory), while others might target Artistic aspects (such as Artistry, Interpretation, Expressiveness, Structural Strength, Melodic *vs* Harmonic Balance, or Tone Quality), and still others might simply say very little (yet actively engage in playing the music section by section).

I point out that, although a few studies may have used a similar protocol, many different methods were actually put into place for the current study. One study, Bangert et al. (2015), did have players participate in a single session in which they first Sight-Read a piece of music, then practised, and finally performed the piece.

However, in that study the participants provided both concurrent and retrospective verbal protocols. Further, the researchers continually probed them about their thought processes being verbalized. For example, they asked: 'Can you explain that further?' Or: 'What do you mean?' In addition, Bangert et al. instructed the players as follows: 'If you fall silent for an extended period of time I may prompt you to keep talking. You don't need to justify things and you don't need to speak in complete sentences: just think aloud.' In the current study I did not verbally interject or impose on the players who were left alone to their own devices and thought processes. Baggert et al. also employed a practice period up to 45 minutes whereby the researchers left the players alone in the room. In the current study all players were solely offered up to 10 minutes while the researcher was present throughout. Finally, Bangert et al. allowed the players to mark up the score with comments, directives, and symbols, whereas in the current study no markings were allowed. See below for a discussion on this point.

The following two vignettes illustrate the great variances among the participating players in the current study. The first vignette is fairly brief (3:08 minutes), while the second is a much longer complex monologue (9:30 minutes).[1] Readers should be aware that while talking aloud, all musicians played their instrument; these occurrences are documented by using the word '*plays*' surrounded by ellipses within a pair of square brackets: *[. . . plays . . .].*

(30y, F, vn)   *I think mainly about what I missed. But I think the second dynamic wasn't really there. I struggled a little bit with the shift. I stopped using the shoulder rest last week, so I decided to try it out. Some little things which I'm still struggling with there. I wasn't light enough with my left hand going up this passage. Dynamics in [Bar] 19 weren't good. I did a silly Bow in [Bar] 25, which meant I was a bit long in the Bow to Pizzicato. I twinned the last chord, so I won't be doing that again. Certainly strange, much bigger dynamic. I didn't read the Leggiero in [Bar] 29 until Bar 30 (I looked back) and wasn't perhaps light enough, so I lightened up a bit. I got carried away at [Bar] 36 with the chords and played louder. [Bar] 37 the dynamics weren't defined enough, accents weren't defined in [Bar] 37. Chords at the end could have been better in tune [. . . plays . . .].*

TOTAL PRACTICE TIME: 03:08

(55y, M, bn)   *The rhythm needs to be more accurate. The notes aren't that difficult, but I have to work on a couple spots [. . . plays . . .]. That seems to be all. Maybe just clean up my Articulation here [. . . plays . . .]. There are a few things I rushed. I know this is an easy passage [. . . plays . . .]. Remind myself that it answers itself [. . . plays . . .]. Coming on to a Syncopation, so now the next time I look at it I'll know that it's there. You know the beginning [. . . plays . . .]. I come back to the Do [C] again [. . . plays . . .]. A little surprise there, so I have to remind myself [. . . plays . . .]. That's easy for me, the rhythm part, subdividing, keeping my cool there. I have to do this again [. . . plays . . .], and really remind myself the D♭ there [. . . plays . . .]. Was I in Alla Breve the first time [beat = 100+]? I made a little mistake in the 2/4 Alla Breve [. . . plays . . .]. All that's under control now. Now this is easy because it doesn't give me any surprises [. . . plays . . .]. Maybe try to get rid of the downbeat so I can show the Syncopation [. . . plays . . .] to [. . . plays . . .]. I like to do that on it. I look at the piece, I try to interpret something [. . .*

[1] Readers can view the music piece for each individual instrument in Appendix A.

plays . . .]. If he's [the Composer] gonna do it, it's sort of stupid, but if he's gonna do it, he wants to say something, that's his problem. My problem is overdoing it a little bit, because why not! Now this is just a little bit confusing, difficult for the Bassoon. It's a hand thing; I have to change my fingering from what I used before . . . used a full fingering [. . . plays . . .], which doesn't work for the G#–F# coming back up again [. . . plays . . .]. So, I have to use a different, I have to remind myself to use simpler fingering that doesn't sound as good but it would be easier [. . . plays . . .]. That's not a pleasant Bassoon moment [. . . plays . . .]. Any time you play anything in sharp keys, I know that note, that area has never been comfortable, my entire career [. . . plays . . .]. The thing between the little finger and the thumb, you know the forefinger, never a nice thing you know [. . . plays . . .]. You know, do I want to tongue it anyways, even though it doesn't do a tongue? I wouldn't do it that way—Legato—completely. If I saw the Composer I'd complain a bit. But if he wants it [. . . plays . . .]. It's a hard interval [. . . plays . . .]. I like the Trio (Triplet) like that. I enjoy playing Alla Breve 3-over-2, that's fun to do [. . . plays . . .]. Now I have to remind myself that it's Tenor Clef. Actually, it's not! I made a mistake looking at it just now. I went into Tenor Clef already [. . . plays . . .]. Stupid mistake. Now it's sort of a bullet of being annoyed at the guy who wrote it! Because you wouldn't put Bassoon in G Clef. It should have been in Tenor clef; bassoon is never in G Clef. So, already I am 'pissed off' at the Composer—for laziness on the Composer's side. The Composer should have known better. For Cellos and Bassoons this goes in Tenor Clef, not G Clef [. . . plays . . .]. First of all, I'm annoyed it's a G that shouldn't be a G. And then I have to jump way back down to F. It is annoying [. . . plays . . .]. Now I realize it is actually the same thing [. . . plays . . .]. Not pleasant fingering up top [. . . plays . . .]. Change the fingering to easier fingering. [. . . plays . . .]. Expressivo. It's sort of nice, feels good, no Sharps or Flats. Easy on Bassoon [. . . plays . . .]. I'll play it again. Maybe . . . why not. But, Metta Mosso at [Bar] 94, Mezzo Piano, Expressivo, I like this guy's style. It goes easy [. . . plays . . .]. Question: Does he want it to be two C#s or a C [natural]? I'd assume he wants a regular Do (C) [. . . plays . . .]. Under a Slur, he should have put a natural on it. It's laziness! So, when I play things like this, and read things, I get annoyed. The notes weren't exact, he should have known better. There are certain things here, and I'm gonna play it, and make something out of it, because that's my job. To make music out of whatever [the Composer] does. But I am already annoyed. You [the audience] are sitting here, and you're gonna say you're paying me money. To do something with this [on the stage], or on a recording session. I have to sit down and make sense out of it quick [. . . plays . . .]. Classic . . . [. . . plays . . .]. Now what does he mean? You know, you can't do it [. . . plays . . .]. It's under a Legato. Is that what he wants? [. . . plays . . .]. Or, he probably wants [. . . plays . . .]. I'm gonna make an adjustment. What I feel is right, because otherwise it's stupid. I don't know the composer, but I presume the rhythmical thing he is working on, he wants [. . . plays . . .]. He is writing everything pretty straight. It is all on Off-Beats [. . . plays . . .]. Do I like it? Not really [. . . plays . . .]. At this point it's in my hand, not in his hands, so I'll make a decision [. . . plays . . .].

TOTAL PRACTICE TIME: 09:30

9.5 Analytic Procedure

A digital audio recording of the Think Aloud Protocol was undertaken for every musician. Each verbal recording was transcribed verbatim (i.e., word for word). While only a few interviews were conducted in the Hebrew language, portions of these conversations (e.g., music idioms and music-related nomenclature) were detailed in English to begin with. They were translated from Hebrew to English as close as possible to the original. Nonetheless, it is acknowledged that when transferring an oral verbal means of communication (i.e., spoken Hebrew) to a more formal means of communication involving printed text (i.e., transcribed English), such a process of linguistic analysis may be intuitive, and perhaps even interpretative.

A qualitative analysis of all documents was conducted. The analysis included: Segmentation, Coding, Conceptualization, Classification, and Categorization. Such procedures enriched the research by identifying themes leading to an improved understanding of meaning illuminating further interpretation.

Table 9.4 Levels of Verbal Report

Themes	Description
I	Problem Recognition
II	Evaluation of Performance
III	Choice of Strategies

Data Source: Nielsen (1997a 1997b)

Over 50 years ago, Nielsen (1997a, 1997b) used a coding schema based on three Main Themes in a single-case study on music practice with a Church Organist. See Table 9.4. Later studies (e.g., Duke et al., 2009; Hallam et al., 2012; Pitts & Davidson, 2000) investigated characteristics of practice behaviours and the development of practice strategies among young(er) players. But none of those above-mentioned present models for coding DP are appropriate for samples of professional full-time contract Symphony Orchestra musicians. Therefore, a unique method of coding was developed and employed based on two previously known independent schemas. One coding scheme was an adaptation of Chaffin and colleagues (2001, 2002/2012) which employed 4 Main Themes with 21 Subthemes (see Table 9.2). The second coding scheme was adapted from Yoshie et al. (2009a, 2009b), employing 2 Main Themes with 10 Subthemes. It should be pointed out that Yoshie et al. developed their coding scheme within a study on Music Performance Anxiety (MPA) among Piano majors during assessment procedures involving a recital performance. See Table 9.5.

Table 9.5 Codes for Music Performance Analyses

Item	Main Themes	Subthemes
I	Technical Strategies	1. Accuracy 2. Dexterity 3. Tempo and Rhythm 4. Memory
II	Artistic Strategies	5. Artistry 6. Interpretation 7. Expressiveness 8. Structural Strength 9. Melodic/Harmonic Balance 10. Tone Quality

Data Source: Yoshie et al. (2009a, 2009b). Reprinted with permission

Table 9.6 Codes for TAPs Analyses in the Current Study

Main Themes		Subthemes
A	Basic Technical Performance Strategies (BTPS)	1. Accuracy 2. Dexterity 3. Tempo and Rhythm 4. Memory 5. Attention
B	Artistic Interpretational Strategies (AIS)	1. Phrasing 2. Dynamics 3. Expression 4. Musical Structure 5. Melodic/Harmonic Balance 6. Tone Quality
C	Metacognitive Strategies (MCS)	1. Self-Evaluation 2. Learning Processes 3. Slow Practice 4. Editorial Finesse
D	Kinaesthetic Engagement (KE)	1. Play Instrument: Section 2. Plays Instrument: Whole Piece 3. Claps/Sings: Section

For the current study, an innovative configuration for coding TAPs transcriptions was brought forward. This codex consists of 4 Main Themes with 18 Subthemes. See Table 9.6. All the 18 Subthemes are potential practice strategies. Although the Main Themes and Subthemes are rather straightforward, I would like to bring out the following:

- Accuracy (A1) also refers to Reading (notation) and Playing instrument (intonation)
- Dexterity (A2) also refers to producing musical sound including Blowing (wind instruments), Bowing (string instrument), Fingering (string instruments, finger numbers), and Hammering (percussion instruments, right–left sticking)
- Tone Quality (B6) also refers to Articulation
- Self-Evaluation (C1) also refers to Self-criticism and Stress (MPA, tension about presence of someone else in room)
- Learning Processes (C2) also refers to *in vivo* performance conditions (lighting, seated or standing posture, physical area)
- Editorial Finesse (C4) also refers to disagreements with the notated score, as well as criticism of the Composer (style writing and/or Orchestration)
- Claps/Sings: Section (D3) also refers to Fingering the instrument without making an audible musical sound (touching fingerboard without a Bow, depressing the lever-keys/valves without Blowing through a mouthpiece or reed).

9.5.1 Validation of the Codex

TAPs transcripts were evaluated for each of the 18 practice strategies (i.e., Subthemes in the Codex) as seen in Table 9.6. The full verbatim commentaries of all players were collated. In total, $N = 46$ transcripts were converted to 230 individual exemplars. Each item was assigned to 1 of 18 practice strategies. The exemplars were evaluated by an external assessor; a retired professor of Music Education with previous training and experience as an Orchestra player. Each exemplar was either confirmed as befitting the Subtheme it had been assigned or reassigned to a more appropriate category. Out of 230 exemplars, only 9 (3.9%) were indicated as needing reassignment. This seemed to confirm a high level of reliability for the codification system, especially when based on an external expert who was not a partner in the study (i.e., involved in neither data collection nor Thematic Analysis). The classification system was thus endorsed. Metaphorically speaking, such a level of validity would be $\alpha > 0.90$. Further, the external assessor reviewed each exemplar, selecting specific items deemed to be the most *characteristic* for each practice strategy. The judge was unaware that 150 items (65% of 230 items) had already been marked by the researcher as typically distinctive. The judge chose 81 items (35% of the original 230 items); 49 (33%) of these were matching those the researcher had previously selected. The correspondence was as follows:

- BTPS: $M = 0.327$ (33%)
- AIS: $M = 0.543$ (54%)
- MCS: $M = 0.410$ (41%)
- KE: $M = 0.80$ (80%)

All 49 items that matched appear in the texts below (section 9.7). These reflect 81% of the 60-item characterizing statements for the 18 Subthemes of the Codex, as conveyed by 32 players reflecting 70% of the sample.

Thereafter, the 230 exemplars were tabulated by frequency, an overall proportion of use, and then analysed for interactions. From the outset, the study planned to explore the possibility that specific practice strategies would be more frequently found among a particular subgroup within the sample. The subgroups that come to mind are: *instrument* (e.g., String players *versus* Wind players), and *age* (e.g., Young(er) Players *versus* Seasoned Musicians).

9.6 The Dataset

9.6.1 Participants

The data of the Think Aloud Protocol (TAP) was collected from $n = 46$ professional full-time contract Symphony Orchestra players. This dataset reflects 89% of the full (N = 52) omnibus corpus: 4 players had cancelled their interview, the recording of 1 Harp player was accidentally deleted, and the data of another player was removed because of a more hostile non-compliant attitude during the *in vivo* music-performance task. The participating players were on average 48 years old (SD = 9.99, Mdn = 51, Range 27–64); they were 59% male.

9.7 The Findings

9.7.1 Strategies of Deliberate Practice (DP)

Employing TAPs the study investigated semi-conscious cognitions and insights that surfaced during DP. The study targeted activities that experts engage in when they evaluate ways to further improve a performance. The study expected to find differences of approach between subgroups based on their instrument, as well as on their age. It was assumed that Young(er) Players would be more focused on aspects of Basic Technique (Table 9.6, Theme A) while Seasoned Musicians would be more focused on aspects of Artistry (Table 9.6, Theme B).

9.7.1.1 Demonstrating Main Themes and Subthemes

Below are 60 exemplars from the players. Of these, 49 (81%) were confirmed by an external assessor. Their comments account for the 4 Main Themes and 15 Subthemes. I point out that while there are indeed 18 Subthemes (as seen in Table 9.6), 3 of these do not account for verbal content but rather are kinaesthetic motor-related action aspects of music performance. I also note that while many players conveyed verbal responses as ongoing unfolding details, often they repeat the same practice strategy—albeit counted as singular. The sections below are presented in an effort to substantiate the Codex. I reiterate that the vignettes are presented in ascending order with the youngest player presented first and oldest player presented last.

A. Basic Technical Performance Strategies (BTPS)
A1. Accuracy (including Reading notation and intonation)

(33y, M, va)   *All the accidentals [... plays ...]. Check that was a C# [... plays ...]. Check the B [... plays ...]. Just practising that intonation. [... plays ...]. Just sort of working out different Bowing that this brings up [... plays ...].*

(47y, M, hn)   *I'm going to look more at the Key Changes. [... plays ...]. Next thing I'm looking at is low notes. First off, I'm only playing high notes, so they are slightly a tiny bit out of my comfort zone.*

(47y, F, vn)   *This piece doesn't make sense to me, and so it's a little bit hard to get some good music out of it. I had some problems with the high notes there. I would think about the position I want to play there, and I missed a B. I have to correct this, and I want to think about the whole thing. What kind of music is this, and Tempo! OK, this was almost the right Tempo I guess. And about the Dynamics, this is OK. Yes. that's what I'm trying to [... plays ...]. This is not very clean, but it's [... plays ...].*

(49y, M, vn)	*First of all, I look at the directives written in the score that I might have missed the first time through. For example, Dynamics (clearly, I missed them). Changing clefs (which I missed except for the first Bar). And Double Stops. Then, I look for fingerings, and rhythms [sings]. Other indications that I missed; some things longer or shorter, or accents.*
(55y, F, fl)	*Well first of all I'm looking at the notes, the rhythms. That's a horrible bit there. I hate anything with that finger [laughs . . . plays . . .]. Now it's a difficult bit because it's not apparent whether I'm supposed to be playing an E or an E♭ [. . . plays . . .].*
(55y, M, db)	*I have been looking at things that are more technical. Truthfully, these are less musical features. I was looking at Sharps, and other symbols. Thinking of fingerings, to understand what I am doing, and where am I doing it. The rhythm. Here is C# and F# [. . . plays . . .] It is not so clean [. . . plays . . .].*
(57y, F, vc)	*OK. I would first look at the section where there is a Clef change and 3 Sharps. That seems to be the most difficult section. I also think it is the fastest (Tempo = 120). So, I would work on that section, both the Tonality and the Tempo [. . . plays . . .] Also, the introduction with the Double Stops is a bit problematic with poor Intonation. So, I need to work on that a bit [. . . plays . . .].*

A2. Dexterity (including Fingering, Bowing, Blowing [embouchure], and Sticking)

(43y, F, db)	*Just decide on where I wanna split the Bow, because there's not enough Bow. Just find the A♭ at the top as well [. . . plays . . .]. That's always a nasty shift to the C#—always a weird one [. . . plays . . .]. So, I would probably go there for the less elegant but safer option if it was in the Orchestra. If I was playing that on my own, I would spend a lot of time in getting that F# shift right [. . . plays . . .]. So that's slightly less elegant [. . . plays . . .]. So, you'd look for a fingering, that you'd shift back on to the A♭ with a second finger so that that's already in position, so you're not jumping to that [. . . plays . . .]. These Double Stops are just not possible on the Bass [. . . plays . . .].*
(60y, M, bn)	*There is an alternative fingering which I could use for this second B, which I would do because it's nice. That is not easy to start on.*

A3. Tempo and Rhythm

(33y, F, bn/dbn)	*OK so first, making the rhythm [sings and snaps fingers]. So, this is making problems for me; rhythm is not my favourite, the 3rd Bar. I have to organize the rhythm right there. The Tempo? Like how fast I'm gonna go. I'm searching for the Tempo of Mozart [sings and snaps fingers to a Mozart melody]. This is 20 [bpm] to the Half [note]. So, it's a little bit slower than that [sings and taps foot and snaps]. Next to the 3rd Compass [a term for 'phrase'] [sings and taps]. OK, I know in this compass I'm gonna go in Quarters, just to be sure that the rhythm is right [sings and taps syncopations]. I noticed now that on page 2, the Tempo is half of the first [page]. So, it's 94, and before it was 100, but it's a Quarter. Right? And this is a Quarter, this other is a Half (so that would be like 200). Right? And it would be like half slow. And I didn't see it before. So, it's [sings] before it's Half [sings]. If these are my Halves, now it's [sings]. OK? So, this is important [. . . plays . . .].*
(39y, F, cl)	*I really hesitate in this Bar with the rhythm for some strange reason [. . . plays . . .]. Yeah. I'm gonna try these rhythms again, 'cause I know what's gonna let me down most. It's where I'm feeling most panic [. . . plays . . .].*
(64y, M, tpt)	*The Tempo that I took was not the Tempo that [the Composer] listed (130bpm). I was down around 120bpm [uses a digital metronome]; maybe not 120. At [Bar] 48 I don't think I was accurate: in [Bar] 48 there was a 5/8 section. I don't think I was completely accurate, I think I was closer to 6/8 [whistles the part while tapping out beat]. Yeah, at least the first 2 measures (48–49) I was probably closer to 6/8 than*

was to 5/8. I just wasn't accurate in my subdivisions. I didn't subdivide properly in organizing the rhythmic patterns. I didn't really do that coming out of the 3/4 measure. So, if I take 3 measures before [sings], it was probably between 5/8 and 6/8.

A4. Memory

(43y, F, db)   *At this point I would write something [on the notation], because that's unusual you know. Talking about memory, to retain that that's a F [natural] for the next 9 notes has always been a problem with me. So, I would write something there [. . . plays . . .].*

(60y, M, cl)   *Maybe this is a symptom of age because I find myself highlighting more Sharps than before [marking in the score]. By highlighting the score, I put the changes more into the motor memory than relying on my general working memory. So, that would assist my level of security (not relying on my memory). Here I am in an environment of Flats, and then when I play it correctly, it sounds to me like a mistake. So, highlighting the score assists me [. . . plays . . .]. When I was younger 10 years ago, I didn't need to highlight so much. I have learned to highlight as a coping strategy.*

A5. Attention

(52y, M, db)   *That means E major chord. E major is [. . . plays . . .]. I have E, a B and a G#. Oh, it's also Pizzicato [. . . plays . . .]. Actually, I don't' know how to play it. But this isn't the hardest thing. I think I should have a look at the [. . . plays . . .]. I forgot that I can see better [if] I use glasses. I [should] have to write in the fingerings. But here it's clear; it's only in the last measure when G# is a G natural.*

(64y, M, tpt)   *Writing in B^b is no problem—if I had a B^b Trumpet! My Trumpet is the ordinary C Trumpet used in the Orchestra. In the Orchestra we [use] C, B^b, D, E^b, F, and A Trumpets. [But] we usually play always on the same C Trumpet. So, it's just a matter of transposition; you'd take a look at it once beforehand.*

B. Artistic Interpretational Strategies (AIS)

B1. Phrasing

(41y, M, va)   *I would guess that some of the phrasing is obviously intended to be very long. The long Bow over [Bars] 14–15. I wouldn't alter the phrasing, but I would make it easier to do the phrasing as the Composer wants.*

(60y, M, cl)   *Maybe I would exaggerate the Leggiero as that would cause a better flow of the melody. To improve the piece, I would look at uncomfortable sections in the higher register around Bar 25, and Bar 37 where there is a Fermata (to sit on that a little bit), take some air and breath. Perhaps even relate to the next section much different than the previous one.*

B2. Dynamics

(40y, F, vn)   *Along the way I'm gonna try to pick up the Dynamics [. . . plays . . .]. Here there are two challenges. First are the Thirds which are notoriously difficult to get into. Then, on top of everything, it is a Pianissimo which makes it even more tricky. I will first practise it a little bit louder, and then I'm going to work on the [. . . plays . . .].*

(54y, F, vc)   *Also, there's a misleading very strange dynamic here. There's a dynamic marking Piano Expressivo, and then there's a Diminuendo to Mezzo Forte. I am assuming it doesn't Diminuendo down to Mezzo Forte, but Diminuendo down to Pianissimo and then to something much louder. I am assuming that is what it means.*

(54y, M, va)   *Another thing which one could do is pay more attention to Dynamics. There is a game between Forte and Piano in this piece both in the same line. One need make more contrast there. Like [. . . plays . . .]. And pay more attention to the accents there.*

(55y, M, db)	*Now I realize that I paid little attention to Dynamics. Now I am looking at them. Here it comes back to Largo (something a bit faster) [sings] and finishes in a Piano Pianissimo [... plays ...].*

B3. Expression

(33y, M, va)	*I like the piece. It's a nice little piece, isn't it! [... plays ...]. And now ... this is a modern piece. I'm just wondering what style to play it in. Whether to have it little 'taunt' or whether more [... plays ...]. My instinct is to make it more of a dance [... plays ...].*
(36y, F, tpt)	*Gotta make sure the C#s down, 'cause it tends to be Sharp. And just looking along the Dolce passage. So, I wanna change the sound there; it's gotta be much softer, much as I think 'hot-ear' rather than a 'cold-ear'. And then [... plays...]. Finding the centre note for the next strip [... plays ...]. And that should be, more sort of 'cheeky' [... plays ...].*
(43y, F, db)	*And then to make the contrast there between the 'punchiness' of the previous stuff and the 'lyrical', like that [... plays ...].*
(56y, F, vn)	*I note that the character is Cantabile. I am thinking of Bows and Ties for a mini-Polyphonic piece [... plays ...]. Suddenly, there are Flats in C major; how does one play that? What does that mean? Something is going on here. And here the Composer (on top of the Flats) writes Dolce. How does one play that?*
(60y, M, cl)	*Try to heighten the character of sections with Staccato to give them more inflection [... plays ... from beginning, but stops short]. I am looking for the style. Where to put the inflection; the 'spices'! This also raises one's self-confidence. I would expect any artist to do the same. This is what raises one from the level of reading notes to the level of playing music.*
(61y, M, fl/picc)	*Well, the first thing I'm thinking here is I've not put any expression into it. That's because I'm grabbing the notes. The notes in Bar 3, I didn't actually figure out the rhythm there because [claps rhythm]. It should have been like that! [claps and sings].*

B4. Musical Structure

(41y, M, vc)	*There's a certain degree of getting what's going on. Obviously, the thing I need to look at is [... plays...]. Which is just weird because it doesn't particularly follow what Harmony you're expecting after this [... plays...].*
(43y, F, db)	*That's an unusual Modulation there [... plays...]. And there was something nasty just in the first bit, with a Modulation. A Minor [... plays...]. That needs to be made really clear. So that doesn't just carry on the way it's been going [... plays...].*
(47y, M, trb)	*The ending? I said it had a funny ending. Because the Tonality doesn't make sense to me [... plays...]. It sounds like C Major, and the F, F Major. I just don't like the musical style of the ending. I don't know, what is the, I tried to play it, and not to make too many mistakes, and give the piece a musical meaning.*
(53y, M, vn)	*OK! I'll play it again—for me! First the whole thing one time. To get an impression of the piece, of the structure. Because the first time you don't get it. The first time I didn't know what will come. Now I know what to expect!*
(54y, M, va)	*The piece is built on an A–B–A Structure; a slow melody. Pretty straightforward, then it develops. In the middle there's a fast section, and goes back to a slow melody.*
(56y, F, vn)	*First of all, I think of Form—the Structure. There are three sections: A–B–A. The first section, the middle section of Triplets, and then a sort of Reprise in Bar 42. Thinking about the architecture, the 'golden point' where the maximum artistic focus is found (which should be about the distance of three-quarters though the piece), is roughly at Bar 15 or Bar 25.*

B5. Melodic/Harmonic Balance

(43y, F, db)   *And this Chord can't be done at all [... plays ...]. You certainly can't sustain it. You'd have to break it up and it wouldn't sound [... plays ...]. Oh! it's Pizzicato, isn't it? Oh yeah [... plays ...]. Well in that case we could [... plays ...]. Could do something like [... plays ...].*

(52y, M, vc)   *Then the other thing is to look for some underneath message, something else people might be looking for.*

B6. Tone Quality (including Articulation)

(33y, M, va)   *Slide or not [... plays ...]. No! Probably not [... plays ...].*

(44y, F, vn)   *Shouldn't really use an Open String there. It doesn't sound very good [... plays ...].*

(57y, F, vn)   *I would also look for the character of the sound required, something much more melodic [... plays ... mumbling to self]. Can it really be like this? I try to stay away from Open String especially in Pianissimo, because if they are not tuned well you can't correct them as you can with a fingered note. Also, you can't do a vibration on an Open String. You are much more limited. Also, the colour is different. But maybe because the sound is not Forte. In Forte I would not attempt to play an Open String [... plays ...].*

C. Metacognitive Strategies (MCS)

C1. Self-Evaluation (including Self-criticism, Stress [Anxiety])

(43y, F, db)   *That doesn't work. That's impossible. The main problem as you could hear is Intonation, because I'm standing up and I've been sitting all day. So, the height of the instrument is slightly different. That always causes a problem for a few minutes [... plays ...].*

(47y, M, vc)   *There's no indication as far as [Double Stops] [... plays ...]. I am quite happy with that. Maybe that would be more in keeping with the title: 'Melody'. I am going to stick to that [... plays ...]. The problem [... plays ...], is that [... plays ...]. It shouldn't be too much of a problem. Then [... plays ...]. I must say it's been about 20 years since someone's heard me Sight-Read like that. It is surprisingly nerve-racking!*

(59y, M, va)   *I would like to play perfectly, I would have to practise a bit more than this [... plays ...].*

(61y, F, vn)   *I think I made a few mistakes. I need to learn alone. Not in front of people!*

C2. Learning Processes (including *in situ* or *in vivo* conditions)

(27y, F, ob)   *I must say it is hard for me to talk about all of this while I am trying to learn the piece. In general, when I have sections that are technically difficult, I play them over and over with different rhythmic variations [... plays ...]. If these were my notes, I would've been writing on them.*

(40y, F, vn)   *So now I am going to work on Intonation a little bit. This is a tricky place [... plays ...]. This is one of those places you'd need to learn to be more efficient. Twenty years ago I wouldn't have approached it this way. I would've gone right to the problem. I would've just gone over this spot, playing it over and over again. And now I am analysing it a little bit more. What my arms have to do, and how I have to react; to get from here to there [... plays ...]. That is something I wouldn't have done 20 years ago. I'd just keep playing the full section over and over again, without leaning in on it [... plays ...].*

(56y, F, vn)   *So, my way of working is to see what is important, what isn't important, and then discover where the focus needs to be. To make music!*

(64y, M, tpt)   *I'll tell students: 'You got something this problematic, look at it first! Check the rhythms, do the fingers. By the time you've done it, you looked at it, you go through the fingers, then you've already learned—and did not waste your face [the embouchure and oral muscles].'*

C3. Slow Practice

(52y, M, db)   *This is too fast at the moment. I have to practise it slowly again to remember the fingers.*

(54y, M, va)   *I think that the major problem of the piece is the Triplets in the middle [section, Bars 29–41]. One would like to get them more precise. I think it'll be nice to practise it slowly. And there's also a part in the fast section with the Triplets—the part with Double-Stopping. So, maybe just to do it once [. . . plays . . . slowly].*

(60y, M, cl)   *The minute I need to play it again, I would pay more attention to the Rests (for example in Bar 3) [sings rhythmically]. You see, I don't even need to play it with my instrument. The minute I sing it out [sings], even if it is not audible (in my head), then I can play it, and feel it! I would most likely do this in my studio. I'd try to play it slower, and then even identify a quick Tempo for performance [. . . plays . . . from beginning, but stops short!]. Here what I would usually do is mark (in bold) the new Accidentals. In an environment of Flats, I would highlight the Sharps.*

(61y, F, vn)   *Had I been at home I would have played through it all—at a slower tempo! That way it will be more familiar to my fingers [. . . plays . . . slow tempo]. I need to play the whole thing again for me, a little slower than as written (in the metronome markings) [. . . plays . . . full piece].*

C4. Editorial Finesse (including critique of Composer, Orchestration, or the Music)

(43y, F, vn)   *Oh, yeah, the pattern in Bar 34 [. . . plays . . .] is unexpected. Going to the C# in the 2nd beat [. . . plays . . .]. The notes are really weird. It's like it's not in any actual key [. . . plays . . .]. Which is that? That's obviously deliberate, isn't it? It messes up your brain [. . . plays . . .]. There's something that's not clear in the music. You've got Mezzo Piano Dolce in Bar 9, and then you've got a Diminuendo in [Bar] 17 too. Now unless it means super-tone Mezzo-Forte, so [. . . plays . . .], and then [. . . plays . . .], which is unusual. You can't erase anything, can you! But that, I think that will be questioned by a player in the Orchestra! Because it's like: if I'm Diminuendo-ing, should I have gone louder than mf before it? Because you can't Diminuendo from mp down to mf. I don't like this person [i.e., the composer]. It's a stupid piece [laughs, . . . plays . . . full piece].*

(43y, F, db)   *With all due respect to the Composer, that's not very good writing for Bass.*

(44y, F, vn)   *Funny Key, it's seems like a funny Key, because it seems as if it's in D major but it's actually got an A major Key Signature [. . . plays . . .].*

(57y, F, vn)   *By the way, can I change to Legato, or do I have to play what is written? This note is a Half note? It looks a very strange 5th (interval) [. . . plays . . .].*

(64y, M, tpt)   *Down here I have to play B♭ Trumpet. He's written F# down at bottom measure 36. I can't play this on this C Trumpet. And as a result, and what I did just now, I played an F#⁻ sounding F# instead of a sounding E natural—which is about the note the F# written as a Whole Tone lower than this Trumpet can play. So, what I am saying is that the Composer wrote a note that I can't physically play on this [C] Trumpet. Had I had a B♭ Trumpet I could have played it. [Author's Note: The piece was scored for B♭ Trumpet.]*

D. Kinaesthetic Engagement (KE)

D3. Claps/Sings: Section (including Fingering instrument without audible sound)

(27y, F, ob)   *In general, I sing it out loud before I play the instrument [sings piece rhythmically from the beginning]. I think I will be the first [player] who uses the full 10 minutes [sings rhythmically].*

(29y, F, vn)   *Sometimes it helps that I don't play with a Bow, just make sure the left hand knows which string I'm on.*

| (33y, F, bn/dbn) | *Compass 5 [i.e., 5th phrase]: I'm gonna have a look at the [she fingers the lever-keys without blowing]. I'm not allowed to make some markings! No? Am I allowed to play? [... plays ... sings and taps].* |
| (61y, M, fl/picc) | *So, I'm just singing it to myself, rhythmically [claps and sings]. And then of course there's expression of the notes. What I often do is just finger it quietly, just thinking about the finger patterns [fingers the lever-keys without blowing].* |

To summarize, the above 60 vignettes illustrate the Codex developed for the current study. These vignettes substantiate all 4 Main Themes and 16 Subthemes. On average there were 4 examples per Subtheme (M = 3.75, SD = 1.65, Range 2–7). The *Thematic Analysis* allowed for further quantitative probing (see below, sections 9.7.2, 9.7.3, and 9.7.4); these delineate issues related to practice duration time, the incidence of specific Subthemes, and the evaluation of interactions between Main Themes or Subthemes with subgroups based on *instrument* or *age*.

9.7.2 Practice Duration

The current study found that practice duration for all 46 participating players was roughly 8 minutes (M = 408.35s, SD = 188.91, Mdn = 372s, Range 148–846s). It should be pointed out that players were not limited to a specific period of time. However, they were told they could practise for roughly ±10 minutes. Nonetheless, no timer was ever present; that is, there was no clock in the room during practice sessions. Then, the data was collapsed into categories of 2 subgrouping variables for further analyses.

9.7.2.1 Instrument Type
The analysis of *instrument* was undertaken in an effort to evaluate if differences of duration time surfaced based on features of musical instruments. The subgroups were: *Strings* (n = 29, 63%), *Winds* (combined Woodwinds and Brass, n = 15, 33%), and *Other* (Harp and Keyboard Percussion, n = 2, 4%). In the final dataset used for this analysis, all players from instrument families other than Strings or Winds were excluded. Hence, data from n = 44 musicians were entered into the analysis. The findings showed no statistically significant differences of DP duration: $M_{Strings}$ = 392.17s, SD = 170.87, Range 148–796s; M_{Winds} = 415.53s, SD = 225.51, Range 196–846s; Δ = 24s; t = .3849, df = 42, p = 0.70. This finding indicates that all participant-players, regardless of their instrument, engaged in DP for nearly the same duration of time.

9.7.2.2 Age of Players
The analysis of *age* was undertaken in an effort to evaluate if differences of duration time surfaced between age subgroups. The subgroups were: *Young(er) Players* less than or equal to age 45 (LTE45) (n = 16, 35%, M_{Age} = 36.8, SD = 5.37, Range 27–44) versus *Seasoned Musicians* greater than or equal to age 55 (GTE55) (n = 16, 35%,

M_{Age} = 58.0, SD = 2.71, Range 55–64). In the final data set used for this analysis, all other players between ages 46 and 54 (n = 14, 30%) were excluded from the analyses in an effort to nullify overlapping that might confound results. Hence, data from n = 32 musicians were entered in the second analysis based on age. Foremost, main effects (differences) between the two groups based on age (LTE45 *versus* GTE55) were statistically significant: t = 14.13, df = 30, p < 0.0001, d = 5.05 (a large effect size); meaning the age subgroups were significantly contrasting. However, no statistically significant differences of DP duration time surfaced between the two age subgroups: M_{LTE45} = 419.63s, SD = 192.47, Range 148–786s; M_{GTE55} = 437.88s, SD = 177.99, Range 180–846s; Δ = 18s; t = .2784, df = 30, p = 0.78. This finding indicates that all participant-players, regardless of their age, were engaged in DP for nearly the same duration time.

Both of these above analyses demonstrate that Seasoned Musicians are just as efficient as far as duration time is concerned as the Young(er) Players.

9.7.3 Incidence of Items

A further analysis of the transcripts for all 46 players found that the total number of strategies (i.e., 18 Subthemes of the Codex) mentioned per player—either voiced aloud (e.g., mentioned verbally) or kinaesthetically enacted upon (e.g., behavioural motor action) was roughly 30 items (M_{Items} = 28.59, SD = 17.37, Mdn = 24, Range 9–103). Then, the data was collapsed into 2 categories of subgrouping variables allowing for evaluation of differences based on instrument or age.

9.7.3.1 Instrument Type
In this analysis, *instrument* (Strings *versus* Winds) served as a group variable. No statistically significant difference surfaced between the 2 subgroups: $M_{Strings}$ = 26$_{Items}$, SD = 14.86, Range = 9–66; M_{Winds} = 34$_{Items}$, SD = 21.96, Range = 13–103; Δ = 8.67; t = 1.488, df = 42, p = 0.144. This finding indicates that all participating players conducted DP roughly in the same manner regardless of the instrument. Albeit, Wind players did verbalize and engage in explicit motor action slightly more than String players; that finding is consistent with other intersectional differences concerning subvocal activity while reading music notation (e.g., Brodsky et al., 1999).

9.7.3.2 Age of Players
In the second analysis, *age* (LTE45 *versus* GTE55) served as a group variable. There were 16 (35%) Young(er) Players LTE45 (M_{Age} = 36.8, SD = 5.37, Range 27–44), and 16 (35%) Seasoned Musicians GTE55 (M_{Age} = 58.1, SD = 2.67, Range 55–64). All players between ages 46 and 54 (n = 14, 30%) were excluded from the analyses in an effort to nullify overlapping that might confound results. Hence, data from n = 32 musicians were entered in the second analysis based on age. The analysis

found no statistically significant differences of item frequency between the age sub-groups (M_{LTE45} = 34$_{Items}$, SD = 12.34, Range 13–66; M_{GTE55} = 29$_{Items}$, SD = 22.70, Range 9–103; Δ = 5.0; t = .6872, df = 30, p = 0.497). This finding indicates that all participating players conducted DP in roughly the same manner regardless of their age.

The above two analyses indicate that players from both String and Wind instrument sections, and players of both age subgroups, mentally perceived, verbally mentioned, and actively engaged in DP in a similar manner. Yet, we do need to understand that such conclusions may be valid when exclusively examining the overall total set of 4 Main Themes. Perhaps, statistically speaking, significant differences could surface in a between-subgroups analysis for each independent Main Theme or Subtheme. Finally, as a thought for the future we might consider if there are significant differences between what the participant-players *said* (i.e., the actual verbal statements made here in Chapter 9) and what they actually *did* (i.e., the music behaviours as rated and observed by external independent judges in a double-blind adjudication procedure, described in Chapter 10).

9.7.4 Evaluation of Independent Main Themes and Subthemes

The data of all 4 Main Themes, as well as the 18 Subthemes, were collated. See Table 9.7. As can be seen in Table 9.7, the average number of incidences (represented as a proportion) are presented for the total sample as well as for each age subgroup.

Table 9.7 can be summarized as follows:

- Basic Technical Performance Strategies (BTPS) represent an average 36% of all strategies mentioned or enacted upon. Although the Young(er) Players engaged in BTPS less than the Seasoned Musicians (33% *versus* 36%, respectively), that difference is not statistically significant.
- Artistic Interpretational Strategies (AIS) represent an average 13% of all strategies mentioned or enacted upon. Although the Young(er) Players engaged in AIS more than the Seasoned Musicians (15% *versus* 13%, respectively), that difference is not statistically significant.
- Metacognitive Strategies (MCS) represent an average 19% of all strategies mentioned or enacted upon. Although the Younger Players engaged in MCS less than the Seasoned Musicians (16% *versus* 21%, respectively), that difference is not statistically significant.
- Kinaesthetic Engagement (KE) represents an average 32% of all strategies mentioned or enacted upon. The Young(er) Players did actually engage in KE more often than Seasoned Musicians (36% *versus* 29%, respectively), and this difference is statistically significant: t = 2.14, df = 30, p = 0.041, d = 0.76 (a moderate effect size).

Table 9.7 Thematic Analyses of TAPs Items: Total Sample and Comparisons by Age Subgroup

Main Themes[1] Subthemes	Total Musicians (N = 46)		Young(er) Players LTE45 (n = 16)		Seasoned Musicians GTE55 (n = 16)		Sig p^2
	M	SD	M	SD	M	SD	
A: BTPS	**0.355**	0.105	**0.326**	0.099	**0.362**	0.118	
A1	0.157	0.082	0.142	0.067	0.136	0.093	
A2	0.091	0.071	0.101	0.074	0.095	0.067	
A3	0.077	0.065	0.063	0.075	0.100	0.061	
A4	0.003	0.010	0.002	0.008	0.008	0.015	
A5	0.026	0.039	0.018	0.030	0.024	0.041	
B: AIS	**0.134**	0.117	**0.150**	0.123	**0.132**	0.134	
B1	0.010	0.023	0.005	0.013	0.016	0.030	
B2	0.037	0.050	0.040	0.045	0.017	0.027	
B3	0.041	0.056	0.050	0.050	0.057	0.072	
B4	0.025	0.036	0.023	0.024	0.030	0.048	
B5	0.006	0.021	0.003	0.011	0.000	0.000	
B6	0.016	0.039	0.028	0.055	0.013	0.031	
C: MCS	**0.191**	0.095	**0.160**	0.126	**0.214**	0.080	
C1	0.067	0.063	0.055	0.074	0.074	0.051	
C2	0.066	0.050	0.066	0.060	0.064	0.039	
C3	0.011	0.020	0.011	0.019	0.012	0.025	
C4	0.047	0.046	0.028	0.034	0.065	0.036	**
D: KE	**0.321**	0.098	**0.364**	0.094	**0.291**	0.098	*
D1	0.267	0.113	0.320	0.099	0.232	0.124	*
D2	0.018	0.037	0.004	0.009	0.020	0.035	
D3	0.036	0.087	0.040	0.098	0.039	0.084	

[1]A: BTPS = Basic Technical Performance Strategies; B: AIS = Artistic Interpretational Strategies; C: MCS = Metacognitive Strategies; D: KE = Kinaesthetic Engagement
[2]$* = p < 0.05$; $** = p < 0.01$

Table 9.7 indicates that much more time was spent on speaking about honing Basic Technical aspects (i.e., Accuracy, Dexterity, Tempo and Rhythm, Memory, Attention), than mentioning Artistic Interpretation (i.e., Phrasing, Dynamics, Expression, Musical Structure, Melodic/Harmonic Balance, Tone Quality), or raising Metacognitions (i.e., Self-Evaluation, Learning Processes, Slow Practice, Editorial Finesse). In a longitudinal case study research by Chaffin and colleagues (2001, 2002/2012), performing musician Gabriela Imreh clearly focused more on Basic Technical and structural features of the music. Commenting on Chaffin et al.'s report, Bangert et al. (2015) claimed that it makes sense for musicians to focus on basic issues particularly when the piece is technically difficult or when they have limited practice time. This was certainly true in the current study. For example, when comparing the three main verbal strategies within a Repeated Measures Analysis of Variance (ANOVA), statistically significant differences surfaced between the practice strategies: $M_{BTPS} = 36\%$, $M_{AIS} = 13\%$, $M_{MCS} = 19\%$; $F_{(2, 90)} = 39.83$, $MSe = 0.0152$, $p < 0.000$, $n_p^2 = 0.47$ (considered a large effect size). Namely, the participating players demonstrated significantly more attentiveness to Basic Technical tactics than to Artistic Interpretations or Metacognitions. Then when pooling together all three 'voiced' strategies (Main Themes A, B, and C) *versus* kinaesthetic 'motor' activity (Main Theme D), a Repeated Measures ANOVA found statistically significant differences: $M_{Verbal} = 68\%$, $M_{Kinaesthetic} = 32\%$; $F_{(1, 45)} = 154.08$, $MSe = 0.0192$, $p < 0.000$, $n^2_p = 0.77$ (considered a large effect size). This finding indicates that during the ±10-minute period of DP the participating players expressed themselves verbally to a much greater extent than they actually employed motor *kinaesthetic* engagement.

Then, a Repeated Measures ANOVA of all 4 Main Themes with age placed as a grouping variable (i.e., proportion of practice strategy used x age) was implemented. The findings did not indicate 2-way interactions: $F_{(3, 90)} = 1.623$, $MSe = 0.0162$, $p = 0.1895$. Nor did the total number of incidences across all 4 Main Themes (i.e., either mentioned or engaged) with age (i.e., number of practice strategies x age) find 2-way interactions: $M_{LTE45} = 34$, $SD = 12.34$; $M_{GTE55} = 29$, $SD = 22.69$; $F_{(1, 30)} = 0.4722$, $MSe = 333.61$, $p = 0.4973$. Therefore, it would seem that the above findings are valid regardless of the players' age. These outcomes contradict those of Bangert et al. (2015) which suggested variances based on experience and levels of expertise.

In summary, the participating musicians were compliant in voicing their thoughts as a strategic manoeuvre to improve the music piece for the 2nd Post-Practice performance. It needs to be pointed out that they were never told: 'It is better to talk than to play the instrument.' Music performance is, after all, about playing a musical instrument! Therefore, one can only assume that for professional full-time contract Symphony Orchestra players, practice is just as much—if not more—*mental rehearsal* than actual *kinaesthetic engagement*. This result confirms findings by other researchers (e.g., Suzuki & Mitchell, 2022) who assert that practice strategies do not necessarily need to involve physically playing an instrument, but rather must engage expert music performers through their mind.

9.8 Discussion and Summary

It is indeed reasonable for research psychologists within the field of Music Performance Science to struggle with the challenge of uncovering the mental processes for decision-making that sway professional Orchestra musicians in preparation for their performances. Not often have research studies been able to reliably access under controlled empirical conditions, Symphony Orchestra players' choices of strategies (e.g., the action sequences) they undertake in DP. Clarke (2002) contended that "there have been comparatively few systematic studies of the psychological processes involved in practice and rehearsal" (p. 65). One exception may be Biasutti (2013) who employed a consultation discussion format for the Conductor and performers to express their views of rehearsal strategies. The current use of *Think AloudProtocols* (TAPs) offers a strong methodology to achieve such a research goal.

DP may truly be an experience based on honed skills that are particular to highly expert performers. Suzuki and Mitchell (2022) state that players set goals, identify problem areas, and strategically plan their practice to enhance learning efforts. Accordingly: "experienced musicians have developed a wide repertoire of practice strategies to utilize, while less advanced students have a more limited toolkit" (p. 613). Namely, although less experienced players may undoubtedly expend much time rehearsing the part of a music composition they intend to perform, and during such preparation they will no doubt also enlist the use of exercises and training drills in an effort to increase their proficiency, their selection of performance-related features and practice strategies may be much more haphazard than that of expert performers.

The current study demonstrates that TAPs reduce the opportunity to theorize and rationalize about what players do, and keep the time-delay between processing and verbalizing to an absolute minimum. For the most part, the participant-players spoke openly and frankly without too much filtering of the verbal flow:

(36y, F, tpt)	*Well first I was just thinking about the opening Bar, to get each note absolutely in the middle, 'cause there's a tendency just to hit slightly Sharp or slightly Flat. So, you know, I've got to try and make sure every single one's in its slot [... plays...]. Yeah, that's mostly in the centre. The bad bit is from the middle F# down to the low F#, which caught me up really. 'Cause it's so [... plays...]. The low F# is the lowest note on the instrument so it's always gonna be a bit dodgy [... plays...].*
(54y, F, vc)	*First thing I looked at was Key Signature, Time Signature, Metronome Marking, Dynamics, Bowings—which I didn't get right in some of the places—and a few Accidentals on the second page that I didn't see straight away [... plays...].*

From the transcripts it can be seen that TAPs allowed participants to say everything that came to their minds while engaged in the task. Yet, sometimes the verbal communication (i.e., the actual phonological expression of ideas) was slashed, broken down, and incomplete. In this connection, the behaviours of the Symphony Orchestra musicians were very similar to what Chaffin et al. (2002/2012) revealed about Concert Pianist Gabriela Imreh:

Although she was not able to mention each decision in full words, let alone the reasons for why she chose what she did, the rest of the story is told by what actually went on at the keyboard. (p. 164)

In the context of the current study, while each player's verbalized thoughts might reflect an evolving mental representation of working memory during the task performance, the direct flow of ideas quickly shifted back and forth between the oral phonological mode of expression and the manual kinaesthetic mode of expression—that is, the instrument they held in their hand. These transitions were ongoing, immediate, and without any time-lag. It seems like a 'handover' (*pun intended!*) from the mind to the fingers *as if* the musical instrument itself was supplementing one's online working memory:

(33y, M, va)   *That's a Subito Mezzo Forte. So I need to [... plays ...] get down below it and then [... plays ...]. And probably that was too loud on that top note, but [... plays ...].*

(43y, F, vn)   *I'm anticipating the positions [... plays ...]. You can do those both [Double Stops] in the 1st Position, but then if I did the 3rd one there, there's a horrible shift. So now I would do [... plays ...]. If I practised it, I'd do the first two probably in the 1st Position [... plays ...], and then [... plays ...], just for 3 notes, and then [... plays ...]. Like an echo, but a sudden 3-note, weirdly sort of [... plays ...]. So I'm looking at those now [... plays ...]. Now, I'm gonna look at Bowing for this bit because of the [... plays ...]. It's better to be on that long note with an up-Bow for the Pizzicato afterwards. In order to make that 5th sound neater. And then it's whether you're on an open A or not [... plays ...]. I think I'd rather not!*

(52y, M, db)   *Sure. I have to think about phrases in the beginning, when it looks easy, but I don't [... plays ...]. I can do, perhaps like this [... plays ...]. I wonder how to play this [... plays ...].*

In addition, there are many thought processes which are not verbalized in working memory, either because they are quite automatic (such as recognition of familiar words and images) or because their 'intermediate' processing passes through so quickly that there is no time to verbalize it (Davis & Bistodeau, 1993; Ericsson & Simon, 1980). Certainly, highly skilled and expert music performance involves cognitive processes that are largely automated. TAPs seem to reveal thoughts that subconsciously come to mind; these may, then, illustrate what knowledge is activated. For example, which parts of cognitive processing are automated, as well as deliberate analytical thinking that is involved in specific tasks.

(27y, F, ob)   *There was a place I played $E^\flat$ instead of E in Measure 15 [... plays ...]. Measure 19, I was confused there [... plays ...]. Also, I had problems of intonation [... plays ...]. High C#. I am checking out how to play that [... plays ...].*

(43y, F, vn)   *This particular Chord in [Bar] 42 is horrible because of [... plays ...]. Holding any 5th on a stringed instrument is really [... plays ...] difficult for Intonation. I'd go to that position rather than the position that I was in the first time. Because the 5th [interval with open string] in 1st Position is a fourth finger which is really horrible.*

(44y, F, vn)   *I wasn't quite sure about the Key Signature [... plays ...]. And then there was a Rit here that I didn't get [... plays ...]. And then I did play Pizzicato, but it looked as if it should be Arco. But the Arco doesn't come till later. So, I just want to look at this last bit [... plays ...]. So, I'm doing a Rit. there, and it doesn't say Rit. [... plays ...].*

(47y, M, hn)   *I couldn't think of the fingerings very, very quickly [... plays ...]. The reason I keep playing that is because I am worried about the tuning of the F# plus a B. I haven't got very good fingering for this Horn—it's a $B^\flat$ Horn. So, I'm gonna have to sort of bend that note a bit because it's going to be sharp.*

(50y, M, vn)   *Here and there are a few notes I accidentally played Sharps or Flats that I need to work out [... plays ...]. I remember that I missed it, there's a jump somewhere that I didn't have time before to work it out. I don't know how to get at it. I'll try it again. The passage towards the end wasn't so solid [... plays ...]. OK, yeah, there was a wrong note there.*

(54y, M, cl/bcl)   *Oh, that was wrong as well. So I noticed that I didn't play a C# here or on those bits. So I'll do that again. I'll have a look at that, what were the bits that went wrong? There is a Sharp here, I didn't play F# last time.*

(55y, M, perc)   *I'm misreading that. I thought that was Tied, but it's just a Slur. And that was throwing me as well [... plays ...]. There are still some bits in that, I know I was fudging. One* *of them is Bar 49: it's two D^bs [. . . plays . . .]. And the F#s which I haven't got [on this Vibraphone]. Sorry! The G#, which I had got is above the notated note pitch; so, I'll just it like that. That's what he means anyway [. . . plays . . .]. And then down to the D#. The easy bits are the Quarter and Eighth Notes. But then the 3rd Bar, I couldn't work it out—and it's so easy! Why I didn't see that, I don't know. The other bit that threw me, Bar 15, I couldn't work out the rhythm. Then the 3/2 (Bar 23); well that was just all over the shop in relation to what speed I had been playing. So, I'll have to work it out. It's basically just 2/2 going into a three (Triplet) rhythm. So, I would say it's necessary to do it again—to work on the speed and the pulse. I need to think about it as a more 4, not as a 2.*

(59y, M, fl/picc)   *Here the intervals are much larger than expected. And, I forgot E^b last time [. . . plays. . .]. Now I see better, and remind myself not to forget the E^b in Bar 14 [. . . plays. . .]. I think I will play through it one more time and I am ready.*

Unlike what has been reported in the literature (e.g., Barkaoui, 2011), the current study did not find that verbal encoding and vocalization of information interfered with task performance. Further, only one player referred to 'thinking aloud' with adversity (See C2 above: 'I must say it is hard for me to talk about all of this while I am trying to learn the piece'). Therefore, it might seem that TAPs did not hamper the players too much even though there might have been an increased load on working memory—making it difficult to keep up with the flow of information they were attending. However, occasionally some comments were made about the research context itself, or the presence of the researcher in the practice room. For example:

(49y, F, vn)   *First of all, I realize that I am not alone.*

(53y, M, vn)   *Not ready for the final yet. I know it's research, but it is still music!*

(54y, M, cl/bcl)   *Basically, if you weren't here [then] I'd just play it all the way through again and again. That's what I'd do [. . . plays . . .].*

(56y, M, va)   *That was Sight-Reading. Well every player who has to learn something very quickly (like in this experiment), would choose sections they need to play. So, I choose to go over the passage in Measure 29 to see the fingering and everything else that I am not sure of there. For example, I am not sure of the Bowing [. . . plays . . .]. I need to practise more on [Bars] 35–36 [. . . plays . . .], and [Bar] 29 again [. . . plays . . .].*

It is interesting to note that some of the comments made by the musicians show disapproval and even condemnation of the quality of the score sheet (i.e., the notation), or the actual music piece itself, or the Composer (i.e., Zorman's proficiency as a musician-orchestrator). This has been noted previously by Weick et al. (1973). Such discontent seemingly serves as a cynical—albeit in players' minds it is somewhat more of an acceptable form of—reaction to vent their stress and frustration. This more *passive aggressive* format is customary for Orchestra musicians, who use criticism of music objects (e.g., the piece, the Composer, the Conductor, the instrument) to mask disappointment with their own performance. Yet, it must be noted that a few players were more positive about the composition itself.

(35y, F, vn)	*Why the pp at the end? It is interesting, because there is a Diminuendo to a pp. Well because from [Bar] 42 it says pp and then all the way to the end, and then a Diminuendo to a pp. So, then something should have happened. That caught my eye! Did I miss something?*
(38y, M, bn/dbn)	*There are lots of Accidentals [. . . plays . . .]. The nature of the instrument means that it's just a lot of extra keys. Here no keys, and then there's extra keys. So, any other key is a combination and finger-position, and that's quite awkward. It's just a kind of register issue where you're going from one part of the instrument to another. That Bar 17, there are ultimate fingerings, so I just have to decide which [. . . plays . . .]. If I was to write it up, I'd just say: 'Use that fingering for that.' I'd normally use what you call a 'long fingering' on the C#. So, there I just have to choose which C# fingering just happens to work a little happier. I'm not really sure why the Composer did that. I mean normally there would probably be [. . . plays . . .]. It's more common for it to be written in Tenor Clef rather than Treble Clef. I don't know, it sometimes happens in French music that they write Treble Clef rather than Tenor Clef. Maybe just to catch us. And that Trill is really [. . . plays . . .]. Maybe that's one of his famous pitfalls. That's quite an intense thing to do [. . . plays . . .].*
(41y, M, vc)	*There is a light shining glare [from the plastic sleeve]; I can't see the notes. Which probably has something to do with the fact that I missed more notes on page 2. I think one of the things we do as Orchestral players is to get used to playing from bad notes.*
(47y, M, vc)	*Basically, two lines are problematic. What's interesting is he's put little [. . . plays . . .]. I assume they're little traps.*
(52y, M, vc)	*About Bar 36 it's hard to distinguish where I actually am because there is a minimal gap between the ledger lines. So, it all looks like it's one big block.*
(53y, M, hrp)	*The author [composer] that did this [. . . plays . . .]. That's terrible Harp phrasing [. . . plays . . .]. That's the leap down that makes up the Chord [. . . plays . . .]. It's tricky [. . . plays . . .].*
(54y, F, vc)	*In a Cello-istic sense, it's not particularly comfortable to do this Chord.*
(55y, M, db)	*Why is this written like this? It is not written for Double Bass. [He] is a Composer, isn't he? Someone who knows better! Is there a possibility to do it like this? [. . . plays . . .]. Let's say most Double Bass players wouldn't be able to play this interval [a minor 6th] with their hand.*
(56y, F, vn)	*The piece is not so difficult. I think I even played a bit faster than 120bpm [. . . plays . . .]. Maybe a student player would need to practise from Bar 30 more than other sections [. . . plays . . .]. Please don't tell the Composer, but his notation is incorrect. He wrote Tenuto in the text [Bar 29] but also wrote Leggiero underneath the text. I can play you the difference [. . . plays . . .]. So, one should ask him what he really wants (Tenuto or Leggiero).*
(57y, F, vn)	*First of all, it says 120 = Quarter Beat. So, I figured it has to be fast. But that changes my interpretation, because 120 is quite different. Nonetheless, there are melodic lines here that I would have played much slower to bring out. Maybe the second section is 120. OK, now I see lines and I thought it was Staccato. Up to now, I was searching for a phrase or expression. A line. An appropriate sound. Dolce. Here it says Leggiero [. . . plays . . .]. There are not such great difficulties here [. . . plays . . .].*
(58y, M, va)	*I see the piece as a nice melody, and one could invest much in affect. The size of the font is not so good for me [. . . plays . . .].*
(60y, M, bn)	*Yeah, I knew there would be Treble Clef [not the usual Clef for a Bassoon part]. I'm not good with Treble Clef. We don't have to use it that often. Try that slur and there is that aspect with the trill at the end. C# to D is rather noisy, and there is no alternative than to do [. . . plays . . .]. Well actually, I suppose [. . . plays . . .]. It would be nicer if it were from a D#, and it does not specify if it's a turn-around or a semi-turn, so I'll play a turn.*

The current study, then, can be seen as targeting the Expert Performance Approach (Ericsson, 1996, 2004, 2015; Ericsson & Smith, 1991). Ericsson and colleagues characterize expertise as the capability to demonstrate reproducible superior performance on representative tasks in a specific domain. Clearly, the highest expertise level is achieved when individuals are able to go beyond mastery, and contribute their creative ideas and innovations to the task at hand (van de Wiel, 2017). Although years of practice and experience are needed to become an expert, skilled performance and experience alone may not be enough. Van de Weil claims that routine behaviour and full automaticity should be counteracted by gaining high-level control of performance that allows further improvements to be made.

(30y, M, vn)	*Just thinking about not Pizzing [Pizzicato] from too far away from the strings. So, keeping it in control [. . . plays . . .].*
(43y, F, db)	*On the second page it's just a question of really reading ahead. I mean this is a very typical passage that we will play a lot of the time. Looking at the accents, just to work out the Articulation which I completely skipped [. . . plays . . .].*
(53y, M, vn)	*I want to have a look at this passage [. . . plays . . .]. I talked about little less technical things [. . . plays . . .]. It's not Country Fiddle [Laughs about Double Stops with Open Strings], here it has to be [. . . plays . . .].*
(55y, F, fl)	*That's Double-Tonguing [. . . plays . . .]. But that front of the note is the Articulation [. . . plays . . .].*
(61y, F, vn)	*I am not looking for specific things. I intuitively feel them! There is a specific section Leggiero that is a little like Bach—then again it sounds like Brahms [. . . plays . . .].*

The vignettes presented in this chapter demonstrate the expertise of Symphony Orchestra musicians; they have well-developed knowledge-based abilities that are finely tuned for music-performance tasks. The players targeted the problems they encountered in a 1st *prima vista* Sight-Reading performance, and engaged in a practice regime to achieve greater proficiency for the 2nd Post-Practice performance. Although their experience allows for fast and accurate performance in routine situations of their skill set, in a more puzzling situation—such as within an empirically related *in vivo* music-performance task—they were challenged to apply knowledge while trying to understand new content concurrently to taking further action.

(29y, F, vn)	*I have to be careful, I have to shift here. Otherwise it's a bit uncomfortable with the string crossing.*
(33y, M, va)	*Understanding the Structure is the next thing, and I see that it repeats itself [. . . plays . . .]*
(35y, F, vn)	*I want to look at the Double-Stoppings [. . . plays . . .]. And I hadn't got that position working at [Bar] 43, the 2nd Position [. . . plays . . .]. That wasn't in tune [. . . plays . . .]. In that Bar, deciding which finger to shift to. Deciding on [Bar] 28, where we play Pizzicato [. . . plays . . .]. How to spread it, I don't know [. . . plays . . .]. I don't like the Bowing there [. . . plays . . .]. Leggiero on this line [. . . plays . . .]. Fourth finger on the C# [. . . plays . . .]. There's something wrong [. . . plays . . .].*
(41y, M, va)	*No, that doesn't work. I am just trying to work out a way of accommodating that long Bow between [Bars] 14–15. Sometimes 3rds will work where you can accommodate them in the same position, but not here [. . . plays . . .].*

(47y, M, trb)	*I just found a big mistake in the 5/8 Bar 48. I didn't play 5/8, I played 6/8. [sings]. I'll practise this 5/8 Bar to get the rhythm right [... plays ...]. This varies between 6/8 and 3/4. To me, it's like a Quarter Note in 130 [bpm] [snaps fingers and sings].*
(52y, M, db)	*When I make the [jumps and 6ths] in Measure 16 [... plays ...]. It's Sharp but, I don't know [... plays ...]. It is heavy and perhaps, I don't know how to play it [... plays ...].*
(54y, F, vc)	*I need to see where the Bows go. There's a little bit I'm still not on top of [... plays ...]. I'm just going to work that little bit out, and choose my fingers [... plays ...].*
(60y, M, bn)	*I'll have a look at the Flats. I'll start with the 2nd line. Just making sure I got that D^b in Bar 5. Slurs. Just making sure that those work OK [... plays ...], and I got some Sharps [... plays ...]. I don't think I got those right to start with. Making sure that the slur from a C# to G# goes. It's not an easy Slur at all, but I will always try and slur it. Triplet I got right. But this top note, B to C# is quite tricky [... plays ...]. There's quite a few intonation issues as well there, getting Bs correct. I would spend longer on that if I had more time. G is far too Sharp, and C is probably too Flat [... plays ...]. I find it quite difficult to get the breath right; to get those intonations [... plays ...]. I think I played an E^b in Bar 43 the first time.*
(60y, M, cl)	*The first thing I am looking at is the Tempo and Metre. I see the common time Alla Breve, so I need to think about counting twos. I see the Clef (2 Sharps). I see that Half = 100, so that gives me an impression of the speed. Also written Leggiero mp and that immediately tells me about the atmosphere that I should play. I think I wasn't exactly at 100; I was little slow. So, this was the natural pace that I took. Then in the Meno Mosso, I was not so stable until I understood the Triple Metre. I didn't feel the Metre as the melody requires. Maybe it is the composition itself, or the melody. I'd rather not comment of that! I am looking at the Meno Mosso (Bar 94) that says Quarter Note = 94, and before that there was Half Note = 100.*
(61y, M, fl/picc)	*And then at [Bar] 13 it's [claps and sings]. Well it's printed out [laughs]. That speed [claps and sings]. So, I'm just thinking through the rhythm here basically. It's rhythmically quite difficult to sort out.*

Perhaps we *should* be sceptical of any first-person account describing their own behaviour and thought processes. And most certainly, this may be highly pertinent for rapid overlearned actions such as those involving music performance. Yet, in the current study the verbal reports which surfaced swiftly do seem to be clear and accurate. Therefore, it seems cogent to focus on players' immediate awareness of how they felt rather than explore the Post-Practice performance by recall, explanation, retrospective reporting, or probing (see Table 9.3). For example:

(27y, F, ob)	*Let's just say my prima vista Sight-Reading was never great! Wow, this is stressful [... plays ...]. But I am a perfectionist [... plays ...].*
(41y, M, va)	*There's something I'm noticing. The more I practise it, the less accurate I'm being about the Rhythm. That bit that I started learning wrongly on page 2 and a Rhythm in Bar 16 that I started [... plays ...]. I'm starting to hear something in my head, and it's not necessarily the same as what's on the page. That's quite strange. I'm just going to try a bit to see if I can get the Bow better. I am tempted to say: 'Let's go for it before it gets any worse.' It's probably because I haven't played properly for a week or more. The more you practise in that beginning phase, more things you notice that are wrong. Then you get to the point [... plays ...]. Not an excuse, just something I've noticed over the years.*
(47y, M, vc)	*So, the question of course is when I come to do it again, under pressure, without writing some of the fingerings in [on the score], I probably will make a lot of mistakes again, but then I am of course talking myself in to a corner—aren't I [... plays ...].*
(55y, F, fl)	*Oh, I can't get that [... plays ...]. I'll probably muck that bit up. But that's nothing new. That's something I've always done. [Laughs.] Well, what I want to say is that because I know this is the final performance, I'm gonna be jittery and probably the first play-through will be better than this one [... plays ...].*

(59y, M, fl/picc)   *To tell you the truth, if I had to do this for the Orchestra, I would have worked on it once, and then put it aside [. . . plays . . . full piece]. At first when I get a piece I only look at the notes. But once I get the notes under control, then I look at (and work on) the expressivity.*

At this juncture, we need to ask one more question: What do the current findings offer the overall investigation package on Seasoned Musicians? I reiterate that previous research on the ill effects of age(ing) within the context of music performance have most often recruited samples of amateur musicians. For example, Krampe and Ericsson (1996) found that old(er) amateur musicians performed comparable to young(er) amateur musicians. They found that relatively small amounts of practice and task-related experience (of an amateurish level of engagement) were sufficient to illustrate age-related stability in several skill-components. But in later studies, Krampe (2002) demonstrated that music-performance skills also caused age-related declines among the normal population. Hence, Krampe concluded that the role of DP not only serves one to acquire expertise, but may also be a platform to maintain proficiencies in fine motor skills across the lifespan. Accordingly, as playing an instrument increases the cortical representations of the hand and fingers, there is a correlation to years of music training. Yet, I wonder: Does this conceptual proposition apply to professional full-time contract Symphony Orchestra players? Especially when differentiating between age subgroups (with age variances roughly 25–35 years apart), are such assumptions still relevant? These questions will be explored further in Chapter 10.

Thus far, the current Think Aloud Protocol study brings forth the following points:

- Seasoned Musicians are just as efficient as Young(er) Players regarding the duration-time of DP.
- Seasoned Musicians are just as efficient as Young(er) Players regarding the frequency and types of practice strategies employed. There are no differences for Basic Technical Performance strategies, Artistic Interpretational strategies, or Metacognitive strategies. Nonetheless, Young(er) Players do engage with their instrument more, while Seasoned Musicians tend to verbalize thoughts and employ mental rehearsal more often.
- There were no differences between the Seasoned Musicians *versus* the Young(er) Players concerning specific efforts invested to improve performances, including: Accuracy, Dexterity, Tempo and Rhythm, Memory, Attention, Phrasing, Dynamics, Expression, Musical Structure, Melodic/Harmonic Balance, Tone Quality, Self-Evaluation, or Learning Processes.

In summary, the current study raises the wide-ranging possibility that although Young(er) Players are more often considered to entertain superior adaptabilities and musical instrument competencies compared to Seasoned Musicians, such assumptions might not actually be a valid representation of the truth.

10
Performing Music, Part B

Music Performance Evaluation

10.1 Introduction

This is the second chapter exploring music performance among Symphony Orchestra musicians. Previously, Chapter 9 examined *Think Aloud Protocols* that occurred during a ±10-minute period of DP in an effort to improve the 2nd music performance. This current Chapter 10 evaluates the actual music performances themselves.

Throughout the more active research sessions, the participating players repeatedly asked: 'Why do we need to perform? What is the purpose? How is <u>that</u> related to the research questions?' My answer was always the same:

> *I am doing this research for my book. So, let's just say that when the book is published, you purchase a copy and read it. You might feel that some parts were more interesting than others. After all, a lot of professional full-time contract players from five different Orchestras in three different countries participated. You might even agree with some things the other players said. And, you might also accept some of my interpretations of the statements they made. But perhaps when you're done with the book, you'd eventually think to yourself: 'Hey! Did you ever hear those musicians play?' I mean when all is said and done, it's not really about the questionnaire booklets, or the assessment measures, or the narrative stories (of their childhood, their Music Calling, and their intended professional career path). Nor, is it about their perceived ability to play. Or, how they feel in their heart to be as young as they were 20 years earlier. Nor, is it about their estimates of Deliberate Practice across their lifetime. Or, their conception about how they seem to have preserved their music skills in spite of aging. Nor is it about having developed a higher level of adaptation and resilience to the stresses of the music-performance profession. Of course, all of those are important factors that need to be examined in order to understand professional Symphony Orchestra players. But the main thing that really matters when investigating music performers, especially when considering ageing, is: How do they play!*

At the time of this writing I am not aware of any other comprehensive study that targets professional musician performers involving a music-performance task. There are a few investigations examining Music Performance Anxiety (MPA) that recruited students in a Music College, amateurs, or semi-professional musicians. In addition,

Seasoned Musicians Playing Beyond the 5th Decade. Warren Brodsky, Oxford University Press. © Oxford University Press (2025). DOI: 10.1093/9780198956501.003.0010

there are a host of studies focusing on a single Pianist during a Sight-Reading task (e.g., Kopiez et al., 2006; Lehmann & Ericsson, 1993, 1997, 1998; Meinz, 2000).

10.2 Musical Maturity

During the single 2-hour interview session the participating Orchestra musicians mentioned the notion of *musical maturity*. Most of the participating players stated that as far as they are concerned, the ill effects of ageing are considerably much more limited because of their years of experience, continued intensive training, and practice. Scientific literature does claim that cognitive-motor expertise affords individuals to accumulate task-relevant experience over years or decades. The ease at which expert music performers demonstrate skills, even at very advanced ages, is certainly undeniable; these highlight a lack of age-related decreases for both cognitive and motor functioning (Krampe, 2002). For example, in a study reported in the *Journal of Experimental Psychology*, researchers Krampe and Ericsson (1996) showed that trained musicians continue to play at an extraordinarily high level throughout their career to a much older age—provided that they continue to practise. According to Frost (2000), the findings of Krampe and Ericsson were highly novel at the time of its publication; after all, as we age our muscles lose strength, coordination, and the ability to recover from hard work.

For the most part, the participating players viewed *musical maturity* as a derivative of experience. Namely: 2-to-3 Decades of experience with Orchestras, Conductors, and the repertoire. The players with the most experience were the old(er) more seasoned musicians. Hence, they are definitely more of an asset than a liability. Accordingly, they are the ones who set the pace and the tone; they are the ones who provide the sound. As stated below by a young(er) 36-year-old female trumpet player: 'It's not the young(er) more acrobatic players that make the Orchestra sound as *The Orchestra*, but rather the musicality that comes from the old(er) players.' Even if the old(er) players might be undermined by a tiny lack of technical clarity here and there (e.g., mishaps of note accuracy or speed), they are the ones who are able to bring out a certain type of musicality that the young(er) players just don't have. That is, the aspects that old(er) players have mastered certainly overcompensate for losses. One question that needs to be asked, is: How much is a tiny lack of technical clarity here and there? How much musicality is actually brought out that supposedly overcompensates for losses? These questions are raised below by the Music Performance Analysis. Subsequently, findings are presented below as empirical evidence to answer them.

Musical Maturity seems to mean playing with better Phrasing, Articulation, Dynamics, and Expression. Most of the Young(er) Players noted that the Seasoned Musicians have learned to see behind the notes. They are the ones who are aware of the bigger overall picture; they are the ones who see the emotional content that needs to be played. Yet, some players did not agree with the defined age-related subgroup categories employed in the study. Namely, they didn't accept the notion that Young(er) Players are *less than or equal to 45 years old* (LTE45), while Seasoned Musicians are *greater than or equal to 55 years old* (GTE55). Yet, such a phenomenon has also been documented previously by Gembris (2013; Gembris & Heye, 2014; Gembris et al., 2018) in their study of N = 2,536 professional musicians from 133 orchestras in Germany. They reported that the participants clearly felt that levels of musical performance rise sharply at young(er) ages, peak in the years between 35 and 40, and then decline relatively quickly. The data shows self-perceptions of musicians between 40 and 50 years of age change significantly. For example, when asked whether they perceived they belonged to the young(er) or old(er) group of players, almost all the musicians LTE40 years felt they belonged to the *younger group*, while almost all the musicians GTE50 years considered themselves to belong to the *older group*. These data confirm there is a critical period of transition between 45 and 55 years—described earlier in Chapter 1 (see section 1.1), as well as outlined by Manturzewska (1990, 2006). In a later paper, Gembris (2023) claimed that the biggest change in the assessment of the ability to achieve musical excellence occurs between 40 and 45 and then again between 50 and 55 years of age; accordingly, while 36% of the musicians surveyed still considered musical excellence possible between the ages of 40 and 45, 11% expected musical performances to peak between the ages of 50 and 55.

Some players in the current study could not even perceive why Science and Academic researchers should be astonished by Symphony Orchestra musicians who undoubtedly perform past the 5th Decade. They perceive it is natural! So *what* is all the 'to do' about; *why* is there any fuss about professional performing musicians to begin with?

(30y, F, vn)	*I do feel that there are effects of ageing on performance in general. I feel that the older players are more of a liability than an asset. That doesn't mean they're not valuable. There'll be places where their contribution is far greater and more useful than others. But then, there'll be that one moment of 'putting in a spare' (a note or chord in the wrong place). But I would not agree that there is a certain age where musicians should 'hang up' their instrument. Certainly not coerced! It's not 'cut and dry'.*
(33y, M, va)	*The older players are definitely more of an asset than a liability. Yet, we do 'Cut the Dead Wood and throw them out!' We all kind of [think] that it's all for the good of the Orchestra. It might be necessary, and it does rejuvenate. For example, we got this fresh new young Section Leader; the section has never sounded better, and there's a better morale. But, the old Principal is still within the section sitting further back. But, when there's too many older players who are not at the top of their game, that is not beneficial. Once they start losing their technique, it will start affecting the overall sound of the Orchestra. Some do carry on past 65; they are still at the top of their ability. We have a Timpanist who retired, and still comes in. We had a few Violinists that kept coming in past their retirement day; they were great! I think the youth can learn from the elders who have a lot of experience to pass on. But if you get too many, the mix is wrong.*
(36y, F, tpt)	*One thing that I have noticed about older players, is when they've got a Solo, they've got 'all the time in the world'. They can make a Solo stand like there's no pulse; almost like time stands still. They just have this ability to make the phrase linger; a little bit more music. That's something that the young players can't do! So, they're more of an*

asset than a liability. They are what makes the Orchestra! The younger players may be more agile, technical, and mechanical. It's not the young acrobatic players that make the Orchestra sound as the Orchestra. The musicality comes from [the older players]! I think Society in general is too preoccupied with image. I mean if a PR expert [suggested that in an effort to win back the younger subscription-buying public that we should furlough all players above 55 years of age], then of course that means 'How you look' rather than 'How you sound'! But musically, if I listen to the top guys in the field, most of them are in their 50s or 60s.

(40y, F, vn)   *If the more experience a player is the better they are, then why do some Orchestras want to get rid of the older players? Well the myth is it's because younger players sound better. Certainly, this is not necessarily the case. I'd expect an older player to sound better musically. I think it's also maturity, and not just experience! Musical Maturity means that you learn to see behind the notes. You learn to see the emotional content of what you're playing. I think somebody who's 15 [years old] cannot play the Brahms Violin Concerto [in D major, Op. 77, written in 1878 by German composer Johannes Brahms,1833–1897]; even though they might be technically [great], they would not be able to perform the emotional depth it needs. So, why would [management] want to get rid of them? Well, some people don't want to see older people onstage! I think that audiences would be happier if we all played from behind a curtain. They'd even prefer to see younger better-looking people on an album CD cover or event poster— with a lot of blond-haired blue-eyed girls in the Orchestra. Just recently I saw an ad for the New York Philharmonic with Joshua Bell [GRAMMY Award-winning American Violinist, b.1967] holding his [Gibson ex Huberman 300-year-old] Stradivarius Violin [c.1713] wearing tight skinny-fitted slacks, titled: 'Bell: Rocking The Leather Pants'.*

(41y, M, vc)   *I don't feel that there is a certain maturity that only comes with years. You have people who are infinitely mature (musically) at the age of 23. Equally you have people who have been playing for years—past the 5th Decade—and don't have a clue. They still don't really listen to themselves, understand what they're doing or how they fit in. What I am saying is that a player could be 'seasoned' already at 26. Music Maturity isn't necessarily connected to age, but rather to experience.*

(41y, M, va)   *I think that older players aren't a liability, but rather they are an asset! They add certain qualities that the younger players don't have. So even though they might be faltering on some aspects compared to the younger players, what they master certainly overcompensates the losses.*

(52y, M, vc)   *I think seasoned players might have a better interpretation and are more expressive. But, they would find it harder to adapt. They might say: 'I did this at [a specific] tempo with Georg Solti [1912–1997, Hungarian-British Conductor, Music Director for 22 years with the Chicago Symphony Orchestra], so I'm not going to move [to a slower or faster pace]. It just feels like the wrong tempo.' A younger 28-year-old player just wouldn't know; they'd do whatever they were asked to do. So, what do you want from a 60-year-old? A lot of it is based on experience. Players often perceive to know what is 'right' or what has worked 'better' before.*

(53y, M, hrp)   *I do see differences between the younger versus the older players. I would not consider older players above 50 to be more of a liability, but more of an asset to the Orchestra. Because what they bring in experience and maturity is an asset! Even if they might be undermined by a tiny lack of technical clarity here and there, they bring out a certain type of musicality that the younger players don't have. What I am saying is that I don't feel older players have lost anything. But yet, I don't really think there's a difference between players [aged] 35–50.*

(54y, F, vc)   *Honestly, I am not sure if a 30-year-old player is 'young'. By the time you're 30, you have matured quite a bit (musically). My gut feeling is that all Orchestra players are instinctively 'good players'. Some people just seem to have a sort of 'inner awareness' of what constitutes being a good Orchestra player. So I think people can be mature players at [age] 30. By then they would have been in an Orchestra 6 years (after music college). I think that I learned a lot when I moved to a front desk position; I was a Rank-&-File player before 30. On the other hand, some people never seem to acquire the skills.*

Although they can play their notes, they never really quite get the hang of playing the right Bow, or breathing with everybody else. I'd definitely say a younger player is under [age] 30, but I would not consider 35 years old to be a 'younger' player. So, the assumption that 50 and above will actually be different than 40 and below, is not necessarily correct.

(55y, M, bn)   *A more seasoned player would be better able to Articulate (the emotion) of what the Composer had in mind. I'd expect a younger player to be more powerful. I would hope that the older player had a little more understanding to produce all the different sounds of different pieces [in different periods of Music History]. Whereas the younger player would be more involved at playing it right; perfectly in tune. But I don't think that younger players are less expressive. I suspect that today I know better what to do with certain pieces. Older players bring knowledge of pieces that younger players would not have. Playing with an Orchestra for over 30 years is definitely an advantage.*

(59y, M, va)   *I think there are good players, bad players, and average players. Maybe I'd expect older ones to play a bit less accurate. The standard of all Orchestra candidates is very high today. I wouldn't say that there's a big difference between the young and old. Every one of us has a maximal level; our best finger-skill technique was just after graduation from college. And from then on it's always going down a bit. But not by a lot! I think the problem is that Orchestra managements conceive of a 35[-year-old] person as being an 'Old Man'. If you want to get a job you have to be younger than 35. The best thing is to have young people who want to expand themselves, as well as older people who want to pass on their experience. The mix is best.*

(60y, M, cl)   *None of the other players understand [that I feel inadequate] or see I have aged. So, it is clear that my ability to perform music has not really been compromised. I feel that over the years my experience and musical insight have contributed to my overall level. I can now express myself even better than when I was younger. This week one of my compatriots said: 'When you played your Solo in that Partita, you reminded me of the place that I came from.' That is a most touching compliment! It was not: 'You played really well.' But rather: 'You were able to express some cultural ideal of place and time.' In my opinion, this is the benefit of a Seasoned Musician. If only we could combine the great expressive insight of someone who is 70 [years old] with the bodily ability of a younger fellow. As we age the body isn't disabled, injured, or handicapped. Rather, sometimes the body places restrictions or limitations on us. Maybe these were within the body already at age 40, but we didn't experience them. With ageing, these conflicts seem to surface.*

(60y, M, bn)   *I do feel that I play better now than I did 25 years ago. Like getting to the heart of the music. In a sense, I would say that having older players is more of an asset than a liability. Years ago we did this 4-week tour of America. It was wonderful playing in the Hall of the Boston Symphony Orchestra. On the walls there were photos, [pictures of the band] year by year. I said to our Manager: 'See if you can spot anyone under 50?' The Boston Symphony Orchestra is this fantastic Orchestra, and they were full of really, really, really old Seasoned Players!*

(61y, F, vn)   *I hear more often from colleagues of my own age that nowadays they know much more how to express the music. They finally feel 'ripe'. They have come to a certain maturity. The more you play, the more you know how to play, and the more you know what needs to be expressed in the music. I am not sure I know what is the age of 'coming to maturity'; not sure if it has to do with 'age' or 'experience'. I started to feel that way after 20 years of being in this Orchestra (when I was 52 years old). That was when I felt I had the intuitive understanding of interpreting the music correctly. Knowing what to play! Not just which notes to play at the right time, not just to be in sync with the Conductor and my section. But rather how to be emotionally 'in tune' with the others and the music.*

(64y, M, tpt)   *The more seasoned you are, the more experience you have, the more times you've played pieces, and the more Conductors you've gone through. You are then actually more of an asset to the Orchestra—even if it's only for another 10 years [till retirement]. By taking in a younger player [they will] have a lot to learn for 20 years. The guys coming out of Music Colleges today are incredible. There is a certain amount of the physical side there; they are stronger on some instruments (like Trumpet), and that makes a difference. So, from the side of Management, they'd get many more years out of a younger player (measured in 'dollars & cents'). Hence, they justify auditioning younger players versus older players. The break-off [age period] is probably around 35.*

10.3 *In Vivo/In Situ* Music Performances

The rest of the chapter will cover all topics related to the *in vivo/in situ* music performances. Foremost, the Method of the study is set out, including: (1) descriptive information about the participating Orchestra players and the blind-judges; (2) portrayal of the environmental and acoustic setting for the *in vivo/in situ* performance; (3) description of the procedure for the music performance; (4) details of the recording gear, and procedure of constructing audio files that were sent to the judges; (5) description of the music composition; and (6) outline of the Music Performance Evaluation assessment measure. Then, the Results of the study will be delineated.

A description of two exploratory probes presented to the players immediately after the performances follows. Initially the players were asked to self-evaluate their own two performances; after that, the players were asked to predict the grading of performance feature components (and constituents) as based on age (e.g., LTE45 *versus* GTE55). Namely, the players were asked to imagine how blind-adjudicators might judge the music performances <u>if</u> they had been aware of the performer's age. Finally, the Music Performance Evaluations of both the *prima vista* Sight-Reading and the Post-Practice performances are detailed. The performances were evaluated by two professional full-time contract Symphony Orchestra musicians serving in a double-blind adjudicating process. I note here that during the interviews a few players revealed that some of their colleagues in the Orchestra declined to join the study simply because of the performance-task requirement. Obviously players had spoken among themselves several months before the active research sessions. Some of the participating players mentioned that there had been an uneasy feeling among other colleagues, knowing that their recorded performances would be judged. Nonetheless, I must say that this is exactly the lifestyle of a performing musician! There are numerous adjudications from Elementary School throughout High school and Music College, work-related auditions, extended trials, and even consistent evaluations of performance levels as a full-time contract player in an Orchestra.

(36y, F, tpt)   *I think if you take the [research study] performances we just did now, a listener would know instantly that I'm a younger Trumpet player. They'd know because I'm still full of this Testosterone-type playing. I haven't yet mellowed out. I think part of the problem with this study is that you're asking people to play. Players like myself never play a Solo. I never stand up like this. That's just alien to me for the last 13 years. In the end, it wasn't very difficult. OK, it was a bit of a challenge because it's brand new, and it's on the spot. I understand why people said: 'No!' [i.e., not willing to participate]. They're afraid to be recorded. But I think that's ridiculous.*

(54y, M, cl/bcl)   *Unfortunately, not too many players over 50 agreed to come to the study. I mean I suppose we all feel vulnerable. Particularly when you ask us to play and be assessed by [other players as judges]. I know this isn't an audition. But I mean, the very fact that one's out of one's comfort zone. For Orchestra musicians that's quite tough. Quite scary. We're never really on the spot like that. In an Orchestra, you're constantly surrounded by people who are better. And so you can raise your game. Yet, if we had to Sight-Read something, we could probably get through it.*

To reiterate, there seems to be a gap in the literature; only a few studies have implemented a music-performance task with professional musicians. Nonetheless, one study that should be mentioned is Bangert et al. (2015). Bangert et al. proclaimed that most previous music-performance research studies have solely analysed data either obtained concurrently during practice or retrospectively following performance. Specifically, they mention Chaffin and Imreh (2001)—described in depth in Chapter 9 (see section 9.3). Therefore, they claim to have explored a more novel approach which they described as 'categorizing decisions made while performing'; these were either *deliberate* (e.g., based on comments made during practice and clearly marked on the score) or *intuitive* (e.g., based on no comments made and there being no markings on the score). Performers' decisions were assessed from recordings judged retrospectively of the recitals. The research team asserted that Sight-Reading is a time-pressured task requiring immediate decision-making; it captures rapid responses to the musical score that are wholly intuitive. By contrast, decisions made during practice, as those reported in *Think Aloud Protocols* (TAPs) and represented by score markings, would be considered deliberate as based on analysis and reflection. Nonetheless, and in spite of their criticism of previous research initiatives, Bangert et al. themselves exclusively collected data during practice and retrospectively following performances. Specifically, they examined the implementation of *performance intentions* rather than evaluating the *actual music performances*. On this topic, Stones and Baker (2020) recalled Ericsson, who considered that "most real-world forms of creative achievement have not yet been successfully measured by objective methods" (p. 2). The current study, then, is an attempt to fill this gap in Music Performance Science literature by implementing a real-world form of creative accomplishment in music performance within a rigorously controlled empirical context.

10.3.1 Method

10.3.1.1 Participants

a) *Participating Orchestra Players.* The data from the Music Performance Analysis was collected from $n = 48$ professional full-time contract Symphony Orchestra players from five Orchestras in three countries (Britain, Germany, Israel). This dataset reflects 92% of the full corpus ($N = 52$). Four players missing from the dataset had cancelled their interview; yet, prior to their withdrawal from the interview they had submitted an 11-measure 12-page questionnaire booklet (as found in Chapters 2 and 11). Unfortunately, these players could not be rescheduled during the active research session in the specific country of the hosting Orchestra. The remaining participating players were on average 48 years old ($SD = 9.80$, $Mdn = 51$, Range 27–64). They were 56% males. The dataset consisted of 30 (63%) String players, 11 (23%) Woodwind players, 4 (8%) Brass players, 2 (4%) Harp players, and 1 (2%) Percussion (Vibraphone) player. The analyses that compared the two age subgroups employed the same procedure used previously in Chapters 8–9; there were 16 Young(er) Players LTE45 (33%, $M_{Age} = 36.8$, $SD = 5.37$, Range 27–44), *versus* 17 Seasoned Musicians GTE55 (35%, $M_{Age} = 58.1$, $SD = 2.67$, Range 55–64). All players between the ages 46 and 54 ($n = 15$, 31%) were excluded from the analyses in an effort to nullify overlapping that might confound results. Each player received financial compensation of $55 (£40, €50) for participating in the study.

b) *Adjudicators.* The audio files were evaluated by two full-time contract Symphony Orchestra musicians serving in a double-blind adjudicating process. The judges were either close to retirement age or already retired ($M_{Age} = 62$, $SD = 8.46$). Each had served roughly 36 years ($SD = 0.71$) as a full-time contract Orchestra player; each held the position of Principal Section Leader. Both judges were males. Each had already functioned as an Adjudicator of music performance for auditions and performance assessments at least 500 times throughout their career ($M = 650$, $SD = 212$, Range 500–800). The adjudicators were not cognizant about the goals of the study. Nor were they informed about performers' identity (i.e., country location, sex, or Orchestra affiliation). Further, the judges had no knowledge of music rendition version (i.e., 1st *prima vista* Sight-Reading [performance 'A'] or 2nd Post-Practice [performance 'B']). Each judge evaluated the recordings (pairs A–B) based on their instrument of expertise; one judge evaluated all String players, while the other evaluated all Wind players (i.e., combined Woodwind–Brass). The 'other' instruments (Harp and Vibraphone) were evaluated by the adjudicator of the Wind instruments. The judges received financial compensation of $54 (£43, €50) per pair of recorded performances.

10.3.1.2 Music Performances

The music performances were conducted during the single 2-hour interview session which took place on-site at one of five venues (in three countries). The rooms used for the recordings were the same rooms where the interviews themselves were carried out: Rehearsal Halls, a *Green Room*, an isolated Management Office, and a large Instrument Storage space. As these rooms were never intended for music performance, it should be noted that neither the chairs nor the ceiling lighting were similar to those found on the Concert Platform of the hosting Orchestra. The music recordings were conducted completely in private, employing an unobtrusive digital audio recorder. The first performance occurred prior to the ±10-minute period of DP, while the second was implemented after a ±10-minute DP. Therefore, the 1st performance was a *prima vista* Sight-Reading, while the 2nd performance was considered a more *polished* rendition version.

The performances were digitally audio recorded with a *H2 Handy Portable Stereo Digital Recorder* (ZOOM). This model was fully described in Chapter 1 (see section 1.6.3.1). The microphone was positioned so as to enable clear audio recording of the music performance. Nonetheless, I note that the recordings were predisposed to local noise, room acoustics, and ambiance of a space that was not designed for music performance or audio recording. The recordings were captured 'live'; in one take, without any mixing, sound editing, or enhancement. Recordings were cropped and trimmed from the 2-hour interview using *SoundForge XP 4.5c Express Audio* (Real Networks) or *WavePad 6.64 Sound Editor* (NCH Software). The procedure assured that no other sounds could be heard. For example, a performer's voice might have alerted a judge to the sex or native tongue (i.e., country of origin) of a participant-player. Sound files were exported in .wav format. A total of 96 audio files (48 participant-players × 2 performances) were prepared for music-performance analyses. All files were reassigned name labels using numbers by employing an algorithm which positioned numeric digits as 'place fillers' in a system designed to camouflage participants' IDs. Therefore, the adjudicators were not able to associate one counterpart (of the paired performances) to the other. The audio files were presented on a flash drive as a list in sequential ascending order; placement of rendition version (A–B or B–A) was counterbalanced across the list.

10.3.1.3 Evaluation Measures

Evaluating musicians' ability is complex. There is no systematic methodical or even pragmatic form of examination. For example, in Ruthsatz et al. (2008), band members' rank was employed as an estimation of *musical achievement*. While I myself have not ever seen the use of Orchestra position employed as a dependent variable or proxy for musical achievement—especially as 'rank' certainly reflects contractual hierarchy—Ruthsatz et al. emphasize that many previous studies in the literature "have typically relied on this type of evaluation for reporting levels of musical achievement, and the validity of music instructors as raters of musical achievement is well-accepted" (p. 333).

At this point, perhaps it is most pertinent to ask: *What do music performers do?* The most basic requirement is that performers play the correct notes, rhythms, dynamics, etc. of a musical idea as they are written out in the notation of a music score. Namely, for the most part, we might see *accuracy* as an appropriate reference point against which a certain level of correctness is measured. Nonetheless, performers are also expected to go beyond the notation; to place great effort on the ability to *articulate* the collective culturally accepted expressions of emotion, as well as their own personal interpretation. Music performance is not a standardized procedure among research initiatives. Thompson and Williamon (2003) claimed that

Table 10.1 Assessment Measure of Music Performance

Main Factors	Subcomponents
I Instrumental Competence	1. Technical Security 2. Rhythmic Accuracy 3. Tonal Quality and Spectrum
II Musicality	4. Musical Understanding 5. Stylistic Accuracy 6. Interpretative Imagination 7. Expressive Range
III Communication	8. Communicative Ability 9. Deportment Onstage 10. Deportment with Instrument 11. Communication of Emotional Commitment and Conviction 12. Ability to Cope with Stress of the Situation
IV Overall Quality of Performance	

Data Source: Thompson and Williamon (2003)

musical performances are simply not open to the reliable and consistent scrutiny that most other research initiatives require. As an example, Clarke (2005) solely distinguished between two varieties of *expressive* features in performance; one was regarded as the unconscious depictions of underlying cognitive processes, while the other was the result of deliberate interpretative choices. Maybe, Clarke's resourceful insight was the spark that inspired Bangert et al. (2015) to study *intuitive* versus *deliberate* decisions in music performance? Long ago, Thompson and Williamon developed an assessment measure to evaluate music performances among Solo players with an Accompanist; their measure consisted of 3 Main Factors comprised of 12 Subcomponents—as well as a mark for the Overall Performance Quality. See Table 10.1.

Thompson and Williamon asserted that when evaluating music performance much depends on the performer's stage of development (e.g., age), as well as on the actual context in which the music performance is being assessed (e.g., early childhood Music Conservatoire, Music-specialist High school, Music Academy College, or professional audition). Further, they claim that most studies target one individual Solo performance, while only a few focus on a performance of a Soloist with an Accompanist or even a Chamber Music Ensemble; the latter explore communication and synchrony between participants. But, the music-performance assessment as developed by Thompson and Williamon would not have been appropriate to investigate the performances in the current study among professional Symphony Orchestra players (without an Accompanist). In another study, Smith and Barnes (2007) developed an Orchestra Performance Rating Scale. This measure was based on 7 Factors comprised of 25 items, including: Bow, Ensemble, Left Hand, Presentation, Position, Rhythm, and Tempo). But, that measure was specific for Secondary School Orchestras rather than professionals.

Table 10.2 Music Performance Evaluation (*MPE*)

Principal Feature Components		Constituents
[A]	Artistic Strategies	Expressiveness
		Organization
		Tone Quality
		Articulation
		Dynamics
		Phrasing
[B]	Temporal Accuracy	Tempo
		Rhythm
[C]	Technical Accuracy	Technique
		Tone (Intonation) Accuracy

Therefore the current study adapted a measure partially brought forward by Yoshie et al. (2009a, 2009b) known as the *Music Performance Evaluation* (*MPE*). See Table 10.2. As can be seen in Table 10.2, *MPE* targets 3 main Principal Feature Components comprised of 10 Constituents. The *MPE* was employed by the participant-players to retrospectively self-rate their own performances—referred to hereafter as *MPsE*. In addition, The *MPE* was employed by the external independent blind-judges to evaluate the actual music performances.

a) *Music Performance Self-Evaluation* (*MPsE*). The players used a 10-point scale to retrospectively self-evaluate their own performances for each of the 10 *MPE* Constituents. The response scale used was:

$$-5 \quad -4 \quad -3 \quad -2 \quad -1 \quad 0 \quad +1 \quad +2 \quad +3 \quad +4 \quad +5$$

The players understood that they were not assessing absolute values of a particular Constituent, but rather comparing between two rendition versions of the same piece. That is, the main issue was not to indicate 'good' or 'bad' per se, but rather to compare between *you* and *yourself* on two repeated performances of the same piece. Therefore, the importance of the *MPsE* was not necessarily to rate a specific numerical value, but rather to evaluate the *direction* of change (or no change), and then to estimate *how far* along the outcome the player reached in the 2nd Post-Practice performance compared to the 1st *prima vista* Sight-Reading performance. The players indicated a zero ('0', nought) to represent *no change* of implementation for a performance feature constituent (i.e., same quality); a negative number ('–', minus) to represent an *inferior* implementation of a performance feature constituent (i.e., decline in quality); a positive number ('+', plus) to represent a *superior* implementation of a performance feature constituent (increase in quality). Individual scores for each of the 10 constituents were computed. Further, accumulative scores were calculated for all 3 Principal Feature Components (i.e., Artistic Expression [A], Temporal Accuracy [B], Technical Accuracy [C]), as well as a combined score of Accuracy [B+C/2], and a more global *MPsE* Total score.

b) *Double-Blind Music Performance Evaluation.* Two external independent judges in a double-blind adjudication process used a 5-point Likert scale to rate the music-performance *level* for each Constituent of the *MPE* assessment measure (1 = Inferior, 5 = Superior). One judge listened to audio recordings free-field (Focusrite *18i8* interface with M-Audio *BX8a* speakers) while the other heard the audio recordings fixed-field (JBL *Tune 500BT* wireless headphones). The judges were instructed as follows:

1. Listen to each performance twice.
2. Designate individual ratings for each of the 10 Constituents on the *MPE* rating form.
3. Place markings on the music notation score for each performance by circling the precise locations (notes) where mishaps of melodic notes or rhythmic patterns occurred, and also underline sections (bar measures) where the unfortunate execution of articulations occurred.
4. Listen to each performance a 3rd time while further examining the evaluation ratings and score markings.
5. After judging all performances of all players, listen again to each performance for a 4th last time—and adjust rating scores accounting for the overall levels of the whole sample.

The analyses computed individual scores for each of the 10 Constituents, accumulative scores for all 3 Principal Feature Components (i.e., Artistic Expression [A], Temporal Accuracy [B], Technical Accuracy [C]), as well as for a combined score of Accuracy [B+C/2], and a more global *MPE* Total score. In addition, the difference between the two performances (i.e., ratings for the 2nd Post-Practice performance *minus* the ratings for the 1st *prima vista* Sight-Reading), referred to as Delta-Δ scores, were determined. Finally, the judges' inscriptions on the actual music notation scores were tallied; these were recoded as a percentile (i.e., %) accounting for the total number of bar measures performed without mishaps. This is referred to as a *Music Notation Score Analysis* (MNSA). This later analysis served as another measure of Accuracy (*triangulation*). The judges were not given any instructions regarding the order by which they were to rate specific Constituents on the *MPE* rating form (Table 10.2).

10.3.1.4 Music Composition
The current study employs an original music piece specifically composed for the study by Symphonic Composer Moshe Zorman (described in the Cover Note preceding Part III). See Appendix A. There were three versions of similar quality and difficulty used in the study. Each was perceived as an independent stand-alone

miniature piece. The music scores presented to the players consisted of notation and articulation markings for 1 of 5 instrument families (Strings, Woodwinds, Brass, Harp, and Keyboard Percussion). In total, 15 music scores were prepared as individual parts: Strings (Violin, Viola, Cello, Double Bass); Woodwinds (Flute, Oboe, Clarinet in B^b, Bassoon); Brass (Horn in F, Trumpet in B^b, Alto Saxophone, Trombone, Tuba); Harp; and Percussion (Xylophone). The scores consisted of an average 60 bar measures. In performance tempo (crochet/quarter note = 120bpm) the duration of each piece was roughly 2:30 minutes.

10.3.1.5 Procedure

Approximately 75 minutes after the onset of the single 2-hour interview session, each player was asked to retrieve their musical instrument that was situated nearby in an instrument case. First they spent a few minutes checking the instrument (e.g., tuning strings, fitting a reed, or placing a mouthpiece). Most players performed seated in a chair as they do in the Orchestra; 3 players stood in an upright position *as if* emulating a Solo performance. The players were allowed to use any performance-related item in their possession, including: Bows, Mallets, Metronomes, Mouthpieces, Pads, Pillows, Reeds, Rosin, or Shoulder Pads. Nonetheless, the players were not allowed to mark up the music notation scores (e.g., notate with comments, directions, or symbols, for Articulation, Bowing, Breathing, Fingering, Pedalling, Phrasing, or Sticking). The reason for this restriction was simply because the same music notation score-parts were viewed by all players of the same instrument in all Orchestras across three countries. Although that procedure was installed for methodological rigour, in retrospect it might have been more adaptive to have provided an individual copy of the same piece for each player to mark up as they saw fit.

When each player verbally noted that they were ready for the music performance task, a music score was placed in front of them on a music stand; the stand had previously been positioned at a suitable reading distance. The scores were viewed on two A4-size pages. The 1st performance was played *prima vista* as an unseen text; the players played the piece at first sight, never having had prior access to 'glance over' the music notation. They did not even have the opportunity to visually scan ('eyeball') the score beforehand. Then, after a period of ±10 minutes for DP, each player played the piece a 2nd time as a more polished performance.

Chaffin et al. (2002/2012) demonstrated that music experts have honed their practice strategies for performance success through self-regulation of practice. Accordingly, the process requires them to plan, control, and monitor learning efforts during DP. While there was some discussion among a number of players who subsequently declined participation in the study because of the specific performance task requirement, Suzuki and Mitchell (2022) point out that the majority of players are accustomed to preparing for concerts through mock performances; these occasions give them ample opportunities to learn how to conceptualize a piece as a whole, and to know how to work at developing an interpretation.

(55y, M, perc)   *While I look at myself as [someone who] can play like when I was younger, I do think I'm even better now. Although that probably didn't show at all [in the prima vista performance]. But the powers of Sight-Reading have never been proved. I have to work at things to get them accurate. We have a repertoire in an Orchestra, and you get to know that repertoire really well. So, it's just a matter of 'brushing up'.*

10.3.2 Results

10.3.2.1 Music Performance Self-Evaluation (*MPsE*)

Immediately after each player completed the Post-Practice performance, they were asked to self-evaluate their implementation. For this task, they employed the *MPsE*. As can be seen in the vignettes below, some players felt that *self-evaluation* is actually a highly difficult undertaking for performing musicians to begin with. Generally, performing musicians are raised solely to consider the sentiments and judgements of their mentor-coach. Second, performance achievements of musicians are usually underrated—unlike achievements of athletes and sportsmen. Finally, some felt that differences between music performances are not as great in one's later years as they may have been in earlier periods of time. Namely, after many years of experience, and coming to Musical Maturity, players no longer expect there to be great variances between performances. Once a specific performance standard has been reached, performance levels are highly predictable, and believed to remain quite stable. Unfortunately, the data of one Seasoned Musician (a String player) was corrupted. Hence, only $n = 47$ were entered to *MPsE* analyses.

(30y, F, vn)   *I probably absorbed more of the notation and markings on the page on the 2nd pass. I don't think there would be huge differences in Organization [between] the 1st and 2nd [performances]. Expressiveness? I wouldn't go either way because I think some players would find something in it while other players won't. I don't think that's an 'age' thing. This particular piece didn't give huge opportunities of expression. That's not to say you can't find it. There's something to think about in every bit. I can see exactly what YOU are doing; every section of the piece has its pitfall. I am sure some players fall into those while other players don't.*

(33y, F, bn/dbn)   *A musician needs to be very critical. That's part of learning how to be a musician. But I know it's a problem. Look: As you're growing up, you play in front of others. Your teacher is there. Everybody's clapping, and saying it's great. Then you just walk up to the teacher, and the first thing you say is: 'What did I do wrong?' As a rule, musicians have a lot of trouble evaluating themselves. They need somebody else to tell them what they did (wrong). This is just the way musicians grow up. It's not the same for athletes. A basketball player can throw the ball to the basket 20 times in the game, and then if he gets it in twice everyone would say: 'Wow, that was great!' [But yet, that incidence is only a 20% success rate.] We play 20,000 notes, and then when just 1 goes wrong, we'd say: [But] 'I got one wrong.' So, we are not raised to look at the 19,999 notes you play right, but only the 1 out of 20,000 you got wrong. [Author's Note: Musicological research indicates that a 90-minute Symphony consists of roughly 350,000 notes.] Even today, when I played the performance piece, I didn't say: 'Oh great, I got 350 notes correct—and it was prima vista Sight-Reading.' Even when you [the researcher] complimented me, my response was: 'But, I got one note wrong.' Why should we be like that? And, after I worked on it for 10 minutes, and played through the whole thing—and clearly it was much better. But, I rated myself much lower than I should have. The scores should've been 3s and 4s and not 1s and 2s. So that means that I expected much more. But maybe that's what makes one a great player; you don't accept a little bit of change from practice, you expect a lot of change, and keep working till it happens.*

(47y, M, hn)   *What I thought about when I did that [performance] was that there wasn't much improvement. I think that I would have improved more when I was younger. You just reach a standard, and find it quite hard to do much better even after practising it. I was disappointed with the second time round; I had felt quite confident that I was gonna do more or less a perfect performance. In both there were slip-ups. I didn't get on top of my Keys. I just think that maybe somebody younger would have done more than me. But I suppose, when I was younger I might have had some bigger accidents. I mean the first reading wasn't great, but it wasn't a massive disaster either. So, it's a bit like an old guy driving a car around a twisted road; there might be a slip somewhere, but he's not gonna go off the road!*

MPsE data was tallied for all 10 Constituents. Accumulated scores were calculated for all 3 Principal Feature Components (i.e., Artistic Expression [A], Temporal Accuracy [B], Technical Accuracy [C]), as well as for a combined score of Accuracy [B+C/2], and a more global *MPsE* Total score. See Table 10.3, left-side column panel.

As can be seen in Table 10.3 (left-side column panel), the total sample of players self-estimated their 2nd Post-Practice Performance as having greatly improved.

Table 10.3 Music Performance Self-Evaluation (*MPsE*): Total Sample and Comparisons Between String Players *Versus* Wind Players

Principal Feature Components and Constituents	Total Musicians (N = 47)			Strings (n = 29)		Winds (n = 15)		Sig
	M	*SD*	Range	*M*	*SD*	*M*	*SD*	p^1
[A] Artistic Expression								
Expressiveness	2.34	1.32	−2–5	2.38	1.21	2.13	1.51	
Organization	2.30	1.14	−1–5	2.31	1.11	2.20	1.26	
Tone Quality	1.30	1.35	−2–4	1.55	1.41	0.87	1.13	
Articulation	1.98	1.38	−1–5	2.41	1.48	1.40	0.74	*
Dynamics	2.23	1.48	0–5	2.27	1.39	1.93	1.54	
Phrasing	1.96	1.29	0–5	2.07	1.25	1.80	1.08	
Total A %	**20.2**	**10.0**	**−5–42**	**21.67**	**10.34**	**17.22**	**8.58**	
[B] Temporal Accuracy								
Tempo	1.13	1.47	−3–4	1.10	1.26	1.67	1.29	
Rhythm	1.85	1.37	−1–4	1.69	1.29	2.20	1.57	
Total B %	**14.9**	**11.9**	**−10–40**	**13.97**	**11.29**	**19.33**	**11.48**	
[C] Technical Accuracy								
Technique	1.83	1.26	−2–4	2.28	1.07	1.13	1.30	**
Intonation	1.66	1.17	−1–4	1.83	1.14	1.27	1.03	
Total C %	**17.5**	**10.2**	**−5–40**	**20.52**	**10.03**	**12.00**	**8.82**	**
[B+C/2] Total Accuracy %	**16.2**	**8.60**	**0–35**	**17.24**	**9.05**	**15.67**	**7.93**	
***MPsE* Tot %**	**36.4**	**16.80**	**5–72**	**38.91**	**18.03**	**32.89**	**14.80**	

[1]Level of significance: * = $p < 0.05$; ** = $p < 0.01$

Readers should note that a number of players did actually self-evaluate their 2nd Post-Practice performance inferior to their 1st Sight-Reading performance (as can be seen in the range of scores). Table 10.3 shows the largest performance improvement was for the Feature Component Artistic Expression [A] (estimated as a 20% improvement). The improvement for Temporal Accuracy [B] and Technical Accuracy [C] was slightly lower (15% and 18%, respectively). When testing differences between the main two Principal Component Features (Expression [A] 20% *versus* Accuracy [B+C/2] 16%) the analyses found statistically significant greater self-estimated improvements for Expressiveness ($t = 3.40$, $df = 46$, $p < 0.01$; $d = 0.12$, a moderate effect size). Finally, as seen in Table 10.3 (left-side column panel), the overall estimated performance improvement (after a ±10-minute period of DP) was a 36% increase in performance quality. The analyses then explored variances of *MPsE* based on two subgrouping variables. The two subgroups that come to mind are: *instrument* and *age*.

The first analysis targeted *musical instrument*. There were 3 instrument subgroups: *Strings* ($n = 29$, 62%), *Winds* (a combined Woodwind and Brass, $n = 15$, 32%), and *Other* (e.g., Harps and Vibraphone, $n = 3$, 6%). In the final dataset, players of instruments other than Strings or Winds were excluded. Hence, data from $n = 44$ musicians were entered in this analysis. See Table 10.3, right-side column panel. As can be seen in Table 10.3 (right-side column panel), the String players self-estimated their improvement for the 2nd Post-Practice performance higher than the Wind players for all 6 Constituents of the Feature Component Artistic Expression [A]. But most of these were not statistically significant; the only exception was Articulation. On the other hand, the Wind players self-evaluated their 2nd Post-Practice performance to be superior for the 2 Constituents of the Feature Component Temporal Accuracy; but these differences were also not statistically significant. While the String players self-estimated the Feature Component Technical Accuracy [C] to have greatly improved beyond how the Wind players envisioned their 2nd Post-Practice performance, and self-estimates of improvement for Technique were statistically significantly higher compared to the Wind players, when collapsing the data for a combined score of Accuracy [B+C/2], all statistically significant differences between the instrument subgroups ceased to surface. Finally, as can be seen in Table 10.3 (right-side column panel), overall improvements of the 2nd performance (*MPsE* Total) were estimated higher for the String players than the Wind players (by 6%), but this difference was not statistically significant: $t = 1.11$, $df = 42$, $p = 0.273$. In summary, self-estimated improvements for specific Principal Feature Components might somewhat depend on the instrument being played, but from a wide-ranging assessment (e.g., *MPsE* Total scores) no significant difference of improvement for performances surfaced between the instrument subgroups.

The second analysis targeted *age*. From the outset, there was a notion that the old(er) players would perform with more Artistic Expression [A] than the Young(er) Players; by conception, this difference should have already been apparent in the 1st *prima vista* Sight-Reading. See Table 10.4, right-side column panel. Such a notion

Table 10.4 Music Performance Self-Evaluation (*MPsE*): Total Sample and Comparisons Between Young(er) Players *Versus* Old(er) Players

Principal Feature Components and Constituents	Total Musicians (N = 47)			Young(er) Players LTE45 (n = 16)		Seasoned Musicians GTE55 (n = 16)		Sig
	M	*SD*	Range	*M*	*SD*	*M*	*SD*	*p*
[A] Artistic Expression								
Expressiveness	2.34	1.32	−2–5	2.13	1.59	2.38	1.31	
Organization	2.30	1.14	−1–5	2.25	1.13	2.13	1.20	
Tone Quality	1.30	1.35	−2–4	1.38	1.54	1.19	1.43	
Articulation	1.98	1.38	−1–5	1.88	1.46	2.00	1.10	
Dynamics	2.23	1.48	0–5	1.78	1.34	2.19	1.60	
Phrasing	1.96	1.29	0–5	2.00	1.27	1.69	1.35	
Total A %	**20.2**	10.0	−5–42	**18.96**	10.52	**19.27**	10.20	
[B] Temporal Accuracy								
Tempo	1.13	1.47	−3–4	1.31	1.14	1.50	1.46	
Rhythm	1.85	1.37	−1–4	1.63	1.36	1.88	1.59	
Total B %	**14.9**	11.9	−10–40	**14.69**	9.91	**16.88**	13.77	
[C] Technical Accuracy								
Technique	1.83	1.26	−2–4	1.94	1.61	1.56	1.15	
Intonation	1.66	1.17	−1–4	1.88	1.15	1.50	1.16	
Total C %	**17.5**	10.2	−5–40	**19.06**	12.14	**15.31**	9.03	
[B+C/2] Total Accuracy %	**16.2**	8.60	0–35	**16.86**	9.20	**16.09**	10.16	
***MPsE* Tot %**	**36.4**	16.80	5–72	**35.83**	17.65	**35.37**	19.23	

was based on insights that were repeatedly mentioned in the interviews (described in Chapters 3–7). Hence, there was an expectancy that a *ceiling effect* would surface, and that self-estimated improvements among Seasoned Musicians would either be *nought* '0' (i.e., remaining the same), or perhaps exclusively improve for the Feature Components of Temporal Accuracy [B], Technical Accuracy [C], or the combined Accuracy [B+C/2] score. As was employed in previous age-related analyses (in Chapters 8–9), 2 age subgroups were employed: *Young(er) Players* LTE45 (n = 16, 34%, M_{Age} = 36.75, SD = 5.37, Range 27-45) and *Seasoned Musicians* GTE55 (n = 16, 34%, M_{Age} = 58.25, SD = 2.70, Range 55-64). Therefore, data from n = 32 musicians were entered in analyses.

As can be seen in Table 10.4 (right-side column panel), self-evaluated improvements for the 6 Constituents of the Feature Component Artistic Expression [A] were split evenly between the 2 age subgroups. LTE45 players perceived to have performed better for 3 out of 6 constituents (i.e., Organization, Tone Quality, and Phrasing), while GTE55 players perceived to have performed better for the other 3 out of 6 constituents (i.e., Expressiveness, Articulation, and Dynamics). Yet, none of these differences were statistically significant. Further, the mechanical aspects of performance were also split between the 2 age subgroups: LTE45 players perceived to have improved more for Technical Accuracy [C] (i.e., Technique and Intonation), while GTE55 players perceived to have improved more for Temporal Accuracy [B] (i.e., Tempo and Rhythm). Again, none of these differences were statistically significant. Finally, perceived total improvement scores (i.e., *MPsE*) were similar for both age subgroups. In summary, after a ±10-minute period of DP, self-evaluated self-estimated improvements of performance features do not surface as dependent on age.

Both of the above analyses demonstrate that self-evaluated estimates of improvement in music performance were no different for any professional full-time contract Symphony Orchestra player regardless of their musical instrument or their age. Structured quality judgements represent an interesting research tool. According to Thompson and Williamon (2003) such judgements have taken on a larger role as the focus of research interest has gradually shifted towards understanding and explaining real-world performance issues. They claim that applied research is more often:

> concerned with improving musical performance itself, investigating practice and memorization strategies, and trying to deduce the factors that make one performer appear more successful than another in a real performance environment. [. . .] It seems important for researchers to have access to performance assessments that are not only reliable and consistent but able to specify differences between two or more performances, be they given by several performers or by the same performer over a period of time. (p. 22)

In general, the participating players of the current study estimated that after a ±10-minute period of DP their 2nd Post-Practice performance was roughly 36% more efficient than their 1st *prima vista* Sight-Reading. But yet, these findings do not align with the statements conveyed by the Young(er) Players in the interviews about their old(er) aged colleagues. Therefore, a second probe was initiated to further explore such attitudes.

10.3.2.2 Likelihood of Music Performance Considering Age Subgroup

After the participating players completed their *MPsE* self-evaluation, they were asked to consider the following imaginary story:

> There was a blind-audition procedure in which two players performed the same piece from behind a screen. Both received the same rating scores from the judges. But one player was a 30-year-old while the other was a 50-year-old. Given these age differences, would you envisage that the internal sub-scores for Performance Features would have been different? That is, do you presume the young(er) player would have received higher scores for specific features, while the old(er) player would have received higher scores for other features?

It should be noted that the performance features mentioned in the above hypothetical are the same Principal Feature Components and Constituents employed by the participating players for their own *MPsE* self-evaluation (just a minute earlier). See Table 10.2. From the outset, several players stated that there should be no differences between the 2 players in the depiction. They assume that players aged 30–35 years old would not be considered *young* because by then they would have had between 7 and 10 years' experience in an Orchestra. Nonetheless, most other players did have some preconceived ideas about how Orchestra players of different ages perform. Hence, they were asked to forecast the likelihood of typical adjudicator scores for music performances as based on 3 age subgroups (LTE45, 46–54 years old, and GTE55). See Tables 10.5, 10.6, and 10.7. No doubt that to some extent such perceptions not only reflect real-life experiences, but also echo stereotypical intuitions reflecting *ageism*. It should be noted that Tables 10.5, 10.6, and 10.7 present items in descending order, from the most frequently mentioned to the least frequently mentioned. In addition, the tables present a percentage (%) for the frequency of mention (as a reference guide). Finally, the reader should note: Table 10.5 conveys depictions from players LTE45 (*n* = 16); Table 10.6 conveys depictions from players between ages 46 and 54 (*n* = 15); Table 10.7 conveys depictions from players GTE55 (*n* = 17).

Table 10.5 Music Performance as Perceived by Players LTE45 (*n* = 16)

Young(er) Players LTE45				Seasoned Musicians GTE55			
Superior	**%**	**Inferior**	**%**	**Superior**	**%**	**Inferior**	**%**
Technical Accuracy	31	Tempo Control	13	Expression	31	Technical Accuracy	19
Tone Quality	19	Phrasing	13	Dynamics	25	Rhythm	13
Energy	13	Understanding	6	Tone Quality	13	Intonation Precision	13
Attention Technique	13	Fit in with Others	6	Tempo Control	13	Tempo Control	6
Rhythm	6			Phrasing	13	Motor Ability	6
Involved	6			Artistic/Musical	13		
Invested	6			Articulation	13		
Intonation Precision	6			Organization	13		
Expression	6			Understanding	6		
Cleaner	6						
Articulation	6						
Agile	6						

a) *Players LTE45*

(29y, F, vn)   *It's difficult to judge if Expression, playing in time, technical aspects, competence, playing in tune, Intonation, etc. change with age. But if you're asking about Accuracy, then I think once people reach a certain level they stay stable. Whereas sometimes when it comes to musical aspects of playing (like emotions) I found that those who are bored just sit back in their chairs. So, my guess would be that some younger players would play with more musical and personal involvement. But again, that's not always the case. I can think of 1–2 people my age or slightly older, that play exactly the same as a*

60-year-old. So, it doesn't have to be the case that there is a difference between a 55-year-old player and someone who is 30. I've been really impressed with some of my colleagues who are above 50 years old; they still perform really well, and definitely like a 35-year-old player.

(30y, F, vn)   *Speaking from experience, I'd say that the younger player would tend to be less rhythmically secure, but probably with more energy. I think an older player is probably more aware of that, and would not rush so much. I guess I'm generalizing, imagining someone fresh out of college versus someone over 50. The young person would generally have better Tone Quality. I think the older players would score better with things like Dynamics and Articulation.*

(33y, M, va)   *But 35 isn't that young, and 55 isn't that old. So [I don't agree with the] two age groupings. Yes! I would probably imagine differences. I would probably say Tempo and Rhythm would be lower for the older people, and probably Technical Accuracy as well. The Intonation would be higher, Tone Quality, the type of sound that they want to play, and probably Dynamics more than younger players. I don't know about Phrasing. Expressiveness might be a bit more 'cause they have got more life experience. So, you might say that the older Seasoned Musicians have more to give on an 'art' level.*

(35y, F, vn)   *No differences for Expressiveness, Dynamics, Tempo, or Rhythm. The only thing that I think might be different would be Technique and Articulation. There are different generations of players; different schools of performance. Things do change technically. On one hand, that seems to have nothing to do with the age. But if you learned how to play 30 years ago, techniques would be slightly different. That doesn't mean the younger players have an advantage today, it's just different.*

(36y, F, tpt)   *I hear people coming straight from college and there's a lot of things that they seem to be able to cope with. They just seem to have more stamina. They just got the ability to deliver all the time! Yet, we've got a Horn player who is coming up for retirement; you just cannot see an end to this guy. Actually, musicians sound better as they get older. But still, the younger players are more agile. Yet, I wouldn't have been able to do [then] what I do now in my Orchestra job. I've adapted my playing to suit the environment. If a young player (25 years old) comes to the Orchestra as a substitute, you'd expect them to be more technically competent than the older players. Certainly a Brass player would have more Testosterone, just a bit more brash. Also, perhaps their concept of sound is different. I would rate the older player for higher Expressiveness than the younger player; Articulation may be better in the younger player; Phrasing would be better in an older player; Technique Accuracy could be better in the younger player; and Intonation Accuracy would be better in the older player. I think Dynamics, Tempo, and Rhythmic Accuracy would be similar.*

(37y, M, va)   *The older player might be just as good or even better, but they'd get less scores in Precision of Intonation, Technique, and Motor Abilities. I think Seasoned Players bring something to the Orchestra that younger players can't. The younger ones might play all of the notes perfectly, and perhaps even understand nuances of music for each period [of Music History], but they can't play with others.*

(38y, M, bn/dbn)   *I wouldn't necessarily think there would be any difference [based on age]. I think that some things are just personal style. Possibly younger players are inexperienced. But, they can 'fly' around their instrument—they are technical wizards. I can't see how age would be a factor.*

(39y, F, cl)   *I would have thought that even two 35-year-olds are different. That their internal marks could be quite different. I find it hard to say in terms of ageing. I would not imagine that an older player would be better at specific features, and that a younger player would be better at others. If we're talking about someone who's in College, then I may be willing to make a generalization that the older player would score better in Expressiveness (because of the experience). [But] for somebody who's professional (and in my view that would also be a 35-year-old), it would just depend on the individual player.*

(40y, F, vn)   *The chances are that both [players] would know what to do in the excerpts. But maybe not! I remember hearing a story from Finland. There was this young woman who played an excerpt. The judges said: 'Very well. Now look at the key signature.' Apparently she played the whole excerpt half a step up. An older player would've known the repertoire. But that also says something about the person who isn't very careful. So in the context of the story, it was not the fact that she auditioned in a different key, but that she didn't pay attention to details. I can't imagine any [performance] features that would be different for younger versus older players. Perhaps, just a few points better among the older ones in Expressiveness.*

(41y, M, va)   *I would say the younger player would be better at Expressiveness, Tone Quality, and Phrasing. Probably Technique. The younger player would probably play more in tune. The older player would have better Rhythm, more consistent Tempo, pay more attention to Dynamics, be more Organized, and probably better Articulated.*

(44y, F, vn)   *I would expect the younger player to take slightly longer sussing the piece out. I think the younger player's tone would be pretty much the same throughout, and probably more accurate with the Rhythm and the notes. Not necessarily Phrasing. [That is] the technical side rather than the expressive side. I do think that the more mature player would be further away from Technique; more involved in producing an end piece of music. So, the older player would have higher scores in Expressiveness, and slightly more for Tone Quality. The younger player would have better Technique, Rhythm, Tempo, and Articulation. I think [the young player] would play a cleaner depiction of the piece, but not necessarily more interesting. You might say that these are the liabilities of the older player. But there are also assets of being the older player; general understanding of the music is much higher having had more life experience.*

Table 10.6 Music Performance as Perceived by Players 46–54 Years Old (*n* = 15)

Young(er) Players LTE45				Seasoned Musicians GTE55			
Superior	**%**	**Inferior**	**%**	**Superior**	**%**	**Inferior**	**%**
Tone Quality	13	Tempo Control	7	Tempo Control	13	Tone Quality	7
Clearer Articulation	7			Rhythm	7	Vibrato	7
Tone Accuracy	7			Expression	7		
Note Accuracy	7			Dynamics	7		

b) *Players Between Ages 46 and 54*

(47y, M, vc)   *I do not believe that [a judge would] be able to hear the difference of age. I've heard maybe 400 auditions; performance had nothing to do with age per se. I've offered jobs to people in their 20s and to people in their 40s; 90% of interest in an Orchestra position comes from people under the age of 30. My personal story is that there was a Principal Cello position open in Munich (Germany). I reckoned I had the right credentials and experience. I sent [in] my application and one question was sent back: 'How old are you?' I was 38, in the prime of my life, at my physical and musical peak! But, they just said: 'You're too old!' I do think that there are no differences based on age, although the internal scores of an older player might be different than the younger player. If you take 10 players that are below 45, and 10 players who are above 55, all professional Orchestra players, they will all have about the same total scores.*

(47y, M, trb)   *We have a lot of auditions, but we never have people who are 40+; they are always young. But if both played the same Trombone Concerto, and both practised it, then: Yeah! There would be differences. Perhaps a younger player would be better in Tone Quality. The older player would perhaps be more precise than the younger one in Temporal Accuracy (like the tempo rhythm). This is perhaps the only feature where the older player could have an advantage.*

(47y, F, vn)   *I suppose that Tone Quality may be better for the younger player. On average, older people don't have a nice tone. But, the older ones would be really good with Tempo and Rhythm; understanding the Tempo and getting the Rhythm right would be easier for someone with more experience. So, I believe that a mixture (50%–50%) of younger and older players in the Orchestra is better.*

(52y, M, db)   *I don't think one can hear a difference between an older versus younger player on Bass. I don't believe that one would have a better Technique or Tone Quality. It's more a question of character. Even a young player can sound very 'old', while an older player can sound very 'young'.*

(53y, M, hrp)   *Dynamics and Expressiveness would be higher for the older more experienced Seasoned Players. I'm thinking the younger string players might have scored better on Tone Accuracy. I don't really see why either should score better or worse for Tempo. The younger players do have clearer Articulation.*

(54y, M, va)   *Does age have anything to do with Interpretation, Intonation, and Expressivity? [A very long period of silence.] When I listen to the older players above 60, I don't feel they are less expressive than younger players. But I do think their interpretation is far better because they have more experience.*

(54y, F, vc)   *I have sat in several auditions. I am not certain that I would have expected older players to play [in one way] and younger players to play in another way. Yet, simply from what I've witnessed, I think some older players are just not able to keep quality a sound for Vibrato.*

(54y, M, cl/bcl)   *I don't know in my heart if there would be a difference. I suppose technically the younger player would be better just getting the notes in the right place. But, I wouldn't necessarily say I'd expect the older players to have a better Tone and the younger players to have a better Technique. When I was 24 and my boss was 56, I felt that I had a lot to learn from him, but I didn't feel we were any different.*

Table 10.7 Music Performance as Perceived by Players GTE55 (*n* = 16)

Young(er) Players LTE45				Seasoned Musicians GTE55				
Superior	%	Inferior	%	Superior	%	Inferior	%	
Technical Accuracy	38	Tempo Control	13	Expression	38	Sound Clarity	13
Temporal Accuracy	25	Expression	6	Dynamics	31	Technical Accuracy	6
Intonation Precision	19	Rhythm	6	Articulation	25		
Rhythm	19			Tone Quality	19		
Reading	13			Phrasing	13		
Faster Pacing	13			Organization	13		
Articulation	6			Tempo Control	6		
Organization	6			Artistic/Musical	6		
				Understanding	6		
				Sound Quality	6		
				Interpretation	6		
				Rhythm	6		
				Intonation	6		

c) *Players GTE55*

(55y, F, fl)   *Hopefully, the 50-year-old would be better at Phrasing, Dynamics, Tone Quality, and Expressiveness. The 30-year-old would be better at everything else. Because when you're young you're concentrating more on the actual notes. Maybe when you're older you slow down a bit, and you see different things as important. It's possible that you could get a 55-year-old who could get a 100% in all [Components]. Certainly the way I see it is that the older you get, the more Expressive and musical you get (but less Technical and mechanical), while the younger you are, the more you have a Technical and mechanical command (but you're not as involved musically).*

(55y, M, perc)   *I think I would see the older fellow better at Expressiveness and Organization; also possibly Tone Quality, Articulation, and Dynamics. I think the younger guy would get [higher scores for] Technique, Technical Accuracy, and maybe Rhythm (more accurate). I know I said that the older ones wouldn't be as accurate, and wouldn't have the same technique. But, what they lack in technique, the sound that they produce [is superior] such as: Phrasing, Articulation, Dynamics, and Expressiveness. So, they will overcome [compensate]. Technique isn't everything; it is a means to an end. What I'm saying is that older players are the ones making the music; the younger players are the ones cramming all the notes in. The older players are the ones who can see the overall picture; the piece in regards of Expressiveness, Articulation, Phrasing, and Organization. They might not play a couple notes, maybe not have the technique, nor the speed, nor accuracy. But, they can see the bigger picture!*

(55y, M, bn)   *I don't think that age makes any difference as far as these types of judgements. I wouldn't expect a younger player to be better at 'X', and an older player be better at 'Y'. When you go to an audition you expect everybody to know how to play. I think that someone who has a good sound gets worse as they age. Most players expect a younger player to be more Technically Accurate than an older player, and expect an older player to be more Expressive than a younger payer. I'd also like to think that way, but I don't know it's true. I'd expect an older player to really know what the piece is all about because of previous experience.*

(55y, M, db)   *Age doesn't really have any connection to musical features. Then again, there is something to say for experience. I wouldn't agree with the myth that younger players are more Technically Efficient and that older players are more Expressive.*

(57y, F, vc)   *I think the older one would have much more experience that allows for better Rhythm, Dynamics, and Articulation. I think the younger player would be able to read notes with more Accuracy. I don't think that age is an issue. Technique does decrease with time. Yet, I play technically better now than I did when I was younger.*

(60y, F, vc)   *I am not so sure that I'd expect the younger one to be better at certain things, while the older player would be better at others. Maybe concerning Tempo, the younger might be able to play faster tempi. But I don't think that younger players are technically better. But, Expressiveness is more difficult to consider; I would expect older musicians to be more experienced and mature. Actually, I think that it is better for an Orchestra to have just as many Seasoned Musicians as Younger Players.*

(60y, M, bn)   *I suppose these are sort of stereotypes. I've always been against speed. I think quite often younger people to be faster. I'm not so interested in just speed, there are other things going on. Time to be able to get a bit of Phrasing. Younger players also are better at Accuracy; older players play less accurately. There is a certain naïveté of a young player in the sense that they are so focused on one specific thing (like accuracy) that they just don't see all the other variables on the musical spectrum like Articulation.*

(60y, M, cl)   *Older players would be able to express themselves more appropriately with a level of intensity of Expression that younger players would not even know how much Expression to express. The older player will be much more capable of Articulating the music. I am not so sure about the Sound Quality. Technique could be better in younger players (vitamins and steroids). The older player will be much more appropriate with levels of performing Dynamics. The younger player would be less stable in Tempo and Rhythm. Technical fine-tuning will be much higher among the younger players. But as far as*

Intonation is concerned, the real story is not how pure the note is, but rather how fast do you respond and fix the out-of-tune note; that happens quicker among older players.

(61y, M, fl/picc)   *Very often younger players are more technically proficient than older players. Older players always say: 'The young players who come in, can play anything—but they haven't got the music in them.' It's a common complaint. So very often you would expect a younger player to be better at Technique, and better Sight-Reading. Whereas an older player would have more of the musical aspects. Expressiveness might come more intuitively with an older player. Tone Quality, Articulation, Dynamics, possibly Phrasing, and Temporal accuracy. Sometimes younger players get the tempos wrong.*

To summarize thus far, as can be seen in Tables 10.5, 10.6, and 10.7, most professional full-time contract Symphony Orchestra musicians did feel that Young(er) Players perform with higher Technical Accuracy, Tone Quality, Intonation Precision, and Articulation—but with less control over Tempo. On the other hand, the same players felt that Seasoned Musicians perform with higher Expression, and control over Tempo and Dynamics. Solely based on personal insight, LTE45 players felt that Young(er) Players are altogether superior to Seasoned Musicians by 11% (75% *versus* 64%, respectively), and players between ages 46 and 54 also felt that Young(er) Players are superior to Seasoned Musicians by 13% (80% *versus* 67%, respectively). But GTE55 players maintained that Seasoned Musicians are far better Orchestra players than Young(er) Players by 14% (87% *versus* 73%, respectively). It is interesting to note that when comparing the above depictions for LTE45 and GTE55 players, there is actually much overlap:

- Young(er) Players perform with higher Technical Accuracy and Tone Intonation Precision—but with less control over Tempo
- Seasoned Musicians perform with higher Expression, control over Tempo and Dynamics, Tone Quality, Phrasing, Organization, Understanding, and Artistic Musicality—but with less Technical Accuracy

Going forward then, the main research question is:

Does the depiction that surfaces from self-evaluated performance estimations (as in Tables 10.3, 10.4), and in forecasts highlighting performance differentials based on age (as in Tables 10.5, 10.6, 10.7), also come to light in objective music-performance analyses by external independent judges in a double-blind adjudication process?

10.3.2.3 Adjudication of Music Performances

The rating scores of two external independent judges in a double-blind adjudication process were tallied for all Principal Feature Components and Constituents of music performance for both performances of all players. It should be noted that the one String player whose probing data (*MPsE* and Likelihood Forecast) was corrupted, did in fact record both music performances. Hence, the data of that additional participant was entered in all further music-performance analyses ($n = 48$). See Table 10.8. Scores for all 3 Principal Feature Components (i.e., Artistic Expression

Table 10.8 Music Performance Evaluation (*MPE*): Comparisons Between 1st *Prima Vista* Sight-Reading *Versus* 2nd Post-Practice Final Performance for Total Sample

Principal Feature Components and Constituents	1st *Prima Vista* Sight-Reading (N = 48)			2nd Post-Practice Music Performance (N = 48)			MΔ	Sig p^1
	M	*SD*	Range	*M*	*SD*	Range		
[A] Artistic Expression								
Expressiveness	3.31	1.08	1–5	4.00	0.86	1–5	0.69	****
Organization	3.29	1.11	1–5	4.35	0.79	1–5	1.06	****
Tone Quality	3.42	1.03	1–5	4.02	0.89	1–5	0.60	***
Articulation	3.63	0.87	1–5	4.27	0.67	1–5	0.65	****
Dynamics	2.90	1.15	1–5	3.65	1.02	1–5	0.75	****
Phrasing	3.58	1.03	1–5	4.25	0.86	1–5	0.67	****
Total (A) %	**67.1**	17.6	23–100	**81.8**	12.8	60–100	**14.7**	****
[B] Temporal Accuracy								
Tempo	3.40	1.22	1–5	3.98	1.04	1–5	0.58	**
Rhythm	3.60	0.94	1–5	4.19	1.07	1–5	0.58	**
Total (B) %	**70.0**	18.3	40–100	**81.7**	17.1	20–100	**11.7**	****
[C] Technical Accuracy								
Technique	3.21	1.11	1–5	3.98	0.86	1–5	0.77	****
Intonation	3.23	1.15	1–5	4.15	0.83	1–5	0.92	****
Total (C)%	**64.4**	20.1	20–100	**81.3**	14.7	50–100	**16.9**	****
[B+C/2] Total Accuracy %	**67.2**	16.7	30–100	**81.5**	14.2	45–100	**14.3**	****
***MPE* Total %**	**67.1**	16.5	28–100	**81.6**	12.7	57–100	**14.5**	****

[1] Level of significance: * = $p < 0.05$; ** = $p < 0.01$; *** = $p < 0.001$; **** = $p < 0.0001$

[A], Temporal Accuracy [B], Technical Accuracy [C]), a combined score of Accuracy [B+C/2], as well as a more global *MPE* Total Score, were all calculated. Further, the differences between both performances (Delta-Δ scores) were determined. It should be noted that an analysis for Reliability (Cronbach's Alpha), that is consistency of Constituents of the two main *MPE* Components, was demonstrated to be acceptable for the 1st *prima vista* Sight-Reading ($\alpha_{[A]}$ = 0.92, $\alpha_{[B+C/2]}$ = 0.74, α_{MPE} = 0.93) as well as for 2nd Post-Practice Performance ($\alpha_{[A]}$ = 0.84, $\alpha_{[B+C/2]}$ = 0.73, α_{MPE} = 0.86).

As can be seen in Table 10.8, the 2nd Post-Practice performance statistically significantly improved for all Principal Feature Components and Constituents thereof, as well as for *MPE* Total Score; these were demonstrated by a series of dependent *t*-tests. Moreover, Table 10.8 indicates that both Constituents of Organization (Artistic Expression [A]) and Intonation (Technical Accuracy [C]) were rated as the greatest of all improvements (see: *M*Δ scores). All other Constituents improved similarly. While the Feature Component of Technical Accuracy [C] was rated to have improved more than the others (17% *versus* 12%–14%), when both Technique precision and Temporal accuracies were collapsed into a combined score of Accuracy [B+C/2], the two main Feature Components (i.e., Expression and Accuracy) were found to have improved equally (14.7% *versus* 14.3%).

Then, 5 Repeated Measures Analyses of Variance (ANOVAs) were conducted with the 1st and 2nd rendition versions serving as the variable of 'time' for all Feature Component scores and for *MPE* Total score. The results of these ANOVAs indicate large effect sizes when considering $n_p^2 \geq 0.14$.

- Artistic Expression [A] significantly improved by 15%: $F_{(1, 47)}$ = 39.65, *MSE* = 131.17, $p < 0.0001$, n_p^2 = 0.50.
- Temporal Accuracy [B] significantly improved by 12%: $F_{(1, 47)}$ = 19.36, *MSE* = 168.79, $p < 0.0001$, n_p^2 = 0.29.
- Technical Accuracy [C] significantly improved by 17%: $F_{(1, 47)}$ = 33.76, *MSE* = 202.46, $p < 0.0001$, n_p^2 = 0.42.
- Accuracy [B+C/2] significantly improved by 14%: $F_{(1, 47)}$ = 41.21, *MSE* = 118.61, $p < 0.0001$, n_p^2 = 0.47.
- MPE Total Score significantly improved by 15%: $F_{(1,47)}$ = 46.17, *MSE* = 109.25, $p < 0.0001$, n_p^2 = 0.50.

In sum, external independent blind-judges indicated that music performances improved after a ±10-minute period of DP similarly to the self-evaluation estimates. Yet, it must be noted that the players did truly overestimate their improvement. Namely, the players evaluated their own improvements to be much higher than the actual ratings of the adjudicators; the players actually estimated their improvements twice as high as those of the external judges (36% *versus* 15%, respectively). However, one could argue that adjudicator ratings, even though they are evaluation scores by experts in the domain, may also be somewhat subjective as they are based on personal impression. One well-known research team, Sam Thompson and Aaron

Williamon (2003) from the Royal College of Music (London), astutely raised the question if adequate levels of inter-rater reliability and consistency can even be established when evaluating music performances? Namely, can the use of discriminant criteria be justified, and if so, what are the most suitable criteria? Can a single evaluation method be generally applied across all instrumental groups? After all, most systems are criterion-based and require the adjudicators to judge aspects of the performance, or the whole piece, relative to a set of written criteria. Further, Wesolowski et al. (2016) confirmed that "psychometric concerns exist in raters' precision in the use of task-specific criterion" (p. 662). As was the case in the current study, the common practice is that judges themselves are typically experienced performers who tend to rely on their own personal abilities for their performance assessments whereby they offer consistent judgements of music-performance quality. Yet, as Wesolowski et al. pointed out: "raters significantly vary in severity, [and] items significantly vary in difficulty, and rating scale category structure significantly varies across raters" (p. 662).

Thompson and Williamon (2003) question if experienced musicians are able to distinguish between different aspects of a performance such as technique and interpretation. Aren't these two components enmeshed in ways that cannot be disentangled? Perhaps, then, a more objective measure might be to analyse representative cryptograms (e.g., signs and symbols) written by judges on the music notation itself; marks that indicate the precise location where mistakes and mishaps occurred. I refer to a *Music Notation Score Analysis* (MNSA). Accordingly, I asked the judges to place markings on the music notation to account for: *Accuracy* (e.g., inaccuracies such as a missing note, omitted accidental sharp # or flat $\flat$, poor intonation, or corrupted rhythmic figure); and *Expressiveness-Articulation* (e.g., inattention to expressive directions, ornaments, or dynamic instructions). In this fashion, the music-performance assessment could be systematically based on observable data for the purposes of documentation within an empirical environment. Then, the marks were tallied, and calculated as the number (% percentage) of bars/measures performed without flaws. See Table 10.9.

Table 10.9 Music Notation Score Analysis (*MNSA*): Comparisons Between 1st *Prima Vista* Sight-Reading *Versus* 2nd Post-Practice Final Performance for Total Sample

MNSA Factors	1st *Prima Vista* Sight-Reading ($N = 48$)			2nd Post-Practice Music Performance ($N = 48$)				Sig
	%[1]	*SD*	Range	%[1]	*SD*	Range	*M*Δ	p[2]
Accuracy (Notes and Rhythm)	81.3	9.00	62–98	89.5	6.89	70–100	8.17	****
Expressiveness (Articulation)	89.5	5.32	76–100	92.7	5.37	80–100	3.28	****
MNSA **Total Score**	85.4	5.9	73–96	91.1	5.06	81–100	5.72	****

[1]% Correct (%)
[2]Level of significance: *= $p < 0.05$; **= $p < 0.01$; ***= $p < 0.001$; ****= $p < 0.0001$

As can be seen in Table 10.9, a series of dependent t-tests demonstrated statistically significant improvements for both *MNSA* Factors (Accuracy and Expressiveness) and for *MNSA* Total Scores. Further, the table indicates that the participating players performed at a rather 'good' (81%) level for *Accuracy* already in the 1st *prima vista* Sight-Reading performance, while the 2nd Post-Practice improvements brought the players to an 'excellent' (90%) level of correct notes, intonation, and rhythms. Further, the players exhibited an 'excellent' (90%) level of *Expressiveness* already in the 1st *prima vista* Sight-Reading performance; perhaps there was a *ceiling effect* with 2nd Post-Practice performances having improved only minimally (3%).

Subsequently, 3 Repeated Measures ANOVAs were conducted with the 1st and 2nd rendition versions serving as the variable of 'time' for both *MNSA* Factors and the Total Score. The results indicate large effect sizes when considering $n_p^2 \geq 0.14$.

- Accuracy (Notes and Rhythm) significantly improved by 8%: $F_{(1, 47)} = 50.92$, $MSE = 31.46$, $p < 0.00001$, $n_p^2 = 0.52$.
- Expressiveness (Articulation) significantly improved by 3%: $F_{(1, 47)} = 19.39$, $MSE = 13.34$, $p < 0.0001$, $n_p^2 = 0.31$.
- *MNSA* Total Score significantly improved by 6%: $F_{(1, 47)} = 70.83$, $MSE = 11.10$, $p < 0.0001$, $n_p^2 = 0.60$.

To sum up thus far, the judges' marks on the music notation scores themselves indicate that after a ±10-minute period of DP the participating professional full-time contract Symphony Orchestra players performed 94% of a newly composed never-before-seen piece of music without flaw. This level of performance reflects an overall 6% improvement in performance quality for the second pass.

At this point it would be cogent to question if *MPE* (the rating of Principal Feature Components of music performance) is positively associated with *MNSA* (a score mark-up indicating the percentage of inaccuracies and mishaps observed during a music performance). For this analysis 3 *Pearson Correlation Coefficients* were employed. *Pearson* is a degree of association between 2 sets of data, with the ratio between covariance presented in a linear relationship with potency normalized between −1 and +1. The first matrix illustrates relationships between data for the 1st *prima vista* Sight-Reading. See Table 10.10.

As can be seen in Table 10.10, the main Feature Components of *MPE* were found to be positively associated with the *MNSA* Factor scores. Albeit, not all associations were strong enough to achieve statistical significance. The second matrix exemplifies relationships between data for the 2nd Post-Practice performance. See Table 10.11.

Table 10.11 shows that the main Feature Components of *MPE* were found to positively associate with *MNSA* Factors scores. Albeit, not all associations were strong enough to achieve statistical significance. The third matrix examines the outcomes of DP indicating improvement for the 2nd Post-Practice performance (i.e., Δ) considering the 1st *prima vista* Sight-Reading. See Table 10.12.

As can be seen in Table 10.12, *MPE* Component Δ scores of DP were found to be positively associated with the *MNSA* Factor Δ scores. Albeit, not all associations were strong enough to achieve statistical significance. While the adjudicators' rating scores (*MPE*) and their music notation score mark-ups (*MNSA*) are not identical, they do seem to be measuring a similar—and highly correlated—behaviour. Perhaps, an explanation for these differences of covariance is that they are disparities between what the judges may have *felt* in their hearts (or in their minds, which is

Table 10.10 Correlation Matrix of Performance Features: *MPE* with *MNSA* for 1st *Prima Vista* Sight-Reading

MPE	*MNSA*		
	Expressiveness Articulation	Accuracy	Total Score
Artistic Expression [A]	**.31**[*1]	.37**	.42***
Accuracy [B+C]	.19	**.24**	.27
***MPE* Total**	.26	.32*	**.36***

[1]Level of significance: *= $p < 0.05$; **= $p < 0.01$; ***= $p < 0.001$

Table 10.11 Correlation Matrix of Performance Features: *MPE* with *MNSA* for 2nd Post-Practice Final Performance

MPE	*MNSA*		
	Expressiveness Articulation	Accuracy	Total Score
Artistic Expression [A]	**.13**	.08	.13
Accuracy [B+C]	.25	**.24**	.27*[1]
***MPE* Total**	.20	.18	**.23**

[1]Level of significance: *= $p < 0.05$

Table 10.12 Correlation Matrix of Outcome Improvement (Δ): *MPE* with *MNSA*

MPE	*MNSA*		
	Expressiveness Articulation	Accuracy	Total Score
Artistic Expression [A]	.28	.41**[1]	.50***
Accuracy [B+C]	.28	**.40***	.50***
***MPE* Total**	.30*	.42**	**.53***

[1]Level of significance: *= $p < 0.05$; **= $p < 0.01$; ***= $p < 0.001$

a more subjective impression) and what they seemingly *observed* with their ears (and cognitive brains, which is a more objective detection). That is an important, and highly related, difference for adjudicators. Finally, there is every possibility that a larger sample than 48 players may have increased the statistical power of some of the above positive associations in the correlational analyses between *MPE* with *MNSA*.

The last leg of in the current investigation package was to explore possible differences of music performance based on subgrouping variables. I ask: Is it possible that a subgroup variable intervened and/or even obstructed certain performance scores or outcomes? The two variables that come to mind are *instrument* and *age*. The first analysis targeted *musical instrument*. There were 3 instrument families: *Strings* (n = 30, 63%), *Winds* (a combined Woodwind and Brass, n = 15, 32%), and *Others* (e.g., Harps and Vibraphone, n = 3, 6%). In this analysis, data from players of instruments other than Strings or Winds were excluded. Hence, data from n = 45 musicians were entered in the analysis. See Table 10.13. Table 10.13 indicates that String players were judged higher than Wind players for the 1st *prima vista* Sight-Reading. Employing a series of independent *t*-test analyses, the Constituents of Phrasing (Artistic Expression [A]) and Rhythm (Temporal Accuracy [B]) were found to be statistically significantly more efficient. Moreover, String players were also evaluated higher than Wind players for the 2nd Post-Practice performance. A series of independent *t*-test analyses indicated statistically significantly higher ratings for the Constituents of Expressiveness, Tone Quality, Articulation, Phrasing (Artistic Expression [A]), and Technique, and Intonation (Technical Accuracy [C]). The overall total *MPE* score was also statistically significantly higher for the String players.

Nonetheless, we might need to ask if *inter-rater reliability* confounded these findings? Namely, one cannot completely rule out the possibility that comparisons between the instrument types are erroneous. After all, each instrument type (Strings *versus* Winds) was judged by a single adjudicator. The question is: Could the differences as found in Table 10.13 simply reflect variances for 'degree' of judgement when using a 5-point Likert rating scale (1 = inferior, 5 = superior)? While one judge may have used the numerical value '4' to indicate a *good* level of performance, the other judge might have used the numerical value '3' for the same performance level. A second variable that could have confounded the results in the above table is: *statistical power*. To begin with, the sample size was rather limited (n = 48). Then, when engaging in a more comparative analysis, the overall cell size became even smaller. In the current case, there are twice the number of String players as there are Wind players (30 *versus* 15, respectively). So, it might be the case that there are issues of 'power' tainting the findings (e.g., statistical significance or null-findings) in Table 10.13. And finally, it needs to be reiterated that the music compositions themselves are not identical. Each one was artfully composed; designed to be similar in music quality and performance difficulty. But they are different! See Appendix A. Could the compositions themselves be a confounding variable? Is it possible that the music piece

Table 10.13 Music Performance Evaluation (MPE) of Rendition Versions: Comparisons Between Instrument (String Players *Versus* Wind Players)

Principal Feature Components and Constituents	1st *Prima-Vista* Sight-Reading					2nd Post-Practice Final Performance					
	String Players (n = 30)		Wind Players (n = 15)		Sig p^1	String Players (n = 30)		Wind Players (n = 15)		Sig p
	M	SD	M	SD		M	SD	M	SD	
[A] Artistic Expression										
Expressiveness	3.47	1.07	3.20	1.01		4.33	0.66	3.33	0.72	****
Organization	3.37	1.10	3.40	1.06		4.47	0.73	4.13	0.83	
Tone Quality	3.30	1.02	3.53	1.06		4.20	0.89	3.53	0.74	**
Articulation	3.60	0.89	3.73	0.88		4.47	0.57	3.80	0.68	**
Dynamics	2.83	1.23	3.13	1.06		3.70	1.12	3.53	0.92	
Phrasing	3.90	0.92	3.20	0.94	*	4.63	0.49	3.53	0.83	****
Total A %	**68.2**	18.0	**67.3**	17.5		**86.0**	11.0	**72.9**	11.1	***
[B] Temporal Accuracy										
Tempo	3.57	1.28	3.40	0.91		3.93	1.17	4.07	0.80	
Rhythm	3.90	0.89	3.20	0.86		4.40	1.10	3.73	0.96	
Total B %	**74.7**	18.3	**66.0**	14.5	**	**83.3**	18.6	**78.0**	14.2	
[C] Technical Accuracy										
Technique	3.33	1.16	3.10	1.06		4.17	0.83	3.60	0.63	*
Intonation	3.23	1.28	3.00	0.85		4.43	0.73	3.46	0.64	****
Total C %	**65.7**	22.5	**61.3**	18.1		**86.0**	14.0	**70.6**	10.3	***
[B+C/2] Total Accuracy %	**70.2**	17.6	**63.7**	14.8		**84.6**	14.9	**74.3**	10.5	*
MPE Total %	**69.1**	17.2	**65.5**	15.5		**85.3**	12.4	**73.6**	9.5	**

^{1}Level of significance: * = $p < 0.05$; ** = $p < 0.01$; *** = $p < 0.001$; **** = $p < 0.0001$

played by String players was less complex than the other music pieces performed by Wind players (the piece of either the Woodwind or Brass players)?

In light of the issues raised above, it seems that perhaps a more reliable analysis would be to compare interaction effects of improvement (Delta-Δ Scores) of the players. Such an analysis would replace the previous *between* groups outcome in the comparison with a more rigorous *within* groups outcome. It is important to note here, that: (1) judges were not aware which performance was paired (i.e., counterpart) to another performance; and (2) all items of the same instrument category were judged by the same adjudicator, and hence improvements between the two performances (if there were any at all) would not be biased by inter-rater variances between adjudicators, or the music contents of compositions, or the sample size. Consequently, 5 ANOVAs were implemented with 'instrument-type' serving as a grouping variable for *MPE* Principal Feature Component Delta-Δ Scores x Instrument.

- Artistic Expression [A]: $M_{\Delta\text{-Strings}}$ = 17.7%, SD = 14.5; $M_{\Delta\text{-Winds}}$ = 5.56%, SD = 16.2; $F_{(1, 43)}$ = 6.55, MSE = 227.91, p = 0.014, n_p^2 = 0.13 (a moderate effect size, considering $n^2{}_p$ > 0.14 is a large effect size).
- Temporal Accuracy [B]: $M_{\Delta\text{-Strings}}$ = 8.66%, SD = 16.3; $M_{\Delta\text{-Winds}}$ = 12.0%, SD = 19.4; $F_{(1, 43)}$ = 0.37, MSE = 302.02, p = 0.55.
- Technical Accuracy [C]: $M_{\Delta\text{-Strings}}$ = 20.3%, SD = 21.3; $M_{\Delta\text{-Winds}}$ = 9.33%, SD = 16.7; $F_{(1, 43)}$ = 3.06, MSE = 395.12, p = 0.09.
- Accuracy [B±C/2]: $M_{\Delta\text{-Strings}}$ = 14.5%, SD = 14.4; $M_{\Delta\text{-Winds}}$ = 10.7%, SD = 16.6; $F_{(1, 43)}$ = 0.64, MSE = 229.32, p = 0.43.
- MPE Total: $M_{\Delta\text{-Strings}}$ = 16.1%, SD = 13.6; $M_{\Delta\text{-Winds}}$ = 8.11%, SD = 15.2; $F_{(1, 43)}$ = 3.24, MSE = 199.13, p = 0.08.

These findings continue to indicate advantages for String players. Namely, statistically significant improvements (by 12%) for Artistic Expression [A]. Moreover, the findings indicate nearly significant differences of String players for Technical Accuracy [C] and *MPE* Total Score. In summary, when targeting instrument type, adjudicator ratings for Principal Component Factors of music performance— as found by *MPE*—indicate significantly more effective Post-Practice Performance levels for String players compared to Wind players.

The music-performance assessment then turned to the representative cryptograms data (e.g., signs and symbols) that judges marked on the music notation (*MNSA*). See Table 10.14. As can be seen in Table 10.14, the music score markings indicate that the Wind players were statistically significantly more efficient in their performances. Namely, the Wind players performed both 1st *prima vista* Sight-Reading and 2nd Post-Practice performance with a higher percentage of flawless bar-measures. A series of independent *t*-tests found the differences between the Wind players and the String players, and these differences were statistically significantly higher.

Table 10.14 Music Notation Score Analysis (*MNSA*) of Rendition Versions: Comparisons Between Instrument (String Players *Versus* Wind Players)

MNSA Factors	1st *Prima Vista* Sight-Reading					2nd Post-Practice Final Performance				
	String Players (n = 30)		Wind Players (n = 15)		Sig p^1	String Players (n = 30)		Wind Players (n = 15)		Sig p
	M	SD	M	SD		M	SD	M	SD	
Accuracy Notes and Rhythm	77.6	8.43	88.6	5.61	****	87.5	6.52	94.6	3.36	***
Expressiveness Articulation	87.6	4.99	93.2	3.54	***	90.6	5.49	96.0	2.35	***
MNSA Total	82.6	5.02	90.9	3.21	****	89.0	4.63	95.3	2.26	****

[1]Level of significance: * = $p < 0.05$; ** = $p < 0.01$; *** = $p < 0.001$; **** = $p < 0.0001$

Consequently, Delta-Δ Scores (i.e., improvement between the 1st and 2nd performances) were placed into 3 ANOVAs with *instrument* type serving as a grouping variable: *MNSA* Factor Delta-Δ Scores x Instrument. The findings indicated that there were no statistically significant differences between the two instruments. That is, players of both instrument types improved the piece (i.e., number of flawless bar-measures played) for the second pass in a similar fashion:

- Accuracy (Notes and Rhythm): $M_{\Delta\text{-Strings}} = 9.87\%$, SD = 8.65; $M_{\Delta\text{-Winds}} = 5.96\%$, SD = 4.95; $F_{(1, 43)} = 2.69$, $MSE = 58.39$, $p = 0.11$.
- Expressiveness: $M_{\Delta\text{-Strings}} = 3.00\%$, SD = 5.48; $M_{\Delta\text{-Winds}} = 2.85\%$, SD = 4.66; $F_{(1, 43)} = 0.008$, $MSE = 26.73$, $p = 0.90$.
- *MNSA* Total Score: $M_{\Delta\text{-Strings}} = 6.43\%$, SD = 5.24; $M_{\Delta\text{-Winds}} = 4.40\%$, SD = 3.62; $F_{(1, 43)} = 1.81$, $MSE = 22.71$, $p = 0.19$.

The above two analyses demonstrate differences between the players. If differences between the players of instrument types are based on *MPE* ratings, then Artistic Expression (Expressiveness, Tone Quality, and Articulation) was a more efficient feature that String players implemented for the 2nd Post-Practice performance. But, if differences between the players of instrument types are based on *MNSE* score markings, then Wind players were clearly more proficient at implementing the 2nd Post-Practice performance at a higher level. At this point, I would like to suggest that the differences that surfaced are indeed within the acceptable scope of music-performance adjudication. Ultimately, there are disparities between what impressions are *felt* in one's heart *versus* what is *observed* and detected with one's ears. Such variances are often the case in Music Performance Auditions, International Music Competitions, and even professional Evaluation Assessment Procedures. Taking a broad look at the above analyses on instrument type, it does seem that professional full-time contract Symphony Orchestra players of both instrument types (Strings and Winds) performed just as well, and indeed both seem to have improved to the same extent after a ±10-minute period of DP.

The second analysis targeted the variable of *age* based on 2 subgroups: Young(er) Players LTE45 ($n = 16$, 33%, $M_{\text{Age}} = 36.8$, $SD = 5.37$, Range 27–44), *versus* Seasoned Musicians GTE55 ($n = 17$, 35%, $M_{\text{Age}} = 58.1$, $SD = 2.67$, Range 55–64). See Table 10.15.

As can be seen in Table 10.15 a series of independent *t*-tests indicated that the judges rated the Young(er) Players as more efficient than the Seasoned Musicians for almost every Principal Feature Component and Constituent thereof of both 1st *prima vista* Sight-Reading and 2nd Post-Practice performance; most of these are statistically significant. Further, the grand-mean difference between the age subgroups for overall *MPE* Total scores was 17% higher for the Young(er) players (22.3% *versus* 11%, respectively).

Nonetheless, the above outcome effects were quite the contrary when examining Post-Practice improvements (i.e., Delta-Δ Scores). Five ANOVAs were implemented with *age* serving as a grouping variable: *MPE* Component Factor Delta-Δ Scores x

Table 10.15 Music Performance Evaluation (*MPE*) of Rendition Versions: Comparisons Between Age Subgroups (Young(er) Players *Versus* Seasoned Musicians)

Principal Feature Components And Constituents	1st *Prima Vista* Sight-Reading					2nd Post-Practice Final Performance				
	Young(er) Players LTE45 (*n* = 16)		Seasoned Musicians GTE55 (*n* = 17)		Sig p^1	Young(er) Players LTE45 (*n* = 16)		Seasoned Musicians GTE55 (*n* = 17)		Sig *p*
	M	*SD*	*M*	*SD*		*M*	*SD*	*M*	*SD*	
[A] Artistic Expression										
Expressiveness	4.00	0.73	2.82	1.13	**	4.32	0.70	3.65	0.93	*
Organization	4.06	0.85	2.88	1.05	**	4.56	0.73	4.18	0.88	
Tone Quality	3.81	0.75	3.18	1.13	*	4.38	0.81	3.65	0.79	*
Articulation	4.06	0.57	3.41	1.06	**	4.44	0.73	3.89	0.60	*
Dynamics	3.69	1.01	2.47	1.10	**	4.19	0.83	3.24	0.97	**
Phrasing	4.25	0.68	3.11	1.11	**	4.50	0.73	3.82	0.95	*
Total A %	**79.5**	12.3	**59.6**	18.7	**	**87.9**	12.4	**74.7**	9.90	**
[B] Temporal Accuracy										
Tempo	4.00	0.97	2.88	1.04	**	4.31	0.60	3.94	0.96	
Rhythm	4.13	0.80	3.18	0.95	**	4.19	1.28	4.12	0.78	
Total B %	**81.3**	15.9	**60.59**	13.9	***	**85.0**	16.3	**80.5**	11.4	
[C] Technical Accuracy										
Technique	4.06	0.85	2.59	1.00	***	4.50	0.63	3.53	0.72	***
Intonation	4.00	0.89	2.64	1.05	***	4.31	0.79	4.00	0.87	
Total C %	**80.6**	14.8	**53.4**	17.5	***	**88.1**	11.7	**75.3**	12.8	**
[B+C/2] Total Accuracy %	**80.9**	12.7	**56.5**	13.0	****	**86.6**	13.3	**77.9**	10.3	*
MPE Total %	**80.3**	11.3	**58.0**	15.2	****	**87.3**	12.4	**76.3**	8.90	**

[1] Level of significance: * = *p* < 0.05; ** = *p* < 0.01; *** = *p* < 0.001

Age. To reiterate, the judges were not aware of which performances were performed by which player, and they were blind to sex, age, and geographical location. It should be noted that large effect sizes are interpreted when $n_p^2 > 0.14$.

- Artistic Expression [A]: $M_{\Delta\text{-LTE45}} = 8.33\%$, SD = 16.1; $M_{\Delta\text{-GTE55}} = 15.10\%$, SD = 15.2; $F_{(1, 31)} = 1.54$, $MSE = 244.53$, $p = 0.22$.
- Temporal Accuracy [B]: $M_{\Delta\text{-LTE45}} = 3.75\%$, SD = 17.5; $M_{\Delta\text{-GTE55}} = 20.0\%$, SD = 16.6; $F_{(1, 31)} = 7.52$, $MSE = 289.52$, $p = 0.01$, $n_p^2 = 0.26$.
- Technical Accuracy [C]: $M_{\Delta\text{-LTE45}} = 7.5\%$, SD = 14.4; $M_{\Delta\text{-GTE55}} = 22.9\%$, SD = 19.9; $F_{(1, 31)} = 6.45$, $MSE = 304.93$, $p = 0.016$, $n_p^2 = 0.17$.
- Accuracy [B±C/2]: $M_{\Delta\text{-LTE45}} = 5.6\%$, SD = 12.9; $M_{\Delta\text{-GTE55}} = 21.5\%$, SD = 1614.6; $F_{(1, 31)} = 10.91$, $MSE = 189.74$, $p = 0.0024$, $n_p^2 = 0.26$.
- *MPE* Total: $M_{\Delta\text{-LTE45}} = 7.0\%$, SD = 13.3; $M_{\Delta\text{-GTE55}} = 18.3\%$, SD = 14.3; $F_{(1, 31)} = 5.52$, $MSE = 190\text{–}92$, $p = 0.025$, $n_p^2 = 0.15$.

The findings show an overall improvement for the *MPE* Total score by 11% in favour of the Seasoned Musicians. That is, the old(er) players statistically significantly enhanced their performance levels for the Principal Feature Components of Temporal Accuracy [B] and Technical Accuracy [C]. Further, the Seasoned Musicians achieved higher improvements (Δ scores) for Artistic Expression [A]; more than double the Young(er) Players, albeit that difference was not statistically significant. In short, it would seem that Seasoned Musicians demonstrated to be more effective in applying a ±10-minute period of DP.

The music-performance evaluation then examined score mark-up data (*MNSA*) for comparisons between the age subgroups. See Table 10.16. As can be seen in Table 10.16, a series of independent *t*-tests indicated that judges did not mark performances differently for any age subgroup. Explicitly, there were no statistically significant differences of *MNSA* Factors for either the 1st *prima vista* Sight-Reading or the 2nd Post-Practice Performance.

Finally, 3 ANOVAs were implemented to explore interaction effects of age with performance improvements: *MNSA* Factor Delta-Δ Scores x Age. These analyses strengthen the findings previously presented (in Table 10.16) indicating no statistically significant differences between the age subgroups for adjudicators' markings on the music notation.

- Accuracy (Notes & Rhythm): $M_{\Delta\text{-LTE45}} = 6.68\%$, SD = 5.80; $M_{\Delta\text{-GTE55}} = 6.96\%$, SD = 8.28; $F_{(1, 31)} = 0.011$, $MSE = 51.69$, $p = 0.91$.
- Expressiveness: $M_{\Delta\text{-LTE45}} = 3.65\%$, SD = 4.27; $M_{\Delta\text{-GTE55}} = 3.08\%$, SD = 6.71; $F_{(1, 31)} = 0.083$, $MSE = 32.03$, $p = 0.76$.
- *MNSA* Total Score: $M_{\Delta\text{-LTE45}} = 5.17\%$, SD = 3.71; $M_{\Delta\text{-GTE55}} = 5.02\%$, SD = 5.19; $F_{(1, 31)} = 0.01$, $MSE = 20.58$, $p = 0.93$.

Table 10.16 Music Notation Score Analysis (*MNSA*) of Rendition Versions: Comparisons Between Age Subgroups (Young(er) Players *Versus* Seasoned Musicians)

MNSA Factors	1st *Prima Vista* Sight-Reading						2nd Post-Practice Final Performance					
	Young(er) Players LTE45 (*n* = 16)		Seasoned Musicians GTE55 (*n* = 17)		Sig		Young(er) Players LTE45 (*n* = 16)		Seasoned Musicians GTE55 (*n* = 17)		Sig	
	M	*SD*	*M*	*SD*	*p*		*M*	*SD*	*M*	*SD*	*p*	
Accuracy Notes and Rhythm	84.1	8.63	81.6	7.39			90.8	4.50	88.6	8.46		
Expressiveness Articulation	91.0	5.21	83.3	5.92			94.7	3.85	91.4	5.84		
MNSA Total	87.6	5.94	85.0	5.39			92.7	3.57	90.0	5.82		

To sum up, the above music-performance analyses based on *age* are much more complex than previous analyses (e.g., examining instrument type). If the issue centres on what adjudicators *felt* in their heart (rated by *MPE*), then clearly the Young(er) Players were 17% more efficient in their performance. Nonetheless, when looking at level of improvement, the Seasoned Musicians were 11% more effective in applying a ±10-minute period of practice to increase the level of performance proficiency. I suggest here that perhaps more than anything else, the above findings show distinctions of age not only for the *product* (e.g., the final performance score) but also for the *process* (e.g., targeting the most appropriate features and components necessary to drill in an effort to improve the music performance).

Are Seasoned Musicians more of an asset or a liability?[1] To some extent, for the majority the 'evidence' may simply be a subjective feeling—even when using a standardized rating assessment measure like *MPE*. But, when examining what the judges detected with their ears, Seasoned Musicians were not more prone to missing a note or accidental, or as having decreased intonation, or demonstrating more incidences of corrupted rhythmic figures. Further, Seasoned Musicians were not found to have a higher frequency for inattention to instructions of music expressive ornaments or dynamics. All of these were apparent from *MNSA*. Hence, perhaps there is little (if any) performance difference between Young(er) Players and Seasoned Musicians.

Ironically, a little-mentioned study conducted almost 20 years ago, pointed to similar conclusions about age subgroups in the Orchestra. Recruiting a representative sample of professional Orchestra players ($N = 150$; $M_{Age} = 40$; 60% Strings, 40% Wind; 70% male), Olbertz (2006) surveyed perceptions concerning the vocation, orchestral lifestyle, job-satisfaction, and skill set. Olbertz was very surprised to find no differences among the players who were between the ages 35 and 50, nor for players who were younger (< 30) or older (> 50) than the main age subgroup. It is a shame that Olbertz never saw the need to collect actual performance data from Orchestra musicians based on age subgroups. The current study, then, attempted to 'fill the gap'.

10.4 Discussion and Summary

This book opened with a main overriding question:

How do Orchestra musicians retain their high level of functional music abilities well beyond the 5th Decade?

That question will be discussed in more depth in Chapter 11. But perhaps before addressing the question of *HOW* musicians might achieve such feats, there seems

---

[1] See Chapter 13 for a more detailed discussion of this issue.

to be a need to demonstrate that Orchestra musicians actually *DO* retain their high level of music abilities beyond the 5th Decade.

From the onset of the study the concept of implementing an *in vivo/in situ* music performance was key. Others had previously mentioned that such a methodology was critical—but no study implemented a platform embracing a music-performance analysis. For example, Hambrick and Ticker-Drob (2015) concluded that "future research should [. . .] develop more sensitive multidimensional measures, efforts to make use of rating systems and objective tests, rather than simple self-report scales [. . . and] measure both accomplishment and skill in musicians" (p. 119).

On the first page of this current chapter, the employment of music-performance analyses was clearly stated. The only thing that really matters, is: How do Seasoned Musicians play! For the current investigation, music pieces were commissioned from Symphonic Composer Moshe Zorman. This action was taken to ensure that none of the musicians could have had previous exposure or experience performing the music (*anonymity*), and to guarantee the performance piece would be suitable for professional full-time contract orchestra musicians. On the one hand the intention was to employ a piece that would be technically challenging to professional Symphony Orchestra musicians, while on the other hand a piece that could realistically be improved within a ±10-minute period of Deliberate Practice (*ecological validity*). Three music pieces, similar in performance quality and content complexity, were employed as stimuli for the investigation. Each was presented with appropriate notation and performance markings for 1 of 5 instrument families (Strings, Woodwinds, Brass, Harp, and Keyboard Percussion). There were 2 performances: a 1st *prima vista* Sight-Reading and a 2nd Post-Practice performance. The players were asked to *self-evaluate* their execution. For the most part, the players estimated an overall 36% improvement. The self-evaluated improvement was quite similar regardless of the instrument each player performed, and irrespective of the performers' age.

The players contemplated how an adjudicator might rate performances based on age subgroup of performers. To this conundrum, most players mentioned what seems to resemble an *urban legend*—a stereotypical typecast bias that reflects *ageism*. Certainly, members of any vocational group might have concerns (and some might even mention a caricaturistic satirist-like ridicule) about work-related proficiencies corrupted by variables, such as: Age, Sex, Gender, Ethnicity, Religion, Culture, or even Place of Birth. In the current study, young(er) Orchestra musicians clearly depicted Seasoned Musicians as performing with higher Expression and control over Tempo, Dynamics, Tone Quality, Phrasing, Organization, Understanding, and Artistic Musicality—but lacking the Technical Accuracy necessary to continue performing in the Orchestra. Unfortunately, such perceptions seem to be accepted by many Orchestra managements and Music Directors. Therefore, one issue posed in the current study was to clarify if the actual ratings of independent double-blind adjudicators would fall in line with such perceptions.

The music-performance analysis employed two measures: *Music Performance Evaluation* (*MPE*) and *Music Notation Score Analysis* (*MNSA*). *MPE* was found to have acceptable reliability, and there were positive associations between the two. When looking at the total sample of participating players, the findings indicate that the 2nd performances significantly improved between 6% and 15% (*MNSA* and *MPE*, respectively). This itself is quite a feat as there was only a ±10-minute period of DP. Then, when considering differences between players based on instrument type or age subgroups, the picture became somewhat more complex. Foremost, employing *MPE*, the judges rated String players higher than Wind players for both 1st *prima vista* Sight-Reading and 2nd Post-Practice performance (by 4% and 12%, respectively). But, this was quite opposite when employing *MNSA* score markings: Wind players more efficiently reproduced the music with a higher number of bar-measures played without any flaw for both 1st *prima vista* Sight-Reading and 2nd Post-Practice performance (by 8% and 6%, respectively). As mentioned earlier, these differences may reflect distinctions representing what judges *felt* in their heart versus what they *observed* with the ears. Such a situation has often been reported in the media about international music competitions (e.g., Gardner, 2019; Isacoff, 2015; Johnson, 2009). Nonetheless, it would seem that players of both instrument types performed just as well, and improved to the same extent after a ±10-minute period of DP. Then again, employing the *MPE* to examine differences between the age subgroups, the judges rated Young(er) Players as performing on a higher level than Seasoned Musicians for both the 1st *prima vista* Sight-Reading and 2nd Post-Practice performance (by 29% and 11%, respectively). Nonetheless, Seasoned Musicians demonstrated to be more effective (by 13%) in applying the ±10-minute period of DP. I would like to point out that the judges did not mark notation scores differently in either 1st or 2nd performances for either age subgroup. Therefore as suggested earlier, distinctions of age for the *product* (i.e., final reproduction) are just one aspect of performance evaluation, while the *process* (i.e., strategically utilizing DP to improve performance) is another aspect which is no less important to consider! To summarize, the adjudicators did not find differences between the age subgroups for inaccuracies or for inattention to instructions.

The music-performance analysis described here found very small differences in performance (if any at all) between the Seasoned Musicians and the Young(er) Players—who were at times more than 20 years younger, and typically considered to entertain superior adaptabilities and more efficient competencies on their musical instrument.

PART IV

SEASONED MUSICIANS

Part IV offers a profile of Seasoned Musicians, looks back in retrospect at a Symphony Orchestra musician's career, summarizes the complete investigation package, and offers some insights on the findings.

Chapter 11 focuses on Orchestra players' self-evaluation of their skills and abilities (motor, inner-hearing, inter-musical, and intra-musical), mood and emotion, as well as at stress and orchestral life. Then, a behavioural inventory of positive ageing including an assessment of Life-Longing (i.e., regretful sentiment for a solo career lost) is presented. Feelings of success, reaching potential, and satisfaction in the occupational domain are detailed. Finally, the social circle involving currently employed players as well as retired players is formalized—specifically looking at the incidence of Dementia or Alzheimer's disease.

Chapter 12 reports interviews from six retired Orchestra players; they look back at their career and years of involvement. Explicitly, these retired players discuss the Orchestra profession as a vocation of longevity, maintaining their career including DP, issues of gender, the value of experience, thoughts about Seasoned Musicians, retirement, and the subject of aging as a (taboo) topic of discussion.

Chapter 13 closes the book. First the chapter examines the Orchestra as a profession among the *50-Top Professions* with the highest rate of workers over age 65. Attempting to target the reasons *how* musicians are capable of such longevity, the chapter scrutinizes ageing among Orchestra players. The focus is not simply on the effects of intensive training from early childhood, but rather specifically on Orchestra Lifestyle. Within this context, the 2-Component Model of Intellectual Functioning is put in place, outlining one reason resilience is so common among Orchestra players—perhaps even to a greater extent than among the general population. The findings of the music-performance analyses (Chapter 10) are brought to the forefront, and new perspectives are offered.

11

Positive Ageing and Creative Resilience

11.1 Introduction

In my 2011 article titled 'Rationale behind investigating positive aging among symphony orchestra musicians: A call for a new arena of empirical study', published in the journal *Musicæ Scientiæ*, I presented the following exemplar:

> When he was 80 years old, the concert pianist Arthur Rubinstein was asked by a television interviewer how he managed to maintain such a high level of expertise in his piano playing. Rubinstein laughed, and then hinted that he employed three strategies, saying: (1) Play fewer pieces; (2) Practise these specific pieces more often; and (3) Use a kind of impression management by playing more slowly before the fast segments in order to make the music appear much faster.

I stated that I had uncovered this vignette among the writings of Baltes (Baltes & Baltes, 1990; Baltes et al., 1999a, 1999b) as an illustration of his theory on Positive Ageing referred to as *Selection, Optimization, and Compensation*. Accordingly, the narrative demonstrates how Arthur Rubinstein (1887–1982, a Polish-American virtuoso pianist) consciously an counteracted age-related losses for motor declines by playing fewer pieces (Selection), practising them more often (Optimization), and inserting a ritardando (decreasing tempo) just prior to faster segments as an effort to produce greater contrasts, heightening the impression of an accelerated pace for the subsequent passage (Compensation). Baltes et al. (1999b) claimed that this example illustrates adaptation to age-related declines in plasticity associated with the biology of ageing. Clearly, the exemplar was not found among the annals of Music Performance Science. But, had Rubinstein been the target of an interview study by a Music Psychologist investigating Seasoned Musicians, then the discussion could have led to a widening of awareness regarding Positive Successful Ageing among professional music performers. Further, the interview might have made strides on examining music development within a Lifespan Psychology approach. At the very least, other insights could have been gained by exploring musical expertise and Deliberate Practice; stage-related music-performance career patterns; age-linked discrepancies between general and domain-specific knowledge and skills; age-related music-performance compensatory behaviour; and intactness of long-term working musical memory.

Seasoned Musicians Playing Beyond the 5th Decade. Warren Brodsky, Oxford University Press. © Oxford University Press (2025).
DOI: 10.1093/9780198956501.003.0011

(60y, M, bn)   *I think that adaptation means having to choose what you're going to do that's different. You have to select between choices, you have to optimize conditions, and you have to compensate all the time. It's going on all the time. Of course, the dots are written out, every single little hieroglyphic there, every Slur, or accent, every Sforzando. So much information going on. But you do your best to do all those sorts of things, so it's incredibly hard having to get it right. Of course, there's interpretation like the amount of Sforzando, or the amount of Legato. But you also have to do it the way he wants you to do it (i.e., that guy waving his arms around). And the way that the Violins are playing that bit, and the guy who's doing the Timps over there, and the way the Double Bass is playing, how that Pizzicato works. And I've got to make a reed work at the same time. And it's not just that. You could be in a different Hall or outside. There are just a million things.*

This chapter presents a conceptual—solely theoretical—model of *Positive Ageing* among Symphony Orchestra players. The model is based on several psychological mechanisms. Foremost, Baltes and colleagues' theory of Successful Ageing known as: *Selection, Optimization, and Compensation*. That theory also includes the *Life-Longing* module. Then, *Life Management in the Occupational Domain* is put in place, including *Self-Evaluation of Vocation-Related Skills and Abilities*. Affect, emotion, mood (*Positive and Negative Affect Schedule*) and burnout (the *Orchestra Musicians Survey*) are integrated as modules within the overall conceptual theory as can be seen in Figure 11.2. The chapter comes to an end by discussing 'creative resilience' and the extent to which Orchestra players are afflicted with Dementia and/or Alzheimer's disease.

11.2 Positive Ageing

11.2.1 Selection, Optimization, and Compensation

Research on the effects of ageing suggests that some abilities may diminish particularly at the upper limits of performance. Old(er) individuals often experience performance declines in sensory mechanisms, strength, speeded performance, as well as information synthesis and separation tasks. One well-known approach of Lifespan Psychologists and Gerontologists is *successful ageing*. According to Abraham and Hansson (1995), Lifespan Gerontologists have conceptualized successful ageing as effective adaptation to developmental change. We might view successful ageing as a person's capability to reach a potential level of physical, social, and psychological well-being in old(er) age. One common barrier to successful ageing is decreased performance in cognitive abilities such as executive function and working memory tasks. Due to age-related cognitive declines, these might include: decreased processing speed, limited working memory capacity, and decreased performance on inhibitory tasks. The landmark work of Paul B. Baltes, former director of the Center for Lifespan Psychology at the Max Planck Institute for Human Development (Germany), and founder of the Max Planck International Research Network on Aging, is explicitly important here.

Margret and Paul Baltes (Baltes & Baltes, 1990; Baltes et al., 1999a, 1999b) developed a model involving three related strategies: *Selection, Optimization, and Compensation (SOC)*. Accordingly, this concept can be seen as an overall orientation—a lifelong developmental process—that is strategically useful whenever developmental losses and challenges predominate over gains. *SOC* was defined as maximizing positive desired outcomes while minimizing negative undesired outcomes. The model provides a context for developmental change and resilience across the lifespan, accounting for the possibility that throughout one's life people encounter opportunities while experiencing limitations in resources—and hence, subsequently there is a need for adaptation.

Baltes et al. (2006) claimed that development, from the perspective of Lifespan Psychology, is a constantly evolving dynamic of change in terms of psychological gains, deterioration, and stability. The relationships between gains and losses versus stability, change over time. At a young age the gains are typically far greater than the losses. But during the course of maturation, the ratio is gradually overturned, and may even be reversed in older age—including the loss of capacities and skills. Engaging in *SOC* behaviour helps old(er) individuals successfully adapt to the increasing age-related declines that surface in later life—by offsetting losses. *SOC* strategies could take on particular importance when people experience declines in biological, mental, or social reserve capacity (Baltes & Staudinger, 1996).

Selection (SOC) involves restricting or narrowing one's range of activities to fewer important domains. *Optimization (SOC)* refers to strategies by which a person augments their developmental reserves to maximize their capabilities. If we take the two together, we would see individuals selectively optimizing those capabilities that are most important. Finally, *Compensation (SOC)* refers to the use of pragmatic strategies to make up for developmental losses. Compensation may be seen as a response to the dissonance between actual or perceived skills *versus* environmental demands—such as involving the development of existing skills by utilizing substitute skills, or even by re-evaluating one's goals and aspirations (Abraham & Hansson, 1995). Baltes (Baltes & Baltes, 1990; Baltes et al., 1999a, 1999b) suggested that *SOC* principles are in fact coping strategies for age-related constraints.

(53y, M, hrp)   *As I've grown older I've learned to use strategies of adapting. For example, on the day of a concert I have to do 'this or that'. And a couple hours before the Concert I have to do 'that'. I mean it's got practical bases, but it's definitely superstitious rituals. For example: Before the Concert starts I have to have the music [score] exactly in the right order, and everything facing the right way. [Laughs.] And then when it's finished, it's all turned over on to the left-hand side, and then closed with everything kept in the same order. It is superstition in a way because I've got plenty of time to spot the notation in the middle of the Concert. But, maybe it's not really superstition? In a sense, this makes you have a certain type of awareness and order that lowers the risk of anything happening. Sure, it takes just 2 seconds to put the pages in the right order during a Concert. There's no problem! But, it just throws you off a little bit. [Laughs.] It does force me to look at the order, and make sure that I haven't forgotten any music.*

(61y, M, fl/picc)   *The danger can be that you can grow tired of it. You say 'this is really hard work'. And you tend to default to a safer option if you're not careful. You know you have to keep your standards up, and it's that keeping your standards up which is a difficult part of it. How do you do that? You keep practising. Keep acquiring [knowledge] about how to do things to maintain the standards. I think it's human nature to be lazy: Is there an easier way of doing it. Well sometimes the easier way is actually a more efficient way. I find ways of doing things which 25 years ago I couldn't play—but I can now. I found a way of coping with the technical difficulties. Very often people think: Well maybe I'll just get away with a bit less. I think often that may be the case. I don't mean to play less notes. But rather vary a tone production or vary an intonation. There are degrees of doing that. You can play with a fairly nice sound, or you can play with a really super sound. And to get the really super sound means you've got to do all your various exercises to produce that tone production. And that means putting in time to do the work. And sometimes you think: Should I warm up for this one? To warm up may mean to get your muscles into trim; for a wind player [that means to] get an embouchure sorted out! Some people may feel: Do I need my absolutely best gold-plated sound for this one? People do become a little bit lazier—that can happen as you get older. I think the really good older players are those who still do that 15 minutes to warm up—to get the best product.*

So the main question is: When you come out of [Music] College and have those top [music] skills, are you going to rely on these for the rest of your career? Or: Do skills get better and better as you go along? When I joined the Orchestra I was way above the rest. But [there were also] many things I was below. I couldn't do them. That wasn't because I was physically incapable of doing them, but I just lacked experience. I think it's probably a fair comment to say that my technique is the same; it didn't get better! But, my ability to utilize my technique got better. So, it may well be if my technique was 120% [20% above the rest when I joined the Orchestra at age 27], then when I leave [retire] it might be 99% [1% below the others]. Hopefully, I will find ways of compensating for that. Because I think: Aha, yeah I know a trick fingering there. Or, sometimes I miss notes if it's a difficult passage. I think: Well, I know what the Composer's trying to achieve here, what he's trying to say. For example, there are some bits in Shostakovich 10 [Symphony No. 10, E minor, Op. 93, premiered in London 1953, written by Soviet Russian composer Dmitri Shostakovich, 1906–1975] where there are these very fast Chromatic Scales sounding like a Glissando. And I think: Well, there isn't time to play that many notes—and a C major scale will do just fine—and no one's gonna tell [the difference]! Up till now I'd played it many, many times, and I've always done a C major scale in one of the moves [movements]. Only one Conductor ever noticed it; he just looked at me, winked, and never said anything. Because the effect was there. So, there are ways of 'cheating'. Cheating is the wrong word. Maybe it is more like rewriting what the Composer was trying to get at. A composer wants an effect and he may not have known the best way of doing it. He thought: Well I'll write this down. And, I think: Ah. I understand what you were trying to achieve. But there's an easier way for me to do that. It's quite common that people find a way to adapt for the context and part. A lot of people just rewrite things, or they miss out the odd note—and sometimes play a different note. It's surprising what you can get away with. But there are ways of making the effect. Another example is in the famous Prokofiev Classical Symphony [Symphony No. 1, D Major, Op. 25, written 1916–1917 by Russian composer Sergei Prokofiev, 1891–1953]. In the last movement, 2 flutes are 'fighting around' with a very difficult thing [part] alternating between the two of them. And it's technically very hard, as well as quite unusual. But, if the 1st Flute would say: 'You play that E and I'll play the G'—it all works out. The same notes have been played by 2 players, but one's doing one note and the other's doing the other note. The effect comes across very well, and Conductors will always say: 'Wonderful!' They don't know; they won't hear the difference. But this is the way of adapting and compensating. It is a proactive process of selecting techniques to adapt and compensate for poorly written music parts. Others may see this as a form of interpretation. So, you find ways of doing that. So yeah, I might think actually when I was 20 I could play this as [written] on the part. But, I can't now. Yet, I can just adapt a bit, and do this new trick-fingering, or twist my mouth a bit, and it will sound the same. That's how you survive as you age.

The question being raised here is: Are professional full-time contract Symphony Orchestra musicians, as a group, more prone to *SOC* behaviour? Namely, does musical development from early childhood, prompt musicians to employ strategies of *SOC* more than others who have not engaged in developing music skills? If so, then *SOC* might be a factor partially answering the initial question raised in Chapter 1:

How do Orchestra musicians retain their high level of functional music abilities well beyond the 5th Decade?

Gembris (2013) wisely points out that developmental changes occur simultaneously in all areas of human life—including those related to music (such as developed musicality and skills for music performance). Accordingly, the gains in one area (e.g., through practice) can occur at the same time as losses in other areas (e.g., age-related impairments). Baltes (1997) contended that while information processing speed, memory, and problem solving may start to decrease in the 3rd Decade of life, other knowledge, experience, wisdom, and social skills seem to increase with time. As Lifespan Psychology underlines the plasticity and modifiability of development and cognitive functioning, it would seem that both young(er) and old(er) adults possess a considerable amount of potential which is not used, and can perhaps be activated by training (referred to as *reserve capacity*). Gembris argued that all individuals possess a musical reserve capacity (i.e., more-or-less extensive musical potential which is for the most part underutilized), which can be activated by musical learning and practice.

Below is a closer look summary at what was originally articulated by Baltes and colleagues (Baltes, 1997; Baltes & Baltes, 1990; Baltes et al., 1999a, 1999b; Freund, 2008; Freund & Baltes, 1998, 2002; Krampe, 2002; Krampe & Baltes, 2003) on successful lifelong developmental processes:

a) Selection. Throughout the lifespan, biological, social, and individual opportunities and constraints specify a range of alternative domains of functioning. From this large number of options, and in collaboration with other forces like parents, children select a subset of options such as choosing a musical instrument on which to focus their resources in the specific domain of music performance. Selection of personal goals gives direction to the overall development of abilities, skills, and talents (leading to mastery) in the specific domain by guiding behaviour across situations across time; this has been referred to as *Elective Selection* (ES). Yet, selectivity can also be a consequence of adaptive responses to losses that threaten one's goals; this has been referred to as *Loss-Based Selection* (LBS).

b) Optimization. To achieve higher levels of functioning that are conducive to goal attainment, the child musician has to acquire and refine activities applied in the selected domain. Baltes called the acquisition of such means, Optimization. An example of Optimization may be practising scales when starting to learn to play an instrument; such training procedures enable one to acquire flexibility in finger movements and other techniques. Which means are best suited for achieving goals also depends on the social and cultural context (e.g., parents, teachers, coaches, peers, learning environments), all of which make some means more accessible than others. Personal characteristics might also weigh in on various opportunities (such as age, gender, socio-economic background, residential location).

c) Compensation. When losses or declines threaten one's level of functioning, then it is necessary to invest resources in an effort to counteract and maintain a given level of function. For example, seeking a different fingering to play a specific passage. The process of finding such alternative means is referred to as Compensation. Which means are best suited for compensating transient or permanent losses may also depend on social and cultural contexts, as well as personal characteristics.

(27y, F, ob)   *I am not sure I feel I am a 'professional musician'. Albeit, I am a full-time Orchestra player. I began when I was 6 years old, and transferred to a Woodwind instrument at age 15. I guess the question is how can I explain that 40% of the players in a Symphony Orchestra are above age 48. Myself, I began playing in Orchestras at [age] 16. I had played with several Orchestras as a Freelance player before this one. I am now one year here as a Principal player—No. 2 [on two instruments]. By the time I will be [age] 48 I will have been here 20 years, and that is 30 years after first playing professionally as an Orchestra musician. That is, I could conceivable continue for another 20 years (placing me at 50 years old), or the 5th Decade as a professional. I have seen Woodwind players above 50 years [old] still in the Orchestra. I have no way to know if they play like they did when they were young. But they are still here. Yet, their motor abilities are not the same. They compensate with a set of 'tricks'. Not that they play every other note (although I think some are doing just that), but almost like that. [Laughs.] I have a friend who plays Clarinet. He received a score from someone in another world-class Orchestra. It was Ravel's Daphnis [Daphnis et Chloé, a 'symphonie chorégraphique' ballet in one act, premiered in 1912, written by French composer Maurice Ravel, by Russian composer Serg1875–1937]. In the notation there was a big 'X' over the Clarinet solo. That solo is very difficult with lots of notes and lots of movement, but it is not heard over the other parts of the Orchestra that mask it. On top of the notes was a handwritten text: 'Clean the Clarinet here!' So perhaps it was not worth the added motor work to learn the section. Or perhaps, that player [who wrote that comment on the score] was older, and this was the way to play it safe. But my friend didn't do that—he did a lot of quick Staccato, tied the notes more, and maybe used other tricks of Articulation to compensate not playing all of the written notes that no one hears anyhow.*

(33y, F, bn/dbn)   *[When] I was a student and there [would be] a problem, I'd practise 6 hours without stopping; without analysing the problem, but just playing! In getting older, you get experience, and it's easier finding solutions. I do think there are people who can't find solutions; somehow, they're stuck. They're not flexible in their brain to even look for solutions. Sometimes I do get stuck, like I'm in a forest and I don't see the trees. And then I begin to think, there's an important point here [that I've missed].*

(40y, F, vn)   *I have learned by experience, to accommodate and adapt; maybe because of maturity and getting older. For example, when I was in my mid-20s my back started to hurt very badly. That was also one of the things that made me exercise regularly. That's something I would tell a younger player today: get in the habit of exercising every day. Make sure your muscles are strong; make sure your muscles are flexible; support muscles that you think have nothing to do with playing. I now do just about anything: Aerobics and Kick-Boxing. [They] work on all the muscles in the body—especially the ones we need in the upper back. There's stretching involved, coordination, and a lot of other skills one needs for playing an instrument. So I do feel that one has to consider the future as involving aches and pains, and the way it'll affect the way you're playing. So, it's best to stay limber through exercise. I wouldn't say that techniques of playing (e.g., certain types of Bowing or Trilling) have become more difficult—as if fingers aren't moving the same way. In fact, I found a more efficient way of playing. I like to analyse how I shift, how I move my Bow arm, what happens in the back? I've become more analytical and much more aware from a kinaesthetic [perspective]. If I didn't do those things there might have been more of a decline.*

(49y, F, vn)   *There are pieces in the Orchestra that the kinaesthetic memory of the fingers comes back even if I have not played them for 8 years. Perhaps in one place I will change the fingerings because today I have a different style of fingering. It is because of my age. As far as fingering is concerned, I think I am wiser today than before. Not because I have trouble with positions, but rather now I seek out fingerings for musical interpretations.*

(50y, M, vn)   *There is an element that you just get better at it because you develop a way to read. Sort of like driving! Many players need new glasses; I changed glasses because I didn't like the multifocals. Actually, the ones I use for reading are slightly stronger than the ones I use for seeing the music and the conductor. I guess I've learned to adapt as a way to cope with visual problems. That is something that's happened in the last few years—adapting to ageing.*

Baltes et al. (1999a, 1999b) examined various statements made by representative samples of the general population (in Germany) indicating *SOC* behaviours; from these they constructed a questionnaire. A 12-item version of the *SOC* questionnaire developed by Baltes et al. consists of the 2 aspects of Selection (Elective and Loss-based), Optimization, and Compensation. Each of the 4 Components are represented by 3 items. Each item in the questionnaire consists of 2 dichotic statements ('A' or 'B'), presented in 2 columns side by side (on the right and left sides of a page), either reflecting the intentional 'target' behaviour or an alternative non-*SOC* related as a 'lure' behaviour (referred to in empirical psychology studies as a 'distracter'). See Table 11.1. The reader should note that Table 11.1 only presents target stratagems. First the respondents choose <u>which</u> of the two behaviours ('A' or 'B') is more 'like them'. Then, they assess <u>how much</u> ('conviction') of the chosen behaviour is 'like them' using a 4-point Likert response scale (1 = 'Very Little Like Me'; 4 = 'Very Much Like Me'). Non-*SOC* behaviour is potentially scored as 'zero' (0 = Nought). The overall average of *SOC* Total frequency (the sum of all 4 Components) is between 0 and 12; the overall average *SOC* power scores for each Component ranges between 1 and 16. Freund and Baltes (1998) reported *SOC* scores for target behaviours as approximately 48% (M_{ES} = 1.3, SD = 1.1; M_{LBS} = 1.4, SD = 0.8; M_O = 1.6, SD = 1.1; M_C = 1.5, SD = 1.1; M_{SOC} = 5.8, SD = 3.2). Baltes et al. (1999a) demonstrated the *SOC* measure as psychometrically valid and reliable, with moderate level coefficient alphas: α_{ES} =.61; α_{LBS} =.64; α_O =.65; α_C =.61; α_{SOC} =.81. Finally, Weise et al. (2000) demonstrated Test-Retest Reliability between .70 and .80 for each Component and *SOC*-Total.

In an effort to replicate and extend previous norms of *SOC* among new diverse samples (such as professional Classical musicians), as well as to add further occupational work setting to the list of vocational groups covered by the *SOC* measure (e.g., Symphony Orchestra), the current study employed the *SOC* Questionnaire with all players in the omnibus sample (*N* = 52, see Chapter 1, section 1.6.2).

Table 11.1 Selection, Optimization, and Compensation: 12-Item Questionnaire

I	**SELECTION (S)**
	A. Elective Selection (ES)
1	I concentrate all my energy on few things.
2	I always focus on the one most important goal at a given time.
3	I think about what I want in life, I commit myself to one or two important goals.
	B. Loss-Based Selection (LBS)
1	When things don't go as well as they have in the past, I choose one or two important goals.
2	When I can't do something important the way I did before, I look for a new goal.
3	When I can't do something as well as I used to, I think about my priorities and what exactly is important to me.
II	**OPTIMIZATION (O)**
1	I keep working on what I have planned until I succeed.
2	I make every effort to achieve a given goal.
3	If something matters to me, I devote myself fully and completely to it.
III	**COMPENSATION (C)**
1	When things don't go as well as they used to, I keep trying other ways until I can achieve the same result I used to.
2	When something in my life isn't working as well as it used to, I ask others for advice or help.
3	When it becomes harder for me to get the same results as I used to, it is time to let go of that expectation.

Data Source: Baltes et al. (1999a). Reprinted with permission

The measure was presented within the 11-measure 12-page questionnaire booklet (see Chapter 1, section 1.6.3.3, Table 1.3 [Q6]). The frequency of *target* items chosen by participants was 7.25 out of 12 items (60.42%). See Table 11.2, left-side column panel, part A. The average frequency of the *S* subcomponents (*ES* and *LBS*) was very similar ($\Delta = 0.05$); no statistically significant difference surfaced ($t = 0.41, df = 51, p = 0.68$). But, in an analysis between the 3 *SOC* subcomponents, statistically significant differences did surface: $O > S$ ($t = 3.56, df = 51, p < 0.0008, d = 0.59$ a moderate effect size); and $O > C$ ($t = 3.19, df = 51, p < 0.002, d = 0.56$ a moderate effect size). Yet, no statistically significant differences were found for *S versus C* ($t = 0.30, df = 51, p = 0.77$). That is, Optimization was found to be a more common behavioural strategy for Orchestra players than Selection or Compensation. Then, the analyses examined the *power* of the target items chosen (range = 1–4). See Table 11.2, left-side column panel, part B. As can be seen, the average power of the *S* subcomponents (*ES* and *LBS*) was very similar ($\Delta = 0.23$); no statistically significant difference surfaced ($t = 1.41, df = 51, p = 0.16$). But, in an analysis between the 3 *SOC* subcomponents, statistically significant differences did surface: $O > S$ ($t = 4.23, df = 51, p < 0.0001, d = 0.60$ a moderate effect size); and $O > C$ ($t = 3.47, df—51, p < 0.001, d = 0.57$ a moderate effect size). Yet, no statistically significant difference was found for *S versus C* ($t = 0.35, df = 51, p = 0.73$). Again, Optimization was not only found to be a more common behavioural strategy for Orchestra players, but players

Table 11.2 Selection, Optimization, and Compensation: Total Sample and Comparisons Between Young(er) Players *Versus* Seasoned Musicians

Sub component	Total Musicians (N=52)			Young(er) Players LTE45 (n = 19)		Seasoned Musicians GTE55 (n = 18)		Sig
	M	SD	Range	M	SD	M	SD	p
A Targets								
ES	1.64	1.21	0–3	1.58	0.96	1.95	1.16	
LBS	1.69	0.90	0–3	1.68	0.75	1.78	1.11	
S[1]	1.67	0.89	0–3	1.63	0.76	1.86	1.07	
O	2.21	0.94	0–3	2.16	0.90	2.28	1.02	
C	1.71	0.83	0–3	2.00	0.82	1.44	0.86	
Total Targets	**7.25**	2.45	1–11	**7.42**	2.24	**7.44**	2.90	
B Power								
ES	1.76	1.37	0–4	1.58	1.20	2.13	1.44	
LBS	1.53	1.04	0–4	1.51	0.89	1.81	1.35	
S[1]	1.65	1.07	0–4	1.55	0.99	1.97	1.31	
O	2.35	1.27	0–4	2.19	1.10	2.66	1.30	
C	1.71	0.94	0–3.3	1.97	0.89	1.54	1.07	
Total Targets	**7.35**	3.29	1–14	**7.25**	2.84	**8.15**	3.77	

[1] = Selection (S) = (ES + LBS)/2

were also affiliated with Optimization items with more 'conviction' (i.e., increased 'like me' answers) than the other items reflecting Selection or Compensation.

Finally, an analysis was implemented to compare between the Young(er) Players and the Seasoned Musicians. See Table 11.2, right-side column panel. As can be seen in Table 11.2, 2 age subgroups were put forward: Younger Players LTE45 (n = 19, 36.5%, M_{Age} = 36.8, SD = 5.53, Range 27–44) *versus* Seasoned Musicians GTE55 (n = 18, 34.6%, M_{Age} = 58.4, SD = 2.83, Range 55–64). All Orchestra players between these two age subgroups (n = 15, 28.9%, 46–54 years old) were not considered in this analysis in an effort to nullify overlapping that might confound results. As can be seen in Table 11.2 (right-side panel), although Seasoned Musicians generally indicated using *SOC* behaviours to a greater extent than the Young(er) Players, and their conviction of *SOC* behavioural strategies was also higher, all of these differences were not statistically significant. Hence, the only main conclusion that surfaces thus far is: *SOC* is a frequent and intensive behavioural strategy among Symphony Orchestra players, and is not necessarily related to age.

One question that needs to be answered is: Do *SOC* strategies reflect a more idiosyncratic behavioural repertoire for professional Symphony Orchestra musicians than other individuals from the general public? To answer the question, an analysis was implemented comparing the current findings with data previously published by Baltes and colleagues from several studies among samples of the general

Table 11.3 Selection, Optimization, and Compensation: Comparison Between General Public (in Germany) *Versus* Professional Symphony Orchestra Players

	Targets	# Items		Comparisons with Orchestra Players[1]				
	%	*M*	*SD*	*t*	*df*	*SE*	*p*	*CI 95%*
1[2]	48	5.80	3.20	3.04	252	0.48	0.003	2.39–0.51
2[3]	59	7.08	2.10	0.67	530	0.31	0.500	0.83–0.40
3[4]	45	5.40	1.60	6.62	256	0.28	0.000	2.40–1.30

[1] = Orchestra Players in current sample: $N = 52$, Targets = 60.4%, $M_{\#Items} = 7.25$, $SD = 2.45$)
[2] = Data Source: Freund and Baltes (1998, $N = 202$)
[3] = Data Source: Baltes et al. (1999a, $N = 480$)
[4] = Data Source: Bajar and Baltes (2003, $N = 206$)

public in Germany. See Table 11.3. As can be seen in Table 11.3, the current sample of professional full-time contract Symphony Orchestra musicians were significantly more affiliated with *SOC*-related behaviours than the general public in Germany. Do *SOC* scores, which can perhaps be looked upon as long-term acquired behaviours and an overall orientation for adapting to the environment, partially answer the question: *How do Orchestra musicians retain their high level of functional music abilities well beyond the 5th Decade?* Certainly, some researchers feel that this may be a portion of the answer! For example, Gembris (2006) asserted that *SOC* strategies "are more apt to explain outstanding musical achievements than the talent concept" (p. 16).

Long-term adaptation processes through an individual's resource investments in a specific domain do represent a universal element for developing high achievements in that domain. Namely, the selection of personal goals, the optimization of achievements by practice, and the compensation for weaknesses make it possible to reach and maintain achievements. Krampe (2006) viewed *SOC* as a stable inter-individual characteristic across one's lifespan. Previously, Krampe and Baltes (2003) stated that the *SOC Model* is a framework for Lifespan Development that can define which behaviours target regulation or *adaptive mastery*. Within the context of the music vocation: Selection may mean prioritizing commitments for a music-performance career; Optimization may relate to goal-relevant means such as practice; and Compensation may denote the use of alternatives to maintain performance in the face of losses.

(60y, F, vc)   *I think being highly critical helps you, as you get older, to maintain your motor skills and your memory. That can help you survive. If you're not critical then you start to go down. That means that one of the strategies of how you're able to minimize the effects of ageing is to maintain a highly critical self-evaluation of how you prepare and how you perform. Whereas if you weren't like that, as you get older things do start to become a little bit weaker. You would just say: It's good enough, I'm 60. But I have finally determined that the Orchestra is just part of my life. I continue to play as a Soloist, with small Chamber Music ensembles, and of course teaching. I also married for the first time (6 years ago). I have a family life with my husband's children [from a previous marriage]. That's a very important change, having little children around at my home, and it's a very significant opening-up of my life!*

(60y, M, cl)   *Looking at some of my mental abilities I do feel that I have a problem more so than I did 10 years ago. But it is very strange to me that other players who I have discussed this [with], do not acknowledge my feelings; they do not see or hear anything different about my playing. But I do! For example, I can't take the same risks as I did before because the levels of Pianissimo virtuosity is not there anymore. But I would have wanted to take those risks. This is very much what happens to me in real life. When I was 20 years old, I loved sports. In retrospect, I just can't believe that I placed myself at such crazy risks—perhaps even beyond the level of endangering my professional career. Today, I don't necessarily see [abstaining from high-risk extreme sports] as a negative thing; it is a strategy of survival. On the one hand your bodily control and abilities have changed (compared to when you were younger), while on the other hand your viewpoint about what can happen to you becomes more concrete.*

There is clearly an issue of Lifelong continuous investment of resources in expertise abilities. Nevertheless, old(er) age certainly causes adaptation and compensation among the players. Accordingly, old(er) players invest a relatively smaller amount of practice time compared to the efforts they dedicated to DP when they were young(er) (see Chapter 2, section 2.2.1.2). This decline may reflect a need to spend more time on health care, especially maintaining bodily functions, than was necessary previously.

(54y, F, vc)   *For the last 10 years I've been practising outside the Orchestra about 3 hours a week. I can't practise every day anymore. Especially since having a child, my whole way of practice has revolved around using 5 minutes here and there in the most productive way. You just learn how to adapt. I didn't learn how to practise properly until I was in my 30s. I just did not have a clue. I mean I played 4 hours a day, and I called it 'practice'. Along the way, the available practice time gets shorter, and you just have to make the best possible use of it. And certainly, when my daughter was only a couple of months (and even later on), I had to breastfeed her before I went to work. If you've got 5 minutes you'd better use it really well! I would have never been able to do that 20 years ago.*

(55y, M, db)   *If I pointed to anything about surviving as a performing musician throughout till pension, I would say: 'Practice'. Most of us cease to practise. This is something that needs to be considered: Why do players stop practising? Maybe they feel they know all the material? Or they have already discovered the principle! Our belief is that making music itself is our practice. That 4–5 hours per day (of rehearsals) are enough practice to maintain yourself as an Orchestra player (especially after 25 years in the Orchestra profession). But yet, there are some things that one has to configure outside of the Orchestra rehearsals. So I do also look at scores and work through fingerings before rehearsals. This allows me to 'save face' (and embarrassment) in front of my colleagues in the section. Now this is quite different for Principal players who need to continue to develop their Soloistic levels of technique for the performance. But for most musicians (i.e., Tutti players) that is not the case. The problem with us, and ageing does affect this, is fitting in with all of the others. You can't be an individual, nor allow individual nuances that might develop along the way to keep you from sounding like the others. That is why I play Jazz outside of the Orchestra; it is a compensation for such regimental performance styles. The Orchestra is one way of playing, and Jazz offers me something else. As the years go by I think my skills get better! Well perhaps not really better than when I was practising many hours. But, I think there is a compensation that allows one to function better. You understand music better. You understand your position as a player in the Orchestra better.*

As pointed out by Abraham and Hansson (1995), developmental losses in the workplace (such as stress, loss of control, and job dissatisfaction), heighten *SOC* strategies even more. Therefore, Orchestra musicians operating near reserve capacity limits might even apply *SOC* principles more to enhance Orchestra work-roles in an effort to be more effective performers.

(33y, M, va)   *To some extent every artist performer has to be a bit narcissistic and egotistical: I want centre stage. That's what the Academies teach you; to be a little bit flashy. They train you to be a Soloist. Not just in the skills, but also in developing a certain temperament and personality. But with self-confidence comes arrogance. You have to have that self-belief in order to get a job. If you don't have that self-belief and self-confidence you won't get to that professional standard that is needed. Nevertheless, I do think that one has to learn how to adapt in order to maintain an Orchestra career. I see people who have left (or are in the process of leaving) because they struggle to fit in; they struggle for their independence. Some of them are really good players. But they just didn't like the Orchestra enough to fit in. To be able to be in the Orchestra you have to adapt to be a team player.*

(38y, M, bn/dbn)   *As you get older you need to adapt! As you're getting older perhaps you're less tolerant of travelling. [You are now more aware that] the seats are causing problems, or need to consider your eyesight and dentures. I've already done things like having had something adjusted on my Bassoon because it actually physically catches on things. There are things that with time you become aware of. Look: I wanted to sit on this chair to play [for the in vivo performance] because it is actually one of our studio chairs. I have to look after myself to be more aware of my own posture. I move the instrument to me rather than move myself to the instrument.*

(39y, F, cl)   *Because of duff seats that [are in] many concert halls, I have a special cushion. I try to get rid of the effect of sitting all day. I sort of adapt with all kinds of different things to try to overcompensate for losses. I think I adapt to those environmental elements that I'm gonna find difficult.*

(52y, M, vc)   *My focus is on doing my job whether the public is there or whether it's just microphones. Yet, I might be inclined to take fewer instrumental risks if there was public there. It also has to do with what kind of recording we're doing. If we're doing a CD, then I can take as many risks as I like, because I can always go back over it. A bit of 'tinkle factor' excitement. But, if it is a live performance, then I only take minimal risks. But, that is not age-related. The only thing I'd consider to be age-related is the kind of risks one would be inclined to take. In addition, I might consider if I've done a lot of practice in recent weeks. As I get older I depend more on the technical aspects that I've stored up over previous years rather than on immediate practice.*

(55y, M, perc)   *I have always been lucky (with this baby face) not looking my age. I don't really have to watch what I eat, and I don't drink beer—only wine. When I was in [Music] College because I never drank, I was an object of ridicule. But now looking back at some of those guys who I had played with, 10 years later some of them had to retire because they couldn't play anymore. They burnt themselves out on booze. One died of AIDS— so he obviously hadn't looked after himself. Out of four Percussion players, only one of them is playing now! He was a Principal, but now is No.4. I can honestly say that I can play all of these [20 Percussion] instruments much better than when I was studying and playing [i.e., practising] every day. My concentration, attention, and memory are all better! And I'm still inspired and motivated.*

(57y, F, vn)   *In the past few years, I have had a Sleep Disorder. That has seemed to have affected my memory; I don't remember the pieces that I need to perform or those I am performing this week. I have been told that problems of sleep are related to hormonal changes subsequent to my age. So, I need to be more dependent on the kinaesthetic memory of my hands. I need to prepare much more outside of formal Orchestra rehearsals. If I don't do that, then when I see my part, it feels as if I am reading the notes for the first time. My situation is not a usual one; my Sleep Disorder is very severe. Even in a concert, if I don't practise outside of the Orchestra, then it seems as if I don't know what to do onstage. I try all kinds of tricks. Maybe the word 'trick' is not the best word. It is more 'adaptation'. A way to deal with the difficulty of my problem and survive is to practise 2 hours a day outside of Orchestra rehearsals.*

11.2.2 Lifespan-Longing for a Soloist's Career

One novel construct in Lifespan Psychology is *Lifespan-Longings* (Baltes et al., 2006; Scheibe, 2005). Lifespan-Longings (L-L) are emotional and mental representations. Scheibe and Freund (2008) contend that the characteristics of *L-L* include: feelings of incompleteness and imperfection, reflecting the idea of development as a lifelong process never reaching completion, with depictions full of rich imagery involving personal ideals of optimal life. Consistent with this notion is that individuals hold subjective beliefs about their own optimal development, and that development always involves both gains and losses. *L-L* focuses on life by considering one's past, present, and future; this is referred to as *tri-time*. *L-L* cause one to reflect and self-evaluate their own life from a retrospective standpoint—relative to some other optimal developmental projectory or to another person(s). *L-L* may be perceived as functionally facilitative towards regulating losses and incompleteness. Accordingly, thinking about, and striving for, one's personal idea (or ideal) of an optimal life, is basic to human development; albeit at the same time, recognizable as unattainable simply because not everything one aspires to achieve can be reached. Therefore, *L-L* reflect a form of personal utopia that also reveals an awareness regarding losses or unfeasible goals; longing for the missing pieces that are believed to make one's existence perfect. These feelings are typically bitter-sweet. They are 'bitter' because of feeling that something is lacking, yet 'sweet' because feelings are connected to positive fantasies of the past or to an ideal future. In a study by Scheibe et al. (2007), 299 participants aged 18–81 rated the extent to which their 3 most important longings were related to 13 life-domains, such as: Education, Health, Relationships, and Vocational Occupation. Responses of all age subgroups suggested a focus of *L-L* was on past unattained developmental tasks, or on specific missed opportunities. However, both middle-aged and old(er) participants also implied that there were many tasks that had been already attained, but then were compromised or even lost altogether during their lifespan.

Long ago, Olbertz (2006) implemented a study among Orchestra players ($N = 150$; $M_{Age} = 40$; 60% Strings, 40% Winds; 70% male). Although it has always been more or less considered somewhat of a *myth*, the findings actually document (to my knowledge for the first time in the academic literature) that players specifically revealed sentiments of 'loss' once they entered an Orchestra. Namely, they expressed the notion that they left their Soloist benchmark behind—be it knowingly or unknowingly. In the current study, such sentiments were also mentioned by players—albeit many others continually contend that such feelings are only among just a 'rare' few. It must be understood that in the circumstance of a Symphony Orchestra player, longing does not function as a positive adaptive behaviour. Rather, longing focuses on aspects of one's incomplete lifestyle involving previous aspirations of being a Virtuoso Soloist.

(37y, M, va)   *Even now I want to be a Soloist. I was once a Concertmaster [actually the Principal] Leader of my section in a student Orchestra [at a Music Academy]. There I discovered qualities about myself that never came out before. The members of my section were very happy. Even internationally well-known players seemed to be impressed. But when I came to audition [4 years ago] they offered me to sit in the last seat [of a string section]. I did an audition to move up for a Principal Leader position of the section [2 years ago, but wasn't successful].*

(61y, F, vn)   *I don't think that from an emotional standpoint (and perhaps also talent) I was not built to be a Soloist. Every player receives talent in one or two of the features necessary to be a professional musician. But Soloists have talent in all of the required features. Those features include technique and expressiveness among others.*

As a matter of fact, several studies (e.g., Baltes et al., 2006; Scheibe & Freund, 2008; Scheibe et al., 2007) found a negative relationship between *L-L* and *well-being*; *L-L* can compromise feelings of happiness. Scheibe and Freund claim that "Life-longings may be quite maladaptive, bearing resemblance with dysfunctional obsessions or prolonged grief" (p. 123). Hence: "focusing on unreachable desires [are] a source of frustration [. . .] with negative consequences for well-being" (p. 127). Moreover, *L-L* seem to be linked with a more critical self-reflection about one's development. In short, obsessions of Lifespan-Longings can allow one to diminish their present life circumstances as they are expressions of unfulfilled personal utopias.

The current study adapted the concept of Lifespan-Longings considering a sample of Symphony Orchestra players. This adaptation was formatted as regretful sentiment for a Soloists career lost. See Table 11.4. The appraisal was presented within the 11-measure 12-page questionnaire booklet (see: Chapter 1, section 1.6.3.3, Table 1.3 [Q8]). Each player was asked to read the complete text as a story-like narrative—paragraph by paragraph. I note here that the right-hand column in Table 11.4 (labelled 'Characteristics') was never presented to the participants, but I add it here for the convenience of the reader. The participants were asked to judge each paragraph *as if* revealing a personal sentiment, and rating each paragraph using a 4-point Likert response scale: 1 = 'Not at All Like Me'; 4 = 'Highly Like Me' to reflect their conviction (belief) in the statement. See Table 11.5. As can be seen in Table 11.5 (left-side column panel), the average *L-L* statement score was below the 50% *midline* of the response scale (i.e., 2). The summed Total *L-L* score was only 38.5% of the full range (*Max* = 24). The 4th statement was highest of all; expressing the idea that performing as a Soloist has to do with 'freedom', 'endless time', and 'being close to God/nature'. Being a Soloist may be somewhat symbolic of a more 'spiritual' nature. Spiritual in the sense that Solo performances may be envisioned as fulfilling a higher more intensive level of passion than what is achieved when performing every day as a section player in an Orchestra. Then, in an effort to compare the Young(er) Players and the Seasoned Musicians, 2 age subgroups were put forward. The findings in Table 11.5 (right-side column panel) show that the LTE45 players rated themselves with higher levels of regret and longing for a Soloist's career than did the GTE55 players; but these differences were not statistically significant.

Table 11.4 Prototype Example of a Lifespan-Longing for a Soloist's Career

	Statement Text	Characteristics
1	*I always wanted a Soloist career. It is the missing piece in my life.*	**Personal utopia, incompleteness:** As long as my lifespan-longings are unfulfilled, something essential is missing for me.
2	*I enjoy imagining myself waiting in the Green Room, walking on to the Concert Platform in between the Orchestra players, and taking my position next to the Conductor. Then, hearing the sounds of the audience and Orchestra in anticipation of my first notes. I imagine myself playing the Solo passages with technical bravura and emotional prowess. Then, the roar of applause, a confirmation of the audience and Orchestra's admiration. Yet, I know that real life will never be that perfect, and this makes me sad.*	**Non-realizability of personal utopia, and ambivalent emotions:** I am longing for something too perfect to be true. My feeling of lifespan-longings is both painful and pleasurable.
3	*Solo performance has been part of my childhood, and it symbolizes something missing in my life today.*	**Tri-time focus:** My lifespan-longings have to do with persons or events from my past, present, and future.
4	*It has to do with freedom, endless time, and being close to God/nature.*	**Symbolic 'spiritual' nature:** What I am longing for is heavily filled with meaning.
5	*I wonder: Could I have lived out a Soloist's career?*	**Reflection:** My lifespan-longings often make me start thinking intensively about myself and my life.
6	*In a way, I would hope that my own children or students would be able to be renowned Soloists.*	**Continuing presence of personal utopia, tri-time focus:** Of personal utopia and tri-time focus.

Adapted from: Scheibe (2005)

Table 11.5 Lifespan-Longing for a Soloist's Career: Total Sample and Comparisons Between Young(er) Players *Versus* Seasoned Musicians

Statement	Total Musicians (N=52)			Young(er) Players LTE45 (n = 19)		Seasoned Musicians GTE55 (n = 18)		Sig
	M^1	SD	Range	M^1	SD	M^1	SD	p
1	1.46	0.80	1–4	1.58	0.84	1.55	0.98	
2	1.42	0.83	1–4	1.53	0.91	1.55	0.98	
3	1.44	0.78	1–4	1.74	0.87	1.33	0.77	
4	1.96	1.10	1–4	2.37	1.17	1.89	1.08	
5	1.50	0.87	1–4	1.53	1.02	1.56	0.92	
6	1.33	0.90	1–4	1.63	1.10	1.55	1.04	
Total	**9.23**	4.08	6–24	**10.34**	5.02	**9.44**	4.08	

[1] = Average Conviction

(41y, M, vc)   *I really didn't like the example about the old player in the questionnaire booklet [i.e., the L-L survey. Author's Note: It was not written, nor implied verbally, that the sentiments captured in the L-L were stated by an older male player.] I thought it was awful. But what I really disliked about it, was that it was all about 'him' and 'his ego'. We make music in the Orchestra for something that's outside ourselves. It was just dreadful what he said: 'I always wanted a Soloist career. It is the missing piece in my life.' ... Everything about him is ego-driven. It's all about Solo playing. Yes, there is a myth that players who join the Orchestra do so out of compromise; not being able to continue to be a Soloist. Yes, the thing is, that is not entirely wrong. Lots of people do that. But the truth is that that's the problem with Music Education. And it's also a problem about how people fit. How people make those sorts of compromises. But, there was nothing in there that sort of gave the point that it's possible to change one's mind about all of those things; to find what's actually worthwhile. There might be something artistically worthwhile being an Orchestra player. What bothers me is the artificial distinction between 'Soloists' and 'Orchestra Players'. Or between 'Soloists' and 'Chamber Ensemble Players'. And there should be a way of teaching you to be a musician which then embraces all of those things. That attitude about Soloists is damaging. If you are taught to be a Soloist, then you just go and do your own little thing. It's all about you, your ego, and expressing yourself.*

(60y, F, vc)   *I don't feel that as I get older I have less satisfaction from the job in the Orchestra. But, I'm not so much connected to that term [job]. All along I knew pretty much what is going on in the Orchestra [as previously I was a Soloist with several Orchestras]. I'm not disappointed anymore. Yet in the beginning I did expect much more. And then I saw that I had to make it part of my life, and to put it up to the level I want to live. But it's not about generally playing in Orchestras. It's difficult to play in an Orchestra because of all the different people. And, the danger of mediocrity; you have to prepare each week a different programme, and things which can't be developed in a deep profound way [as one does as a Soloist]. In the Orchestra other people decide and choose the programmes, the Conductor, and the Soloists. No, I wouldn't say I should still stay in the Orchestra cause that's my life. The Orchestra has relatively been my life especially because it permits me to live as a musician. So, it is a compromise! I could have been a famous soloist!*

11.2.3 Life Management in the Occupational Domain

Compared to other occupational groups and professional organizations, little is known about Symphony Orchestra players.[1] The overall consensus is that they are hard-working, ambitious, self-absorbed, introspective, and introverted creative individuals. The general public often views Symphony Orchestra players as those with strong inner-driven working careers who are self-selected and enjoying what many people sitting in the venue Concert Hall as the audience romanticize as a glamorous life with opportunities for self-expression and self-actualization. Ironically, even when musicians themselves first embarked on their performance career they expected to live out rich and creative lives. However, such promises almost always fall short, and these fables may never be fulfilled as imagined. Foremost, musicians are trained from early childhood as Soloists. Hence Orchestra work may be seen as a disappointment (both on personal and professional vocational levels). Orchestra musicians do often view themselves as *artists* who are simply paid to perform what others want to buy (see Chapter 5, section 5.2.2). Subsequently, such perceptions

[1] This material has been adapted from a paper previously published by Brodsky (2006). Reprinted with permission.

lead to a high percentage of players viewing their position in the Orchestra as more of a 'job' than the fulfilment of their passion (see Chapter 7, sections 7.3.2 and 7.3.4). In fact, for some players an Orchestral contract may be the ultimate trade-off for debased artistic standards (see Chapter 7, section 7.4.2).

Indeed, the careers of Symphony Orchestra players begin with musical training in the early years of their life. These eventually lead to a highly disciplined acquisition of skill on a musical instrument throughout the teenage years. Thereafter, the focal point of formal training occurs in a tertiary College-level environment known as the Music Academy. However, the curriculum there is not calculated to give a rounded education, but rather to create polished musicians (Persson, 1996a, 1996b). One could assume that although the *conservatory culture* (e.g., Kingsbury, 1988/2001) does successfully serve to initiate musicians into their professional guild and vocation, it also functions to prevent *musicians-to-be* from being anything else but a performing musician. Nonetheless, many do settle for a life of Studio Teaching of instrument instruction, Teaching General Music in a classroom, or even a non-music-related profession rather than a long-term career involving the Concert Stage (see Chapter 2, section 2.1.1 and Table 2.1). The above situation raises questions about the eventual contentment of Symphony Orchestra players towards their profession.

Smith and Murphy (1984) surveyed six *American Symphony Orchestra League* (ASOL) Orchestras; they found several raisons d'être for musicians to choose to be in an Orchestra. They further noted that success in one respect was often reported to compete with success in another. For example, success at the top of the profession was often dwarfed by being deprived of the rewards of its practice. So great was the embitterment at this occurrence that many players reported to give up the prestige and potential income associated with a *first-class* organization (in Germany referred to as an 'A' Orchestra) by accepting a position with a subordinate organization, simply because the latter provides more interesting musical work. Smith and Murphy reckoned that the Orchestra "is a setting in which the successful development of a career is too often a matter of sorting through and accommodating to various contradictions and trade-offs among these rewards" (p. 150). They claim this is what makes Symphony players so interesting to investigate—both as a phenomenon and as a field of study! It is ultimately the way in which the potential rewards, along with the various musical frustrations, are mixed together as the foundation of a highly distinctive setting that is overwhelmingly incomparable to all other occupational milieus. Freund and Baltes (2002) found evidence that persons with higher levels of associated *SOC* behavioural strategies also reported higher levels of occupational comfort—that is job competence and job satisfaction.

Over three decades ago, in a different interview study (albeit with some of the same Orchestras that participated in this current study), several players spoke about the lack of opportunities for professional creativity within the existence of being an Orchestra musician (Brodsky, 2006). Players must put aside their *individual voice* in order to successfully achieve the *blend* required for a group performance. Further, being a member of a Symphony Orchestra is not always 'all it is cracked up to be'. It is interesting to note that several players claimed to have read (perhaps in a blog, or *The Classical Musician* magazine) about the level of general job satisfaction reported by Symphony Orchestra members. Accordingly, these were reported to be even far below levels of general job satisfaction as recounted by Federal Prison Guards. One of the factors that was raised (see Brodsky, 2006) about players' job satisfaction was financial compensation. Several players stated that even if you win an orchestra job, more than likely you will not get paid enough to make a living to own a home, or to buy a new car, or to send your kids to college. I point out that these sentiments also surfaced in the current study (see Chapter 7, sections 7.3.1 and 7.4.2).

Weise and Freund (2005) note that in today's job market individuals have to respond proactively to changing demands to maintain employability. Therefore, not only do they direct their professional activities to achieve the goals they set, but they also define their own success criteria. Accordingly, work-related proactivity implies that one does not only react to the explicit demands of the work environment, but rather self-initiates behaviour beyond immediate pressures. The researchers highlight evidence indicating that people involved in the pursuit of personal goals demonstrate higher subjective well-being. Within a Lifespan Psychology approach, it is altogether more adaptive to choose goals that converge with societal demands, individual capacities, and personal motives. The point being made here is that different contexts (such as work *versus* family) may interfere with each other—and such variances surface at different phases of life. In addition, an individual's development in one domain (like an occupational career) can interrelate—either positively as an asset or negatively as a liability—with the development in other domains (like intimate relationships and domestic responsibilities).

Successful *Life Management in the Occupational Domain* (*LMOD*) was assessed with a 3-item measure from Weise et al. (2002). An adapted version of the measure was presented within the 11-measure 12-page questionnaire booklet (see Chapter 1, section 1.6.3.3, Table 1.3 [Q9]). See Table 11.6. The participants were asked to judge the extent that each *LMOD* statement reflects their attitude about professional life in the Symphony Orchestra. The measure employed a 7-point scale for players' responses (1 = 'Not at All', 7 = 'Absolutely'). See Table 11.7. As can be seen in Table 11.7 (left-side column panel), the extent to which the players in the current sample perceived they were successful in pursuing and achieving their occupational goals in the Symphony Orchestra (Item #1) was roughly 66%. That percentage is roughly the same extent to which they were satisfied with how they managed their life as a professional Symphony Orchestra musician (Item #3).

The above-mentioned finding can be interpreted as reflecting a higher level of satisfaction for the profession. In an earlier study, Franziska Olbertz from the Institute for Research on Musical Ability at the University of Paderborn (Germany) recruited $N = 148$ contract players from A-Class Orchestras in Eastern Germany. The sample consisted of 58% Strings and 37% Winds; 70% male; with an average age of 43 years old. Olbertz (2006) found the overriding majority (80%) to be content with their

Table 11.6 Life Management in the Occupational Domain

	Text
1	How close did you come to achieving your goals in the occupational domain this past year?
2	How successful have you been so far in pursuing your occupational goals?
3	How satisfied are you with your life management in the occupational domain?

Data Source: Weise et al. (2002)

Table 11.7 Life Management in the Occupational Domain: Total Sample and Comparisons Between Young(er) Players *Versus* Seasoned Musicians

Item	Total Musicians (N=44)			Young(er) Players LTE45 (n = 19)		Seasoned Musicians GTE55 (n = 14)		Sig
	M^1	SD	Range	M^1	SD	M^1	SD	p
1	4.61	1.35	1–7	4.42	1.43	4.71	1.33	
2	4.72	1.16	1–7	4.53	1.31	4.86	1.10	
3	4.46	1.30	1–7	4.47	1.47	4.50	1.02	
Total	13.84	3.33	5–19	13.42	3.85	14.07	2.76	

^{1} = Average Contentment

jobs; the players even noted that they would choose the profession all over again. Olbertz found no differences between players of instrument (String and Wind) or age subgroups (< 35 years young, between 35 and 50 years, > 50 years old).

Then, in an effort to examine differences based on age, 2 age subgroups were put forward: Young(er) Players LTE45 ($n = 19$, 36.5%, $M_{Age} = 36.8$, $SD = 5.53$, Range 27–44) *versus* Seasoned Musicians GTE55 ($n = 14$, 26.9%, $M_{Age} = 58.5$, $SD = 3.06$, Range 55–64). All other players between these two age groups were not considered in an effort to nullify overlapping that might confound results. It should be noted that unfortunately *LMOD* data was not collected for 4 Seasoned Musicians (hence: $n = 14$). See Table 11.7 (right-side column panel. Although the Seasoned Musicians rated their contentment higher than the Young(er) Players, these differences were not statistically significant. Therefore, it can be assumed that perceived success and positive attitudes related to Life Management in the Occupational Domain of Symphony Orchestra players are not necessarily related to age.

11.3 Self-Evaluation of Skills and Abilities

In their study on ageing among a sample of professional and amateur players in a community orchestra in Western Sydney (Australia), MacRitchie and Garrido (2019) employed a 12-item music-performance-related self-efficacy assessment.

Their questionnaire examined players' confidence in coping with various challenges of playing such as: technical difficulties, expressive and interpretative challenges, playing to the best of one's ability, general challenges of rehearsals and concerts, and enhancing the Orchestra. In addition they asked about the overall confidence they have with their instrument. But the data of that sample did not cover full-time contract professional Symphony Orchestra players. Yet, the idea of assessing music skill and abilities is quite valuable when investigating professional Orchestra musicians.

The current study implemented the *Self-Evaluation of Skills and Abilities* (SESA). Originally this assessment was developed by Brodsky in 1994 (Brodsky, 1995, 2006) for Symphony Orchestra musicians while investigating a music-based cognitive-behavioural therapeutic intervention for Music Performance Anxiety (MPA). In the current study, the measure was presented within the 11-measure 12-page questionnaire booklet (see Chapter 1, section 1.6.3.3, Table 1.3 [Q4]). *SESA* evaluated perceived competence accounting for four dynamic proficiencies. These were:

a) Motor Abilities: skills related to playing a musical instrument
b) Hearing Abilities: skills related to score-reading with an instrument, as well as the inner hearing of the score from music notation
c) Inter-Musical Abilities: skills related to being able to synchronize with other players in a group effort to reproduce a music composition
d) Intra-Musical Abilities: skills related to one's personal interpretation and expression of an emotion during the reproduction of a music composition.

Each player self-rated their overall level of confidence as a music performer on a 10-point scale (1 = Lacking, 10 = Practically Perfect). See Figure 11.1. Self-evaluation scores for each music-performance ability and skill set were tallied. See Table 11.8. As can be seen in Table 11.8 (left-side column panel), the competency scores of proficiencies indicate that:

1	2	3	4	5	6	7	8	9	10
lacking		limited		reasonable		natural-born		extra sensitive	
	under developed		okay		good		very good		practically perfect

Figure 11.1 Response Scale of Confidence in Music Skills and Abilities

Source: Brodsky (1995, 2006). Reprinted with permission.

- Motor Abilities > Hearing Abilities: $t = 3.69$, $df = 51$, $p < 0.01$, $d = 0.52$ (a moderate effect size)
- Inter-Musical Abilities > Motor Abilities: $t = 5.35$, $df = 51$, $p < 0.0001$, $d = 1.15$ (a large effect size)

Table 11.8 Self-Evaluation of Music Abilities: Total Sample and Comparisons Between Young(er) Players *Versus* Seasoned Musicians

Proficiency	Total Musicians (N=52)			Young(er) Players LTE45 ($n = 19$)		Seasoned Musicians GTE55 ($n = 18$)		Sig
	M^1	SD	Range	M^1	SD	M^1	SD	p^1
Motor	7.19	1.48	4–10	6.90	1.49	7.39	1.69	
Hearing	6.12	2.20	2–10	6.16	1.80	6.56	2.50	
Inter-Musical	8.17	1.31	5–10	7.84	1.26	8.44	1.38	
Intra-Musical	7.82	1.53	5–10	7.47	1.58	8.56	1.42	*
Total %	73.4	12.6	48–100	70.9	11.4	77.4	14.9	

[1] * = p < 0.05

- Inter-Musical Abilities > Hearing Abilities: $t = 7.37$, $df = 51$, $p < 0.00001$, $d = 1.43$ (a large effect size)
- Intra-Musical Abilities > Motor Abilities: $t = 3.31$, $df = 51$, $p < 0.01$. $d = 0.42$ (a moderate effect size)
- Intra-Musical Abilities > Hearing Abilities: $t = 1.75$, $df = 51$, $p < 0.00001$, $d = 0.90$ (a large effect size)
- Inter-Musical Abilities = Intra-Musical Abilities (no statistically significant differences)
- Overall Total Score (%) was calculated by averaging the mean scores of all four proficiencies (multiplied by a factor of 10); the Total scores for competence in proficiencies were roughly 73%.

Then, in an effort to examine differences based on age, two age subgroups were put forward: Young(er) Players LTE45 ($n = 19$, 36.5%, $M_{Age} = 36.8$, $SD = 5.53$, Range 27–44) *versus* Seasoned Musicians GTE55 ($n = 18$, 34.6%, $M_{Age} = 58.5$, $SD = 3.06$, Range 55–64). All other players between these ages were not considered in an effort to nullify overlapping that might confound results. As can be seen in Table 11.8 (right-side column panel), the findings demonstrate that the Young(er) Players appraised their proficiencies lower than the Seasoned Musicians; but for the most part these differences were not statistically significant. The one exception was Intra-Musical Abilities ($t = 2.19$, $df = 35$, $p = 0.035$, $d = 0.73$ a moderate effect size). This finding indicated that Seasoned Musicians perceive their capability to interpret and express the necessary emotions of the music being performed to a much higher extent than the Young(er) Players.

(49y, F, vn) *At my age it is just so much more simple to play in the Orchestra. I say that because it has finally become very natural—without thinking about it. Things happen and you are just in focus. People around me are playing, and I am so much inside the element that I don't even need or look at the Conductor. I don't look at the players either. I just feel it! Over 25 years ago, when I was in a student Orchestra, I felt very strange. I couldn't hear my own sound. I felt that the colour of my sound didn't fit the mixture. I was more preoccupied with the materials. At the time I was a Soloist, played in Chamber Ensembles, and also taught music students.*

One troublesome finding here is that the players' overall level of confidence in their music-performance-related abilities (i.e., Total Score) is just below 75%. Arguably, this is not what would have been expected from world-class music performers. In a previous study, among UK Symphony Orchestra players, Brodsky (2006) also found that while just under half of the sample rated their skills as 'good' or 'extra-sensitive' (i.e., ranging between 6 and 9 on the same 10-point response scale in Figure 11.1), there were almost as many players who rated their skills as 'limited' or 'reasonable' (i.e., ranging between 3 and 5 on the 10-point scale). When considering both studies, perhaps Symphony Orchestra players are individuals who are not aware of the distinction between *self-assessment* and *self-criticism*. Self-criticism among professional music performers is perhaps highly important, but unfortunately that often includes *self-condemnation*. Certainly, even 'perfectionist' qualities do not necessarily have to turn into 'self-purgatory ideations'.

11.4 Affect, Emotion, Mood, and Burnout

11.4.1 Positive and Negative Affect

The terms 'affect', 'emotion', and 'mood' are seemingly interchangeable. Yet, *affect* refers to the internal mental feeling that surfaces from emotional experiences; it varies in the direction of the valence (from 'unpleasant' to 'pleasant'), as well as in the strength of the arousal (from 'disengaged' to 'highly active'). On the other hand, *emotion* is more physical in the sense that it is founded on a number of basic constituents, including: cognitive appraisal and basic emotional categories (or emotional states). Finally, *mood* can be distinguished from affect and emotion in both duration and intensity; mood is more 'persistent' and less intense than emotion—as well as more 'stable' than affect. It is interesting to note that many dimensional approaches exist which reduce affect and emotion to either 'positive' or 'negative' states. The most popular of all measures, especially for research purposes, is: the *Positive and Negative Affect Schedule* (*PANAS*) developed by Watson et al. (1988). It must be noted, however, that as is the case with all self-report questionnaires, *PANAS* is not as objective as seems to be reported in the literature. For example, there may be respondents who find it difficult to assess their own affect accurately, while some may either understate (underestimate) or overstate (overestimate) their emotions or mood states.

Two dominant dimension factors of self-rated affect (as found in *PANAS*) are *Positive Affect* (PANAS-PA) and *Negative Affect* (PANAS-NA). Although the expressions 'positive' and 'negative' could suggest that these two dynamic aspects are actually contrary to each other (e.g., opposites as far as associations are concerned), long-standing research has demonstrated that while each is distinct and meaningful on its own, they are not contradictory (Watson et al., 1988). Accordingly, the *PANAS-PA* sub-scale reflects the extent to which a person feels enthusiastic, active, and alert. Higher *PANAS-PA* is a state of high energy, full concentration, and pleasurable engagement; lower *PANAS-PA* is characterized by sadness and lethargy. On the other hand, the *PANAS-NA* sub-scale is a more general dimension of subjective distress and unpleasurable engagement. Higher *PANAS-NA* consists of aversive states such as anger, contempt, disgust, guilt, fear, and nervousness; lower *PANAS-NA* is characterized as a state of calmness and serenity. It is important to point out that *PANAS* represents *states* rather than *traits*.

The *PANAS* version employed in the current study is a brief 20-item measure. *PANAS* was presented within the 11-measure 12-page questionnaire booklet (see Chapter 1, section 1.6.3.3, Table 1.3 [Q5]). There are 10 descriptors for each affect. The *PANAS-PA* sub-scale consists of the following 10 adjectives (alphabetically): Active, Alert, Attentive, Determined, Enthusiastic, Excited, Inspired, Interested, Proud, and Strong. The *PANAS-NA* sub-scale consists of the following 10 adjectives (alphabetically): Afraid, Ashamed, Distressed, Guilty, Hostile, Irritable, Jittery, Nervous, Scared, and Upset. *PANAS* employs a 5-point Likert Scale to reflect 'how often' one feels a specific adjective (1 = 'Never', 5 = 'Always'); hence, sub-scale scores range from 10 to 50. In general, *PANAS-PA* sub-scale scores are usually higher than *PANAS-NA* sub-scale scores. Higher *PANAS-PA* sub-scale scores indicate increased positive affect with an average score of about 30 ($M_{\text{PANAS-PA}} = 33.3$, $SD \pm 7.2$). Lower *PANAS-NA* sub-scale scores indicate decreased negative affect with an average score of about 15 ($M_{\text{PANAS-NA}} = 17.4$, $SD \pm 6.2$). Watson et al. (1988) reported adult norms for the general population, as follows: $M_{\text{PANAS-PA}} = 35.0$, $SD = 6.4$; $M_{\text{PANAS-NA}} = 18.1$, $SD = 5.9$.

PANAS-PA and *PANAS-NA* sub-scale scores were calculated for the current total sample. See Table 11.9, left-side column panel. The analysis found that professional Orchestra musicians perceived themselves as having higher levels of *PANAS-PA* than *PANAS-NA*, and this difference was statistically significant: $t = 10.33$, $df = 51$, $p < 0.00001$, $d = 2.16$ (a large effect size). Namely, much like other members from the general public (e.g., Watson et al., 1988) the current sample of professional contract Symphony Orchestra players perceived themselves as feeling more energy and concentration than lethargy and sadness.

Then, in an effort to examine differences based on age, two age subgroups were put forward: Young(er) Players LTE45 ($n = 19$, 36.5%, $M_{\text{Age}} = 36.8$, $SD = 5.53$, Range 27–44) *versus* Seasoned Musicians GTE55 ($n = 18$, 34.6%, $M_{\text{Age}} = 58.5$, $SD = 3.06$, Range 55–64). All other players between these ages were not considered in an effort to nullify overlapping that might confound results. As can be seen in Table 11.9

(right-side column panel), the findings demonstrate that Young(er) Players reported less *PA* and more *NA* than the Seasoned Musicians; but these differences were not statistically significant.

(30y, F, vn)   *The first few years after I came here (6 years ago) I was very enthusiastic. I just got out of College. You sort of retain a certain amount of distance from different colleagues because you're excited and you simply want to do your job. And then you start to absorb a little; you begin to make decisions with other players. I would say that about 50% of all players become cynical and burnt out, and that environment affects [your mood].*

(60y, F, vc)   *I see difficulties of ageing among other people—but not myself! For example, some are less interested. They put their instrument in a locker behind the stage and do not practise at home (which then affects the level of their playing). They're simply waiting for the year of pension to arrive. But I don't know if this is connected to age, or if this is something players do automatically when coming to the Orchestra (because I also see it among younger players). It's a question of personal motivation. Also, I see that older musicians get more easily impatient, and sometimes depressed. Maybe this occurs when they sit in the Orchestra at the end [back rows] of a section. Perhaps [it is] years passing without too much contact in their surroundings. There are people who come in the morning, and are rather isolated in the Orchestra. Then they go home. That's all there is! I have heard several players say: 'For more than 40 years, this Orchestra has been my life. Now pension!' Maybe, they never developed anything else outside of the Orchestra.*

Freund and Baltes (1998) found positive correlations between *PANAS-PA* and *SOC* behavioural strategies. They employed a German translation of the same 20-item *PANAS* version used in the current study. Albeit, Freund and Baltes only presented the 10-item *PANAS-PA* sub-scale among $N = 202$ members from the general population. The *PANAS-PA* scores were: $M_{\text{PANAS-PA}} = 32.70$ ($M_{\text{Item}} = 3.27$), $SD = 0.55$. They found correlations between *PANAS-PA* with *SOC* Subcomponents (see Table 11.1) as follows: $r_{\text{SOCTot}} = .29$ ($p < 0.01$); $r_{\text{ES}} = .05$; $r_{\text{LBS}} = .17$ ($p < 0.05$); $r_{\text{O}} = .37$ ($p < 0.01$), $r_{\text{C}} = .27$ ($p < 0.01$). It does seem pertinent here to indicate that the current sample of full-time contract Symphony Orchestra musicians demonstrates higher levels of *PANAS-PA* as seen in Table 11.9 (left-side column panel) than did the general German population recruited by Freund and Baltes. Such a difference is statistically significant: $t = 2.13$, $df = 252$, $SE = 0.09$, $p = 0.04$, CI 95% 0.012–0.348, $d = 0.33$ (a small effect size).

Table 11.9 Positive and Negative Affect: Total Sample and Comparisons Between Young(er) Players *Versus* Seasoned Musicians

Affect Sub-Scale	Total Musicians (N=52)			Young(er) Players LTE45 ($n = 19$)		Seasoned Musicians GTE55 ($n = 18$)		Sig
	M	*SD*	Range	*M*	*SD*	*M*	*SD*	*p*
PA Positive	34.5	5.41	21–46	33.2	6.07	35.4	5.44	
NA Negative	19.9	7.87	10–46	20.5	7.03	19.0	7.93	

11.4.2 Occupational Burnout

Chronic stress can be emotionally draining, leading to burnout. *Burnout* is a symptom of Emotional Exhaustion, Depersonalization, and reduced Personal Accomplishment (see Chapter 5, sections 5.2.2 and 5.3.2). The consequences of Symphony Orchestra player burnout are potentially very dangerous for the musicians themselves, the Orchestra, the organization management, and for the audience (who purchase yearly subscriptions). For example, Burnout can lead to deterioration in the quality of care for rehearsals, performances, and recordings. Burnout correlates with physical health, such as: headaches, gastrointestinal disorders, muscle tension, hypertension, episodes of cold and flu, and sleep disorders. Burnout correlates with mental health, such as: exhaustion and fatigue, behavioural symptoms, and decreased work performance (including: negative attitudes, low morale, absenteeism, and job turnover). Burnout also seems to correlate to self-reported increases of alcohol and drug abuse.

The *Maslach Burnout Inventory* (MBI) developed by Maslach and Jackson (1981/1986) was produced as a tool for Counsellors, Teachers, and Occupational Designers (i.e., Human Resources). *MBI* seems to be considered a first-choice application to identify potential sources of Occupational Burnout. *MBI* is a 22-item survey consisting of three Components which assess distinct aspects of Burnout:

- Emotional Exhaustion (MBI-EE, 9-item sub-scale, scores range 0–54)
- Depersonalization (MBI-DP, 5-item sub-scale, scores range 0–30)
- Personal Accomplishment (MBI-PA, 8-item sub-scale, score range 0–48)

Respondents use a 7-point Likert Scale (from 0 to 6) to indicate how often they have perceived feeling each of the 22 item statements (0 = Never, 3 = A Few Times a Month, 6 = Every Day). *MBI* is self-administered in roughly 22 minutes. Burnout is conceptualized as a continuous variable ranging from Low-Burnout (consisting of low-*MBI-EE*, low-*MBI-DP*, high-*MBI-PA*), through Mid-Burnout (consisting of mid-*MBI-EE*, mid-*MBI-DP*, mid-*MBI-PA*), to High-Burnout (consisting of high-*MBI-EE*, high-*MBI-DP*, low-*MBI-PA*). See Table 11.10. Maslach and Jackson published norms with $N = 11,067$ individuals from the general public between the ages of 25 and 65 years. These are: $M_{MBI-EE} = 20.99$ ($SD = 10.75$); $M_{MBI-DP} = 08.73$ ($SD = 5.89$); and $M_{MBI-PA} = 34.58$ ($SD = 7.11$). *MBI* is a highly valid and reliable measure. Burnout is associated to greater role conflict, work pressure, lower degrees of peer support, and a lack of promotion opportunity (Tuuli & Karisalmi, 1999). In addition, factors such as personality, personal expectation, and motivation, all seem related to levels of Burnout. Higher levels of Burnout have been connected to 'withdrawal' behaviours as coping strategies (such as getting away from people and/or shutting off thoughts about the job); Lower levels of Burnout have been connected to 'social' coping strategies (such as talking and getting advice).

Table 11.10 Levels of Occupational Burnout

	Low Burnout	Average Burnout	High Burnout
EE	≤ 16	17–26	≥ 27
DP	≤ 06	07–12	≥ 13
PA	≥ 39	38–32	≤ 31

Data Source: Maslach & Jackson (1981/1986)

Although *MBI* had specifically been developed for Human Services and Education occupations, Maslach and Jackson (1981/1986) suggested that future research with other occupational groups is welcome, but would necessitate having to revise the wording of items to be more ecologically valid (as stated on p. 15 of the manual). In that spirit, in 1993 I adapted *MBI* for Symphony Orchestra musicians (Brodsky, 1995, 2006; Brodsky & Sloboda, 1997a, 1997b). My assumption, back then, was that the use of the word 'Burnout' might have adverse negative repercussions (including non-compliance). Therefore, the 1993 adapted *MBI* version was simply titled: *Orchestra Musicians Survey*. See Table 11.11. It should be noted that the headings (in the 'bold' font of Table 11.11) were neither presented to the participants in the 1994 study nor in the current study. I add these headings here solely for the convenience of the reader.

Within the Orchestra setting, *MBI* suggests the following conceptions:

- *MBI-EE* reflects feelings of being emotionally overextended and exhausted by work in the Orchestra
- *MBI-DP* reflects unfeeling and impersonal responses towards the Orchestra members, the Conductor, Management, and the Audience
- *MBI-PA* reflects lacking feelings of competence and successful achievement in the Orchestra.

In the 1994 study Brodsky recruited $N = 54$ professional Orchestra musicians (Brodsky, 1995, 2006; Brodsky & Sloboda, 1997a, 1997b). They were from four British contract Symphony Orchestras ($n = 44$, 82%), and six British freelance Orchestras ($n = 10$, 18%). All participants resided in north-west England. The findings were as follows: $M_{MBI-EE} = 21.16$, $SD = 09.59$; $M_{MBI-DP} = 07.19$, $SD = 06.02$; and $M_{MBI-PA} = 27.62$ $SD = 08.51$. Based on published norms (see Table 11.10), these scores reflected Mid-to-High Occupational Burnout.

In the current study, taking place 27 years after the above described 1994 study, the same *Orchestra Musicians Survey* was presented within the 11-measure 12-page questionnaire booklet (see Chapter 1, section 1.6.3.3, Table 1.3 [Q7]). Unfortunately, *MBI* data was not collected for 8 participants (hence note: $n = 44$). See Table 11.12. As can be seen in Table 11.12 (left-side column panel), the professional full-time contract Symphony Orchestra players demonstrated Low Occupational Burnout (consisting of low-*MBI-EE*, low-*MBI-DP*, and high-*MBI-PA*). Then, in an effort to examine differences based on age, two age subgroups were put forward: Young(er) Players LTE45 (n = 19, 36.5%, M_{Age} = 36.8, SD = 5.53, Range 27–44) *versus* Seasoned Musicians GTE55 (n = 14, 26.9%, M_{Age} = 58.5, SD = 3.06, Range 55–64). All other players between these ages were not considered in an effort to nullify overlapping that might confound results. As can be seen in Table 11.12 (right-side column panel), the Seasoned Musicians reported lower *MBI-EE*, higher *MBI-DP*, and higher *MBI-PA* scores compared to the Young(er) Players; but these differences were not statistically significant. These findings indicate levels of Low Burnout.

In an interesting comparison between Orchestra players from the same British Symphony Orchestras—having participated in both the 1994 and this current study—data from the *Orchestra Musicians Survey* (adapted *MBI*) provide a very unique picture about levels of Burnout. To my knowledge, this depiction has never before been seen in the scientific journal literature (neither in the fields of Music

Table 11.11 The Orchestra Musicians Survey

Emotional Exhaustion (EE)

1	I feel emotionally drained from my work with the Orchestra.
2	I feel used up at the end of the day's rehearsal or performance.
3	I feel fatigued when I get up in the morning and have to face another day on the job with the Orchestra.
4	Working with musicians and conductors all day is really a strain for me.
5	I feel burned out from my work with the Orchestra.
6	I feel frustrated by my job with this Orchestra.
7	I feel I'm working too hard on my job.
8	Working with musicians and conductors directly puts too much stress on me.
9	I feel like I am at the end of my rope.

Depersonalization (DP)

1	I feel I treat some musicians, conductors, and Orchestra managers as if they were impersonal objects.
2	I've become more callous towards people since I signed a contract with this Orchestra.
3	I worry that a performance career is hardening me emotionally.
4	I don't really care what happens to some Orchestra members.
5	I feel some Orchestra members blame me for some of their problems and mistakes.

Personal Accomplishment (PA)

1	I can easily understand how other Orchestra members feel about things.
2	I deal very effectively with the problems that may arise during rehearsals and onstage.
3	I feel I'm positively influencing other people's lives through music performances.
4	I feel very energetic.
5	I can easily create a relaxed atmosphere with members of the Orchestra or my section.
6	I feel exhilarated after working closely with members of the Orchestra or my section.
7	I have participated in many worthwhile performances with this Orchestra.
8	During rehearsals or on stage, I deal with emotional problems very calmly.

Source: Brodsky (1995). Adapted from MBI (Maslach & Jackson 1981/1986)

Science nor in the Public Health sector). In the spirit of full transparency I must acknowledge that not all of the same players participated in both studies (which were more than 25 years apart). However, roughly 50% of the participants were in both studies. See Table 11.13. As can be seen in Table 11.13, a subset of players selected from the same two Orchestras who were found to have High Burnout in 1994 (consisting of high-*MBI-EE*, mid-*MBI-DP*, low-*MBI-PA*) demonstrated Low Burnout in the current study 25 years later (consisting of: low-*MBI-EE*, low-*MBI-DP*, high-*MBI-PA*). It can be seen that the differences for the *MBI-EE* and *MBI-DP* subcomponents were statistically significant. These findings could be interpreted as an indication of increased awareness for Mental Health and Well-being promoted among Symphony Orchestras, or improved policies of Orchestra managements over the past 30 years. Namely, compared to yesteryear, both musicians and music-performance managements may have learned more potent coping strategies to efficiently decrease the psychological experience and fallout of Occupational Burnout.

Table 11.12 Orchestra Musicians Survey: Total Sample and Comparisons Between Young(er) Players *Versus* Seasoned Musicians

MBI Component	Total Musicians (N=44)			Young(er) Players LTE45 (n = 19)		Seasoned Musicians GTE55 (n = 14)		Sig
	M	*SD*	Range	*M*	*SD*	*M*	*SD*	*p*
EE	15.0	10.1	2–44	15.1	10.6	14.3	8.07	
DP	4.66	4.26	0–17	4.37	4.02	5.36	4.36	
PA	31.2	7.77	12–47	28.8	8.08	32.9	7.44	

Table 11.13 Twenty-Five+ Years Comparison of Burnout Scores: Professional Contract Players from Two British Orchestras

MBI Component	1993–1994 UK Study (n = 30)		Current Study (n = 27)		Sig				
	M	*SD*	*M*	*SD*	*t*	*df*	*SE*	*p*	*d*[1]
EE	22.86	10.65	15.81	10.92	2.47	55	2.86	0.017	0.65
DP	08.68	06.93	04.30	04.23	2.84	55	1.54	0.006	0.76
PA	26.33	08.31	29.84	08.18				NS	

[1] = Moderate Effect Size for Cohen's *d* (0.3–0.79)

11.5 Conceptual Model of Successful Positive Ageing

Below I present a conceptual model as a framework of *Successful Positive Ageing* among professional full-time contract Symphony Orchestra players. The model incorporates *Selection, Optimization, and Compensation* (SOC) that reflects specific behavioural repertoires. *Lifespan-Longings* (L-L) have been entered, as well as *Life Management of the Occupational Domain* (LMOD), and the *Self-Evaluation of Skills and Abilities* (SESA). A more successful positive ageing should occur with higher scores of *SOC, LMOD*, and *SESA*—and lower scores of *L-L*. Two more emotional-behavioural characteristics that have been entered as components in to the model, are: Affect (*Positive and Negative Affect Schedule*, PANAS) and Burnout (*The Orchestra Survey* [adapted from the *Maslach Burnout Inventory*, MBI]). Theoretically, a more successful positive ageing should occur with higher scores for positive affect (high-*PANAS-PA* with low-*PANAS-NA*)—and lower scores for Burnout (high-*MBI-PA* with low-*MBI-DP* and low-*MBI-EE*). See Figure 11.2.

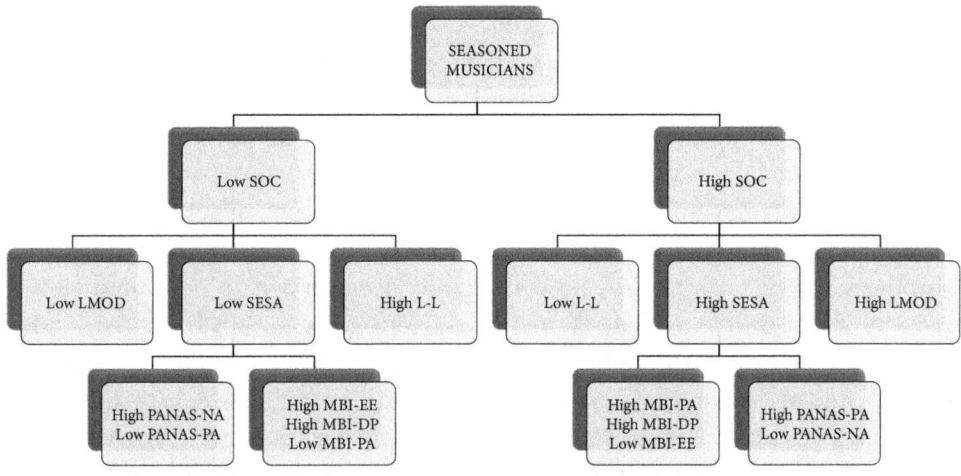

Figure 11.2 Conceptual Interface of Successful Positive Ageing

At the time of this writing, the *Conceptual Interface of Successful Positive Ageing* is solely a theoretical model. Certainly, the size of the current sample is very limited, and statistical power is of great consideration. While some of the components indicate associations for the expected outcomes, others only denote associative trends. For example, positive trends were found for *SOC* with *LMOD* ($r = .29$) and *SOC* with *PANAS-PA* ($r = .17$), while negative trends were found for *SOC* with *L-L* ($r = -.16$) and *SOC* with *PANAS-NA* ($r = -.16$). Further, positive trends were found for *PANAS-PA* with *MBI-PA* ($r = .27$); while negative trends were found for *PANAS-PA* with *MBI-EE* ($r = -.26$), and for *PANAS-NA* with *MBI-PA* ($r = -.21$). However, statistically significant negative correlations did surface for *SOC* with *MBI-EE* ($r = -.31$, $p < 0.05$), and statistically significant positive correlations surfaced between *PANAS-NA* and *MBI-EE* ($r = .38$, $p < 0.05$).

Although the above associative findings do not convey the empirical evidence needed to demonstrate psychometric validity of the proposed model, these initial results are very encouraging from a theoretical conceptual vantage point. It is obvious that additional research with larger samples of professional full-time contract Symphony Orchestra players is required.

11.6 Creative Resilience

Ackerman (2014) points out that with increasing age during adulthood, numerous changes in sensory, perceptual, motor, and intellectual capacities take place. But, few of these seem to occur in a more positive direction. Baltes et al. (1999b) defined development as selective age-related change in an adaptive capacity; whereby different functions in a variety of domains progress without cohesiveness, and trade-offs between gains and losses are more of the rule than an exception. Moreover, the extent and rate of decay of ageing is highly variable per each individual. Hence, factors such as *lifestyle* and *well-being* may contribute to disparities. Most specifically, the degree of engagement in mentally stimulating activities seems to be highly significant. Therefore, one overriding question is: To what extent does variability in ageing reflect processes relating to *Differential Preservation*? The concept of Differential Preservation seeks to explain the degree to which cognitive and motor performance is preserved by some individuals across their lifespan compared with others. As an example, music-making has been shown to be a predictor of variability for cognitive ageing (Hanna-Pladdy & Gajewski, 2012; Hanna-Pladdy & MacKay, 2011; Hanna-Pladdy & Menken, 2020), as well as a positive resource for health and well-being (Gembris, 2013; Perkins & Williamon, 2014). That is, experts seem to have acquired mechanisms which permit the circumvention of specific limitations—especially for tasks and activities that are relevant to their domain of expertise (Krampe, 2002). This is considered maximal adaptation to specific constraints. Evidence from neuropsychological studies show that musical training and lifelong musicianship enhance the maintenance of cognitive abilities. For example, Alain et al. (2014) point out that old(er) musicians aged 45–65 perform better than age-matched controls on a host of measures, including auditory working memory tasks, phonemic fluency, verbal working memory, verbal immediate recall, visuospatial judgement, and motor dexterity. Other evidence indicates that musical training contributes to cognitive reserves that delay age-related declines in non-musical tasks (e.g., Amer et al., 2013; Parbery-Clark et al., 2012, 2013). In general, musical training has been linked to shaping structural brain development (e.g., Hyde et al., 2009), and a host of neuroscience studies point to music engagement as a platform promoting brain plasticity (e.g., Wan & Schlaug, 2010), as well as alleviating age-related declines (e.g., Vromans & Postma-Nilsenova, 2016).

Nonetheless, there is also a possibility that individuals who are more mentally active, are likely to have had higher levels of cognitive functioning throughout their lives—and that such innate differences are preserved across the lifespan. This alternative is termed *Preserved Differentiation*. The concept of Preserved Differentiation seeks to explain current levels of mental activity as determined by a third more stable factor which is evident during one's lifespan (Moussard et al., 2016). Krampe (2002) felt that experts of any age are superior in general cognitive speed and intelligence, as well as for expertise-relevant abilities (such as musical talent and finger dexterity), in a way that their advantages might be attributed to inter-individual differences with long-term stability that already existed prior to acquisition of expertise. In this connection, investigations often target personality characteristics, temperaments, and typologies, as well as participation in leisure activities; in addition there are psychogenic features of developing expertise (e.g., intelligence, higher ability, and talent).

Specifically concerning performing musicians, one factor that has repeatedly been investigated is Deliberate Practice. DP is consistently seen as the criterion for acquiring superior performance level and expertise (see Chapter 2, section 2.2.1.2) rather than viewing masterclass proficiencies as based on innate ability and talent. Nonetheless, other areas of investigation include age of onset (see Chapter 2, section 2.2.1), intelligence, personality, as well as genes (i.e., heritability). One might wonder if such factors not only explain why Orchestra musicians are different than others in the general population (as far as developing aural and motor proficiencies, and performance-related skills), but also shed light on how Symphony Orchestra musicians seem to maintain cognitive abilities that alleviate age-related declines. Psychological resilience may, then, be a variable that allows us to understand why some individuals are able to withstand, and even thrive on, the pressures they experience in their lives. Namely: musical training and lifelong musicianship "protect an individual from the stressors they encounter, and distinguish between those who adapt to the circumstances and those who yield to the demands" (Fletcher & Sarker, 2013, pp. 12–13).

One mental constituent, with subsequent behavioural derivatives, that has repeatedly surfaced as a factor accountable for variances among individuals is *cognitive fluency*. Salthouse (2006) found the Symphony Orchestra profession as one offering the greatest longevity of expertise to its members—and this observation was borne out by comparisons with other groups of experts such as Chess Grandmasters, and with additional occupations including Architects, Athletes, College Professors, Pilots, and Physicians. While this finding may seem quite unexpected, previous research did point to this conclusion roughly two decades earlier (see Chapter 1, section 1.2). Yet most certainly, ageing does ultimately take a significant toll on performance. For example, Ackerman (2014) asserts that no older-aged elite performer can possibly compete against someone who is 20 years younger, and this applies to all fields of performance:

When performance requires speed of intellectual processing, increasing age in adulthood is typically associated with reduced performance, even when the individuals perform the task daily [. . .] there are declines in performance, on average, for such tasks too. Of course, some individuals are more resilient in the face of aging than others—but anyone who believes that at age 90 (when he retired from performing heart surgeries), the pioneering heart surgeon Michael DeBakey had the same steady hands that he had at age 40, is deluding themselves. (p. 9)

Therefore, the observation that old(er) aged Symphony Orchestra musicians maintain elite levels of cognitive and psychomotor performance proficiencies—which are no more than superhuman mental, intellectual, perceptual, mechanical, structural, and spiritual abilities—despite oncoming age-related declines, is even more of a dilemma than meets the eye. Are Symphony Orchestra musicians a select group of individuals who demonstrate an above-average adaptiveness in developing cognitive reserves? Is such overall competence linked to the delay of age-related declines?

Kenny et al. (2018) could not find disadvantages for old(er) Seasoned Musicians above 55 years of age, compared to Young(er) Players between 18 and 30 years old. However, the researchers did note that the older(er) musicians represent a rather smaller cohort in Orchestras, and when considering the decline in their numbers after age 55, they may simply be viewed as those who were better able to manage and sustain longer careers than the others—who have in the meantime retired or deceased. Kenny et al. deduced that, given these circumstances, such individuals are

survivors either by virtue of being resilient both physically and psychologically at the onset of their careers, or by acquiring those skills required to sustain a long musical career as they progressed through their careers. (p. 45)

11.6.1 Dementia and Alzheimer's Disease Among Symphony Orchestra Players

In the year 2000 it was estimated that approximately 4.8 million individuals suffered from Alzheimer's disease (AD) in the USA alone. In 2001, AD was the 7th leading cause of death among older individuals; the prevalence of AD among older individuals was as high as 10%. In 2015, almost two-thirds of those with AD required assistance in personal care. Given the public-health burden and individual consequences of AD, investigators have long sought to identify modifiable risk factors, hoping ultimately to postpone or prevent disease onset. Grant and Brody (2004) projected that by 2050, the number of those afflicted will likely reach 10.5 million (in the USA alone). Wolff et al. (2023) claim that it is estimated that 416 million people fall along the AD continuum, with up to 32 million suffering from the later stages of Dementia. While the beneficial effects of attaining higher education are not completely uniform across research studies, most investigations have found *protective effects* from intensive cognitive activities that enhance reserves or synaptic connections, and these might even be a factor for delaying AD. One mechanism that could account for this protective role based on cognitively stimulating activities involves music training, music performance, and a music performer's lifestyle.

As the incidence of Dementia surges with increasing age, identifying protective factors is critical. For example, many studies (such as Verghese et al., 2003) report associations between reduced Dementia and participation in leisure activities. Indeed, there is increasing interest in identification of modifiable lifestyle factors that may enhance the cognitive vitality of older adults. Further, there is the notion that these may possibly delay the onset of Dementia or Alzheimer's disease (Hanna-Pladdy & Gajewski, 2012; Hanna-Pladdy & MacKay, 2011). Nonetheless, as yet there is no clear account for whether specific activities such as playing a musical instrument afford a significantly cognitively stimulating effect that can account for prevention of age-related cognitive declines. Moreover, it is only an assumption that frequent participation in such cognitively stimulating activities involving music may reduce the risk of Dementia and Alzheimer's disease.

Long ago Halpern (2012) placed such a notion on the mantle (so to speak) as the *challenge* for future research. Hence, Hanna-Pladdy and MacKay (2011) attempted to evaluate how engagement with a musical instrument throughout the lifespan may influence cognitive ageing. That is, they attempted to explore how numerous years of musical activity might predict cognition in advanced age. The researchers evaluated neuropsychological performance in low- *versus* high-activity musicians. They claim that "musical participation is easily quantified in terms of number of years of training or participation, and there is data supporting differential brain organization for amateur musicians" (p. 378). But yet, the sad truth is that even today, after many years of *Music Neuroscience* investigation, little is known about the lifetime effects of musical instrument experience on health, cognition, and ageing. In an early unpublished paper, and based on initial observations, Brody et al. (ND) suggested a lower rate of Dementia among orchestra musicians. They proposed a prospective pilot study examining the direct and indirect effects of playing a musical instrument on health and ageing focusing on cognition. Accordingly, these were based on the cognitive demands and attributes of playing a musical instrument. Brody et al. suggested an association between the frequency of music exposure and the risks for developing Alzheimer's disease. Because playing a musical instrument requires effectively integrating a variety of cognitive demands throughout the lifespan, they proposed that music engagement could effectively develop cognitive reserves, and that those reserves could manifest as protecting against cognitive decline (e.g., Dementias and AD) in later life. Grant and Brody (2003, 2004) pointed at the effects of music exposure (i.e., playing an instrument) as resulting in either larger brains and greater numbers of neurons, or more efficient use of the brain's developed net-works, or better use of alternative pathways—all of which have since been found in neuroanatomical comparisons of musicians and non-musicians. Brody et al. felt these mechanisms would be consistent with what might be seen as a *preventive effect* of playing a musical instrument throughout one's lifespan:

> *Orchestral performance requires near perfection and achieving an extraordinary degree of concentration during practice and performance over many years. Few cognitive activities require concentration over such long periods as that required to play a musical instrument at a professional level. We hypothesize that older musicians will have higher levels of cognitive functioning and will experience less decline over time in cognitive functioning. Musical training also develops these reserves, and higher levels of cognitive reserves will translate into lower rates of cognitive decline (and ultimately Alzheimer's disease risk).* (Author's Note: There are no page numbers in the document for a citation).

In an effort to further their hypothetical theory about the protective outcomes of playing a musical instrument across one's lifecycle, Brody et al. (ND) designed a major research package[2] that detailed the participation of retired professional musicians between 70 and 88 years old—all of whom would have been emeritus members of the International Conference of Symphonic and Orchestral Musicians (ICSOM) or life members of the Chicago Federation of Musicians Union, as well as both amateur musicians and a group of older-aged individuals from a retirement community (as comparison groups). Unfortunately, the proposed study did not materialize.[3]

Verghese et al. (2003) reported a 21-year prospective study in the *New England Journal of Medicine* suggesting that among leisure activities involving either a cognitive component (e.g., board games or cards, crossword puzzles, group discussions, reading books or newspapers, writing for pleasure), or a physical component (e.g., bicycling, bowling, dancing, golf, exercise, housework, swimming, tennis, walking), or playing a musical instrument (for 5 years or more), all seem to delay and/or prevent the onset of Dementia. In their synthesis of the evidence published as a literature review, Stern and Munn (2010) claimed that "participating in mentally stimulating leisure activities was associated with an overall risk reduction of 50%" (p. 15). Nonetheless, in their follow-up study ($N = 2,702$), Verghese et al. found various types of Dementias among 187 (7%) of the same participants, and AD among 61 (2.3%) participants. Most interesting of all was the data that they presented after controlling for Age, Sex, Education, Medical Illnesses, Blessed Information Memory-Concentration Test Score, and participation in other leisure activities. Specifically, when they examined subgroups who played a musical instrument, of the 452 participants who reported to play a musical instrument less than once per week, 120 had developed Dementias. However, among the 17 who reported to play a musical instrument several times per week, only 4 had developed Dementias.

---

[2] This document was prepared as a proposal for research funding to be submitted to the NIH (USA).
[3] The study was perhaps abandoned because Alice G. Brandfonbrenner (1931–2014), one of the principal research team members, became terminally ill.

Accordingly, those who played more 'frequently' had a lower *hazard-risk ratio* of 0.31 (CI 95% = 0.11–0.90) for the incidence of Dementia compared to those who 'rarely' played or did not play a musical instrument at all.

Grant (Grant & Brody, 2003, 2004; Brody et al., ND) clearly points out that playing a musical instrument makes multiple simultaneous cognitive demands. Few cognitive activities involve the same level of continual feedback and exercise on one's working memory as does music performance. Additionally, a musical instrument requires much attention towards perfecting the sound (e.g., involving the development of many techniques as well as one's aesthetic musicality). Moreover, playing a musical instrument requires appreciable proprioceptive input that must be integrated with other aspects of playing—from Sight-Reading to Music Performance. Grant and Brody felt that there is every possibility that music training and music performance protect against the development of Neurodegenerative Diseases that affect the Plaques and Neurofibrillary Tangles of AD, as well as enhance cognitive reserves that might delay clinical expression of Dementia.

There is much evidence for anatomic cerebral differences between musicians and non-musicians. Differences have been noted in reorganization of the Sensory Cortex, larger anterior halves of the Corpus Callosum and Cerebellar volumes, as well as Planum Temporal Asymmetry—all involved in music perception. Investigations have suggested that the musician's brain is a model of *neuroplasticity*, at least in auditory and motor domains. Jancke (2009) points out that musical activity seems to counteract age-related reductions of Grey Matter in those areas that are involved in musical activities. In summary, perhaps the cognitive demands associated with music have protective effects against Dementia, and even if the relationship is viewed as casual (at this point in time when writing the current book), then playing a musical instrument may certainly reduce the risk of developing Dementia at an older age.

Few cognitive activities require concentration over such long periods of time as does playing a musical instrument in a Symphony Orchestra. Therefore, we might ask: Is an *Orchestral Lifestyle*, that initially begins at an early age in childhood and continues throughout later years in Music College, more likely to protect music performers from cognitive decline (and associated diseases such as Dementia and AD) by developing neuronal and cognitive reserve capacities? It is of particular importance to note a research report (Grant & Brody, 2003, 2004) in which N = 23 retired Orchestra musicians were interviewed; the participants were on average 77 years old (SD = 6.8, Range 65–87). Among a host of other issues discussed, these retired musicians contemplated if they have knowledge of any living former colleague from any Orchestra who may be afflicted with Dementia or AD. I want to bring out that as far as I am concerned, one specific finding is highly unsettling! I say that simply because it has been <u>overlooked</u> for more than 2 decades! That is: 20 years ago, Grant and Brody (2004) published the following finding in the journal *Aging Clinical and Experimental Research*:

No participant was aware of a living current former Orchestra member with either reported or suspected Dementia or AD. (p. 404)

This is simply: AMAZING! Not just the finding itself, but that we (the collective 'we' research community) have missed noticing the finding altogether. The researchers claimed that, given the demographics, they would have expected the 23 musicians in their sample to have mentioned between 8 and 9 players with Dementia or AD—whereby at least 4 would have been described as moderately to severely cognitively impaired.

Along these lines, Balbag et al. (2014) considered music's potential role as a non-pharmacological, non-invasive, and protective health modifier against cognitive impairment and Dementia. Although they could not speak about causal mechanisms, they did suggest that the cognitive benefits associated with musical ability may grant old(er) musicians better maintained cognitive reserve, or at the very least provide them with compensatory abilities to mitigate age-related cognitive declines. Balbag et al.'s study looked at 27 pairs of twins, where at least one twin was defined as a musician. In 17 pairs, the musician-twin was cognitively intact; in 6 pairs the musician-twin was Demented or cognitively impaired. Accordingly, this finding confirmed the hypothesis that among those who played a musical instrument in older adulthood, there was a 64% lower likelihood of developing Dementia and a cognitive impairment (e.g., compared to the co-twin who did not play an instrument). In another study by Manzano and Ullen (2018) from the Department of Neuroscience at the Stockholm Karolinska Institutet (Sweden), the researchers examined monozygotic (identical) twins to study expertise-dependent effects on neuroanatomy—using musical training as model behaviour; essentially they controlled for genetic factors and shared environment of upbringing. Manzano and Ullen found that the musically active twins had greater Cortical Thickness in the auditory-motor network of the left hemisphere, and more developed White Matter microstructure in relevant tracts in both hemispheres as well as the Corpus Callosum. Furthermore, the volume of Grey Matter in the left Cerebellar region was greater for the co-twins who played an instrument. All of these findings claim to have provided the first clear support that a significant portion of the differences in brain anatomy between experts and non-experts depends on causal effects of training. The effects of individual musical expertise on brain and cognitive functions can be of great significance with regard to brain ageing. These findings have been interpreted in relation to *reserve capacity*. That is, brain reserve is thought to be related to the structural characteristics of the individual nervous system, and cognitive reserves (CR). CR, or the more efficient configuration of the neural network (Piccirilli et al., 2020), serve as a protective layer for delay of age-related declines or the onset of Dementia and Alzheimer's disease. Nonetheless, while Wolff et al. (2023) indicate that music engagement is a potential proxy for CR, and that across long periods of time music engagement may help to mitigate cognitive decline because performing music involves several forms of activity requiring in-depth training of specialized cognitive functions leading to mastery and expertise, a more serious ecologically valid empirically reliable assessment of the role of music in cognitive reserve—or music-generated cognitive reserve as a proxy to delay or prevent the onset of Dementia or AD—still remains to be seen!

In an effort to present a non-biased treatise, I offer here a study that sheds light on quite the opposite position than the one that has been put forward above. Tuire Kuusi from the Sibelius Academy at the Helsinki University of the Arts (Finland) and colleagues, examined the cause of death among professional musicians in the Classical genre of music in Finland between 1981 and 2016. They accounted for fatalities from Cardiovascular Disease, Cancer, Neurodegenerative Disease, and Alcohol-Related Diseases (Kuusi et al., 2019). All data was obtained from official national Statistics of Finland. Accordingly, the sample consisted of Church musicians (N = 22,368, 80%) as well as Orchestral musicians and other performing artists (5,780, 20%, including Freelance players of Radio & Television Broadcasting, Theatre venues, and the Opera). The musicians were 57% female. While the findings suggest Standard Mortality Rates (SMR) between 0.59 and 0.75 (e.g., indicating a form of protective effect of music on health), the data also indicate that professional musicians were not protected from Neurodegenerative Diseases. Specifically: although there was no difference between Church musicians and the general population, both Orchestra players and Freelance performers demonstrated higher SMRs (1.29) for Neurodegenerative Diseases (such as Dementia) compared to the general population. The research team comment that while their study raises the question whether or not music can really ameliorate Dementia, and hence their data does present a rather different picture than what has been presented in the literature, for certain most other studies about the effects of music training on brain structure and function have targeted young musicians (with an average age of 23 years). Nevertheless, Kuusi et al. also raised limitations in their studies by there being no information in their data regarding music engagement and music activity; perhaps some of those deceased had spent more time Teaching music than actually Performing music.

11.6.1.1 Surveying the Social Circle

The current study, then, attempted to explore the notion that long periods of music engagement may help to mitigate cognitive decline and Neurodegenerative Disease. All players in the sample (N = 52) were asked to recall details of their Social Circle to pinpoint the incidence of Dementia or Alzheimer's disease. Thirteen questions were presented as a survey within the 11-measure 12-page questionnaire booklet (see: Chapter 1, section 1.6.3.3, Table 1.3 [Q10]). The participating players claimed that they were acquainted with roughly 90 full-time practising Orchestra musicians (M = 90.79, SD = 57.86, Range 30–300). These players were roughly 30–50 years old. Out of these, roughly 4 (5%) were considered to be performing on an 'impaired level'; 2 players (M = 1.97, SD = 3.87, Range 0–20) demonstrated significant loss of tone (pitch) accuracy, while 2 players (M = 1.72, SD = 3.99, Range 0–20) demonstrated

significant loss of rhythmic abilities. Yet, all of these players were still performing on an acceptable standard as required by their Orchestra. Further, the players
claimed that they were acquainted with about 30 full-time Orchestra musicians
aged 50–60 years old (M = 29.5, SD = 14.49, Range 5–70). Out of these, roughly
5 (17%) were considered to be performing on an 'impaired level'; 3 players (M =
2.91, SD = 5.03, Range 0–20) demonstrated significant loss of tone (pitch) accuracy,
while 2 players (M = 1.91, SD = 3.98, Range 0–20) demonstrated significant loss of
rhythmic abilities. Yet, even these were still performing nightly, and maintaining the
more acceptable standards required by their Orchestra. Finally, each player claimed
that they were acquainted with roughly 12 professional full-time contract Orchestra musicians who are currently retired aged 65+ years old (M = 11.75, SD = 8.99,
Range 1–50). Out of these, just 1 (8%) player was considered to be functioning on
an 'impaired level' with significant loss of memory (M = 0.18, SD = 0.49, Range 0–2),
or loss of motor control (M = 1.15, SD = 3.21, Range 0–20). Yet, in less than 2% of
the cases—namely, not even 1 retired Orchestra player acquaintance of any participating player—was known to have presently (or had in the past) either Dementia
(M = 0.16, SD = 0.43, Range 0–2) or Alzheimer's disease (M = 0.11, SD = 0.38, Range
0–2). Below is a vignette of a player who claims to have an acquaintance with a few
hundred players in several Symphony Orchestras, many who have retired, but can
think of only 1 former player of her current Orchestra afflicted with a Neurodegenerative Disease. For the sake of comparison, these same Symphony Orchestra players
claimed that they have other contacts with roughly 23 retired people (M = 23.4, SD
=27.31 Range 1–150) aged 65+ years old from outside the music vocation; only 1
or 2 (7%, M = 1.30, SD = 1.71, Range 0–5) were known to have been afflicted with
either Dementia or Alzheimer's disease.

(30y, F, vn)   *I also have an acquaintance with about 100 people that have retired over the years.*
Only one of these has Dementia. He was an Orchestra player. He played Clarinet, and
worked here some years ago. He also has Parkinson's.

11.7 Discussion and Summary

This chapter offers a profile of Seasoned Musicians with an emerging theoretical
conceptual model of successful maturation across the lifespan. The model consists of a behavioural inventory of positive ageing (*Selection, Optimization, and
Compensation*, SOC) including an assessment of regretful sentiment for a Soloist's
career lost (*Life-Longings*, L-L). Further added were feelings of success and reaching one's potential in the occupational domain (*LMOD*), as well as evaluating
job-relevant skills (e.g., motor, aural, inter-musical, and intra-musical abilities,
SESA). Then, mood and emotion (*Positive and Negative Affect Schedule*, POMS),
and satisfaction in the occupational domain (*Orchestra Musicians Survey* adapted
from the *MBI*) were brought forward. All of these were juxtapositioned to form

the 'Conceptual Interface of Successful Positive Ageing Among Orchestra Players' (see Figure 11.2). Finally, the chapter explored *Creative Resilience*—an idea putting forth the possibility that factors within Orchestral Lifestyle, which ultimately account for an overall existence from early childhood based on a regimen of music practice and performance, support Neuroprotective processes that prevent or delay the onset of cognitive impairment such as Dementia and Alzheimer's disease. This then may just help to answer one of the two critical questions raised by the investigation package: *What can Seasoned Musicians tell us about lifelong music engagement?*

SOC as a behavioural inventory of Positive Ageing among Symphony Orchestra players has been viewed by others as an appropriate model for professional musicians. For example, Gembris (2008) suggested the following musical strategies as compensation for age-related declines among music performers.

- Practise more often
- Develop more efficient practice techniques
- Focus more often on more difficult parts
- Engage in shorter durations of practice
- Reduce the number of musical pieces, activities, and engagements
- Decrease musical demands
- Simplify difficult parts and notes
- Play only suitable pieces
- Leave difficult parts to others
- Play more slowly
- Skip fast passages and single tones
- Play from the score instead of memory
- Give up soloist play.

Some of these suggested strategies have also been raised by the current participant players. Nonetheless, it must be said that several of these points do not jive with being a Symphony Orchestra musician.

(55y, M, perc)   *I adapt to my deficiencies. That might well be what has been able to keep me playing as well as I did when I was younger. I think I play better now than when I was younger. I'm more focused and better in technique. But, it does take me a long time for my brain to get the things right. I'll go over it several times. I'll have to slow it right down, and build it up from scratch. So that I know exactly what my right is doing and what my left [is doing]. I can't give anything to chance, otherwise it'll be a disaster. So I always have to write in [notation] which stick I'm using, and the shape. Anything to help me. I would never have done that in the beginning; I would have been too shy to mark up the part. But I've seen other players write in everything. And I thought that's a great idea! If I photocopy it from the library, I can keep a record, have my own part; I can emphasize things, highlight notes, put 'spectacles' [a graphic icon of optical lenses] when things are coming up. But it's not just all experience. For example, I write cues in the part, so I know when X–Y–Z, is coming up. I will write down anything so I don't miss the entry. I didn't do that when I was in my 20s or 30s. I started doing that only in the past 10–15 years.*

I don't think that as you get older you get more fatigued or bored, nor have less satisfaction. I'm even more inspired now than I was. I'm more mature! So I know how to deal with my deficiencies much better than when I was young. You just have to accept that that's the way you are. So, some things I'm good at. Sight-Reading is shockingly bad! I remember my [College] teacher saying: 'Look, you don't need to be a good Sight-Reader to be in an Orchestra. What you need to do is to be prepared!' That's true! I've learned that you only need to be a good Sight-Reader if you're going into the [recording] session game. But, that would be a scary way to make an income. I much prefer being in the Orchestra where you can see what's coming up, and then prepare yourself weeks and months in advance.

In the current study the Orchestra musicians were found to choose *SOC* target behaviours in more than 60% of all items; Optimization as a behavioural strategy was found to be a more frequent behavioural repertoire among Orchestra players not related to age subgroups. The study also found professional Orchestra musicians to demonstrate significantly higher *SOC* scores than the general public in Germany. Employing *SOC* behaviours among professional musicians has been 'somewhat' reported previously. For example, Bennet and Hennekam (2018) conducted multiple case studies ($N = 108$) with professional musicians; unfortunately, only 10 of the participants were Classically trained. Yet, the researchers examined working practices in the early, middle, and late stages of the career. They investigated if *SOC* strategies were used to adapt to changing working conditions, or to maintain their performance. The results showed that in the early-career phase, players considered the performance as the primary criterion for success to optimize their potential. Then, in the mid-career phase they realized that they had underestimated the fierce competition of music performance as a vocation, and hence engaged in Teaching and Administration for financial income. Bennet and Hennekam point out that these changes in evaluating the field of activity, adjusting goals, and subsequently refocusing activity, all reflect the importance of *SOC* behaviours among music performers.

The current study found that *Lifespan-Longings* for Symphony Orchestra musicians was very low. This was to be expected given that musicians who chose a Symphony Orchestra career would have had to successfully resolve the emotional dissonance that comes to the surface when giving up passionate childhood aspirations of being a virtuosi Soloist.

The chapter looked at the players' confidence in their skills and abilities. It is somewhat disconcerting to find that among a sample of professional contract full-time Orchestra players, recruited from five Symphony and Philharmonic Orchestras in three countries, the confidence in their skills was perceived at a 73% level. This level of confidence was similar across both age subgroups with one exception: Seasoned Musicians believed in their capability to interpret and express emotions significantly more than Young(er) Players. Further, the professional Symphony Orchestra musicians rated themselves with higher levels of Positive Affect than Negative Affect, and lower levels of occupational Burnout surfaced.

Therefore, the model that is presented clearly reflects possible components signifying a more successful and positive Ageing (especially for Seasoned Musicians). Hypothetically this concept can only be empirically proven if access was assured to Symphony Orchestra players who left their contract position prematurely (e.g., between ages 40 and 55)—as a comparison control group. The model is comprised of various constituents, including:

- Engaging in specific non-music related behavioural repertoires as adaptive strategies (*SOC*)
- Higher confidence in music skills and abilities (*SESA*)
- Lower emotional dissonance regarding choice of vocation (*L-L*)
- Perceived success in reaching potential in the occupational domain (*LMOD*)
- Feeling higher levels of personal accomplishment, as well as lower levels of depersonalization and emotional exhaustion in the occupational domain (*MBI*)
- Feeling higher levels of positive affect, and lower levels of negative affect (*PANAS*).

Finally, the chapter raised the question: *Is Orchestral Lifestyle, that initially begins at an early age in childhood throughout later years of music college, more likely to protect music performers from cognitive decline and associated Neurodegenerative diseases such as Dementia and AD, by developing neuronal and cognitive reserve capacities?* Anecdotal evidence from the participating players certainly seems to point to this conclusion. All participants claimed that, looking at their social circle (roughly 100 retired Orchestra musicians per player), are not aware of any player afflicted with Dementia or AD—and if so then it would be 'just 1' (i.e., 1 out of 100).

Yet, in this current study I was not able to differentiate between the *music* itself versus the *music performance*, or the *music-performance career* versus *Orchestra Lifestyle*. These are all important distinctions, which together make Orchestra musicians a unique group of professionals. One study that comes to mind here is Laurin et al. (2001). To explore the association between physical activity and the risk of cognitive impairment and Dementia, the research team collected data from $N = 9,008$ randomly selected men and women 65+ years with a cognitively normal baseline—whereby 4,615 (51%) also completed a 5-year follow-up. The results found 3,894 (84% of the follow-up sample) remained without cognitive impairment, 436 (9.5% of the follow-up sample) were diagnosed as having cognitive impairment but no Dementia, and 285 (5.5% of the follow-up sample) were diagnosed as having Dementia. High levels of physical activity were associated with reduced risk of cognitive impairment, Dementia of any type or Alzheimer's disease. That is, they found the protective edge of exercise on cognitive loss persisting throughout a 5-year follow-up period. The research team emphasized that several mechanisms may underlie the potentially protective effects of physical activity on cognitive function. For example, Laurin et al. found that physical activity:

- Sustains Cerebral Blood Flow by decreasing blood pressure
- Lowers Lipid levels
- Inhibits Platelet aggregability
- Enhances Cerebral metabolic demands.

There is also evidence that exercise may provide Aerobic capacity and Cerebral nutrient supply. Yet, Laurin et al. clearly assert that it could be argued that regular physical activity does not per se serve a protective function on cognition and cognitive disorders, but rather it "can be viewed merely as a marker of good health, being itself related to lower risk of cognitive impairment and Dementia" (p. 503), especially as the findings cannot account for other variables (including environmental factors, diet, lifestyle habits) or preclinical states.

In the case of Symphony Orchestra players, given a lifetime engagement in *music* (receptive listening from early childhood), *music performance* (daily practice, music-making as an individual and with other music-performance groups from early childhood throughout adulthood), developing a *music-performance career* (based on learning, beyond 10,000 hours of DP, and hundreds of experiences in performing live onstage), having been offered a contract as an Orchestra member, and partaking in an intense full-time existence (Orchestra Lifestyle), there is no assurance that it is solely the performance 'exercise' component which serves the protective function. Perhaps, we need to look at the full package, which to a certain degree is the total-sum for *resilience* among Symphony Orchestra players.

12
Looking Back from Retirement

12.1 Introduction

What can those who played throughout up to the 5th Decade, and then retired from active service in a Symphony Orchestra, tell us? Many young(er) players have specific concepts about Seasoned Musicians. The terms *old guard* and *dead wood* often surfaced in the narratives of Chapters 3–7 and 10. On the other hand, there is recognition that the old(er) players do emulate constancy and exemplify 'year-old traditions' of music-performance organizations of which they are proud to be a member.

(30y, F, vn)   *There are players here who are over 60 years old and still here. Some over 65. I know some are pensioners [but not all]. I think their playing has gotten worse. They are much more unstable as far as rhythm is concerned. And, they are far less connected to the rest of their Orchestra section. I'm thinking about two specific players. I mean, the only thing is, they are not players who have a reputation of being tremendously sectional [at least] since I've been here. The old guard! They're gonna retire soon anyhow. These [players] are still a product of an old time. Not that I would want them gone. It's just a different age.*

(35y, F, vn)   *In our Orchestra there are a lot of older members in the 2nd Violins, while the 1st Violins are all younger members. So, there is kind of a balance. I am not implying that the older members don't play as well as younger members. There is a hearsay anecdote that as players get older, they sometimes move further to the back; or they move from the 1st Violin section to 2nd Violin section. But not so in our Orchestra. The [players in] 2nd violins have been there for a long time while [those in] 1st Violins have come and gone quicker. The difference is just another way of approaching the music. Although as a musician you have to be as competent to play in each section, technically some of the music in 1st Violins is more difficult; because it is the nature of the part while the nature of the player would be the same. I would say that the older players are more of an asset than a liability. Foremost, there's a sort of stability. And because they offer experience, there is a certain type of pleasure that somehow goes through the whole Orchestra. Moreover, there's a history that goes along with their experience. The Orchestra plays in a certain style because of those players who have been around 40 years ago. The older players make up the core of the performance. But I do suppose the younger players bring on the [bravura].*

This chapter discusses a second interview study, a telephone survey study, with an additional sample of Seasoned Musicians. The participants had retired from one of the Symphony Orchestras taking part in the omnibus sample. The idea of gaining access to a limited focus group of retired Symphony Orchestra players was part of an overall effort to explore the question of Lifelong music engagement. Not many studies about retirement within the music profession can be found in the literature—especially regarding Classical music trained Symphony Orchestra musicians. Perhaps the first was Smith (1988, 1989) who interviewed 14 retired

Seasoned Musicians Playing Beyond the 5th Decade. Warren Brodsky, Oxford University Press. © Oxford University Press (2025). DOI: 10.1093/9780198956501.003.0012

Orchestra members between the ages of 55 and 90 (see Chapter 1, section 1.2). Those musicians had been Orchestra players for an average 41 years, of which the last 35 years were with the Chicago Symphony Orchestra. A second study by Oakland (2014)—sponsored by the Musicians Union (UK)—was an attempt to understand the experiences of Symphony Orchestra musicians as they approached retirement. Oakland interviewed 13 players between the ages of 55 and 66, who all reported their length of service with an Orchestra to be between 25 and 43 years. Oakland found:

a) Career longevity is supported by a more balanced approach. Players needed to develop a comfortable 'fit' with the job. The participants either managed to appropriate the vocation into their personal lives, or altered their perceptions and expectations of being an orchestral player.

b) The musicians viewed themselves as those who had managed a high-profile playing career until retirement. They felt they should have been seen as having a wealth of information for young(er) players, but the lack of hierarchy in the career structure of an Orchestra generated a perception that age and experience are not valued.

c) The players had been highly fixated on the more concrete issues of retirement, and had less insight about how such a change in musical status might have affected them on a more personal level (e.g., the role of music performance in their everyday lives).

For this telephone survey study, the names and the contact information of retired players were provided by the managements of two British Symphony Orchestras. Ten musicians were initially contacted by telephone; subsequently six players (60%) agreed to schedule a telephone conversation interview. This format was employed because many of the participants had no access to transportation to travel to the Rehearsal Halls where the field research with the main sample was being carried out. My overall feeling at the time was that these players were genuinely excited and happy to speak about their ±30-year Symphony Orchestra position as a contract player. Their first reaction was simply astonishment; they were dumbfounded that someone was sincerely interested to hear about their long-term music career. The standard opening statement made was as follows:

Hello. I am looking at how players were able to continue to play past the age of 50; reflecting roughly 25–30 years of a career in the music-performance profession. Compared to some 70 or more years ago, we're living longer, and our careers last longer. The more we study the ageing process, the more we find that unlike other professions demanding physical performance and motor endurance, Orchestra players are performing on the stage at an extremely high level—even past the age of 60. This defies what we know about ageing. We simply don't understand how Orchestra players can outperform other professionals in other vocations to such lengths. The Orchestra management you previously worked with offered me your name and contact number as someone who retired from the band after many years of service. This is a great opportunity for me.

Initially, each player was asked to describe themselves.

(63y, M, db)	*I'm 63, retired at 60. I played Double Bass. I was No. 2 for most of my time, but then Principal for the last 10 years of my employment in the Orchestra. Altogether I was there for 37 years.*
(64y, F, va)	*I am 64, retired at 58. I played [in the Orchestra] for 27 years (but had already played with five other Orchestras before that for 15 years). I started Piano at 9 years old, but moved to Viola at age 13.*
(67y, M, vc)	*I am 67, retired at 60. I played Cello (Tutti) with the Orchestra for 34 years. I started playing at 12 years old. Before that I was a Choirboy.*
(69y, F, va)	*I am 69, retired at 60. I played Viola as a Rank-&-File player with the Orchestra for 23 years. I began Piano at age 7, Violin at age 8, and moved over to Viola at about age 25. I was already a professional from day 1!*
(72y, F, fl/picc)	*I'm 72, retired at 58. I played 2nd Flute (Piccolo and Alto Flute) with the Orchestra for 25 years. I had played in four Orchestras before that. I began playing at 12 years old, but didn't have a Flute teacher till I was 17. At 18 I went to an Academy.*

As previously described (Chapter 1, section 1.6.2), the second sample of $N = 6$ retired musicians consisted of 4 females and 2 males, who were mostly String players. They were on average 67 years old ($SD = 3.39$, Range 63–72), had retired between the ages of 58 and 63 ($M_{Age} = 60$, $SD = 1.9$), and had been employed as a full-time contract Symphony Orchestra player for roughly 31 years ($SD = 6.25$, Range 23–37). These musicians began learning to play music in early childhood ($M_{Age} = 7.3$, $SD = 1.53$, Range 6–9), but had switched to their principal instrument by age 15 ($M_{Age} = 15.6$, $SD = 5.4$, Range 12–25).

In a study with Orchestra players, Sergeant and Himonides (2019) noted that they found 12 male players having served in an Orchestra between 40 and 51 years, and only 1 woman player who had been employed 40 years. They mention that women tended to leave the orchestra earlier than males. Accordingly, such behaviour certainly affects the balance of sex-representation in Orchestras. Even if all appointments to vacant positions were to be equally distributed between the sexes, because of the more extended length of service of males, logistically an Orchestra would always include a greater number of men than women. In addition, the fact that ladies leave earlier also increases the numbers of old(er) male players remaining in the Orchestra for sustained periods. Sergeant and Himonides bring out that career patterns of male and female instrumentalists differ; in general women remain in the Orchestra for approximately 16–20 years, while men remain for approximately 20–25 years. Smith (1988) had observed that Woodwind and Brass players retired earlier than the String players (6th Decade between 50 and 60 years old *versus* 7th Decade between ages 60 and 70, respectively). As regards such longevity, Gembris (2013) astutely pointed out that because of age-related restrictions and health problems that affect work routines, only those musicians who are more resilient to the ill effects of ageing remain in the orchestra until an old(er) age.

12.2 The Interviews

In the interviews, the discussions targeted several topics. Foremost, the Orchestra profession as a vocation of longevity was mentioned. Longevity and maintaining an Orchestra career were examined, and within that context Deliberate Practice was a specific focus. Given the time period in which these players were active performers—a time when male players dominated the profession—one issue that surfaced related to the presence of female players in the Orchestra. When conversations turned to the value of *experience* as a feature among players, Seasoned Musicians were described as players who are 'cherished'. Finally, conversations targeted 'ageing' and 'retirement'. These topics are usually considered *off-limits* for discussion. The interviews closed with each player being asked to recollect the incidence of Dementia and Alzheimer's disease among Orchestra players from their social circle of friends and acquaintances.

12.2.1 The Orchestra Profession as a Vocation of Longevity

At first the players reflected on my opening statement (above), offering their initial thoughts about the Orchestra profession as a vocation allowing longevity of activity. The main point brought up was that an Orchestra is a group of like-minded people. Yet, when the social unit is put aside, truly the non-verbal engagement with music comes to the surface. The Orchestra is not only a functional environment for people who have the skills to partake in active music making, but also furnishes a milieu supporting those who have a principal orientation with the world (both internal and external) through the aural modality (see Chapter 2, section 2.1).

(64y, F, va)   *What kept people going was this tremendous camaraderie among the players. Not necessarily that everybody's friendly with everybody, but people had their own [group]; they would do things together. And I think, when things were economically tough, and we nearly went under, people kept their spirits up collectively. People developed deep strong affections for each other. The Orchestra has a consistency over a period of more than 25 years; at least a quarter of the Orchestra remains at any one time. In many businesses, no sooner has somebody been appointed then they're looking for work somewhere else. The Orchestra is completely opposite! I had one [music-stand] partner who I sat with for 14 years. He used to introduce me to people by saying: 'This is the woman who sees more of me than my wife!' Youngsters who get appointed to the Orchestra may have better skills, but get fatigued much more as they don't have the stamina. So many don't even get through that first [trial] period. I've played almost every day for 45 years.*

(67y, M, vc)   *The secret in growing old in the Orchestra is adapting. It has to do with changing along with different Conductors, different repertoires, and staying enthusiastic. I think the biggest problem of Orchestral players is becoming disillusioned. If it becomes a habit, you lose the enthusiasm; you can only do it if you find the inspiration as the passion of music that keeps you young at heart. I would say that there's something about Orchestral life and the Lifestyle that keeps Orchestral players young. I liked travelling, and my Orchestra travelled a lot. But I do think it was a physically wearing life. Orchestral players are under pressure just as much after 30 years as they are after 1 (that first) year. I think that wears people down; many Orchestral players don't survive.*

(69y, F, vc)   *I agree with the statement that there's something about Orchestra life that allows musicians to go on until a very late age, when in many other professions you just can't. In other jobs you wouldn't have so many like-minded friends. That's the basic thing; it's one big community. People are doing the same as you, and thinking the same as you. Maybe the intensity of Orchestra life is one of the reasons that many players develop relationships and marry other players. I didn't marry anybody; I was married to my Cello. Thirty-seven years in the same job. But [everyday] different music, Conductors, and venues. My impression is that these days there's less commitment to the Orchestra than in my day. [Today] it's more of a job rather than a family affair. I get the impression that players move about more. If they got a job with the Orchestra, they'd say it's a good place to move on from.*

(72y, F, fl/picc)   *Well, an Orchestra is a social unit. In a way it has nothing to do with music; you tour and you go around with people. The Orchestra is rather incestuous. But I don't know if there are as many liaisons as people like to make out of it! Yet, in the early days when we were on tour, there was always noise in the corridors, doors slamming, and all the rest of it. It was all a party! But, it's now much more serious. We used to drink at lunchtime. But not anymore! I think all of that took a toll on us as we were getting older—the bed-hopping and drinking! By the time I got married that wasn't a part of my particular life. My husband was a Schoolmaster at a regular school; that was very different as most of the players married other players. After I got married, I had kids and left for 6 years. It was quite difficult coming back after that big gap. By then my kids were probably about 4 and 6. I had not practised all that time. I had to work very hard to get my music-performance level back up to par to get accepted again to my position.*

12.2.2   Longevity and Maintaining an Orchestra Career

The players considered the performance skills they had maintained during their more than 30-year career. Some spoke about mental abilities (e.g., concentration and attention), others spoke about motor skills (e.g., hand positioning, finger agility, and Bowing), and still others spoke about the sound quality produced on their instrument (e.g., expression and articulation). Players expressed the notion that they feel there was relatively no decline over the years—not even on their final day in the Orchestra—the day they retired! Nonetheless, one did admit to have succumbed to performance nerves with physical symptoms. Finally, several talked about emotional constitutions (e.g., resilience), mood (e.g., involvement and inspiration), as well as passion for music and music performance.

(63y, M, db)   *I know I am not very good at mental abilities. Yet, I think I became better than when I was 30 [years old]. I certainly remember thinking at the time [when I was younger] that my mind is all over the shops. While I couldn't remember somebody's name, I could remember the music and the notation of every piece that came up. But in this Orchestra, we were getting new pieces all the time. So, there was no question of remembering because we read! When I started in the Orchestra about 30 years old I wasn't aware of musical grammar (i.e., conventions of how things should be notated). My speed and motor skills (accuracy to play the notes) improved. My biggest problem has always been in coordination; that's what limits how fast I can play—it's not how fast I move my fingers. I think that's something that improves with age. Yet there may be a time when it starts to fall off. There is a certain element of not getting excited any more about the music. But that is minimized in an Orchestra by the wide range of repertoire. As far as chronic illness of ageing goes, an awful lot of us have had aches and pains over the years. A lot of people in every Orchestra have been off sick with muscular skeleton problems. We sort of go along to the doctor, and expect the doctor to put us right. But, that's 'crap' because doctors don't know what to do about it. Some people were natural child prodigies; but, then when tensions start to creep in, they just didn't know what to do about it.*

(64y, F, va) *I found that I knew exactly where the really tricky things were, and I could cope with the difficult passages. While some people would complain that the rehearsals were boring, I used to attempt to mentally work on my own playing [during rehearsals]: my Bow-arm, the precision of my fingers, the way I was using finger shapes [e.g., hand positions]. But I found that just keeping my motor skills fit on the instrument became progressively more difficult. About age 40 I felt my fingers were stiff; I began having a little bit of Arthritis. It was more difficult to achieve the speed that I used to be able to play. I felt I had to work harder to just maintain what I had had. I said to people: It's like swimming against the stream, against the current. You can just swim, and swim, and if you're lucky you stay in one place and don't go backwards. Many people didn't keep up their skills; eventually they were asked to leave. At first they were criticized, and in some cases they were given a warning. At one time we had a system where somebody might be given a warning, and were told they had to take lessons to improve and regain the standard that they had. My husband was a Principal [Woodwind player] for 31 years; he had survived a lot of criticism to maintain all that. So, some players will have the resilience to survive the criticism. Some survive and some don't! There was one woman who took lessons; she reauditioned twice, and she survived. She only recently retired! Nonetheless, there was a Horn player who started to shake so much from nerves that every time he lifted the Horn to his face he couldn't play. And other people who've had disorders just broke down by the comments that they were getting.*

Feeling involved and inspired depended a lot on the Principal Conductor and the general mood of the Orchestra. When we were working for a Conductor who was very strongly disliked, it was much harder to keep attention going. If you had a foreign Conductor who was trying to conduct local English music, you'd think he didn't even know how this piece goes. He'd be trying to force the Orchestra to play in a way that you say [to yourself]: Damn it, we've been playing this piece since the Composer wrote it. I was very, very involved with the work; I felt that I was a totally committed musician. But, under those conditions, I was emotionally withdrawn. Yet at the same time, I would attempt to be professional and play my absolute best. I did have a bad patch for few years where I didn't enjoy it. Partly [because of] the Conductor, and partly because I'd began to feel I was not appreciated—especially after being demoted. At that point, I thought I'm either going to sit here getting bitter and resentful, or I need to start a new focus on something else. As a result, I began studying a new non-music skill that proved to completely take over when I retired.

(67y, M, vc) *I did not feel that it was becoming more difficult to concentrate or pay attention until the last year. I am very fit and healthy for my age. I personally wasn't aware that I was slowing down, and couldn't control my hands anymore. There was no difference of coordination, and my motor skills were fine. [During my career] I was less inclined to move around [to other Orchestras] because this was my home town. I do feel that as I got older I was less inspired in the rehearsals (unless there was an outstanding Conductor, or if it was a great piece of music). But concerts were different. I mean: You know damn well that if your present Principal Conductor doesn't feel you're pulling your weight, you might get pushed towards the door. So, you have this paranoia throughout your years in the Orchestra—even if you've been there 30 years or more!*

(69y, F, va) *I always wanted to be in an Orchestra. But, I didn't join till I was 38 [years old]. Before that I taught General Music in two schools. After I was married, I freelanced for 5 years as a Viola player and taught instrument lessons. All the time I was playing Chamber Music, and was in an amateur Orchestra. I didn't go to [Music] College; so nobody in the music world knew me. I did an audition for the Orchestra but didn't get in. Then, I was offered some extra work with them. That helped me a lot. And about 2–3 years later, I applied again; that's when I got in. When I joined the Orchestra, I just loved it! So, how did I keep going? Well, you practise! We would assume that motor skills begin to slow down at a certain age. Don't forget I went to [age] 60, and I was still playing on spot! But I did notice towards the end that my brain and my fingers didn't necessarily coordinate the way they had done before. That happened in fast passages. I would take [the score] home and practise it. Then when I got into the Orchestra I found I lost a lot of it. That worried me, and I'd get a block there! You see these black notes coming. That's when the 'rot' sets in. You have to pretend. You have to keep on going. You can't stop! Actually, I didn't stop making sounds during those passages. I probably got two to three notes per passage. I always tried to play it. So, I was happy to retire. I'd enjoyed it. I felt so privileged to have played in the Orchestra. But I was relieved in the end. Worried that eventually somebody would catch on, and it would be an embarrassment. Had I been a Solo Wind player, I would have been forced to retire even earlier. But as a Rank-&-File String player I could hide behind a massive sound to a certain extent!*

One also needs stamina; lots of energy to just go on and on and on. Particularly, when you're on tour it's quite physically demanding. By the time you're there for 10 years you feel very competent. But, because I came late to the profession, I always felt I had a lot of catching up to do. My ability to Sight-Read remained intact even towards the end. I was able to hear the notes from the page; you have to do that. If I look at a piece of music, I can hear it.[1] I still felt just as inspired, just as excited, and just as motivated when I got older. I didn't become more intolerant of Conductors, but I was 'cheesed off' with people in the Orchestra when they moaned about things. And it got worse as I aged. Those kinds of players were always giving off negative vibrations. And I became more intolerant of them.

I was playing at a time period when there were various behaviours which were acceptable—that nowadays are not. Such as: drinking, boozing, bed-hopping, and things like that. There were stories in the daily tabloids which claimed these behaviours were essentially coping mechanisms for the pressures of stage performances. Though looking back, I would say that they were all just social behaviours. My assumption would be that all Orchestras did the same kind of things. Even trashing hotel rooms! We didn't do too much of that! Still, there were UK Orchestras who were banned from certain hotels. But, I can definitely say that various other types of behaviour did go on— like couple-swapping. Well, actually, I had an affair with somebody in the Orchestra, and when we were on tour we stayed together. It wasn't really partner (wife-) swapping. I mean my marriage went pear-shaped, and I just fell in love. He was also in the Orchestra. We were together all the time when we were at work. That made work even more exciting! But, having said that, it's hard being on tour. On average, we did three tours a year, each for roughly 5–14 days. There were also many overnighters. Drinking after a concert was a terrific release. You've done something together as a team, and while it may have been very enjoyable, it was also very stressful. So, as a group you go to a pub after a concert. You're keyed up, and then you have this release, and it's a very nice way of winding down together.

During my 23 years in the Orchestra, especially in my older years, I took care of the physical strains of music performance with Alexander lessons. That was very helpful with my shoulder, the muscles of my neck, and everything else. I don't remember having any mental strains or stress problems. But, I was very ill when I was 48 years old; I was off for maybe 4 months. Also, I probably began to wear glasses sooner than I might have done had I not had to read music all the time. Finally, sitting in front of Trumpets and Trombones hurt my ears; apparently I've lost more hearing [% of threshold] compared to others [of my age group] because of [a Noise-Induced Hearing Loss].

(69y, F, vc)   *I did it, I loved it, there was no problem! Some say that as one gets older they become a little bit more forgetful. They have difficulties with attention and focus. One would think that as we get older, our abilities to continue and control those finely developed motor skills don't go on that long. I can tell you I didn't feel a scrap from when I joined the Orchestra. Not a scrap! As I was getting older I didn't feel less inspired or less emotionally involved. Some Conductors were less inspiring than others, but I didn't become disillusioned or cynical. The more experience you have, the more you can detect which Conductors don't really know what they're doing. But, being a professional, I would still pay attention. Touring was one of the best things; that did not become more difficult as I aged.*

---

[1] Most players intuitively feel they can 'hear' the music. This is referred to as *Notational Audiation*. But actual empirical evidence shows that such skills can only be demonstrated among 30% of expert Orchestra musicians. The findings indicate that players actually do not *hear* anything at all, but rather, the phenomenon is linked to *subvocal phonological* activity (Brodsky et al., 1999, 2003, 2008).

12.2.3 Deliberate Practice (DP)

Each of the six retired players claimed that DP was the primary factor responsible for the maintenance of their skill set. Practice was accountable for how and why they were able to have such a long career (±30 years). All claimed to have practised several hours every day every week. Practice regimens were usually based on the specific repertoire programme of each week. All the players practised outside Orchestra rehearsal time; for the most part they practised at home in the after hours.

(63y, M, db)   *I did practise most days when I was at the Orchestra across my 34-year career, and I still usually do now. We didn't start till 10 o'clock in the morning. I usually aimed to finish breakfast by 8:30, and do a bit of warming up till about 9:15; to tried to keep my hand all the way up till my last year. I don't really consider myself to be retired. I mean, I may have retired from the Orchestra, but I'm working as a Freelancer with different Orchestras at the moment.*

(64y, F, va)   *I was able to keep my skills up to the age of 58 because I practised—up until the second-to-last day at work. [Laughs.] I practised an average of 4 hours a week (considering how hard we worked in the Orchestra). When I was in the Opera, a lot of times we only worked in the evening; back then when I was young I might have done 5 hours' practice during the day before I went to play. I mean some people thought it was enough to play in the Orchestra. Especially women, who were very busy with their families. They would say: 'Oh, it's good practice coming to work!' I used to feel that my playing deteriorated if I didn't do my own practice outside of the Orchestra on a regular basis.*

(67y, M, vc)   *I believe that as long as you keep your playing up and keep practising, then you can make it through. I did practise away from the Orchestra on a regular basis. So, I do feel that that's more or less the key. I feel I was able to continue to play [in my 60s] the same as when I was in my 30s.*

(69y, F, va)   *My practising varied according to the music; but in general, it was 2 hours a week. Doesn't sound much, but I practised 2 hours a week—all the time throughout my [23-year] career up until when I retired at [age] 60. We're not talking about rehearsal with the Orchestra, but what's called Deliberate Practice at home.*

(69y, F, vc)   *I sometimes practised outside Orchestra rehearsals, but not every day. I have no idea how many hours. When I had to, and when I could. It varied as there was no set schedule. If I had a piece that needed attention, then I had to get stuck into it and make the time. I would say that the secret is extra practice outside of rehearsal. But the trouble is, when you play in an Orchestra, it's a pretty full-time job!*

(72y, F, fl/picc)   *The fact that some Conductors want a piece performed in a different way, they might be rehearsing other people [sections] all the time. You have to sit there not really doing much while other people are rehearsing. I found my position different than a lot of my String player friends [who] complained at the end of the rehearsal; they were exhausted! But if I am to keep my fingers working, I've got to practise. I did lots of practice, and I found it very hard. I kept on doing it in my house every day! I did sound-blowing and just getting my lip going before I came. It would be hours every day just to keep the fingers going.*

12.2.4 Gender in the Orchestra

The four retired female players all recalled a time period when women were kept out of Orchestras. There was a time when Orchestras were more often seen as a *men's club*. The retired players spoke of changing times; nowadays the proportion of women to men is evenly split (50%–50%). Today, women players often get married, have children, receive maternity leave, and return to the same Orchestra, to the same position as they had before giving birth. Having said that, some did infer that being able to return to the acceptable standard of performance, after giving birth and being at home with a baby for some time, was extremely difficult (see Chapter 4, section 4.1; Chapter 5, section 5.2). The process of having to prepare to reaudition in front of a jury panel of players required much DP, which unfortunately could not always be fulfilled while caring for children younger than 4 years old.

One issue raised that is not often spoken about in an open manner, is relationships among Orchestra players (albeit, see Chapter 5, section 5.2.4.1). The players spoke about characteristic differences between the sexes concerning such affairs. For example, the women players tended to have relationships with other musicians *within* the Orchestra, while the men players more often sought relationships with other musicians *outside* the Orchestra. Many men players also sought partners from outside the music-performance vocation. One of the retired players mentioned that while being married to someone in the Orchestra was quite an advantage as far as many aspects of the relationship are concerned. It was also clear that should the marriage go sour, then one of the partners would have to leave their job in the specific Orchestra of which they are both active members on the permanent roster of players and relocate elsewhere in another Orchestra.

(64y, F, va)   *I would say that about 90% of women players did marry other Orchestra musicians, whereas the men players tended to also find partners among the non-musician community. I think it's only a male musician who would tolerate a woman being out; not being at home, not in there to cook the meals, and so on. As it was, we worked together, so we operated as a team. Having said that, I didn't get married till I was nearly 40 [years old]. It was very entertaining [laughs] when we went on tour together. Yes, we felt we were extremely fortunate from that point of view. Certainly, we were able to keep an eye on each other; we had both been in relationships [with Orchestra players] before we were married. And put it this way: if you are married and you work together, and you do everything together, then you have to make it work on all fronts. If it's not gonna work, then one of you will have to leave the Orchestra. But, I would say, it's 100% from my point of view; but [laughingly] maybe my husband might say something different! We went into it with our eyes open. His parents had a business together, they worked and lived together; he was used to that kind of attitude.*

(69y, F, va)   *When I joined in 1978 it was already much more acceptable for women to play in the String section. Maybe it was more acceptable for women to be in this Orchestra back then. But, it was still a problem with some other Orchestras who were quite slow to accept women players.*

(69y, F, vc)   *I keep saying 'ladies', but that doesn't mean I had no social ties with the men players. But the men couldn't come into the Ladies' Changing Room. Today, the Orchestra is more or less 50–50, but when I joined the Orchestra, female players were very far and few between. Partly it was because when you got married you pretty much automatically left. Certainly, in those days if you had a family you left. I don't remember anyone in the Orchestra having children—which is what's happening nowadays. They're off for maternity, and then come back if they want to. But I don't remember anyone doing that in the 60s. It was sort of a Men's Club. But yet this [specific] Orchestra was never like that. They'd welcome anybody, and everybody, who could play well enough. When I joined there were a lot of older ladies who'd been in since before the war time [World War II].*

(72y, F, fl/picc)   *I must admit I never had difficulty being a female in the Orchestra back in those days. Because in my earliest days in the Orchestra there were one to two females who had infiltrated the Wind section; most of the females were in the String section. As it happens, when I got the job at the Orchestra I wasn't the one token female; there was even a married couple playing in the section. So, I wasn't on my own at all. Eventually there was one, two, and then three female Wind players. Now it's about 50–50. I think that for a long time many Orchestras just had a policy to refuse to admit women. But then when they let one in, the policy couldn't stay. Certainly, in my time that it all changed!*

12.2.5 The Value of 'Experience' as a Feature Among Players

The six retired players were quite adamant that long years of experience are a most valued feature for any Orchestra musician. Specifically, that Seasoned Musicians are an asset because of their vast years of experience—well beyond what any young(er) more technically proficient player could offer. Accordingly, experience can actually counterbalance the lack of instrumental prowess of an old(er) player. An interesting point made below is that perhaps the Orchestra vocation is one of the only professions in which age, job experience (duration and seniority), and tenure (terms of a permanent contract) are not reflected in the hierarchical levels of work (e.g., chain of command).

(67y, M, vc)   It is true that usually one would think of people who are 63 as being a little bit forgetful, perhaps even getting a bit slower. But if that were the case, older Orchestra players would be counterbalanced by the extra experience they might have. Where a youngster might wonder what the hell to do if a pianist got lost, you'd know to listen carefully and jump about to catch them. So, experience counterbalances lack of youth. Now I did mention that in most other professions, years of experience are reflected in your rank in the organization. But the Orchestra doesn't necessarily reflect that at all. You can have a young kid who's been around for only 5 years as your Principal. So, age and experience are not reflected in the workings of the organization. The Orchestra may not be the only organization that works like that—but certainly it is among a minority of vocations that do work like that. So actually, age makes no difference in the Orchestra. Many of the younger players do respect the older players because of their experience. Yet, some also look at them as being 'dead wood'—and of course some of them are dead wood! Ultimately the only thing that makes a difference in the Orchestra is: skill. So you could have a younger player in a more advanced position, and an older player in the back—or vice versa. You would assume that everybody has some respect for each other because of skill and not because of age (or experience).

Orchestral life has changed over the years. For the most part the changes have been for the better. But, from my perspective, some changes are not for the better. For example, drinking as a norm is frowned upon now. I feel that my first 10 years of experience in the Orchestra invoked much more of a feeling of camaraderie as a family and a team. My experience of the last 10 years [with] the Orchestra is that it became a lot more competitive. It was once that each player complemented the other; where one has a weakness the other one has a strength. You were there to help each other! Today, a lot of the younger players see the faults and limitations and criticize other players. So, [in my opinion] the drinking made it more friendly and sociable. When the drinking was cut out, to some degree that also changed some social behaviours as well—especially when on tour! There was a period of time that when on tour Orchestra players behaved in ways that weren't acceptable (e.g., trashing up hotels). But generally, the lads behaved well.

    I have said that in my first 20 years in the Orchestra there were more players that had been there for a long period. It was more stable then. Now, there's a lot more turnover in the last 20 years [of my career]). Some feel that is because the music has become harder, and the skills required are on a higher level. But I don't think that that was the case! The greater movement is because more people are prepared to move; they have more ambition so they move to different Orchestras to get more senior posts.

(69y, F, va)   *I think the older players are more an asset than a liability. They bring experience to the Orchestra. Experience means that they've sat in an Orchestra for many years. They're good to begin with. So, they know a lot of music—especially the standard repertoire. We always had new music thrown at us which we had to learn very quickly. Hence, it's not just having had experience and knowing the music, but it's a question of knowing how to deal with music, and how to deal with the practice and preparation of music.*

(72y, F, fl/picc)   *It's quite true that older musicians are valued in lots of ways, because they have the experience. If you sit in an Orchestra where there's an awful lot of repertoire, some of the things you'd play a load of times. And when you're young and learning all the pieces, you have to learn what to listen for and what to do. But a lot of the young people get bored. They just came out of College, and absolutely have no problem in playing all the notes. But yet they haven't a clue about sitting day after day after day in an Orchestra. They can't adapt to a Conductor who wants to do it in a different way that was rehearsed [previously] the day before.*

12.2.6 Seasoned Players

The vignettes illustrate the notion that the Seasoned Musicians bring much more to the Orchestra than simply having had previous experience with the repertoire. Rather, Seasoned Musicians have a more mature attitude and musicality of music performance than Young(er) Players. The old(er) Seasoned Musicians know how to *fit in* with the collective sound more effectively. This has long ago been referred to as *Orchestral Timbres* (Pressnitzer et al., 1996). On the other hand, two out of six players pointed out that a 30-year-old player would not in their opinion be considered a *young* player. Namely, that any 10-year period of music-performance experience within an Orchestra will offset differences in familiarity and performance capabilities between the players that might be hypothetically conceptualized by researchers (like me!) to be related to age(ing).

    I point out that for the purposes of empirical investigation, many researchers have defined age categories contrarily. On the one hand, age subgroups simply serve as a means to split the sample for statistical data analyses; these somewhat depend on sample size and the range of ages among the participants recruited. On the other hand, the sample size and the range of ages among the participants have everything to do with the inclusion criterion used for recruits to enter the sample. For example, Zendel and Alain (2012, 2013) defined musicians as: "having advanced musical training (e.g., university degree, Royal Conservatory Grade 8, College diploma, or equivalent), and continued practice on a regular basis until the day of testing" (p. 505). Yet, we might consider that there are differences in advanced music training in Musicology and Music Education (e.g., a college diploma or university degree) *versus* a Music Conservatory and Academy of Music *versus* an 'equivalent'. In addition, what would it mean to practise on a regular basis when considering someone who is in their late 70s or early 80s? Zendel and Alain classified age subgroups as follows: young(er) musicians were between 23 and 33 years old (*M* = 28) while old(er) musicians were those between 61 and 84 years old (*M* = 69). Perhaps had they recruited only currently working professional musicians, then such classifications might have been altered. A second example is Parbery et al. (2012) who defined young(er) musicians as those between 18 and 32 years old while old(er) musicians were those between 45 and 65 years old.

(67y, M, vc)   *What do the younger players have that the more experienced seasoned players don't? Well, they are obviously physically stronger. And, while they should be more aware of the fact that they're lucky to be in an Orchestra, that isn't always the case! We [the older players] do take it for granted after a while. That is the danger when you've been in one place for so long! I mean I don't want to sound like a bitter old man, but when I joined the Orchestra, for the first 6 months I didn't dare open my mouth. I was honoured and delighted to be in the Orchestra. I kept my mouth shut and my eyes open to see what was going on. But, as time progressed, it came to be less and less the norm. A lot of youngsters come and join in the Orchestra now, with an attitude: 'The Orchestra is lucky to have me in it!'*

(69y, F, vc)   *I think technique was stressed less in my days than it is today. Young players now are technically brilliant. But not so musical! The more seasoned players would be more musical because experience offers you not just the knowledge of a repertoire, but various other fashions how to play or express it. If you are a younger player of 30 [years old] you haven't had life experience either. I didn't grow up until I was [age] 50. I mean I really didn't start to live until I was 50; the same thing goes for my musical life. My feeling is that Seasoned Musicians, the players who are 55 and above, are more of an asset than a liability.*

(69y, F, va)   *If I focus on what kind of musical elements or characteristics older players bring to the Orchestra, I'd have to say it's just an overall plus. If we were all just playing Solos, you might not notice any difference. Maybe [a younger versus older player] would sound different, but they'd be exactly as competent. Then again, I'd say that in an Orchestral setting, players have to fit into a section. Fit the intonation and know how to blend. The more experience you have, the easier it is to fit into a section. I mean as a Soloist, the younger player might be able to whizz around the instrument more because they've just come from College; they've spent the last 3-5 years practising. But, perhaps after 10 years in the Orchestra (at age 30) all other aspects would even out. What I'm saying is that a player who is 30, which some might consider to be a young professional, as far as the Orchestra's concerned, that's not young at all! Ten years' experience is really enough for them to be a competent Orchestra player. So, in my mind, the conception of age 30 being 'young' is incorrect. I mean that's young in 'people years'. But if they already have 10 years' experience, then, that's not young in 'Orchestra years'. Once you've done all the pyrotechnics, you then have to learn your trade of sitting in an Orchestra. Certainly, a lot of people won't know much repertoire when they come to an Orchestra. I don't necessarily believe the myth that a younger player has more technical abilities, while an older player has more musical abilities.*

12.2.7 Retirement

Manturzewska (1990, 2006) presents findings showing that musicians are rather late in retiring:

Most of them began retirement after 70, some continuing professional activity till a very late age. There have been personas in our sample continuing their jobs after 90 years of age. (p. 37)

Yet, most of the musicians in the Manturzewska study were not professional Symphony Orchestra players. I reiterate that the players in the current telephone interview study retired between the ages of 58 and 63 ($M_{Age} = 60$, $SD = 1.9$), and had been employed as a full-time contract Symphony Orchestra player for roughly 31 years ($SD = 6.25$, Range 23–37). Each player presented their own perception of retiring from the Orchestra. Some felt it was just time to retire; they had been a loyal member of a music-performance team. But now there were other things they wanted to do while they were still fit to do so! Others noted that their playing had declined to a point whereby they felt it was time to end a performance career before they embarrassed themselves in public.

(63y, M, db)   *The Orchestra always used to chuck you out when you were 60. That's when the pension kicks in. So, I took the money and ran. I thought I wanted to get out and do something else while I still felt I was young enough to do so. I wanted to do Period Instrument work [referred to as 'Early Music' generally comprising Medieval music between 500 and 1400, Renaissance music between 1400 and 1600, and Baroque music between 1600 and 1750]. I've been interested in that for about 30 years. I'm now doing a certain amount of work. Quite a lot of opera—which is the other thing I wanted to do. So, I didn't leave the performance side, but just changed the type of work I do.*

(69y, F, va)   *I was a Rank-&-File player for 23 years in the Orchestra. I retired when I was [age] 60 as that was mandatory. My brain and fingers stopped being able to coordinate. Maybe that happens with most players. Or maybe it is something that happens to some players. Actually, I never talked about it before, because when you're in an Orchestra you don't admit that there are things you can't do. It is kind of funny that everybody knows, but nobody talks about it! I was aware of those around me playing every single note in very fast passages, while myself I was not playing as well. I probably looked fine from a distance, but I was aware that I wasn't playing as well as I should have been. I had that feeling for about 18 months to 2 years before I retired. It's very difficult to pinpoint because I don't really know when it started.*

(69y, F, vc)   *I was quite proud to be in the Orchestra. When I was 61 [years old], the official age for retirement was 64. But actually I wanted to leave early because playing was becoming quite a problem. Not mentally, not finger-related, but my legs were really objecting to it. It was just a physical thing in my legs that after 37 years I didn't feel that I had to go on until the absolute bitter end. I could have stayed longer from the point of view of skills. It's just sitting and playing was less than comfortable for me.*

(72y, F, fl/picc) *I retired about [age] 58. By the time I left, they had wanted me to go. I think things were getting on top of me. Yet, it was upsetting that they asked me to go. Looking back, they were quite right. But it's always a blow because you think you're doing a reasonably good job.*

12.2.8 Ageing as a Topic of Discussion

In the early 1990s I had noticed many themes of conversation were simply *taboo* with Orchestra players (Brodsky, 1995). Some topics and issues were *off-limits* for research-related discussions—even with an external person. For example, at that time Music Performance Anxiety (referred to as 'Stage Fright') was a dominant research theme acknowledged as a topic that is 'not to be mentioned openly'. There was fear among the musicians that perhaps a player could lose their position as a result of 'opening up' in an interview. The message conveyed was that players should 'suffer in silence'. British citizens refer to this behaviour as *keeping a stiff upper lip*; not expressing feelings when upset. Great performers of the not-so-distant past—such as Vladimir Horowitz (1903–1989), Constantin Lipatti (1917–1950), Gina Bachauer (1913–1976), Claudio Arrau (1903–1991), and Arturo Benedetti Michelangeli (1920–1995)—were always seen as strong, invincible, fearless, and charming heroes whose eccentricities were not only accepted and emphasized, but often invented as a publicity device. These masters of yesteryear could not have admitted to hand pains, physical injuries, Music Performance Anxieties (Stage Fright), or mental breakdowns. At best, they could announce early retirement, go to a sanatorium, or leave for the country. Such an attitude was then (and is perhaps even today) still looked upon by many to be a positive attribute especially in remaining resolute and unemotional when faced with adversity. Having said that, some more modern players understood how much help they could get in return for 'opening up'. For example, the public had witnessed the likes of Leon Fleisher (1928–2020) and Gary Graffman (b. 1928) who exposed their painful career-wrecking hand injuries and revealed the treatments they underwent, or André Watts (1946–2023) who exposed his paralysing Performance Anxiety and described the therapeutic interventions he employed to conquer it. But, while it may seem acceptable for musicians to appear more *human*—and that means that music performers are revealed to the public as being less *superhuman* and therefore slightly more imperfect in the process of achieving the extraordinary, the effects of such a new depiction of the performing musician-artist may not be considered so positive in the eyes of professional musicians.

There is no evidence that *ageing* should be seen as a topic that is taboo to discuss openly. Every human matures throughout their lifetime. Each one of us can (and does) see tasks that were once easier to accomplish at a young(er) age than now years later. The current study specifically placed much focus on 'positive resilience' and 'preservation of expertise' sustained across a lifetime of music development—rather than targeting declines and inabilities of music performance. Having said that, not all players were open to the notion of discussing the effects of ageing on music performance.

(69y, F, vc)   *Why do I think players in the Orchestra do not [wish] to speak about ageing? Why is it such a taboo subject? Maybe there's a perception that you become less good as a player as you get older. And if you do, then others might think it's time for you to leave. I presume that about 70% of the players prefer not even to speak about it.*

(72y, F, fl/picc)   *You know Richard really thought of writing his book on this subject: ageing. But he is very clear-headed, and he reckoned that he would have to interview his own colleagues in his own Orchestra. And although he did do that for his book, he did not [dare] to speak to them on the subject of ageing. [See R. Davis, 'On Becoming An Orchestra Musician', de la Mare Pubishers, 2004.] He always said nobody would want to open themselves up. Nobody does! And of course, he realized that [ageing] wasn't something you could ask people about.*

12.2.9 Dementia and Alzheimer's Disease Among Orchestra Players

Finally, in a similar fashion as was done in the main study (see Chapter 11, section 11.6.1), all the retired musicians were asked to recall other retired musicians from their personal social circle who might be afflicted with Dementia or Alzheimer's disease—or perhaps had been afflicted before they passed away. For the most part, these retired musicians could not recall retired elderly Orchestra musicians with such conditions. Sometimes, just 1 out of 100 (1%) of retired Orchestra musicians were mentioned as having been diagnosed with Dementia or Alzheimer's disease.

(63y, M, db)	*I've was in the Orchestra for nearly 40 years, so there's [at least] 70 people that have retired. I mean a lot of them are dead now. How many of them has (or had) Alzheimer's or Dementia? I'm honestly not aware of any of these that had that. I know a few with Parkinson's (i.e., trembling problems). In general I know many less non-musician retired people; I'm thinking of neighbours, say roughly 30. Certainly two (including dead people) had Alzheimer's or Dementia.*
(64y, F, va)	*I probably know about 80–100 retired Orchestra musicians. I think only one had Dementia or Alzheimer's. I probably also have 20 non-musician acquaintances, and again only one comes to mind with Dementia or Alzheimer's.*
(69y, F, va)	*I think I know about 10 retired full-time players. How many of them have Dementia or Alzheimer's disease? None! How many non-musician retired professionals do I think I know? Maybe I know 20. Only one has Dementia or Alzheimer's disease; but if you count the dead, then another two.*
(69y, F, vc)	*I probably know half a dozen retired full-time players. I am not aware of any of those who developed Dementia or Alzheimer's disease. I know about 50 non-musicians who have retired. I suppose there are at least four with Dementia or Alzheimer's.*
(72y, F, fl/picc)	*Well I know about 100 or so players from a few Orchestras. I can think of only one who had Dementia—or maybe it was Alzheimer's. I also know about 100 retired non-musicians; none that I can think of have Dementia.*

12.3 Discussion and Summary

This chapter reports a recruitment of six retired players from two Symphony Orchestras. These ex-Orchestra musicians did not interview face to face on-site in the rehearsal halls of the hosting organization. Therefore, they were not part of datasets from the computerized Psychomotor Tapping Tasks, *in vivo/in situ* music performances, or Think Aloud Protocols during a ±10-minute period of Deliberate Practice. In addition, they did not complete the 11-measure 12-page Questionnaire Booklet. These players simply agreed to speak over the telephone for 60 minutes about their past career. The retired players were exceptionally happy to reminisce about their previous career lifestyle, and seemed very gratified to have had the honour of occupying a place in a world-class Symphony Orchestra throughout an average 31-year career (with some enduring even more, throughout 37 years). As representing those professional musicians who would have been labelled as having achieved Successful Positive Ageing in the Symphony Orchestra, it does seem important to incorporate their recalled memories of times past and insights on topics that can be seen from their perspective of time.

(69y, F, va)   *I suppose it's the music that makes Orchestra playing so different than any other team-oriented profession. Well, I mean most people in the Orchestra love the music, and all are interested in their instrument. In this Orchestra, every week there was always something new in the repertoire. It kept you going for many years. So, I would imagine that players of an Orchestra that only do the standard 'box office' hits could burn out sooner. And of course, the skills that each brings to the collective is great! When you've got a skill on the instrument, you want to play the music. It's not some obsession with the instrument per se. It's the fact that you have the instrument and you want to play the music. I mean the instrument is the vehicle on which we can do something great with other people. What we do is to play music! In this Orchestra a lot of people stay for quite a long time. There's a certain passing population, but most people stay for a long time. So, I just valued having people around me who I knew and were like-minded. Some players do say that if they couldn't play in an Orchestra they couldn't do anything else. I think that's because we have concentrated on it from such an early age. We specialize in one, and only one, thing! Some do it from age 3–4; I started when I was 7 years old. What I'm saying is, it's not just that everybody has a musical skill and we all play, but that we're much more like-minded.*

I think it's the music. Very few people can really comprehend anything about it. The Orchestra spends hours together every day for years rehearsing, and then travelling. It's sort of like a family. It's like being locked up together for a long period of time, and I think that's very different—even from other music groups like Pop bands, Jazz bands, Big Bands, or Choirs. And I suppose that's what makes the bond! Orchestra Life is very different than just playing together. In a way, it rules your life. Perhaps that's why most of the players rarely have had any significant relationships with people who weren't musicians. I think it's the common understanding of what music is, and what making music is all about. I think if you're not in that, then, it's almost impossible to explain to somebody who you are. So, why do musicians think they're so special? I think it's something to do with the fact that nobody else really understands—intimately understands—what we're doing. I think it's because musicians are non-verbal people. Music is a different language. And your heart and your emotions are connected to that. So, for someone else to connect to your heart, whether that be romantically or otherwise, how can they do that if they don't speak your language?

(72y, F, fl/picc)   *I think that those who survive, do so because they're able to adapt! If I wouldn't have adapted, I would have been given the boot! I don't think that as I was getting older in the Orchestra I found it more difficult to concentrate, pay attention, or to focus. But, I did start to get very nervous (which I hadn't before). After all, I was sitting between two players [under consideration for dismissal]. But yet, these players were marvellous! They had no trouble with fingers, whereas I myself was definitely having slight motor problems. I was good enough in the early days as 2nd Flute, but then I did start feeling that perhaps I wasn't quite as good. As the 2nd Flute, I was quite conscientious not to be myself, but to play to the person [1st Flute] next to me. But, it's very difficult when they get the push [dismissed]. Then, you have to play to somebody else with a totally different intonation and approach. You have to change everything! But, I think that this is the way I survived!*

Music has to be your life passion. You hear it all the time, you have to practise it, you have to teach it. I mean it does take over your whole life! There's very little in life that is not music once you're in an Orchestra. Nonetheless, I think that after a bit, quite a few players see it as just a 'job'. Perhaps the energy levels do change. I think I felt that way too. I was always able to cope with it—up until the very end.

What I'm saying is that as you get older you have to be able to learn how to cope and move on. You have to play naturally, you have to be able to sense when people are coming in, sense the pitch. As soon as you worry about things like pitch, you begin doubting yourself. There were quite a lot of Conductors who liked me in the Orchestra; but then suddenly, I felt there were one or two who didn't! So, by the time I was asked to leave, I was really ready to leave. I would have wished it came from me. But. it wouldn't have occurred to me to ask to leave for a couple more years.

13

Finale

Musical Gerontivity

13.1 Introduction

The study depicted in this book explored ageing among music performers. Certainly, I was not the first to investigate old(er) aged musicians. For example, Krampe and Ericsson (1996) document the following:

> *Wilhelm Kempff, the famous pianist, decided to give up public performances when he felt his finger dexterity deteriorating and his memory becoming less reliable. At this point in his career he was no less than 85 years old. Numerous musicians continue in old age to amaze their audiences with performances that are far beyond the reach of most persons of any age. How are such extraordinary achievements possible for these individuals of advanced age?*
> (p. 331)

Yet, unlike Wilhelm Kempff (1895–1991), the current study specifically highlights full-time contract Symphony Orchestra players. The study does not examine the negative ill effects of ageing as they may be in the circumstances that cause players to leave the Symphony Orchestra. But rather, the investigation examined the more positive effects of music and Orchestra Lifestyle that have weight in supporting players to maintain skills and remain in the Orchestra beyond the 5th Decade (till 60–65 years old and sometimes even longer). Such an approach focuses on behavioural strategies as well as personality traits that portray lifespan changes within the domain and vocation of Classical Music performance. One reason that Music Science should be concerned with this phenomenon is because of the recognition that there is almost no other profession in which people persist with expert proficiencies in their domain *as if* they were 20 or 30 years younger (a time when they entered the field). Specifically, the highly tuned sophisticated motor-skills and mental abilities that formulate music expertise.

In 2017, Chris Wilson of *Time Magazine* reported the *50 Top Professions* with the highest rate of workers over age 65. See Table 13.1. As can be seen in the table, the vocations listed are in descending order of frequency with the highest percentage of members above age 65 listed at the top. Wilson examined a 5-year period from the US Census Bureau's American Community Survey measuring every occupation with those still in the labour force after age 65. Table 13.1 clearly indicates that professional Musicians and Singers are among the *Top 10* of the list. Musicians and

Seasoned Musicians Playing Beyond the 5th Decade. Warren Brodsky, Oxford University Press. © Oxford University Press (2025). DOI: 10.1093/9780198956501.003.0013

Singers are also collectively one of three vocations that demand highly refined expert motor-skills and mental abilities (in addition to Dentists, and Physicians and Surgeons). Yet, unlike professional Orchestra musicians, the impact of hand tremors on health professionals (such as Surgeons) most likely causes them to 'subcontract' the more practical work to substitutes, medical residents, and trainees as the dedicated service provider. It must be pointed out that other professions requiring microsecond response-time performance (including Acrobats, Air Pilots, Athletes, Dancers, Motor-Racing Drivers, and Sportsmen) are not even presented in Wilson's *Time Magazine* list. As an example, Lufthansa Airlines not only mandated the pilots of their *Airbus A380* to retire at age 60 (Brandfonbrenner, 2003), but began awarding a $38,000 bonus to those who voluntarily retired by age 55 (Loh, 2021). This policy may have surfaced because of age-related ill effects with reaction time among old(er) pilots, leading to previous recommendations that *take-off* and *landing* controls be delegated to young(er) co-pilots. Table 13.1 is obviously of interest to professionals from the domain of *Industrial Gerontology*—which is the study of ageing and work, the ageing workforce, and processes involving employment and retirement (Sterns & Miklos, 1995). In their 'Preface' to the book *Aging and Work in the 21st Century*,

Table 13.1 50 Top Professions with Workers over Age 65

1. Tax Preparers	26. Library Assistants and Clerical Workers
2. Clergy	27. Personal Care Aides
3. Farmers, Ranchers, and Agricultural Managers	28. Artists
4. Bus and Ambulance Drivers, and Attendants	29. Librarians
5. Real Estate Brokers and Sales Agents	30. Teachers and Instructors
6. Psychologists	31. Secretaries and Administrative Assistants
7. Barbers	32. Janitors and Building Cleaners
8. Musicians and Singers	33. Social and Community Service Managers
9. Taxi Drivers and Chauffeurs	34. Construction and Building Inspectors
10. Dentists	35. Interviewers (Except Eligibility and Loan)
11. Chief Executives and Legislators/Public Administration	36. Personal Financial Advisers
12. Property, Real Estate, and Community Association Managers	37. Receptionists and Information Clerks
	38. Retail Salespersons
13. Post-secondary Teachers	39. Cost Estimators
14. Sales and Related Workers	40. Driver/Sales Workers and Truck Drivers
15. Physicians and Surgeons	41. Architects (Except Naval)
16. Lawyers, Judges, Magistrates, and Judicial Workers	42. Word Processors and Typists
17. Appraisers and Assessors of Real Estate	43. Hairdressers, Hairstylists, and Cosmetologists
18. Couriers and Messengers	44. Civil Engineers
19. Door-to-Door Sales Workers, News and Street Vendors	45. Wholesale and Retail Buyers
	46. Office Clerks
20. Writers and Authors	47. File Clerks
21. Bookkeeping, Accounting, and Auditing Clerks	48. Sales Representatives, Wholesale and Manufacturing
22. Management Analysts	49. Editors, News Analysts, Reporters, and Correspondents
23. Insurance Sales Agents	50. Pharmacists
24. Entertainment Attendants and Workers	
25. Security Guards and Gaming Surveillance Officers	

Data Source: Wilson (2017)

editors Shultz and Adams (2009) declare that among the most important, but far less obvious, issues of the ageing workforce are: maintaining competence and occupational health, facilitating adaptation to new technologies, and managing boundaries between personal and work-life.

What is it about Symphony Orchestra musicians who continue to play beyond age 55, claiming to perform as well as they did when they were 20 or 30 years younger? I ask: When an Orchestra musician asserts they play *just as well* as they did years ago, are they actually denying that they see, or hear, or feel any discrepancy at all? Or rather, is what they mean: The variance between today's performance level and yesteryear's performance level is simply negligible—less than 5%? After all, had their current performance levels declined by 20% or 30%, they wouldn't have been able to remain in the Symphony Orchestra. There is evidence that old(er) experts show normal age-graded declines in general measures of processing speed and performance in a similar fashion to non-expert controls. But there is little, if any, age-related decline in efficiencies or the speed at which they perform skill-related tasks (Krampe, 2002, 2006).

Since the 1990s there have been many reports that musicians demonstrate differences of brain anatomy and hormone levels compared to non-musicians (e.g., Altenmuller et al., 1997; Brochard et al., 2004; Gaab & Schlaug, 2003; Gaser & Schlaug, 2003; Herholz & Zatorre, 2012; Janata, 2005; Jancke et al. 2000; Koelsch & Skeie, 2020; Meister et al., 2005; Moreno & Farzan, 2015; Nakamura et al., 1999; Otte et al., 2001; Pascual-Leone, 2003; Samson et al., 2001; Schlaug, 2003, 2015; Schlaug et al., 1995; Skoe & Kraus, 2012; Sluming et al., 2007; Zatorre, 2003; for a review, see Cuddy et al., 2020). Twenty years ago, Norton et al. (2005) presented a review of studies having explored the brains of individuals with exceptional and highly specialized sensorimotor skills, auditory skills, and auditory-spatial skills. Norton et al. showed that specifically among *musicians*, certain regions of the brain were larger or had more volume: the anterior Corpus Callosum, the medial portion of Heschl's Gyrus, the inferior frontal Gyrus, the Cerebellum, and the Intrasulcal length of the precentral Gyrus (which is a parameter of primary motor cortex size). In addition, musicians with Absolute Pitch were seen to have greater left-sided asymmetry of the Planum Temporale. Further, Mansens et al. (2018) point out that research studies with adult musicians show musical training as changing the brain. That is, professional musicians have a significantly larger anterior part of the Corpus Callosum. Accordingly, all these above-mentioned changes relate to the onset age of training; those who started with musical training before 7 years of age had significantly larger changes, including enhanced Hippocampal volume (which is associated with increased fluid intelligence in musically trained people).

Altenmuller and James (2020) claim that the unique neuroanatomical findings among musicians illustrate the potential for musical training to generate architectural and functional modifications across various brain structures and their connections. Nonetheless, some researchers (e.g., O'Brian et al., 2015; Rodrigues et al., 2013) state that we do not yet really know: Did atypical brain structures exist prior to music training, and hence predispose some children to choose and engage in music training? Or: Does musical development and skill acquired over long periods of highly specialized music training, prompt later changes in neuro-configurations? Moreover, we may wonder if these modifications are actually manifestations of music learning *per se* (referred to as *cortical plasticity* as a response to the training), or might they be the result of some other distinctive more 'eccentric' environment-related variable and/or lifestyle? The truth is that perhaps we are still at a loss in differentiating between the two when investigating musicians' behaviour or brain functions. For example, Krampe (2002, 2006) found that while their performance in general measures of cognitive speed was quite similar to that of all normal old(er) adults in their 6th or 7th decade of life, there was little decline among old(er) music experts in speed and accuracy of skill-related performance tasks. Indeed, the findings of the current music-performance analyses (outlined in Chapter 10) strengthen the outcomes described by Krampe. But as yet, even the current investigation does not offer distinctive explanations differentiating between the 'music', the 'music performance', the 'music performer', and 'Orchestra Lifestyle'. Nonetheless, in this chapter I will attempt to fill the gap with a descriptive explanatory discussion.

(47y, M, hn) *Ageing has not taken the toll! Not on me personally, nor on other players my age [or older]. I honestly believe that my focus of attention, concentration, and motivation haven't changed that much. Neither have my motor skills, the physical restraints and the challenge of the instrument. Though, I do have to work harder, I'm telling you I still think I can do it. I understand that it is not just me. People who assess my abilities, such as my employers, are satisfied. So, it's not just because players [like me] say they can do it. Yet, it doesn't make sense because the split-second reaction time which is something that I have to do, should change [with age]. So, how do I explain that? What is it about an Orchestra player? [Different from] a Soloist, a Piano player, a Rock 'n' Roller, or Jazz/Pop player, that allows you to keep very superman-like skills straight up to when you're 65 or 68 [years old]—and some play even past 70 if they're still allowed. How do we do it? And, I'm not talking about one person. I never really thought about 'why'. I've always seen it in orchestras; always a few guys over 60 years old—usually [they are] String- or Wooden-players [Woodwinds]. If you don't fall down all the trapdoors, you can keep going. My mind is always thinking about how can I not collapse into one of these doors.*

William J. Dawson, a symphonic Bassoonist and hand surgeon who was a past president of the American *Performing Arts Medicine Association*, formerly from the Feinberg School of Medicine at Northwestern University (USA), described problems of maturing musicians. Dawson (1993) claimed that making music can be a lifelong activity, and unlike many other occupations, an instrumental performance career could last as long as 50–60 years! However, Dawson recognized that although physical and mental capabilities are expected to change with normal processes of ageing, some conditions are nonetheless classified as pathological diseases. Both Gembris (2013) as well as Hargreaves and Lamont (2017) assert that all performers go through similar kinds of age-related changes during their lifespan. In contrast to athletes, dancers, and sportsmen—who all have a much more limited period of active performance—musicians enjoy a professional career of 30 years or more. Yet, Symphony Orchestra musicians are indeed likely to experience health problems and challenges at different points in their extended career. Therefore, Dawson wondered: How do professional musicians deal effectively with these changes? And: How do they continue to perform for as long as they do? In this early 1990s paper, Dawson listed a range of manifestations for ageing among musicians. All of these were deficits that could potentially become fatal for players in maintaining the required standards of Orchestra performance:

a) Sight: Presbyopia; Cataract; Glaucoma
b) Hearing: Presbycusis and Noise-Induced Hearing Loss; Conductive (middle-ear) loss; Sensorineural (inner-ear and hearing nerve deafness) loss
c) Musculoskeletal: Osteoarthritis (degenerative joints, wear-and-tear arthritis); Osteoarthritis (spinal stiffness limiting flexibility); decreased ability to side-turn or lift up head; Low back pain and stiffness; Osteoporosis (bone change, more easily fractured and broken); Degenerative tendinitis (movement pain).

It should be noted that while Dawson's article was highly insightful at the time of publication, it is far from exhaustive. Nor does Dawson touch on other areas of human development and behaviour, such as mental, motor, emotional, musical, or environmental considerations of ageing for a music-performance professional. I note here that many other publications of the same time period (e.g., Smith, 1992) were quite similar.

At this point I reiterate the main question posed in Chapter 1:

How do Orchestra musicians retain their high level of functional music-performance abilities well beyond the 5th Decade—despite the ill effects of ageing?

13.2 Ageing Among Orchestra Players

One issue in the ageing literature that has yet to result in a definite answer concerns the association between age, experience, and performance. For example, Salthouse (2006) presented studies in the domains of Architecture, Medicine-Physicians, Music, Pilot Communication, and Sports-Baseball Players. Accordingly, these studies generally failed to find Age x Experience interactions with measures of domain-relevant performance. While there were positive associations between amount of experience in the relevant activity and various measures of domain-specific performance, there were few (if any) interactions that would indicate experience as moderating the relations between age and cognition. Salthouse questioned: If people continue to accumulate relevant experience with increasing age, perhaps they might perform better on domain-related cognitive tasks than they would have performed without that boost in experience. Salthouse specifically stated: "To the extent that continuously increasing experience serves to maintain performance that would decline in the absence of that experience, one might predict the relations between age and measures of cognitive functioning would be more negative if the amount of experience was controlled by statistical procedures" (p. 78). In an interesting anecdote, Salthouse mentions:

> *There has been considerable interest in the age-cognition relations among academics, because professors like to believe that they live in a constant state of mental stimulation, and therefore if the mental-exercise hypothesis is correct, they might be able to look forward to less pronounced age-related declines in cognitive functioning than people in less stimulating occupations. Unfortunately, most of the empirical evidence has not been consistent with this optimistic expectation.* (p. 76)

Nonetheless, there is indeed evidence that higher levels of experience in a domain minimize, and perhaps even eliminate, normal age differences in domain-related tasks (Meinz, 2000; Meinz & Salthouse, 1998). For example, Mansens et al. (2018) point to a large body of research that provides evidence for the prevention of cognitive decline in several domains through participation in mentally stimulating leisure activities, such as: Board or Card Games, Crossword Puzzles, Reading, and Writing. Further, Groussard et al. (2020) substantiated the same notion for activities involving Theatre and Music. But, when specifically considering 'music', Mansens et al. debated if it is explicitly the *music* itself that benefits cognitive function? The more receptive aural music experience involving a host of music elements, including: Dynamics, Harmony, Melody, Metre, Pitch, Rhythm, Structure, Tempo, Texture, Timbre, and Tonality. Or: Is it the *music performance*? Making music together with others onstage in front of an audience requires one to do multiple things at the same time, such as remembering notes, listening to assess if it all sounds right, coordinating breathing with hands (and feet), and keeping rhythm.

Long ago an article published in the *APA Monitor*[1] pointed out that little evidence existed for age-related causes of work deterioration (Azar, 1998). Previously, Sterns and Miklos (1995) outlined a report by the Commonwealth Fund (published in 1993), titled 'Untapped Resource'. That report was about Americans over 55 in the workforce. Accordingly, already in the 1990s, over 14 million people beyond 55 years of age were employed consistently, and received high ratings on work performance.

---

[1] The official magazine of the American Psychological Association (APA).

More current case studies also indicate old(er) workers as being highly flexible, trainable, and cost-effective. But modifications in sensory, perceptual, motor, and intellectual capacities clearly occur throughout normal maturation—and therefore it would be logical that ageing would ultimately take its toll on work performance. Azar asserted that old(er) workers have always found it hard to compete with younger workers, especially in tasks that require psychomotor and procedural speed. These tasks account for most of the differences between young(er) *versus* old(er) workers. The notion was quite apparent for Ericsson (2000) who stated: "Older expert performers (age 60–70) are often found to be able to perform at levels vastly superior to those of younger untrained adults [. . .] [however] older expert performers are rarely able to match the performance of young expert performers—especially in activities demanding maximal speed and power" (p. 370). Accordingly, Ericsson found that older *master athletes* train less often and with less intensity than do young *elite athletes*. So, he questioned: Is it the 'age' or the 'lack of training' (i.e., practice regimes)? In agreement with this line of thinking is Ackerman (2014) who notes that we would never see an elite performer in their 5th Decade winning an international performance competition against an elite performer 25–30 years younger; and rarely would we ever see a world record being broken by a performer in their 5th Decade. Yet, as Azar pointed out, old(er) workers are perfectly capable of learning new tasks, and while their productivity may certainly lag behind their young(er) counterparts, they tend to be highly consistent. Moreover, if companies are solely concerned with productivity, then younger workers are an asset. But, if companies are concerned with accuracy, then older workers are more than adequate; the ratio of successful ideas to total tries is relatively consistent.

The typical approach taken in research examining diversity among workers, employs tasks that emphasize speed or response time (RTs). Shammi et al. (1998) felt that such studies miss many critical features of performance—such as *consistency*. Here I ask: Why is there only limited (if any) impact of ageing on job-related music-performance tasks among Seasoned Musicians in the Orchestra? I reiterate that this was clearly seen in the findings of the current investigation package, including: Psychomotor Tapping (Chapter 8), Think Aloud Protocols (Chapter 9), and Music Performances (i.e., a double-blind adjudication process, Chapter 10). Perhaps examining RTs is not as pertinent as might have been thought previously by Music Performance Science studies. The current investigation demonstrates, through a large number of variables, that difference in domain-specific expertise-related tasks between subgroups of players younger than 45 years old *versus* players older than 55 years old is very small, if it exists at all. I suggest here that one possible reason for the phenomenon is that most tasks in the music-performance domain (at least as far as Classical Music is concerned) rely on *crystallized* knowledge and experience rather than on *fluid* cognitive skills. I discuss this point in more detail below.

The comprehensive investigation package described in this book attempts to shed light on Ageing in the Symphony Orchestra—most specifically Positive Ageing among Seasoned Musicians. While such a sample may have been discussed before, unfortunately the scientific literature is frequented with rather complex—and at times convoluted—findings. For example, one researcher who has made groundbreaking progress in focusing on old(er)-aged instrumental musicians is Brenda Hanna-Pladdy, formerly from the Landon Center on Aging, Department of Psychiatry and Behavioral Sciences, University of Kansas Medical Center (USA). Hanna-Pladdy and MacKay (2011) boldly stated that relatively few studies have evaluated the non-musical cognitive functions of instrumental musicians, and while most of these were correlational studies of young musicians or young adults who played an instrument, none really offer information as far as *ageing* is concerned. On the whole, and while the collective findings are inconsistent, the literature acknowledges musicians as having cognitive advantages. These include: enhanced Verbal Memory abilities and Language functions, as well as benefits in Auditory Processing and Visuospatial abilities. Hence, Hanna-Pladdy and MacKay designed a prima facie study to evaluate whether (or not) differences in cognitive functioning in advanced ages surface. They evaluated if old(er) individuals who engaged in at least 10 years of musical experience displayed better cognitive performance than other individuals (matched for Age and Education, but yet self-reported to have had less musical experience). Given that such empirical designs are based on comparing between subgroups, we would expect the highest possible level of ecological validity in defining inclusion criteria and recruiting participants. In this connection, I ask: Is 10 years of musical experience (referred to in the literature as *The 10-Year Rule*) an acceptable marker for defining 'musicians' as a research sample? That is: Does playing an instrument between 1st and 10th Grade (i.e., ages 5–15) reflect 'music engagement over one's lifespan'? Or: Would it be more acceptable as a marker for *The 10-Year Rule* if engagement had been between ages 15 and 25? If we do not ask the question to begin with, then future research studies may simply perpetuate such practices (e.g., Fancourt et al., 2022; Gray & Gow, 2020; Strong & Mast, 2019). In their review paper examining the definition of 'who is a musician' for samples in empirical science studies, Zhang et al. (2020) critiqued a variety of criteria that have been put forward in the literature. Among these were: 'Years of Training', 'Years of Formal Music Lessons', 'Accumulated Hours of Deliberate Practice', 'Final Tertiary Degree', and 'Accumulative Years of Experience'. Given the last, we might wonder: What constitutes music experience? Does a decade of naïve, amateur, or semi-professional levels of music performance mirror the developmental trajectory that is characteristic for mastery as found among music experts? Unfortunately, Zhang et al. claimed that the most robust standard found in the literature is: 'at least 6 years of music expertise' (referred to as *The 6-Year Rule*). Finally, some researchers (e.g., Mansens et al., 2018) simply recruited samples of musicians as based on 'Frequency of Musical Activity', which they defined as: 'at least once every 2 weeks'. I would clearly like to declare my opposition to these! I do not accept *6 years*, *10 years*, or *once every 2 weeks* as a 'proxy' for an ecologically reliable inclusion criterion targeting professional musicians as a research sample. It is imperative that investigations with participants defined as 'professional music performers with lifelong learning of a musical instrument and music making' are actually *these specific kind of people*. As an example, in their review paper, Wolff et al. (2023) presented 'key evidence for cognitive advantages in older adult musicians'. The sample (item) sizes are very small indeed. But, as can be seen in the descriptives of Wolff et al.'s Table 1, only one out of four studies listed actually recruited valid participants (e.g., musicians having had 46–80 years of music training and practice), whereas all other studies had recruited participants with 1–10 years of playing a musical instrument! So I wonder: What exactly can we learn about cognitive advantages in older adult musicians from this review paper? The issue is even more relevant in a study focused on ageing among professional Symphony Orchestra players.

Kenny et al. (2018) claimed that "relatively little scientific literature exists on the physical and psychological health characteristics of professional orchestral musicians as they age, or what factors may be associated with longevity in the orchestral workplace" (p. 39). Accordingly, the researchers noted that at least as far as Australia is concerned, there is a very low representation of old(er) musicians in orchestras. They suggest that as a group, Seasoned Musicians are musical *survivors*—either by virtue of having been both physically and psychologically resilient at the outset, or by having acquired adaptive skills necessary to sustain a long musical career as they progressed through the vocation. Playing a musical instrument is likely to be affected by age-related declines in function including: physical, cognitive, psychological, and organ-related changes. Ageing has many repercussions for professional musicians, although its impact can vary greatly between them. While it would seem logical that the reality of age-related changes leads to a performance decline in a wide number of players from middle age, Kenny et al. reported that musculoskeletal examinations indicated intact strength, flexibility, and dexterity. Namely, Symphony Orchestra musicians were not necessarily affected by age-related declines, and were still playing professionally.

> *Contrary to expectations, we did not find significant disadvantages in the older age groups of professional orchestral musicians, either in terms of their physical function, performance-related pain, effort exerted while playing, psychological measures assessing social anxiety, [. . .] music performance anxiety, depression, core self-concept, days lost from work, or workplace satisfaction.* (pp. 44–45)

13.2.1 Orchestra Lifestyle and Ageing

The current study explored a host of themes that need to be considered when examining the ageing processes among Symphony Orchestra players. Orchestral

Lifestyle and environment were explored within the context of age-related ill effects on mental, motor, emotional, music-performance, and environmental skills. From the onset of the study, the basic contention was that ageing might cause havoc with focus of attention, concentration, stamina, mental agility, and information processing. Namely, that ageing might serve as a trigger for increased errors, slips, and memory failures; or contribute to boredom and fatigue. The findings show that players do not feel their mental skills have weakened, deteriorated, or were compromised as they aged. But rather, they have become better with time! They do not necessarily experience declines in their mental skill set involving concentration, focus of attention, attention span, score-reading, Sight-Reading, memory, eye–hand span, mental flexibility, automaticity, and mental stamina. Moreover, a third of the players claimed that ageing has not in the least afflicted their physical abilities or their motor skill set; most specifically, their kinaesthetic memory has not declined, and expression of affect is just as fluid as ever. Accordingly, their abilities to control and maintain tempo in a steady state, as well as follow tempo fluctuations, are completely intact. Finally, pitch accuracy, hand positioning, and finger agility are all on the same level as they were at age 25.

Nonetheless, many Symphony Orchestra players did mention age-related ill effects and declines. The vignettes clearly indicate that the old(er) Orchestra musicians feel they have come to an age where there is weaker eyesight and an overall increase in general fatigue. Tiredness is experienced in practice, daytime Orchestra rehearsals, and night-time stage venues. They find themselves needing *more time*: more time to learn a new music piece, more time to warm up before a rehearsal and concert, and longer durations for breaks at rehearsals and concerts to refresh themselves (and relieve their bladder). In addition, they require more time for post-concert recovery (Post-Performance Arousal); an increased duration of time to calm down from high levels of adrenaline, and to relax their lips and hand muscles.

Players often spoke about the increasing difficulty of sitting in a chair. As they aged, it has become more problematic to sit at the edge of the seat for long periods of time, to remain in an optimal seated posture in order to hold a musical instrument. Aches and pains are more frequent: backaches, musculoskeletal aches, twinges of the buttocks, stiffness of the body, and pains in finger joints. There is a general lack of agility and flexibility; a more general decrease in natural power and physical strength. Some mentioned a decrease in stamina, weaker muscles, slowing down, and decrease of control over tongue and lips (embouchure). Wind players clearly spoke about the difficulty in producing higher-range notes, while String players discussed problematic synchrony between the Bow (right hand) and the fingers (left hand). There is an ever-increasing inability to physically relax effectively prior to repetitive movements (such as when preparing for a Tremolo, Vibrato, or Trill). Sometimes players avoid adjacent pitches in multiple-note fast-paced passages. Moreover, there may be changes in sound quality. Nonetheless, almost all players admit that while the accuracy of a score may be slightly less than what is written, performances are still between 90% and 97% true to text! Finally, some players of advanced ages may demonstrate slower reaction times as seen in flawed entrances; those lags have been estimated to be between a 64th and a 32nd note. But yet, even when considering all of the above, as one player so eloquently portrayed the situation:

Ageing, among Symphony Orchestra players, just seems to have caused a situation whereby yesteryear's elite Olympic athletes simply remain to be expert professional sportsmen.

Therefore, the overall picture does seem to be one in which most Symphony Orchestra players, including the more Seasoned Musicians (above 55 years of age), perform at a more than acceptable level and retain their positions. Seasoned Musicians play very well! The evidence for this can be seen in the actual performance assessments as evaluated by judges in a double-blind adjudication procedure (Chapter 10, and reflected upon in section 13.3). If there is any decline at all, then it would be estimated as roughly 1%–5%. That is, even if an old(er) aged Orchestra player self-reported experiencing the ill effects of ageing on their music-performance capacities, they are still executing their performance capabilities between 95% and 99% of proficiency—after 35 years or more in a highly vigorous motor-demanding profession.

Symphony Orchestra musicians speak about maintaining passion, motivation, involvement, and satisfaction within the context of ageing. In addition, they discuss discipline, artistic integrity, commitment, and conviction. They express a sense of responsibility, dedication, and pride to be in an Orchestra. But yet, they also strongly recognize the fact that all their skills and vocation can be lost at any time because of wear and tear. One of the more unique topics that players bring up is camaraderie, orchestral allegiance and devotion, and relationships (e.g., coupling) among players. Sometimes they note how one's personal existence and Orchestra Lifestyle collide in ways that do not occur in any other profession. The majority mention having an intense intimate bond with their musical instrument. While discussing spirituality, creativity, and emotional communication within music performance, players clearly stated that there is a need for age-related adaptation to emotions. They speak about performance nerves, Drugs and Alcohol, Burnout, Chronic Fatigue, failing to reach their potential, Fear of Failure, and Fear of Success. On the one hand, they seem to be more open to verbalizing their thoughts on these topics than they might have been in previous years, but they still very much admit that all these topics are taboo for open discussion in the *Green Room*. It is rather surprising to note how many players perceived listening to music outside the orchestra as an indication of well-being; there is a feeling that players who are detached from listening to music beyond Orchestra activity, are no less than burned-out musicians.

Music-performance aspects of the vocation need to be considered when examining issues of ageing. The participating players were steadfast that an orchestra musician's skill set is not necessarily their ability to play the notes *per se*, but rather their capability to 'fit in'. Foremost is the coordinated effort to match one's desk partner, then the instrument section, and then the Orchestra. It is the ability to blend, in an effort to contribute to the group's overall sound. The players saw this as related to flexibility and an awareness about cohesiveness of the Orchestra. Yet this essential mindset is also at the expense of giving up one's self-perceived expectations of achieving one's potential. The players talk about the costs of staying in the same orchestra for many years. On the one hand much effort is invested in maintaining skills, but on the other hand most realize that they will simply remain in the same place at the same level as was offered to them in their first initial contract some 20–30 years earlier. They mention that few players ever move forward and upward in an Orchestra; Rank-&-File players seldom become Sub-Leaders or Principals, few move from 4th Desk to 1st Desk, and rarely do players transfer from the 2nd Violins to 1st Violins. The majority stated outright that after the age of 35, they are not even accepted for audition procedures—maybe with the exception of their own Orchestra. Therefore, Symphony Orchestra players learn very early on within their career track that they have little to aspire to as far as reaching any further higher levels of actualizing any potential; the very best that one can attain is their coveted tenured contract.

All Symphony Orchestra players speak about becoming a collaborator—a bandmate and team member. This ultimately means taking directions from a Conductor. All 80–120 players of an Orchestra (Sinfonietta, Symphony, or Philharmonic-sized Orchestra) continually need to acclimatize and adjust their performance exclusively for one sole personality. That is the ethos that needs to be satisfied day after day, night after night, week after week, month after month, and year after year! So, we might ask: As players age, does it become easier for them to forfeit their hard-earned knowledge (both theoretical and applied information), gained through years and even decades of music-performance experience? Namely: As the years go by, do Orchestra musicians develop more mature attitudes and perspectives towards leadership and authority allowing for the presence of different but equally worthy artistic interpretations? Although the old(er) players did claim that they feel they have matured as more tolerant and compliant professionals, many young(er) players assert that they have observed the exact opposite behaviour among the Seasoned Musicians.

The work environment, working conditions, orchestral position, and job security are highly potent issues. The players are very candid about these as being quite harsh, and to some extent trigger frailties that resurface during the 5th Decade. These can turn to disabling emotions. Much was said about working schedules, evening hours, and lost weekends. In addition, during the later years of professional life, travel—overnight venues and touring—seems to create a more destructive and even hostile atmosphere. Nevertheless, the most problematic element (as far as work employment conditions are concerned) is the periodic performance evaluations. Most players perceive these as insulting and offensive—if not causing an even greater rift between management than is usually the case in most other professions. Hierarchical rankings in the Orchestra, advancement, and mobility are especially hot topics of contention. Finally, personal and social perspectives about Symphony Orchestra lifestyles often cause turmoil in a way that simply does not exist in any other occupation. The Orchestra profession has undergone many changes throughout History—alternating between being *cherished* to being *guffawed at*. Societal perceptions of the music-performance vocation most certainly affect music performers—and sometimes even more so at old(er) ages in the 5th Decade.

13.2.2 The 2-Component Model of Intellectual Functioning

In their pioneering study applying intellectual functioning within a Lifespan Psychology Ageing-related context, Baltes et al. (1999b) highlighted the three goals of development as: Growth, Maintenance, and Regulation of Loss.

a) Growth is an indication of the decreasing allocation of resources (i.e., behaviours) aimed at reaching higher levels of adaptive functioning.
b) Maintenance or resilience is an indication of resources invested in maintaining levels of adaptive functioning when new challenges surface (i.e., the normal ill effects of ageing), or in an effort to return to previous levels subsequent to losses.
c) Regulation of Loss, which increases with ageing, is an approach that one uses to organize adaptive functioning at lower levels when recovery from age-related losses is no longer viable.

These three goals clearly parallel the *SOC* model of behavioural strategies. I point out here that the current sample of Symphony Orchestra musicians reported higher levels of *SOC* than other samples of the general public (see Chapter 11, section 11.2.1). Baltes et al. noted that there is empirical evidence about individuals who more often report *SOC* strategies as also reporting higher indications of Successful Ageing. Yet, as described above, there are inevitable changes of physical and mental capabilities among performing musicians.

Krampe and Ericsson (1996) outlined the assumption that most age-related differences in speeded performance have a single common cause, and are mediated by age-related reductions in processing speed. Accordingly, this is referred to as a general slowing or *cognitive ageing*. That is a global decline in performance with increasing age consisting of a reduction in capacities of working memory, deceleration of processing speed, weakening of neural interconnectedness, and lessening of ability to ignore irrelevant information. The speed of cognitive operations is considered the more *fluid* component of intelligence. On the other hand, as Krampe and Ericsson point out, some areas of cognitive functioning may be less affected than others; for example, the more *crystallized* acquired components of intelligence involving a large range of extensive accumulated knowledge that does not change with age. In this connection, Baltes (1997; Baltes et al., 1999b) highlights the 2-Component Model of Cognitive Intellectual Operation. The 2-component model views *Cognitive Mechanics* as opposed to *Cognitive Pragmatics*. Accordingly, the mechanics of cognition relates to fluid elementary processing operations, such as reasoning, spatial attention, and perceptual speed. Namely, intellectual cognitive mechanical functioning is founded on speed and accuracy of information processing, and the coordination of working memory, especially when transferring information from short-term memory buffers. It also includes new innovative learning. Hence, neurobiology is ultimately of great importance, while the ill effects of ageing (i.e., declines in stability, age-associated insults to the brain, and neuro-dysfunction) certainly influence these operations and competences. Baltes et al. indicated a linear decline in the mechanics of cognition during adulthood towards the inevitability of increased deterioration in old age. On the other hand, the pragmatics of cognition is crystallized, involving acquired information such as verbal knowledge, semantics, and numerical ability. Cognitive Pragmatics is rich content-based information determined by culture and lifelong experience; some knowledge is subsequent to individualized practice, while other contents are maintained pragmatic information. Baltes and colleagues indicate that the pragmatics of cognition remains fairly intact throughout one's lifespan, well into the 6th and 7th Decade, after which it also begin an inescapable decline in old age.

Perhaps, then, here is an essential explanatory basis that might account for *Positive Successful Ageing among Seasoned Musicians*: Cognitive Pragmatics is essentially knowledge which can be used to make up for losses in Cognitive Mechanics—especially within the specific domain of expertise of Classical Music Performance. Content-rich acquired knowledge is fundamental for ageing individuals with domain-specific abilities to counteract the ill effects of age-related losses, while expertise within a specific domain involving a wide range of declarative and procedural knowledge is rarely altered by ageing because the mechanics of cognition is resilient for knowledge within the specific domain of proficiency. So, is it a possibility that Symphony Orchestra players may be more resistant to the ill effects of ageing than other individuals, simply because they have had lifelong music training from early childhood (before age 7), and they have engaged in the performance vocation as a full-time contract player within a work-life environment referred to as Orchestra Lifestyle for 35 (or more) years?

13.2.3 Resilience and Cognitive Reserve

In their literature review on Psychological Resilience, David Fletcher and Mustafa Sarker of Loughborough University (UK) claim that it is important to distinguish between *protective* factors and *promotive* factors—the former indicate shielding or insulation from potential negative effects while the latter essentially denote adaptive mental and behavioural processes that promote personal assets to alter responses that predispose maladaptive outcomes (Fletcher & Sarker, 2013). They contend that:

> Individuals operating in a demanding performance environment on a daily basis would be deemed to exhibit resilience if they evaluated stressors as an opportunity for develop-ment and, consequently, received peer recognition for their work. In contrast, if individuals operating in a similar environment did not react as positively and their work suffered and, subsequently, sought social support from their colleagues, this would be an example of coping. (p. 16)

As more and more current Gerontological work concentrates on *plasticity* and *quality of life*, we wonder: How is Resilience and Successful Positive Ageing defined or measured? There seem to be as many definitions and theoretical models as there are research papers (for a review, see Windle, 2011). Yet, one measure that has been used repeatedly in empirical research studies is the *Connor-Davidson Resilience Scale* (*CD-RISC*, Connor & Davidson, 2003). The *CD-RISC* scale consists of 25 items. But then as a further development, an adapted reduced 10-item version (*CD-RISC-10*) was put forward and validated by Campbell-Sills and Stein (2007). Among the items are:

- I believe I can achieve my goals, and I am able to adapt to change
- I can deal with whatever comes, and I tend to bounce back after hardship
- I can handle unpleasant feelings, and I see the humorous side of things
- I think of myself as strong person, and I am strengthened by coping with stress
- I am not easily discouraged by failure, and I think clearly when under pressure.

The adapted version was employed by Kegelaers et al. (2021) with 64 musicians: 36 (56%) were students (either Undergraduate finalists or Year-1 MA Master students from the Amsterdam Conservatorium, M_{Age} = 23, *SD* 3.43, 53% male, $M_{YrsInst}$ = 13), and 28 (44%) were professionals (from one of the international Orchestras in the Netherlands, M_{Age} = 34, *SD* = 13.70, 61% female, $M_{YrsInst}$ = 24). It is interesting to note that Kegelaers et al. did not find statistical differences of *CD-RISC-10* scores between the student musicians and professional Orchestra players. No doubt these two subgroups could also be seen as variegated by age: late teens to early 20s (M_{Age} = 35, *SD* = 5.2) *versus* late 20s to mid-40s (M_{Age} = 38.9, *SD* = 5.0).

Perhaps we might ask: How do Resilience and age-related changes interact with Successful Positive Ageing? In their special issue editorial titled 'Successful aging 2.0: Resilience and beyond' published in the *Journal of Gerontology: Social Sciences*, Prunchno and Carr (2017) note that resilience is a *process*, while Successful Positive Ageing is a *state* (see model: Chapter 11, section 11.5, Figure 11.2). The researchers claim that core aspects of Resilience play a prominent role in the *SOC* model proposed by Baltes and colleagues. Indeed, during the last decade, there has been huge interest in assessing the impact of lifestyle choices on Successful Ageing. Accordingly, older adults who engage in physical activity demonstrate superior performance on cognitive tasks. Alain et al. (2014) presented evidence suggesting increased Cardiovascular fitness may be related to increased Brain volume and to enhanced cognitive performance. Further, that higher educational and occupational achievements attenuate the negative effects of ageing on cognitive abilities (Moussard et al., 2016). Namely, that many enriched experiences generate *Cognitive Reserves* (CR) that delay age-related cognitive decline (Scarmeas & Stern, 2003).

Wolff et al. (2023) outline CR as an active mechanism that optimizes neural processes through compensatory cognitive strategies. Music engagement is noted for its role in promoting CR, albeit perhaps music's role in Brain Reserve and Brain Maintenance may be more indirect than is put forward by research studies in the literature. Alain et al. affirmed that musicians are an excellent sample to study aspects of CR—especially in terms of age-related declines. Parbery-Clark et al. (2012), were highly explicit:

> *Lifelong musical experience is analogous to a long-term auditory training program, in that precise subcortical response timing is sustained through the maintenance of intricately balanced excitatory and inhibitory subcortical neural networks. A broader significance: musical experience protects against age-related degradation in neural timing, highlighting the modifiable nature of these declines.* (pp. 1483.e4)

Therefore, if the continued engagement in stimulating activities across one's lifetime acts to maintain CR, then is there a possibility that specific kinds of eccentric lifestyles—such as being a Classical Music Symphony Orchestra player—might boost CR mitigating age-related declines? This is the ultimate question I have raised: What can Seasoned Musicians tell us about lifelong music engagement? Hence: Does lifelong musical development, with a more formal music training initiating in early childhood before age 7, eventually acclimatizing to a lifestyle as a full-time professional contract Symphony Orchestra musician, have a major impact on human resilience that is consequently experienced as positive successful ageing?

13.3 The Proof is in the Pudding

There is an old metaphor that means the value, quality, or truth of something must be judged based on direct experience with it. Namely: 'The Proof is in the Pudding'. Originally this expression was: '*The proof of the pudding is in the eating.*' That is: Things must be considered by trying them yourself, or by seeing them in action through direct observation rather than relying on hearsay anecdote. I would like to apply this expression within the context of offering evidence for a particular 'dispute' that has frequented the pages of this book: 'Are Seasoned Musicians More of an

Asset or a Liability?' Readers certainly experienced sections of previous chapters as having presented diverging, opposing, and even heated viewpoints on this issue. But, for some players (and note the age of the player below) there was really no issue at all:

(52y, M, vc)   *The older players aren't any more of an asset than younger players. It's a commu-nity. Each orchestra has its own little tradition of the way it plays, the ways it sounds. It's very hard to change that. It's the community as a whole that makes it. We have all got different skills. Younger players bring different skills. Older players have dif-ferent skills. Younger players may just have a little bit more energy, may be more technical, more secure in terms of instrumental playing, probably a little less guess-work involved. The chances of missing a shift in a younger player might be less than it is in an older player (who probably hasn't practised properly for a few weeks or months). But then the older player has a more stable mental approach, because they've been there, they've done that, they've seen it. They don't need to get all flus-tered if the tempo is faster than it was two weeks ago. They will have brought that experience from somebody else, 20 different Conductors who lead that piece. And they have all played it in a consistently accurate, solid, and secure manner. The younger players will fit into that, but they will also bring their youthful enthusi-asm to the performance. So, we're a community of older, younger, middle, very old, and very young people—all contributing our little bit according to experience. It's a community, and each musician within that group has something. Some have great rhythmic skills, others have great lyrical skills, others have great harmonic skills, and others can hear longer lines of music. We all bring our little bit of inspiration together.*

13.3.1 The Psychomotor Facilities of Seasoned Musicians

Krampe (2002) claimed that the production of rhythmic patterns demonstrates age-specific deterioration in sequencing capacity. That is, with increased complexity older adults demonstrate a higher number of errors, which indicate lack of distinc-tion in relative target duration within the same rhythmic cycles. Perhaps Krampe's intention was 'complex rhythms' such as *Cross-Rhythms* or *Poly-Rhythms*. In the cur-rent study, there were no deteriorations among the Seasoned Musicians concerning their capacities to control fine motor movements. The current study employed five isochronous tapping tasks (see Chapter 8, section 8.2.2.2), including: (a) self-paced tapping at a spontaneous rate of speed; (b) self-paced tapping at preferred rate of speed; (c) speeded uni-manual single-finger tapping for the right hand; (d) speeded uni-manual single-finger tapping for the left hand; (e) speeded bimanual alternate-finger tapping. As far as *pace* is concerned, Seasoned Musicians performed all tapping tasks just as fast as Young(er) Players. When assessing variability or *consis-tency* of motor performance (i.e., deviations of tapping), the current study found that the variability of spontaneous and preferred finger-tapping tempos were within sim-ilar ranges, and that Seasoned Musicians were just as consistent. Finally, the old(er) players demonstrated even better indices of symmetry. In short, the *proof of the pud-ding* is that no negative effects of age were found for Seasoned Musicians regarding domain-specific expertise-related psychomotor facilities.

13.3.2 The Performance Facilities of Seasoned Musicians

John Rink, a specialist in music-performance studies at Cambridge University (UK), Director of Studies in Music at St John's College, and former director of the AHRC Research Centre for Musical Performance as Creative Practice, stated that performance-related analysis can be divided into two principal categories: (a) analysis prior to a given performance; and (b) analysis of the performance itself (Rink, 2002). Regarding the former, Rink claimed that such an analysis

> primarily takes place as an interpretation is being formulated and subsequently re-evaluated—that is, while one is practising rather than performing. This does not deny its potential influence on actual performance or that new discoveries are sometimes made during performances. (p. 39)

Although music performance is typically a public experience, preparation for a performance usually takes place in private—and often in complete isolation. The starting point for performances of Classical Music is normally a score: a text with instructions for the performer to translate what the Composer might have had in mind into an audible sound. Rink outlined six processes that most performers implement. See Table 13.2. Reid (2002) felt that decoding a score requires considerable interpretative input and insight from the performer. Even the simplest passage will be shaped according to the performer's understanding of how it fits. Rink claimed that such decisions might be intuitive and unsystematic, as most performers consider how the music unfolds in time, and how they need overcome conceptual and mechanical challenges. In the current study, all participating players were asked to perform a newly composed piece at first sight—never before having had access to the text—not even visually scanning the score. This is referred to as a *prima vista* performance (see Chapter 10, sections 10.3.1.2 and 10.3.1.5). Then, before playing the piece a second time, each player received a standard ±10:00 minutes for Deliberate Practice. DP was the time used to rehearse and resolve performance elements or sections perceived as being difficult. Namely, players spent their time attempting to overcome glitches and snags that surfaced to improve malfunctions, anomalies, and near errors of fingering or articulation. Each player was asked to speak aloud throughout the full duration—known as a *Think Aloud Protocol* (TAP). The study employed an innovative configuration for coding TAPs transcriptions. Unlike the six techniques outlined by Rink in Table 13.2, the *codex* used in the current study consisted of four Main Themes with 18 Subthemes (see Table 9.6), all of which are potential practice strategies or techniques. The current study found that the participating players, regardless of their instrument (Strings or Winds) or their age (LTE45 or GTE55), all mentally perceived, verbally mentioned, and actively engaged in DP in a similar manner. The Seasoned Musicians were just as efficient in implementing strategic manoeuvres required to improve the music piece. Further, DP duration time was similar for all players, and the number of strategies employed to improve

Table 13.2 Intuitive Processes Implemented During Practice for Music Performance

	Techniques
1	Identifying Formal Divisions and Basic Tonal Plan
2	Graphing Tempo
3	Graphing Dynamics
4	Analysing Melodic Shape and Constituent Motifs/Ideas
5	Preparing a Rhythmic Reduction
6	Re-Notating the Music

Data Source: Rink (2002, p. 41)

the piece were each recognizably linked to aspects of Accuracy, Dexterity, Tempo-Rhythm, Memory, Attention, Phrasing, Dynamics, Expression, Musical Structure, Melodic–Harmonic Balance, and Tone Quality.

The second form of music-performance analysis outlined by Rink (2002) has to do with the performance itself. In the current study, music-performance data was collected from 48 professional full-time contract Symphony Orchestra players. There were two performances per player: The first occurred prior to a ±10-minute period of Deliberate Practice (a *prima vista* Sight-Reading), while the second was implemented post-practice (a more *polished* rendition-version). The performances were audio-recorded and sent to expert judges in a double-blind adjudicating procedure (see Chapter 10, section 10.3). The external independent blind-judges rated the 2nd music performances as having improved between 6% and 15% depending on the assessment measure used for evaluation. Previously I suggested that the differences between the two measures ultimately reflected disparities between what judges *felt* in their heart (a more subjective impression) and what they *observed* with the ears (a more objective detection). One fascinating result of the music-performance analyses was the following: If the issue of music-performance evaluation centres on aspects of the *product* (e.g., the final performance score), then the Young(er) Players performed more efficiently by an average 17%. Nonetheless, if the issue of music-performance evaluation centres on aspects of the *process* (e.g., employing the most appropriate Feature Components and Constituents while practising the music to improve performance, that is, the overall post-practice improvement seen in Delta-Δ scores), then the Seasoned Musicians were more effective by 11%. Finally, when evaluating performances for *flawlessness*, that is the percentage of exact precision for the second pass, it could be seen that while the Young(er) Players performed 85% error-free, the Seasoned Musicians performed 90% error-free—albeit these differences were not statistically significant, and therefore do not indicate that one subgroup significantly outperformed the other. Namely, all players regardless of their age subgroup were equally similar in performance! Therefore: Are Seasoned Musicians More of an Asset than a Liability? The *proof of the pudding* is that little (if any) difference between Young(er) Players and Seasoned Musicians surfaces. So, my answer to the query that has entered the text of this book as having been insinuated in the interviews (and vignettes) by many players, is simple. The evidence clearly shows that

Seasoned Musicians are no more of a liability for performing at expert performance levels than are Young(er) Players!

13.4 Discussion and Summary

A Symphony Orchestra career is often looked upon with awe by the public.[2] A contract position with a well-known Orchestra is highly regarded, and often the target of competitive auditions. Yet, Orchestra Lifestyle is easily misconceived by outsiders. While only a few researchers have ever been able to penetrate group barriers to gain the confidence of Orchestra members, most do not report emotions and cognitions pertinent to occupational development, career aspirations, vocational motivations, and performance experiences. Certainly, none have implemented psychomotor tasks (e.g., computerized trials involving Finger Tapping), a period of Deliberate Practice (employing Think Aloud Protocols), or an *in vivo/in situ* music-performance analysis. In a very early study, perhaps the one that I would view as a first psychosocial research investigation among Orchestra players, Westby (1960) infiltrated an Orchestra milieu by spending six weeks just getting to know the players. Westby claimed that this time frame was necessary to lay the groundwork for the development of trust, and stated: "Symphony musicians are an occupational group exhibiting considerable anxiety over their jobs on a number of dimensions [...] gaining the confidence of the musicians in the interview situation was therefore crucial for the elicitation of unthreatened responses" (p. 223).

The general public perceive full-time contract Symphony Orchestra players as being hard-working, ambitious, self-absorbed, introspective, and introverted creative individuals. Actually, 30 years of investigation led Kemp (1996) to outline Symphony Orchestra players as individuals who exhibit: higher motivation, persistence, and enthusiasm; depth of emotionality and creativity; independence and self-confidence; as well as individuality and inventiveness. Further, Kemp demonstrated that they tend to be emotionally open (imaginative and intuitive), less bound by conventional beliefs and restraints, prefer complexity (ambiguity and multidimensionality), and are characteristically exhibitionistic (able to transmit emotions at will and to thrill others). Moreover, they are able to dare to risk success or failure, and possess the courage to tolerate lack of appreciation by external judges. Finally, Orchestra players are regarded as possessing a high degree of work satisfaction, and their passion for the vocation is enhanced by a sensory pleasure in exercising superior skills and capacities for music performance. Another researcher, Sternbach

---

[2] Portions of this section were adapted from Brodsky (2006). Reprinted by permission.

(1993, 1995), stated that Symphony Orchestra players are usually seen as individuals with strong inner-driven working careers who are self-selected, and enjoy what we all romanticize as a glamorous life with opportunities for self-expression and self-actualization. Yet, none of these perceptions, or personological studies of temperament, have made any strides in uncovering the journey that musicians actually make to become a professional Symphony Orchestra player, nor have they detailed the immense efforts players invest in maintaining their skill set to preserve their presence in the Classical Music performance profession. Specifically, there has not as yet been a case study of Symphony Orchestra Lifestyle. Hence, compared to other occupational groups and professional organizations, little is known about Symphony Orchestra players. The current study, then, was an attempt to fill that gap.

Long ago Steptoe (1989) examined Orchestral Lifestyle through a postal survey with 65 players in two British organizations—the Royal Philharmonic Orchestra and the London Philharmonic Orchestra. I note that these two performance organizations were not participants in the current investigation. Steptoe found that the more positive aspects of the vocation were: Variety of the job; Travelling; Performing to audiences; Social life in the musical world; and Status as an artist. The more negative aspects of the vocation were: Monotony of rehearsals; Uncertainty about schedule; Irregular hours; Travelling; Separation from family; Competition and Back-stabbing among colleagues; and Financial weakness. It would seem that Steptoe's findings foretold a number of similar points that have been disclosed in the vignettes of this current study, as if predicting the storylines that would be revealed from the Orchestra musicians 50 years later.

In an earlier study by Brodsky (2006), a sample of full-time contract Symphony Orchestra players were asked to respond to the question: 'Why do musicians want to be a full-time contract professional Symphony Orchestra player?' That query came on the coat-tails of the participants offering a far more negative set of motives renouncing the profession than positive ones in favour of joining the profession. It did seem that for many players, the music-performance vocation was rather undesirable. But for the majority, the incentives for a Symphony Orchestra career were: Socializing with like-minded people, Camaraderie, Solidarity, and Teamwork. Namely, players do view the Symphony Orchestra as "the place where they can do what they do best, and with others who do it just as well" (p. 687). But truth be told, already then I saw Orchestra Lifestyle as an outer shell, somewhat protecting all those on the inside from the realities of the outside world. Orchestra Lifestyle seemed to serve as architectural scaffolding, an adhesive-like casing, bonding and banding together all of those who engage in collective music-making. There is no room for anything else but life among the Orchestra. I had concluded:

Orchestral Lifestyle entails a somewhat parallel reality to what other mortals experience, and the way of life within a contract orchestra is an all-encompassing structure leaving no room for a partial involvement. (p. 686)

My final question to the players at that time, was: 'Why do Symphony Orchestra musicians even want to perform onstage?' After all, there is a lot of tension, anxiety, and a live stage performance is not without its risks. I remember many of the players looking at me . . . and then there was always a moment of silence! What had been said after the silence was broken was rather unpretentious and down to earth. What I heard was: "The concert platform provides an arena for the exhibition of technical mastery, and this public display of expertise influences each and every musician's psychological equilibrium. They do it because they can, and for most musicians, there is no alternative" (p. 687).

13.4.1 Coda

Researchers interested in advancing the science of expert performance need to rise above specific disciplinary differences and develop theories and models that account for as many potentially relevant explanatory factors as possible. These might include, but are not limited to: Deliberate Practice, environmental variables, and heritable traits, as well as situational factors. Hambrick et al. (2014) claimed that some of these might moderate performance. They claimed that: "An open-minded exchange of ideas among researchers with diverse theoretical and methodological perspectives will make this possible and shed fresh light on the origins of expert performance" (p. 43). Unlike investigations on Lifespan Development of everyday abilities, studies on exceptional performance have generally focused on the conditions by which exceptional people have been able to develop, and are able to exhibit at will, super-human levels of mastery (Ericsson, 2000). Hence, perhaps, the study of professional full-time contract Symphony Orchestra players is somewhere in the middle. After all, Orchestra players are remarkably uniquely different from other people simply on the basis of their performance skills and music persona-identity. Yet they are more commonplace than Virtuosi Soloists in the sense that they work in a contracted position within a vocational setting on a daily basis. Habibi et al. (2014) are perhaps the only research team to have considered differences between several modes of music performance; specifically, whether the music activity is individual or centred on a group collaboration. "Given that playing music in a group requires musicians to pay close attention to auditory and sensorimotor output as well as to the emotional state of other players, it is reasonable to expect that collective music making may improve pro-social behavior and strengthen group cohesion" (p. 9). I would take the association between music training and development of emotional/social skills as co-dependent on the type of music engagement, even a step further. I would consider Symphony Orchestra musicians as inherently distinctive from all other performing musicians—explicitly because of Orchestra Lifestyle.

Today we do face unprecedented population changes resulting from human ageing. As a result there is a great need to identify those factors that might promote healthy cognitive ageing, and may even protect against age-related neurodegenerative conditions such as Dementia and Alzheimer's disease. Balbag et al. (2014) feel that almost all past attention has focused on the cognitive effects of playing a musical instrument (as a child, youngster, teenager, and young adult); musical engagement is indeed viewed as a protective factor in later life cognition, and as delaying neurodegenerative decline and illness. Yet, thus far, most studies present fairly inconsistent findings—based on unreliable samples as proxies for musicians—that are at best simply projective by nature. At the time of writing, the current case study stands alone in depth, breadth, and reliability compared to any other published description of professional full-time contract Symphony Orchestra players. Most specifically, the investigation package in the book puts forth the conceptions and perceptions of how music performers adapt to the ill effects of ageing, and these perhaps reveal a picture illustrating higher levels of resilience than usually depicted among the general population.

Appendix A

Original music by Israeli Symphonic Composer Moshe Zorman (b. 1952). Three versions—each an independent complete stand-alone *miniature*—consist of the appropriate notation and performance markings for one of five instrument families: Woodwinds, Brass, Keyboard Percussion, Harp, and Strings. There were 15 scores for all orchestra instruments as individual parts:

1	Flute
2	Oboe
3	Clarinet in B♭
4	Bassoon
5	Horn in F
6	Trumpet in B♭
7	Alto Saxophone
8	Trombone
9	Tuba
10	Xylophone
11	Harp
12	Violin
13	Viola
14	Cello
15	Double Bass

Flute

melody for w.w

Moshe Zorman

2

Flute

Oboe

melody-oboe

Moshe Zorman

2

Oboe

Clarinet in B♭

melody-w.w

Moshe Zorman

Bassoon

melody- w.w

2

Horn in F

melody- horn in f

Moshe Zorman

2   Horn in F

Trumpet in B♭

melody-trumpet

Moshe Zorman

2   Trumpet in B♭

Alto Saxophone

melody- alto sax

Moshe Zorman

2

Alto Saxophone

Trombone

melody-trombone

Moshe Zorman

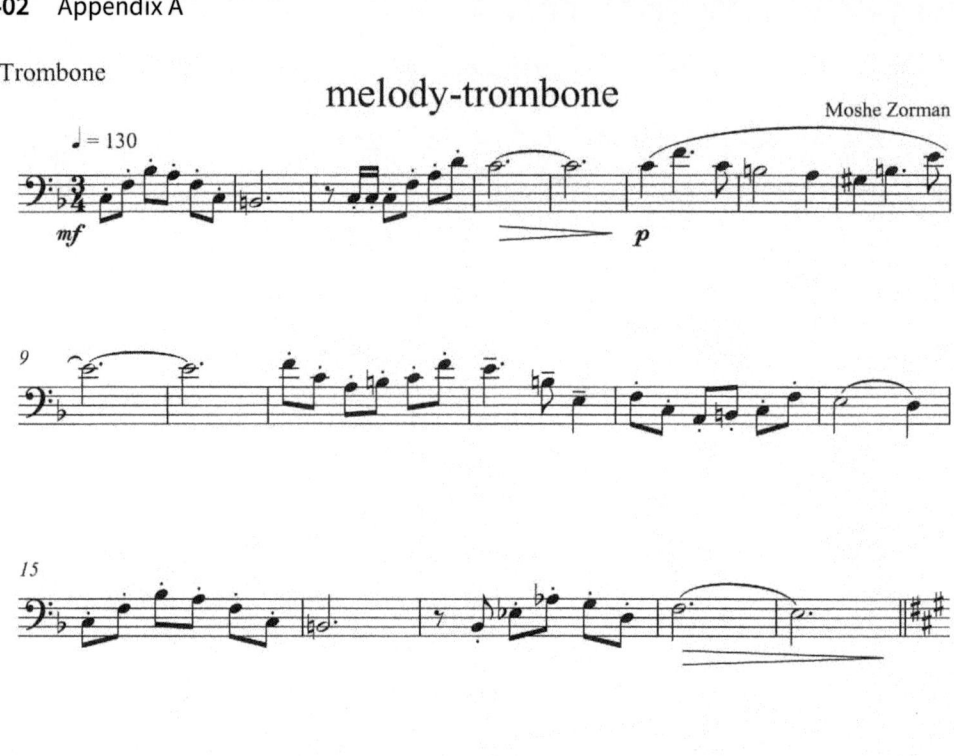

2   Trombone

Tuba

melody-tuba

Moshe zorman

2   Tuba

Xylophone

melody for xylophone

Moshe Zorman

2

Xylophone

Harp

melody-harp

Moshe Zorman

2   Harp

Violin

melody-violin

Moshe Zorman

2   Violin

Viola

melody-viola

Moshe Zorman

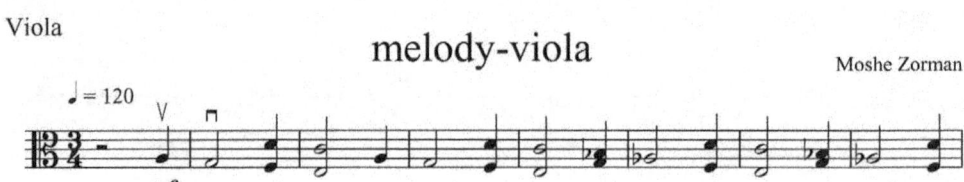

2

Viola

Violoncello

melody-cello

Moshe Zorman

2   Violoncello

Contrabass

melody-bass

Moshe Zorman

2   Contrabass

Appendix B

The *Keele Assessment of Auditory Style* (Brodsky, 1995, 2004) was developed by Warren Brodsky and John A. Sloboda of the Unit for the Development of Musical Skill and Development in the Department of Psychology at Keele University (Staffordshire, UK). KAAS is a 61-item self-report questionnaire targeting behaviours based on retrospective memory across three critical periods of human development:

Child-Youngster, 4–12 years old
Teenager, 13–18 years old
Adult, >18 years old

KAAS employs a five-point Likert scale to rate responses ('Never' = 1; 'Always' = 5), with an option to mark 'naught' (zero = 0) for items the respondent couldn't remember or those items that did not seem relevant. Among the total 61 items there is a 38-item subscale reflecting more general behaviours related to sound; these items and subscale are referred to as the *Auditivity Scale*. In addition, there is a second 23-item subscale for specific music engagement such as playing an instrument.

KEELE ASSESSMENT OF AUDITORY STYLE (KAAS)

AS A PRIMARY MODE OF PSYCHOLOGICAL ORIENTATION AND DEVELOPMENT

Warren Brodsky and John A. Sloboda (1993)

Please fill in the blank space of each statement below by indicating one of the numbers from the 5-point scale which describes YOU during the specified period of your lifetime. You can indicate answers such as 'don't know', 'can't remember', or 'not relevant' with a zero (0). Please do not leave any questions blank. In this questionnaire the meaning of the words 'instrument' and 'music activity' should also include voice, composing, and conducting. The indicators are:

5 = ALWAYS 4 = OFTEN 3 = SOMETIMES 2 = RARELY 1 = NEVER

AS A CHILD/YOUNGSTER (5–12) . . .

1. When I listened to music I _____ found myself unable to sit still.
2. Music _____ caused me to move in a rhythmic way (e.g., tap fingers, stamp feet, move head, sway body).
3. I _____ liked stories more than nursery rhymes and songs.
4. I _____ preferred stories and book reading at night-time above lullabies and songs.
5. I _____ remember feeling afraid when I heard loud noises.
6. I was _____ comforted by a familiar tune or melody when sad.
7. I _____ discovered myself making noise (such as humming, singing, or beating) or moving rhythmically throughout the day.
8. I _____ found it easier to follow a written text if I or someone else read it aloud.
9. I _____ found it both easy and enjoyable to fall asleep while on a train, bus, or motor car.
10. I _____ found myself suddenly humming a piece of music or melody without realizing that I'd started.
11. I would _____ hum bits and pieces of music while walking along the way not especially aware of their source.
12. I _____ felt as if I could experience my emotions far better through music than through speech.
13. I was _____ aware that I felt and heard things in music that I could not articulate verbally.
14. I _____ felt drawn to repeat and re-experience musical events that affected me.
15. The role models I most wanted to be like were _____ music performers.

AS AN ADOLESCENT (13–18) . . .

16. I was _____ aware of the similarities and/or differences in intonation (tone qualities) between my voice and my parents' voices.
17. I _____ imagined music in my mind when bored.
18. I _____ identified myself as having a special gift for music.
19. I _____ felt more comfortable within other social groups than musical social settings such as ensemble and choir.
20. When listening to piece of music I _____ imagined that I too was among the performers.

AS AN ADULT (18±) . . .

21. I am _____ very sensitive to the sound quality of other people's voices.
22. Voice tone is _____ a major influence on whether I am attracted to someone.
23. I find I _____ tend to trust people more if their voices are pleasing to me.

24. When I choose names (e.g., children, pets) I _____ pay attention to their rhythmic and musical sound.
25. The external sound environment (soundscape) is _____ a major factor for me when choosing neighbourhoods where to live.
26. When I find myself in new surroundings I am _____ first aware of the landscape before the soundscape.
27. I _____ become anxious when I become aware of a soundless environment (total quiet).
28. During conversation I _____ find myself listening or attending to the other person's speech patterns and vocal inflections more than the actual content itself.
29. I _____ find silences in conversation more difficult to tolerate than actual differences of opinion.
30. I am _____ aware of an emotion depicted on the television/movie screen via the soundtrack before the screenplay action is revealed.
31. I _____ feel as if there is a piece of music going through my mind.
32. I have _____ felt that when I am away from my significant other(s), the mere sound of their voice will relieve me from melancholy and loneliness.
33. When I listen to music I _____ experience and perceive a kinaesthetic body 'feeling' the music in addition to my ear 'hearing' the music.
34. When improvising or humming to myself, I can _____ decide whether I composed an original piece (phrase) or simply repeated one that I had heard previously.
35. I have _____ felt that I must protect my hearing as it is my most important link to the outside world.
36. I have _____ noticed that I depend often on my sense of hearing for gaining information regarding where things might be (location).
37. I _____ prefer to hear the news via the radio than the television.
38. I find that I _____ fall asleep more easily when there is music playing in the background.

AS A CHILD/YOUNGSTER INVOLVED IN MUSICAL ACTIVITY (4–12) . . .

39. It _____ felt to me as though I was playing the instrument of my choice.
40. I _____ had feelings of being different from the other children who were not learning an instrument.
41. I _____ spent time producing expressive sounds on my instrument.
42. I _____ had a certain 'feeling of power' when I produced some sounds with my instrument.
43. I _____ had a 'feeling of comfort' when I produced some sounds with my instrument.
44. I _____ attempted to imitate sound qualities of other performers with my instrument.
45. I _____ attempted to imitate sound qualities of nature with my instrument.
46. I _____ liked to show off through the sounds I could produce on my instrument.

AS AN ADOLESCENT INVOLVED IN MUSICAL ACTIVITY (13–18) . . .

47. I _____ felt that the degree to which I was able to master a piece or technique, influenced the degree to which I felt I was in control of my life.
48. I _____ felt my parents' approval of me was dependent on my success as a musician.
49. I _____ identified more with ensemble performers than soloists.
50. I _____ found myself playing on my instrument at times of sadness, loneliness, fear, or apprehension.
51. I had _____ felt that the reason I was never really motivated to attempt to overcome frustrations of peer interactions and academic challenges, was because I could always escape into my own world of music (sound) making.
52. I had _____ felt that because I had such an intense interest with music I was not inclined to become involved with any other pursuits.

AS AN ADULT INVOLVED IN MUSICAL ACTIVITY (18±) . . .

53. I am _____ uncertain if I actually heard a musical sound (motif or phrase) rather than imagining it.
54. When I imagine seeing music notation, I _____ imagine hearing the notes.
55. When I cannot hear my instrument during a performance, I _____ feel 'I am lost'.
56. I can_____ tolerate inexactness of musical pitch.
57. I _____ feel assaulted by eighth and quarter tones.
58. I _____ enjoy improvising with sound sonorities on my instrument.
59. I _____ feel that through playing my instrument I reconnect with the child in me.
60. When I practise by myself I _____ find that my mouth has fallen open and/or my eyes have closed.
61. My understanding of another person is _____ heightened when we perform music together.

References

Abels, H., & Hafeli, M. (2014). Seeking professional fulfilment: US symphony orchestra members in schools. *Psychology of Music, 42*(1), 35–50.

Abraham, J. D., & Hansson, R. O. (1995). Successful aging at work: An applied study of selection, optimization, and compensation through impression management. *Journal of Gerontology: Psychological Sciences, 50B*(2), 94–103.

Abrahan, V. D., Shifres, F., & Justel, N. (2019). Cognitive benefits from musical activity in older adults. *Frontiers in Psychology: Emotion Science, 10*(March), Article 652.

Ackerman, P. L. (2014). Nonsense, common sense, and science of expert performance: Talent and individual differences. *Personality and Individual Differences, 45*, 6–17.

Aggleton, J., Kentridge, R., & Good, J. (1994). Handedness and musical ability: A study of professional orchestral players, composers and choir members. *Psychology of Music, 22*(2), 148–156.

Alain, C., Zendel, B. R., Hutka, S., & Bidelman, G. M. (2014). Turning down the noise: The benefit of musical training on the aging auditory brain. *Hearing Research, 308*, 162–173.

Ali, S. (2010). Understanding our students' self-regulation during practice: Verbal protocol as a tool. *Journal of Singing, 66*(5), 529–536.

All-Party Parliamentary Group on Arts, Health and Wellbeing Inquiry (2017). *Creative health: The Arts for health and wellbeing.* Found at: https://www.culturehealthandwellbeing.org.uk/appg-inquiry/.

Allmendinger, J., Hackman, J. R., & Lehman, E. V. (1996). Life and work in symphony orchestras. *The Musical Quarterly, 80*(2), 194–219.

Altenmuller, E., Gruhn, W., Parlitz, D., & Kahrs, J. (1997). Music learning produces changes in brain activation patterns: A longitudinal DC-EEG study. *International Journal of Arts Medicine, 5*(1), 28–33.

Altenmuller, E., & James, C. E. (2020). The impact of music interventions on motor rehabilitation following stroke in elderly. *In* L. L. Cuddy, S. Belleville, & A. Moussard (Eds.), *Music and the aging brain* (pp. 407–432). London, UK: Academic Press, Elsevier.

Amer, T., Kalender, B., Hasher, L., Trehub, S. E., & Wong, Y. (2013). Do older professional musicians have cognitive advantages? *PLOS ONE, 8*(8), Article e71630.

American Geriatrics Society (2007). Trends in the elderly population. Health and ageing resources on the web, chapter 2. Found at: http://www.healthinageing.org/ageingintheknow/.

Andrews, M. W., Dowling, W. J., Halpern, A. R., & Bartlett, J. C. (1998). Identification of speeded and slowed familiar melodies by younger, middle-aged, and older musicians and nonmusicians. *Psychology and Aging, 13*, 462–471.

Ascenso, S., Perkins, R., & Williamon, A. (2018). Resounding meaning: A PERMA wellbeing profile of classical musicians. *Frontiers in Psychology (Performance Science), 9*, Article 1895, 14 pages.

Ascenso, S., Williamon, A., & Perkins, R. (2017). Understanding the wellbeing of professional musicians through the lens of positive psychology. *Psychology of Music, 45*(1), 65–81.

Azar, B. (1998). Little evidence that old age causes work deterioration. *APA Monitor, 29*(July)

Babin, A. (1999). Orchestra pit sound level measurements in Broadway shows. *Medical Problems of Performing Artists, 14*(4), 204–209.

Bajor, J. K., & Baltes, B. B. (2003). The relationship between selection optimization with compensation, contentiousness, motivation, and performance. *Journal of Vocational Behavior, 63*, 347–367.

Balbag, M. A., Pedersen, N. L., & Gatz, M. (2014). Playing a musical instrument as a protective factor against dementia and cognitive impairment: A population-based twin study. *International Journal of Alzheimer's Disease*, Article ID 836748, 1–6.

Baltes, P. B. (1997). On the incomplete architecture of human ontogeny: Selection, optimization, and compensation as foundation of developmental theory. *American Psychologist, 52*(4), 366–380.

Baltes, P. B., & Baltes, M. M. (1990). Psychological perspectives on successful aging: The model of selective optimization with compensation. *In* P. B. Baltes & M. M. Baltes (Eds.), *Successful aging: Perspectives from the behavioral sciences* (pp. 1–34). Cambridge, UK: Cambridge University Press.

Baltes, P. B., Baltes, M. M., Freund, A. M., & Lang, F. (1999a). *The measurement of selection, optimization, and compensation (SOC) by self report.* Technical Report Nr. 66. Berlin: Max Planck Institute for Human Development. Found at: https://doi.org/10.48644/mpib_escidoc_33564.

Baltes, P. B., Lindenberger, U., & Staudinger, U. M. (2006). Life span theory in developmental psychology. *In* R. M. Lerner (Ed.), *Handbook of child psychology: Theoretical models of human development* (6th ed., Vol. 1, pp. 569–654). Hoboken, NJ: Wiley.

Baltes, P. B., & Staudinger, U. M. (1996). Interactive minds in a life-span perspective: prologue. *In* P. B. Baltes & U. M. Staudinger (Eds.), *Interactive minds: Life-span perspectives on the social foundation of cognition* (pp. 1–34). Cambridge, UK: Cambridge University Press.

Baltes, P. B., Staudinger, U. M., & Lindenberger, U. (1999b). Lifespan psychology: Theory and application to intellectual functioning. *Annual Review of Psychology, 50,* 471–507.

Bangert, D., Fabian, D., Schubert, E., & Yeadon, D. (2014). Performing solo Bach: A case study of musical decision-making. *Musicæ Scientiæ, 18*(1), 35–52.

Bangert, D., Schubert, E., & Fabian, D. (2015). Practice thoughts and performance action: Observing processes of musical decision-making. *Music Performance Research, 7,* 27–46.

Barkaoui, K. (2011). Think-aloud protocols in research on essay rating: An empirical study of their veridicality and reactivity. *Language Testing, 28*(1), 57–75.

Barry, N. H. (1992). The effects of practice strategies, individual differences in cognitive style, and gender upon technical accuracy and musicality of student instrumental performance. *Psychology of Music, 20*(2), 112–123.

Bartel, L. R., & Thompson, E. G. (1995). Coping with performance stress: A study of professional orchestral musicians in Canada. *The Quarterly Journal of Music Teaching and Learning, 5*(4), 70–78.

Barton, R. (2004). The ageing musician. *Work, 22,* 31–38.

Behar, A., Wong, W., & Kunov, H. (2006). Risk of hearing loss in orchestra musicians: Review of the literature. *Medical Problems of Performing Artists, 21,* 164–168.

Behroozi, K. B., & Luz, J. (1997). Noise-related ailments of performing musicians: A review. *Medical Problems of Performing Arts, 12*(1), 19–22.

Bennett, A., & Hodkinson, P. (Eds.) (2012). *Ageing and youth cultures: Music, style and identity.* London, UK: Berg.

Bennett, D., & Hennekam, S. (2018). Lifespan perspective theory and (classical) musician's careers. *In* C. Dromey & J. Haferkorn (Eds.), *Routledge research in creative and cultural industries management: The classical music industry* (pp. 112–125). London, UK: Routledge, Taylor & Francis.

Biasutti, M. (2013). Orchestra rehearsal strategies: Conductor and performer views. *Musicæ Scientiæ, 17*(1), 57–71.

Bonneville-Roussy, A., Lavigne, G. L., & Vallerand, R. J. (2011). When passion leads to excellence: The case of musicians. *Psychology of Music, 39*(1), 123–138.

Botstein, L. (1996). The future of the orchestra. *The Musical Quarterly, 80,* 189–193.

Boucher, M., Creech, A., & Dubé, F. (2019). Video feedback and the self-evaluation of college-level guitarists during individual practice. *Psychology of Music, 49,* 159–176.

Brandfonbrener, A. G. (1997). Orchestral injury prevention intervention study. *Medical Problems of Performing Arts, 12*(1), 9–14.

Brandfonbrener, A. G. (2003). Old musicians never die: Issues of ageing in orchestra musicians. *Medical Problems of Performing Artists, 18,* 135–136.

Bright, R. (1980). *Music in geriatric care.* Wahroonga, NSW: Musigraphics.

Brochard, R., Dufour, A., & Depres, O. (2004). Effect of musical expertise on visuospatial abilities: Evidence from reaction times and mental imagery. *Brain and Cognition, 54,* 103–109.

Brodsky, M. (1995). Blues musicians' access to health care. *Medical Problems of Performing Artists, 10,* 18–23.

Brodsky, W. (1990). Disassociative ego functions of the creative musician. *The Creative Child and Adult Quarterly, 15*(4), 183–188.

Brodsky, W. (1995). Career stress and performance anxiety in professional orchestra musicians: A study of individual differences and their impact on therapeutic outcomes. [Unpublished doctoral dissertation]. Keele University, Staffordshire, UK.

Brodsky, W. (1996). Music performance anxiety reconceptualized: A critique of the current research practices and findings. *Medical Problems of Performing Artists, 11*(3), 88–98.

Brodsky, W. (1997). Auditivity—a cognitive and psychological orientation based on sensory preferences for audition. *In* A. Gabrielsson (Ed.), *Proceedings of the Third Triennial ESCOM Conference (European Society for the Cognitive Sciences of Music)* (pp. 317–322). Uppsala, Sweden: Department of Psychology, Uppsala University.

Brodsky, W. (1999). Auffuhrungsangste bei Musikern als musikbezogenes Phanomen: Ein neues Konzept (Reconceptualizing music performance anxiety as a music-related phenomenon). *Musikphysiologie und Musikermedzin* (Journal of Music Physiology and Music Medicine), *6*(March), 14–18.

Brodsky, W. (2000). Post-Exposure effects of music-generated vibration and whole-body acoustic stimulation among symphony orchestra musicians. *Psychology of Music, 28*(1), 98–115.

Brodsky, W. (2004). Developing the Keele Assessment of Auditory Style (KAAS): A factor-analytic study of cognitive trait predisposition for audition. *Musicæ Scientiæ, 8*(1), 83–108.

Brodsky, W. (2006). In the wings of British orchestras: A multi-episode interview study of symphony players. *Journal of Occupational and Organizational Psychology, 79*(4), 673–690.

Brodsky, W. (2011). Rationale behind investigating positive aging among symphony orchestra musicians: A call for a new arena of empirical study. *Musicæ Scientiæ, 15*(1), 3–15.

Brodsky, W. (2015). *Driving with music: Behavioural-cognitive implications.* Boca Raton, FL: CRC Press, Taylor & Francis Group.

Brodsky, W., Henik, A., Rubinstein, B. S., & Zorman, M. (1999). Inner hearing among symphony orchestra musicians: Intersectional differences of string players versus wind players (Chapter 20). *In* S. W. Yi (Ed.), *Music, mind, and science* (pp. 370–392). Seoul: Seoul National University Press.

Brodsky, W., Henik, A., Rubinstein, B.-S., & Zorman, M. (2003). Auditory imagery from musical notation in expert musicians. *Perception & Psychophysics, 65*(4), 602–612.

Brodsky, W., & Kessler, Y. (2017). The effects of beam slope on the perception of melodic contour. *Acta Psychologica, 180*, 190–199.

Brodsky, W., Kessler, Y., Rubinstein, B.-S., Ginsborg, J., & Henik, A. (2008). The mental representation of music notation: Notational audiation. *Journal of Experimental Psychology: Human Perception & Performance, 34*, 427–445.

Brodsky, W., & Sloboda, J. A. (1997a). Clinical trial of a music generated vibrotactile therapeutic environment for musicians: Main effects and outcome differences between therapy subgroups. *Journal of Music Therapy, 34*(1), 2–32.

Brodsky, W., & Sloboda, J. A. (1997b). The effects of whole-body acoustic stimulation on subjective relaxation, verbalisation, and visual imagery among professional orchestra members. *In* A. Gabrielsson (Ed.), *Proceedings of the Third Triennial ESCOM Conference (European Society for the Cognitive Sciences of Music)* (pp. 232–328). Uppsala, Sweden: Uppsala University, Department of Psychology.

Brodsky, W., Sloboda, J. A., & Waterman, M. G. (1994). An exploratory investigation into auditory style as a correlate and predictor of music performance anxiety. *Medical Problems of Performing Artists, 9*(4), 101–112.

Brodsky, W., & Sulkin, I. (2011). Handclapping songs: A spontaneous platform for child development among 5–10-year-old children. *Early Child Development and Care, 181*(8), 1111–1136.

Brody, J. A., Grant, M. D., Brandfonbrenner, A. G., Nyenhuis, D., & Rathouz, P. (ND). Music cognition and ageing: A pilot study. Unpublished Grant Proposal.

Bruhn, H. (2002). Music development of elderly people. *Psychomusicology, 18*, 59–75.

Bugos, J. A., Perlstein, W. M., McCrea, C. S., Brophy, T. S., & Bedenbaugh, P. H. (2007). Individualized piano instruction enhances executive functioning and working memory in older adults. *Aging & Mental Health, 11*(4), 464–471.

Bullerjahn, C., Dziewas, J., Hilsdorf, M., Kassl, C., Menze, J., & Gembris, H. (2020). Why adolescents participate in a music contest and why they practice—the influence of incentives, flow, and volitation on practice time. *Frontiers in Psychology, Performance Science, 11*(561814), 17 pages.

Burwell, K., & Shipton, M. (2013). Strategic approaches to practice: An action research project. *British Journal of Music Education, 30*(3), 329–345.

Butler, J., & Kern, M. L. (2016). The PERMA-Profiler: A brief multi-dimensional measure of flourishing. *International Journal of Wellbeing, 6*(3), 1–48.

Campbell, P. S. (1998). *Songs in their heads*. Oxford, UK: Oxford University Press.

Campbell-Sills, L., & Stein, M. B. (2007). Psychometric analysis and refinement of the Connor-Davidson Resilience Scale (CD-RISC): Validation of a 10-item measure of resilience. *Journal of Traumatic Stress, 20*(6), 1019–1028.

Carter, F. (1995/1996). Dear Orchestra . . . a tour of South America with the RPO. *Performing Arts Medicine News, 3*(4), 9–11.

Carterette, E. C., & Kendall, R. A. (1996). Acoustical analysis of natural and emulated orchestral instrument signals. Paper presented at the 4th ICMPC (International Conference on Music Perception and Cognition), Faculty of Music, McGill University, Montreal, Quebec, 11–15 August 1996.

Cavanaugh, J. C. (1997). *Adult development and ageing*. Pacific Grove, CA: Brooks/Cole.

Cepeda, N. J., Kramer, A. F., & de Sather, J. (2001). Changes in executive control across the life span: Examination of task-switching performance. *Developmental Psychology, 37*(5), 715–730.

Chaffin, R., & Imreh, G. (2001). A comparison of practice and self-report as sources of information about the goals of expert practice. *Psychology of Music, 29*(1), 39–69.

Chaffin, R., Imreh, G., & Crawford, M. (2002/2012). *Practicing perfection: Memory and piano performance* (2nd ed.). Hove, Sussex: Psychology Press, Taylor & Francis.

Chaffin, R., & Lemieux, A. F. (2004). General perspectives on achieving musical excellence. *In* A. Williamon (Ed.), *Musical Excellence* (pp. 19–40). New York, NY: Oxford University Press.

Charcur, K., Serrat, R., & Villar, F. (2022). Older adults' participation in artistic activities: A scoping review. *European Journal of Aging, 19*(4), 931–944.

Charters, E. (2003). The use of think-aloud methods in qualitative research: An introduction to think-aloud methods. *Brock Education, 12*(2), 68–81.

Chasin, M. (2006a). On music and hearing loss. *The Hearing Review, 13*(3).

Chasin, M. (2006b). Hearing aids for musicians. *The Hearing Review, 13*(3).

Chasin, M., & Chong, J. (1992). A clinically efficient hearing protection program for musician. *Medical Problems of Performing Artists, 7*(2), 40–43.

Christman, S. D. (1993). Handedness in musicians: Bimanual constraints on performance. *Brain and Cognition, 22*, 266–272.

Clarfield, A. M. (2023). Joni Mitchell and me: My heart, her brain. *Journal of the American Geriatrics Society, 1–3*, 3 pages.

Clarke, E. F. (2002). Understanding the psychology of performance. *In* J. Rink (Ed.), *Musical performance: A guide to understanding* (pp. 59–72). Cambridge, UK: Cambridge University Press.

Clarke, E. F. (2005). Creativity in performance. *Musicæ Scientiæ, 9*(1), 157–182.

Clift, S., Hancox, G., Morrison, I., Hess, B., Kreutz, G., & Stewart, D. (2010a). Choral singing and psychological wellbeing: Quantitative and qualitative findings from English choirs in a cross-national survey. *Journal of Applied Arts and Health, 1*, 19–34.

Clift, S., Nicol, J., Raisbeck, M., Whitmore, C., & Morrison, I. (2010b). Group singing, wellbeing and health: A systematic mapping of evidence. *The UNESCO Journal, 2*(1), 24–pages.

Coffman, D. D. (2002). Banding together: New horizons in lifelong music making. *Journal of Ageing and Identity, 7*, 133–143.

Coffman, D. D., & Adamek, M. (1999). The contribution of wind band participation to quality of life of senior adults. *Music Therapy Perspectives, 17*, 27–31.

Coffman, D. D., & Levey, K. M. (1997). Senior adult bands: Music's new horizon. *Music Educators Journal, 84*, 17–22.

Cohen, S., & Bodner, E. (2019). The relationship between flow and music performance anxiety amongst professional classical orchestra musicians. *Psychology of Music, 47*(3), 420–435.

Cohen, S., & Ginsborg, J. (2021). The experience of mid-career and seasoned orchestral musicians in the UK during the first COVID-19 lockdown. *Frontiers in Psychology, 12*, Article 645967, 16 pages.

Connolly, C., & Williamon, A. (2004). Mental skills training. *In* A. Williamon (ed.), *Musical excellence* (pp. 221–246). New York, NY: Oxford University Press.

Connor, K. M., & Davidson, J. R. T. (2003). Development of a new resilience scale: The Connor–Davidson Resilience Scale (CD-RISC). *Depression and Anxiety, 18*, 76–82.

Cottrell, S. (2004). *Professional music-making in London: Ethnography and experience.* Aldershot, UK: Routledge, Taylor & Francis (Ashgate).

Creech, A., Hallam, S., Varvarigou, M., McQueen, H., & Gaunt, H. F. (2013). Active music making: A route to enhanced subjective well-being among older people. *Perspectives in Public Health 133,* 36–43.

Cuddy, L. L., Belleville, S., & Moussard, A. (2020). *Music and the aging brain.* London, UK: Academic Press, Elsevier.

Daatland, S. O. (2005). Quality of life and ageing. *In* M. L. Johnson (Ed.), *The Cambridge handbook of age and ageing* (pp. 371–377). New York, NY: Cambridge University Press.

Danziger, D. (1995). *The orchestra: The lives behind the music.* London, UK: Harper Collins Publishers.

Davidson, J. (2002). Developing the ability to perform. *In* J. Rink (Ed.), *Musical performance: A guide to understanding* (pp. 89–101). Cambridge, UK: Cambridge University Press.

Davidson, J. W. (1999). Self and desire: A preliminary exploration of why students start and continue with music learning. *Research Studies in Music Education, 12*, 30–37.

Davidson, J. W., Howe, M. J. A., Moore, D. G., & Sloboda, J. A. (1996). The role of parental influences in the development of musical ability. *British Journal of Developmental Psychology, 14*, 399–412.

Davidson, J. W., McNamara, B., Rosenwax, L., Lange, A., Jenkins, S., & Lewin, G. (2014). Evaluating the potential of group singing to enhance the well-being of older people. *Australian Journal of Ageing, 33*(2), 99–104.

Davidson, J. W., Sloboda, J. A., & Howe, M. J. A. (1995–1996). The role of parents and teachers in the success and failure of instrumental learners. *Council for the Bulletin of Research in Music Education, 127*(Winter), 40–44.

Davies, J. B. (1994). Seeds of false consciousness: Peer commentary to Sloboda et al. (1994) 'Is everyone musical'. *The Psychologist, 7*(7), 355–356.

Davis, J. N., & Bistodeau, L. (1993). How do L1 and L2 reading differ? Evidence from thinking aloud protocols. *Modern Language Journal, 77*(4), 459–472.

Davis, R. (2004). *Becoming an orchestral musician: A guide for aspiring professionals.* London, UK: de la Mare Publishers Limited.

Dawson, W. J. (1993). Problems of aging (the mature musician)—Arts medicine for the double reed player. *Journal of the International Double Reed Society, 21*, 89–91.

Dawson, W. J. (1999). Upper extremity problems of the mature instrumentalist. *Medical Problems of Performing Artists, 14*, 87–92.

Deliege, I., & Sloboda, J. A. (1996). *Musical beginnings: Origins and development of musical competencies.* Oxford, UK: Oxford University Press.

Deniz, J. (2012). Video recorded feedback for self-regulation of prospective music teachers in piano lessons. *Journal of Instructional Psychology, 39*(1), 17–21.

Détári, A., Egermann, H., Bjerkeset, O., & Vaag, J. (2020). Psychosocial work environment among musicians and in the general workforce in Norway. *Frontiers in Psychology (Performance Science), 11,* Article 1315, 11 pages.

Dillinger, N. J. (1997). Experiences of professional orchestra musicians with chornic conditions. *Medical Problems of Performing Artists, 12*(4), 122–126.

Dobrow, S. R. (2013). Dynamics of calling: A longitudinal study of musicians. *Journal of Organizational Behavior, 34*, 431–452.

Dobrow, S. R., & Tosti-Kharas, J. (2011). Calling: The development of a scale measure. *Personal Psychology, 84*(4), 1001–1049.

Dobson, M. C., & Gaunt, H. F. (2015). Musical and social communication in expert orchestral performance. *Psychology of Music, 43*(1), 24–42.

Drake, C., Jones, M. R., & Baruch, C. (2000). The development of rhythmic attending in auditory sequences: Attunement, referent period, focal attending. *Cognition, 77*, 251–288.

Duke, R. A., Simmons, A. L., & Cash, C. D. (2009). It's not how much; it's how: Characteristics of practice behavior and retention of performance skills. *Journal of Research in Music Education, 56*(4), 310–321.

Eaton, S., & Gillis, H. (2002). A review of orchestra musicians' hearing loss risks. *Canadian Acoustics, 30*(2), 5–14.

Einhorn, K. (2006). The medical aspects of noise induced otologic damage in musicians. *The Hearing Review, 13*(3).

Elliott, R. (2019). Aging and popular music. In D. Gu & M. E. Dupre (Eds.), *Encyclopedia of gerontology and population aging* (pp. 1–6). Cham, Switzerland: Springer Nature.

Emmerich, E., Rudel, L., & Richter, F. (2008). Is the audiologic status of professional musicians a reflection of the noise exposure in classical orchestra musicians? *European Archives of Oto-Rhino-Laryngology, 265*, 753–758.

Ericsson, K. A. (1996). The acquisition of expert performance. *In* K. A. Ericsson (Ed.), *The road to excellence* (pp. 1–50). Mahwah, NJ: Lawrence Erlbaum Associates.

Ericsson, K. A. (1997). Deliberate practice and the acquisition of expert performance: an overview. *In* H. Jorgensen & A. C. Lehmann (Eds.), *Does practice make perfect? Current theory and research on instrumental music practice* (Vol. 1, pp. 9–52). Majorstua, Norway: Norges musikkhøgskole (The Norwegian State Academy of Music).

Ericsson, K. A. (1998). The scientific study of expert levels of performance: General implications for optimal learning and creativity. *High Ability Studies, 9*(1), 75–100.

Ericsson, K. A. (2000). How experts attain and maintain superior performance: Implications for the enhancement of skilled performance in older individuals. *Journal of Aging and Physical Activity, 8*, 366–372.

Ericsson, K. A. (2004). Deliberate practice and the acquisition and maintenance of expert performance in medicine and related domains. *Academic Medicine, 79*(10), S70–S81.

Ericsson, K. A. (2015). Acquisition and maintenance of medical expertise: A perspective from the expert-performance approach with deliberate practice. *Academic Medicine, 90*(11), 1471–1486.

Ericsson, K. A., Krampe, R. T., & Tesch-Romer, C. (1993). The role of deliberate practice in the acquisition of expert performance. *Psychological Review, 100*(3), 363–406.

Ericsson, K. A., & Lehmann, A. C. (1996). Expert and exceptional performance: Evidence of maximal adaptation to task constraints. *Annual Review of Psychology, 47*, 273–305

Ericsson, K. A., & Simon, H. A. (1980). Verbal reports as data. *Psychological Review, 87*(3 May), 215–251.

Ericsson, K. A., & Simon, H. A. (1993). *Protocol analysis: Verbal reports as data* (rev. ed.). Cambridge, MA: MIT Press.

Ericsson, K. A., & Smith, J. (Eds.). (1991). *Toward a general theory of expertise: Prospects and limits.* Cambridge, UK: Cambridge University Press.

Fancourt, D., Geschke, K., Fellgiebel, A., & Wuttke-Linnemann, A. (2022). Lifetime musical training and cognitive performance in a memory clinic population: A cross-sectional study. *Musicæ Scientiæ, 26*(1), 71–83.

Farnam, A. L. (2016). *Characteristics of lifelong musicians.* [Unpublished Master's Thesis in Music Education (#1865)]. University of Arkansas, Fayetteville, AR.

Fassang, A. (2006). Recruitment in symphony orchestras: Testing a gender neutral recruitment process. *Work, Employment and Society, 20*(4), 801–809.

Felger, J. C. (2014). The immune response to stress in orchestra musicians: Setting the stage for naturalistic paradigms. *Brain, Behavior, and Immunity, 37*, 21–22.

Fetter, D. (1993). Life in the orchestra. *Maryland Medical Journal, 42*(3), 289–292.

Fletcher, D., & Sarkar, M. (2013). Psychological resilience: A review and critique of definitions, concepts, and theories. *European Psychologist, 8*(1), 12–23.

Freund, A. M. (2008). Successful aging as management of resources: The role of selection, optimization, and compensation. *Research in Human Development, 5*(2), 94–106.

Freund, A. M., & Baltes, P. B. (1998). Selection, optimization, and compensation as strategies of life management: Correlations with subjective indicators of successful aging. *Psychology and Aging, 13*(4), 531–543.

Freund, A. M., & Baltes, P. B. (2002). The adaptiveness of selection, optimization, and compensation as strategies of life management: Evidence from a preference study on proverbs. *Journal of Gerontology: Psychological Sciences, 57B*(5), P426–P434.

Frost, J. (2000). Aging and the musician; Musicians' assistance program. *Allegro, 100*(2). Found at: https://www.local802afm.org/allegro/articles/aging-and-the-musician/.

Fry, H. J. H. (1986a). Incidence of overuse syndrome in the symphony orchestra. *Medical Problems of Performing Arts, 1*(2), 51–55.

Fry, H. J. H. (1986b). Incidence of overuse syndrome in the symphony orchestra. *Medical Problems of Performing Artists, 1*(2), 51–55.

Gaab, N., & Schlaug, G. (2003). Musicians differ from nonmusicians in brain activation despite performance matching. *In* G. Avanzini, C. Faienza, D. Minciacchi, L. Lopez, & M. Majno (Eds.), *The Neurosciences and Music* (Vol. 999, pp. 385–388). New York, NY: The New York Academy of Sciences.

Gagne, F., & McPherson, G. (2016). Analyzing musical prodigiousness using Gagne's Integrative Model of Talent Development. *In* G. McPherson (Ed.), *Musical prodigies: Interpretations from psychology, education, musicology, and ethnomusicology* (pp. 3–114). Oxford, UK: Oxford University Press.

Galvao, A. (2000). Practice in orchestral life. Paper presented at the Sixth International Conference on Music Perception and Cognition, Keele, UK (5–10 August 2000).

Gardner, C. (2019). Are competitions inherently problematic? *The Strad* (11 February). Found at: https://www.thestrad.com/debate/are-competitions-inherently-problematic/8365.article.

Gaser, C., & Schlaug, G. (2003). Brain structures differ between musicians and non-musicians. *The Journal of Neuroscience, 23*(27), 9240–9245.

Gaunt, H. F., & Dobson, M. C. (2014). Orchestras as 'ensembles of possibility': Understanding the experience of orchestra musicians through the lens of communities of practice. *Mind, Culture, and Activity, 21*(4), 298–317.

Gembris, H. (2006). *Musical development from a lifespan perspective*. Frankfurt, Germany: Peter Lang GmbH.

Gembris, H. (2008). Musical activities in the third age: An empirical study with amateur musicians. In Alison Daubney, Elena Longhi, Alexandra Lamont, and David Hargreaves (Eds.), *Musical development and learning*: 2nd European Conference on Developmental Psychology of Music (pp. 103–108). Hull, UK: GK Publishing.

Gembris, H. (2013). Music making as lifelong development and resource for health. In R. MacDonald, G. Kreutz, & L. Mitchell (Eds.), *Music, health, and wellbeing* (pp. 367–382). Oxford, UK: Oxford University Press.

Gembris, H. (2023). Maria Manturzewska's model of the lifespan development of professional musicians in the light of recent research and cultural changes. *Musicæ Scientiæ, 27*(4), 827–841.

Gembris, H., & Heye, A. (2014). Growing older in a symphony orchestra: The development of the age-related self-concept and self-estimated performance of professional musicians in a lifespan perspective. *Musicæ Scientiæ, 18*(4), 371–391.

Gembris, H., Heye, A., & Seifert, A. (2018). Health problems of orchestral musicians from a life-span perspective: Results of a large-scale study. *Music & Science, 1*(1), 1–20.

Getzmann, S., Jasny, J., & Falkenstein, M. (2017). Switching of auditory attention in 'cocktail-party' listening: ERP evidence of cueing effects in younger and older adults. *Brain and Cognition, 111*, 1–12.

Gibbons, A. C. (1988). A review of the literature for music development/education and music therapy with the elderly. *Music Therapy Perspectives, 5*, 33–40.

Gobet, F., & Campitelli, G. (2007). The role of domain-specific practice, handedness, and starting age in chess. *Developmental Psychology, 43*(1), 159–172.

Goldin, C., & Rouse, C. (2000). Orchestrating impartiality: The impact of 'blind' auditions on female musicians. *American Economic Journal, 90*(4), 715–741.

Goodchild, M., Wild, J., & McAdams, S. (2019). Exploring emotional responses to orchestra gestures. *Musicæ Scientiæ, 23*(1), 25–49.

Gordon, E. E. (1975). *Learning theory, patterns, and music*. Buffalo, NY: Tometic Associates.

Gordon, E. E. (1993). *Learning sequences in music—Skill, content, and patterns*. Chicago: GIA Publications, Inc.

Gordon, S. (2006). *Mastering the art of performance: A primer for musicians*. Oxford, UK: Oxford University Press.

GOScience (2008). *Foresight mental capital and wellbeing project*. London, UK: The Government Office for Science.

Grant, M. D., & Brody, J. A. (2003). *Playing a musical instrument, cognition, and Alzheimer's disease—A conceptual framework*. Unpublished Research Report.

Grant, M. D., & Brody, J. A. (2004). Musical experience and dementia: Hypothesis. *Aging Clinical and Experimental Research, 16*(5), 403–405.

Gray, R., & Gow, A. J. (2020). How is musical activity associated with cognitive ability in later life? *Aging, Neuropsychology, and Cognition, 27*(4), 617–635.

Greene, L. S., & Williams, H. G. (1993). Age related differences in timing control of repetitive movement: Application of the Wing–Kristofferson model. *Research Quarterly of Exercise and Sports, 64*, 32–38.

Grondahl, D. (1987). *Thinking processes and structures used by professional pianists in keyboard learning*. [Hovedfagseksamen (Master's Degree) in Music Education]. Oslo, Norway: Norges musikkhøgskole (The Norwegian State Academy of Music).

Groussard, M., Coppalle, R., Hinault, T., & Platel, H. (2020). Do musicians have better mnemonic and exucutive performane than actors? Influence of regular musical or theater practice in adults and in the elderly. *Frontiers in Human Neuroscience, 14*, Article 557642, 11 pages.

Gruhn, W. (2021). Musical processing across the life span. *In* A. Creech, D. A. Hodges, & S. Hallam (Eds.), *Routledge international handbook of music psychology in education and the community* (pp. 86–100). London: Routledge, Taylor & Francis.

Guss, C. D. (2018). What is going through your mind? Thinking aloud as a method in cross-cultural psychology. *Frontiers in Psychology, 9*(13 August), Article 2192, 1–11.

Habibi, A., Ilari, B., Crimi, K., Metke, M., Kaplan, J. T., Joshi, A. A., Leahy, R. M., Shattuck, D. W., Choi, S. Y., Halder, J. P., Ficek, B., Damasio, A., & Damasio, H. (2014). An equal start: absence of group differences in cognitive, social, and neural measures prior to music or sports training in children. *Frontiers in Human Neuroscience, 8*, Article 690, 1–11.

Hallam, S., Creech, A., Varvarigou, M., McQueen, H., & Gaunt, H. F. (2012). Perceived benefits of active engagement with making music in community settings. *International Journal of Community Music, 5*(2), 155–174.

Hallam, S., Rinta, T., Varvarigou, M., Creech, A., Papageorgi, I., Gomes, T., & Lanipekun, J. (2012). The development of practicing strategies in young people. *Psychology of Music, 40*(5), 652–680.

Halpern, A. R. (2012). Dementia and music: Challenges and future directions. *Music Perception, 29*(5), 543–545.

Hambrick, D. Z., Oswald, F. L., Altmann, E. M., Meinz, E. J., Gobert, F., & Campitelli, G. (2014). Deliberate practice: Is that all it takes to become an expert? *Intelligence, 45*, 34–45.

Hambrick, D. Z., & Tucker-Drob, E. M. (2015). The genetics of music accomplishment: evidence for gene-environment correlation and interaction. *Psychonomic Bulletin & Review, 22*, 112–120.

Hamilton, L. H. (1995). Personality and occupational stress in elite performers. *Medical Problems of Performing Arts, 10*(3), 86–90.

Hanna-Pladdy, B., & Gajewski, B. (2012). Recent and past musical activity predicts cognitive aging variability: Direct comparison with general lifestyle activities. *Frontiers in Human Neuroscience, 6*, Article 198, 1–11.

Hanna-Pladdy, B., & MacKay, A. (2011). The relation between instrumental musical activity and cognitive aging. *Neuropsychology, 25*(3), 378–386.

Hanna-Pladdy, B., & Menken, M. (2020). Training-induced cognitive and neural changes in musicians: Implications for healthy aging. *In* L. L. Cuddy, S. Belleville, & A. Moussard (Eds.), *Music and the aging brain* (pp. 221–243). London, UK: Academic Press, Elsevier.

Hannu, K., & Pallab, P. (2002). A comparison of concurrent and retrospective verbal protocol analysis. *American Journal of Psychology, 113*(3), 387–404.

Hargreaves, D. J. (1994). Musical education for all: Peer commentary to Sloboda et al. (1994) 'Is everyone musical?'. *The Psychologist, 7*(7), 357–358.

Hargreaves, D. J., & Lamont, A. (2017). *The psychology of musical development*. Cambridge, UK: Cambridge University Press.

Harper, B. S. (2002). Workplace and health: A survey of classical orchestral musicians in the United Kingdom and Germany. *Medical Problems of Performing Artists, 17*(2), 83–92.

Hart, C. W., Geltman, C. L., Schupbach, J., & Santucci, M. (1987). The musician and occupational sound hazards. *Medical Problems of Performing Artists, 2*(1), 22–25.

Hasson, D., Theorell, T., Liljeholm-Johansson, Y., & Canlon, B. (2009). Psychosocial and physiological correlates of self-reported hearing problems in male and female musicians in symphony orchestras. *International Journal of Psychophysiology, 74*, 93–100.

Hays, Y., Bright, R., & Minichiello, V. (2002). The contribution of music to positive ageing: A review. *Journal of Ageing and Identity, 7*, 165–175.

Hearn, H. A. (1972). Aging and the artistic career. *The Gerontologist, 12*(4), 357–362.

Hendricks, K. S. (2014). Changes in self-efficacy beliefs over time: Contextual influences of gender, rank-based placement, and social support in a competitive orchestra environment. *Psychology of Music, 32*(3), 347–365.

Henoch, M., & Chesky, K. (1999). Hearing loss and ageing: Implications for the professional musician. *Medical Problems of Performing Artists, 14*, 76–79.

Henson, M. (1994). Orchestral employment practices. *Performing Arts Medicine News* (September/October), 17–19.

Herholz, S. C., & Zatorre, R. J. (2012). Musical training as a framework for brain plasticity: Behavior, function, and structure. *Neuron, 76*, 486–502.

Herman, R., & Clark, T. (2023). It's not a virus! Reconceptualizing and de-pathologizing music performance anxiety. *Frontiers in Psychology, 14*(1194873), 29 pages.

Hillman, S. (2002). Participatory singing for older people: A perception of benefit. *Health Education, 102*, 163–171.

Holst, G. J., Paaup, H. M., & Baelum, J. (2011). A cross-sectional study of psychological work environment and stress in the Danish symphony orchestras. *International Archives of Occupational and Environmental Health, 85*(6), 639–649.

Hoppmann, R. A., & Ekman, E. F. (1999). Arthritis in the ageing musician. *Medical Problems of Performing Artists, 14*, 80–84.

Horvath, J. (2010). *Playing (less) hurt: An injury prevention guide for musicians.* New York, NY: Hall Leonard Publishers.

Horvath, J. (2019). Challenges for the aging musician. *www.Interlude.HK* (23 November), 6 pages. Found at: https://interlude.hk/challenges-for-the-aging-musician/.

Howe, M. J. A. (1998). Early lives: Prodigies and non-prodigies. *In* A. Steptoe (Ed.), *Genius and the mind* (pp. 97–110). Oxford, UK; Oxford University Press.

Howe, M. J. A., Davidson, J., Moore, D., & Sloboda, J. A. (1995). Are there early childhood signs of musical ability? *Psychology of Music, 22*, 162–176.

Howe, M. J. A., Davidson, J. W., & Sloboda, J. A. (1998). Innate talents: Reality or myth? *Behavioral and Brain Sciences, 21*, 399–442.

Howe, M. J. A., & Sloboda, J. A. (1991a). Young musicians' accounts of significant influences in their early lives: 1. The family and musical background. *British Journal of Music Education, 8*, 39–52.

Howe, M. J. A., & Sloboda, J. (1991b). Early signs of talents and special interests in the lives of young musicians. *European Journal of High Ability, 2*, 102–111.

Hyde, K. L., Lerch, J., Norton, A., Forgead, M., Winner, E., Evens, A. C., & Schlaug, G. (2009). Musical training shapes structural brain development. *The Journal of Neuroscience, 29*(10), 3019–3025.

Imreh, G. & Crawford, M. (2002). In the words of the masters: Artists accounts of their experiences. *In* R. Chaffin, G. Imreh, & M. Crawford (Eds.), *Practicing perfection: Memory and piano performance* (pp. 26–65). Mahwah, NJ: Lawrence Earlbaum Associates, Ltd.

Isacoff, S. (2015). Competition judging: Keeping evil out of the jury room. Musical America Worldwide (3 February). Found at: https://www.musicalamerica.com/news/newsstory.cfm?storyID=33290&categoryID=7.

James, I. (1984). Most players admit stress symptoms, survey shows orchestral musicians often suffer from tension and anxiety, nearly 10 per cent drink before playing, and over half mention the harm caused by bad conductors. *Classical Music, 17*, 7.

James, I. (2000). The causes and effects of stress in the orchestra player. *Musical Performance*, 2(4), 1–5.

Janata, P. (2005). Brain networks that track musical structures. *Annals of the New York Academy of Sciences, 1060* (The Neurosciences and Music II: From Perception to Performance), 111–124.

Jancke, L. (2009). Music drives brain plasticity. F1000 Biology *Report*, 1(78), 6 pages.

Jancke, L., Schlaug, G., & Steinmetz, H. (1997). Hand skill asymmetry in professional musicians. *Brain and Cognition, 34*, 424–432.

Jancke, L., Shah, N. J., & Perters, M. (2000). Cortical activations in primary and secondary motor areas for complex bimanual movements in professional pianists. *Cognitive Brain Research, 10*, 177–183.

Jeffri, J. (2007). Information on artists IV: Aging performing artists: Executive summary. Found at: http://arts.tc.columbia.edu/rcac/images/rcacimages/ioa4_shortsummary.pdf.

Jellison, J. A. (2000). *How can all people continue to be involved in meaningful music perception? Vision 2020.* The National Association for Music Education (MENC). Found at: http://www.menc.org/publication/vision2020/.

Jennings, R., & Gardner, A. (Eds.) (2012). '*Rock on': Women, ageing and popular music.* Farnham, UK: Ashgate.

Johnson, J. K., Louhivuori, J., & Siljander, E. (2017). Comparison of well-being of older adult choir singers and the general population in Finland: A case-control study. *Musicæ Scientiæ, 21*(2), 178–194.

Johnson, M. (2009). The dark side of piano competitions. The New York Times (7 August). Found at: https://www.nytimes.com/2009/08/08/opinion/08iht-edjohnson.html.

Jones, M. R. (1976). Time, our lost dimension: Toward a new theory of perception, attention, and memory. *Psychological Review, 83*, 323–355.

Jones, M. R. (1990). Learning and the development of expectancies: An interactionist approach. *Psychomusicology, 9*(2), 193–228.

Jones, Q. (2022). *12 notes: On life and creativity.* New York, NY: Harry N. Abrams Publishers.

Jordan, C. (2019). When I'm 64: A review of instrumental music-making and brain health in later life. *Experimental Gerontology, 123*, 17–23.

Joseph, D., & Southcott, J. (2018). Music participation for older people: Five choirs in Victoria, Australia. *Research Studies in Music Education, 40*(2), 176–190.

Kadrmas, E. F., Dyer, J. A., & Bartley, G. B. (1996). Visual problems of the ageing musician. *Survey of Ophthalmology, 40*, 338–341.

Kahari, K. R., Axelsson, A., Hellstrom, P.-A., & Zachau, G. (2001). Hearing development in classical orchestra musicians: A follow-up study. *Scandinavian Audiology, 30*(3), 141–149.

Kahn, A. P. (1999). *Keeping the beat: Healthy ageing through amateur chamber music playing.* Evanston, IL: Wordscope Associates, Inc.

Keele, S. W., Pokorny, R. A., Corcos, D. M., & Ivry, R. (1985). Do perception and motor production share common timing mechanisms: A correlational analysis. *Acta Psychologica, 60*, 173–191.

Kegelaers, J., Schuijer, M., & Oudejans, R. R. D. (2021). Resilience and mental health issues in classical musicians: A preliminary study. *Psychology of Music, 49*(5), 1273–1284.

Kemp, A. E. (1995). Aspects of upbringing as revealed in the personalities of musicians. *The Quarterly Journal of Music Teaching and Learning, 5*(4), 34–41.

Kemp, A. E. (1996). *The musical temperament: Psychology and personality of musicians.* Oxford, UK: Oxford University Press.

Kemper, S., Herman, R. E., & Lian, C. H. T. (2003). The costs of doing two things at once for young and older adults: Talking while walking, finger tapping, and ignoring speech or noise. *Psychology and Aging, 18*(2), 181–192.

Kenny, D., & Ackermann, B. (2015). Performance-related musculoskeletal pain, depression and music performance anxiety in professional orchestral musicians: A population study. *Psychology of Music, 43*(1), 43–60.

Kenny, D. T., & Ackermann, B. J. (2017). Hitting the high notes: Healthy aging in professional orchestral musicians. *In* A. Stamatios-Alexandrou, R. Burke, & C. L. Cooper (Eds.), *The aging workforce: Individual, organizational and societal challenges* (pp. 355–376). Bingley, UK: Emerald Publishing.

Kenny, D., Driscoll, T., & Ackermann, B. (2014). Psychological well-being in professional orchestral musicians in Australia: A descriptive population study. *Psychology of Music, 42*(2), 210–232.

Kenny, D. T., Driscoll, T., & Ackermann, B. J. (2016). Is playing in the pit the pits? Pain, strength, music performance anxiety, and workplace satisfaction in professional musicians in stage, pit, and combined stage/pit orchestras. *Medical Problems of Performing Artists, 31*(1), 1–7.

Kenny, D. T., Driscoll, T., & Ackermann, B. J. (2018). Effects of aging on musical performance in professional orchestral musicians. *Medical Problems of Performing Artists, 33*(1), 39–46.

Kingsbury, H. (1988/2001). *Music, talent, and performance.* Philadelphia, PA: Temple University Press.

Kivimaki, M., & Jokinen, M. (1994). Job perceptions and well-being among symphony orchestra musicians: A comparison with other occupational groups. *Medical Problems of Performing Arts, 9*(3), 73–76.

Knight, D. B. (2006). Geographies of the orchestra. *GeoJournal, 65,* 33–53.

Koch, M. (2006). Musical career: Dream or nightmare? *In* H. Gembris (Ed.), *Musical development from a lifespan perspective* (pp. 107–118). Frankfurt, Germany: Peter Lang GmbH.

Koelsch, S., & Skeie, G. (2020). The musical brain. *In* L. L. Cuddy, S. Belleville, & A. Moussard (Eds.), *Music and the aging brain* (pp. 1–40). London, UK: Academic Press, Elsevier.

Kopiez, R., Weihs, C., Ligges, U., & Lee, J. I. (2006). Classification of high and low achievers in a music sight-reading task. *Psychology of Music, 34*(1), 5–26.

Krampe, R. T. (2002). Ageing, expertise and fine motor movement. *Neuroscience and Behavioral Reviews, 26,* 769–776.

Krampe, R. T. (2006). Musical expertise from a lifespan perspective. *In* H. Gembris (ed.), *Musical development from a lifespan perspective* (pp. 91–106). Frankfurt, Germany: Peter Lang GmbH.

Krampe, R. T., & Baltes, P. B. (2003). Intelligence as adaptive resource development and resource allocation: A new look through the lenses of SOC and expertise. *In* R. J. Sternberg & E. L. Grigorenko (Eds.), *The psychology of abilities, competencies, and expertise* (pp. 31–69). New York, NY: Cambridge University Press.

Krampe, R. T., Engbert, R., & Kliegl, R. (2001). Age-specific problems in rhythmic timing. *Psychology and Aging, 16,* 12–30.

Krampe, R. T., Engbert, R., & Kliegl, R. (2002). The effects of expertise and age on rhythm production: Adaptations to timing and sequencing constraints. *Brain and Cognition, 48,* 179–194.

Krampe, R. T., & Ericsson, K. A. (1995). Deliberate practice and elite musical performance. *In* J. Rink (Ed.), *The practice of performance: Studies in musical interpretation* (pp. 84–104). Cambridge, UK: Cambridge University Press.

Krampe, R. T., & Ericsson, K. A. (1996). Maintaining excellence: Deliberate practice and elite performance in young and older pianists. *Journal of Experimental Psychology: General, 125,* 331–359.

Krampe, R. T., Kliegl, R., Mayr, U., Engbert, R., & Vorberg, D. (2000). The fast and the slow of skilled bimanual rhythm production: Parallel versus integrated timing. *Journal of Experimental Psychology: Human Perception and Performance, 26,* 206–233.

Krampe, R. T., Mayr, U., & Kliegl, R. (2005). Timing, sequencing, and executive control in repetitive movement production. *Journal of Experimental Psychology: Human Perception and Performance, 31*(3), 379–397.

Kuusi, T., Haukka, J., Myllykangas, L., & Jarvela, I. (2019). Causes of death of professional musicians in the classical genre. *Medical Problems of Performing Artists, 34*(2), 92–97.

Kvale, S. (1996). *InterViews: An introduction to qualitative research interviewing.* Thousand Oaks, CA: SAGE Publications, Inc.

Lamont, A., Murray, M., Hale, R., & Wright-Bevans, K. (2018). Singing in later life: The anatomy of a community choir. *Psychology of Music, 46*(3), 424–439.

Langer, E., Russell, T., & Eisenkraft, N. (2009). Orchestral performance and the footprint of mindfulness. *Psychology of Music, 37*(2), 125–136.

Langerdorfer, F., Hodapp, V., Kreutz, G., & Bongard, S. (2006). Personality and performance anxiety among professional orchestra musicians. *Journal of Individual Differences, 27*(3), 162–171.

Langner, D. (2004). Flawed expertise: Exploring the need to overcome the discrepancy between instrumental training and orchestral work—the case of string players. *In* J. W. Davidson (Ed.), *The music practitioner: Research for the music performer, teacher and listener* (pp. 251–263). Aldershot, UK: Ashgate Publishing Ltd.

Laurin, D., Verreault, R., Lindsay, J., MacPherson, K., & Rockwood, K. (2001). Physical activity and risk of cognitive impairment and dementia in elderly persons. *Archives of Neurology, 58*(March), 498–504.

Lederman, R. J. (1999). Ageing and the instrumental musician. *Medical Problems of Performing Artists, 14*, 67–75.

Lehmann, A. C., & Ericsson, K. A. (1993). Sight-reading ability of expert musicians in the context of piano accompanying. *Psychomusicology, 12*(2), 182–195.

Lehmann, A. C., & Ericsson, K. A. (1997). Research on expert performance and deliberate practice: Implications for the education of mature musicians and music students. *Psychomusicology, 16*(1-2), 40–58.

Lehmann, A. C., & Ericsson, K. A. (1998). Preparation of a public performance: The relation of practice and performance. *Musicæ Scientiæ, 2*(1), 67–94.

Levitin, D. (2012). What does it mean to be musical? *Neuron, 73*, 633–637.

Liljeholm-Johansson, Y., & Theorell, T. (2003). Satisfaction with work task quality correlates with employee health: A study of 12 professional orchestras. *Medical Problems of Performing Artists, 18*(4), 141–149.

Loh, C. (2021). Lufthansa incentivising early retirement for A380 crews. Simple Flying (10 July). Found at: https://simpleflying.com/lufthansa-a380-crew-early-retirements/.

London, S. J. (1963). The ecology of aging in musicians. *The Gerontologist, 3*(4), 160–165.

Lyness, J. M. (2017). Lessons from the lives of celebrated musicians: What Armstrong, Cash, Dylan, Ellington, Fitzgerald, and Sinatra can teach us about creative resilience and aging. *American Journals of Geriatric Psychiatry, 25*(12), 1295–1299.

MacDonald, R. A. R., Hargreaves, D. J., & Miell, D. (Eds.). (2002). *Musical identities*. Oxford, UK: Oxford University Press.

MacNamara, Á., Holmes, P., & Collins, D. (2006). The pathway to excellence: The role of psychological characteristics in negotiating the challenges of musical development. *British Journal of Music Education, 23*(3), 285–302.

Macnamara, B. N., Hambrick, D. Z., & Oswald, F. L. (2014). Deliberate practice and performance in music, games, sports, education, and professions: A meta-analyses. *Psychological Science, 25*(8), 1608–1618.

MacRitchie, J., & Garrido, S. (2019). Ageing and the orchestra: Self-efficacy and engagement in community music-making. *Psychology of Music, 47*(6), 902–916.

Mansens, D., Deeg, D. J. H., & Comijs, H. C. (2018). The association between singing and/or playing a musical instrument and cognitive functions in older adults. *Aging & Mental Health, 22*(8), 964–971.

Manturzewska, M. (1990). A biographical study of the life-span development of professional musicians. *Psychology of Music, 18*, 112–139.

Manturzewska, M. (2006). A biographical study of the lifespan development of professional musicians. *In* H. Gembris (Ed.), *Musical development from a lifespan perspective* (pp. 21–54). Frankfurt, Germany: Peter Lang GmbH.

Manzano, O. de, & Ullén, F. (2018). Same genes, different brains: Neuroanatomical differences between monozygotic twins discordant for musical training. *Cerebral Cortex, 28*(1), 387–394.

Marchant-Haycox, S. E., & Wilson, G. D. (1992). Personality and stress in performing artists. *Personality and Individual Differences, 13*(10), 1061–1068.

Maslach, C., & Jackson, S. E. (1981/1986). *Maslach burnout inventory* (2nd ed.). Palo Alto, CA: Consulting Psychologists Press, Inc.

Maslach, C., & Leiter, M. P. (2008). Early predictors of job burnout and engagement. *Journal of Applied Psychology, 93*(3), 498–512.

Mathews, J. A., & Mathewa, W. (1993). A survey of rheumatic disorders in orchestral musicians. *Medical Problems of Performing Arts, 8*(1), 14–15.

Matziorinis, A. M., Gaser, C., & Koelsch, S. (2022). Is musical engagement enough to keep the brain young? *Brain Structure and Function, 228*, 577–588.

Maury, S., & Rickard, N. (2022). The benefits of participation in a choir and an exercise group on older adults' wellbeing in a naturalistic setting. *Musicæ Scientiæ 26*(1), 144–171.

McAuley, J. D., Jones, M. R., Holub, S., Johnston, H., & Miller, N. S. (2006). The time of our lives: Lifespan development of timing and event tracking. *Journal of Experimental Psychology: General, 135*, 348–367.

McBride, D., Gill, F., Proops, D., Harrington, M., Gardiner, K., & Attwell, C. (1992). Noise and the classical musician. *British Medical Journal, 305*, 1561–1563.

McPherson, G. (Ed.) (2016). *Musical prodigies: Interpretations from psychology, education, musicology, and ethnomusicology.* Oxford, UK: Oxford University Press.

Meinz, E. J. (2000). Experience-based attenuation of age-related differences in music cognition tasks. *Psychology and Aging, 15*(2), 297–312.

Meinz, E. J., & Salthouse, T. A. (1998). The effects of age and experience on memory for visually printed music. *Journal of Gerontology: Psychological Sciences, 53B*(1), 60–69.

Meister, I., Krings, T., Foltys, H., Boroojerdi, B., Muller, M., Topper, R., & Thron, A. (2005). Effects of long-term practice and task complexity in musicians and non-musicians performing simple and complex motor tasks: Implications for cortical motor organization. *Human Brain Mapping, 25*, 345–352.

Middlestadt, S. E., & Fishbein, M. (1989). The prevalence of severe musculoskeletal problems among male and female symphony orchestra string players. *Medical Problems of Performing Artists, 4*(1), 41–48.

Mills, J. (2004). Working in music: Becoming a performer-teacher. *Music Education Research, 6*(3), 245–261.

Mills, J., & Smith, J. (2006). Working in music: Becoming successful. *In* H. Gembris (Ed.), *Musical development from a lifespan perspective* (pp. 131–140). Frankfurt, Germany: Peter Lang GmbH.

Moreno, S., & Farzan, F. (2015). Music training and inhibitory control: A multidimensional model. *Annals of The New York Academy of Sciences 1337* (The Neurosciences of Music V), 147–152.

Moussard, A., Bermudez, P., Alain, C., Tays, W., & Moreno, S. (2016). Life-long music practice and executive control in older adults: An event-related potential study. *Brain Research, 1642*, 146–153.

Nakamura, S., Sadato, N., Oohashi, T., Nishina, E., Fuwamoto, Y., & Yonekura, Y. (1999). Analysis of music–brain interaction with simultaneous measurement of regional cerebral blood flow and electrocenphalogram beta rhythm in human subjects. *Neuroscience Letters, 270*, 222–226.

Nass, M. L. (1971). Some considerations of a psychoanalytic interpretation of music. *Psychoanalytic Quarterly, 40*, 303–316.

Nass, M. L. (1975). On hearing and inspiration in the composition of music. *Psychoanalytic Quarterly, 44*, 431–447.

National Institute on Aging, US National Institutes of Health (2006). *Greater proportion of older men, women working, according to updated Federal report.* Updated Statistical Report on Ageing (July).

Nelson, C. (2017). Is popping pills the sure way to beat performance nerves? The Strad (February) (online), Article #3133. Found at: https://www.thestrad.com/is-popping-pills-the-sure-way-to-beat-performance-nerves/3133.article.

Nielsen, S. G. (1997a). Verbal protocol analysis and research on instrumental music practice. Paper presented at the Third Triennial ESCOM Conference, Uppsala University, Uppsala, Sweden, 7–12 June 1997.

Nielsen, S. G. (1997b). Self-regulation of learning strategies during practice: A case study of a church organ student preparing a musical work for performance. In H. Jorgensen & A. C. Lehmann (Eds.), *Does practice make perfect? Current theory and research on instrumental music practice* (pp. 109–122). Majorstua, Norway: Norges musikkhøgskole (The Norwegian State Academy of Music).

Niquette, P. (2006, March 6). Hearing protection for musicians. *The Hearing Review, 13*(3).

Nisbett, R. E., & Wilson, T. D. (1977). Telling more than we can know: Verbal reports on mental processes. *Psychological Review, 84*(3), 231–259.

Norton, A., Winner, E., Cronin, K., Overy, K., Lee, D. J., & Schlaug, G. (2005). Are there pre-existing neural, cognitive, or motoric markers for musical ability? *Brain and Cognition, 59*, 124–134.

Noy, P. (1968). The development of musical ability. *Psychoanalytic Study of the Child, 23*, 332–347.

Noy, P. (1990). Form creation in art: An ego psychological approach to creativity. *In* S. Feder, R. L. Karmel, & G. H. Pollock (Eds.), *Psychoanalytic explorations in music* (pp. 209–231). Madison, CT: International University Press.

Oakland, J. (2014). *Ageing and retirement: Towards an understanding of the experiences of symphony musicians as they approach retirement*. University College, London, UK. Found at: http://doi.org/10.1314/RG.2.1.1385.8408.

Oare, S. (2012). Decisions made in the practice room: A qualitative study of middle school students' thought processes while practicing. *Update: Applications of Research in Music Education, 30*(2), 63–70.

O'Brian, J. L., Nikjeh, D. A., & Lister, J. J. (2015). Interaction of musicianship and aging: A comparison of cortical auditory evoked potentials. *Behavioral Neurology* (4 October), Article ID 545917, 1–12.

Olbertz, F. (2006). Job satisfaction of professional orchestra musicians. *In* H. Gembris (Ed.), *Musical development from a lifespan perspective* (pp. 55–72). Frankfurt, Germany: Peter Lang GmbH.

Otte, A., Juengling, F. D., & Kassubek, J. (2001). Exceptional brain function in musicians and the neural basis of music processing. *European Journal of Nuclear Medicine, 28*(1), 130–131.

Palmer, M. (1989). Music therapy in gerontology: A review and projection. *Music Therapy Perspectives, 6*, 52–55.

Papaioannou, A., Theodorakis, Y., Ballon, F., & Auwelle, Y. V. (2004). Combined effect of goal setting and self-talk in performance of a soccer-shooting task. *Perceptual and Motor Skills, 98*(1), 89–99.

Parasuraman, S., & Nachman, S. A. (1987). Correlates of organizational and professional commitment: The case of musicians in symphony orchestras. *Group & Organizational Studies, 12*(3), 287–303.

Parasuraman, S., & Purohit, Y. S. (2000). Distress and boredom among orchestra musicians: The two faces of stress. *Journal of Occupational Health Psychology, 5*(1), 74–83.

Parbery-Clark, A., Anderson, S., Hittner, E., & Kraus, N. (2012). Musical experience offsets age-related delays in neural timing. *Neurobiology of Aging, 33*(7), 1483.e1481–1483.e1484.

Parbery-Clark, A., Strait, D. L., Hittner, E., & Kraus, N. (2013). Musical training enhances neural processing of binaural sounds. *The Journal of Neuroscience, 33*(42), 16741–16747.

Park, A.-L. (2015). Can musical activities promote healthy ageing? *International Journal of Emergency Mental Health Resilience, 17*(1), 258–261.

Parncutt, R., & McPherson, G. E. (Eds.) (2002). *The science and psychology of music performance: Creative strategies for teaching and learning*. New York, NY: Oxford University Press.

Parry, C. B. W. (2004). Managing the physical demands of musical performance. *In* A. Williamon (ed.), *Musical excellence* (pp. 41–60). New York, NY: Oxford University Press.

Pascual-Leone, A. (2003). The brain that makes music is changed by it. *In* I. Peretz & R. J. Zatorre (Eds.), *The cognitive neurosciences of music* (pp. 396–409). Oxford, UK: Oxford University Press.

Perkins, R., & Williamon, A. (2014). Learning to make music in older adulthood: A mixed-methods exploration of impacts on wellbeing. *Psychology of Music, 42*(4), 550–567.

Persson, R. S. (1996a). Studying with a musical maestro: A case study of common-sense teaching in artistic training. *Creativity Research Journal, 9*(1), 33–46.

Persson, R. S. (1996b). Concert musicians as teachers: On good intentions falling short. *In* A. J. Cropley & D. Dehn (Eds.), *Fostering the growth of high ability: European perspectives* (pp. 303–318). Norwood, NJ: Ablex Pub. Corp.

Peters, M. (1985a). Performance of a rubato-like task: When two things cannot be done at the same time. *Music Perception, 2*(4), 471–482.

Peters, M. (1985b). Constraints in the performance of bimanual tasks and their expression in unskilled and skilled subjects. *The Quarterly Journal of Experimental Psychology, 37*(2) 171–196.

Piccirilli, M., Palermo, M. T., Germani, A., Bertoli, M. L., Ancarani, V., Buratta, L., Dioguardi, M. S., Scarponi, L., & D'Alessandro, P. (2020). Music playing and interhemispheric communication: Older professional musicians outperform age-matched non-musicians in fingertip cross-localization test. *Journal of the International Neuropsychological Society, 27*(3), 1–11.

Piperek, M. (1981). *Stress and music—Medical, psychological, sociological, and legal strain factors in a symphony orchestra musician's profession*. Vienna, Austria: Wilhelm Braumuller.

Pitts, S. E., & Davidson, J. W. (2000). Developing effective practise strategies: Case studies of three young instrumentalists. *Music Education Research, 21*(1), 45–56.

Platz, F., Kopiez, R., Lehmann, A. C., & Wolf, A. (2014). The influence of deliberate practice on musical achievement: A meta-analysis. *Frontiers in Psychology, 5*(June), Article 646.

Pressnitzer, D., McAdams, S., Winsberg, S., & Fineberg, J. (1996). Roughness and musical tension of orchestral timbres. Paper presented at the 4th ICMPC (International Conference on Music Perception and Cognition), Faculty of Music, McGill University, Montreal, Quebec, 11–15 August.

Pruett, K. D. (1991). Psychological aspects of the development of exceptional young performers and prodigies. *In* R. T. Sataloff, A. G. Brandfonbrenner, & R. J. Lederman (eds.), *Textbook of performing arts medicine* (pp. 337–350). New York, NY: Raven Press.

Pruett, K., D. (2004). First patrons: Parenting the musician. *Medical Problems of Performing Artists, 19*(4), 154–159.

Prunchno, R., & Carr, D. (2017). Successful aging 2.0: Resilience and beyond (Editorial). *Journal of Gerontology: Social Sciences, 72*(2), 201–203.

Radford, J. (1994). Variations of a musical theme: Peer commentary to Sloboda et al (1994) 'Is everyone musical?'. *The Psychologist, 7*(7), 359–360.

Reid, S. (2002). Preparing the performance. *In* J. Rink (Ed.), *Musical performance: A guide to understanding* (pp. 102–112). Cambridge, UK: Cambridge University Press.

Ricket, D. L., Barrett, M. S., & Ackermann, B. J. (2013). Injury and the orchestral environment: Part I. The role of work organisation and psychosocial factors in injury risk. *Medical Problems of Performing Artists, 28*(4), 219–229.

Ricket, D. L., Barrett, M. S., & Ackermann, B. J. (2014a). Injury and the orchestral environment: Part II. Organisational culture, behavioral norms, and attitudes to injury. *Medical Problems of Performing Artists, 29*(2), 94–101.

Ricket, D. L., Barrett, M. S., & Ackermann, B. J. (2014b). Injury and the orchestral environment: Part III. The role of psychosocial factors in the experience of musicians undertaking rehabilitation. *Medical Problems of Performing Artists, 29*(3), 125–135.

Rink, J. (Ed.) (2002). *Musical performance: A guide to understanding*. Cambridge, UK: Cambridge University Press.

Robson, C. (1993). *Real world research: A resource for social scientists and practitioner- researchers.* Oxford, UK: Blackwell Publishers.

Rodrigues, A. C., Loureiro, M. A., & Carmelli, P. (2013). Long-term musical training may improve different forms of visual attention ability. *Brain and Cognition, 82*, 229–235.

Rogenmoser, L., Kernbach, J., Schlaug, G., & Gaser, C. (2019). Keeping brains young with making music. *Brain Structure and Function, 123*, 17–23.

Rosenthal, R., Durairaj, M., & Magann, J. (2009). Musicians' descriptions of their expressive musical practice. *Bulletin of the Council for Research in Music Education, 181*(summer), 37–49.

Ruthsalz, J., Detterman, D., Griscom, W. S., & Cirullo, B. (2008). Becoming an expert in the musical domain: It takes more than just practice. *Intelligence, 36*, 330–338.

Salthouse, T. A. (1996). The processing-speed theory of adult age differences in cognition. *Psychological Review, 103*, 403–428.

Salthouse, T. A. (2006). Mental exercise and mental aging: Evaluating the validity of the 'use it or lose it' hypothesis. *Perspectives on Psychological Science, 1*(1), 68–87.

Samson, S., Ehrl, N., & Baulac, M. (2001). Cerebral substrates for musical temporal processes. *Annals of the New York Academy of Sciences, 930*, 166–176.

Santucci, M. (1990). Musicians can protect their hearing. *Medical Problems of Performing Artists, 5*(4), 136–138.

Santucci, M. (2006). Please welcome on stage . . . personal in-the-ear monitoring. *The Hearing Review, 13*(3).

Sataloff, R. T. (1992). Vocal ageing: Medical considerations in professional voice users. *Medical Problems of Performing Artists, 7*, 17–21.

Scarmeas, N., & Stern, Y. (2003). Cognitive reserve and lifestyle. *Journal of Clinical and Experimental Neuropsychology, 25*(5), 625–633.

Scheibe, S. (2005). *Longing ('Sehnsucht') as a new lifespan concept: A developmental conceptualization and its measurement in adulthood.* [Unpublished doctoral dissertation]. Center for Lifespan Psychology at the Max Planck Institute of Psychology and Ageing, The Free University of Berlin. Found at: http://dx.doi.org/10.17169/refubium-16215.

Scheibe, S., & Freund, A. M. (2008). Approaching Sehnsucht (life longings) from a life-span perspective: The role of personal utopias in development. *Research in Human Development, 5*(2), 121–133.

Scheibe, S., Freund, A. M., & Baltes, P. B. (2007). Toward a developmental psychology of Sehnsucht (life longings): The optimal (utopian) life. *Developmental Psychology, 43*(3), 778–795.

Schlaug, G. (2003). The brain of musicians. *In* I. Peretz & R. J. Zatorre (Eds.), *The cognitive neurosciences of music* (pp. 366–381). Oxford, UK: Oxford University Press.

Schlaug, G. (2015). Chapter 3: Musicians and music making as a model for the study of brain plasticity. *Progress in Brain Research, 217*, 37–55.

Schlaug, G., Jancke, L., Huang, Y., & Steinmetz, H. (1995). In vivo evidence of structural brain asymmetry in musicians. *Science, 267*(5198), 699–701.

Sergeant, D. C., & Himonides, E. (2019). Orchestrated sex: The representation pf male and female musicians on world-class symphony orchestras. *Frontiers in Psychology, Performance Science, 10*(1760), 1–18.

Shammi, P., Bosman, E., & Stuss, D. T. (1998). Aging and variability in performance. *Aging, Neuropsychology and Cognition, 5*(1), 1–13.

Shultz, K. S., & Adams, G. A. (Eds.). (2009). *Aging and work in the 21st century.* New York, NY: Psychology Press, Taylor & Francis Group.

Skoe, E., & Kraus, N. (2012). A little goes a long way: How the adult brain is shaped by musical training in childhood. *The Journal of Neuroscience, 32*(34), 11507–11510.

Sloboda, J. A. (1984). Music performance: Expression and the development of excellence. *In* R. Aiello & J. A. Sloboda (eds.), *Musical perceptions* (pp. 152–172). New York, NY: Oxford University Press.

Sloboda, J. A. (1990). Musical excellence—how does it develop? *In* M. J. Howe (ed.), *Encouraging the development of exceptional skills and talents* (pp. 165–178). Leicester, UK: British Psychological Society.

Sloboda, J. A. (1991). Musical expertise. *In* K. A. Ericsson & J. Smith (eds.), *Toward a general theory of expertise* (pp. 153–171). Cambridge, UK: Cambridge University Press.

Sloboda, J. A. (1992). Empirical studies of emotional response to music. *In* M. R. Riess-Jones & S. Holleran (Eds.), *Cognitive bases of musical communication* (pp. 33–46). Washington, DC: American Psychological Association.

Sloboda, J. A. (1993a). Weighing of the talents. *Nature, 362*, 115–116.

Sloboda, J. A. (1993b). Musical ability. *In* G. Bock & K. Ackrill (eds.), *The origins and development of high ability* (pp. 106–113). Chichester, UK: John Wiley and Sons Ltd.

Sloboda, J. A. (1996). The acquisition of musical performance expertise: Deconstructing the 'talent' account of individual differences in musical expressivity. *In* K. A. Ericsson (ed.), *The road to excellence* (pp. 107–126). Mahwah, NJ: Lawrence Erlbaum Associates.

Sloboda, J., & Davidson, J. (1996). The young performing musician. *In* I. Deliege & J. A. Sloboda (eds.), *Musical beginnings: Origins and development of musical competence* (pp. 171–190). Oxford, UK: Oxford University Press.

Sloboda, J. A., Davidson, J. W., & Howe, M. J. A. (1994a). Is everyone musical? *The Psychologist, 7*(7), 349–354.

Sloboda, J. A., Davidson, J. W., & Howe, M. J. A. (1994b). Musicians: experts not geniuses: Response to peer commentaries by Davies, Hargreaves, Radford, Torff, and Winner to Sloboda et al. (1994) 'Is everyone musical?'. *The Psychologist, 7*(7), 363–365.

Sloboda, J. A., Davidson, J. W., Howe, M. J. A., & Moore, D. G. (1996). The role of practice in the development of performing musicians. *British Journal of Psychology, 87*, 287–309.

Sloboda, J. A., & Howe, M. J. A. (1991). Biographical precursors of musical excellence: An interview study. *Psychology of Music, 19*, 3–21.

Sluming, V., Brooks, J., Howard, M., Downes, J. J., & Roberts, N. (2007). Borca's area supports enhanced visuospatial cognition in orchestra musicians. *Journal of Neuroscience, 27*(14), 3799–3806.

Smilde, R. (2006). *Lifelong learning for musicians.* Paper presented at the 81st Annual Meeting of the National Association of Schools of Music, Boston (20 November 2005). Found at: https://www.hanze.nl/assets/kc-kunst—samenleving/lifelong-learning-in-music/Documents/Publ ic/lifelonglearningformusicians.pdf.

Smilde, R. (2009). Musicians as lifelong learners: Discovery through biography. Utrecht, the Netherlands: Eburon Academic Publishers. Also published in The Hague: Hanze University of Applied Science Groningen and Royal Academy of Fine Arts and Dance. Found at: https://www.hanze.nl/assets/kc-kunst—samenleving/lifelong-learning-in-music/Documents /Public/musiciansaslifelonglearnersdiscoverythroughbiography.pdf.

Smith, B. P., & Barnes, G. V. (2007). Development and validation of an orchestra performance rating scale. *Journal of Research in Music Education, 55*(3), 268–280.

Smith, D. E. (1988). The great symphony orchestra—a relatively good place to grow old. *International Journal of Ageing and Human Development, 27,* 233–247.

Smith, D. E. (1989). Ageing and the careers of symphony orchestra musicians. *Medical Problems of Performing Artists, 4,* 81–85.

Smith, D. E. (1992). Medical problems of orchestral musicians according to age and stage of career. *Medical Problems of Performing Arts, 7*(4), 132–134.

Smith, D. E., & Lipe, A. W. (1991). Music therapy practices in gerontology. *Journal of Music Therapy, 28,* 193–210.

Smith, T. S., & Murphy, R. J. (1984). Conflicting criteria of success in the careers of symphony musicians. *Empirical Studies of the Arts, 2*(2), 149–172.

Southcott, J. E. (2009). 'And as I go, I love to sing': The Happy Wanderers, music and positive aging. *International Journal of Community Music, 2,* 143–156.

Spahn, C., & Richter, B. (2006). The development of the singing voice across the lifespan. *In* H. Gembris (Ed.), *Musical development from a lifespan perspective,* pp. 119–131. Frankfurt, Germany: Peter Lang GmbH.

Steptoe, A. (1989). Stress, coping and stage fright in professional musicians. *Psychology of Music, 17,* 3–11.

Steptoe, A., & Fidler, H. (1987). Stage fright orchestral musicians: A study of cognitive and behavioral strategies in performance anxiety. *British Journal Psychology, 78,* 241–249.

Stern, C., & Munn, Z. (2010). Cognitive leisure activities and their role in preventing dementia: A systematic review. *International Journal of Evidence Based Healthcare, 8*(1), 2–17.

Sternbach, D. (1993). Addressing stress-related illness in professional musicians. *Maryland Medical Journal, 42*(3), 283–288.

Sternbach, D. J. (1995). Musicians: A neglected working population in crisis. *In* S. Sauter & L. Murphy (Eds.), *Organizational risk factors* (pp. 283–302). Washington, DC: APA.

Sternberg, R. J. (1986). A triangular theory of love. *Psychological Review, 93*(2), 119–135.

Sternberg, R. J. (2021). Toward a triangular theory of love for one's musical instrument. *Psychology of Music, 49*(6), 1747–1757.

Sterns, H. L., & Miklos, S. M. (1995). The aging worker in a changing environment: Organizational and individual issues. *Journal of Vocational Behavior, 47,* 248–268.

Steverink, N., & Lindenberg, S. (2006). Which social needs are important for subjective well-being? What happens to them with aging? *Psychology and Aging, 21,* 281–290.

Stones, M. J., & Baker, J. (2020). Editorial: Modeling human potential across the lifespan. *Frontiers in Psychology (Movement Science and Sport Psychology), 11,* Article 106, 3–pages.

Strong, J. V., & Mast, B. T. (2019). The cognitive function of older adult instrumental musicians and non-musicians. *Aging, Neuropsychology, and Cognition, 26*(3), 367–386.

Suzuki, A., & Mitchell, H. F. (2022). What makes practice perfect? How tertiary piano students self-regulate play and non-play strategies for performance success. *Psychology of Music, 50*(2), 611–630.

Theorell, T., Liljeholm-Johansson, Y., Bjork, H., & Ericson, M. (2007). Saliva testosterone and heart rate variability in the professional symphony orchestra after 'public faintings' of an orchestra member. *Psychoneuroendocrinology, 32,* 660–668.

Thompson, E. C., White-Schwoch, T., Tieney, A., & Kraus, N. (2015). Beat synchronization across the lifespan: Intersection of development and musical experience. *PLOS ONE, 10*(6), e0128839(0128831–0128813).

Thompson, S., & Williamon, A. (2003). Evaluating evaluation: Musical performance assessment as a research tool. *Music Perception, 21*(1), 21–41.

Torff, B., & Winner, E. (1994). Don't throw out the baby with the bath water: Peer commentary to Sloboda et al (1994) 'Is everyone musical?'. *The Psychologist, 7*(7), 361–362.

Tuuli, P., & Karisalmi, S. (1999). Impact of working life quality on burnout. *Experimental Aging Research, 25*, 441–449.

van de Wiel, M. W. J. (2017). Examining expertise using interviews and verbal protocols. *Frontline Learning Research, 5*(3, Special Issue), 112–140.

Verghese, J., Lipton, R. B., Katz, M. J., Hall, C. B., Derby, C. A., Kuslansky, G., Ambrose, A. F., & Buschke, H. (2003). Leisure activities and the risk of dementia in the elderly. *New England Journal of Medicine, 348*(25), 2508–2516.

Voltmer, E., Zander, M. F., Fischer, J. E., Kudielka, B., Richter, B., & Spahn, C. (2012). Physical and mental health of different types of orchestra musicians compared to other professions. *Medical Problems of Performing Artists, 27*(1), 9–14.

Vromans, R., & Postma-Nilsenova, M. (2016). Can musical engagement alleviate age-related decline in inhibitory control? *In* A. Papafragou, D. Grodner, D. Mirman, & J. C. Trueswell (Eds.), *Proceedings of the 38th Annual Conference of the Cognitive Science Society* (pp. 2807–2812). Austin, TX: Cognitive Science Society.

Wan, C. Y., & Schlaug, G. (2010). Music making as a tool for promoting brain plasticity across the life span. *The Neuroscientist, 16*(5), 566–577.

Watson, D., Clark, L. A., & Tellegen, A. (1988). Development and validation of brief measures of positive and negative affect: The PANAS scales. *Journal of Personality and Social Psychology, 54*(6), 1063–1070.

Weick, K. E., Gilfillan, D. P., & Keith, T. A. (1973). The effect of composer credibility on orchestra performance. *Sociometry, 36*, 435–465.

Weise, B. S., & Freund, A. M. (2005). Goal progress makes one happy, or does it? Longitudinal findings from the work domain. *Journal of Organizational and Organizational Psychology, 78*, 287–304.

Weise, B. S., Freund, A. M., & Baltes, P. B. (2000). Selection, optimization, and compensation: An action-related approach to work and partnership. *Journal of Vocational Behavior, 57*, 273–300.

Weise, B. S., Freund, A. M., & Baltes, P. B. (2002). Subjective career success and emotional well-being: Longitudinal predictive power of selection, optimization, and compensation. *Journal of Vocational Behavior, 60*, 321–335.

Welsh, J. C., Dewhurst, S. A., & Perry, J. L. (2018). Thinking aloud: An exploration of cognition in professional snooker. *Psychology of Sport & Exercise, 36*, 197–208.

Wesolowski, B. C., Wind, S. A., & Engelhard Jr., G. (2016). Examining rater precision in music performance assessment: An analysis of rating scale structure using the multifacted Rasch Partial Credit model. *Music Perception, 33*(5), 662–678.

Westby, D. L. (1960). The career experience of the symphony musician. *Social Forces, 38*, 223–230.

Whelan, M. N. M. (1994). Physical stress in orchestral musicians. *Performing Arts Medicine News* (November/December), 19–30.

Williamon, A. (Ed.) (2004). *Musical excellence: Strategies and techniques to enhance performance.* Oxford, UK: Oxford University Press.

Williamon, A., Ginsborg, J., Perkins, R., & Waddell, G. (2021). *Performing music research: Methods in music education, psychology, and performance science.* Oxford, UK: Oxford University Press.

Wilson, C. (2017). The 50 jobs where people work the longest. *TIME Magazine* (5 April). Found at: https://time.com/4726657/retirement-age-jobs/.

Windle, G. (2011). What is resilience? A review and concept analysis. *Reviews in Clinical Gerontology, 21*, 152–169.

Wise, G. W., Hartmann, D. J., & Fisher, B. J. (1992). Exploration of the relationship between choral singing and successful aging. *Psychological Reports, 70*, 1175–1183.

Wolff, L., Quan, Y., Perry, G., & Thompson, W. F. (2023). Music engagement as a source of cognitive reserve. *American Journal of Alzheimer's Disease & Other Dementias*, *38*, 1–15.

Woolford, D. H., Carterette, E. C., & Morgan, D. E. (1988). Hearing impairment among orchestral musicians. *Music Perception*, *5*(3), 261–284.

Yoshie, M., Kudo, K., Murakoshi, T., & Ohtsuki, T. (2009a). Music performance anxiety in skilled pianists: Effects of social-evaluative performance situation on subjective, autonomic, and electromyographic reactions. *Experimental Brain Research*, *199*, 117–126.

Yoshie, M., Shigemasu, K., Kudo, K., & Ohtsuki, T. (2009b). Effects of state anxiety on music performance: Relationship between the revised Competitive State Anxiety Inventory-2 subscales and piano performance. *Musicæ Scientiæ*, *13*(1), 55–84.

Yueng, E., Chan, W., Pan, F., Sau, P., Tsui, M., Yu, B., & Zaza, C. (1999). A survey of playing-related musculoskeletal problems among professional orchestral musicians in Hong Kong. *Medical Problems of Performing Arts*, *14*(1), 43–46.

Zatorre, R. J. (2003). Music and the brain. *In* G. Avanzini, C. Faienza, D. Minciacchi, L. Lopez, & M. Majno (Eds.), *The neurosciences and music* (Vol. 999, pp. 4–14). New York, NY: The New York Academics of Sciences.

Zendel, B. R., & Alain, C. (2012). Musicians experience less age-related decline in central auditory processing. *Psychology and Aging*, *27*(2), 410–417.

Zendel, B. R., & Alain, C. (2013). The influence of lifelong musicianship on neurophysiological measures of concurrent sound segregation. *Journal of Cognitive Neuroscience*, *25*(4), 503–516.

Zhang, J. D., Susino, M., McPherson, G., & Schubert, E. (2020). The definition of a musicians in music psychology: A literature review and the six-year rule. *Psychology of Music*, *48*(3), 389–409.

Index

For the benefit of digital users, indexed terms that span two pages (e.g., 52–53) may, on occasion, appear on only one of those pages.

Tables, figures, and boxes are indicated by an italic *t*, *f*, or *b*.